Rosenzweig

Statistical Methods for Psychology

Statistical Methods for Psychology

David C. Howell
University of Vermont

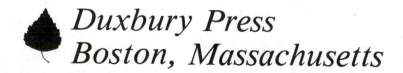

Duxbury Press
Boston, Massachusetts

PWS PUBLISHERS

Prindle, Weber & Schmidt · ✿ · Willard Grant Press · ᴡɢ · Duxbury Press · ♠
Statler Office Building · 20 Providence Street · Boston, Massachusetts 02116

PWS Publishers is a division of Wadsworth, Inc.

ISBN 0-87872-269-9

Library of Congress Cataloging in Publication Data

Howell, David C
    Statistical methods for psychology.

    Bibliography: p.
    Includes index.
    1. Psychometrics.   I. Title.
BF39.H69   519.5 ′02415   81-9797
ISBN 0-87872-269-9   AACR2

Printed in the United States of America.
    84 85 86 — 10 9 8 7 6 5 4 3

To
Cathy,
Barbara, Lynda, and Stephanie

Cover image ''Proximities XXXIX'' a collage by Robert Kelly. Used with permission of the artist. Cover and text design by Susan London and coordinated by John Servideo. Art drawn by Julie Gecha. Composed in Times Roman by Arrowsmith Ltd. Covers printed by Lehigh Press. Text printed and bound by Halliday Lithograph, Plympton, Massachusetts, U.S.A.

Preface

This text is intended to provide a survey of statistical techniques commonly used in Psychology, Education, and the Behavioral and Social Sciences. It is designed for use with students at the intermediate level or above, but does not assume that the person has had either a previous course in statistics or a course in mathematics beyond high school algebra. Those students who have had an introductory course in statistics will find that the early material provides a good review. The book is suitable for either a one-term or a full-year course, and I have used it successfully for both. Since I have found that students, and faculty, frequently refer back to the book from which they originally learned statistics, I have included some material which will make the book a useful reference for future use. The instructor who wishes to omit this material will have no difficulty in doing so.

My intention in writing this book was to explain the material at an intuitive level. This should not be taken to mean that the material is "watered down," but only that the emphasis is on conceptual understanding. The fact that a student can derive the sampling distribution of t, for example, does not mean that he or she has any understanding of how that distribution is to be used. My aim has been to concentrate on the *meaning* of a sampling distribution and to show the role that it plays in the general theory of hypothesis testing. In my view, the student gains a better understanding of the way a particular test works and of the interrelationship among tests by this approach than by the technical approach.

While no one would be likely to call this book controversial, I have felt it important to express opinions on a number of controversial issues. For example, I have argued that the underlying scale of measurement is not as important as some have suggested, and I have recommended that the Newman-Keuls test is probably the most useful procedure for making multiple comparisons in the general case. I do not expect every instructor to agree with me on every point, and he or she has the opportunity to present an opposing view in class. (In fact it might make the class more interesting.) At the same time, it seems to me that it is unfair and frustrating to the student to present a large number of multiple comparison procedures (which I do) and then to walk away and leave the student with no recommendation about which procedure is best for his or her problem. In addition, it is the controversies which make statistics an interesting discipline.

In the last few years the number of students who have ready access to a computer has increased rapidly, and the use of computer software packages has risen accordingly. Any text in statistics must not only address the issue of how to compute the test statistics we use, but also show the students how to obtain the same solution on a computer and how to interpret the resulting computer output. This book contains numerous examples of solutions obtained by standard software packages (BMDP, MINITAB, and SPSS). These will be useful in the long run even for the student who does not have access to computer facilities. In addition, many of the exercises at the end of chapters either present the student with a sample of a computer output and ask him/her to interpret it, or ask him/her to solve a previous problem by use of one or another software package.

With a few exceptions, the text is organized in a traditional way. Chapters 1, 2 and 4 present the basic material on plotting data, measures of central tendency and dispersion, and the normal distribution. Chapter 3 on the theory of hypothesis testing is an unusual and important one. In a completely general and non-technical way it lays out the concepts of sampling distributions and the null hypothesis, and their use in testing hypotheses. I have found that even those students who have had a previous course in statistics and are able to perform statistical tests, often do not really understand the logic behind what they are doing. They fail to understand that all tests reduce to: (1) a method of calculating the test statistic, (2) the comparison of that test statistic with the sampling distribution of the statistic, and (3) a decision based on that comparison. Chapter 3 is intended to remedy this problem.

Chapter 5 presents the rudiments of probability theory and the binomial distribution, and leads directly into Chapter 6 which covers the Chi-square test.

Chapter 7 is primarily devoted to Student's t, and includes, in addition to the standard coverage, a complete discussion of heterogeneity of variance and the Behrens-Fisher problem, and a brief introduction to the F statistic.

Chapter 8 presents the concept of power, a discussion of the need to estimate the power of any proposed experiment, and a simplified approach to power estimation.

Chapters 9 and 10 are concerned with bivariate correlation and regression. Chapter 9 is devoted to the least squares regression line and Pearson's product-moment correlation, while Chapter 10 presents a collection of alternative correlational techniques, their relationship to Pearson's r, and a variety of measures of association.

The analysis of variance is covered in Chapters 11 through 14. These chapters contain a very complete coverage of one-way, factorial, and repeated-measures designs. They also contain an extended coverage of multiple comparison techniques. Since the analysis of variance plays such an important role in experimental research, and since most people doing research fall back on their old textbook when they come to a problem, I feel that it is important to cover the topic here as thoroughly as possible, and to cover it in such a way that the student understands precisely what he or she is doing.

Chapter 15 is devoted to multiple regression. The coverage is based on the assumption that multiple regression solutions are almost always obtained by use of computer programs. Thus the chapter has relatively little to say about computation and much to say about explanation and interpretation.

Chapter 16 shows the student how the multiple regression procedures covered in Chapter 15 can be applied to the analysis of variance and the analysis of covariance. In many ways this is one of the most important chapters in the book, since it leaves the student better prepared to understand more advanced techniques.

Finally, Chapter 17 presents a brief coverage of nonparametric statistics. It may be covered as a whole, anywhere in the course sequence; it can be integrated into the preceding chapters where appropriate; or it can be omitted altogether, depending upon the orientation of the instructor.

This book owes much to many people who have contributed in a variety of ways. I would like to express my appreciation to three former teachers: Dr. Davis J. Chambliss (who taught me that there is an appealing logic behind statistical procedures), Dr. Edward A. Bilodeau (who taught me much about research, though, to his regret, taught me less about being compulsive), and Dr. David L. Prouty (who taught me that a sentence can be written in more than one way, and that one of those ways may be better than others).

I owe thanks to my colleagues at the University of Vermont and at the University of Durham, England, where I spent a sabbatical year working on this project. Dr. Lawrence R. Gordon has been particularly helpful with his comments and suggestions. I would also like to thank my editor, Pat Fitzgerald, and several anonymous reviewers who read the manuscript with considerable care and offered valuable suggestions.

Most of all I owe a debt to all of those students who suffered through earlier drafts of the book and encouraged me with their comments. This is especially true of Dr. Stephanie H. McConaughy, who identified a depressing number of errors but who insisted that it was all worth doing. Most of all I want to thank my wife, Cathy. She not only offered substantive criticism of the manuscript, but typed the final draft, proofread everything, wrote the index, and did a variety of chores—all on top of her own work.

I am indebted to the University of California Press and the McGraw-Hill Book Company for permission to illustrate computer examples and exercises by means of BMDP and SPSS. Information about the SPSS Batch System is available from SPSS, Inc. I am also indebted to B. J. Winer and William Winkler for permission to use numerical examples from their work. Finally I want to thank the Institute of Mathematical Statistics, the Biometric Society, the American Statistical Society, and the *Biometrika* Trustees for permission to reproduce tables from their journals.

David C. Howell
Burlington, Vermont

Table of Contents

Preface

Statistical Methods for Psychology

1

Basic Concepts

Objective

To examine the kinds of problems we will deal with in this book and the issues which are involved in the selection of a statistical procedure.

Contents

Statistics   The word ***statistics***† is used in at least three different ways, and before beginning any book on the subject it is well that we know what it is we are talking about. As the word is used in the title of this book, it refers to a set of rules and procedures for reducing large masses of data to manageable proportions and for allowing us to draw conclusions from those data. This is essentially what the book is all about.

A second, and very common, meaning of the term is expressed by statements such as "Statistics show that the world's supply of nickel is being consumed at a very rapid rate." In this meaning of the term the word *statistics* is used in place of the much better word "data". For our purposes *statistics* will never be used in this sense.

A third common meaning of the term is used in reference to the result of some arithmetic or algebraic manipulation applied to data. Thus we can speak of the mean (average) of a set of numbers as a statistic. This is a perfectly legitimate usage and will occur repeatedly throughout the book.

We now have two proper uses of the term: (1) the set of rules and procedures and (2) the outcome of the application of those rules and procedures to samples of data. The reader can tell from the context which of the two meanings is intended.

1.1   *Descriptive and Inferential Statistics*

Statistical procedures can be roughly separated into two overlapping areas—descriptive and inferential statistics. With the exception of Chapter 2, this book will be almost entirely devoted to inferential statistics.

Descriptive Statistics

Whenever your purpose is merely to describe a set of data, you are engaged in employing descriptive statistics. The census results from 1980, the number of tons of coffee imported last year from Brazil, and certain summary information concerning grades on an examination in a particular course, are all examples of descriptive statistics.

The descriptive statistician has a wealth of statistical techniques at hand to allow him to do his job efficiently, but an exhaustive elaboration of these techniques lies outside the scope of this book. The most important measures, such as means, variances, and standard deviations, will be discussed in the next chapter, since they are also essential to an understanding of inferential

---

† The words and phrases in the margin represent *key words* which are being highlighted for emphasis and for your convenience.

statistics. The various techniques for graphically presenting data, many of them self evident, will remain largely, but not entirely, untouched.

Inferential Statistics

Most of the statistical work in Psychology and the other social sciences is concerned with inferential statistics. To expand on this point requires that we define the concepts of populations and samples, since the field of inferential statistics is concerned with using samples to infer something about populations.

Population **Populations and samples** A *population* can be defined as the entire collection of events (people's heights, rats' running speeds, and so on) in which you are interested. Thus if we were interested in the IQs of all adult Americans, then the collection of all adult American IQs would form a population—in this case a population of more than 100 million members. If, on the other hand, we were only interested in the collection of IQs of the second grade class in Fairfax, Vermont (a town of fewer than 2000 inhabitants) our population of numbers could quite easily be obtained in its entirety. To go to the opposite extreme consider the set of outcomes of rolling a die. Clearly once you have rolled a die you can always roll it again, and assuming that it never wears out it could be rolled an infinite number of times, thus producing an infinitely large population (mathematicians would prefer the word *uncountable*, but infinite will do).

The point is that a population can range from a relatively small set of numbers which is easily collected to an infinitely large set of numbers which can never be completely collected. Unfortunately for us the populations in which we are interested are usually quite large. The practical consequence is that we will seldom if ever measure entire populations. Instead, we will

Sample be forced to draw only a *sample* of observations from that population, and to use that sample to infer something about the characteristics of the population.

Random sample Assuming that the sample is a truly *random sample*, meaning that each and every element of the population has an equal chance of being included in the sample, we can not only estimate certain characteristics of the population, but can also have a very good idea of how accurate are our estimates. To the extent that the sample is not a random sample, our estimates may be meaningless, since the sample will not accurately reflect the entire population.

Before going on, let us clear up one point that tends to confuse many people. The problem is that one person's sample might be another person's population. For example, if I were to conduct a study into the effectiveness of this book as a teaching instrument, one class's scores on an examination might be considered by me to be a sample, though a non-random one, of the population of scores for all students using, or potentially using, this book. The class instructor, on the other hand, cares only about his own students, and would regard the same set of scores as a population. In turn, someone interested in the teaching of statistics might regard my population (everyone using this book) as a non-random sample from a larger population (everyone using any textbook in statistics). Thus the definition of a population depends upon what you are interested in studying.

The fact that I have here used non-random samples to make a point should not lead the reader to think that randomness is not important. On the contrary, it is the cornerstone of most statistical procedures. As a matter of fact, one could define the relevant population as the collection of numbers from which samples have been randomly drawn.

Inferential statistics   **Inference**   We can now define *inferential statistics* as that branch of statistics dealing with inferring characteristics of populations from characteristics of samples. This statement is inadequate by itself, however, as it leaves the reader with the impression that all we care about is determining population characteristics—for example, the average height of adult American males, the average running speed of second grade school children, and so on. If that were all there were to inferential statistics, it would be a pretty dreary subject. The problem that many students have with statistics is that they do not realize until too late that when we attempt to infer the average reading speed of third grade children taught under one method of instruction, we do not usually have any great interest in what that average is. We only care whether it is larger or smaller than some other average—for example, the average reading speed of a sample of third grade children taught under some other method. Thus in many cases inferential statistics is a tool to estimate characteristics of two or more populations, mainly for the purpose of finding out if those characteristics are different. This explains why someone might conduct a study into the running speed of hooded rats under some schedule of reinforcement. It is obviously not a matter of great national concern just how fast a rat can run. But it might be a matter of some more limited interest whether rats trained under a different schedule of reinforcement will run faster.

1.2 Selection Among Statistical Procedures

On the next page of this book you can see what is known as a decision tree for selecting among the available statistical procedures to be presented in this book. This decision tree also represents a rough outline of the organization of the text, and as such is worth some study at this point. At the top

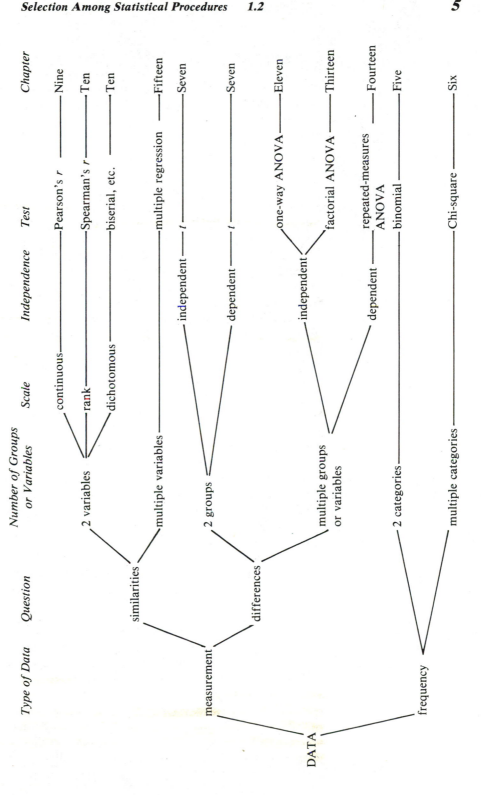

of the tree are a set of labels for decisions to be made, which distinguish one type of test from another. These decisions are relatively simple ones, and the first three will be discussed briefly. Discussion of the fourth decision is better left to a more appropriate time.

Types of Data

Measurement data

Numerical data generally come in two kinds, which we will designate as measurement data and frequency data. By *measurement data* is meant the result of any sort of measurement. For example, a grade on a test, a person's weight, the speed at which a person can read this page, an individual's IQ, and so on. In all cases some sort of instrument (in its broadest sense) has been used to measure something.

Frequency data

On the other hand, *frequency data* consist of things such as "158 people like chocolate bars with almonds and 26 do not," or "John Jones received 38 votes and Bill Smith received 6." Here we have set about counting things and our data consist of totals or frequencies. A city election might be participated in by thousands of people, but the results (data) would consist of only a few numbers—the number of votes for each candidate. However, with measurement data, we might measure these same thousands of people, but would come up with thousands of numbers—one for each person. Whenever the data represent one or more measurements for each subject we will say that we have measurement data. Whenever the data represent a set of total (or subtotal) counts, we will say that we have frequency data.

The two kinds of data are treated in two quite different ways. In Chapters 5 and 6 we will examine frequency data to see how we can determine whether there is or is not a reliable difference between, for example, the preferences for two different candy bars. In Chapter 7 and those which follow we are going to be concerned chiefly with measurement data. Using measurement data we have to make a second distinction, not in terms of the type of data, but in terms of the questions we will ask.

Differences vs. Relationships

Difference

Relationship

Most statistical questions fall roughly into one of two overlapping categories—differences and relationships. For example one experimenter might be primarily interested in whether there is a *difference* between smokers and non-smokers in terms of their performance on a given task. A different experimenter might be interested in whether there is a *relationship* between the numbers of cigarettes smoked per day and scores on this same task. Although these two questions obviously overlap, they are treated by what, on the surface, appear to be quite different methods. Chapters 7 and 8 and 11 to 14 will be concerned primarily with those cases in which we ask if there are differences between two or more groups, while Chapters 9, 10, and 15 will deal with cases in which we are interested in examining relationships between two or more variables. Finally Chapter 16 will show that we have been using the same kind of statistical procedure throughout, although we have been asking somewhat different questions and phrasing our answers in distinctively different ways.

Numbers of Groups or Variables

As we will see in subsequent chapters, an obvious distinction between statistical techniques concerns the number of groups or the number of variables to which they apply. Thus, for example, what is generally referred to as simple linear regression is restricted to the case of two variables (one criterion and one predictor), while multiple linear regression employs any number of predictor variables. The third decision in our tree concerns the number of groups or variables involved.

The three decisions we have been discussing (type of data, differences versus relationships, and number of groups or variables) allow us to separate most statistical procedures into particular categories. One further criterion which some textbooks use for creating categories of tests, but which is not used in this book, involves the scale of measurement which applies to the data.

1.3 Scales of Measurement

Scales of measurement

The topic of **scales of measurement** is one of those topics which is seen as crucial by some writers and trivial by others. While this book will tend to side with the latter group, it is important that you have some familiarity with the general issue. A side benefit of this discussion is that you will begin to realize that statistics is not merely a cut-and-dried set of facts, but rather a set of facts put together with a variety of interpretations and opinions.

Probably the foremost leader of those who see scales of measurement as crucially important to the choice of statistical procedures was S. S. Stevens.[†] Basically, Stevens defined four types of scales: nominal, ordinal, interval, and ratio. These scales are distinguished on the basis of what relationships exist between items having different scale values.

[†] Chapter 1 in Stevens' *Handbook of Psychology* (1951) is an excellent reference for anyone wishing to go further into the really substantial mathematical issues underlying his position.

Nominal Scales

Nominal scale   In a sense *nominal scales* are not really scales at all, since they do not scale items along any dimension, but rather label them. The classic example of a nominal scale is the set of numbers assigned to football players. Frequently these numbers have no meaning whatsoever other than as convenient labels distinguishing the players from one another. We could just as easily use letters or the pictures of animals.

Ordinal Scales

Ordinal scale   The simplest true scale is an *ordinal scale*, which rank orders people, objects or events along some continuum. An example of an ordinal scale might be the class standings of people graduating from high school. Here the scale tells us which person was best in his class, which was second best, etc. Another, more debatable, example would be the traditional grading system. A student who earns a 95 is generally presumed to know more about the subject matter than a person who earns an 85, who in turn is presumed to know more than someone who earns a 75. Thus we scale people, in terms of knowledge, by their grades.

Ordinal scales do not tell us the whole story, however, because no information is given about the differences between points on the scale. Thus we do not know how different are the levels of knowledge of the student earning a 95 and the student earning an 85, nor do we know if the difference in knowledge between a 95 and an 85 is comparable to the difference in knowledge between an 85 and a 75. Distinctions of that sort must be left to the next type of scale.

Interval Scales

Interval scale   When we move up to *interval scales* we come to a scale where we can legitimately speak of differences between scale points. A common example is the Fahrenheit scale of temperature, where a 10–point difference has the same meaning anywhere along the scale. Thus the difference between 10 and 20 degrees is the same as the difference between 80 and 90 degrees. Notice that this scale also satisfies the properties of the two preceding ones. What we do not have with an interval scale, however, is the ability to speak meaningfully about ratios. Thus we cannot say, for example, that 40 degrees F is one half as hot as 80 degrees F, or twice as hot as 20 degrees F. We will have to move to ratio scales for that purpose.

Ratio Scales

Ratio scale

True zero point

A *ratio scale* is one which has a *true zero point.* Notice that the zero point must be a true zero point, and not an arbitrary one such as 0 degrees Fahrenheit. Examples of ratio scales are the common physical ones of length, volume, time and so on. With these scales we not only have the properties of the preceding scales, but can also speak about ratios. We can say that 10 seconds is twice as long as 5 seconds, that 100 pounds is one third as heavy as 300 pounds and so on.

One might think that it would usually be obvious what kind of scale we are working with. Unfortunately, especially with the kinds of measures we collect in the social sciences, this is not the case. Consider for a moment the situation in which an examination is administered to a group of students. If I were foolish enough I might argue that this is a ratio scale. I would maintain that a person who received a zero knew truly nothing, and that an 80 was twice as good as a 40. Though most people would find this position untenable, with certain examinations I might be able to build a reasonable case. Someone else might argue that it is an interval scale and that while the zero point was somewhat arbitrary—the student receiving a zero knew a little bit but I did not happen to ask the right questions—equal differences in grades represent equal differences in knowledge. Finally, a more reasonable case might be made that the grades represent an ordinal scale. A 95 is better than an 85, which in turn is better than a 75, but the successive differences in grades do not reflect equal differences in knowledge.

Since there is usually no unanimous agreement concerning the scale of measurement employed, it is up to the individual user of statistical procedures to make the best decision she can concerning the nature of the data. All that can be asked of her is that she use a little common sense in coming to her decision.

Importance of the Scale of Measurement

The statement was made earlier that there is a difference of opinion as to the importance assigned to scales of measurement. Some authors have totally ignored the problem, while others have organized whole textbooks around the different scales. It seems to me that the central issue is the absolute necessity of separating numbers from the objects to which they refer. If one subject in a verbal learning study recalled 20 items and another subject recalled 10 items, the number of words recalled was twice as large for the first subject, even though we might not be willing to say that the first subject remembers twice as much about the material studied. Similarly with examination grades one student may be assigned twice as high a grade as another, although this does not necessarily mean that he has learned twice as much. Thus so long as we are referring only to the numbers themselves without references to the objects or events to which those numbers refer (and this is what a statistical test actually does), we may carry out any of the standard mathematical operations. An excellent and highly recommended reference is a very entertaining paper by Lord (1953) entitled "The statistical treatment of football numbers" in which he argues that these numbers can be treated in any way you like, since "the numbers do not remember where they came from" (p. 751).

The rub comes when it is time to interpret the results of some form of statistical manipulation. At that point we must ask if the statistical results bear any meaningful relationship to the objects or events in question. Here we are no longer dealing with a statistical issue, howver, but with a methodological one. There is no statistical procedure which can tell us whether the fact that one group received higher grades than another on a history examination means anything at all in terms of any group differences in underlying knowledge of the subject matter. Moreover, to be satisfied because the measure forms a ratio scale of test performance (50 items correct is twice as many as 25 items correct), is to lose sight of the fact that we set out to measure knowledge of history, which may not increase in any neat way with increases in scores. Our statistical tests can only apply to the numbers which are obtained, and inferences to underlying variables hinge primarily on common sense, and not on the scale of measurement.† For an interesting and important debate on the entire issue the reader is referred to articles by Stevens (1951), Burke (1953), Senders (1953), Lord (1953), Bakan (1966), Baker, Hardyck, & Petrinovich (1966), Jette, Howell, & Gordon (1977), and Gaito (1980).

From the preceding discussion the apparent conclusion, and the one accepted in this book, is that the underlying scale of measurement is not of crucial importance in our choice of statistical techniques. Obviously, a certain amount of common sense is required in the interpretation of the results of these statistical manipulations. Only a fool would conclude that a painting which was judged as excellent by one person and contemptible by another was therefore to be classified as mediocre.

1.4 Variables

Variables

Properties of objects or events which can take on different values are referred to as **variables**. Hair color, for example, is a variable because it is the property

---

† As Cohen (1965) has pointed out: "Thurstone once said that in psychology we measure men by their shadows. Indeed, in clinical psychology we often measure men by their shadows while they are dancing in a ballroom illuminated by the reflections of an old-fashioned revolving polyhedral mirror" (p. 102).

Discrete variables

Continuous variables

of an object (hair) and it can take on different values (brown, yellow, red, etc.). Properties such as height, length and speed are variables for the same reason. We can further discriminate between *discrete variables* (such as sex, marital status, and the number of heads in five flips of a coin) in which the variable can only take on one of a relatively few possible values, and *continuous variables* (such as speed, time, and so on) where the variable could assume, at least in theory, any value between the lowest and highest points on the scale. As we will see later in this book, this distinction plays an important role in some of our procedures.

Independent variables

Dependent variables

In statistics we also dichotomize the concept of a variable in an additional way. We speak of *independent variables* (those which are manipulated by the experimenter) and *dependent variables* (those which are not under the experimenter's control—the data). Common examples of independent variables in psychology are schedules of reinforcement, teaching methods, placement of electrodes, and method of treatment. Common examples of dependent variables are running speed, scores on a test, incidence of lordosis, and so on. Bascially what the study is all about are the independent variables and the results of the study (the data) are the dependent variables. Independent variables may be either qualitative or quantitative, while dependent variables are generally, but not always, quantitative only.

1.5   *Notation*

Any discussion of statistical techniques requires a notational system for expressing mathematical operations. It is thus surprising that no standard notational system has been adopted. While there have actually been several attempts to formulate a general policy, the fact remains that no two textbooks use exactly the same notation.

The notational systems commonly used range from the very complex to the very simple. The more complex systems gain precision at the loss of easy intelligibility, while the simpler systems gain intelligibility at the loss of precision. Since the loss of precision is usually trivial when compared with the gain in comprehension, this book will adopt an extremely simple system of notation.

Notation of Variables

The general rule is that a variable as a whole will be represented by an upper case letter, usually X or Y. An individual value of that variable will then be represented by the letter and a subscript. Suppose for example that we have the following five examination grades.

85   82   75   63   92

This set of scores will be referred to as X. The first member of this set (85) will be referred to as X_1, the second X_2, and so on. When we wish to refer to one member without specifying which one, we will refer to X_i, where i can take on any value between 1 and 5. In practice the use of subscripts is a distraction, and they will generally be omitted where no confusion would be expected.

Summation Notation

Sigma

One of the most common symbols in statistics is the upper case Greek letter *sigma* (Σ), which is the standard notation for summation. It is readily translated as "add up, or sum, what follows." Thus ΣX_i is read *sum the X_is*. To be perfectly correct, the notation for summing all N values of X is

$$\sum_{i=1}^{N} X_i$$

which translates to *sum all of the X_is from $i=1$ to $i=N$*. There is seldom any need in practice for specifying this precisely what is to be done, and in fact in most cases all subscripts will be dropped and the notation for the sum of the X_i will be simply ΣX.

TABLE 1.1

Illustration of Operations Involving Summation Notation

	RUNNING SPEED (X)	AMOUNT REINF. (Y)	X^2	Y^2	$X - Y$	XY
	10	3	100	9	7	30
	15	4	225	16	11	60
	12	1	144	1	11	12
	9	1	81	1	8	9
	10	3	100	9	7	30
Sum	56	12	650	36	44	141

$$\Sigma X = (10+15+12+9+10) = 56$$
$$\Sigma Y = (3+4+1+1+3) = 12$$
$$\Sigma X^2 = (10^2+15^2+12^2+9^2+10^2) = 650$$
$$\Sigma Y^2 = (3^2+4^2+1^2+1^2+3^2) = 36$$
$$\Sigma(X-Y) = (7+11+11+8+7) = 44$$
$$\Sigma XY = (10\cdot3+15\cdot4+12\cdot1+9\cdot1+10\cdot3) = 141$$
$$(\Sigma X)^2 = 56^2 = 3136$$
$$(\Sigma Y)^2 = 12^2 = 144$$
$$(\Sigma(X-Y))^2 = 44^2 = 1936$$
$$(\Sigma X)(\Sigma Y) = (56)(12) = 672$$

There are several extensions of the simple case of ΣX which must be noted and thoroughly understood. One of these is ΣX^2, which is read as *sum the squared values of X*. Another common expression is ΣXY which means *sum the products of the corresponding values of X and Y*. These operations are illustrated in Table 1.1, along with some others that will be discussed shortly.

Examination of Table 1.1 reveals another set of operations of the form $(\Sigma X)^2$. The general rule which always applies is to perform operations within parentheses before performing operations outside of parentheses. Thus for $(\Sigma X)^2$ we sum the values of X and *then* we square the result, as opposed to ΣX^2 where we square the Xs before we sum.

Double Subscripts

A common notational device is to use two or more subscripts to specify exactly which value of X you have in mind. Suppose for example that we were given the data shown in Table 1.2. If we want to specify the entry in

TABLE 1.2
Sample Data

			TRIAL				
		1	*2*	*3*	*4*	*5*	*Total*
	1	8	7	6	9	12	42
Day	2	10	11	13	15	14	63
	Total	18	18	19	24	26	105

the ith row and jth column, we will denote this as X_{ij}. Thus the score on the third trial of Day 2 is $X_{2,3} = 13$. With some notational schemes it is not uncommon to find

$$\sum_{i=1}^{2} \sum_{j=1}^{5} X_{ij},$$

which translates as *sum the X_{ij}s where i takes on values 1 and 2 and j takes on all values from 1 to 5*. The student should be aware of this system of notation, since other books to which he or she refers may use it. In this book, however, the simpler, but less precise, ΣX is used where possible, with ΣX_{ij} coming in only when absolutely necessary, and $\Sigma \Sigma X_{ij}$ never appearing.

A thorough understanding of notation is essential if you are to learn even the most elementary statistical techniques. The student is urged to study Table 1.1 until he or she fully understands all of the procedures involved.

There are a few rules of summation which the reader will find extremely helpful in following the discussion in the text, and these are given below. The demonstration of these rules is left to the student, since their application can be illustrated with very simple examples:

A. $\Sigma(X + Y) = \Sigma X + \Sigma Y$

Constant   **B.** $\Sigma C = NC$, where C is any **constant** and N is the number of times the summation is performed. A specific example which occurs with fair regularity in derivations is $\Sigma \bar{X} = N\bar{X}$, where $\bar{X}$ represents the sample mean, which is a constant for a given sample of data, and N is the number of observations.

C. $\Sigma CX = C\Sigma X$

1.6 Summary

In this chapter we have examined the differences between descriptive and inferential statistics and noted that the bulk of the book will deal with inferential procedures. We have also seen that the choice of which procedure to use depends mainly on the kinds of data we have, the question we wish to ask, and the number of groups or variables under consideration. The problem of the scale of measurement was discussed, and the argument was made that the particular scale on which a variable is measured is far less important than is the use of common sense in drawing inferences from the variables we actually measure (e.g., number of correct trials) to the objects or events we wish to study (e.g., learning ability). Finally, we looked at the concept of a variable and the notational system we will use to represent variables and their values.

Exercises for Chapter 1

1.1   Give an example of a very small population, one of reasonable size, and an infinitely large one.

1.2   Why wouldn't the students in English 208 (Advanced Creative Writing) represent a random sample of students at that university?

1.3   Would the students in English 208 represent a random sample from any population?

1.4   How would you obtain a random sample of students at a given university?

1.5   Give examples of measurement and frequency data.

1.6   Give examples of nominal, ordinal, interval, and ratio data.

1.7   Assume that I can create the perfect test of Sanskrit. What kind of a scale will grades on this test represent?

1.8   I am proposing to use a student's knowledge of Sanskrit as a measure of her teacher's ability to teach. In what way would this change your answer to Exercise 1.7?

1.9   We have trained rats to run a straight–alley maze for food reinforcement, and use speed as a measure of learning. All of a sudden our rat lay down and went to sleep half-way through the maze. What does this say about his knowledge, his motivation, and the properties of our scale?

1.10   Give examples of two independent variables and two dependent variables.

1.11   Give three examples of discrete variables.

1.12   Give three examples of a continuous variable.

1.13   In a hypothetical experiment, Harris, Peabody, and Smith (1992) rated ten Europeans and ten North Americans on a 12–point scale of musicality. The following data are given for the Europeans:

  10   8   9   5   10   11   7   8   2   7

a.   What are X_3, X_5, and X_9?
b.   Calculate ΣX.
c.   Write the summation notation in its most complex form.

1.14   With reference to the preceding question, the data for the North Americans are:

  9   9   5   3   8   4   6   6   5   2

Using the symbol Y for this variable:

a.   What are Y_1 and Y_8?
b.   Calculate ΣY.

1.15   Using the data from Exercise 1.13:

a.   Calculate ΣX, $(\Sigma X)^2$, and ΣX^2.
b.   Calculate $\Sigma X / N$, where N represents the number of scores.
c.   What do you call the thing that you just calculated?

1.16   Using the data from Exercise 1.14:

a.   Calculate ΣY, $(\Sigma Y)^2$, and ΣY^2.
b.   Calculate

$$(\Sigma Y^2 - (\Sigma Y)^2/N)/(N-1)$$

c.   Calculate the square root of the previous answer.

1.17 Using the data from Exercise 1.13 and 1.14:

a. Calculate ΣXY.

b. Calculate $\Sigma X \Sigma Y$.

c. Calculate

$(\Sigma XY - \Sigma X \Sigma Y / N)/(N - 1)$ (where N = the number of *pairs*)

1.18 Use the previous data to demonstrate that

a. $\Sigma(X + Y) = \Sigma X + \Sigma Y$.

b. ΣXY is not equal to $(\neq)$ $\Sigma X \Sigma Y$.

c. $\Sigma CX = C \Sigma X$, where C is any constant (e.g. 3).

1.19 Use the package of computer programs called MINITAB to answer Exercise 1.15*a*. A sample program follows. (Your instructor will have to tell you how to call up the package.)

```
SET THE FOLLOWING DATA INTO C1
10 8 9 5 10 11 7 8 2 7
SUM C1
MULTIPLY --- X --- PUT INTO C2 (where --- represents answer to previous operation)
MULTIPLY C1 X C1    PUT INTO C3
SUM C3
STOP
```

1.20 Use MINITAB to answer 1.17.   *Hint*: start out by:

```
SET THE FOLLOWING DATA INTO C1
10 8 9 ...
SET THE FOLLOWING DATA INTO C2
9 9 5 ...
```

If you don't have a MINITAB Manual, try it anyway, expanding on the previous exercise.

2 Measures of Central Tendency and Dispersion

Objective

To show the ways in which data can be reduced to more interpretable form through the use of graphic representation and measures of central tendency and dispersion.

Contents

Whenever an experimenter collects a set of data, he immediately finds himself faced with the task of trying to make some sense out of a large collection of numbers. Depending on the compulsivity of the experimenter, the data may appear as neat columns of numbers on specially ruled paper, or as a motley collection of numbers on whatever scrap of paper was to be found when it became time to run subjects. Although the latter form of data collection appears to predominate in psychology, the method of recording is actually irrelevant. What is relevant, however, is the fact that raw data are nothing but a collection of numbers, and even the most experienced investigator is usually hopelessly lost when presented with such a collection. He must first organize it and then try to reduce the information to some manageable proportions.

As an illustration, suppose that we asked 200 students to rate the pleasantness of a picture on a scale from 0 to 10, managing in some way to eliminate the usual tendency for ratings to pile up at the center and the extremes of the scale. At the end of the task we will have 200 numbers, one for each student. It should be apparent that we would not learn very much by looking at a jumble of 200 numbers, other than some vague subjective impression that people found the picture pleasant or unpleasant on the whole. We must first organize the data and then reduce them to a few numbers which carry the most relevant information.

2.1 *Plotting Data*

One of the simplest ways to reorganize data so as to make them more intelligible is to plot them. We will briefly discuss several common ways in which data can be represented graphically.

Frequency Distributions

Frequency distribution   As a first step we might wish to make a ***frequency distribution*** of the data. In other words we would count the number of times that each of the 11 numerical ratings was given by our subjects. A possible frequency distribution for this study is shown in Figure 2.1(a).

The distribution shown in Figure 2.1(a) is called a frequency distribution because we have plotted the possible numerical values of the data along the X axis (the abscissa) and the frequency with which each value occurred along the Y axis (the ordinate). Frequency distributions are common in the social sciences, and I cannot stress strongly enough the desirability of making such a distribution for any set of data. It is an extremely useful method of quickly grasping the general character of the data and will prove useful in evaluating the validity of certain assumptions we will require in subsequent chapters.

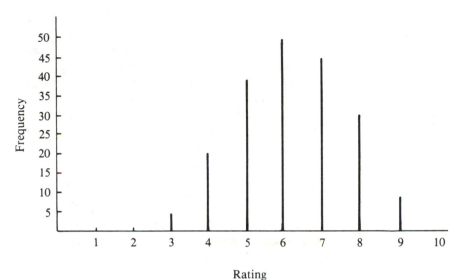

FIGURE 2.1(a)

Frequency distribution
of 200 ratings
of the pleasantness
of a picture

Histograms

Recognizing that forcing a subject to choose an integer value for his rating (he cannot, for example, give a rating of 3.68) forces him to assign a rating of 6 to any subjective value between 5.5 and 6.5, we might choose to graph the data as a series of vertical bars, the width of which represent the intervals containing the underlying subjective ratings. Such a graph is
Histogram   called a **histogram**, an example of which is presented in Figure 2.1(b).

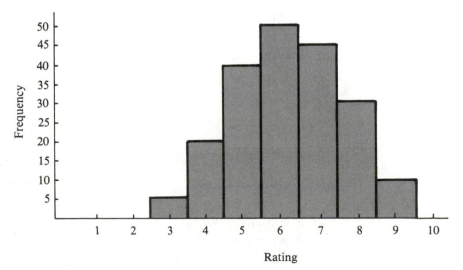

FIGURE 2.1(b)

Histogram of 200
ratings of the
pleasantness of a
picture

The histogram has one interesting feature which generalizes to other methods of plotting distributions. If we arbitrarily define the width of an interval to be one unit, then the area of any segment is equal to the number of scores falling within that interval. Furthermore, the total shaded area is equal to N, the sample size. The same general statement with appropriate changes in wording can be made about many distributions we plot. This is *Area*   the reason why we will repeatedly refer to the area under the curve—**area** and *number* (or *percentage*) *of scores* are interchangeable concepts.

Frequency Polygon

A third method of presenting a distribution would be to connect the tops of the lines in Figure 2.1(a) with a ruler. An example of this resulting *Frequency polygon*   **frequency polygon** is presented in Figure 2.1(c).

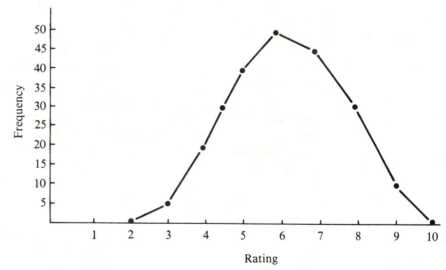

FIGURE 2.1(c)

Frequency polygon of 200 ratings of the pleasantness of a picture

Smoothed Distributions

The final method to be discussed is a simple extension of the frequency polygon. Each of the methods that we have seen so far has shown slight irregularities in the way the curves rise and fall. On the assumption that these irregularities are due to chance (i.e., are unreliable fluctuations unique to our particular sample), we might fit a smoothed curve to the data, making the curve pass as closely as possible to the points. An example of such a curve is shown in Figure 2.1(d).

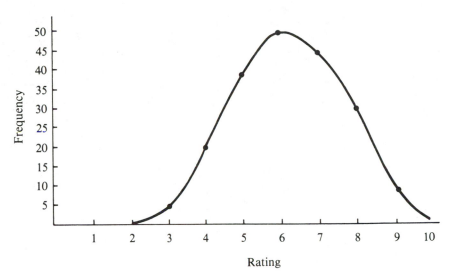

FIGURE 2.1(d)

Smoothed curve fitted
to distribution of
200 ratings of the
pleasantness of a
picture

In this particular case the curve fits extremely well, although in other cases it might represent only a rough approximation. While there are sophisticated statistical techniques for fitting curves to data, if the only purpose is to obtain a general understanding of what the data look like, fitting a curve by hand is almost always adequate.

2.2 Describing Distributions

The distribution of scores illustrated in Figures 2.1(a–d) is a more-or-less regularly shaped distribution, rising to a maximum and then dropping away again rather smoothly. Not all distributions are like this, however, and it is important to understand the terms used to describe different distributions. Consider the two hypothetical distributions shown in Figures 2.2(a) and 2.2(b). Both of these distributions are called ***symmetric*** because they have the same shape on either side of the center. Distribution 2.2(a) is what we will later refer to as the ***normal distribution***. Distribution 2.2(b) is referred to as ***bimodal***, because it has two peaks. The term *bimodal* is used to refer to any distribution which has two predominant peaks, whether or not these peaks are of exactly the same height.

Symmetric

Normal distribution
Bimodal

Next consider Figures 2.2(c) and 2.2(d). Here are two distributions which are obviously not symmetric. Distribution 2.2(c) has a tail going out to the left, while distribution 2.2(d) has a tail going out to the right. We say that 2.2(c) is ***negatively skewed*** while 2.2(d) is ***positively skewed***. Although there are statistical measures of the degree of ***skewness***, they are not commonly used in the social sciences.

Negatively skewed
Positively skewed
Skewness

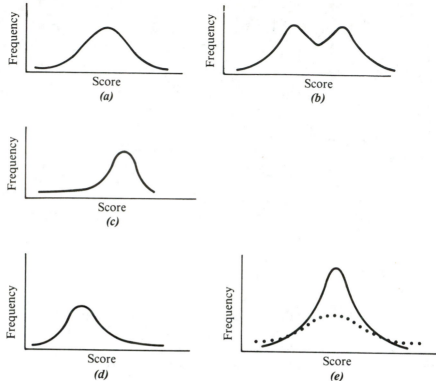

FIGURE 2.2

Shapes of frequency distributions, (*a*) normal, (*b*) bimodal, (*c*) negatively skewed, (*d*) positively skewed, (*e*) platykurtic and leptokurtic

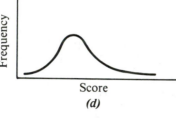

Kurtosis   The last characteristic of a distribution which we will examine is that of kurtosis. **Kurtosis** refers to the degree of *peakedness* exhibited by a distribution. Consider the two distributions represented in Figure 2.2(e). One distribution is relatively low in the tails and peaked in the center, while the other is high in the tails and relatively low in the center. The first is

Leptokurtic   called **leptokurtic** while the second is called **platykurtic**. Distributions such
Platykurtic   as the normal distribution which are neither too peaked nor too flat are
Mesokurtic   called **mesokurtic**.

Skewness and kurtosis, while not commonly used measures in the social sciences, are convenient verbal labels to be used in describing distributions, and play an important role in more mathematical treatments of statistics.

So far almost no mention has been made of the numbers themselves. We have seen how data may be organized and presented in the form of distributions, and have discussed a number of ways in which distributions can be characterized—symmetry or lack of it (skewness), kurtosis, and modality. As useful as this information might be in certain circumstances, it is very inadequate in others. We still do not know whether the subjects generally liked or disliked the picture they rated, or how much unanimity there was among subjects. To obtain this knowledge we must reduce the data to a set of measures which carry the information we need. The questions to be asked refer to location or central tendency and dispersion of the distribution along the underlying ten point scale.

2.3 Measures of Central Tendency

Measure of central tendency

The phrase *measure of central tendency*, or sometimes *measure of location*, refers to that set of measures dealing with where on the scale the distribution is centered. There are three major measures of central tendency (mode, median, and mean) and they will be discussed in turn.

The Mode

Mode

The *mode* (Mo) can be defined simply as the most common score—that score obtained from the largest number of subjects. Thus the mode is that value of X corresponding to the highest point on the distribution. In the example used in Figure 2.1, this value is 6, since more people rated the picture *6* than rated it any other value.

If two *adjacent* ratings occurred with equal (and greatest) frequency, a common convention is to take an average of the two values and call that the mode. If, on the other hand, two *nonadjacent* ratings occur with equal (and greatest) frequency, we would say that the distribution is bimodal and would most likely report both modes.

The Median

Median

The *median* (Med) is defined as the value of the middlemost score, when the data are arranged in numerical order. For example, consider the numbers (5 8 3 7 15). If these numbers were arranged in numerical order (3 5 7 8 15), the middle score would be 7 and would be called the median. Suppose, however, that there were an even number of scores—for example, (5 8 3 7 15 14). Rearranging we obtain (3 5 7 8 14 15) and there is no middle score. In this case, the average (7.5) of the two middle scores (7 and 8) is commonly taken as the median.

It might be pointed out at this time that some textbooks (e.g., Ferguson, 1966) advocate a very laborious procedure for finding the median when there are many ties in the data. The reader will be pleased to learn that that method is no better than the simpler method of taking the middle value. Furthermore, a median value obtained in the more complex way has certain undesirable properties which recommend against its use.

The Mean

Mean   The most common measure of central tendency, and one which really needs little explanation, is the *mean*, or what is generally meant by the word *average*. The mean is defined as the total of the scores divided by the number of scores, and is usually designated as $\bar{X}$ (read X bar).

$$\bar{X} = \frac{\Sigma X}{N}$$ *(2.1)*

As an illustration, the mean of the numbers 3, 5, 12, 5 is

$$(3 + 5 + 12 + 5)/4 = 25/4 = 6.25.$$

Relative Advantages and Disadvantages of Mode, Median, and Mean

Only when the distribution is symmetric will the mean and median be equal, and only when the distribution is symmetric and unimodal will all three measures be the same. In all other cases, and this includes almost all situations dealing with samples rather than populations, some choice must be made. It would be very convenient if we could have a set of rules concerning when to use one measure of central tendency rather than another. This however is not the case. If we are to make intelligent choices among the three measures it is necessary to have some idea of the strengths and weaknesses of each measure.

The mode   As we have seen, the mode is the most commonly occurring score. By definition, then, it is a score that actually occurred, whereas the mean and sometimes the median, may be values which never appear in the data. The mode also has the obvious advantage of representing the largest number of people. Consider, for example, your friendly hardware dealer who is in danger of going bankrupt. He can only stock one size of bolt, and knows from experience that he normally would sell 25 $\frac{1}{4}''$ bolts, 50 $\frac{3}{8}''$ bolts, and 70 $\frac{1}{2}''$ bolts. The mean bolt would be .41″ and he can't even get those. The median bolt would be $\frac{3}{8}''$, and if he stocked those he would sell 50. The modal bolt is $\frac{1}{2}''$ and he would sell 70 of those. If he can only have one size in stock, any reasonable hardware dealer would obviously choose the modal size.

The disadvantage of the mode is that it may not be representative of the set of numbers. This is illustrated in Figure 2.3, where the mode (9) is certainly not a representative value for the distribution.

The median   The major advantage of the median, which it shares with the mode, is the fact that it is unaffected by extreme scores. Thus the medians

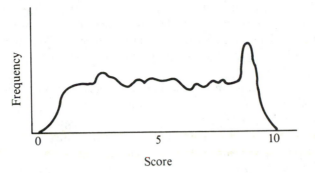

FIGURE 2.3

Illustration of
distribution in
which the
mode is not
representative of
the set of scores

of (5, 8, 9, 15, 16) and (0, 8, 9, 15, 206) are both 9. Many experimenters find this to be extremely useful in studies where abberant scores occasionally occur but have no particular significance. For example, the average trained rat can run down a short runway in somewhere around 1 to 2 seconds. Every once in a while this same rat will inexplicably stop half-way down, scratch himself, poke his nose at the photocells, and lie down to sleep. In this instance it is of no practical significance whether it takes him 30 seconds or 10 minutes to get to the other end—it may even depend on when E gives up and pokes him with a pencil (a common practice). If we ran a rat through three trials per day, and his times were (1.2, 1.3, and 20 seconds), that would have the same meaning to us as if his times were (1.2, 1.3, and 136.5 seconds). Obviously, however, his daily mean would be quite different in the two cases. It is this problem which frequently induces experimenters to work with the median time per day rather than the mean.

The median has another point in its favor, as opposed to the mean, which those writers who get excited over scales of measurement are likely to point out. The calculation of the median does not require any assumptions about the interval properties of the scale. With the numbers (5, 8, and 11), the object represented by the number 8 is in the middle, no matter how close or distant it is from objects represented by 5 and 11. When we say that the *mean* is 8, however, we may be making the implicit assumption that the underlying distance between objects 5 and 8 is the same as the underlying distance between objects 8 and 11. Whether or not this assumption is reasonable is up to the experimenter. This text will work on the principle that if it is an absurdly unreasonable assumption the experimenter will realize that and take appropriate steps. If it is not absurdly unreasonable, then its practical effect on the results will most likely be negligible. This problem of scales of measurement has already been discussed in more detail in Chapter 1.

The mean   Of the three principle measures of central tendency, the mean is by far the most common. It would not be too much of an exaggeration to say that for many people statistics is (unfortunately) nearly synonymous with the study of the mean.

As has already been pointed out, there are certain disadvantages associated with the mean. It is influenced by extreme scores, its value may not actually exist in the data, and its interpretation in terms of the underlying variable being measured requires at least some faith in the interval properties of the data.

The mean has several important advantages, however, which far outweigh its disadvantages. Probably the most important of these from an historical point of view is the fact that it is algebraically tractable. Whatever its faults, the fact that the mean can enter into algebraic equations and be manipulated accounts in large part for its widespread application. There are other very important advantages to the mean which also need to be discussed (unbiasedness and efficiency), but this discussion will be deferred until later in the chapter after we have discussed the principle of estimation.

2.4   *Measures of Dispersion*

We have discussed a number of descriptive labels to indicate the general shape of a distribution (e.g., skewness and modality) and have examined various measures for locating the center of that distribution. It is now time to consider ***measures of dispersion*** which relate to how the scores are distributed about the center of the distribution. Everyone has probably had experience with examinations where all students received approximately the same grade, and with examinations where the scores ranged from excellent to dreadful. Measures referring to the differences between these two types of situations are what we have in mind when we speak of dispersion around the median, mode, or any other point we wish. In general we will be referring specifically to dispersion around the mean.

Measures of dispersion

As an illustration, consider the two sets of the following data. Assume that we have taken two strains of five rats each and deposited them individually on the bottom of a circular box. The floor has been laid off in a grid, and we have counted the number of squares into which each rat stepped in a 30–sec. interval. We have defined this measure as an index of exploratory behavior, and are interested in whether animals in Strain X are more variable in the exploratory behavior they exhibit than animals in Strain Y. The mean level of exploratory behavior is of no interest to us, and in fact the data have been constructed with equal means.

Strain X	5	4	4	6	6
Strain Y	5	1	8	7	4

We could construct distributions of these scores to illustrate the differences between the strains. The two distributions are shown in Figure 2.4.

While it is apparent that rats of Strain Y are more variable than those of Strain X in their responses, some sort of measure is needed to reflect

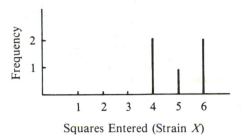

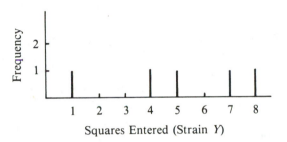

FIGURE 2.4

Distribution of scores for Strains X and Y in terms of the number of grid squares entered

this fact. There are a number of measures that could be used, and these will be discussed in turn, starting with the simplest.

Range

Range

The ***range*** is a measure of distance, namely the distance from the lowest to the highest score. For our sample data the range for Strain X is $(6-4) = 2$, and for Strain Y it is $(8-1) = 7$. The range is an exceedingly common measure and is illustrated in everyday life by such statements as *The price of hamburger ranges from* $1.29 *to* $1.99 *per pound.* The range suffers, however, by its total reliance on extreme values, or what are com-

Outliers

monly called ***outliers***. As a result it may give a very distorted picture of the variability. Another way of saying this is that the range suffers from a lack of what we will shortly term *efficiency*. This means that over repeated samples from the same population, the range itself will vary considerably from sample to sample, depending on whether very extreme scores happen to be included in that sample.

Semi-Interquartile Range

Semi-interquartile range

The ***semi-interquartile range*** represents an attempt to circumvent the lack of efficiency we have just attributed to the range. An interquartile range is obtained by discarding the upper and lower 25 percent of the distribution and taking the range of what remains. The semi-interquartile range is simply half of that difference. We cannot really calculate the semi-interquartile range for our example, since we have only five data points.

In many ways the semi-interquartile range suffers from problems which are just the opposite of those found with the range. Specifically, it discards too much of the data. If we want to know if one strain is more variable than another, it does not make sense to toss out those scores which are most extreme.

Other Range Statistics

There is nothing particularly sacred about the idea of eliminating the upper and lower 25 percent of the distribution before calculating the range. In fact we could eliminate any percentage we wished, so long as we could justify to ourselves and to others what we are doing (preferably such a decision should be made before the data are collected). Dixon & Massey (1957) present a discussion of this issue and suggest that eliminating the upper and lower 7 percent might be a very satisfactory procedure. The advantage of such an approach is that it allows elimination of those scores which we are likely to think of as accidents, without eliminating the variability which we seek to study.

The range statistics have important uses in the area of descriptive statistics, and are in fact the easiest method of conveying information about dispersion to a non–statistical audience. They are not much used in inferential statistics, however, due to the shortcomings mentioned above.

The Sum of the Deviations

Before leading everyone down the garden path to disappointment, it should be pointed out that this measure turns out to be no measure at all. It is mentioned here only to introduce the concept of a deviation, which will be used as a basis for future measures.

At first glance it would seem that if we want a measure of how scores are dispersed around the mean (i.e., deviate from the mean), then the most *Deviation* logical thing to do would be to obtain all of the **deviations** (i.e., $X_i - \bar{X}$) and sum them. The more widely the scores are dispersed, the greater the deviations, and therefore the greater the sum of the deviations—at least at first glance. Consider the data for Strain X from the previous example. These data are reproduced below along with the deviation of each score from the mean.

Data:	5	4	4	6	6	$\bar{X} = 5$
$(X_i - \bar{X}) =$	0	-1	-1	1	1	

You will observe that if you calculate the sum of these deviations $[\Sigma(X - \bar{X})]$, the sum will be zero. The deviations below the mean are balanced by deviations above the mean. In fact, one could define the mean as that value around which the sum of the deviations is zero. Since the sum of the deviations around the mean will always be zero, this measure is certainly not going to turn out to be a satisfactory measure of dispersion.

Since we have raised here the issue of a deviation $(X - \bar{X})$, it should be noted that some textbooks refer to a deviation score with a lower case letter. Thus $x = (X - \bar{X})$. This point must be kept firmly in mind by anyone who has enough sense to consult other sources when and if they fail to understand something in this one.

Mean Absolute Deviation

If you think about the problem we encountered when we tried to get something useful out of the sum of the deviations, you might well be led to suggest that we could solve the whole problem by taking the absolute values of the deviations—i.e., dropping the signs. This suggestion makes sense in light of the fact that we want to know *how much* scores deviate from the mean, without regard to whether they are above or below it. The measure just suggested here is a perfectly legitimate one, and even has a name—the

Mean absolute deviation   ***mean absolute deviation*** (m.a.d.).

$$\text{m.a.d.} = \frac{\Sigma|X - \bar{X}|}{N}. \qquad\qquad (2.2)$$

The vertical lines in Equation 2.2 indicate that we are taking the absolute deviations. The sum of the absolute deviations is divided by N (the number of scores) to yield an average (mean) deviation.

For the data from the two strains of rats, the mean absolute deviations are given as

Strain X	5	4	4	6	6	$\bar{X} = 5$
$|X - \bar{X}|$	0	1	1	1	1	$\Sigma|X - \bar{X}| = 4$

$$\text{m.a.d.} = \frac{\Sigma|X - \bar{X}|}{N} = \frac{4}{5} = .80$$

Strain Y	5	1	8	7	4	$\bar{Y} = 5$
$|Y - \bar{Y}|$	0	4	3	2	1	$\Sigma|Y - \bar{Y}| = 10$

$$\text{m.a.d.} = \frac{\Sigma|Y - \bar{Y}|}{N} = \frac{10}{5} = 2$$

For Strain X the m.a.d. $= .80$, while for Strain Y it is 2. Thus the m.a.d. reflects the differences in dispersion, being larger with greater dispersion.

For all its simplicity and intuitive appeal, the mean absolute deviation has not played an important role in statistics. Why this is so will be discussed later in this chapter, but first we need to examine two more very important measures of dispersion.

The Variance

Variance

The mean absolute deviation was an attempt to circumvent the troublesome minus signs that caused the deviations to sum to zero. The **variance** represents a different approach to the same problem. In this case we take advantage of the fact that the square of a negative number is positive. Thus

Squared deviations

we sum the **squared deviations**, rather than the deviations themselves. Since we want an average, we must next divide this sum by a function of N. For the moment take it on faith that we will divide not by N itself, but by $(N-1)$—the reason will be made clear shortly. The measure just described

s^2

is called the variance and will be denoted s^2, or, to be more specific, s_X^2, where the subscript (X in this case) indicates the variable whose variance we are measuring.

$$s_X^2 = \frac{\Sigma(X - \bar{X})^2}{N - 1}$$

(2.3)

For our example

Strain X	5	4	4	6	6	$\bar{X} = 5$
$(X - \bar{X})$	0	−1	−1	1	1	$\Sigma(X - \bar{X}) = 0$
$(X - \bar{X})^2$	0	1	1	1	1	$\Sigma(X - \bar{X})^2 = 4$

$$s_X^2 = \frac{\Sigma(X - \bar{X})^2}{N - 1} = \frac{4}{5 - 1} = 1.00$$

Strain Y	5	1	8	7	4	$\bar{Y} = 5$
$(Y - \bar{Y})$	0	−4	3	2	−1	$\Sigma(Y - \bar{Y}) = 0$
$(Y - \bar{Y})^2$	0	16	9	4	1	$\Sigma(Y - \bar{Y})^2 = 30$

$$s_X^2 = \frac{\Sigma(Y - \bar{Y})^2}{N - 1} = \frac{30}{5 - 1} = 7.50$$

From the example we see that the variances do reflect the difference in dispersion. Strain Y, which was much more dispersed than Strain X, has a variance of 7.50, whereas Strain X has a variance of 1.00.

Although the variance is an exceptionally important concept, and is one of the most commonly used statistics, it does not have the direct intuitive interpretation one would like. Since it is based on *squared* deviations, the result is in terms of squared units. Thus Strain Y has a mean of 5 units and a variance of 7.5 squared units. But squared units are awkward things to talk about. Fortunately the solution to this problem is simple—take the square root of the variance.

Standard Deviation

Standard deviation   The **standard deviation** is defined as the positive square root of the variance, and is symbolized as *s* (with a subscript identifying the variable) or, occasionally, as S.D.

$$s_X = \sqrt{\frac{\Sigma(X - \bar{X})^2}{N-1}}$$

for our example

$$s_X = \sqrt{s_X^2} = \sqrt{1.0} = 1.0$$

$$s_Y = \sqrt{s_Y^2} = \sqrt{7.5} = 2.74.$$

If you look back at what we have done, you will see that basically the standard deviation is a measure of the average of the deviations. Granted these deviations have been squared, summed, and so on, but at heart they are still deviations. Even though we have divided by $N-1$ instead of N, we have still obtained something very much like a mean or average deviation. Thus we can more or less say that subjects in Strain X deviate, on the average, 1 unit from the mean, while subjects in Strain Y deviate, on the average, 2.74 units from the mean. This rather loose way of thinking about the standard deviation goes a long way toward giving it meaning without doing serious injustice to the concept.

Just as we pointed out that the sum of the deviations around the mean is zero, so also can we point out that the sum of the *squared* deviations around the mean is a minimum. In other words **the sum of the squared deviations about the mean is less than the sum of the squared deviations about any other point**. While this statement sounds like something a statistician might mumble at night instead of counting sheep, it does have importance for us. In fact, since statisticians like quantities which are minima, this is one argument for employing the variance and standard deviation when dealing with means. Equally important, however, is the fact that the sum of the *absolute* deviations around the mean is not a minimum, which is one of the arguments against the use of the m.a.d. (To be a minimum, the sum of absolute deviations must be taken around the *median*. This suggests that if you are interested in working with medians and want a measure of dispersion, use the mean absolute deviation.)

Computational Formulae for the Variance and Standard Deviation

The previous expressions for the variance and standard deviation, while perfectly correct, are incredibly unwieldy given any reasonable amount of data. While they are excellent definitional formulae, we will now consider a more practical set of calculational formulae.

We start with the expression

$$s_X^2 = \frac{\Sigma(X - \bar{X})^2}{N - 1}$$

expanding this we get

$$s_X^2 = \Sigma(X^2 + \bar{X}^2 - 2X\bar{X})/(N - 1).$$

From the rules given for summation in Chapter 1 (page 4) we have

$$s_X^2 = (\Sigma X^2 + \Sigma\bar{X}^2 - \Sigma 2X\bar{X})/(N - 1)$$

$$= (\Sigma X^2 + N\bar{X}^2 - 2\bar{X}\Sigma X)/(N - 1).$$

Substituting $\bar{X} = \Sigma X/N$

$$s_X^2 = \left[\Sigma X^2 + \frac{N(\Sigma X)^2}{N^2} - \frac{2(\Sigma X)^2}{N}\right] \Big/ (N - 1)$$

$$s_X^2 = \frac{\Sigma X^2 - \dfrac{(\Sigma X)^2}{N}}{N - 1} \tag{2.5}$$

which is the computational formula for the variance.

You are strongly encouraged to memorize this final solution (Equation 2.5). This equation, or parts of it, will reoccur again and again throughout this book, and will crop up in the most unlikely places.

Applying this formula to our example we obtain

Strain X	5	4	4	6	6	$\Sigma X = 25$
X^2	25	16	16	36	36	$\Sigma X^2 = 129$

$$s_X^2 = \frac{\Sigma X^2 - (\Sigma X)^2/N}{N - 1} = \frac{129 - 25^2/5}{4} = \frac{129 - 125}{4} = \frac{4}{4} = 1.0$$

Strain Y	5	1	8	7	4	$\Sigma Y = 25$
Y^2	25	1	64	49	16	$\Sigma Y^2 = 155$

$$s_Y^2 = \frac{\Sigma Y^2 - (\Sigma Y^2)/N}{N - 1} = \frac{155 - 25^2/5}{4} = \frac{155 - 125}{4} = \frac{30}{4} = 7.5$$

You will note that these answers are exactly the same as the ones obtained earlier.

Calculating the standard deviation requires only that we take the square root of the variance. Thus

$$s_X = \sqrt{\frac{\Sigma X^2 - \frac{(\Sigma X)^2}{N}}{N-1}}.$$ **(2.6)**

For our data $s_X = \sqrt{1.0} = 1.0$ and $s_Y = \sqrt{7.5} = 2.74$.

The Influence of Extreme Values on the Variance and Standard Deviation

It is important to note that the variance and standard deviation are very sensitive to extreme scores. To put this differently, extreme scores play a disproportionate role in determining the variance. Consider the situation where a set of data range from roughly 0 to 10, with a mean of 5. From the definitional formula for the variance (Equation 2.3), you will see that a score of 5 (the mean) contributes nothing to the variance, since the deviation score is zero. A score of 6 contributes $1/(N-1)$ to s^2, since $(X - \bar{X})^2 = (6-5)^2 = 1$. A score of 10, however, contributes $25/(N-1)$ units to s^2, since $(10-5)^2 = 25$. Thus while 6 and 10 deviate from the mean by 1 and 5 units respectively, their contributions to the variance are 1 and 25. This is what we mean when we say that large deviations are disproportionately represented. You might keep this in mind next time you use a measuring instrument which is "OK because it is only unreliable at the extremes." It is just those extremes which may be important.

2.5 *Estimation and Ways of Describing Estimators*

Estimates
Statistics
Parameters
Population mean
Mu (μ)

Mention has already been made of the fact that we generally calculate measures such as the mean and variance for the purpose of using them as *estimates* of the corresponding measures in the populations. Characteristics of samples are called *statistics* and are designated by Roman letters (e.g., $\bar{X}$). Characteristics of populations, on the other hand, are called *parameters* and are designated by Greek letters. Thus the *population mean* is symbolized by μ (*mu*). In general, then, we use statistics as estimates of parameters.

If the purpose of obtaining a statistic is to use it as an estimator, then it should come as no surprise to find that our choice of a statistic (and even how we define it) is partly a function of how well that statistic functions as an estimator of the parameter in question. In fact the variance (s^2) is defined as it is specifically because of the advantages which accrue when s^2 is used to estimate the population variance, signified by σ^2 (sigma^2).

There are two properties of estimators that are of particular interest to statisticians and heavily influence our choice of the statistics we compute. These properties are unbiasedness and efficiency.

Unbiasedness

Expected value

Suppose that we have a population for which we somehow know the mean (μ). If we were to draw one sample from that population and calculate the sample mean ($\bar{X}_1$), we would expect that $\bar{X}_1$ would be reasonably close to μ, since it is an estimator of μ. Now suppose we draw another sample and obtain its mean ($\bar{X}_2$). (The subscript is used here to differentiate the means of successive samples.) This mean would probably also be reasonably close to μ. If we were to keep up this procedure and draw sample means *ad infinitum*, we would find that the average of the sample means would be precisely equal to μ. Thus we say that the ***expected value*** (i.e., the long range average) of the sample mean is equal to μ, the population mean. We denote this by writing $[E(\bar{X}) = \mu]$, where $E(\bar{X})$ is the expected value of $\bar{X}$. An estimator whose expected value equals the parameter to be estimated

Unbiased estimator

is called an ***unbiased estimator,*** and this is a very important property for a statistic to possess.

Efficiency

Efficiency

Estimators are also characterized in terms of what is called ***efficiency***. Suppose that our population is symmetric. In this case the values of the mean and median will be equal. Now suppose that we want to estimate the mean of this population (or, equivalently, its median). If we drew many samples and calculated their means, we would find that the means ($\bar{X}$s) clustered closely around μ. If, instead, we used sample medians as our estimators, they would cluster more loosely around μ, although the median is also an unbiased estimator in this situation, since $E(\text{Med}) = \mu$. The fact that the sample means cluster more closely around μ than do the sample medians, means that the mean is more *efficient* as an estimator (in fact it is the most efficient estimator of μ). Since the mean is more efficient than the median, this implies that for any particular sample the mean is more likely to be closer to μ (i.e., a more accurate estimate) than is the median. While it should be obvious that efficiency is a relative term (a statistic is more or less efficient than some other statistic), it is common to come across the statement that such and such a statistic is *efficient*. In this usage of the term we really mean that the statistic is more efficient than all other statistics as an estimate of the parameter in question.

The three advantages of the mean and variance (algebraic tractability, unbiasedness, and efficiency) are sufficient to guarantee them a major role in statistics. For the rest of this book these statistics will play the major role.

The Sample Variance as an Estimator of the Population Variance

The sample variance offers an excellent example of what was said in the discussion of unbiasedness. Suppose for the moment that you have in front of you data on an entire population, and want to find its variance. Since you have the entire population, the mean that you calculate from these scores will be the population mean (μ). Since you have μ you do not need

Population variance   to estimate it from the sample. The variance in this case will be the **population variance** (σ^2), and we will define it as

$$\sigma^2 = \frac{\Sigma(X - \mu)^2}{N}.$$

(2.7)

Notice that the denominator here is N, rather than $N-1$. The reason for this is that the deviations are taken around μ rather than around an estimate of μ (namely $\bar{X}$). This is the only case, some introductory texts notwithstanding, where we will use N as the denominator in calculating a variance. Whenever you have a sample rather than a population, and you almost always will, the appropriate denominator is $N-1$.

There are two ways of explaining why sample variances require $N-1$ as the denominator. The first approach deals with what has already been said about the sample variance (s^2) as an unbiased estimate of the population variance (σ^2). Assume for the moment that we had an infinite number of samples (each containing N observations) from one population, and that we knew the population variance. Suppose further that we were foolish enough to calculate sample variances as $\Sigma(X - \bar{X})^2/N$. If we took the average of these samples variances we would find

$$\text{average}\left(\frac{\Sigma(X - \bar{X})^2}{N}\right) = E\left(\frac{\Sigma(X - \bar{X})^2}{N}\right) = \frac{(N-1)\sigma^2}{N}.$$

Thus the expected value of $\Sigma(X - \bar{X})^2/N$ is not σ^2, which we hoped to estimate, but instead $\sigma^2(N-1)/N$. Thus we are estimating the wrong thing and have a biased estimate of σ^2. The above result does provide us with a basis for estimating σ^2, however.

$$E\left[\frac{\Sigma(X-\bar{X})^2}{N}\right] = \frac{\sigma^2(N-1)}{N}$$

$$E\left[\frac{\Sigma(X-\bar{X})^2}{N} \cdot \frac{N}{N-1}\right] = \sigma^2$$

$$E\left[\frac{\Sigma(X-\bar{X})^2}{N-1}\right] = \sigma^2$$

The preceding algebraic manipulations show us not only how to find an estimate of σ^2, but also that this estimate is unbiased.

2.6 *Degrees of Freedom*

Degrees of freedom

The foregoing discussion is very much like saying that we divide by $N-1$ *because it works*. While some people will find this a perfectly good answer, others will not, wishing to know why it works. The answer to that question requires a discussion of **degrees of freedom** (df). Consider that you have three numbers in front of you. The numbers are 6, 8, and 10, and their mean is 8. You are now informed that you may change any of those numbers, so long as the mean is kept constant at 8. How many numbers are you free to vary? If you say that you are free to vary all three numbers, you are wrong. If you change all three of them in some haphazard fashion, the mean almost certainly will not equal 8. Only two of the numbers can be *freely* changed if the mean is to remain constant. Suppose that you change the 6 to a 7 and the 10 to a 13. Then the remaining number is determined. It must be 4 if the mean is to be 8. If you had 50 numbers with the same instructions, only 49 would be free to vary. Thus we say that you have lost one degree of freedom to the mean.

Now let us go back to the formulae for the population and sample variances and see why we lost a degree of freedom in calculating the sample variances.

$$\sigma^2 = \frac{\Sigma(X-\mu)^2}{N} \qquad s^2 = \frac{\Sigma(X-\bar{X})^2}{N-1}$$

In the case of σ^2, μ is known and does not have to be estimated from the data. Thus no df are lost and the denominator is N. But in the case of s^2, μ is not known and must be estimated from the sample mean ($\bar{X}$). Once you have estimated μ from $\bar{X}$ you have fixed it for purposes of estimating variability. Thus you lose that degree of freedom which you lost above and have only $N-1$ df left ($N-1$ scores free to vary). We lose this one degree of freedom *whenever* we estimate a mean. It follows that the denominator (the number of scores on which your estimate is based) should reflect this restriction. For an interesting geometrical interpretation of degrees of freedom, the reader is referred to Walker (1940).

2.7 *The Effect of Linear Transformations on Data*

It is more common than one might at first suppose that there are occasions on which we wish to transform data in one way or another. For instance we may wish to convert feet into inches, inches into centimeters, Fahrenheit degrees into degrees Celsius, test grades based on 79 questions to grades based on a 100 point scale, 4–5 digit incomes into 1–2 digit incomes, and so on. Fortunately all of these transformations fall within a set of *Linear transformations* transformations called ***linear transformations***, meaning that we multiply each X by some constant (possibly 1) and add a constant (possibly 0).

$$X_{\text{new}} = bX_{\text{old}} + a$$

where a and b are our constants. An example of such a transformation is the formula for converting Celsius to Fahrenheit:

$$F = \tfrac{9}{5}(C) + 32.$$

As long as we content ourselves with linear transformations there are a set of simple rules which define the mean and variance of the observations on the new scale in terms of their means and variances on the old.

1. Adding (or subtracting) a constant to (or from) a set of data adds (or subtracts) that same constant to (or from) the mean.

    $$\bar{X}_{\text{new}} = \bar{X}_{\text{old}} \pm a\,; \text{ for } X_{\text{new}} = X_{\text{old}} \pm a$$

2. Multiplying (or dividing) a set of data by a constant multiples (or divides) the mean by the same constant.

    $$\bar{X}_{\text{new}} = b\bar{X}_{\text{old}}; \text{ for } X_{\text{new}} = bX_{\text{old}}$$
    $$\bar{X}_{\text{new}} = \bar{X}_{\text{old}}/b\,; \text{ for } X_{\text{new}} = X_{\text{old}}/b$$

3. Adding or subtracting a constant to (or from) a set of scores leaves the variance and standard deviation unchanged.

    $$s^2_{\text{new}} = s^2_{\text{old}}\,; \text{ for } X_{\text{new}} = X_{\text{old}} \pm a$$

4. Multiplying (or dividing) a set of scores by a constant multiplies (or divides) the variance by the square of the constant and the standard deviation by the constant.

    $$s^2_{\text{new}} = b^2 s^2_{\text{old}} \text{ and } s_{\text{new}} = bs_{\text{old}}; \text{ for } X_{\text{new}} = bX_{\text{old}}$$
    $$s^2_{\text{new}} = s^2_{\text{old}}/b^2 \text{ and } s_{\text{new}} = s_{\text{old}}/b\,; \text{ for } X_{\text{new}} = X_{\text{old}}/b$$

The following example illustrates these rules. In each case the constant used was 3.

Addition of a constant:

			OLD						NEW			
	Data		$\bar{X}$	s^2	s			**Data**		$\bar{X}$	s^2	s
4	8	12	8	16	4		7	11	15	11	16	4

Multiplication by a constant:

			OLD						NEW			
	Data		$\bar{X}$	s^2	s			**Data**		$\bar{X}$	s^2	s
4	8	12	8	16	4		12	24	36	24	144	12

2.8 Summary

In this chapter we have examined a number of procedures for reducing a set of data to measures which make them more interpretable. We first considered alternative methods of plotting data and saw that this gave at least a general idea of the nature of the data. We then dealt with ways of describing the shapes of the distributions which we have plotted. The three major measures of central tendency (mean, mode, and median) were introduced as indicators of the center of the distribution, and the range, variance, and standard deviation were introduced as measures of the dispersion of scores within the distribution. We then touched briefly on the fact that a statistic, which is a characteristic of a sample, is used as an estimator of a parameter, which is a characteristic of a population, and examined ways in which we could describe properties of estimators. Finally, we looked at the question of degrees of freedom and at the effect of various linear transformations on the data.

Exercises for Chapter 2

2.1 Children differ from adults in that they tend to recall stories in terms of a sequence of actions, rather than in terms of an overall plot. This means that their descriptions of a movie are filled with the phrase "and then . . .". An experimenter with supreme patience has asked 50 children to tell her what a given movie was about. Among other variables she counted the number of "and then . . ." statements. The data are given below:

$$
\begin{array}{cccccccccc}
18 & 15 & 22 & 19 & 18 & 17 & 18 & 20 & 17 & 12 \\
16 & 16 & 17 & 21 & 23 & 18 & 20 & 21 & 20 & 20 \\
15 & 18 & 17 & 19 & 20 & 23 & 22 & 10 & 17 & 19 \\
19 & 21 & 20 & 18 & 18 & 24 & 11 & 19 & 31 & 16 \\
17 & 15 & 19 & 20 & 18 & 18 & 40 & 18 & 19 & 16
\end{array}
$$

a. Plot a frequency distribution for these data.
b. Plot a histogram for the data.
c. What is the general shape of the distribution?

2.2 As part of the same study described in Exercise 2.1, the experimenter then obtained the same kind of data for adults. Their data are below:

$$
\begin{array}{cccccccccc}
10 & 12 & 5 & 8 & 13 & 10 & 12 & 8 & 7 & 11 \\
11 & 10 & 9 & 9 & 11 & 15 & 12 & 17 & 14 & 10 \\
9 & 8 & 15 & 16 & 10 & 14 & 7 & 16 & 9 & 1 \\
4 & 11 & 12 & 7 & 9 & 10 & 3 & 11 & 14 & 8 \\
12 & 5 & 10 & 9 & 7 & 11 & 14 & 10 & 15 & 9
\end{array}
$$

a. Plot a frequency distribution for these data.
b. Overlay this frequency distribution on the one from Exercise 2.1.

2.3 *a.* Calculate the mode, median and mean for the data in Exercise 2.1.
b. Plot these three measures on the frequency distribution.

2.4 *a.* Calculate the mode, median and mean for the data in Exercise 2.2.
b. Plot these three measures on the frequency distribution.

2.5 What is the range and the interquartile range for the data in Exercise 2.1?

2.6 What is the range and the interquartile range for the data in Exercise 2.2?

2.7 What are the variance and standard deviation for the data in Exercise 2.1 using the computational formulae?

2.8 What are the variance and standard deviation for the data in Exercise 2.2 using the computational formulae?

2.9 Randomly draw (close eyes and point) 10 sets of 5 scores each from the data in Exercise 2.1. Plot the frequency distribution of the means of these 10 samples as a demonstration that means of samples cluster more tightly than individual observations. (Group the means into appropriate intervals.)

2.10 Write a statement comparing the data in Exercises 2.1 and 2.2.

2.11 A manufacturer of a well-known imported car claims that his cars have excellent mileage ratings when properly tuned. Unfortunately these cars go out of tune easily.

a. Draw a hypothetical frequency distribution for a study of the mileage for several hundred of these cars.

b. What would the direction of skew be?

c. What would the manufacturer have to do to produce a symmetric distribution for these data?

2.12 What kind (shape) of a distribution would we expect to obtain if we recorded the number of cigarettes smoked per day for each of the next 200 people who came through the door?

2.13 A group of 15 rats running a straight alley maze produced the following number of trials to criterion:

Trials to criterion:	18	19	20	21	22	23	24
Number of rats (freq.):	1	0	4	3	3	3	1

a. Calculate the mean number of trials to criterion for this group.

b. Calculate the standard deviation for these data.

2.14 Given the following set of data demonstrate that subtracting a constant from every score reduces the mean by that constant.

12 8 5 9 7 3

2.15 Using the data in Exercise 2.14 demonstrate that dividing by a constant divides the variance by the square of that constant and divides the standard deviation by the constant.

2.16 The following data have a mean of 6 and a standard deviation of 2.27.

10 7 3 4 8 5 5 6

Demonstrate for future reference that if you subtract $\bar{X}$ from each score and divide each result by the standard deviation, the new distribution will have a mean of 0 and a standard deviation of 1.

2.17 Use the following MINITAB computer printout to answer Exercises 2.1, 2.3, 2.5, and 2.7. What information is missing?

```
-- HISTOGRAM FOR DATA IN C1

    MIDDLE OF      NUMBER OF
    INTERVAL       OBSERVATIONS
       8.            0
      12.            3     ***
      16.           13     *************
      20.           27     ***************************
      24.            5     *****
      28.            0
      32.            1     *
      36.            0
      40.            1     *


-- MEDIAN C1
   MEDIAN =       18.000

-- DESCRIBE C1
   C1        N =  50     MEAN =     18.900    ST.DEV. =    4.50
```

2.18   Use MINITAB to reproduce the results in Exercises 2.2, 2.4, 2.6, and 2.8.

2.19   Use SPSS to complete Exercises 2.1, 2.3, 2.5, and 2.7.

2.20   Use the following SPSS computer printout to answer Exercises 2.2, 2.4, 2.6, and 2.8. (The "Adjusted freq" column would ignore missing data if there were any.)

```
- - - - - - - - - - - - - - - - - - - - - - - - - - - - - - - -


                                      Relative  Adjusted   Cum
                             Absolute   freq      freq     freq
Category label        Code     freq    ( % )     ( % )     ( % )

                       1.       1        2.0       2.0      2.0

                       3.       1        2.0       2.0      4.0

                       4.       1        2.0       2.0      6.0

                       5.       2        4.0       4.0     10.0

                       7.       4        8.0       8.0     18.0

                       8.       4        8.0       8.0     26.0

                       9.       7       14.0      14.0     40.0

                      10.       8       16.0      16.0     56.0

                      11.       6       12.0      12.0     68.0

                      12.       5       10.0      10.0     78.0

                      13.       1        2.0       2.0     80.0

                      14.       4        8.0       8.0     88.0

                      15.       3        6.0       6.0     94.0

                      16.       2        4.0       4.0     98.0

                      17.       1        2.0       2.0    100.0
                              ------    ------    ------
                      Total    50      100.0     100.0


Mean        10.200    Std err     0.481    Median     10.125
Mode        10.000    Std dev     3.405    Variance   11.592
Kurtosis     0.286    Skewness   -0.295    Range      16.000
Minimum      1.000    Maximum    17.000

Valid cases    50     Missing cases    0


- - - - - - - - - - - - - - - - - - - - - - - - - - - - - - - -
```

3

Sampling Distributions and Hypothesis Testing

Objective

To lay the groundwork for the procedures discussed in this book by examining the general theory of hypothesis testing as it applies to all statistical tests.

Contents

In the last chapter we examined a number of *descriptive statistics* and how these might be used to describe a set of data. While description of data is important, it is not sufficient to answer many of the most interesting problems we encounter. Descriptive statistics will not tell us, for example, whether a finding that 30 percent of a sample of females and 33 percent of a sample of males prefer sugarless gum really means that more males than females in the general population prefer sugarless gum. These percentages may or may not differ merely by chance, and it is important to consider techniques for making some decision as to whether or not this difference is really a chance difference.

To take a different example suppose that a consumer research group found that on eight out of ten items sampled Store *X* charges more than Store *Y*. Can this difference be explained by normal variability in prices or does it represent a real difference between stores? In other words, would they obtain the same kind of difference if they reran the study on ten different items?

Hypothesis testing

We have just seen two examples of the kinds of questions which fall under the heading of **hypothesis testing**. This chapter is intended to present the theory of hypothesis testing in as general a way as possible, without becoming involved in the specific techniques or properties of any particular test.

The theory of hypothesis testing is so important in all that follows that a thorough understanding of it is essential. Many students who have had one or more courses in statistics and know how to run a number of different statistical tests still do not have a basic knowledge of what it is they are doing. As a result they have difficulty interpreting statistical tables and have to learn every new procedure in a step by step rote fashion. This chapter is designed as a way to avoid that difficulty by presenting the theory in its most general sense. Professional statisticians might well fuss over the looseness of the definitions, but any looseness can be set right in subsequent chapters. Others may object that we are discussing hypothesis testing before we discuss any statistical procedures. That is partly the point. The material covered here cuts across all statistical tests and can be discussed independently of them. Moreover, by separating the material in this way, the student is free to concentrate on the underlying principles without worrying about the mechanics of calculation.

3.1 *Sampling Distributions*

Sampling distribution

The most basic concept underlying all statistical tests is that of the **sampling distribution** of a statistic. It is fair to say that if we did not have sampling distributions we would not have any statistical tests. Roughly speaking, sampling distributions tell us what values we might (or might not) expect *types*

binomial

hyper geometric

poisson

normal

for a particular statistic under a set of predefined conditions. As such, they provide the opportunity to evaluate the likelihood (given a sample statistic) of whether or not such predefined conditions actually exist.

Basically the sampling distribution of a statistic can be thought of as the distribution of values obtained for that statistic over repeated sampling. Although sampling distributions are almost always derived mathematically, it is easier to understand what they represent if we consider how they could, in theory, be derived empirically.

We will take as an illustration the sampling distribution of the mean, since it is the most easily understood. The sampling distribution of the mean is nothing but the distribution of means of an infinite number of samples all drawn from some specified population. Suppose, for example, that we have a population with a known mean ($\mu = 100$). Further suppose that we draw a very large number (theoretically an infinite number) of samples from this population, each sample consisting of 10 scores. For each sample we will calculate its mean, and when we finish drawing all of our samples we will plot the distribution of these means. Such a distribution would be a sampling distribution of the mean, and might look like the one presented in Figure 3.1.

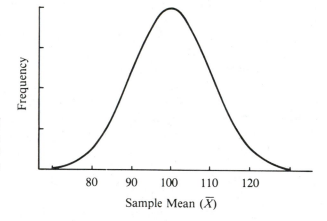

FIGURE 3.1

Distribution of sample means, each based on $n = 10$ scores

As we will see in Chapter 7, statisticians know exactly what this distribution will look like without drawing even one sample, but the actual shape is not important here. What is important is that after plotting the sampling distribution we have an excellent idea of what kinds of sample means to expect from this population. We know, for example, that if we sample 10 scores from this population, a sample mean in the neighborhood of 95 is reasonably likely (cf. Figure 3.1). We also know that it is extremely unlikely that we would draw from this population a sample of 10 observations which has a mean as low as 20, although there is some (incredibly small) probability of doing so. The fact that we now know the kinds of values we might expect for the mean of a sample drawn from this population is now going to allow us to turn the question around and ask if an obtained sample mean can be taken as evidence in favor of the hypothesis that we are actually sampling from this population.

3.2 Hypothesis Testing

We do not go around obtaining sampling distributions, either mathematically or empirically, simply because they are interesting to look at. We have important reasons in mind for doing so. The usual reason is that we want to test some hypothesis. Consider the example of an experimenter who has collected a sample of data with a mean of 60. For certain theoretical reasons she wants to test the hypothesis that this sample came from a population whose mean is 100. Logically the only way she can test such an hypothesis is to have some idea of the probability of obtaining a sample mean of 60 if she were actually sampling from a population where $\mu = 100$. The answer to this question is precisely what a sampling distribution is designed to provide. Suppose that our experimenter obtains (constructs) the sampling distribution of the mean for a population whose mean $(\mu) = 100$, and then determines that probability of a sample mean as low as 60. For the sake of argument we will say that this probability was .002. Her argument can then go as follows: "If I in fact did sample from a population with $\mu = 100$, the probability of obtaining a sample mean as low as 60 is only .002, a rather unlikely event. Since a sample mean this low is unlikely to be obtained from this population, I can reasonably conclude that this sample probably came from some other population (whose mean was not 100)."

It is important to realize just what has been done in this example, since it is typical of the logic of most tests of hypotheses. The actual test consisted of several stages.

1. Our hypothetical experimenter had a sample mean and wished to test the hypothesis that it came from a population with $\mu = 100$.

Null hypothesis 2. She set up the hypothesis (called the **null hypothesis** (H_0)) that the sample was in fact drawn from a population with $\mu = 100$.

3. She then obtained the sampling distribution of the mean under H_0 (i.e. the sampling distribution of the mean from a population with $\mu = 100$).

4. Given the sampling distribution, she calculated the probability of a mean *at least as extreme* as her actual sample mean.

5. On the basis of this probability she either rejected, or failed to reject, H_0. In the present case it was rejected. Since H_0 states that $\mu = 100$, rejection of H_0 represents a belief that $\mu \neq 100$, although the actual value of μ remains unspecified.

That discussion is oversimplified in the sense that in practice we would also need to take into account (either directly or by estimation) the value of σ^2, the population variance, and N, the sample size. However the logic of the approach is representative of the logic of most, if not all, of our statistical tests. In each case we will set up the null hypothesis, construct the sampling distribution of the particular statistic on the assumption that H_0 is true, compare our sample statistic to that distribution, and reject or retain H_0 depending upon the probability, under H_0, of a sample statistic as extreme as the one we have obtained.

Up to this point we have discussed only the sampling distribution of the mean. In fact, there is a sampling distribution for every statistic, although some of these might not be known. To work through a second example with a different statistic, consider the sampling distribution of the variance. This could be obtained either empirically or, as is done in practice, mathematically. To obtain the distribution empirically one would draw an infinite number of samples from a specified population, calculate the variance for each sample, and plot the distribution of these sample variances. In Chapter 6 we will see what this distribution would look like. To test the hypothesis that a particular sample came from a population whose variance (σ^2) is equal to some specified value, call this value σ_0^2, we would first set up the null hypothesis that $\sigma^2 = \sigma_0^2$ (or, equivalently, that $\sigma^2 - \sigma_0^2 = 0$). We would then construct the sampling distribution of the variance when the population variance is in fact $= \sigma_0^2$. Finally we would compare our sample variance with this sampling distribution, and either reject or retain H_0 depending upon the results of that comparison.

3.3   *The Null Hypothesis*

As we have seen, the concept of the null hypothesis plays a crucial role in the testing of hypotheses. Students are frequently puzzled by the fact that we begin by setting up an hypothesis that is directly counter to what we hope to show. For example, if we hope to demonstrate that college students do not come from a population with a mean IQ of 100, we immediately set up the null hypothesis that they do. Or, if we hope to show that the means (μ_1 and μ_2) of the populations from which two samples are drawn are different, we state the null hypothesis that the population means are equal (or, equivalently, $\mu_1 - \mu_2 = 0$). (The phrase *null hypothesis* is most easily seen in this second example where it refers to the hypothesis that the difference between the two population means is *null*.)

There are several reasons why we use the null hypothesis. The philosophical argument, used by Fisher when he first introduced the concept, is that we can never prove something to be true, but we can prove something to be false. Observing 3000 people with one head does not prove the statement "everyone has only one head." However finding one person with two heads does disprove the statement beyond any shadow of a doubt. While one might argue with Fisher's basic position, and many people have, the null hypothesis retains its dominant place in statistics.

A second, and more practical, reason for employing H_0 is that it provides us with a starting point for any statistical test. Consider, for example, the case where you wish to show that the mean IQ of college students is greater than 100. Suppose further that you were magnanimously granted the privilege of proving (or at least accepting) the truth of some hypothesis. What hypothesis are you going to test? Shall you test the hypothesis that $\mu = 101$, or maybe the hypothesis that $\mu = 112$, or how about $\mu = 113$? The point is that you do not have a specific hypothesis in mind, and without one you can not construct the sampling distribution you need. However, if you assume H_0: $\mu = 100$, you can immediately set about obtaining the sampling distribution given $\mu = 100$, and then, with luck, reject that hypothesis and conclude that the mean IQ of college students is greater than 100, which is what you wanted to show in the first place.

The student should be aware that there is not universal agreement on the wisdom of testing H_0, or at least with Fisher's original formulation of the problem. For a criticism of Fisher's views see the work of Neyman & Pearson (summarized in Pearson (1966)) and for a criticism of the whole concept of hypothesis testing see Edwards, Lindman, & Savage (1963), although be forewarned that these are not easy papers to read. A somewhat easier set of papers on this topic can be found in Heerman & Braskamp (1970).

Test statistics

We have been discussing the sampling distribution of two very common statistics, the mean and the variance. There are a large number of other statistics for which we know the sampling distribution, and these statistics are of a slightly different kind. They are what might be called *test statistics*, since they are associated with specific statistical tests. Examples of such statistics are chi square, t, F, and r, of which you should have at least some vague awareness from other sources. (If you don't, don't worry about it.) This is not the place to go into a detailed examination of any of these statistics or their sampling distributions. It is the place, however, to point out that their sampling distributions are obtained and used in essentially the same way as the sampling distributions of the mean and variance.

As an illustration, consider the sampling distribution of the statistic t, which will be discussed further in Chapter 7. For those who have never heard of the t test, it is sufficient to point out that it is often used to answer the question whether two samples were drawn from the same or different population(s). Let μ_1 and μ_2 represent the means of the populations from which the two samples were drawn. The null hypothesis is then the H_0: $\mu_1 = \mu_2$ (or $\mu_1 - \mu_2 = 0$). If you were extremely patient you could empirically obtain the sampling distribution of t when H_0 is true by drawing an infinite number of pairs of samples all from one population (in which case H_0 must be true because μ_1 and μ_2 are the same thing), calculating t for each pair of samples (by methods discussed in Chapter 7), and plotting the resulting values of t. The resulting distribution is the sampling distribution of t when H_0 is true. If we then had a sample of data which produced a particular value of t, we would test the null hypothesis by comparing our sample t to the sampling distribution of t obtained under the null hypothesis.

The preceding paragraph could be rewritten substituting chi square, F, r, or any other statistic in place of t, with only minor changes dealing with how the statistic is calculated. Thus we see that all sampling distributions could be obtained in basically the same way (calculate and plot an infinite number of statistics by sampling from a known population (i.e., under H_0)). Once this fact is understood, the rest of this book is merely the elaboration of methods for the calculation of the desired statistic.

If you have a sound grasp of the logic of testing hypotheses by the use of sampling distributions, the remainder of the course is relatively simple. For any new statistic to be encountered only two basic questions need to be asked. The first is *how and with what assumptions is it calculated* and the second is *what does its sampling distribution look like under H_0*. If we know the answers to these two questions, our test is accomplished by calculating the test statistic for the data at hand and comparing the statistic to the sampling distribution.

It would be misleading if you thought that the preceding paragraph implied that the remainder of the book was essentially a cookbook of recipes (formulae) and sampling distributions. It is not. There is a great deal to be learned about the assumptions underlying the use of formulae, the appropriateness of specific tests for answering specific questions, and the design of experiments which answer those questions which need to be answered. Nonetheless, a thorough understanding of sampling distributions and their use makes the rest of the material immeasurably easier to understand.

3.4 Tabled Sampling Distributions

Through this chapter we have been speaking as if we commonly obtain sampling distributions by actually calculating statistics on large numbers of samples. Fortunately, this is not the case. For all the statistics we will cover in this book the sampling distributions are either known or can be derived by very simple calculations.

At the end of the book are a large number of tables. Most of these are in fact sampling distributions, or at least the most important information to be drawn from those distributions. Although discussion of the specific attributes of each distribution will be left to the appropriate chapter, the distributions have one thing in common that should be mentioned at this point.

As we have already seen, the sampling distribution of any statistic plots *Abscissa* all possible values of that statistic on **the *abscissa* (the horizontal axis)** against *Ordinate* the probability of occurrence of those values on **the *ordinate* (the vertical axis)**. In actual practice, however, we are not interested in all of the possible values of the statistic. As you will discover in the next chapter, what we are interested in are the values which cut off specific extreme percentages (e.g., 5%, 1%, .5%, etc.) of the distribution. If we want to reject H_0 whenever our statistic lies in the extreme 5% of the distribution (as diagrammed in Figure 3.2) all that we really need to know is what point on the abscissa cuts off that extreme 5%. Either our obtained statistic is less than this value or it is greater than it, and this information is sufficient to allow us to reject or fail to reject H_0.

FIGURE 3.2

Hypothetical sampling distribution for some unspecified statistic, illustrating regions of rejection and non-rejection

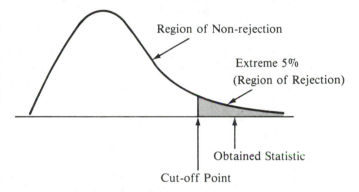

The tables in the back of the book are designed to give us the information we need. Instead of tabling the entire sampling distribution, which would be an incredibly cumbersome task, the tables give us only the critical values for certain specified percentages of the distributions. We then have only to ask if our obtained value is larger or smaller than the critical value given in the table.

3.5 Summary

The purpose of this chapter has been to examine the general theory of hypothesis testing without becoming involved in the specific calculations required to actually carry out a test. We first considered the concept of the sampling distribution of a statistic, which merely represents the distribution that the statistic in question would have if it were repeatedly computed from an infinite number of samples under certain specified conditions. The sampling distribution basically tells us what kinds of values are reasonable to expect for the statistic if the conditions under which the distribution was derived are met. We then examined the null hypothesis and the role it plays in hypothesis testing. We saw that we can test any null hypothesis by asking what the sampling distribution of the relevant statistic would look like if the null hypothesis were true, and then comparing our particular statistic to that distribution.

Exercises for Chapter 3

3.1   Suppose that I told you that last night's NHL hockey game resulted in a score of 26—13. You would probably be inclined to suspect that I had made an error and was not really reporting a hockey game score. In effect you have just tested (and rejected) a null hypothesis. Outline this hypothesis test using the logic described in this chapter.

3.2   Over the past two years a friend of mine has run five miles 150 times. He runs that course in about 35 minutes give or take a minute or two.

a.   Draw a rough sketch of what that particular distribution probably looks like.

b.   If he came in today and told me that he just ran five miles in 34 minutes should I believe him?

c.   Explain the logic involved in answering part 3.2*b*.

3.3   On the way to winning fame and fortune one of my colleagues has just invented a new test and has named it the E test. This test is designed to compare the ranges of two samples, and E is the ratio of the larger range over the smaller. Describe how he could obtain the sampling distribution of E.

3.4   In Exercise 3.3 it turns out that the sampling distribution of E depends on the number of scores in each sample for which a range is computed. My colleague only wants to reject H_0 if he has a value of E which would occur less than 5% of the time if H_0 were true. Describe what the *tabled* distribution of E might look like.

3.5   Describe how you might go about proving the hypothesis that the average weight of a grain of sand is .013862 grams.

1 tailed vs 2 tailed

Based on rejection rule; rejecting one or both ends of distribution
based on theory or idea of directiorality. 2 tail= cut α to .025.
Harder to reject HO when using 2 tailed. Extremes of distribution or
prediction of expected difference use 1 tail.

Type 1 vs Type 2

Specifiy probability of being in error. 1=α= probability of rejecting HO.
when should be retained. 2=β= probability of retaining HO when should be rejected. when raise
type 1 you lower type 2.

Null vs research hypothesis

HO = theres is no relationship between the variables or the regression=0;etc
HO is assumed true and under test. (FISHER; WKOFF) nullifiablility, can't prove a
theory). Ha= based on theory, nature of relationship of variables under study. If data
significantly different than HO, reject HO, acept HA.

Standard error vs Standard score

standard error, $\sigma_{\bar{x}}$, standard deviation of a sampling distribution of means, average variablility
about mean, standard score, Z, distance form which score differs from the mean measured in
standard deviatiations.

===

Canonical vs Discrimiinate Function

Both are regresion equations, canonical= sets of independent on sets of dependant.
Two least square composites are formed. Can.= correlation between these two. Discriminant=
dependent variables is group menbership. Used to discrimiate groups from each other based
on a set of measures. Assign indivsual to group based on score.

===

Factorial analysis vs Factor analysis

Factorial= experimental design in which every level of every variable is paired with every
other variable. Usually seperate groups recieve different treatments, takes into account
interaction. Factor= statistical technique, examines groups of independent factors to measure
extent to which they belong together and measure same construct.

F test vs T test

F test= anoua, significant effects of variables, uses MS instead of means,
sums across means; T test= difference between 2 means.

===

Between subjects vs Within subjects

Between= variance= systematic difference between groups of measures= treatment effect=.
Part of Y explained by treatment effects.= Explained.
Within= error variance= variation of measures due to chance= how each score deviates from
group mean= unexplained.

i vs Posthoc

Apriori= comparisons decided before collecting or examining data. Greater power for an effect
at any level of α Bonferroni Dunn, or orthogonal or linear comparisons, post hoc= comparisons
after examination of data and difference noted. accumulating type 1 error, loss of power
cheffe, Tukey, Newman, Keiel.

4 The Normal Distribution

Objective

To develop the concept of the normal distribution and show how it can be used to draw inferences about observations and to test simple hypotheses.

Contents

From what has been said in the preceding chapters, it is apparent that we are going to be very much concerned with distributions—distributions of data, hypothetical distributions of populations, and sampling distributions. Of all the possible forms which distributions can take, the class known as **the *normal distribution*** is by far the most important for our purposes. There are several reasons for this.

Normal distribution

1.   Many of the dependent variables with which we deal are commonly assumed to be normally distributed in the population. That is to say that we frequently assume that if we were to measure the whole population, the resulting distribution would closely resemble the normal distribution.

2.   More importantly, the sampling distributions of some important statistics tend to be normal for reasonable sample sizes. For example, we know that if we took a very large number of samples of 30 scores each from some population (of any shape), the distribution of the means of these samples would be remarkably normal.

3.   Most of the statistical procedures which we will employ have, somewhere in their derivation, an assumption of normality, either of the population from which the samples come, or of the sampling distribution of some statistic.

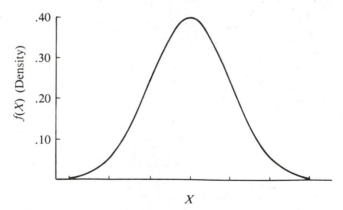

FIGURE 4.1

A characteristic normal distribution with values of X on the abscissa and density on the ordinate

The distribution shown in Figure 4.1 is a characteristic normal distribution. It is a symmetric, unimodal distribution, frequently referred to as bell shaped and has limits of $\pm\infty$. The abscissa represents different values of X while the ordinate is referred to as the ***density***, and is related to (but not the same as) the frequency or probability of occurrence of X. We use *density* on the ordinate when dealing with a continuous variable, and use *probability* or *frequency* on the ordinate when dealing with a discrete variable.

Density

4.1 The Normal Distribution Function

Mathematically, the normal distribution is defined as

$$f(X) = \frac{1}{\sigma\sqrt{2\pi}} (e)^{\frac{-(X-\mu)^2}{2\sigma^2}} , \qquad\qquad (4.1)$$

where π and e have their traditional meaning ($\pi = 3.1416$ and $e = 2.7183$). Given that μ and σ are known, the ordinate $[f(X)]$ for any value of X is obtained simply by substituting μ, σ, and X in Equation 4.1 and solving the equation. In practice one is unlikely to ever have to do this, since the distribution is tabled, but it is nice to know that it could be done.

Those of you who have had a course in calculus will realize that the area under the curve between any two values of X (say X_1 to X_2), and thus the probability of randomly drawing a score and having it fall within that interval, could be found by integrating the function over the range from X_1 to X_2. Those who have not had such a course can take comfort from the fact that tables are readily available in which this work has already been done for us—or by use of which we can easily do it ourselves.

Two-parameter function

Examination of Equation 4.1 reveals that it contains two parameters, μ and σ, and is thus what is called a ***two-parameter function***. This means that there will be a different normal distribution for each combination of μ and σ, and thus the area under the curve between any two points on the abscissa (X_1 and X_2) will depend upon the values of both parameters. Obviously this will never do as far as the people who create tables are concerned. They cannot reasonably be expected to make up a new set of tables for every pair of μ and σ that come along. And yet we can not really do much of anything unless we have the necessary tables.

4.2 The Standard Normal Distribution

Standard normal distribution

The solution to the problem of tabling the normal distribution was quite simple. What we have tabled is what is called the ***standard normal distribution*** which has a mean of 0 and a standard deviation and variance of 1. Such a distribution is often referred to as $N(0, 1)$, where N refers to the fact that it is normal, 0 is the value of μ, and 1 is the value of σ^2. Thus the more general expression is $N(\mu, \sigma^2)$. Given the standard normal distribution in the tables, and a set of rules for transforming any normal distribution to standard form, we can use the tables to find the areas under any normal distribution.

Consider the distribution shown in Figure 4.2. This is a distribution with a mean of 50 and a standard deviation of 10. It might, for example,

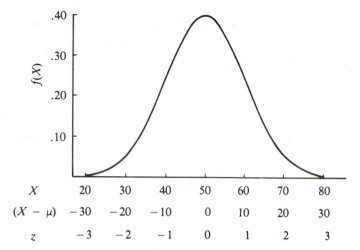

FIGURE 4.2

A normal distribution
with various
transformations on
the abscissa

represent the theoretical distribution of scores on some particular examination. Since the only tables that are readily available are those of the standard normal distribution, we must first transform the distribution in Figure 4.2 (or at least specific points along the distribution) to $N(0, 1)$. That is, we want to be able to say that a score of X_i from $N(50, 100)$ is comparable to a score of z_i from $N(0, 1)$. Then anything which is true of z_i is also true of X_i, and z and X are comparable variables.

From Chapter 2 we know that subtracting a constant from a set of scores reduces the mean by that constant. Thus if we subtract 50 (the mean) from all of our values for X, the new mean will be $50 - 50 = 0$. (More generally, the distribution of values of $(X - \mu)$ has a mean of 0.) The effect of this transformation is shown in the second set of values for the abscissa in Figure 4.2. We are half way there since we now have our mean down to zero, although the standard deviation (σ) is still 10. We also know from Chapter 2 that if we divide all values of a variable by a constant we divide the standard deviation by that constant. Therefore if we divide $(X - \mu)$ by 10, the standard deviation will now be $\frac{10}{10} = 1$, which is just what we wanted. We will call this transformed distribution z and can define it, on the basis of what we have done, as

$$z = \frac{X - \mu}{\sigma} \tag{4.2}$$

For our particular case where $\mu = 50$ and $\sigma = 10$.

$$z = \frac{X - \mu}{\sigma} = \frac{X - 50}{10}$$

The third set of values (labeled z) for the abscissa in Figure 4.2 show the effect of this transformation. Note that aside from a linear transformation of the numerical values, the data have not been changed in any way. The distribution has the same shape and the observations continue to stand in the same relation to each other as they did before the transformation.

It is important to realize exactly what converting X to z has accomplished. A score which used to be 60 is now 1. That is, a score which used to be one standard deviation (10 points) above the mean is now given a new value of 1. A score of 45, which was .5 standard deviations *below* the mean *z score* is now given the value of $-.5$, and so on. In other words, a *z score* represents the number of standard deviations X_i is above or below the mean—a positive z score being above the mean and a negative z score being below the mean.

Equation 4.2 is completely general. We can transform any distribution to a distribution of z scores simply by application of Equation 4.2. However, what must be kept in mind is that the shape of the distribution is unaffected by the transformation. That means that if the distribution was not normal before it was transformed, it will not be normal afterward. Many people who should know better still believe that they can *normalize* (in the sense of producing a normal distribution) their data by transforming them to z. "It just ain't so."

Use of the Tables of the Standard Normal Distribution

As has already been mentioned, the standard normal distribution is extensively tabled. Such a table can be found in Appendix (z).

Consider the distribution represented in Figure 4.3. Suppose that we wish to know the area above 1 standard deviation from the mean, if the total area under the curve is taken to be 1.00. We have already seen that z scores represent standard deviations from the mean, and thus we know that we want to find the area above $z = 1$. From Appendix (z) we can see that the area from the mean to $z = 1$ is .3413, that the area in the *larger portion* is .8413, and the area in the *smaller portion* is .1587. If we visualize

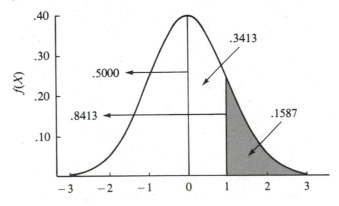

FIGURE 4.3

Illustrative areas under the normal curve

the distribution being divided into the segment below $z = 1$ and the segment above $z = 1$, the meaning of the terms *larger portion* and *smaller portion* becomes obvious, and we can see that the answer to our original question is .1587. Since we have already equated the terms area and probability, we can now say that if we sample at random from a normal population, the probability that our observation will be more than one standard deviation above the mean of the population is .1587. This last point is an illustration of why we care about areas in the first place—they lead directly to probability statements.

Now suppose that we want the probability that a score will be more than one standard deviation from the mean *in either direction*. This is a simple matter of the summation of areas. Since we know that the normal distribution is symmetric, then the area below $z = -1$ will be the same as the area above $z = +1$. This is why the table does not contain negative values of z—they are not needed. We already know that the areas in which we are interested are each .1587. Then the total area outside $z = \pm 1$ must be .1587 + .1587 = .3174.

To extend this last procedure, consider the situation in which we want to know the probability of falling between 1.3 standard deviations below the mean and 1.7 standard deviations below the mean. This situation is diagrammed in Figure 4.4.

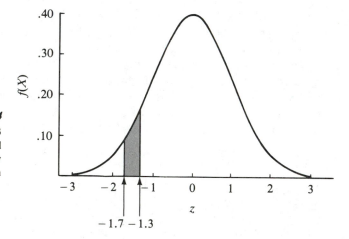

FIGURE 4.4

Area between 1.3 and 1.7 standard deviations below the mean

From Appendix (z) we know that the area from the mean to $z = -1.7$ is .4554, and from the mean to $z = -1.3$ is .4032. The difference in these two areas must represent the area between $z = -1.7$ and $z = -1.3$. This area is .4554 − .4032 = .0522. Thus the probability that an observation drawn at random from a normally distributed population will lie between 1.7 and 1.3 standard deviations below the mean is .0522.

Simple Confidence Limits on an Observation

For a final example, consider the situation in which we want to specify limits within which we have some specified degree of certainty that a given score sampled at random will fall. In other words we want to make a statement of the form "I am 95% sure that if I draw a score at random from this population it will lie between ____ and ____." From Figure 4.5 you can see the limits we want—the limits which include 95% of the scores in the population.

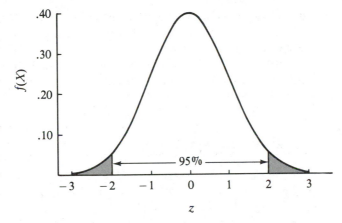

FIGURE 4.5

Values of z which enclose 95% of the scores

If we are looking for the limits within which 95% of the scores fall, we are also looking for the limits beyond which the remaining 5% of the scores fall. If we want to rule out this remaining 5%, then we want to find that value of z which cuts off 2.5% in each tail. (We would not need to use symmetric limits, but we always do.) From the appendix we see that these values are $z = \pm 1.96$. Thus we can say that we are 95% sure that a score sampled at random will fall between 1.96 standard deviations above and 1.96 standard deviations below the mean.

However if our problem requires answers in terms of raw scores rather than z scores, we have a little more work to do. To obtain the raw score limits we simply work Equation 4.2 backward, solving for X instead of z. Thus if we want to state the limits within which 95% of the population falls, we want to find those scores which are 1.96 standard deviations above or below the mean of the population. This can be written as

$$\pm z = \frac{X - \mu}{\sigma}$$

$$X - \mu = \pm z\sigma$$

$$X = \mu \pm 1.96\sigma$$

where the values of X corresponding to $\mu + 1.96\sigma$ and $\mu - 1.96\sigma$ represent the limits we seek.

If we were dealing with something like Graduate Record Examination scores, where the mean and standard deviation used to be 500 and 100, respectively, then the limits would be

$$\text{limits} = 500 \pm (1.96)(100)$$
$$= 500 \pm 196.$$

Thus the probability is .95 that a score (X) chosen at random would lie within the limits $304 \le X \le 696$.

What we have just discussed is closely related to, but not quite the same as, what we will later consider under the heading of confidence limits. The only major difference is that here we knew the population mean and were trying to estimate where X will fall. When we discuss confidence limits we will have a sample mean (or some other statistic) and will want to set confidence limits which have a .95 probability of bracketing the corresponding parameter.

Important Values of z

There are certain areas under the normal distribution which are of particular interest to us. For example, the upper 1% of the distribution is cut off by $z = 2.33$. The following list contains these particularly useful values. While it is not necessary to memorize these, it will be to your advantage to be able to recognize them for what they are when they appear again later. The value $z = 1.96$ is especially important in this regard.

z	$area > z$	$area > \pm z$
1.65	.05	.10
1.96	.025	.05
2.33	.01	.02
2.57	.005	.01

Measures Related to z

Standard scores We have already seen that z, as defined by Equation 4.2, will convert a distribution with any mean and variance to a distribution with a mean of 0 and a standard deviation (and variance) of 1. We frequently refer to such transformed scores as *standard scores*. There are, however, other transformational scoring systems with particular properties, some of which are used every day without anyone realizing what they are.

A good example of such a scoring system is the common IQ. The scores from an IQ test have already been transformed to a distribution with mean =100 and standard deviation =15 (or 16 in the case of the Binet). Knowing this, you can readily convert an individual's IQ (e.g. 120) to his position in terms of standard deviations above or below the mean (i.e. you can calculate his z score). Since IQ scores are more or less normally distributed, you can then convert z into a percentile measure by use of Appendix (z). The working of this example is left to the student.

Some other very common examples are the nationally administered examinations such as the Graduate Record Exam. In these cases the raw scores are transformed by the producers of the test and reported as coming from a distribution with a mean of 500 and a standard deviation of 100 (at least initially). Such a scoring system is very easy to devise. We start by. converting raw scores to z scores (on the basis of the raw score mean and standard deviation), we then convert the z scores to the particular scoring system we have in mind. Thus

new score = new S.D. (z) + new mean

for Graduate Record Exam: new score = $100(z) + 500$

An additional example is what we call T scores (note that T is always capitalized). T scores are nothing but a distribution of scores with a mean of 50 and a standard deviation of 10.

$$T = 10(z) + 50$$

The only real advantage of T scores (or any of the examples just mentioned) over z scores is that they seem to be more easily understood by most people. Having once given back a set of examinations with the grades reported as z scores, I will never be that foolish again. People seem to be willing to accept and more-or-less understand a T score of 40, they can even handle an exam grade of 65, but that same paper with a z score of -1 produces all manner of complaints; and yet the grades are exactly equivalent. In common statistical procedures we work almost exclusively with z. But in reporting test results to people outside of statistics we are inclined to use one of the other measures, even though the technical meaning is exactly the same.

4.3 *Using the Normal Distribution to Test Hypotheses*

One of the chief uses of the normal distribution is the testing of hypotheses. It can be used to test hypotheses both about individual observations and about sample statistics such as the mean. In this chapter we will deal with individual observations, leaving the question of testing sample statistics until later chapters.

To take a simple example, assume that we know that the mean rate of finger tapping of normal adults is 100 taps in 20 seconds, with a standard deviation of 20, and that tapping speeds are normally distributed in the population. Assume further that we know that the tapping rate is slower among patients with certain clinical abnormalities. (Actually it is the difference in rate between the two hands that is important, but the example is simpler if we speak in terms of the speed of one hand.) Finally, suppose that an individual has just been sent to us who taps at a rate of 70 taps/20 seconds. Is his score sufficiently below the mean for us to assume that he did not come from a population of clinically normal people? This situation is diagrammed in Figure 4.6, where the arrow indicates the location of our piece of data (our patient's score).

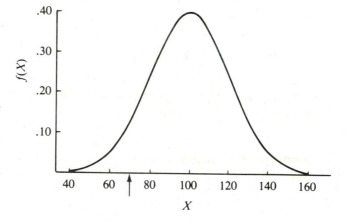

FIGURE 4.6

Location of patient's score on distribution of scores of clinically normal people

The logic of the solution to this problem is the same as the logic of hypothesis testing in general, which we discussed in Chapter 3. We will begin by assuming that the individual does come from the population of normals. This is the null hypothesis (H_0). If H_0 is true we know automatically the mean and standard deviation of the population from which he was supposedly drawn (100 and 20, respectively). With this information we are in a position to calculate the probability that a score such as his would be obtained from this population. If this probability is very low, we can reject H_0 and conclude that he did not come from the healthy population. On the other hand, if the probability is not particularly low, then the data represent a reasonable result under H_0, and we would have no reason to doubt its validity, and thus no reason to doubt that the patient is healthy.

The individual had a score of 70. What we want to know is the probability of obtaining a score *at least as low as* 70 if H_0 is true. This is something we already know how to find—it is the area below 70 in Figure

4.6. All we have to do is convert the 70 to a z score and then refer z to Appendix (z).

$$z = \frac{X - \mu}{\sigma} = \frac{70 - 100}{20} = \frac{-30}{20} = -1.5$$

From the appendix we see that the probability of a z score of -1.5 or below is .0668.

We now have to decide if an event with a probability of .0668 is sufficiently unlikely to cause us to reject H_0. Here we have to fall back on arbitrary conventions which have been established over the years. The rationale for these conventions will become clearer as we go along, but for the time being we must keep in mind that they are merely conventions. One convention suggests that we reject H_0 if the obtained probability under H_0 is less than or equal to .05 ($p \leq .05$), while another, more conservative and suggests setting the rejection level at $p \leq .01$. For the purposes of setting a standard level of rejection for this book we will use the .05 level, while keeping in mind that some people would consider this too lenient. When we come to Chapter 8 it will be more apparent why this particular level was chosen over its competitors.

For this particular situation we have obtained a probability value of .0668, which is obviously greater than .05. Since we have specified that we will not reject H_0 unless the probability of our data under H_0 is less than .05, we must conclude that we have no reason to decide that our patient did not come from a population of healthy people. More specifically, we conclude that a finger tapping rate of 70 could reasonably have come from a population of scores with mean $= 100$ and standard deviation $= 20$. It is important to note that we have not shown that our patient is healthy, but only that we have insufficient reason to believe that he is not. It may be that he is just acquiring the disease and therefore is not quite as different from normal as is usual for his condition. This is an example of how we can never say that we have proved the truth of the null hypothesis—we only know that he isn't sufficiently ill for his illness to be statistically detectable.

4.4 *Type I and Type II Errors*

Whenever we reach a decision in statistics we run the risk of that decision's being in error. While this is true of almost all decisions, statistical or otherwise, the statistician has one point in her favor that other decision-makers lack. She not only makes a decision by some rational process, but she can also specify the probability of that decision being in error. In everyday life we make decisions with only the subjective feeling that we probably made the right choice. On the other hand, the statistician can state quite precisely the probability that she erroneously rejected H_0 when in fact it was true. This ability to specify the probability of error follows directly from the logic of the test employed.

Consider the previous finger tapping example, this time ignoring the score obtained from our patient. The situation is diagrammed in Figure 4.7, where the distribution is the distribution of scores from normal subjects, and the shaded portion represents the lowest 5% of the distribution.

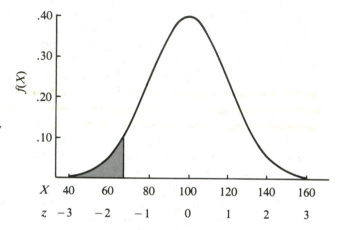

FIGURE 4.7

Lowest 5 percent of scores from clinically normal people

If we are working at the .05 level, as discussed previously, then we will reject H_0 whenever an individual's score falls in the shaded area, i.e., whenever a score as extreme as his has a probability of .05 or less of coming from the population of normals. Yet by the very nature of our procedure, 5% of the normals will themselves fall in the shaded portion. Thus if we have actually sampled a person who was normal, we stand a 5% chance of his being in the shaded tail of the distribution, causing us to erroneously reject H_0. This kind of error (rejecting a true H_0) is called a ***Type I error***, and its probability is designated as α (***alpha***), the size of the rejection region. In the future, whenever we represent a probability by α, we will be referring to the probability of a Type I error.

Type I error

Alpha (α)

You might feel that a 5% chance of making an error is too great a risk to take, and suggest that we make our criterion much more stringent—for example by rejecting only the lowest 1% of the distribution. This is a perfectly legitimate procedure, but realize that the more stringent you make your criterion, the more likely you are to make another kind of error—failing to reject H_0 when it is in fact false. This type of error is called a ***Type II error***, and its probability is symbolized by β (***beta***).

Type II error

Beta (β)

The major difficulty in terms of Type II errors stems from the fact that if H_0 is false we almost never know what the true distribution would look like for the population from which our data came. We only know the distribution of scores under H_0. Put in the present context, this is to say that we know the distribution of scores from normals, but not from non-normals. It may be that non-normals, on the average, tap considerably more slowly than normals, or it may be that, again on the average, they tap only a little more slowly than normals. This latter situation is exemplified in Figure 4.8, where the distribution labeled *NN* represents our hypothetical distribution of non-normals, while *N* represents the distribution of normals. Remember that the curve *NN* is only hypothetical, we do not really know the location of the non-normal distribution, other than that it is lower (slower speeds) than distribution *N*.

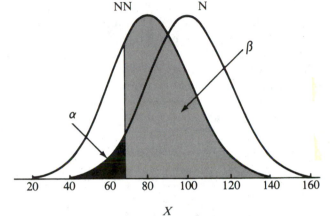

FIGURE 4.8

Areas corresponding to α and β for tapping speed example

The lightly shaded portion of Figure 4.8 represents the probability (β) of a Type II error. This is a situation in which a subject was actually drawn from the non-normal population but his score was not sufficiently low for us to reject H_0.

In this particular situation illustrated in Figure 4.8 we can in fact calculate β. The cutoff point we have set is 67, which corresponds to a z score of -1.65. The mean of the non-normals is 80, and we will assume that its standard deviation and shape are like that of the normal subjects (viz. 20 and normal). Then all we have to do is ask ourselves what percentage of a normal distribution with a mean of 80 and a standard deviation of 20 lies above a score of 67. Converting to z

$$z = \frac{X - \mu}{\sigma} = \frac{67 - 80}{20} = \frac{-13}{20} = -.65.$$

From Appendix (z) we find that the area above $z = .65$ is .7422. Thus for this example 74% of the time when we have a patient who is actually non-normal, we will make a Type II error by failing to reject H_0 when it is false.

From Figure 4.8 you can see that if we were to reduce our level of α (the probability of a Type I error) from .05 to .01, this would reduce our Type I errors, but would increase our Type II errors. Setting α as .01 would mean that $\beta = .908$. Thus you can see that there is room for debate over what level of significance to use. The decision rests primarily on your opinions concerning the relative importance of Type I and Type II errors. If it is important to avoid Type I errors (such as telling someone that he has a disease when he does not), then you would set a stringent (i.e. small) level of α. If on the other hand you want to avoid Type II errors (telling someone to go home and take an aspirin when in fact he needs immediate treatment) then you might set a fairly high level of α. (Setting α at .20 in this example would reduce β to .44.) Unfortunately, in practice most people choose an arbitrary level of alpha, such as .05, and simply ignore β. In some cases this is probably all you can do. In other cases, however, there is much more to be done, as we will see in Chapter 8.

It should be stressed again that Figure 4.8 is hypothetical. We could only draw that figure because we arbitrarily decided that non-normals were distributed as $N(80,400)$. In most everyday situations we do not know the mean and variance of the non-normals and can only make educated guesses, thus providing only crude estimates of β.

4.5   One- and Two-Tailed Tests

The previous discussion brings us to a consideration of one- and two-tailed tests. In the previous example we knew that the non-normals tapped more slowly than normals, and therefore we decided to reject H_0 only if a subject tapped too slowly. However suppose that our subject had tapped at 180 times/20 seconds. Although this is an exceedingly unlikely event to observe from a normal subject, it does not fall in our rejection region, which consists solely of low rates. As a result we find ourselves in the position of not rejecting H_0 in the face of a very unlikely piece of data.

The question then arises as to how we can protect ourselves against this type of situation (if protection is thought necessary). The answer is to specify before we run the experiment that we are going to reject a given percentage (say 5%) of the extreme outcomes, both those which are extremely high and those which are extremely low. But if we reject the lowest 5% and the highest 5%, then we would in fact reject H_0 a total of 10% of the time when it is actually true—i.e. $\alpha = .10$. However we usually do not like to work with α as high as .10, we would prefer to see it set at .05, for example. The only way around this is to reject the lowest 2.5% and the highest 2.5%, making a total of 5%.

One-tailed test   The situation in which we reject only the lowest (or only the highest) tapping speeds is referred to as a *one-tailed test*, since our rejection region is located in only one tail of the distribution. When we reject extremes in
Two-tailed test   either tail, we have what is called a *two-tailed test*. It is important to keep in mind, however, that while we gain something with a two-tailed test (the

ability to reject extreme scores in either direction), we also lose something. A score that would fall in the rejection region of a one-tailed test may not fall in the rejection region of a two-tailed test, since now we only reject 2.5% in each tail.

In the finger tapping example, the decision between a one- and a two-tailed test might seem reasonably clear cut. We know that people with a given disease tap more slowly, and therefore we only care about rejecting H_0 for slow scores—high scores having no diagnostic importance. There are many other situations, however, when we do not know which tail of the distribution is important, and need to guard against extremes in either tail. This situation might arise when we are considering a new teaching method. We might find that the new method was better than the standard method, or we might find that it was worse. In either case we want to reject H_0.

In general, two-tailed tests are far more common than one-tailed tests. There are several reasons for this. First of all, the investigator may have no idea what the data will look like and therefore has to be prepared for any eventuality. Although this situation is rare, it does arise in some exploratory work.

A common reason for preferring two-tailed tests is that the investigator is reasonably sure that the data will come out one way, but wishes to cover himself in the event that he is wrong. This type of situation arises more often than you might think. A frequent question which arises when the data may come out in the other way around is "Why not plan to run a one-tailed test and then, if the data come out the other way just change your test to a two-tailed test?" This kind of question arises from people who have no intention of being devious, but just do not understand the logic of what they are doing. If you start an experiment with the extreme 5% of the left hand tail as your rejection region, and then turn around and reject an outcome in the extreme 2.5% of the right hand tail, then you are really working at the 7.5% level. Here you have a situation where you will reject 5% of the outcomes in one direction (assuming the data fell in the expected tail) and are also willing to reject 2.5% of the outcomes in the other direction (when the data are in the unexpected direction). There is no denying that 5% + 2.5% = 7.5%. This is why the choice between a one- and a two-tailed test is made before the data are collected, and is also one reason why two-tailed tests are usually chosen.

Robustness   The last reason for using a two-tailed test concerns what is called the *robustness* of a test. You will recall, for example, that we had to assume that the distribution of finger tapping speeds was a normal distribution, since we wanted to use the tables of the standard normal distribution. The robustness of a test refers to the degree to which we can violate the assumptions of a test and yet leave the validity of the test more-or-less unaffected. A number of empirical studies have shown that the common statistical tests which we shall be considering are remarkably robust when they are run as two-tailed tests, but are not always so robust when run as one-tailed tests. Since we frequently violate assumptions to some extent in most of our procedures, we owe it to ourselves to take the more cautious route and choose to run two-tailed tests.

While the above discussion argues in favor of two-tailed tests, and while in this book we will generally confine ourselves to such procedures, no hard and fast rule can be formulated. The final decision depends upon what you already know about the experimental situation, the questions you want to answer, and the relative severity of different kinds of errors. It is important to keep in mind that with respect to a given tail of a distribution, the difference between a one- and two-tailed test is that the latter just uses a different cutoff. A two-tailed test at $\alpha = .05$ is actually more liberal than a one-tailed test at $\alpha = .01$.

4.6 Summary

This chapter has dealt with the concept of the normal distribution and what we know about the characteristics of this distribution. We saw how any normal distribution can be reduced to the standard normal distribution, and how the standard normal distribution can be used to provide answers to a number of questions. We then used the properties of the normal distribution to test simple hypotheses, a process which represents the first application of the material covered in Chapter 3. Having tested an hypothesis, we were then in a position to consider the concepts of Type I and Type II errors and one- and two-tailed tests.

Exercises for Chapter 4

4.1   Assuming that we have a distribution in which $\mu = 0$ and $\sigma^2 = 1$, use Equation 4.1 to find $f(X)$ for $X = 0$, 1, and -1. (*Hint*: recall that $X^{-1/2} = 1/\sqrt{X}$)

4.2   For those with a calculator which can deal with non-integer powers, use Equation 4.1 to find $f(X)$ for $X = 1.5, 2.5,$ and -3.5.

4.3   **a.**   Plot the following data

$$X = 1 \quad 2 \quad 2 \quad 3 \quad 3 \quad 3 \quad 4 \quad 4 \quad 4 \quad 4 \quad 5 \quad 5 \quad 5 \quad 6 \quad 6 \quad 7$$

Assume that the above data represent a population with $\mu = 4$ and $\sigma = 1.63$.
b.   Convert the distribution in Exercise 4.3a to a distribution of $X - \mu$.
c.   Convert the distribution in Exercise 4.3b to a distribution of z.

4.4   Using the distribution in Exercise 4.3, calculate z scores for $X = 2.5$, 6.2, and 9. Interpret these results.

4.5 Suppose that we want to study the errors found in the performance of a simple task. We take a large piggy bank containing somewhere around $10.00 in pennies and ask a large number of subjects to count the pennies. We find that the mean number of pennies reported is 975 with a standard deviation of 15. Assume that the distribution of counts is normal.

a. What percentage of the counts will lie between 960 and 990?
b. What percentage of the counts will lie below 975?
c. What percentage of the counts will lie below 990?

4.6 *a.* Using the example from Exercise 4.5, what two values of X (the count) would encompass the middle 50% of the results?
b. 75% of the counts would be less than ____.
c. 95% of the counts would be between ____ and ____.

4.7 The chairman of my department has just finished counting the pennies and he claims that there are only 950 pennies in the pile. What can we conclude?

4.8 A set of reading scores for 4th grade children has a mean of 25 and a standard deviation of 5. A set of scores for 9th grade children has a mean of 30 and a standard deviation of 10. Assume that the distributions are normal.

a. Draw a rough sketch of these data, putting both groups in the same figure.
b. What percentage of 4th graders score better than the average 9th grader?
c. What percentage of 9th graders score worse than the average 4th grader?

4.9 Under what conditions would the answers to Exercise 4.8 *b* and *c* be equal?

4.10 A certain diagnostic test is indicative of problems only if a child scores in the lowest 10 percent of all those taking the test. If the mean score is 150 with a standard deviation of 30, what would the diagnostically meaningful cutoff be?

4.11 A dean must distribute salary raises for next year. He has decided that the mean raise is to be $1500, the standard deviation of raises is to be $300, and that the distribution is normal.

a. 10% of the faculty will have a raise equal to or greater than $____.
b. The 5% of the faculty who do nothing useful will receive no more than $____ each.

4.12 We have sent everyone in a large Introductory Psychology course out to check whether people use seatbelts. They have each been told to look at 100 cars and count the number of people wearing seatbelts. The number found by any given student is considered that student's score. The mean score for the class is 40 with a standard deviation of 7.

a. Diagram this distribution.

b. Our laziest student reported finding 20 users (out of 100). What can we conclude?

4.13   A friend has just produced a diagnostic test of language problems. To obtain a score for her scale you simply count the number of constructions (e.g., plural, negative, passive) which the student produces correctly in response to specific prompts from the person administering the test. Unfortunately the test has a mean of 48 and a standard deviation of 7. Parents have trouble understanding the meaning of a score on this scale, and my friend wants to convert the scores to a mean of 80 and a standard deviation of 10 (to make them more like the kinds of grades parents are used to). How should she go about this task?

4.14   Unfortunately the whole world is not built upon the principle of a normal distribution. In the preceding example the real distribution is badly skewed because most children do not have language problems and therefore produce all constructions correctly.

a. Diagram what this distribution might look like.

b. How would you go about finding the cutoff for the bottom 10% if the distribution is not normal?

4.15   Grant me the assertion that of all students who study for an exam in Statistics 182 the mean grade is 85 with a standard deviation of 5.

a. If I want to work at the 5% (one-tailed) level, what is the cutoff for deciding that a particular student did not study.

b. Describe what a Type I error would mean in this situation.

4.16   I have a diagnostic test of mental development which I give to all students. I declare anyone scoring in the bottom 5% to be "mentally undeveloped."

a. Does the notion of a Type I error apply here?

b. How would the answer to part *a* of this question differ from the answer to part *b* of Exercise 4.15?

4.17   Go back to Exercises 2.1 and 2.2 for Chapter 2.

a. For purposes of this question, declare the variance of those distributions to be the average of their separate variances. What is this value and that of the corresponding standard deviations?

b. Plot the two distributions on the same figure in schematic form.

c. Assume that we are testing the null hypothesis that a given score came from a child and are using a one-tailed test. Indicate on this figure the areas for α and β.

4.18 For the data in Exercise 4.17

a. What is the magnitude of β for $\alpha = .05$?
b. What is the magnitude of β for $\alpha = .01$?

4.19 What would the answers to Exercise 4.18 be if we were using a two-tailed test?

4.20 Suppose that I could magically shrink the standard deviations of the two distributions referred to in Exercise 4.17. What would be the effect on α and β?

main effects v interaction

In factorial analysis of variance main= effects of variables taken individually , eg, dif. gp1 vs gp2. Interaction= 2 groups behave different under different levels of variable. Gp1 and G2 differ under treatments 1 ,2 ,3 ,.

==

Multicolinearity

Independent variables are highly correlated, means beta values unstable from sample to sample the R^2 may change little. Closer determinant = 0, greater collinearity=greater redundancy in data=impresise stimate of regression coeffiecient.

Inverse v Transpose of Matrix

cannot use standard mathematical procedures with matrices, therefore to divide one must use an inverse definition given A and B, 2 square matrices, if AB=i, thene i= identity matrix then A= inverse of B. Transpose is found by exchanging rows and columsn and is written A'.

Statistical Test of Significance Versus Measure of Association

test of sig = whether obtained statistical was achieved by chance or departure is extreme enough to be significant. Measure of assoc. = variables are sorted on basis of membership in group. Different numbers are nominal, might see an association between variables.

==

Beta coefficient Y b

Y= A+ $B_2 x_2$..+ e;. B= for 1 unit of increase in x, y will increase that amount, weighting for x's, observed slope, estimates B with estimated standard error=S_b=Sy .x /$\sqrt{Sxy}$. In order to assess relative contributions to the equation, standardize b's which= beta, Beta= hypothetical slope value.

==

Regression vs Residual

M Regression= how well a set of x variables will predict a value of Y=. how will points cluster around regresion line. Residual =% of deviation of cluster= error= y-Y= observed expected.

==

Covariance vs Variance

Covariance =% to which 2 variables values vary together. variance= % to which values of 1 variable varies among themselves.

==

In the first four chapters of this book the word *probability* has been used repeatedly. In fact probability theory forms the basis for all statistical procedures. While this chapter will not deal with probability theory in depth, it is important that we cover a few of the major topics in this area. We need to have a definition of what is meant by the word *probability*, we need to know something about the basic laws and terminology of probability, and we need to have some idea about the ways in which probabilities can be used to answer the kinds of questions we are likely to be called on to answer.

5.1 Probability

Probability

Analytic

The concept of **probability** can be viewed in several different ways and there is not even general agreement as to what we mean by the word *probability*. The oldest and most common definition of a probability is what is called the **analytic** view. I have a bag of caramels hidden in the drawer of my desk. (It is hidden because my colleagues are not to be trusted.) This bag contains 85 of the light caramels which I like and 15 of the dark ones which I save for candy-grubbing colleagues. Being hungry, I reach into the bag and grab a caramel at random. What is the probability that I will pull out a light colored caramel? Since 85 out of 100 caramels are light and since I am sampling at random, the probability (p) of drawing a light caramel is $85/100 = .85$. This example illustrates a definition of probability. If an event can occur in A ways and fail to occur in B ways, and if all possible ways are equally likely, then the probability of its occurrence is $A/(A+B)$, and the probability of its failing to occur is $B/(A+B)$. Since there were 85 ways of drawing a light caramel (one for each of the 85 light caramels) and 15 ways of selecting a dark caramel, $A = 85$, $B = 15$, and $p(A) = 85/(85+15) = 0.85$.

Relative frequency

An alternative view of probability is the **relative frequency** approach. Suppose that we keep drawing caramels from this bag, noting the color on each draw. In conducting this sampling study we sample with replacement, meaning that each caramel is replaced before the next one is drawn. If we made a very large number of draws we would find that (approximately) 85% of the draws would result in a light caramel. Thus we might define probability as the limit of the relative frequency of *light* which we approach as the number of draws increases.

Subjective

There is yet a third concept of probability which is advocated by a large number of theorists, and that is the **subjective** approach. By this definition probability represents an individual's subjective belief in the likelihood of the occurrence of an event. Thus, for example, the statement "I think that tomorrow will be a good day" is a subjective statement of degree of belief which probably has very little to do with the long-range relative frequency of occurrence of good days, and in fact may have no mathematical basis whatsoever. This is not to say, however, that such a view of probability has no legitimate claim for our attention. Subjective probabilities play an extremely important role in human decision making and govern all aspects of our behavior. At the same time, statistical decisions can generally be stated with respect to more mathematical approaches, although even here the interpretation of these probabilities has a strong subjective component.

While the particular definition of probability which you or I prefer may be important to each of us, any of the definitions will lead to essentially the same result in terms of hypothesis testing (although those who favor subjective probabilities may not agree with the general hypothesis testing orientation). In actual fact most people use the different approaches interchangeably. When we say that the probability of losing at Russian roulette is $\frac{1}{6}$, we are referring to the fact that one of the gun's six cylinders has a bullet in it. When we buy a particular car because *Consumers' Report* said that it has a good repair record, we are responding to the fact that a high proportion of these cars have been *successes*. When we say that the probability of the Yankees winning the pennant is high, we are stating our subjective belief in the likelihood of that event. But when we reject a null hypothesis because the probability is very low that the data would have been obtained if the null had been true, it is not important which view of probability we hold.

5.2 *Basic Terminology and Rules*

Event   The basic bit of data for a probability theorist is what is termed an ***event***. When we speak of something as simple as flipping a coin, the event is the outcome of that flip—either a head or a tail. When we draw caramels out of a bag, the possible events are light and dark.

Independent events   Two events are said to be ***independent*** when the occurrence (or non-occurrence) of one event has no effect on the occurrence or non-occurrence of the other. Thus the voting behavior of two randomly chosen subjects would normally be assumed to be independent, especially with a secret ballot, since how one person votes could not be expected to influence how the other will vote. However, the voting behavior of two members of the same family would probably not be independent events, since those people share many of the same beliefs and attitudes.

Mutually exclusive   Two events are said to be ***mutually exclusive*** if the occurrence of one event precludes the occurrence of the other. Thus the two possible outcomes of flipping a coin (head and tail) are mutually exclusive because it could not come up both heads and tails in the same toss. Finally a set of events is said *Exhaustive*   to be ***exhaustive*** if they include all possible outcomes. Thus on a true-false test item the outcomes True and False are mutually exclusive and exhaustive because you must give one response or the other (exhaustive) and can not give both (mutually exclusive).

Joint and Conditional Probabilities

Joint probability

It is important to define two types of probabilities which will be referred to in subsequent sections of this book and which play an important role in statistical analyses. These are joint probabilities and conditional probabilities. A *joint probability* is defined simply as the probability of the simultaneous occurrence of two or more events. For example, the probability that you and I are both over six feet tall is a joint probability. Similarly, the probability that the next six people to enter a theater are all wearing brown shoes is also a joint probability. Given two events *A* and *B*, their joint probability is denoted $p(A, B)$.

Conditional probability

A *conditional probability* is the probability that one event will occur *given* that some other event has occurred. The probability that you will have an automobile accident given that you are drunk is an example of a conditional probability. The probability of the Yankees winning the World Series given that they win the pennant is another. With two events, *A* and *B*, the conditional probability of *A* given *B* is denoted $p(A|B)$.

It is important not to confuse joint and conditional probabilities. The probability that you have one child who is three and one who is six is a joint probability. On the other hand the probability that you have a six year old *given* that you have a three year old is a conditional probability. In this case the conditional probability is probably higher than the joint probability, because if you have a three year old you are at least in the right age group to also have a six year old.

Basic Laws of Probability

There are two very important theorems of probability which are central to the discussion of what follows. These are what are often referred to as the additive and multiplicative rules.

Additive law of probability

The additive rule To illustrate the additive rule we will complicate the previous example by eating some of the light caramels and replacing them with wooden cubes. We now have 30 light caramels, 15 dark caramels, and 55 rather tasteless wooden cubes. Given these frequencies, we know that $p(\text{light}) = 30/100 = .30$, $p(\text{dark}) = 15/100 = .15$, and $p(\text{wooden}) = 55/100 = .55$. But what is the probability that I will draw a caramel, either light *or* dark, rather than a wooden cube? Here we need the **additive law of probability**:

> Given a set of mutually exclusive events, the probability of occurrence of one event or another is equal to the sum of their separate probabilities.

Thus $p(\text{light or dark}) = p(\text{light}) + p(\text{dark}) = .30 + .15 = .45$. Notice that we have imposed the restriction that the events must be mutually exclusive, meaning that the occurrence of one event precludes the occurrence of the other. About one half of the population of this country are female and about one half of the population have traditionally feminine names. But the probability that a person chosen at random will be female *or* will have a feminine name is obviously not $.50 + .50 = 1.00$. The two events are not mutually exclusive.

The multiplicative rule   Now suppose that we go back to the original bag of caramels when $p(\text{light}) = .85$ and $p(\text{dark}) = .15$. Suppose that I draw two caramels, replacing the first before drawing the second. What is the probability that I will draw a light one the first time *and* a light one the second? Here we need to invoke the *multiplicative law of probability*:

Multiplicative law of probability

==The probability of the joint occurrence of two or more independent events is the product of their individual probabilities.==

Thus $p(\text{light, light}) = p(\text{light}) \times p(\text{light}) = .85 \times .85 = .7225$.   Similarly   the probability of a light caramel followed by a dark one is $p(\text{light, dark}) = p(\text{light}) \times p(\text{dark}) = .85 \times .15 = .1275$. Notice that we have restricted ourselves to independent events, meaning that the occurrence of one event has no effect on the occurrence or non-occurrence of the other. Because of the fact that sex and name are not independent it is *in*correct to state that $p(\text{female with feminine name}) = .50 \times .50 = .25$.

Finally, we can take a simple example which illustrates both the additive and the multiplicative laws. What is the probability that over two trials (with replacement) I will draw one light caramel and one dark one, ignoring the order in which they are drawn? First we use the multiplicative rule to calculate

$p(\text{light, dark}) = .85 \times .15 = .1275$

$p(\text{dark, light}) = .15 \times .85 = .1275.$

Since these two outcomes satisfy our requirement (and since they are the only ones which do), we now need to know the probability that one or the other of these outcomes will occur. Here we apply the additive rule

$p(\text{light, dark}) + p(\text{dark, light}) = .1275 + .1275 = .2550$

Thus the probability of obtaining one caramel of each color on two draws is .2550.

Permutations and Combinations

The special branch of mathematics dealing with the number of ways in which objects can be put together (e.g., the number of different ways of forming a 3 person committee with 5 people available) is known as

Combinatorics   **combinatorics**. While there are not many instances in this book when we need a knowledge of combinatorics, there are enough of them to make it necessary to define very briefly the concepts of permutations and combinations and to give formulae for their calculation.

Permutations   Suppose that we are designing an experiment using slides as stimuli, and we are concerned that the order of presentation of the slides is important. Given that we have six slides, how many different ways can *Permutations*   these be arranged? This is a question of *permutations,* and we want to know the permutations of six slides taken six at a time. Alternatively, suppose that we have six slides, but any given subject is only going to see four of them. Now how many orders can be used? This is a question about the permutations of six slides taken four at a time.

The calculation of permutations is rather straightforward although the arithmetic can become laborious. The number of permutations of N things taken X at a time is

$$p_X^N = \frac{N!}{(N-X)!}$$ **(5.1)**

N Factorial   where the symbol $N!$ is read N **factorial** and represents the product of all integers from N to 1. (In other words, $N! = N(N-1)(N-2)\ldots(1)$.) By definition, $0! = 1$. For our first problem in which subjects are presented with all six slides we have

$$p_6^6 = \frac{6!}{(6-6)!} = \frac{6!}{0!} = \frac{6 \cdot 5 \cdot 4 \cdot 3 \cdot 2 \cdot 1}{1} = 720,$$

and thus there are 720 different ways of arranging six slides. For our second problem where we have six slides but only show four to any one subject, we have

$$p_4^6 = \frac{6!}{(6-4)!} = \frac{6!}{2!} = \frac{6 \cdot 5 \cdot 4 \cdot 3 \cdot \cancel{2} \cdot \cancel{1}}{\cancel{2} \cdot \cancel{1}} = 360.$$

If we want to present all possible arrangements to each subject we would need 360 trials, a result which may be sufficiently large to lead us to modify our design.

Combinations   When we were dealing with permutations we worried about the way in which each set of slides was arranged; that is, we worried about all possible orders of arrangements. Suppose that we no longer care about the order of the slides within sets, but we need to know how many different sets of slides we could form if we had six slides but took only four *Combinations*   at a time. This is a question of *combinations*. The combinations of N things taken X at a time is given by

$$C_X^N = \frac{N!}{X!(N-X)!}.$$ **(5.2)**

Thus for six slides taken four at a time we have

$$C_4^6 = \frac{6!}{4!(6-4)!} = \frac{\overset{3}{\cancel{6}} \cdot 5 \cdot \cancel{4} \cdot \cancel{3} \cdot \cancel{2} \cdot \cancel{1}}{\cancel{4} \cdot \cancel{3} \cdot \cancel{2} \cdot \cancel{1} \cdot 2 \cdot 1} = 15.$$

If we wanted every subject to get a different set of four slides, but did not care about the order within a set, we would need 15 subjects.

5.3   *The Binomial Distribution*

We now have all of the information on probabilities and combinations that we need for understanding one of the most common probability distribu-

Binomial distribution   tions—the **binomial distribution**. This distribution will be discussed very briefly, and we will see how it can be used to test simple hypotheses.

The binomial distribution deals with the situation in which each of a number of independent trials results in one of two mutually exclusive

Bernoulli trial   outcomes. (Such a trial is called a **Bernoulli trial** after a famous mathematician of the same name.) The most common example of a Bernoulli trial is flipping a coin, and the binomial distribution could be used to give us the probability of, for example, 3 heads out of 5 tosses of a coin. The binomial distribution is an example of a discrete, rather than a continuous, distribution, since one can flip coins and obtain 3 heads or 4 heads, but not 3.897 heads, for example.

Mathematically, the binomial distribution is defined as:

$$p(X) = C_X^N p^X q^{(N-X)} = \frac{N!}{X!(N-X)!} p^X q^{(N-X)}, \tag{5.3}$$

where

$p(X)$ = the probability of X successes

N = the number of trials

p = the probability of a success on any one trial

$q = (1-p)$ = the probability of a failure on any one trial

C_X^N = the number of combinations of N things taken X at a time

Success   The words **success** and **failure** are used as arbitrary labels for the two
Failure   alternative outcomes. We will require that the trials be independent of one another, meaning that the result of trial$_i$ has no influence on trial$_j$.

To illustrate the application of Equation 5.3, assume that we wish to know the probability of 9 (X) heads out of 10 (N) flips of a coin. If we assume that the coin is fair, then p = probability of a head on any one toss = .50, and q = probability of a tail = .50. From Equation 5.3 we have

$$p(X) = \frac{N!}{X!(N-X)!} p^X q^{(N-X)}$$

$$p(9) = \frac{10!}{9!1!}(.50^9)(.50^1)$$

$$10! = 10 \cdot 9 \cdot 8 \cdots 2 \cdot 1 = 10 \cdot 9!$$

$$p(9) = \frac{10 \cdot 9!}{9!1!}(.50^9)(.50^1)$$

$$= 10(.001953)(.50) = .0098.$$

Thus the probability of obtaining 9 heads out of 10 tosses with a fair coin is rather remote, occurring approximately one time out of every one hundred tosses.

This simple example actually incorporates what you have already learned about joint probabilities, additive and multiplicative laws, and combinations (conditional probabilities and permutations are not involved in the binomial distribution). We are concerned with the probability of obtaining 9 heads (and 1 tail) out of 10 flips of a coin. One outcome which satisfies our criterion would be 9 heads followed by 1 tail, and the probability of this particular outcome is the *joint probability*

$$p(H, H, H, H, H, H, H, H, H, T) = (.50^9)(.50^1) = p^X q^{(N-X)}.$$

This illustrates the application of the multiplicative law. However, there are a number of other outcomes which include exactly 9 heads (e.g., *H, H, H, H, H, H, H, H, T, H*) and the additive law tells us that we can sum the probabilities of each of these to obtain the total probability of 9 heads and 1 tail. But instead of enumerating all possible 9–1 splits, calculating their probabilities (which will be $p^X q^{(N-X)}$ in each case), and summing; it is easier to calculate how many ways we could select 9 heads out of 10 tosses, and multiply $p^X q^{(N-X)}$ by that number. This is where the formula for combinations comes in, because we really want to know the number of combinations of 10 things taken 9 at a time without regard to the order of those 9 things. This value is $C_X^N = C_9^{10} = 10$, and thus our final answer is

$$(C_9^{10})(p^9 q^1) = \frac{10!}{9!1!}(.5^9)(.5^1) = 10(.00098) = .0098.$$

As a second example the probability of 6 heads out of 10 tosses is the probability of any one such outcome $(p^6 q^4)$ times the number of possible 6–4 outcomes (C_6^{10}). Thus

$$p(6) = \frac{N!}{X!(N-X)!}p^X q^{(N-X)} = \frac{10!}{6!4!}(.5^6)(.5^4) = \frac{10 \cdot 9 \cdot 8 \cdot 7 \cdot 6!}{6! \, 4 \cdot 3 \cdot 2 \cdot 1}(.5^{10})$$

$$= \frac{5040}{24}(.000976)$$

$$= .2051$$

Plotting Binomial Distributions

You will notice that the probability of 6 heads is greater than the probability of 9 heads. This is what we would expect since we are assuming a fair coin which should come up heads about as often as it comes up tails. If we were to calculate the probabilities for each outcome between 0 and 10 heads out of 10, we would find the results shown in Table 5.1. You will observe from this table that the sum of those probabilities is 1.00, within rounding error, reflecting the fact that all possible outcomes have been considered.

TABLE 5.1

Binomial Distribution for $p = .50$, $N = 10$

NUMBER OF HEADS	PROBABILITY
0	.001
1	.010
2	.044
3	.117
4	.205
5	.246
6	.205
7	.117
8	.044
9	.010
10	.001
	.998

Now that we have calculated the probabilities of the individual outcomes, we could plot the distribution of the above results, as has been done in Figure 5.1. While this distribution resembles many of the distributions we have seen, it differs from them in two important ways. First you will note that the ordinate has been labeled *probability* instead of *frequency*. This is because Figure 5.1 is not a frequency distribution at all, but rather a probability distribution. The distinction is rather important. With frequency distributions we were plotting the obtained outcomes of some experiment—i.e., we were plotting real data. Here we are not plotting real data, but instead we are plotting the probability that some event or another will occur.

The fact that the ordinate represents probabilities instead of densities as in the normal distribution reflects the fact that the binomial distribution deals with discrete rather than continuous outcomes. With a continuous distribution such as the normal distribution, the probability of any specified individual outcome is near zero. With such distributions we must speak of the probability of falling with a particular interval. For example, we do not really expect to sample at random and find a person who is exactly 5.75382

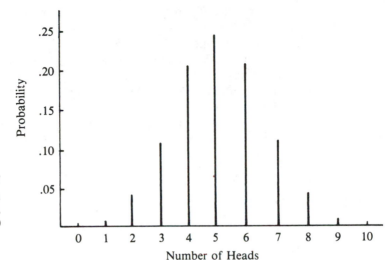

FIGURE 5.1

Binomial distribution
when $N = 10$,
and $p = .50$

feet tall (although the mean height of American males is somewhere around $5\frac{3}{4}$ feet). With a discrete distribution, however, the data fall into one or another of relatively few categories, and probabilities for individual events can easily be obtained. In other words, with discrete distributions we deal with the probability of individual events, whereas with continuous distributions we deal with the probability of intervals of events.

The second way in which this distribution differs from many of the distributions we have discussed is that although it is a sampling distribution, it is one obtained mathematically rather than empirically. The values on the abscissa represent statistics (the number of heads obtained in a given experiment) rather than individual observations or events. We have already discussed sampling distributions in Chapter 3, and what we said there applies directly to what we will consider in this chapter.

The Mean and Variance of a Binomial Distribution

In Chapter 2 we saw that it is possible to describe a distribution in many ways—we can discuss its mean, its standard deviation, its skewness, and so on. From Figure 5.1 we can see the distribution for the outcomes of a fair coin is symmetric. This will always be the case when $p = q = .50$, but not for other values of p and q. Furthermore the mean and standard deviation of the distribution are very easily calculated.

$$\text{mean} = Np \tag{5.4}$$

$$\text{var.} = Npq \tag{5.5}$$

$$\text{S.D.} = \sqrt{Npq} \tag{5.6}$$

For example Figure 5.1 shows the binomial distribution for $N = 10$ and $p = .50$. The mean of this distribution is $10(.5) = 5$ and the standard deviation is $\sqrt{10(.5)(.5)} = \sqrt{2.5} = 1.58$.

We will see shortly that being able to specify the mean and standard deviation of any binomial distribution is exceptionally useful when it comes to testing hypotheses. Before that, however, it is necessary to point out two more considerations.

In the previous examples we dealt with a fair coin where $p = q = .50$. Had we chosen to use a drastically biased coin (if such things are not figments of some probability theorist's imagination), the arithmetic would have been the same but the results would have been different. For purposes of

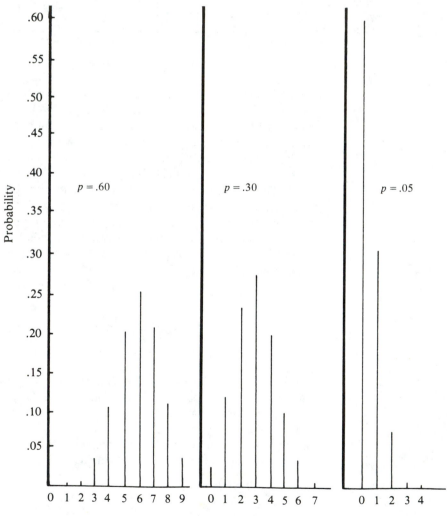

FIGURE 5.2

Binomial distributions for $N = 10$ and $p = .60$, .30, and .05

illustration, three distributions obtained with different values of p are plotted in Figure 5.2. Here you can see that for a given number of trials as p and q depart more and more from .50, the distributions become more and more skewed, although the mean and standard deviation are still Np and $\sqrt{Npq}$, respectively. Moreover, it is important to point out that as the number of trials increases the distribution approaches normal, regardless of p and q. As a rule of thumb as long as both Np and Nq are greater than about 5, the distribution is sufficiently normal for most purposes.

5.4 *Using the Binomial Distribution to Test Hypotheses*

Many of the situations for which the binomial distribution is useful in testing hypotheses are handled equally well by the Chi-square test discussed in the next chapter. For that reason this discussion will be limited to those cases where the binomial distribution has a unique contribution to make.

In downhill skiing the difference between the winner and the runner up is often a matter of a few hundredths of a second, and it is hard to believe that the fact that one person came in ahead of another by that small difference really means that the first is a better skier. But suppose that in the course of a season Sam and Ed are both entered in the same six races and Sam came in ahead of Ed in all six. What is the probability of this result if in fact the two skiers are really equal in ability and the true probability of Sam winning on any race is .50? The statement $p = .50$ represents the null hypothesis in this case. If we consider each race as an independent event then we can use the binomial to calculate the probability of six wins out of six for Sam given that the null hypothesis is true and $p = .50$. Letting X represent the event "Sam wins",

$$p(6) = C_6^6 p^6 q^0$$

$$= \frac{6!}{6!0!}(.5^6)(.5^0) = 1(.015625)(1)$$

$$= .016.$$

Thus the probability of Sam winning 6 out of 6 races *if H_0 is true* ($p = .50$) is only .016. If we consider this probability to be too small for us to maintain our belief in H_0, then we will reject H_0. But how do we define the phrase *too small*? In Chapter 4 we discussed this problem and resolved it by setting arbitrary cutoffs such as $p < .05$ or $p < .01$. This is what we will do here, and for the sake of uniformity we will choose to work at the 5 percent level. Thus whenever the data have a probability of occurrence of less than .05 when H_0 is true, we will reject H_0 in favor of the alternative hypothesis (H_1). Thus since the probability of 6 wins out of 6 races (with H_0 true) is less than .05, we will reject H_0 and conclude that Sam is really a better skier.

As a second example, suppose that the results had come out differently and Sam had won 5 out of 6 races. Here we have to ask about the probability that Sam would win *at least* 5 races if H_0 is true, and this is the probability of 5 wins plus the probability of six wins. Thus we need the sum of $p(5)$ and $p(6)$.

$$p(5) = C_5^6 (.5^5)(.5^1)$$

$$= \frac{6!}{5!1!}(.03125)(.5) = 6(.015625)$$

$$= .094$$

$p(6) = .016$ (from the previous problem)

The probability of *at least* 5 wins $= .094 + .016 = .110$. Since this probability exceeds our cutoff of .05, we will not reject H_0. We do not have sufficient data to conclude that Sam is a better skier. Put another way, the data are not inconsistent with the belief that the two skiers are equal in ability.

A similar use for the binomial would be involved in a study in which we want to demonstrate the effectiveness of drinking coffee as an aid to performance on simple mental tasks. We take 8 students who are studying in the library late at night. We give these students a short test of mental arithmetic problems, then give them a cup of coffee, and then another test. We find that 7 out of 8 students do better after having a cup of coffee.

First consider the null hypothesis in this example. Ignoring tied scores, if the coffee really had no effect, and the level of performance had not changed more than expected by chance, then we would expect about half of the subjects to receive a higher score on the second administration and the rest to receive a lower score. Thus under H_0, $p(\text{higher}) = p(\text{lower}) = .5$. The binomial can now be used to compute the probability of obtaining at least 7 out of 8 improvements if H_0 is true.

$$p(7) = \frac{8!}{7!1!}(.5^7)(.5^1) = 8(.0039) = .031$$

$$p(8) = \frac{8!}{8!0!}(.5^8)(.5^0) = 1(.0039) = .0039$$

Thus the probability of *at least* 7 improvements $= .031 + .0039 = .0349$ if the null hypothesis is true and performance is unaffected by one cup of coffee. Since this probability is less than our traditional cutoff of .05, we will reject H_0 and conclude that performance has improved. Note that this does not necessarily mean that coffee led to the improvement. We might very well be looking at a practice effect. Our result tells us that $p \neq .50$, but it does not tell us why.

5.5 *The Multinomial Distribution*

Multinomial distribution

The binomial distribution which we have just examined is a special case of a more general distribution, the **multinomial distribution**. While there is relatively little to be gained by an extended examination of the multinomial, you should at least know that it exists.

In the case of the binomial distribution we dealt with events that could only have one of two outcomes—a coin could land heads or tails, a student might be classified as attentive or not attentive, and so on. There are, however, many situations in which an event can have more than two possible outcomes—in rolling a die there are 6 possible outcomes, in running a maze there might be three choices (right, left, and center), political opinions could be classified as *For*, *Against*, or *Undecided*. In these situations we must invoke the more general multinomial distribution.

If we define the probability of each of k events (categories) as p_1, $p_2, \ldots, p_k$ and wish to calculate the probability of exactly X_1 outcomes of event$_1$, X_2 outcomes of event$_2$, $\ldots$, X_k outcomes of event$_k$, this probability is given by

$$p(X_1, X_2, \ldots, X_k) = \frac{N!}{X_1! X_2! \ldots X_k!} p_1^{X_1} p_2^{X_2} \ldots p_k^{X_k}, \qquad (5.7)$$

where N has the same meaning as in the binomial. You will note that when $k = 2$ this is in fact the binomial distribution where $p_2 = 1 - p_1$ and $X_2 = N - X_1$.

As a brief illustration, suppose that we had a die with 2 black sides, 3 red sides, and 1 white side. If we were to roll this die, the probability of a black side coming up is $\frac{2}{6} = .333$, the probability of a red is $\frac{3}{6} = .500$, and the probability of a white side is $\frac{1}{6} = .167$. If we rolled it 10 times, what is the probability of obtaining exactly 4 blacks, 5 reds, and 1 white? This probability is given as

$$p(4, 5, 1) = \frac{10!}{4!5!1!} (.333^4)(.500^5)(.167^1)$$

$$= 1260(.333^4)(.500^5)(.167^1) = 1260(.000064)$$

$$= .081$$

At this point, this is all that we will say about the multinomial. It will appear again in the next chapter when we discuss Chi-square, and forms the basis for some of the other tests you are likely to run into in the future.

5.6 *Summary*

In this chapter we have examined the concept of *probability*, the basic terminology for describing probabilities, and two of the most important rules for the manipulation of probabilities (the additive and multiplicative rules). After considering the concepts of permutations and combinations, we combined the previous rules and concepts and dealt with the binomial distribution. We then saw how the binomial distribution can be approximated by a normal distribution under fairly general conditions, and how it can be used to test hypotheses concerning events having dichotomous outcomes. Finally the multinomial distribution was briefly discussed as an extension of the binomial to events having three or more possible outcomes.

Exercises for Chapter 5

5.1   Give an example of a *analytic*, a *frequentistic*, and a *subjective* view of probability.

5.2   Assume that you have bought a ticket for the local fire department lottery, and that your brother has bought two tickets. You have just read that 1000 tickets have been sold.

a.   What is the probability that you will win?
b.   What is the probability that your brother will win?
c.   What is the probability that you or your brother will win?

5.3   Now assume that in the previous question there were only a total of 10 tickets sold and there were 2 prizes.

a.   Given that you don't win first prize, what is the probability that you will win second prize? (The first prize winning ticket is not put back in the hopper.)
b.   What is the probability that your brother will come in first and you will come in second?
c.   What is the probability that you will come in first and he will come in second?
d.   What is the probability that the two of you will take first and second place?

5.4   Which of the parts in Exercise 5.3 dealt with joint probabilities?

5.5   Which of the parts in Exercise 5.3 dealt with conditional probabilities?

5.6   In a five choice task where subjects are asked to choose the stimulus which the experimenter has arbitrarily determined to be correct, the subjects can only guess on the first trial. We have 10 subjects in this experiment. Plot the sampling distribution of the number of correct choices on trial 1.

5.7   Referring back to Exercise 5.6, what would you conclude if 6 of our 10 subjects were correct on trial 1?

5.8 Again referring back to Exercise 5.6, what is the minimum number of correct choices on a trial for you to conclude that our subjects as a group are no longer performing at chance levels?

5.9 In some homes a mother's behavior seems to be independent of her baby's, and vice versa. If the mother looks at her child a total of 2 hours/day, and the baby looks at the mother a total of 3 hours/day, what is the probability that they will look at each other at the same time?

5.10 In Exercise 5.9 assume that the mother and child are both asleep from 8:00 pm to 7:00 am. What would the probability be now?

5.11 In a verbal learning experiment we want to look at recall of different classes of words (nouns, verbs, adjectives, and adverbs). Each subject will see one of each. We are afraid that there may be a sequence effect, however, and want to have different subjects see the different classes in a different order. How many subjects will we need if we are to have one subject per order?

5.12 Referring back to Exercise 5.11, assume that we have just discovered that because of time constraints each subject can only see two of the four classes. The rest of the experiment will remain the same, however. Now how many subjects do we need? (*Warning*: Do not actually try to run an experiment like this unless you are sure that you know how you will analyze the data.)

5.13 In a learning task a subject is presented with 5 buttons. He must learn to press a certain 3 of them in a predetermined order. What chance does that subject have of pressing correctly on the first trial?

5.14 An ice cream shop has 6 different flavors of ice cream, and you can order any combination of any number of them. How many different ice cream cones could they theoretically advertise? (We do not care if the oreo-mint is above or below the pistachio.)

5.15 We are designing a physiological study with six electrodes implanted in a rat's brain. The six channel amplifier in our recording apparatus blew two channels when the research assistant took it home to run his stereo. How many different ways can we record from the rat's brain? (It really makes no difference what goes on which channel.)

5.16 In a study on knowledge of current events, we give a 20–item true-false test to a class of college seniors. One of my not-so-bright students had 11 right. Do we have any reason to believe that he was doing anything other than guessing?

5.17 Some people know things which are true, some don't know anything, and some know things that are actually false. In Exercise 5.16, suppose we wanted to set limits to identify all those who "don't know anything." What limits would we set?

5.18   This question is not an easy one, and requires putting together material in Chapters 4 and 5. Suppose that we make up a driving test which we have good reason to believe should be passed by 60% of all drivers. We administer it to 30 drivers and find that 22 pass it. Is the result sufficiently large to cause us to reject H_0 ($p = .60$)? This problem is too unwieldy to be solved by solving the binomial for $X = 22, 23, \ldots, 30$. But you do know the mean and variance of the binomial, and something about its shape. With the aid of a diagram of what the distribution would look like you should be able to solve it.

6   *Chi-Square*

Z Test versus T Test

if n become large, with t test, d.f. > 30, ca use Z test, as T distribution becomes **normal**. Z test used to assess population means. T Test = Sample means. Z Test can be used to assess whether a given score would not be expected from normal distribution.

Critical Region V Level of Significance

Level of significance, α , sets critical region of rejection. If significance level set a .05 and if obtained score lies in that extreme region, score not obtained by chance.

Binomial Expansion

binomial = has 2 variables, coin toss, expanded notion by nomial experiment = coin toss multiple tries. Tree diagram to trace possible outcomes of experiment:

$$\frac{n!}{x!(n-x)!} \times p^x \times q^{n-1}$$

generates binomial distribution which is a probability not frequencey distribution.

Factor Loadings

final outcomes of factor analysis = factor matrix = table of coefficients that express relations between test & underlying factors. Entries in table = factor loadings. correlation btwn item + factor.
Item – 2 factors = stastic and noise.

Rotation of Axes

used in factor analysis, axis distinguish between factors so that scores of factors cluster around axis so that it maximizes the differences between factors.

Oblique = correlation between factors
Orthoganal = independence between factors.

In the preceding chapter we examined the use of the binomial distribution to test simple hypotheses. In those cases we were limited to situations in which an individual event had one of only two possible outcomes, and we merely asked whether, over repeated trials, one outcome occurred significantly more often than the other.

In this chapter we will expand the kinds of situations that we can evaluate. We will deal with the case in which a single event can have two *or more* possible outcomes, and then with the case in which we have two variables and we want to test null hypotheses concerning their independence. For both of these situations the appropriate statistical test will be the Chi-square (χ^2) test.

Chi-square (χ^2)   The term **Chi-square (χ^2)** has two distinct meanings in statistics, a fact which leads to some confusion among students. In one meaning of the term it is used to refer to a particular mathematical distribution which exists in and of itself without any necessary referent in the outside world. In the second meaning of the term, it is used to refer to a statistical test whose resulting test statistic is distributed in approximately the same way as the χ^2 distribution. When you hear someone refer to Chi-square they usually have this second meaning in mind. You must be familiar with the term in both of its meanings, however, if you are to use the test correctly and intelligently, and have a good understanding of many of the other statistical procedures which follow.

6.1 The χ^2 Distribution

χ^2 distribution   The **χ^2 distribution** is the distribution defined by

$$f(\chi_k^2) = \frac{1}{2^{k/2}\Gamma(k/2)} \chi^{2((k/2)-1)} e^{-(\chi^2)/2}. \tag{6.1}$$

This is a rather messy looking function and most readers will be pleased to know that they will not have to work with it in any arithmetic sense. It does have some features which should be pointed out, however, if you are to understand what the distribution of χ^2 is all about. The first thing that should be mentioned, if only in the interest of satisfying healthy curiosity, is that

Gamma function   the term $\Gamma(k/2)$ in the denominator is what is called a **gamma function** and is related to what we normally mean by factorial. In fact when the argument of gamma (i.e., $k/2$) is an integer, then $\Gamma(k/2) = ((k/2)-1)!$. We need gamma functions in part because arguments are not always integers.

A second, and more important feature of Equation 6.1 is that the distribution has only one parameter (k). Everything else is either a constant or else the value of χ^2 for which we want to find the ordinate [$f(\chi^2)$]. Whereas the normal distribution was a two parameter function, with μ and

σ as parameters, χ^2 is a one parameter function with k as the only parameter. When we move from the mathematical to the statistical world, k will become our degrees of freedom. The fact that the distribution depends upon k means that we will have a different distribution for each value of the degrees of freedom. Note that we signify the degrees of freedom by subscripting χ^2. Thus χ^2_3 is read "χ^2 on 3 degrees of freedom."

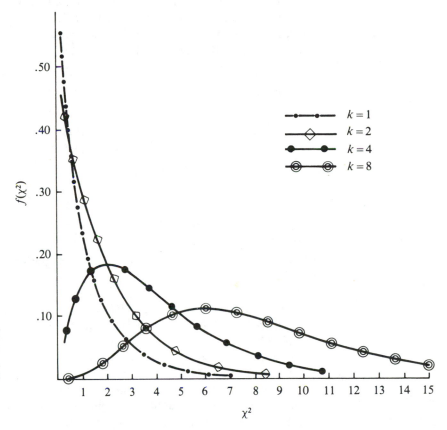

FIGURE 6.1
χ^2 distribution
for $k = 1, 2, 4,$
and 8

In Figure 6.1 are plotted several different χ^2 distributions, each representing a different value of k. From this figure it is obvious that the distribution changes markedly with changes in k, becoming more and more symmetric as k increases. It is also apparent that the mean and variance increase with increasing values of k. It can be shown that in all cases

mean $= k$

variance $= 2k$.

6.2 *Statistical Importance of the χ^2 Distribution*

As I have pointed out above, the χ^2 distribution is a mathematical distribution which exists independently of any particular referent in the outside world. It would obviously have no place in this book, however, if it did not have some degree of relevance to at least one statistical procedure. In fact the χ^2 distribution is in some way related to a great many of the statistics to be covered in this book, of which the Chi-square test is only one. I will now discuss some of these relationships.

Chi-square and z

Assume that we had a normal population with known mean (μ) and variance (σ^2). From this distribution we will sample one observation, calculate

$$z^2 = \frac{(X - \mu)^2}{\sigma^2},$$

record z^2, and repeat the procedure an infinite number of times. When we finish this task we can then plot the distribution of z^2, and we will find that this distribution looks exactly like the χ^2 distribution on 1 df. In fact

$$\chi_1^2 = z^2. \tag{6.2}$$

Those who wish can show that this is true by substituting $k = 1$ in Equation 6.1 and noting that the result will equal Equation 4.1 (*Hint*: $\Gamma(\frac{1}{2}) = \sqrt{\pi}$; $z = N(0, 1)$).

To carry the above example further, assume that instead of sampling one score at a time from our normal population, we sampled N scores at a time. For each individual observation we calculated z^2, and then over the N observations we calculated Σz^2. Again we repeat this procedure an infinite number of times and plot the resulting values of Σz^2. The resulting distribution will be distributed as χ^2 on N df.

$$\chi_N^2 = \sum_{i=1}^{N} z_i^2 = \Sigma\left(\frac{(X_i - \mu)^2}{\sigma^2}\right) \tag{6.3}$$

An important property of χ^2 which is illustrated by this result, together with Equation 6.2, is that the sum of N independent values of χ^2 is itself distributed as χ^2. In this case the degrees of freedom will be equal to the sum of the degrees of freedom for the separate χ^2s.

Two important restrictions on Equations 6.2 and 6.3 are the requirement that the observations are sampled independently of one another and that they are sampled from a normal population. These restrictions will be referred to again when we discuss the Chi-square test.

The usefulness of the above relationships may not be immediately obvious, although a full discussion of their value must await a discussion of the Chi-square test. The most important point to be made here is that Equations 6.2 and 6.3 tell us what would happen *if* we were to draw an infinite number of samples under the specified conditions. In other words we do not ever have to take on the Herculean task of drawing vast numbers of samples, since we already know what the resulting distribution will look like. This is true of most of the sampling distributions we will discuss in this book.

Chi-Square and Variance

One of the important, but little discussed, uses of χ^2 deals with its relationship to population and sample variances. This relationship forms the basis of many of our most important statistical tests, and helps to explain several of the restrictions we will place on the use of these tests.

Assume for the moment that we had a normally distributed population with a known variance (σ^2). From this population we draw an infinitely large number of samples of N observations each, and calculate the sample variance (s^2) for each sample. We could then plot the sampling distribution of the variance—the distribution of sample variances. This distribution would bear a direct linear relationship to the distribution of χ^2.

$$\chi^2_{N-1} = \frac{(N-1)s^2}{\sigma^2}$$

Turning this around we have

$$s^2 = \frac{\chi^2 \sigma^2}{N-1}.$$

Since the fraction $\sigma^2/(N-1)$ is a constant, the distribution of s^2 will differ by only a constant from the distribution of χ^2. Keep in mind that we have assumed we are dealing with normal distributions. (For a more thorough treatment of this topic see Hays, 1963, p. 342ff.)

We have just seen something which will become important later concerning the sample variance. We already knew that s^2 was an unbiased estimate of σ^2, meaning that on the average s^2 will equal σ^2. But we now know that the distribution of s^2 resembles that of χ^2, which we know to be skewed. This means that although the average s^2 will equal σ^2, more than half the time our particular value of s^2 will be smaller than σ^2, no matter how things average out in the end. This fact will become important when we discuss the *t* test in Chapter 7.

6.3 The Chi-Square Test (One-Way Classification)

Chi-square test

Goodness of fit test

To this point we have confined our discussion to the χ^2 distribution, examining its relationship to certain important statistics. We now turn our attention to what is commonly referred to as the **Chi-square test**, which is based on the χ^2 distribution. We will first examine the test as it is applied to one-dimensional tables (often called a **goodness of fit test**) and then as applied to two-dimensional tables (contingency tables).

Consider the situation in which we ask 100 people to taste two brands of coffee and state their preference between the brands. When we have finished with the experiment, the question that we will want to ask is whether people in general prefer one brand of coffee over the other. In other words, do the obtained frequencies in favor of each coffee differ from the 50:50 split which would be expected by chance if the coffees were indistinguishable? The test we will employ to answer this question is the Chi-square test.

From Equation 6.2 we know that

$$\chi_1^2 = z^2 = \frac{(X - \mu)^2}{\sigma^2},$$

where X is sampled from a normal population with mean = μ and variance = σ^2. At the same time we also know that if people are selecting coffees at random, the number of people (X) selecting a particular brand of coffee can be viewed as coming from a binomial distribution with mean = Np and variance = Npq. Furthermore we know that for reasonable sample sizes the binomial is approximately normal. These facts allow us to substitute the mean and variance of the binomial into Equation 6.2, arriving at

$$\chi_1^2 = \frac{(X - Np)^2}{Npq}. \tag{6.4}$$

χ^2 as defined by Equation 6.4 would be distributed exactly as the distribution of χ^2 if N were infinitely large (and therefore if the binomial distribution were exactly normal). For reasonable sample sizes the binomial distribution from which we are sampling would be approximately normal, and the result of Equation 6.4 would very closely approximate the χ^2 distribution.

Observed frequencies

Expected frequencies

A much more common way to write the formula for χ^2 is to let O_i represent the **observed frequencies** and E_i represent the **expected frequencies**. Expanding Equation 6.4 we obtain

$$\chi_1^2 = \frac{(X - Np)^2}{Np} + \frac{(N - X - Nq)^2}{Nq} \tag{6.5}$$

and substituting in Equation 6.5 we obtain

$$\chi^2 = \frac{(O_1 - E_1)^2}{E_1} + \frac{(O_2 - E_2)^2}{E_2}$$

or, dropping the subscripts as being self-evident,

$$\chi^2 = \sum \frac{(O - E)^2}{E} \qquad\qquad (6.6)$$

This last formula is the one commonly given for the Chi-square test. The advantage of the earlier equation (6.5) is that it makes explicit the source of the expected frequencies and serves as a reminder that, in the two category case, the test is based upon the binomial distribution and the restrictions which go with it. We will use the two formulae interchangeably. The nice thing about Equation 6.6 is that it is completely general. Although it was developed on the basis of the binomial, we can now use it as the formula for all situations to which the Chi-square test applies, whether or not that case is also an example of the binomial.

Example 6.1

Orientation in Pigeons

As an illustration of the use of the Chi-square test, consider the situation in which we wish to test whether pigeons can respond to the Earth's magnetic field. We hypothesize, somewhat recklessly, that if this is so, a pigeon dropped into a circular open field will orient itself toward the North. To simplify our task we will record a pigeon as orienting toward the North whenever his head is north of his tail (and will redrop any pigeons who orient themselves perfectly along the East–West axis). This procedure results in one half of the possible positions being classified as *North* and the other half being classified as *South*. Now suppose that we test 100 pigeons in the apparatus and find that 58 orient toward the North and 42 toward the South. Is this difference in favor of the North significant, or would it be likely to occur if the pigeons were insensitive to the Earth's magnetic field and were just orienting themselves at random? To answer this question we will employ the Chi-square test.

The null hypothesis (H_0) is the hypothesis of no differences in the tendencies to turn North or South. In other words H_0 states that there is no difference between p (probability of turning North) and q (probability of turning South) and therefore that $p = q = .50$. In terms of expected values this means that under H_0 we would expect 50 pigeons to orient each way. Since we have used 100 *different* pigeons, the observations should be independent. There is certainly no reason to assume that one pigeon's behavior should have any effect on another pigeon's behavior. This is in contrast to the situation in which we might use one bird 100 times, in which case we might have strong reservations about the independence of observations.

Lastly, since we can think of this situation as being comparable to tossing 100 coins and counting heads and tails, we can conceive of our data as having been sampled from a binomial. Considering the sample size, the distribution of possible outcomes would be essentially normal. Thus we have met the parametric assumptions implicit in the use of Chi-square (independence and normality of the sampling distribution of outcomes).

Since the expected frequencies in each category are equal to 50, we can tabulate the data as in Table 6.1. From Equation 6.6

TABLE 6.1
Hypothetical Data for
Study of Orientation
in Pigeons

| | ORIENTATION | | |
	North	South	Total
Observed Frequency	58	42	100
Expected Frequency	50	50	100

$$\chi^2 = \sum \frac{(O-E)^2}{E}$$

$$= \frac{(58-50)^2}{50} + \frac{(42-50)^2}{50} = \frac{8^2}{50} + \frac{-8^2}{50} = \frac{128}{50}$$

$$= 2.56.$$

The Tabled χ^2 Distribution

Now that we have obtained a value of χ^2, we must refer it to the χ^2 distribution to determine the probability of a value of χ^2 at least this extreme.

Tabled distribution of χ^2

The **tabled distribution of χ^2**, like that of most other statistics with which we will deal, differs in a very important way from the *tabled* standard normal distribution, as was pointed out earlier in Chapter 3. Since many students seem to have difficulty in appreciating this difference and in understanding the use of statistical tables, we will make use of a simple illustration. Consider the distribution of χ^2 for 1 df shown in Figure 6.2. While it is certainly true that we could construct a table of exactly the same form as that for the standard normal distribution, allowing us to determine what percentage of the values are greater than any arbitrary value of χ^2, this would be tremendously expensive and wasteful. We would have to make

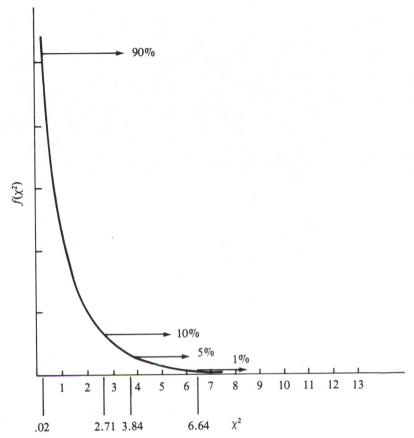

FIGURE 6.2

Areas under the χ^2 distribution

up a new table for every reasonable number of degrees of freedom. And since it is not uncommon for us to want up to 30 df, this would require 30 separate tables, each the size of Appendix (z). Such a procedure would be particularly wasteful since most users would need only a small fraction of each of these tables. If we wish to reject H_0 at the .05 level, all that we really care about is whether or not our value of χ^2 is greater or less than the value of χ^2 which cuts off the extreme 5% of the distribution. Thus for our particular purposes all we need to know is the 5% cutoff point for each df. Others might want the 2.5%, 1%, etc. cutoffs, but it is hard to imagine wanting the 17% values, for example. Thus the tables of χ^2, such as the one given in Appendix (χ^2) are designed to supply only those values which might be of general interest.

Turn for a moment to Appendix (χ^2). Down the left hand margin you will find the degrees of freedom. In each column you will find the critical values of χ^2 cutting off the percentage of the distribution labeled at the top of the column. Thus, for example, you will see that for 2 df, a χ^2 of 5.99 cuts off the upper 5% of the distribution.

Returning to our particular example, we have found a value of $\chi^2 = 3.56$ on 1 df. From the appendix we see that with 1 df a χ^2 of 3.84 cuts off the upper 5% of the distribution. Since our obtained value (χ^2_{obt}) = 2.56 is less than $\chi^2_{.05} = 3.84$, we will not reject the null hypothesis. We will therefore conclude that we do not have reason to doubt that the pigeons are operating at random.

Because the logic of hypothesis testing is so extremely important to an understanding of statistics, it might be well to risk beating a dead horse by considering what we have done from a different angle. Assume for a moment that our *calculated* value of χ^2 had turned out to be 6.00. We would have rejected H_0. What would this have meant? Equation 6.6 states that regardless of what hypothesis is true, if we take the obtained frequency, subtract the *true* value of the expected frequency, square, divide by the *true* value of the expected frequency, and then sum the results over all categories, the answer will be distributed as χ^2—i.e., only 5 percent of the time will we obtain a value of χ^2 greater than 3.84 with 1 df. The null hypothesis in effect states that the *true* value of E, in this example, is (100)(.50) = 50. As a result we took 50 as the expected value and proceeded accordingly. To the extent that H_0 was true, we have inserted the *true* expected value and will have a χ^2 distribution. To the extent that H_0 is false, we have inserted the wrong expected value, and our result will not be distributed as χ^2 (i.e., over an infinite number of replications of the experiment the resulting values of χ^2 will not have a χ^2 distribution).

Extension to the Multicategory Case

In the previous section we concerned ourselves with the situation in which the data fell into one of two categories. We can easily extend this to *Multicategory case* the **multicategory case**, in which data can be classified into 3 or more categories, the number being signified by k. When we leave the two category case, however, we also leave the binomial distribution and must consider our data as coming from a multinomial distribution. Aside from an increase in the difficulty of the derivation, which we will not be concerned with anyway, the nature of the test and its application are left unchanged. Since we have more than two categories, we will have to let $p_1, p_2, \ldots, p_k$ replace p and q, and let $X_1, X_2, \ldots, X_k$ replace X and $N - X$. These are trivial changes, however, and with these in mind we can rewrite Equations 6.5 and 6.6 to read

$$\chi^2 = \sum \frac{(X_i - Np_i)^2}{Np_i} = \sum \frac{(O - E)^2}{E} . \tag{6.7}$$

We will again lose one df, and the result will be distributed as χ^2 on $k - 1$ df.

As an example, let us consider an improvement on our experiment with the pigeons. Instead of simply classifying behavior as North or South, we will lay the circle out in four quadrants—any orientation between North-west and Northeast will be called North, between Northeast and Southeast will be called East, and so on. Thus behavior can be classified as falling into one of four categories. Suppose that we obtained the data shown in Table 6.2. Our procedure for the analysis would be the same as that followed in

TABLE 6.2

Hypothetical Data for Study of Orientation in Pigeons

| | ORIENTATION | | | | |
	North	*East*	*South*	*West*	*Total*
Observed Frequencies	32	23	18	27	100
Expected Frequencies	25	25	25	25	100

the earlier example, the only difference being the number of categories over which we sum our calculations

$$\chi_3^2 = \sum \frac{(O-E)^2}{E}$$

$$= \frac{(32-25)^2}{25} + \frac{(23-25)^2}{25} + \frac{(18-25)^2}{25} + \frac{(27-25)^2}{25}$$

$$= 4.24.$$

From Appendix (χ^2) we see that for $k-1=3$ df, $\chi_{.05}^2 = 7.82$. Our value of 4.24 is less than 7.82, and once again we will not reject H_0. We still have not shown that there is sufficient reason to doubt that pigeons do anything but orient themselves at random.

The thoughtful reader might ask why we analyzed the data this way rather than lumping the categories East, South, and West together under the heading of *Not North*. There is no particularly convincing statistical answer to this question, other than to say that it depends on what you know about the behavior of pigeons and what you expect the results to look like.

6.4 Chi-Square as a Test of the Independence of Two Variables

In the preceding section we examined situations in which there was one independent variable under consideration. A second, possibly more impor-tant, use of Chi-square deals with the situation in which we have two variables and want to determine if these variables are independent of one another. For example, we might wish to know if preference for a political party is independent of sex, whether presence or absence of illness is independent of presence or absence of immunization, or whether preference for different types of music is independent of age. Any two variables can be examined in this way, so long as data on each variable can be classified into categories.

Independence of two variables

In the case in which we wish to ask about the ***independence of two variables***, the data are cast in what we commonly refer to as a ***contingency table***. Thus to evaluate the relationship between hyperkinesis and sex, for example, we would make up a table in which sex appears along one dimension and hyperkinesis appears along the other.

Contingency table

	Female	Male
Hyperkinetic		
Non-hyperkinetic		

Cell

The entries in each ***cell*** represent frequency data, the number of female hyperkinetics, male hyperkinetics, and so on.

In asking the kind of question in which we are now interested, the same underlying procedures are involved as were involved in the earlier examples. The only difference is in the way in which we obtain the expected frequencies, and we will see that even here we are simply extending what we already know.

Example 6.2

The Zeigarnik Effect

As an example, and an extreme one at that, let us consider a study by Lewis & Franklin (1944), based on an earlier study by Zeigarnik (1927). Zeigarnik originally presented subjects with a number of separate tasks, some of which she unobtrusively interrupted, preventing their completion. At the end of the session subjects were asked to list all of the tasks on which they had worked, and Zeigarnik found substantially better recall of uncompleted tasks. Lewis & Franklin (1944) wished to examine whether the presence or absence of the so-called Zeigarnik Effect depended upon the subject's perception of the tasks. They divided 24 subjects into two groups. Group SI (self-involved) was told that the tasks were measures of ability. Group TO (task-oriented) were told that they were simply helping the experimenter to standardize the tasks. Subjects were then presented with the tasks one at a time, some of the tasks were interrupted before completion, and the subjects were later asked for recall of all of the tasks.

The data are presented in Table 6.3, where the cell entries represent the number of subjects in each group recalling more completed (or uncompleted) tasks. Thus, for example, in Group TO 10 subjects recalled more uncompleted tasks than completed ones, and 2 recalled more completed tasks than uncompleted ones.

The only change which must be made in our formula for Chi-square concerns the fact that the data are arrayed along two dimensions instead of one. This means that we will have to refer to X_{ij} and p_{ij} instead of X_i and p_i. In the new designation i indicates the number of the row and j the number of the column. Thus X_{12} is the score in row 1 column 2, i.e., 2. We can now write

$$\chi^2 = \sum \frac{(X_{ij} - Np_{ij})^2}{Np_{ij}} = \sum \frac{(O-E)^2}{E}.$$

TABLE 6.3

Data for Study
by Lewis & Franklin
(1944)

observed

Group	GREATER RECALL *Uncompleted Tasks*	*Completed Tasks*	
TO	10 P_{11}	2 P_{12}	12
SI	1 P_{21}	11 P_{22}	12
	11	13	24

calculate probabilities

$P_{11} = \frac{12}{24} \times \frac{11}{24}$

$P_{12} = \frac{12}{24} \times \frac{13}{24}$

$P_{21} = \frac{12}{24} \times \frac{11}{24}$

$P_{22} = \frac{12}{24} \times \frac{13}{24}$

expected

$n \cdot P_{11}$	$n \cdot P_{12}$
$n \cdot P_{21}$	$n \cdot P_{22}$

Calculation of Expected Frequencies

The only remaining problem is the calculation of Np_{ij}. From Chapter 5 we know that the probability of the *joint* occurrence of two *independent* events is the product of the probabilities of their separate occurrence. Thus the probability of a head on both of two trials is the probability of a head on the first trial times the probability of a head on the second trial ($p = (.5)(.5) = .25$).

If the variables in Table 6.3 are independent, then the probability that a subject is classified as a member of cell$_{11}$ (TO, Uncompleted) is equal to the probability of his being a member of row 1 times the probability of his being a member of column 1. The probability for row 1 is $\frac{12}{24}$, since 12 of the 24 subjects are in row 1. The probability for column 1 is $\frac{11}{24}$, since there are 11 of the 24 subjects in that column. Given these individual probabilities, then, the probability that the subject is in row 1 *and* column 1 (i.e., cell$_{11}$) is

$$p_{11} = \frac{12}{24} \times \frac{11}{24}.$$

While this looks as if it will involve a great deal of arithmetic, in fact it will not. First of all remember that we want Np_{ij}, not just p_{ij}. Secondly, N is the total number of subjects in the experiment, which in this case is 24. Thus

$$Np_{11} = 24 \times \left(\frac{12}{24} \times \frac{11}{24}\right) = \frac{(12)(11)}{24} = 5.5.$$

Row total
Column total
Grand total

If we let the abbreviations *RT*, *CT*, and *GT* stand for **Row Total**, **Column Total**, and **Grand Total**, where it is understood that the particular row or column total in question is the one corresponding to the row or column of the cell whose expected frequency we seek, then

$$E_{ij} = Np_{ij} = \frac{(RT_i)(CT_j)}{GT}. \qquad\qquad (6.9)$$

It is important to note that Equation 6.9 derives directly from the assumption that the two variables are independent, and essentially represents the statement of the null hypothesis. Thus when we say "under H_0," this is equivalent to saying "when Equation 6.9 holds."

Calculation of χ^2

Given Equations 6.8 and 6.9, we can now analyze the data in Table 6.3 by means of a Chi-square contingency analysis. In Table 6.4 appear both the observed and expected frequencies. You will note that the row, column, and grand totals of the table of expected values are the same as those of the table of observed values. This must always hold, since our expectations must account for all of the observations.

TABLE 6.4   Observed and Expected Frequencies for Lewis & Franklin (1944) Study

OBSERVED FREQUENCIES

Group	Uncompleted Tasks	Completed Tasks
TO	10	2
SI	1	11
	11	13

EXPECTED FREQUENCIES

Group	Uncompleted Tasks	Completed Tasks	
TO	5.5	6.5	12
SI	5.5	6.5	12
	11	13	24

The calculation of χ^2 follows directly, now that we have obtained the expected frequencies.

$$\chi^2 = \sum \frac{(O-E)^2}{E} = \frac{(10-5.5)^2}{5.5} + \frac{(2-6.5)^2}{6.5} + \frac{(1-5.5)^2}{5.5} + \frac{(11-6.5)^2}{6.5}$$

$$= \frac{4.5^2}{5.5} + \frac{(-4.5)^2}{6.5} + \frac{(-4.5)^2}{5.5} + \frac{4.5^2}{6.5}$$

$$= 13.594$$

Degrees of Freedom

Degrees of freedom   Before we can compare our value of χ^2 to the tabled value, we must know the **degrees of freedom**. For the analysis of contingency tables, the degrees of freedom are always given by

$$\mathrm{df} = (R-1)(C-1), \tag{6.10}$$

where R is the number of rows and C is the number of columns.

For our particular example with 2 rows and 2 columns, we have $(2-1)(2-1) = 1$ df. While it may seem strange that we have 1 df whether we have two categories or four cells, it would be apparent that given only 1 entry, and the row and column totals, the rest of the entries are completely determined.

Evaluation of χ^2

The critical value of χ^2 for 1 df is 3.84. Since our obtained value of χ^2 is 13.594, we will reject the null hypothesis and conclude that there is a relationship between the orientation of the subject toward the task and the types of tasks he is able to recall. If the tasks are seen as measures of ability, the subject has a strong tendency to recall those which he or she completed. On the other hand if the subject has no personal involvement with the tasks, then uncompleted tasks are more often recalled.

Computer Analyses

As an illustration of the output from a typical computer program, the data in Table 6.3 have been analyzed using MINITAB. The MINITAB output is shown in Table 6.5. Output from other computer programs would have a similar format.

TABLE 6.5
MINITAB Output
for Data from
Table 6.3

```
-- READ DATA INTO C1 AND C2
-- 10  2
--  1 11

-- CHISQUARE ON DATA IN C1 AND C2

EXPECTED FREQUENCIES ARE PRINTED BELOW OBSERVED FREQUENCIES
        I  C1   I  C2   I  TOTALS
-------I-------I-------I-------
   1 I   10 I    2 I     12
     I    5.5I    6.5I
-------I-------I-------I-------
   2 I    1 I   11 I     12
     I    5.5I    6.5I
-------I-------I-------I-------
TOTALS I   11 I   13 I     24

TOTAL CHI SQUARE =

        3.68 +  3.12 +
        3.68 +  3.12 +

              =  13.59

DEGREES OF FREEDOM = ( 2-1) X ( 2-1) =  1
```

Correction for Continuity

Many books advocate that for a simple 2×2 table such as the one presented here we should employ what is called ==Yates' Correction for Continuity,== especially when the expected frequencies are small. (The correction merely involves reducing the absolute value of each numerator by .5 units before squaring.) There is a very large literature on the pros and cons of Yates' Correction, with firmly held views on either side. Although in this book I will end up recommending that you not use the correction, it is important to understand what all the fuss is about.

A glance at Figure 6.1 will show that χ^2 is a *continuous function*, meaning that all values along the abscissa are possible. But if you go back to the preceding example you will discover that there is no way to rearrange the data, *keeping the marginal totals constant*, to come up with a $\chi^2 = 13.596$, for example. In other words, with finite sample sizes the obtained distribution of χ^2 for the Chi-square test is discrete (especially so with small samples) whereas the theoretical χ^2 distribution is continuous. This leads to a certain *mismatch* when we attempt to evaluate a χ^2 statistic against the χ^2 distribution.

This *mismatch* led Yates (1934) to devise a correction to be applied in the case of a 2×2 contingency table. The result of this correction is that the probability of the corrected χ^2, taken from χ^2 tables, is quite close to the *true* probabilities calculated on the basis of the individual probabilities of all possible tables with those marginal totals (the R_i and C_j). Yates' Correction in fact accomplishes his goal quite nicely, and is certainly to be recommended whenever it makes sense to calculate a probability given that the marginal totals are fixed. Unfortunately, to speak about *fixed marginals* implies that if you reran the experiment the individual cell totals might well

*Yates' Correction
for Continuity*

Continuous function

Fixed marginals

change but you would arrive at the same marginal totals. This situation rarely exists, and if it does not exist it seems to make little sense to ask what the probability of the data would be if we assumed that the marginals are fixed. For this reason (the unreasonableness of a fixed-marginal assumption), most recent papers have argued against the use of Yates' Correction (Bradley, Bradley, McGrath, & Cutcomb, 1979; Camilli & Hopkins, 1978, 1979; Overall, 1980). Furthermore, for the cases in which either one or neither marginal is fixed the uncorrected Chi-square provides an excellent approximation to the true probabilities—certainly a better approximation than provided by Yates' Correction.

Chi-Square for Larger Contingency Tables

The previous example involved two variables (task orientation and type of material recalled) each of which had two levels. This particular design is referred to as a 2×2 contingency analysis, and is a special case of the more general $R \times C$ designs, where R and C represent the number of rows and columns. As an example of a larger contingency table, consider a study by Hovland, Harvey, & Sherif (1957). Hovland *et al.* were interested in examining the relationship between the strength of an individual's belief in a cause and his willingness to change that belief. At the time, the State of Oklahoma was discussing the repeal of prohibition. Hovland *et al.* collected 183 people strongly in favor of prohibition (members of the W.C.T.U. and other such organizations) and an unselected sample of 290 college students. (They also found 25 "wets" from among their friends and acquaintances, but their data are not relevant for our purposes.)

The investigators administered to all of their subjects an attitude survey concerning prohibition. They then took subsamples of the "drys" and the unselected subjects and presented them with a communication advocating the repeal of prohibition. The attitude survey was readministered and subjects were classified as to whether they had moved away from or toward the direction of the communication, or had remained unchanged. The data are presented in Table 6.6, and the values in parentheses are the expected cell frequencies. The expected frequencies were obtained just as they were in the previous example. The calculation of χ^2 is:

$$\chi^2 = \sum \frac{(O-E)^2}{E} = \frac{(19-28.714)^2}{28.714} + \frac{(34-24.000)^2}{24.000} + \cdots + \frac{(22-21.714)^2}{21.714}$$

$$= 13.051$$

There are 2 df for Table 6.6, since $(R-1)(C-1) = (2-1)(3-1) = 2$. The critical value of $\chi^2_{.05} = 5.99$. Since our value of 13.051 is larger than 5.99, we are led to reject H_0 and to conclude that it is not true that the willingness to change an opinion in the face of persuasion is independent of the strength

TABLE 6.6		Toward		Unchanged		Away	
Data for Study by Hovland, Harvey, & Sherif (1957)	*Drys*	19	(28.714)	34	(24.000)	16	(16.286)	69
	Unselected	48	(38.286)	22	(32.000)	22	(21.714)	92
		67		56		38		161

of that opinion. On the contrary, the data support the hypothesis that susceptibility to a persuasive communication is a function of the strength of a person's belief.

Alternative Formulae

There are several alternative formulae available for calculating χ^2 for certain special cases. In almost all cases these formulae actually save very little time, in light of the fact that they are a nuisance to remember and must be looked up on each occasion. The general formula is easily remembered and can be applied in every situation.

There is one interesting exception to this general principle. Guilford & Fruchter (1973) mention a formula, which they attribute to S. W. Brown, which allows one to calculate χ^2 for a contingency table without ever actually calculating expected frequencies. When the work is to be done on a desk calculator, this can make for a considerable saving in time and energy, since obtaining and recording all of the expected frequencies can be quite a chore. Letting RT, CT, GT, and X_{ij} have the same meaning they had in Equation 6.8, substituting $(RT)(CT)/GT$ for Np_{ij} in Equation 6.8, and simplifying the expression algebraically, it is possible to show that

$$\chi^2 = \sum \frac{(O-E)^2}{E} = N\left[\sum \frac{X_{ij}^2}{(RT_i)(CT_j)} - 1\right]. \qquad (6.11)$$

The application of this formula can be illustrated using the data from the previous example.

$$\chi^2 = 161\left[\frac{19^2}{(69)(67)} + \frac{34^2}{(69)(56)} + \frac{16^2}{(69)(38)} + \frac{48^2}{(92)(67)} + \frac{22^2}{(92)(56)}\right.$$

$$\left. + \frac{22^2}{(92)(38)} - 1\right]$$

$$= 161(1.081 - 1) = 161(.081)$$

$$= 13.051.$$

Small Expected Frequencies

Small expected frequency

One of the most important requirements for the use of the Chi-square test concerns the size of the expected frequencies. We have already met this problem briefly in discussing corrections for continuity. Before defining more precisely what we mean by *small* we should first examine why a **small expected frequency** causes so much trouble. There are two ways of explaining the difficulty, and they are so closely related, being two sides of the same coin, that it is difficult to speak about one without invoking the other.

First of all consider the basic fact that we are using a mathematical distribution to approximate the distribution of the statistic resulting from a Chi-square test. As you should recall, in deriving the test we first showed that $\chi^2 = \Sigma z^2$ when we sampled observations from a normal population. We then used this relationship to show that Σz^2 could be converted into our familiar Chi-square statistic, invoking the binomial (or multinomial) distribution in the process. We were allowed to use the binomial (or multinomial) because these distributions approach the normal when Np is large. Notice that we have had to take cognisance of the assumption of normality in the process. But neither the binomial or the multinomial produce anywhere near normal distributions for small values of Np. This means that we will have violated the assumption of **normality** for small expected frequencies (small values of Np).

Normality

Suppose we look at the problem from a different angle. If there are only a few possible values of χ^2_{obt}, then the χ^2 distribution can not provide a reasonable approximation to the distribution of our statistic. We cannot fit an extremely **discrete distribution** with a continuous one. But those cases which result in only a few possible values of χ^2_{obt} are the ones with small expected frequencies. (This is directly analogous to the fact that if you only flip a coin three times and there are only four possible values for the number of heads, the resulting sampling distribution can hardly be satisfactorily approximated by the normal.)

Discrete distribution

If the student takes a fixed set of marginal totals for a 2×2 table, selects the marginal totals so as to have at least one small expected frequency, and then constructs all possible data tables for that set of marginals, she will immediately see what the problem is.

We have seen that difficulties arise when we have small expected frequencies, but the question of how small is small remains. What conventions do exist are conflicting and have only minimal claims to preference over the others. I take the rather conservative position that all expected frequencies should be at least 5. Camilli & Hopkins (1979), on the other hand, demonstrate that the test produces few Type I errors in the 2×2 case as long as the total sample size is ≥ 8, but they, and Overall (1980), point to the extremely low power to correctly reject a false H_0 which such tests possess.

6.5 *Summary of the Assumptions of Chi-Square*

Due to the widespread misuse of Chi-square still prevalent in the literature it is important to pull together in one place the underlying **assumptions** of χ^2. For a thorough discussion of the misuse of χ^2, the reader is referred to the paper by Lewis & Burke (1949) and the subsequent rejoinders to that paper. These papers are not yet out of data 30 years after they were written.

The Assumption of Independence

We assumed at the beginning of this chapter that observations were independent of one another. The word *independence* has been used in two different ways in this chapter, and it is important to keep these two uses separate. A basic assumption of χ^2 deals with the independence of *observations* and is the assumption, for example, that one subject's choice among three brands of coffee has no effect on another subject's choice. This is what we are referring to when we speak of an assumption of independence. We have also spoken of the independence of *variables*, as when we discussed contingency tables. In this case independence is what is being tested, whereas in the former use of the word it is an assumption.

It is not uncommon to find cases in which the assumption of independence of observations is violated, usually by having the same subject respond more than once. A typical illustration of violation of the independence assumption occurred recently when an individual categorized five animals as to the level of activity on each of four days. When he was finished he had a table similar to the one below.

| | ACTIVITY | | |
High	Medium	Low	Total
10	7	3	20

This table looks quite legitimate until you realize that there were only five animals, and thus each animal was contributing four tally marks toward the cell entries. This kind of error is quite easy to make, but it is nevertheless an error. The best guard against it is to make certain that the Grand Total equals precisely the number of subjects in the experiment.

Normality

We have already discussed the assumption of normality (and therefore continuity) at length when we spoke of small expected frequencies, and there is nothing more to be said here.

Inclusion of Non-Occurrences

Although this requirement has not yet been mentioned specifically, it is inherent in the derivation. It is probably best explained by an example. Suppose that one of 20 males, 17 were in favor of having Daylight Savings Time in effect the year round. Out of 20 females, only 11 were in favor of Daylight Savings Time on a permanent basis. We want to determine if men are significantly more in favor of DST than are women. One *erroneous* method of testing this would be to set up the following data table.

	Male	Female	Total
Observed	17	11	28
Expected	14	14	28

Non-occurrences

We could then compute χ^2 ($=1.28$) and fail to reject H_0. But the data table above does not take into account the negative responses (what Lewis & Burke, 1949, call ***non-occurrences***). Looking back at Equation 6.5 you will notice that we have to make use of $N - X$ and Nq, as well as X and Np. Thus the data should be cast in the form of a contingency table.

	Male	Female	
Yes	17	11	28
No	3	9	12
	20	20	40

Now $\chi^2 = 4.29$ which is significant at $\alpha = .05$, resulting in an entirely different interpretation of the results.

Failure to take the non-occurrences into account not only invalidates the test, but reduces the value of χ^2, leaving you less likely to reject H_0. Again it is important to be sure that the Grand Total is exactly equal to the number of subjects in the study.

6.6 One- and Two-Tailed Tests

There is considerable confusion among people as to whether Chi-square is a one- or a two-tailed test. This confusion results from the fact that there are different ways of defining what we mean by a one- or two-tailed test. If we think of the sampling distribution of χ^2, we can argue that χ^2 is a one-tailed test due to the fact that we only reject H_0 when our value of χ^2 lies in the extreme right hand tail of the distribution.† On the other hand, if we think of the underlying data on which our obtained χ^2 is based, we could argue that we have a two-tailed test. If, for example, we were using Chi-square to test the fairness of a coin, we would reject H_0 if it produced too many heads *or* if it produced too many tails, since either event would lead to a large value of χ^2.

The above discussion is not intended to start an argument over semantics (I personally could not care less whether you want to think of Chi-square as a one- or a two-tailed test), but rather it is intended to point out one of the weaknesses of the Chi-square test so that this can be taken into account. The weakness is that the test, as normally applied, is a non-directional test. To take a simple example, consider the situation in which you wish to show that increasing amounts of quinine added to an animal's food make it less appealing. You take 90 rats and offer them a choice of three bowls of food, differing in the amount of quinine. You then count the number of animals selecting each bowl of food. Suppose the obtained data were

	AMOUNT QUININE	
Small	Medium	Large
39	30	21

The computed value of χ^2 is 5.4, which, on 2 df, is not significant at $p \le .05$.

The important fact about the data is that any of the six possible configurations of the same frequencies (such as 21, 30, 39) would produce exactly the same value of χ^2, and you receive no *credit* for the fact that the configuration you obtained is precisely the one you predicted. Thus you have employed a *multi-tailed* test when in fact you have a specific prediction of the direction in which the totals will be ordered. The only solution to this problem is to decide *before running the experiment* that you will fail to reject H_0, regardless of the value of χ^2, unless the ordering of the frequencies fits with your prediction. This means that *a priori* you have a probability of only $\frac{1}{6}$ of even calculating χ^2, since the other $\frac{5}{6}$ of the outcomes, if H_0 is true, will

---

† See Hays (1963, pp. 344–345) for an example in which both tails of the distribution may be used.

be in the wrong direction. Since you have restricted yourself to rejecting H_0 only if one particular order appears (out of six possible orders), you can now evaluate χ^2 at the $(6)(\alpha) = (6)(.05) = .30$ level. If H_0 is true, the probability of a Type I error will be $(\frac{1}{6})(.30) = .05$, which is what you originally intended. In this instance we would reject H_0 for this example.

It should be apparent that we do not have to restrict ourselves to the limited case where only one particular ordering will lead to a test. We might set the criterion as the frequency of *small* must be less than the other two frequencies, for example, in which case we are allowing $\frac{2}{6}$ of the possible outcomes and can enter the χ^2 tables at $\alpha = .15$. It is important to keep in mind, however, that the admissible orders must be specified *a priori*, and that H_0 may never be rejected for other orders, regardless of how extreme are the frequencies.

6.7 *Likelihood Ratio Tests*

Likelihood ratios

An alternative approach to the analysis of categorical data is based upon what are called ***likelihood ratios***. These procedures are introduced here for two reasons. First of all there is reason to believe that these tests are less affected by small sample sizes than is the normal Chi-square test when there are two or more degrees of freedom. For very large sample sizes the two are equivalent. The second reason for introducing these tests is that they are heavily used in what are called ***log-linear models*** for the analysis of

Log-linear models

contingency tables. Log-linear models are particularly important when we want to analyze multi-dimensional contingency tables. Although such models are beyond the scope of this book (the interested reader is referred to Goodman (1970) and Bishop, Fienberg, & Holland (1975)), they are becoming more and more important and at least some minimal exposure to maximum likelihood methods is warranted.

Without going into detail, the general idea of a likelihood ratio can be described quite simply. Suppose that we collect some data and calculate the probability or likelihood of the data occurring given the null hypothesis. We also calculate the likelihood that they would occur under some alternative hypothesis (the hypothesis for which the data are most probable). If the data are much more likely for some alternative hypothesis than for H_0, we would be inclined to reject H_0. However if the data are almost as likely under H_0 as they are for some other alternative, we would be inclined to retain H_0. Thus the likelihood ratio (the ratio of these two likelihoods) forms a basis for evaluating the null hypothesis.

Using likelihood ratios it is possible to devise tests for the analysis of one-dimensional arrays and for contingency tables. For the development of these tests the reader is referred to Mood (1950) or Mood & Graybill (1963).

For the one-dimensional case

$$\chi^2_{C-1} = 2\Sigma X_i(\log_e X_i - \log_e p_i) - 2N \log_e N$$

where X_i and p_i are the number of observations and the probability for each cell.

For the analysis of contingency tables

$$\chi^2_{(R-1)(C-1)} = 2N \log_e N + 2\Sigma X_{ij} \log_e X_{ij} - 2\Sigma R_i \log_e R_i - 2\Sigma C_j \log_e C_j$$

where R_i and C_j are the row and column totals, respectively. This statistic is evaluated with respect to the χ^2 distribution on $(R-1)(C-1)$ degrees of freedom.

Likelihood ratio test

As an illustration of the use of the **likelihood ratio test** for contingency tables, consider the data used in the example of sex preferences for Daylight Savings Time. The cell and marginal frequencies are

	Male	Female	
Yes	17	11	28
No	3	9	12
	20	20	40

$$\chi^2 = 2N \log_e N + 2\Sigma X_{ij} \log_e X_{ij} - 2\Sigma R_i \log_e R_i - 2\Sigma C_j \log_e C_j$$

$$= 2(40)(3.6889) + 2[17(2.833) + 11(2.398) + 3(1.099) + 9(2.197)]$$

$$- 2[28(3.334) + 12(2.485)] - 2[20(2.996) + 20(2.996)]$$

$$= 295.11036 + 195.22467 - 246.24121 - 239.65858$$

$$= 4.435$$

This is a χ^2 on 1 df and, since it exceeds $\chi^2_{.05} = 3.84$, will lead to rejection of H_0.

6.8 Summary

This chapter was concerned with the use of the Chi-square test for the analysis of frequency data. After a discussion of the χ^2 distribution, the Chi-square test was introduced to test hypotheses concerning the distribution of outcomes along one dimension. We next examined the use of the Chi-square test for testing the independence of two variables, which is the situation in which it is most commonly used. We then dealt with the effect of small expected frequencies and the general assumptions behind the Chi-square test. Finally, likelihood ratio tests were introduced as an alternative to the Chi-square test, and it was pointed out that these tests will most likely play an increasingly important role in the future.

Exercises for Chapter 6

6.1 The Chairman of a Psychology Department suspects that some of his faculty are more popular than others. There are three sections of Introductory Psychology (taught at 10:00 am, 11:00 am, and 12:00 pm) by Professors X, Y, and Z. The number of students who enroll for each are given below.

Prof. X	Prof. Y	Prof. Z
32	25	10

Run the appropriate Chi-square test and interpret the results.

6.2 The data in Exercise 6.1 will not really answer the question which the Chairman wants answered. What is the problem and how could the experiment be improved?

6.3 I have a theory that if you ask subjects to sort one-sentence characteristics of people (e.g., I eat too fast) into five piles ranging from "not at all like me" to "very much like me", the percentage of items placed in each pile will be approximately 10%, 20%, 40%, 20%, and 10% for the five piles. I have my daughter sort 50 statements and obtain the following data.

    8 10 20 8 4

Do these data support my hypothesis?

6.4 To what population does the answer to Exercise 6.3 generalize?

6.5 In an old study by Clark & Clark (1939), black children were shown black dolls and white dolls and asked to select one to play with. Out of 252 children, 169 chose the white doll and 83 chose the black doll. What can we conclude about the behavior of these children?

6.6 Following up Exercise 6.5, Hraba & Grant (1970) repeated the Clark & Clark (1939) study. The studies were not exactly equivalent, but the results are interesting. They found that out of 89 black children, 28 chose the white doll and 61 chose the black. Run the appropriate Chi-square test on their data and interpret the results.

6.7 Combine the data from Exercises 6.5 and 6.6 into a two-way classification and run the appropriate test. How does the question which the two-way classification addresses differ from the questions addressed by Exercises 6.5 and 6.6?

6.8   From the following MINITAB output, verify the results in Exercise 6.7. Does MINITAB use Yates' Correction?

```
-- READ DATA INTO C1 AND C2
-- 169   83
--  28   61

-- CHISQ ON DATA IN C1 AND C2

EXPECTED FREQUENCIES ARE PRINTED BELOW OBSERVED FREQUENCIES
        I   C1   I   C2   I   TOTALS
-------I-------I-------I-------
    1   I   169  I   83   I     252
        I 145.6I  106.4I
-------I-------I-------I-------
    2   I    28  I   61   I      89
        I  51.4I   37.6I
-------I-------I-------I-------
TOTALS I   197  I  144  I     341

TOTAL CHI SQUARE =

        3.77 +   5.15 +
       10.66 +  14.59 +

              = 34.17

DEGREES OF FREEDOM = ( 2-1) X ( 2-1) =   1
```

6.9   Community Mental Health Centers tend to see a variety of problems, but some Centers seem to see more of one kind of problem than others. Out of the last 100 clients seen by each Center, a count has been made of those classed as having social adjustment problems, problems with living, and other problems. The data are given below.

MENTAL
HEALTH CENTER

	A	B	C	
Social Adjustment	50	40	40	130
Problems with Living	26	34	20	80
Other Problems	24	26	40	90
	100	100	100	300

a.   What null hypothesis would the Chi-square test on this table actually test?
b.   Run the appropriate analysis.
c.   Interpret the results.

6.10   Use the data in Exercise 6.9 to demonstrate how Chi-square varies as a function of sample size.

a.   Cut each cell entry in half and recompute Chi-square.
b.   What does this have to say about the role of the sample size in hypothesis testing?

6.11   In discussing the correction for continuity, reference was made to the idea of *fixed marginals*, meaning that a replication of the study would produce the same row and/or column totals. Give an example of a study in which

a.   both sets of marginal totals (Row and Column) could reasonably be considered fixed

b.   one set of marginal totals is fixed, and

c.   no marginal totals are fixed.

6.12   Howell & Huessy (1979) used a rating scale to classify children as showing or not showing hyperkinetic-like behavior in 2nd grade. They then classified these same children again in 4th and in 5th grade. At the end of 9th grade they examined school records and noted which children were enrolled in remedial English. In the data given below, all children who were ever classed as hyperkinetic have been combined into one group (labeled Hyper).

	Remedial English	Non-Remedial English	
Normal	22	187	209
Hyper	19	74	93
	41	261	302

Does behavior during elementary school discriminate achievement level during high school?

6.13   In Exercise 6.12 the data were collapsed across categories. If we don't collapse we obtain the following data

	Never	2nd	4th	2 & 4	5th	2 & 5	4 & 5	2, 4 & 5
Remedial Eng.	22	2	1	3	2	4	3	4
Non-Rem. Eng.	187	17	11	9	16	7	8	6

a.   Run the Chi-square test.

b.   What would you conclude, ignoring the small expected frequencies?

c.   How comfortable do you feel with these small expected frequencies, and how might you handle the problem?

6.14   Apply Equation 6.11 to the data in Exercise 6.13.

6.15   Use the likelihood ratio approach to analyze the data in Exercise 6.12.

6.16   Use the likelihood ratio approach to analyze the data in Exercise 6.13.

6.17   It would be possible to calculate a one-way Chi-square test on the data in row one of Exercise 6.13. What would be the hypothesis that you would be testing if you did that? How would that hypothesis differ from the one you tested in Exercise 6.13?

6.18 Suppose that we ask a group of 40 subjects whether they favor Monday Night Football, make them watch a game, and then ask them again. We could record the data as follows.

	Pro	*Con*	
Before	30	10	40
After	15	25	40
	45	35	80

a. Why would Chi-square calculated on such a table be inappropriate?

b. McNemar (1969) advocates reorganizing the table as

		AFTER		
		Pro	*Con*	
BEFORE	*Pro*	10	20	30
	Con	5	5	10
		15	25	40

Run a 2×2 Chi-square test on this table.

c. What null hypothesis did you test in Exercise 6.18*b*?

6.19 With reference to Exercise 6.18, I want to know about the effect of having to watch the game. Thus I run a one-way Chi-square test on the $20 + 5 = 25$ subjects who changed their opinion. (This is really McNemar's suggestion.)

a. Run the test.

b. Explain how this tests the null hypothesis that I really wanted to test.

6.20 The Post Office is interested in evaluating the speed of mail delivery. They mail letters (to Washington, D.C.) from a variety of distances, and record the number of days it takes for the mail to arrive. The data are given below.

			DISTANCE		
		50 miles	*150 miles*	*300 miles*	*3000 miles*
Days to deliver	1	5	10	15	5
	2	10	10	5	5
	3 or more	15	5	10	10

a. Run the Chi-square test.

b. Interpret the results.

6.21 From the following SPSS computer printout,

a. Verify the answer to Exercise 6.20a.
b. Interpret all of the entries in the upper left hand cell.
c. Interpret the value for "significance".

```
- - - - - - - - - - - - - - - - - - - - - - - - - - - - - - - - - - - - - - - - - - - -

                    DISTANCE
           Count   :
           Row % :50 MILES 150 MILE 300 MILE 3000 MIL    Row
           Col % :          S        S        ES        Total
           Total % :    1.:      2.:      3.:      4.:
DAYS       --------:--------:--------:--------:--------:
           1.  :     5 :    10 :    15 :     5 :     35
ONE            : 14.3 : 28.6 : 42.9 : 14.3 :  33.3
               : 16.7 : 40.0 : 50.0 : 25.0 :
               :  4.8 :  9.5 : 14.3 :  4.8 :
           -:--------:--------:--------:--------:
TWO        2.  :    10 :    10 :     5 :     5 :     30
               : 33.3 : 33.3 : 16.7 : 16.7 :  28.6
               : 33.3 : 40.0 : 16.7 : 25.0 :
               :  9.5 :  9.5 :  4.8 :  4.8 :
           -:--------:--------:--------:--------:
           3.  :    15 :     5 :    10 :    10 :     40
THREE OR MORE  : 37.5 : 12.5 : 25.0 : 25.0 :  38.1
               : 50.0 : 20.0 : 33.3 : 50.0 :
               : 14.3 :  4.8 :  9.5 :  9.5 :
           -:--------:--------:--------:--------:
        Column     30       25       30       20      105
        Total    28.6     23.8     28.6     19.0    100.0

Chi square =    12.89583 with    6 Degrees of freedom   Significance =  0.0447

- - - - - - - - - - - - - - - - - - - - - - - - - - - - - - - - - - - - - - - - - - - -
```

7 *Hypothesis Tests Applied to Means*

Objective

To introduce the *t* test as an hypothesis testing procedure for use with measurement data, and to show how it can be used with several different experimental designs.

Contents

In the two preceding chapters we have discussed tests dealing with frequency data. In those situations the results of any experiment can usually be represented by a few subtotals—the frequency of occurrence of each category of response. In this and subsequent chapters we are going to deal with a different type of data, that which we have previously termed measurement or score data.

In the analysis of measurement data our interest can either be focused on differences between groups of subjects, or on the relationship between two or more variables. The question of relationship between variables will be postponed until Chapters 9, 10, 15, and 16. The present chapter will be concerned with the question of differences, and the statistic in which we will be most interested will be the sample mean.

Suppose that we collected data on a random sample of 25 children who brushed their teeth with toothpaste X and 25 children who brushed their teeth with toothpaste Y. We found that the first group of children had a mean of 1.58 cavities per child after one year, while the second group had a mean of 2.10 cavities per child. Is the observed mean difference sufficient evidence for us to say that toothpaste X is better than toothpaste Y in terms of cavity prevention? This is the type of question on which we will concentrate in this chapter.

We will typically phrase our questions to ask whether one *mean* is significantly greater than some specified population mean, or whether two means are significantly different from one another. While one occasionally encounters questions about differences between sample variances, these are unfortunately relatively rare. Tests on variances will be dealt with at the end of this chapter. By and large most experiments are designed to examine sample means, and the bulk of this chapter will be devoted to methods for dealing with means and mean differences.

7.1 *Sampling Distribution of the Mean*

Sampling distribution of the mean

Central Limit Theorem

If we wish to perform tests on sample means, it is important that we know something about the ***sampling distribution of the mean***, since this distribution forms the basis for evaluating the likelihood of any particular value of $\bar{X}$. Fortunately all of the important information about the sampling distribution of the mean can be summed up in one vitally important theorem: the ***Central Limit Theorem***. The Central Limit Theorem states:

> Given a population with mean μ and variance σ^2, the sampling distribution of the mean (the distribution of sample means) will have mean μ and variance σ^2/N, and will approach the normal distribution as N, the sample size, increases.

This theorem is one of the most important theorems in statistics, since it not only gives us the mean and variance of the sampling distribution of the mean, regardless of sample size, but also states that ==as *N* increases this sampling distribution approaches normal== *whatever* ==the shape of the parent population.== The importance of this fact will become apparent shortly.

The rate at which the sampling distribution of the mean approaches normal is a function of the shape of the parent population. If the population is itself normal, the sampling distribution of the mean will be normal regardless of *N*. If the population is symmetric, the approach will be quite rapid, especially if the population is unimodal. If the population is markedly skewed, we may require sample sizes of 30 or more before the means closely approximate a normal distribution.

To illustrate the Central Limit Theorem suppose that we take an infinitely large population of random digits evenly distributed between 0 and 100. This population will have what is called a rectangular distribution, every value between 0 and 100 being equally likely. The probability distribution of this population is shown in Figure 7.1. In this case the mean (μ) is 50, the standard deviation (σ) is 28.87, and the variance (σ^2) is 833.33.

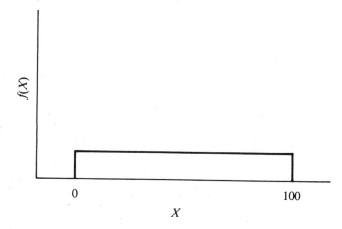

FIGURE 7.1
Rectangular distribution
with $\mu = 50$,
$\sigma = 28.87$

Further suppose that we drew with replacement 10,000 samples of size 4 ($N = 4$) from this population and plotted the resulting sample means. Such sampling can be easily accomplished with the aid of a high speed computer, and in fact the results of just such a procedure are presented in Figure 7.2(a). From this figure it is apparent that the means, while not exactly normally distributed, are at least peaked in the center and trail off toward the extremes. If you were to go to the effort of calculating the mean and variance of this distribution you would find that they are very close to $\mu = 50$ and $\sigma_{\bar{X}}^2 = \sigma^2/N = 833.33/4 = 208.33$. Any discrepancy between the actual and predicted values is attributable to rounding error and the fact that we did not draw an infinite number of samples.

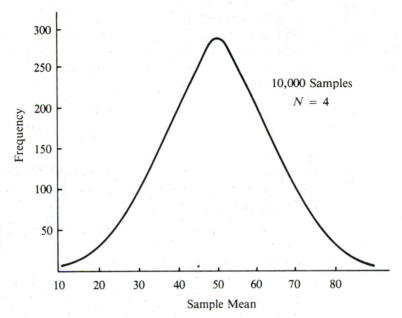

FIGURE 7.2(a)

Distribution of
10,000 means
for $N = 4$

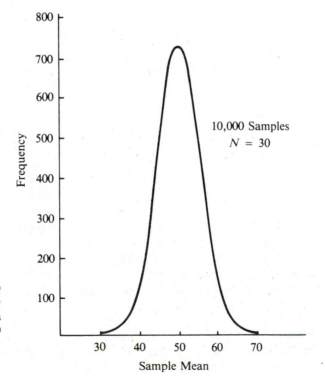

FIGURE 7.2(b)

Distribution of
10,000 means
for $N = 30$

Now suppose that we repeated the entire procedure, only this time we drew 10,000 samples of size 30. Again this has actually been done using a computer and the results are plotted in Figure 7.2(b). Here you see that, just as the Central Limit Theorem predicted, the distribution is approximately normal, the mean is again at $\mu = 50$, and the variance has been reduced to $833.33/30 = 27.78$.

7.2   *Testing Hypotheses about Means*

From the Central Limit Theorem we know the important characteristics of the sampling distribution of the mean. On the basis of this information we are in a position to begin testing hypotheses about the means. For the sake of continuity, however, it might be well to go back to something we discussed in Chapter 4, where we tested the hypothesis that a single score was sampled from a given population. In Chapter 4 we wished to test the hypothesis that a single subject with a finger tapping rate of 70 came from a normal population with $\mu = 100$ and $\sigma = 20$. To test this hypothesis we set up H_0 that the subject did come from this population. We then solved for z

$$z = \frac{X - \mu}{\sigma} = \frac{70 - 100}{20} = -1.5$$

and found that under H_0 our subject was only 1.5 standard deviations below μ. Since this is not an unlikely event (by our conventional definition of *unlikely* as $p < .05$), we failed to reject H_0.

Exactly the same logic applies to the testing of means. The only difference is that instead of comparing an observation to a distribution of observations, we will compare a mean to a distribution of means.

As an example, suppose that a manufacturer of Vitamin C would like to test the hypothesis that people who take Vitamin C differ in their mean IQ from normals. As a result, he collects 25 people who take Vitamin C and obtains IQ scores for them. The mean IQ in his sample is 105. Is this significantly (reliably) greater than the population mean of 100 (the IQ mean in the population)? The only way to answer this question is to have some idea what the distribution of sample means would look like if we were to draw random samples of $N = 25$ from a population of IQ scores. This is precisely the kind of question the Central Limit Theorem is designed to answer.

We know that the population of IQ scores has a mean of 100 and a standard deviation of 15 (a variance of $15^2 = 225$). The Central Limit Theorem states that if we obtain the sampling distribution of the mean from this population it will have a mean of 100, a variance of $225/25 = 9$, and a

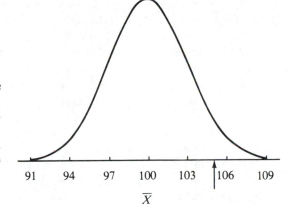

FIGURE 7.3

Sampling distribution
of the mean for
samples of $N = 25$
drawn from
$N(100,225)$ population

91   94   97   100   103   106   109

$\overline{X}$

Standard error standard deviation (usually referred to as the ***standard error*** $[\sigma_{\bar{X}}])$† of $\sigma/\sqrt{N} = 3$. This distribution is diagrammed in Figure 7.3. The arrow in Figure 7.3 represents the location of our sample mean.

Since we know that the sampling distribution is normally distributed with a mean of 100 and a standard error of 3, we can find areas under the distribution by reference to tables of the standard normal distribution. Thus, for example, the area to the right of $\bar{X} = 106$ is simply the area under the normal distribution greater than two standard deviations above the mean. For our particular situation we need the area above $\bar{X} = 105$. We can calculate this in the same way we did with individual observations, with only a minor change in our formula for z.

$$z = \frac{\bar{X} - \mu}{\sigma_{\bar{X}}} = \frac{\bar{X} - \mu}{\sigma/\sqrt{N}}$$

(7.1)

For our data

$$z = \frac{105 - 100}{3} = \frac{5}{3} = 1.67.$$

You will note that Equation 7.1 is of the same form as our earlier formula for z $(z = (X - \mu)/\sigma)$. The only differences are that X has been replaced by $\bar{X}$ and σ has been replaced by $\sigma_{\bar{X}}$. These differences occur because we are now talking about a distribution of means, and thus the data points are now means and the standard deviation in question is now the standard error of the mean (the standard deviation of the means). The formula for z continues to represent (1) a point on the distribution, minus (2) the mean of the distribution, all divided by (3) the standard deviation of the distribution.

---

† The standard deviation of any sampling distribution is normally referred to as a *standard error* of that distribution. Thus the standard deviation of means is called the standard error of the mean (symbolized by $\sigma_{\bar{X}}$), while the standard deviation of mean differences, which will be discussed later, is called the standard error of mean differences and is symbolized by $\sigma_{\bar{X}_1 - \bar{X}_2}$.

From Appendix (z) we find that the probability of a z as large as 1.67 is .0475 and the probability of a deviation as large as 1.67 standard errors in either direction from the mean $= 2(.0475) = .0950$. Thus with a two-tailed test (that people who take Vitamin C have a mean IQ *different* from that of normals), we would not reject H_0 and would conclude that we have no evidence that people who gobble Vitamin C differ in their IQs from normals. (Even had we rejected H_0 we would have no way to tell if Vitamin C increased IQ or if high IQ people were more likely to take Vitamin C.)

The above test of one sample mean against a known population mean is predicated on the assumption that the distribution in Figure 7.3 is normally distributed, or at least that it is sufficiently normal that we will be only negligibly in error when we refer to the tables of the standard normal distribution. Many textbooks will state that we assume that we are sampling from a normal population, but this is not strictly true. All that it is necessary to assume is that the sampling distribution of the mean (Figure 7.3) is normal. This assumption can be satisfied in two ways—either if (1) the population from which we sample is normal, or (2) our sample size is sufficiently large to produce at least approximate normality by way of the Central Limit Theorem. This is one of the great benefits of the Central Limit Theorem; it allows us to test hypotheses even if the parent population is not normal, providing only that N is sufficiently large.

7.3 Testing a Sample Mean When σ is Unknown (The One-Sample t Test)

The previous example was deliberately chosen from among a fairly limited number of situations in which the population standard deviation (σ) is known. In the general case, however, it is rare that we know the value of σ, and we will usually have to estimate it by way of the *sample* standard deviation (s). This poses certain problems with which we will now have to deal: the sampling distribution of s^2, the t statistic, and degrees of freedom.

The Sampling Distribution of s^2

If we are going to use s^2 as an estimate of σ^2, it is important that we first look at the sampling distribution of s^2, since it gives us some insight into the problems we are likely to encounter. From Chapter 6 we know that

$$\chi^2_{N-1} = \frac{(N-1)s^2}{\sigma^2},$$

and thus

$$s^2 = \frac{(\chi^2_{N-1})(\sigma^2)}{N-1}.$$

For any given population and sample size, $\sigma^2/(N-1)$ is a constant. Thus we may write

$$s^2 = \chi^2_{N-1}C$$

where C is our constant. We already know from Chapter 2 that the mean of the distribution of s^2 is σ^2 (that is the definition of an unbiased estimator). We also know from Chapter 6 that the χ^2 distribution is positively skewed, although as N increases the skewness diminishes. But if χ^2 is skewed, then the sampling distribution of s^2 is also skewed, and we can state

$$p(s_i^2 < \sigma^2) > p(s_i^2 > \sigma^2). \tag{7.2}$$

Equation 7.2 says that for any given sample, the obtained value of s^2 is more likely to be too small (relative to σ^2) than too large, even though in the long run s^2 is an unbiased estimator of σ^2.

The t Statistic

The practical result of this skewness in the sampling distribution of s^2 is that if we were to substitute s^2 for σ^2 in our formula for z, our denominator is more likely to be too small than too large. Thus, letting t denote the results when σ^2 is replaced by s^2,

$$t = \frac{\bar{X} - \mu}{\sqrt{\dfrac{s^2}{N}}} = \frac{\bar{X} - \mu}{\dfrac{s}{\sqrt{N}}} \tag{7.3}$$

is not going to be normally distributed, and therefore cannot be evaluated by reference to the tables of the standard normal distribution. (Since $s/\sqrt{N}$ is more likely to be less than $\sigma/\sqrt{N}$, t will be greater than the corresponding value of z more often than it will be less than z. Thus the distribution will have more values in the tails and fewer in the center.) An example of the comparison of z and t is given in Figure 7.4, where t on infinite degrees of freedom is equivalent to z.

As you can see from Figure 7.4, the distribution of t varies as a function of the degrees of freedom. From what we know about χ^2, this is to be expected, since the distribution of χ^2, and thus the distribution of s^2, is a function of the degrees of freedom. As $N \to \infty$, $p(s^2 < \sigma^2) \to p(s^2 > \sigma^2)$. The tendency for s to underestimate σ will disappear, and t will become normally distributed and equivalent to z.

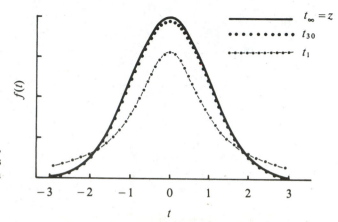

FIGURE 7.4

t distribution for 1, 30, and ∞ degrees of freedom

==While some textbooks advocate using *t* when $N < 30$ and pretending that $t = z$ for $N > 30$, that approach will not be used here.== It seems silly to use *z* as an approximation when the exact distribution (i.e., *t*) is given in the same collection of tables. The only time such a procedure can be justified is when we want something other than the common critical values such as $t_{.05}$ or $t_{.01}$. If for some reason we desire to know the area beyond a particular value of *t*, i.e., if we want more or less exact probabilities for our data rather than a simple statement of significance, then for large samples *z* can reasonably be used as an approximation. *have to go out further on a t-dist. to get smaller tails than a z. t-scores have to be bigger than z scores to be sig.*

Degrees of Freedom

It has been mentioned that the *t* distribution is a function of the degrees of freedom. For the one sample case, df $= N - 1$. The one degree of freedom has been lost because we used the sample mean in estimating σ^2. To be more precise, we calculated the variance (s^2) by calculating the deviations of the observations from their mean $(X - \bar{X})$. Since $\Sigma(X - \bar{X}) = 0$, only $N - 1$ of the deviations are free to vary (the *N*th is determined if the sum of the deviation is to be zero), and ==we have $N - 1$ degrees of freedom for *t*.==

Example 7.1

Is Fresh Air Good for You?

At this point a simple example would be helpful to illustrate the use of *t*. Suppose that the average life span for American males is 70 years and that we are interested in investigating the life span of people who spend most of their life working out of doors, such as loggers, construction workers, and so on. One might argue either that these people would have a longer life expectancy due to the fact that they have a great deal of exercise, or that they will have a shorter life expectancy because of the physical strains under which they work. To investigate the problem we decide to draw a sample of 25 such individuals from medical records and compare their ages at death with the population mean of 70. Before beginning our study we need to decide the level of significance (α) and whether we want a one- or a two-tailed test. Due to the nature of the question (we do not know which way the results will go) and the comments in Chapter 4 about one- and two-tailed tests, a two-tailed test is the more appropriate choice. We will therefore choose to work with a two-tailed test. For reasons of consistency, we will elect to set α at .05. It is to be hoped, however, that an actual experimenter would have a more rational reason for his choice of α than mere consistency.

Since we have set $\alpha = .05$ and are working with a two-tailed test, the critical value of t will be that value which cuts off the extreme 2.5% of each tail of the t distribution. This value is generally denoted as $t_{\alpha/2} = t_{.025}$. (Similarly the two-tailed critical value for $\alpha = .01$ is $t_{\alpha/2} = t_{.005}$.)

We next go to the medical records and collect the necessary data on a random sample of 25 people who have spent most of their adult life working out of doors. To simplify the example we will ignore the raw data and simply say that the sample mean was 75 and the sample standard deviation was 10. From an examination of the data we are satisfied that the population from which they came is sufficiently normally distributed to give us confidence in the normality of the sampling distribution of the mean.

From the data at hand,

$$t = \frac{\bar{X} - \mu}{s_{\bar{x}}} = \frac{\bar{X} - \mu}{s/\sqrt{N}}$$

$$= \frac{75 - 70}{10/\sqrt{25}} = \frac{75 - 70}{2}$$

$$= 2.50.$$

This value will be a member of the t distribution on $25 - 1 = 24$ df if the null hypothesis is true—i.e., if the data were sampled from a population with $\mu = 70$. From the table of t distribution in Appendix (t) we can obtain the critical value of t on 24 df ($t_{.025} = 2.064$). Since $t_{obt} > t_{.025}$, we will reject H_0 at $\alpha = .05$, and conclude that our sample was not drawn from a population with $\mu = 70$. By simple common sense we would further conclude that our data came from a population with $\mu > 70$. This is equivalent to the statement that the mean life span of the population of people who work out of doors is greater than the mean life span of people in general.

7.4 The Mean Difference Between Two Related Samples (The Matched-Sample t)

μ_1
μ_0

Matched-sample t

In the previous example we had one set of scores and wished to test the hypothesis that the mean of the population from which the scores came (μ_1) was equal to some specified population mean (μ_0). A closely related situation is the one in which we have two related (dependent or matched) samples and want to test the hypothesis that the difference between their corresponding population means is zero. In this case we want what is sometimes called the **matched-sample t**.

Consider the situation in which an experimenter runs a number of subjects under one condition, introduces some treatment (such as decreasing the amount of reinforcement) and then runs them again. He is interested in testing whether the mean score for the second testing session is different from the mean score for the first session. To simplify matters we shall let the variable X_1 represent the first set of scores and the variable X_2 represent the second set. Thus the data will look like those shown in Table 7.1.

TABLE 7.1
Illustration of Notational System

Subject	X_1	X_2	$X_1 - X_2$
1	X_{11}	X_{21}	$X_{11} - X_{21}$
2	X_{12}	X_{22}	$X_{12} - X_{22}$
3	X_{13}	X_{23}	$X_{13} - X_{23}$
...	...	...	...
N	X_{1N}	X_{2N}	$X_{1N} - X_{2N}$
Mean	$\bar{X}_1$	$\bar{X}_2$	$\overline{X_1 - X_2} = \bar{X}_1 - \bar{X}_2$

The null hypothesis in this case is the hypothesis that there is no difference between the mean (μ_1) of the population from which the X_1s were sampled and the mean (μ_2) of the population from which the X_2s were sampled. In other words, $H_0: \mu_1 - \mu_2 = 0$.

Difference Scores

While it is possible to view the data as representing two samples of scores, it is also possible, and very profitable, to view the data as one set of scores—the set of differences between X_1 and X_2 for each subject. This set of differences is indicated in the third column of Table 7.1. If in fact the treatment introduced after the first test session had no effect, the average subject's score would not change from session to session. By chance, some subjects would have a higher score on X_2 than on X_1, and some would have a lower score, but on the average there would be no difference. (This is directly analogous to the situation in which we have two identical populations and repeatedly sample pairs of scores, one score from each population. If the populations are identical, or at least both are symmetric and have the same mean, the difference between the two scores will average out to zero.)

If we now think of our data as being the column of difference scores, the null hypothesis becomes the hypothesis that $\mu_{X_1-X_2} = \mu_1 - \mu_2 = 0$. In other words, the mean of differences is equal to the difference of means, and a test on one is equivalent to a test on the other. The statement that $\mu_{X_1-X_2} = \mu_1 - \mu_2$ is expressed in a theorem which states that the mean of the sum of (or differences between) two variables is equal to the sum (or difference) of their means—i.e., $\overline{X_1 \pm X_2} = \bar{X}_1 \pm \bar{X}_2$. The truth of this theorem can be easily demonstrated.

$$\text{Mean } (X_1 \pm X_2) = \overline{X_1 \pm X_2} = \frac{\sum(X_1 \pm X_2)}{N}$$

$$= \frac{\sum X_1 \pm \sum X_2}{N} = \frac{\sum X_1}{N} \pm \frac{\sum X_2}{N} = \bar{X}_1 \pm \bar{X}_2$$

The t Statistic

We are now at precisely the same place we were a few pages back. We have a sample of data (the difference scores) and a null hypothesis, and want to test whether that sample came from a population with a mean (0) specified by H_0. Thus, recalling that t equals the difference between a sample mean and a population mean, divided by the standard error of the mean

$$t = \frac{\overline{X_1 - X_2} - \mu_{X_1-X_2}}{s_{\overline{X_1-X_2}}} = \frac{\overline{X_1 - X_2} - 0}{s_{\overline{X_1-X_2}}}. \qquad (7.4)$$

A more common, but equivalent, way of writing Equation 7.4 is to let the
D   symbol **D** represent the **difference scores** and to write

Difference scores

$$t = \frac{\bar{D} - 0}{s_{\bar{D}}}$$

where, from the Central Limit Theorem, $s_{\bar{D}} = s_D/\sqrt{N}$, **N** being the number of difference scores.

$$S_d = \sqrt{\frac{\sum (d_i - \bar{d})^2}{n-1}}$$

Degrees of Freedom

The degrees of freedom for the matched-sample case are exactly the same as they were for the one-sample case. Since we are working with the difference scores, N will be equal to the number of subjects (or the number of *pairs* of observations). Since the variance of these difference scores is used as an estimate of $\sigma^2_{\bar{X}_1-X_2}$, and since this sample variance relies on the sample mean $(\overline{X_1-X_2})$, we will lose one df to the mean and have $N-1$ df.

Example 7.2

Placebo Effects of Cold Remedies

Suppose we wish to examine the placebo effect of cold preventatives. We take a group of 10 recent cold sufferers and ask them to rate the severity of their cold on a 25–point scale. We then tell them to scurry right back the next time they feel a cold coming on. As they return with their next cold we hand them little yellow pills which we say will reduce the severity of the cold. In fact these little yellow pills are nothing but compressed sawdust, which is not particularly noted for its medicinal properties. When the patients have recovered from their colds, we again ask them to rate its severity on a 25–point scale. The data from this fictitious study are presented in Table 7.2, where X_1 represents the first set of ratings and X_2 represents the second set.

From Table 7.2 you will note that $\overline{X_1-X_2}=\bar{X}_1-\bar{X}_2$, just as was stated above. You will also see that all of the information we need to calculate t is given.

$$t=\frac{\overline{X_1-X_2}-0}{s\,\overline{X_1-X_2}}=\frac{\overline{X_1-X_2}-0}{s_{X_1-X_2}/\sqrt{N}}$$

$$=\frac{1.2-0}{1.4757/\sqrt{10}}=\frac{1.2}{.4667}$$

$$=2.5714$$

On $10-1=9$ df, $t_{.025}=2.262$. Since t_{obt} (2.5714) $>t_{.025}$ (2.262), we will reject the null hypothesis that $\mu_{X_1-X_2}=0$ in favor of the alternative hypothesis. Thus we will conclude that the taking of the placebo affected (in this case reduced) the reported severity of colds. Whether this reduction is to be attributed to a desire on the part of the subjects to please the experimenter, a psychological effect of the placebos, or some real medicinal effect of sawdust, cannot possibly be determined from this experiment—it was not designed to answer those questions. What we do know, however, is that the data demonstrate (at $\alpha=.05$) that placebos do have an effect on reported severity.

The basic assumption underlying the above test is the same as that for the standard one-sample t test. We assume that the sampling distribution of $\bar{X}_1-\bar{X}_2$ is normal.

TABLE 7.2
Hypothetical Data
from Placebo Study

Subject	X_1	X_2	$X_1 - X_2$
1	18	16	2
2	19	16	3
3	17	18	−1
4	15	15	0
5	19	17	2
6	20	18	2
7	22	21	1
8	20	21	−1
9	17	14	3
10	17	16	1
Mean	18.4	17.2	1.2
Variance			2.1778
S.D.			1.4757

Matched Samples

Matched samples

In the previous section we considered the situation in which we have related or dependent samples. Such samples are frequently *matched samples*, which is probably a more descriptive label. Since many people seem to have difficulty keeping in mind the difference between matched or dependent samples and independent samples, which we will discuss in the next section, it would be profitable to examine for a moment just what matched samples are.

In the previous example we tested 10 different subjects twice. Thus we had 10 pairs of measurements, a pair being defined as the two scores for any one subject. It should be apparent that the X_2 observation for any subject is not likely to be independent of his X_1 observation. If a subject tends to think of all colds as severe, he is likely to give relatively high ratings for both X_1 and X_2. On the other hand, a subject who thinks of anything less than double pneumonia as good for his macho image is likely to give low ratings to X_1 and X_2, even though X_1 may be higher than X_2. This tendency for X_1 and X_2 to be correlated forces us to use a test, such as the one just described, which takes this relationship into account.

Matched samples are not limited to the situation in which each subject is tested twice. Another very common design uses pairs of subjects who are matched on some variable, for example age or home environment. In these designs one member of the pair might be given treatment X_1 and the other given treatment X_2. Data collected in this way would also be tested by a matched-sample t, since we would expect that the responses of a pair of subjects on X_1 and X_2 would not be independent. (If we thought that they would be independent there would have been no point in forming matched pairs in the first place.) Another common instance of matched samples occurs when the X_1 and X_2 scores represent the mean or median responses of Groups 1 and 2 on each trial of a learning experiment. Here the first X_1, X_2 pair would represent the responses on Trial$_1$, the second pair would represent the responses on Trial$_2$, and so on.

We have seen three examples of situations in which responses are paired. In the first case they were paired because they came from the same subject, in the second because they came from a pair of subjects, and in the third because they came from the same trial. The general rule is that we will consider that we have matched or dependent samples whenever we can meaningfully think of the data as representing pairs of scores, regardless of the basis on which these pairs are formed.

7.5 Testing the Difference Between the Means of Two Independent Samples (*Two-Sample t*)

One of the most common uses of the *t* test involves testing the difference between the means of two independent groups. For example we might wish to compare the mean number of trials-to-criterion in a simple discrimination task for two groups of rats—one raised under normal conditions and one raised under conditions of sensory deprivation. Or we might wish to compare the mean levels of retention of a group of college students asked to recall active-declarative sentences and a group asked to recall passive-negative sentences. As a final example we might wish to compare the mean reported severity of colds of one group given a placebo and one group not given the placebo.

In conducting any experiment with two independent groups we would most likely find that the two sample means differed by some amount. The important question, however, is whether this difference is sufficiently large to justify the conclusion that the two samples were drawn from different populations—i.e., was the mean of the population of scores from which the placebo scores were drawn different from the mean of the population of scores from which the non-placebo scores were drawn.

Distribution of Mean Differences

Sampling distribution of mean differences

Since we are interested in the difference between sample means it is important that we digress for a moment and examine the ***sampling distribution of mean differences***. Suppose that we have two populations (X_1 and X_2) with means μ_1 and μ_2 and variances σ_1^2 and σ_2^2. We now draw samples of size N_1 from population X_1 and samples of size N_2 from population X_2, and record the means and the differences between the means for each pair of samples. ==Because we are sampling independently from each population, the sample means will be independent.== (Means are paired only in the trivial sense of being drawn at the same time.) Since we are only supposing, we might as well go all the way and suppose that we repeated this procedure an infinite number of times. The results are presented schematically in Figure 7.5. In this figure the first two columns represent the sampling distributions

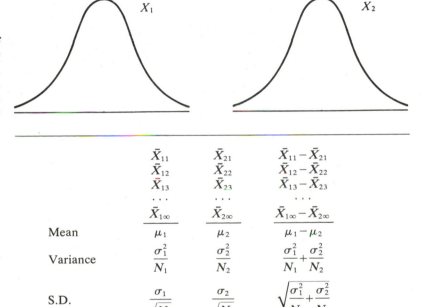

FIGURE 7.5

Hypothetical set of means and mean differences when sampling from two populations

	X_1	X_2	$X_1 - X_2$
	$\bar{X}_{11}$	$\bar{X}_{21}$	$\bar{X}_{11} - \bar{X}_{21}$
	$\bar{X}_{12}$	$\bar{X}_{22}$	$\bar{X}_{12} - \bar{X}_{22}$
	$\bar{X}_{13}$	$\bar{X}_{23}$	$\bar{X}_{13} - \bar{X}_{23}$
	$\cdots$	$\cdots$	$\cdots$
	$\bar{X}_{1\infty}$	$\bar{X}_{2\infty}$	$\bar{X}_{1\infty} - \bar{X}_{2\infty}$
Mean	μ_1	μ_2	$\mu_1 - \mu_2$
Variance	$\dfrac{\sigma_1^2}{N_1}$	$\dfrac{\sigma_2^2}{N_2}$	$\dfrac{\sigma_1^2}{N_1} + \dfrac{\sigma_2^2}{N_2}$
S.D.	$\dfrac{\sigma_1}{\sqrt{N_1}}$	$\dfrac{\sigma_2}{\sqrt{N_2}}$	$\sqrt{\dfrac{\sigma_1^2}{N_1} + \dfrac{\sigma_2^2}{N_2}}$

of $\bar{X}_1$ and $\bar{X}_2$, while the third column represents the sampling distribution of mean differences. It is this third column in which we are most interested, since we are really interested in testing differences between means. The mean of this distribution is $\mu_1 - \mu_2$, from a theorem discussed earlier. The

Variance sum law   variance of this distribution is given by what is commonly called ==the *variance sum law*==, a limited form of which states:

> ==The variance of a sum or difference of two *independent* variables is equal to the sum of their variances.==

The complete form of the law would delete the restriction that the variables be independent, and states that the variance of their sum or difference is

$$\sigma_{X_1 \pm X_2}^2 = \sigma_1^2 + \sigma_2^2 \pm 2r\sigma_1\sigma_2, \tag{7.5}$$

where the notation ± is interpreted as + when we are speaking of their sum and as − when we are speaking of their difference. The term r in Equation 7.5 is the correlation between the two variables and is equal to 0 when the variables are independent. (The fact that $r \neq 0$ when the variables are not independent was what forced us to treat the matched sample case separately.)

Since the variance of the distribution of $\bar{X}_1$ is σ_1^2/N_1 and the variance of the distribution of $\bar{X}_2$ is σ_2^2/N_2, and since the variables are independent, then the variance of the difference of these two variables is the sum of their variances. Thus

$$\sigma_{\bar{X}_1 - \bar{X}_2}^2 = \sigma_{\bar{X}_1}^2 + \sigma_{\bar{X}_2}^2 = \frac{\sigma_1^2}{N_1} + \frac{\sigma_2^2}{N_2}. \tag{7.6}$$

Having found the mean and variance of a set of differences between means, we know most of what we need to know. The sampling distribution of mean differences is presented in Figure 7.6.

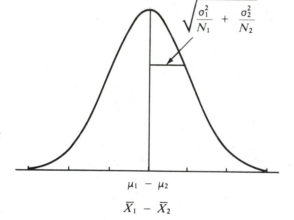

FIGURE 7.6

Sampling distribution of mean differences

The final point to be made about this distribution concerns its shape. An important theorem in statistics states that the sum or differences of two normally distributed variables is itself normally distributed. Since Figure 7.6 represents the difference between two sampling distributions of means, and since we know that the sampling distribution of means is at least approximately normal for reasonable sample sizes, then the distribution in Figure 7.6 must itself be at least approximately normal.

The t Statistic

Given the information we now have about the sampling distribution of mean differences, we can proceed to develop the appropriate test procedure. We have earlier defined z as a statistic (a point on the distribution) minus the mean of the distribution, divided by the standard error of the distribution. Our statistic in the present case is $(\bar{X}_1 - \bar{X}_2)$, the observed difference between the sample means. The mean of the distribution is $(\mu_1 - \mu_2)$, and the ***standard error of mean differences*** is

Standard error of mean differences

$$\sqrt{\frac{\sigma_1^2}{N_1} + \frac{\sigma_2^2}{N_2}}.$$

Thus we can write

$$z = \frac{(\bar{X}_1 - \bar{X}_2) - (\mu_1 - \mu_2)}{\sqrt{\dfrac{\sigma_1^2}{N_1} + \dfrac{\sigma_2^2}{N_2}}}. \tag{7.7}$$

However the above formula is not particularly useful, since we rarely know the necessary population variances. We can circumvent this problem by using the sample variances as estimates of the population variances. This, for the same reasons discussed earlier for the one-sample t, means that our result will be distributed as t rather than z.

$$t = \frac{(\bar{X}_1 - \bar{X}_2) - (\mu_1 - \mu_2)}{\sqrt{\dfrac{s_1^2}{N_1} + \dfrac{S_2^2}{N_2}}}. \tag{7.8}$$

Pooling Variances

While Equation 7.8 is quite appropriate when the sample sizes are equal, it requires some modification for unequal sample sizes. This modification is in the interest of improving our estimate of the population variance. One of the assumptions inherent in the use of t for two independent samples is the assumption that $\sigma_1^2 = \sigma_2^2$—i.e., that our samples come from populations with equal variances (regardless of the truth or falsity of H_0). Such an assumption is generally not altogether unreasonable for most cases. If we think of an experiment as starting out with two groups of subjects who are equivalent, and then doing something to one (or both) group(s) which will raise or lower the scores, it often makes sense to assume that the variances will remain unaffected. Since the population variances are assumed to be equal, this common variance can be represented by the symbol σ^2, without a subscript. We have two estimates of σ^2, namely s_1^2 and s_2^2, and it makes sense to obtain some sort of an average of s_1^2 and s_2^2, on the grounds that this average (called the ***pooled variance***) should be a better estimate of σ^2 than either of the two separate estimates. We do not want to take the simple arithmetic mean, however, since this would give equal weight to the two estimates even if one were based on considerably more observations.

Pooled variance

Weighted average   What we want is a ==**weighted average**, where the sample variances are weighted by their df.== If we call this new estimate s^2 then

$$s^2 = \frac{(N_1-1)s_1^2 + (N_2-1)s_2^2}{N_1+N_2-2}.$$ *(7.9)*

Having defined s^2 we can now write

$$t = \frac{(\bar{X}_1 - \bar{X}_2) - (\mu_1 - \mu_2)}{\sqrt{\dfrac{s^2}{N_1} + \dfrac{s^2}{N_2}}}, \quad or \quad \sqrt{s_p^2\left(\frac{1}{n_1}+\frac{1}{n_2}\right)}$$ *(7.10)*

[handwritten margin note:] $s_p^2 = \dfrac{\sum(x_{i1}-\bar{x}_1)^2 + \sum(x_{i2}-\bar{x}_2)^2}{n_1+n_2-2}$

where s^2 is defined as in Equation 7.9. It is left to the student to show that Equations 7.8 and 7.10 are equivalent when $N_1 = N_2$.

Degrees of Freedom

You will note that two sample variances (s_1^2 and s_2^2) have gone into our calculation of t. Each of these variances is based upon squared deviations about their corresponding sample means, and therefore each sample variance has $N_i - 1$ df. Over the two samples, therefore, we will have $N_1 - 1 + N_2 - 1 = N_1 + N_2 - 2$ df. ==Thus the two-sample t will be based on $N_1 + N_2 - 2$ degrees of freedom.==

Example 7.3

Recall as a Function of Sentence Structure

To illustrate the use of t as a test of the difference between two independent means, we will consider an example from the verbal learning literature. Let us suppose that an investigator wants to determine whether subjects exhibit greater recall for active-declarative sentences (Joe rang the bell) than for passive-negative sentences ("The bell was not rung by Joe"). The experimenter obtains 30 subjects, and assigns them at random to two groups of 15 subjects each. One group (Group A) is read 25 active-declarative sentences, with a recall test after each sentence. The other group (Group P) hears and recalls passive-negative forms of the sentences used for Group A. The number of sentences correctly recalled by each subject are presented in Table 7.3.

Before we consider any statistical test, and ideally before the data are even collected, we must specify several features of the test. First we must decide upon a level of significance (α), and whether we want a one- or a two-tailed test. For reasons given earlier in the book we will choose a two-tailed test with $\alpha = .05$, although there is nothing particularly sacred about these decisions. Finally, we must state the

TABLE 7.3

	GROUP P	GROUP A
	13	17
	18	17
	17	21
	13	18
	14	22
	13	18
	18	16
	19	15
	16	18
	14	20
	13	21
	15	16
	14	15
	16	16
	15	20
Mean	15.2	18.0
Variance	4.170	5.286

null hypothesis. Since we want to test whether or not there is a difference between the means of the populations of scores from which our two samples were drawn, the null hypothesis will be the hypothesis that there is no difference between the population means—i.e., $H_0: \mu_1 - \mu_2 = 0$.† Given the null hypothesis as stated, we can now calculate t. For the sake of a complete example we will pool our variances (by Equation 7.9), although as has been said this is not necessary when $N_1 = N_2$.

$$t = \frac{(\bar{X}_1 - \bar{X}_2) - (\mu_1 - \mu_2)}{\sqrt{\dfrac{s^2}{N_1} + \dfrac{s^2}{N_2}}}.$$

From H_0, $\mu_1 - \mu_2 = 0$, and from Equation 7.9

$$s^2 = \frac{(N_1 - 1)s_1^2 + (N_2 - 1)s_2^2}{N_1 + N_2 - 2}$$

$$= \frac{14(4.170) + 14(5.286)}{15 + 15 - 2} = \frac{58.38 + 74.004}{28}$$

$$= 4.728$$

† It should be pointed out that if we had a good reason for testing the hypothesis that μ_1 was 5 points higher than μ_2, for example, we could set $H_0: \mu_1 - \mu_2 = 5$, although this type of situation is extremely rare.

Then

$$t = \frac{(15.2 - 18) - (0)}{\sqrt{\dfrac{4.728}{15} + \dfrac{4.728}{15}}} = \frac{-2.8}{\sqrt{\dfrac{9.456}{15}}} = \frac{-2.8}{.794}$$

$$= 3.53.$$

For this example we have $N_i - 1 = 15 - 1 = 14$ df for each group, making a total of $N_1 + N_2 - 2 = 28$ df. From the sampling distribution of t in Appendix (t), $t_{.05}(28) = \pm 2.048$. Since our value of t_{obt} far exceeds $t_{\alpha/2}$, we will reject H_0 (at $\alpha = .05$) and conclude that there is a difference between the means of the populations from which our observations were drawn. In other words we will conclude (statistically) that $\mu_1 \neq \mu_2$ and (practically) that $\mu_1 < \mu_2$. In terms of our experimental variables, active-declarative sentences are recalled better than passive-negative sentences.†

7.6 Heterogeneity of Variance (The Behrens-Fisher Problem)

Homogeneity of variance

We have already seen that one of the assumptions underlying the t test for two independent samples is the assumption of *homogeneity of variance* ($\sigma_1^2 = \sigma_2^2 = \sigma^2$). To be more specific, we can say that *when* H_0 is true and *when* we have homogeneity of variance, then, pooling the variances, the ratio

$$t = \frac{\bar{X}_1 - \bar{X}_2}{\sqrt{\dfrac{s^2}{N_1} + \dfrac{s^2}{N_2}}},$$

is distributed as t on $N_1 + N_2 - 2$ df. If we have homogeneity of variance there is no difficulty, and the techniques discussed in this section are not needed. When we do not have homogeneity of variance, however, this ratio is not, strictly speaking, distributed as t. This leaves us with some sort of a problem, but fortunately a solution (or a number of competing solutions) exist.

---

† Since active-declarative sentences are generally shorter than passive-negative sentences, our interpretation of the results could be open to question. Unless our sentences were equated for length, we have no defense against the argument that we have merely shown that shorter sentences are better remembered than longer ones. We have confounded the variables of syntax and sentence length.

Heterogeneous variances

First of all, unless $\sigma_1^2 = \sigma_2^2 = \sigma^2$ it makes no sense to pool (average) variances since the reason we were pooling variances was that we assumed them to be estimating the same quantity. For the case of **heterogeneous variances** we will first dispense with pooling procedures and define

$$t' = \frac{\bar{X}_1 - \bar{X}_2}{\sqrt{\dfrac{s_1^2}{N_1} + \dfrac{s_2^2}{N_2}}},$$

where s_1^2 and s_2^2 are taken to be heterogeneous variances. As we have said, t' is *not* distributed as t on $N_1 + N_2 - 2$ df. But if we knew what the sampling distribution of t' actually looked like, there would be no problem. Fortunately, although there is no universal agreement, we know at least the approximate distribution of t'.

The Behrens-Fisher Problem and Alternative Solutions for the Sampling Distribution of t'

Behrens-Fisher problem

One of the first attempts to find the exact sampling distribution of t' was begun by Behrens and extended by Fisher, and the general problem of heterogeneity of variance has come to be known as the **Behrens-Fisher problem**. Based on this work, the Behrens-Fisher distribution of t' was derived, and is tabled in Fisher & Yates (1953, Table VIa). However this tabled distribution covers only a few degrees of freedom, and is therefore not particularly useful for most purposes.

To provide a more practical approach to the problem, Cochran & Cox (1957) have presented a method of approximating the critical values of the Behrens-Fisher distribution. This method requires that we solve for the critical value of t' against which to compare t'_{obt}.

$$t'_{\alpha/2} = \frac{t_1 \dfrac{s_1^2}{N_1} + t_2 \dfrac{s_2^2}{N_2}}{\dfrac{s_1^2}{N_1} + \dfrac{s_2^2}{N_2}},$$

where t_1 and t_2 are the critical values ($t_{\alpha/2}$) of t for $N_1 - 1$ and $N_2 - 1$ df, respectively.

Satterthwaite's solution

An alternative solution was developed by Satterthwaite (1946) based on a different approach to the problem. **Satterthwaite's solution** is particularly important in that we will refer back to it when we discuss the analysis of variance. Using Satterthwaite's method, one views t' as a legitimate member of the t distribution, but for an unknown number of degrees of freedom. The problem then becomes one of solving for the appropriate

df'

df (denoted **df'**).

$$df' = \frac{\left(\dfrac{s_1^2}{N_1} + \dfrac{s_2^2}{N_2}\right)^2}{\left(\dfrac{s_1^2}{N_1}\right)^2 \Big/ (N_1 - 1) + \left(\dfrac{s_2^2}{N_2}\right)^2 \Big/ (N_2 - 1)}$$

The degrees of freedom (df') are then taken to the nearest integer. The advantage of this approach is that df' is bounded by the smaller of $N_1 - 1$ and $N_2 - 1$ at one extreme and $N_1 + N_2 - 2$ at the other. More specifically

$$\text{Min}(N_1 - 1, N_2 - 1) \le df' \le N_1 + N_2 - 2.$$

Since the critical value of t decreases as df increases, we can first evaluate t' as if df' were at its minimum. If the difference is significant here, it will certainly be significant for the true df'. If the difference is not significant, we can then evaluate t' at its maximum $(N_1 + N_2 - 2)$. If it is not significant at this point, no reduction in the degrees of freedom (by more accurate calculation of df') would cause it to be significant. Thus the only time we even need to actually calculate df' is when the value of t' would not be significant for $\text{Min}(N_1 - 1, N_2 - 1)$ df, but would be significant for $N_1 + N_2 - 2$ df.

In this book we will rely primarily on the Satterthwaite approximation. It has the distinct advantage of applying easily to problems which will arise in the analysis of variance, and is not noticeably more awkward than the Cochran & Cox solution.

Testing for Heterogeneity of Variance

An important question, however, is whether we even have heterogeneity of variance to begin with. Since we obviously do not know σ_1^2 and σ_2^2 (if we did we would not be solving for t), we must in some way test the difference between our two sample variances (s_1^2 and s_2^2). If we define

$$F = \frac{s_L^2}{s_S^2}, \qquad\qquad (7.13)$$

s_L^2 where s_L^2 represents the larger of the two variances and s_S^2 the smaller, then
s_S^2 this statistic (F) is distributed as the F distribution on $N_1 - 1$ and $N_2 - 1$ df.
F The F distribution is tabled in Appendix (F) and will be discussed in more detail later. To use the table you simply enter it at the column corresponding to the df for the numerator and the row corresponding to the df for the denominator. The cell entries correspond to the upper-tail critical values for $\alpha = .05, .025$, and $.01$ respectively. Since we want a two-tailed test (we want to reject H_0 whenever $\sigma_1^2 \neq \sigma_2^2$) these α levels should be doubled. Thus for a two-tailed test at $\sigma = .05$ we would use the tabled critical value at $\alpha = .025$.

TABLE 7.4

Calculations for
Solution with
Heterogeneous Variance

	X_1	X_2
Mean	46.22	42.10
Variance	40.00	10.00
N	15	10

$$F = \frac{s_1^2}{s_2^2} = \frac{40}{10} = 4.00$$

$$F_{.025}(14,9) = 3.77$$

$$t' = \frac{\bar{X}_1 - \bar{X}_2}{\sqrt{\dfrac{s_1^2}{N_1} + \dfrac{s_2^2}{N_2}}} = \frac{46.22 - 42.10}{\sqrt{\dfrac{40}{15} + \dfrac{10}{10}}} = \frac{4.12}{\sqrt{3.67}}$$

$$= 2.15$$

$$df' = \frac{\left(\dfrac{s_1^2}{N_1} + \dfrac{s_2^2}{N_2}\right)^2}{\left(\dfrac{s_1^2}{N_1}\right)^2 \Big/ (N_1 - 1) + \left(\dfrac{s_2^2}{N_2}\right)^2 \Big/ (N_2 - 1)}$$

$$= \frac{\left(\dfrac{40}{15} + \dfrac{10}{10}\right)^2}{\left(\dfrac{40}{15}\right)^2 \Big/ 14 + \left(\dfrac{10}{10}\right)^2 \Big/ 9}$$

$$= \frac{(2.67 + 1)^2}{\dfrac{2.67^2}{14} + \dfrac{1^2}{9}}$$

$$= \frac{(3.67)^2}{.5079 + .1111} = 21.72$$

$$= 22$$

Example 7.4

**Hypothetical Data
with Heterogeneous
Variances**

To illustrate the procedure of working with heterogeneous variances, consider the data in Table 7.4. The upper part of the table presents hypothetical means, variances, and sample sizes. The lower portion of Table 7.4 gives the calculation of F, t', and df'.

The first test shown in Table 7.4 is an F test for heterogeneity of variance. The $F_{obt} = 4.00$ is larger than $F_{.025} = 3.77$ on 14 and 9 df, causing rejection of the null hypothesis of equal population variances.

Having rejected H_0, we know that the resulting test statistic will not be exactly distributed as t, but as t'. We next solve for t', obtaining a value of 2.15. This value would not be significant at the minimum df' (9), but would be for the maximum df' (23), thus requiring us to solve for df' (the number of degrees of freedom with which we will enter the table of t). From Table 7.4 we see that df' = 21.72, which, taken to the nearest integer, is 22. From Appendix (t) we find that the critical value of $t_{.025}$ on 22 df = 2.07. Since $t' > t_{.025}$, we will reject H_0 and conclude that the population means differ.

An important point to be grasped in the last section is that the use of a special formula for the calculation of df' is seldom needed. The only time when there is any serious problem resulting from heterogeneity is when t' falls in that rather narrow region where it would be significant for the maximum df' and not significant for the minimum df'. At all other times the interpretation is straightforward, regardless of whether or not our population variances are equal. This is one of the things we have in mind when we speak about the robustness of t in the face of violations of assumptions. To put it in its simplest terms, whether or not we have heterogeneity of variance, a large value of t is significant and a small one is not. Only when t falls in the borderline region will we worry about heterogeneity of variance.

The Robustness of t

Robust

We have previously referred to the fact that the t test is what is described as ***robust***, meaning that it is more or less unaffected by moderate departures from the underlying assumptions. For the t test for two independent samples, we have two major assumptions and one side condition that must be considered. The two assumptions are those of normality of the sampling distribution of mean differences and homogeneity of variance. The side condition is the condition of equal sample sizes vs. unequal sample sizes. Although we have just seen how the problem of heterogeneity of variance can be handled by special procedures, it is still relevant to ask what happens if we use the standard approach even with heterogeneous variances.

Box (1953), Norton (1953), Boneau (1960), and many others have investigated the effects of violating, both independently and jointly, the underlying assumptions of t. The general conclusion to be drawn from these studies is that for equal sample sizes, violation of the assumption of equal variances produces very small effects—the nominal value of $\alpha = .05$ is most likely within $\pm.02$ of the true value of α. By this we mean that if you set up a situation with unequal variances, *but with H_0 true*, and proceed to draw (and compute t on) a very large number of pairs of samples, you will find that somewhere between 3 and 7% of the sample *t* values actually exceed $\pm t_{.025}$. This level of inaccuracy is not intolerable. The same kind of statement applies to violations of the assumption of normality, provided that the true populations are of roughly the same shape, or else both are symmetric. If the distributions are markedly skewed (especially if in opposite directions), serious problems arise unless their variances are fairly equal.

With unequal sample sizes, however, the results are more difficult to interpret. In Boneau's study, for example, sample variances were pooled in all cases, since this is probably the most common procedure in practice (although it is incorrect for heterogeneous variances). Boneau found that when there was heterogeneity of variance and unequal sample sizes, the actual and normative probability values differed considerably. However keep in mind that Boneau was pooling variances and evaluating *t* on $N_1 + N_2 - 2$ df. We do not know what would have happened had he solved for *t'* and then evaluated *t'* on df' degrees of freedom, although from what we already know from the preceding section it would seem reasonable to predict that in this case the test would have proven to be robust since Satterthwaite's solution does not require the homogeneity assumption.

The investigator who has collected data which she feels may violate one or more of the underlying assumptions is referred to the article by Boneau (1960). This article is quite readable and contains an excellent list of references to other work in the area.

7.7 Heterogeneity of Variance as an Experimental Finding

To this point we have been speaking of heterogeneity of variance as if it were something to be avoided, or at least treated with caution, and have generally ignored the fact that it might be a meaningful result in its own right. While statistical analyses generally deal with means, and view variability as something which only makes our interpretation of means more difficult, there is much to be said for the variance as a measure of the effect of an experimental manipulation. Consider, for example, an individual who wishes to investigate the effects of a tutorial system of teaching, as opposed to the more traditional lecture method. He takes two groups of students, drawn at random from the population of available students, teaches one group by a tutorial method and the other by a traditional system of lectures, and finally administers some sort of an examination at the end of the year. We will assume that an examination which is fair to both groups can be devised. The data from the experiment are given in Table 7.5.

The difference between the means is obviously trivial, and not even worth testing. (Who would care even if a difference of such a small magnitude

TABLE 7.5
Data for Two
Alternative
Teaching Methods

	TUTORIAL	LECTURE
Mean	86.5	85.1
Variance	61.4	19.75
N	20	20

were to be statistically significant?) If our investigator were to conclude, however, that there were no differences between the two methods, he would be missing the most interesting result displayed by these data. Notice that the variance for the tutorial group is more than 3 times the variance for the lecture group. To test this we can compute

$$F = 61.4/19.75 = 3.11$$

on 19 and 19 df. From Appendix (F) with some rough interpolation, $F_{.025}(19,19) = 2.53$. Thus we would reject H_0 and conclude that the variance for the tutorial method is significantly greater (at $\alpha = .05$, two-tailed) than for the lecture method. Apparently the tutorial method is very good for some students, and very bad for others. The lecture method seems to strike a neutral position for all. This finding is very likely of more interest than any differences which might appear between means.

Testing for Heterogeneity with Nonindependent Variances

The F test for the difference between two sample variances which we have just discussed applies only to variances of independent samples. But suppose that we had subjects perform the same task on two successive days, and wished to compare the variances for the two days. Since the same subjects are involved, the variances will not be independent. If we let $F = s_1^2/s_2^2$, $s_1^2 > s_2^2$, $r =$ the correlation between the two sets of scores, and $N =$ the number of subjects, it can be shown that

$$t = \frac{(F-1)\sqrt{(N-2)}}{2\sqrt{F(1-r^2)}} \qquad (7.14)$$

is distributed as t on $N - 2$ df, and is a test of H_0: $\sigma_1^2 = \sigma_2^2$. For the ingenious derivation of this technique the reader is referred to Pitman (1939) or Snedecor & Cochran (1967).

It is of more than passing interest that we have methods for testing the differences between variances. The social sciences have a long tradition of being concerned with mean difference to the exclusion of other types of differences which might exist. In many cases this is quite justifiable, but we must not lose sight of the fact that the variance can also provide considerable insight into the results of experimental manipulations.

7.8 *Combining the Results of Several Experiments*

It occasionally happens that an investigator has run several experiments which are more or less comparable and which all test the same general hypothesis. Suppose that the experimenter finds that the results for each experiment are in the predicted direction, but not one of them quite reaches statistical significance. The obvious question which then arises concerns the probability of this joint set of results if $H_0: \mu_1 - \mu_2 = 0$ is in fact true.

There are several answers to that question, depending upon the experimental design and the number of experiments in question. The simplest solution employs the binomial distribution, but requires at least five separate experiments on no more than two groups. Starting with the logical statement that if H_0 is true, $p(\bar{X}_1 < \bar{X}_2) = p(\bar{X}_1 > \bar{X}_2) = .50$ (or, for the one sample case, $p(\bar{X} < \mu) = p(\bar{X} > \mu) = .50$), one can then ask "What is the probability of finding r out of k experiments with $\bar{X}_1 > \bar{X}_2$?" This question is easily answered by use of the binomial distribution.

A second answer to the question which is not constrained by the experimental design or the number of experiments has the disadvantage of being somewhat impractical in many cases. This solution is based on the fact that a probability can be converted to χ^2 on 2 df.

$$\chi^2 = -2 \log_e p \tag{7.15}$$

Since we have already seen that the sum of k independent Chi-square variables is itself distributed as χ^2 with df equal to the sum of the separate df, then, for k experiments

$$\chi^2 = -2\Sigma \log_e p_i \tag{7.16}$$

will be distributed as χ^2 on $2k$ df. Thus if we could obtain the exact probability of $(t \geq t_{\text{obt}})$ for each experiment, we could then take the natural logarithms of these probabilities, sum, multiply by -2, and evaluate this result against $\chi^2_{.05}$ on $2k$ df. The only problem with this approach is that seldom can we calculate the probability for a given value of t, since most of the tables of t (or whatever the statistic in question is) only have probabilities for the critical values. However, more and more computer programs are now printing out the exact probabilities, and experimenters who need these values can usually obtain them. Thus this method may become more useful in the near future.

The last method to be discussed is the simplest, although it only applies when t is used as the statistical test. Winer (1971) shows that

$$z = \frac{\Sigma t_i}{\sqrt{\Sigma \dfrac{\mathrm{df}_i}{\mathrm{df}_i - 2}}} \tag{7.17}$$

is distributed as the standard normal deviate when each $df_i \geq 10$. To take a simple example, suppose that we had run five experiments, each on 20 df, and obtained the following values of t.

Experiment	1	2	3	4	5
t	1.28	.50	2.01	1.60	1.70

Each of these experiments is independent of the others and all bear on the same general hypothesis. Then

$$z = \frac{(1.28 + .50 + 2.01 + 1.60 + 1.70)}{\sqrt{\frac{5(20)}{18}}}$$

$$= \frac{7.09}{\sqrt{5.56}}$$

$$= 3.01.$$

From the distribution of z we find that the $p(z \geq 3.01) = .0013$. Thus we can reject H_0 at this level of significance and conclude that $\mu_1 > \mu_2$.

It is important to note that all of these tests require the assumption that the separate experiments are independent and that they bear on the same general hypothesis. I know of no practical way to combine the results of non-independent experiments. A more extensive discussion of this whole problem of combining results is found in Rosenthal (1978).

Although the techniques discussed in this section have a useful role to play in statistical analyses, this role should not be overemphasized. While there are some areas of research where a difference, no matter how small, is important, there are many more areas where small differences are not only not important, but in fact simply add confusion to the literature. We will have considerably more to say about this in later chapters when we discuss ways of assessing the magnitude of an experimental effect. Simply because a difference has *statistical* significance does not mean that it is necessarily of *practical* significance. *Significance and importance are two entirely different things.*

7.9   Confidence Intervals

In Chapter 4 we discussed the concept of the confidence interval for a observation, and saw that it is possible to make statements of the form "The probability is .95 that the interval ____ to ____ includes the observation."

Confidence intervals   It is similarly possible to set up **confidence intervals** for means and mean differences, and this section will be concerned with this problem.

To take an example, suppose that we had conducted a study to determine the mean sound level of noise in the middle of a large forest. We have chosen to work in such a setting because we need some idea of what is generally meant by the word *quiet* and a forest typically given as an example of a quiet place. Further assume that we taken readings on 16 randomly selected days and obtained a mean 50 decibels with a standard deviations of 5 db. We now want to set up confidence limits for μ (the true mean loudness level of a forest). From Equation 7.3 we have

$$t = \frac{\bar{X} - \mu}{s/\sqrt{N}}.$$

What we need to find are the smallest and largest value for μ for which we would just fail to reject H_0—for which the data could be considered minimally plausible.

For 16 observations we have 15 df. From Appendix (t) we find that the critical value of $t_{\alpha/2} = t_{.025} = 2.131$. Thus we want the values of μ which will produce values of $t_{obt} = \pm 2.131$. Working backwards to solve for μ instead of t, we obtain

$$\pm 2.131 = \frac{\bar{X} - \mu}{s/\sqrt{N}} = \frac{50 - \mu}{5/\sqrt{16}}$$

$$\pm 2.131 = \frac{50 - \mu}{1.25}$$

$$\mu = 50 \pm 2.131(1.25)$$

$$\mu = 50 \pm 2.664.$$

Therefore

$$47.336 \leq \mu \leq 52.664$$

Thus the probability is .95 that the interval 47.336 to 52.664 decibels includes the mean decibel level of our forest. For this particular study the confidence limits are far more useful than would be the test of some null hypothesis.

From the above we can write the general formula for confidence intervals for

$$\text{CI}(\mu) = \bar{X} \pm t_{\alpha/2}(s_{\bar{X}}), \tag{7.18}$$

where $t_{\alpha/2}$ is the two-tailed critical value obtained from Appendix (t).

The generalization to the two sample case follows directly from what we have already done. Equation 7.19 gives the formula for this interval.

$$\text{CI}(\mu_1 - \mu_2) = (\bar{X}_1 - \bar{X}_2) \pm t_{\alpha/2}(s_{\bar{X}_1 - \bar{X}_2}) \tag{7.19}$$

The student should be able to verify this equation from what has already been said about the one sample case.

As an illustration for the two sample case, suppose that we want to compare the quiet of a forest with the sound level of a typical two-person conversation. We measure the db level for 16 such conversations and find a mean of 65 and a standard deviation of 9. There is no point in testing the difference between the means for the forest and the conversation, since this was not the question at hand and our confidence limits will speak to that issue anyway. What we do want is some idea of the true difference in noise level between the two situations. In other words we want confidence limits for $\mu_1 - \mu_2$.

TABLE 7.6
Data for Sound Levels in Two Environments

	CONVERSATION X_1	FOREST X_2
Mean	65	50
Variance	81	25
N	16	16

$$s^2 = \frac{(N_1-1)s_1^2 + (N_2-1)s_2^2}{N_1+N_2-2} = \frac{15(81)+15(25)}{30} = 53.0$$

$$\text{CI}(\mu_1 - \mu_2) = (\bar{X}_1 - \bar{X}_2) \pm t_{\alpha/2}\sqrt{\frac{s^2}{N_1} + \frac{s^2}{N_2}} = (65-50) \pm 2.042\sqrt{\frac{53}{16} + \frac{53}{16}}$$

$$\text{CI}(\mu_1 - \mu_2) = 15 \pm 2.042(2.574) = 15 \pm 5.26$$

Therefore

$$9.74 \leq (\mu_1 - \mu_2) \leq 20.26.$$

The probability is .95 that the interval between 9.74 and 20.26 db covers the true difference between the sound level of a quiet forest and a two-person conversation.

A word is in order about the interpretation of confidence limits. Statements of the form $p\ (9.74 \leq \mu_1 - \mu_2 \leq 20.26) = .95$ are not to be interpreted in the usual way. The parameter $\mu_1 - \mu_2$ is not a random variable. It does not jump around from experiment to experiment. Rather it is a constant and our interval is what varies from experiment to experiment. Thus we can think of our parameter as a stake and our experimenter as tossing rings at it. Ninety-five percent of the time a ring of specified width will encircle the parameter, and five percent of the time it will miss. A confidence statement is a statement of the probability that the ring has been on target and *not* a statement of the probability that the target (parameter) landed in the ring.

7.10 Summary

We began this chapter by examining the sampling distribution of the mean and what it has to tell us about likely and unlikely values for a given sample mean under specified conditions. From there we examined the way in which the t statistic can be used to test null hypotheses about the mean of a single sample, about the difference between the means of two matched samples, and finally about the difference between the means of two independent samples. We next considered procedures which apply to those cases in which we have problems with heterogeneity of variance, and then discussed the fact that such heterogeneity may be an important result in its own right. Finally, we examined ways of combining results of several experiments and the concept of confidence limits.

Exercises for Chapter 7

7.1 We randomly assigned 9 children to each of two groups, asked them to brush their teeth with Toothpaste X or Toothpaste Y, and counted the number of cavities per child at the end of 6 months. The data are given below.

| Toothpaste X | 3 | 3 | 2 | 2 | 3 | 4 | 3 | 1 | 0 |
| Toothpaste Y | 1 | 3 | 2 | 1 | 0 | 3 | 1 | 0 | 2 |

Run the appropriate t test.

7.2 What is the role of random assignment in Exercise 7.1?

7.3 Suppose that we redesign the study described in Exercise 7.1. Instead of assigning different subjects to each group, we ask 9 children to use Toothpaste X for 6 months, count their cavities, ask them to use Toothpaste Y for the next 6 months, and count cavities again.

| Toothpaste X | 3 | 3 | 2 | 2 | 3 | 4 | 3 | 1 | 0 |
| Toothpaste Y | 2 | 1 | 0 | 1 | 3 | 2 | 3 | 0 | 1 |

Run the appropriate t test.

7.4 *a.* What are some of the flaws with the previous study as it has been described?

b. How might those flaws be corrected?

7.5 A small state college admitted 200 freshmen this fall. They found that the mean SAT verbal score for this class was 490. Assuming that the SAT has a national mean of 500 and standard deviation of 100, is this mean significantly below the national average?

7.6 In actuality, College Board scores have been declining for years, and the national mean is no longer 500. Suppose that the true national mean this year was 470 with a standard deviation of 90. What can this college conclude about the quality of its applicants (at least as measured by the SAT)?

7.7 Construct the 95% and 99% confidence limits for the data in Exercise 7.5. What do these limits mean?

7.8 Construct the 95% and 99% confidence limits for the data in Exercise 7.3. What do these limits mean?

7.9 As part of a study to reduce smoking, a national organization ran an advertising compaign to convince people to quit smoking. To evaluate the effectiveness of their campaign they had 15 subjects calculate the average number of cigarettes smoked per day in the week before and the week after exposure to the ad. The data are given below

Before   45 16 20 33 30 19 33 25 26 40 28 36 15 26 32
After   43 20 17 30 25 19 34 28 23 41 26 40 16 23 34

Run the appropriate *t* test.

7.10 Assume that the data in Exercise 7.9 had come out differently. The new data are given below.

Before   45 16 20 33 30 19 33 25 26 40 28 36 15 26 32
After   59 35 30 40 20 10 20 20 36 46 10 25 8 35 46

Run the appropriate *t* test.

7.11 Compare the conclusions a careful experimenter would draw from Exercises 7.9 and 7.10.

7.12 In a comparison of different programs advocated by two organizations concerned with weight loss, 20 subjects were enrolled in Program *A* and 20 in Program *B*. The amount of weight lost in the next 6 months was recorded. The following data are given in terms of pounds for those people who stuck with the program.

Program A   25 21 8 20 12 30
Program B   15 17 9 12 11 19 14 18 16 10 5 13

Run the appropriate *t* test (taking into account the relevant variances).

7.13 The following data represent alternative data which might have been obtained in the study described in Exercise 7.12.

Program A   25 21 18 20 22 30
Program B   15 7 9 12 11 29 14 8 16 10 5 23

Compare the appropriate df' for both this question and the previous one. Can you make a guess at the major variable controlling the differences in df'?

7.14 In Exercise 7.12 are the means the most important statistics? What else might be considered more important?

7.15 Use F to test the differences in the variances in Exercise 7.12 and 7.13.

Experimenter bias **7.16** Much has been made of the concept of *experimenter bias*, which refers to the fact that data often (honestly) come out the way the experimenter expects them to. Suppose that we use a student as an experimenter and tell him that we hope to show that Drug A facilitates social interaction while Drug B interferes with social interaction. In fact all subjects are given a placebo, but the experimenter is (incorrectly) told for half of the cases that the subject has been given Drug A and told for the other half that he has been given Drug B. The experimenter is then asked to rate the quality of the social interaction in which the subject engages (higher scores are better). The scores assigned by the experimenter are given below for all subjects completing the study.

Drug A	19	15	22	13	18	15	20	25	22
Drug B	14	18	17	12	21	21	24	14	

What would you conclude?

7.17 Suppose that we repeated the preceding question with four other experimenters and obtained the following results:

Experimenter	2	3	4	5
df	15	18	12	15
t	1.4	1.8	1.7	−.10

What would you conclude?

7.18 The following MINITAB output is an analysis of the data from Exercise 7.3.

a. Verify that these answers agree with the answers you found for that exercise.

b. Is this a one-tailed or a two-tailed test?

```
-- READ DATA INTO C1 AND C2

   3 2
   3 1
   ...
   0 1

-- SUBTRACT C2 FROM C1 PUT IN C3

-- TTEST ON MU = 0 FOR DATA IN C3
   C3      N = 9     MEAN =     0.88889      ST.DEV. =     1.05

   TEST OF MU =     0.0000 VS. MU N.E.     0.0000
   T = 2.530
   THE TEST IS SIGNIFICANT AT   0.0353

-- STOP
```

7.19 Use MINITAB or SPSS to analyze the data in Exercise 7.1.

7.20 The following SPSS printout represents both a pooled and an unpooled *t*-test on the data for Exercise 7.12.

a. Locate the *F* test on the variances. Is it significant?

b. What conclusion would you draw from the analysis of the data?

```
                1 RUN NAME        T-TEST FOR QUESTION 7.12 USING SPSS
                2 VARIABLE LIST   GROUP,SCORE
                3 INPUT FORMAT    FIXED(F2.0,F3.0)
                4 INPUT MEDIUM    TDATA2.DAT
                5 T-TEST          GROUPS = GROUP(1,2)/VARIABLES = SCORE

- - - - - - - - - - - - - - - - - - - - - - - - - - - - - - - - - - - - - - - - - - - - -

GROUP 1 - GROUP    EQ      1.
GROUP 2 - GROUP    EQ      2.
```

Variable	Number of cases	Mean	Standard Deviation	Standard Error	*	F Value	2-Tail Prob.	*	T Value	Pooled variance estimate Degrees of Freedom	2-tail Prob.	*	T Value	Separate variance estimate Degrees of Freedom	2-tail Prob.
SCORE					*			*				*			
GROUP 1	6	19.3333	8.140	3.323	*			*				*			
					*	3.96	.054	*	2.14	16	.048	*	1.72	6.30	0.135
GROUP 2	12	13.2500	4.093	1.181	*			*				*			

7.21 Suppose that you were confident of the means and variances in Exercise 7.16. How many subjects would you need (assuming equal *N*s) to have a significant *t*?

8

Power

Objective

To introduce the concept of the power of a statistical test, and to present ways by which we can calculate the power of a variety of statistical procedures.

Contents

Until very recently most applied statistical work as it is actually carried out in analyzing experimental results was primarily concerned with minimizing (or at least controlling) the probability of a Type I error (α). When it comes to designing experiments people generally tend to ignore the fact that there is a probability (β) of another kind of error, labeled Type II errors. Whereas Type I errors deal with the problem of *finding* a difference that is not there, Type II errors concern the equally serious problem of not finding a difference that is there. When we consider the substantial cost in time and money that goes into a typical experiment, one could argue that it is remarkably short sighted of experimenters not to recognize the fact that they may, from the start, have a very small chance of finding the effect they are looking for, even if such an effect does exist in the population.

There are good historical reasons why investigators have tended to ignore Type II errors. Until recently many textbooks ignored the problem altogether, and those books which did discuss the material discussed it in ways which were not easily understood by the average reader (noncentrality parameters and power curves with strange things on the abscissa take considerable thought at first). In the past ten years, however, Cohen has discussed the problem in a very clear and lucid manner in several publications. Cohen (1969) presents a thorough and rigorous treatment of the material. In Welkowitz, Ewen, & Cohen (1971) the material is treated in a slightly simpler way through the use of an approximation technique. Their approach is the one adopted in this chapter. The reader should have no difficulty with either of the sources listed previously, or for that matter with any of the many excellent papers Cohen has published on a wide variety of topics.

Speaking in terms of Type II errors is a rather negative way of approaching the problem, since it keeps reminding us that we might make a mistake.

Power   The more positive approach would be to speak in terms of *power*, which is defined as the probability of correctly rejecting a false H_0. Thus power $= 1 - \beta$. A more powerful experiment is one which has a better chance of rejecting a false H_0 than does a less powerful experiment.

The present chapter will take the approach of Welkowitz, Ewen, & Cohen (1971), and work with an approximation to the true power of a test. This approximation is an excellent one, especially in light of the fact that we do not really care whether power $= .85$ or $.83$, but rather whether it is in the .80s or the .30s. Those who wish a more exact solution are referred to Cohen (1969). For expository purposes we will assume for the moment that we are interested in testing one sample mean against a specified population mean, although the approach immediately generalizes to the testing of other hypotheses.

8.1 *Factors Affecting the Power of a Test*

As might be expected, power is a function of several variables. It is a function of (1) α, the probability of a Type I error, (2) the true alternative hypothesis

(H_1), (3) the sample size, and (4) the particular test to be employed. With the exception of the relative power of independent versus matched samples, we will avoid this last relationship on the grounds that when the test assumptions are met the majority of the procedures discussed in this book can be shown to be the uniformly most powerful tests of those available to answer the question at hand.

The Basic Concept

To review briefly what has already been covered in Chapter 4, consider the two distributions in Figure 8.1. The distribution to the left (labeled H_0) represents the sampling distribution of the mean when the null hypothesis is true and $\mu = \mu_0$. The heavily shaded right hand tail of this distribution represents α, the probability of a Type I error, assuming that we are using a one-tailed test (otherwise it represents $\frac{\alpha}{2}$). This area contains the means which would result in significant values of t. The second distribution (H_1) represents the sampling distribution of the statistic when H_0 is false and the true mean $= \mu_1$. It is readily apparent that even when H_0 is false many of the sample means (and therefore the corresponding values of t) will none-the-less fall to the left of the critical value, causing us to fail to reject a false H_0, thus committing a Type II error. The probability of this error is indicated by the lightly shaded area in Figure 8.1, and is labeled β. Lastly, when H_0 is false and the test statistic falls to the right of the critical value, we will correctly reject a false H_0. The probability of doing this is what we mean by power, and is shown in the unshaded area of the H_1 distribution.

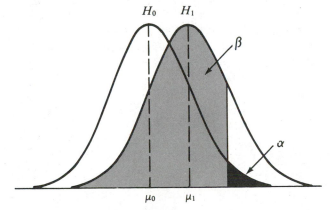

FIGURE 8.1

Sampling distribution of $\bar{X}$ under H_0 and H_1

Power as a Function of α

With the aid of Figure 8.1 it is easy to see why we say that power is a function of α. If we are willing to increase α, our cut-off point moves to the left, thus simultaneously decreasing β and increasing power, although with a corresponding rise in the probability of a Type I error.

Power as a Function of H_1

The fact that power is a function of the true alternative hypothesis [more precisely $(\mu_0 - \mu_1)$] is illustrated by comparing Figures 8.1 and 8.2. In Figure 8.2 the distance between μ_0 and μ_1 has been increased, and this has resulted in a substantial increase in power. This is not particularly surprising, since all that we are saying is that the chances of finding a difference depend on how large the difference is.

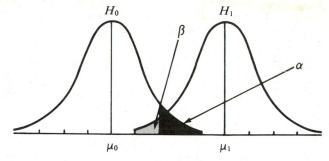

FIGURE 8.2
Effect on β of increasing $\mu_0 - \mu_1$

Power as a Function of N and σ^2

The relationship between power and sample size (and between power and σ^2) is only a little subtler. Since we are interested in means or mean differences, we are interested in the sampling distribution of the mean. But we know that the variance of the sampling distribution of the mean decreases as either N increases or σ^2 decreases, since $\sigma_{\bar{X}}^2 = \sigma^2/N$. Figure 8.3 illustrates

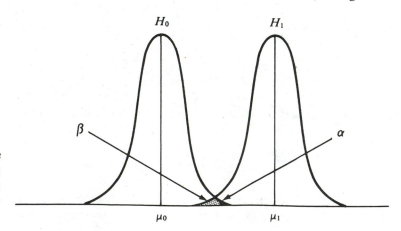

FIGURE 8.3
Effect on β of decrease in standard error of the mean

what happens to the two sampling distributions (H_0 and H_1) as we increase N or decrease σ^2, relative to Figure 8.1. Figure 8.3 illustrates that as $\sigma_{\bar{x}}^2$ decreases the overlap between the two distributions is reduced with a resulting increase in power.

If an experimenter is going to concern himself with the power of a test, then he is most likely going to be interested in those variables governing power which are readily amenable to manipulation. Since N is more easily manipulated than either σ^2 or $(\mu_0 - \mu_1)$, and since tampering with α produces undesirable side effects in terms of increasing the probability of a Type I error, discussions of power are generally concerned with the effects of varying sample size.

8.2 *Effect Size*

As we have seen in Figures 8.1–8.3, power depends upon the degree of overlap between the sampling distributions under H_0 and H_1. Furthermore, this overlap is a function both of the distance between μ_0 and μ_1 and also the standard error. One measure, then, of the degree to which H_0 is false would be the distance $\mu_1 - \mu_0$ expressed in terms of the number of standard errors. The problem with this measure, however, is that it includes the sample size (in the computation of the standard error), when in fact we will usually wish to solve for the power associated with a given N or else for that value of N required for a given level of power. For this reason we will take as our distance measure, or **effect size**

Effect size

$$\gamma = \frac{\mu_1 - \mu_0}{\sigma} \tag{8.1}$$

Gamma (γ) ignoring the sign of γ (*gamma*), and incorporating N at a later date. Thus γ is a measure of the degree to which μ_1 and μ_0 differ in terms of the standard deviation of the parent population. From Equation 8.1 we see that γ is estimated independently of N, simply by estimating μ_1, μ_0, and σ.

Estimating the Effect Size

The first task becomes that of estimating γ, since it will form the basis for future calculations. There are three ways in which this can be done.

1. Prior research: It is commonly found that on the basis of past research we can get at least a rough approximation to γ. Thus we could look at sample means and variances from other studies and make an informed guess at the values we might expect for $\mu_1 - \mu_0$ and for σ. In practice this task is not as difficult as it might seem, especially when you realize that a rough approximation is far better than no approximation at all.

2.   Personal assessment of what difference is *important*: In many cases an investigator is able to say "I am interested in detecting a difference of at least 10 points between μ_1 and μ_0." The investigator is essentially saying that differences less than this have no important or useful meaning, while greater differences do. Here we are given the value of $\mu_1 - \mu_0$ directly, without any necessary knowledge of the particular values of μ_1 and μ_0. All that remains is to estimate σ from other data. As an example, the investigator might say that he is interested in finding a procedure which will raise scores on the Graduate Record Examination by 40 points above normal. We already know that the standard deviation for this test is 100. Thus $\gamma = \frac{40}{100} = .40$.

If, instead of our hypothetical experimenter saying that he wanted to raise scores by 40 points, he said that he wanted to raise them by $\frac{4}{10}$ of a standard deviation, he would have been giving us γ directly. In some cases this type of a statement is possible.

3.   The use of special conventions: When we encounter a situation in which there is no way in which we can estimate the required parameters, we can fall back on a set of conventions proposed by Cohen (1969). Cohen has more or less arbitrarily defined three levels of γ. For a justification of these levels the reader is referred to that reference.

Effect Size	γ
Small	.20
Medium	.50
Large	.80

Thus in a pinch the experimenter can simply decide whether he is after a small, medium, or large effect, and set γ accordingly. It must be emphasized, however, that this solution should only be chosen when the other alternatives are not feasible.

It may strike the reader as peculiar that he is being asked to define what difference he is looking for before the experiment is conducted. Most people would respond by saying "I don't know how the experiment will come out. I just wonder if there will be a difference." Although many experimenters behave in this way, and the present author is no virtuous exception, I think that if you consider this excuse you will start to question its validity. Do we really not know, at least vaguely, what will happen in our experiments, and if so, why are we running them? While there is occasionally a legitimate "I-wonder-what-would-happen-if" experiment, in general "I don't know" really translates to "I haven't thought that far ahead."

Recombining the Effect Size and N

In discussing the effect size (γ) a decision was made to split the sample size from the effect size, so as to make it easier to deal with N separately. The final concept that we will need is a method for combining the effect *Delta (δ)* size with the sample size. For this we will use the symbol δ (*delta*).

$$\delta = (\gamma)(f(N)) \tag{8.2}$$

where the particular function of N [$f(N)$] will be defined differently for each individual test. The nice thing about this system is that it will allow us to use the same table of δ for power calculations for all of the statistical procedures to be considered.

8.3 *Power Calculations for the One-Sample t*

As the first example, we will examine the calculation of power for the one-sample t test. In the previous section we saw that δ is based on γ and some function of N. For the one-sample t that function will be $\sqrt{N}$ and δ will then be defined as

$$\delta = \gamma\sqrt{N}. \tag{8.3}$$

Given δ as defined by Equation 8.3, we can immediately determine the power of our test from the table of power in Appendix (*power*).

As an example assume that a clinical psychologist wants to test the hypothesis that people who seek treatment for psychological problems have a higher IQ than normal. She wants to use the IQs of 25 randomly selected clients and is interested in finding the power of detecting a difference of 5 points between the mean of the general population and the mean of the population from which her clients are drawn. Thus $\mu_1 = 105$, $\mu_0 = 100$, and $\sigma = 15$.

$$\gamma = \frac{105 - 100}{15} = .33$$

then

$$\delta = \gamma\sqrt{N} = .33\sqrt{25} = .33(5)$$

$$= 1.65.$$

Although the clinician expects the sample means to be above average, she plans to use a two-tailed test at $\alpha = .05$ to protect against unexpected events. From Appendix (*power*) for $\delta = 1.65$ with $\alpha = .05$ (two-tailed) we find that power is between .36 and .40. By crude linear interpolation we will say that power = .38. This means that if H_0 is false and μ_1 is really 105, only 38% of the time will our clinician find a significant difference between her *sample* mean and that specified by H_0. This is a rather discouraging result, since it means that if the true mean is 105, 62% of the time our clinician will make a Type II error.

Since our experimenter was intelligent enough to examine the question of power before she began her experiment, all is not lost. She still has the chance to make changes which will lead to an increase in power. She could, for example, set α at .10, thus increasing power to approximately .50, but this is probably unsatisfactory. (Journal editors, for example, generally hate to see α set at any value greater than .05.)

Estimating Required Sample Size

Alternatively the investigator could increase her sample size, thereby increasing power. But how large an N does she need? The answer to that question depends simply on what level of power she desires. Suppose that she wished to set power at .80. From Appendix (*power*) we know that for power = .80, δ must equal 2.80. Thus we have δ and can simply solve for N.

$$\delta = \gamma\sqrt{N}$$

$$N = \left(\frac{\delta}{\gamma}\right)^2 = \left(\frac{2.80}{.33}\right)^2 = 8.40^2$$

$$= 70.56.$$

Since clients generally come in whole lots, we will round off to 71. Thus if the experimenter wants to have an 80% chance of rejecting H_0 when $\gamma = .33$ (i.e., when $\mu_1 = 105$), she will have to use the IQs for 71 randomly selected clients. While she may claim that this is more clients than she can easily test, there is no alternative other than to be willing to settle for a lower level of power.

The reader might be inclined to wonder why we selected power = .80 in the previous example. With this degree of power we still run a 20% chance of making a Type II error. The answer lies in the question of practicality. Suppose for example that we had wanted power = .95. A few simple calculations will show that this would require a sample of $N = 119$, and for power = .99 you would need approximately 167 subjects. These may well be unreasonable sample sizes for this particular experimental situation or the resources of the experimenter. It is important to remember that increases in power are generally bought by increases in N, and at high levels of power the cost can be very high. If one is taking data from data tapes supplied by the Bureau of the Census, that is one thing. It is quite a different matter when you are studying teenage college graduates. Basically the rule is "You pays your money and you takes your choice."

Noncentrality Parameters

At this point it might be well to point out that δ is what most textbooks refer to as a ***noncentrality parameter***. The concept is relatively simple, and well worth considering. We have previously said that

$$z = \frac{X - \mu}{\sigma} \quad \text{or} \quad \frac{\bar{X} - \mu}{\sigma/\sqrt{N}}$$

is normally distributed around zero regardless of the truth or falsity of any null hypothesis, so long as μ is the true mean of the distribution from which the Xs were sampled. If H_0 states that $\mu = \mu_0$ (some specific value of μ) *and H_0 is true*, then

$$z = \frac{\bar{X} - \mu_0}{\sigma/\sqrt{N}}$$

will also be normally distributed about zero. But if H_0 is false and $\mu \neq \mu_0$, then

$$z = \frac{\bar{X} - \mu_0}{\sigma/\sqrt{N}}$$

will not be distributed around zero, since in subtracting μ_0 we have been subtracting the wrong population mean. In fact the distribution will be centered at the point

$$\frac{\mu_1 - \mu_0}{\sigma/\sqrt{N}}$$

which is δ. This shift in the mean of the distribution from 0 to δ is referred to as the degree of noncentrality, and δ is the noncentrality parameter.

The question of power, then, becomes the question of how likely we are to find a value of the noncentral (shifted) distribution which is greater than the critical value that t would have under H_0. In other words, even though larger than normal values of t are to be expected because H_0 is false, we will occasionally obtain some small values by chance. The percentage of these values that happen to lie below $t_{.05}$ is β, the probability of a Type II error. As we know we can easily obtain power from β, since power $= 1 - \beta$.

Cohen's contribution, then can be seen as splitting the noncentrality parameter (δ) into two parts—sample size and effect size. One part (γ) depends solely on parameters of the populations, while the other depends upon sample size. Thus he has separated parametric considerations $(\mu_0, \mu_1,$ and $\sigma)$ about which we can do relatively little, from sample characteristics (N) over which we have more control. While this produces no basic change in the underlying theory, it makes the concept easier to understand and to use.

8.4 Power Calculations for Differences Between Two Independent Means

The treatment of power in the case where we wish to test the difference between two independent means is very similar to our treatment of the case where we had only one mean. In the previous section we obtained γ by taking the difference between μ under H_1 and μ under H_0 and dividing by σ. In the present case we will do basically the same thing, although this time we are going to be working with mean differences. Thus we want to difference between the two population means $(\mu_1 - \mu_2)$ under H_1 minus the difference $(\mu_1 - \mu_2)$ under H_0, again divided by σ. (Recall that we assume $\sigma_1^2 = \sigma_2^2 = \sigma^2$.) But $(\mu_1 - \mu_2)$ under H_0 is zero in all normal applications, so we can drop that term from our formula. Thus,

$$\gamma = \frac{(\mu_1 - \mu_2) - (0)}{\sigma} = \frac{\mu_1 - \mu_2}{\sigma},$$

where the numerator refers to the difference to be expected under H_1 and the denominator represents the standard deviation of the populations. In the case of two samples we must distinguish between experiments involving equal Ns and those involving unequal Ns. We will treat these two cases separately.

Equal Sample Sizes

For the sake of an example assume that we wish to test the difference between two treatments and either expect that the difference in population means will be approximately 5 points or else are only interested in finding a difference of at least 5 points. Further assume that from past data we think that σ is approximately 10. Then

$$\gamma = \frac{\mu_1 - \mu_2}{\sigma} = \frac{5}{10} = .50.$$

Thus we are saying that we are expecting a difference of half a standard deviation between the two means.

First we will investigate the power of an experiment with 25 observations in each of two groups. We will define δ in the two sample case as

$$\delta = \gamma \sqrt{\frac{N}{2}}$$

where $N =$ the number of cases *in any one sample* (there are $2N$ cases in all). Thus

$$\delta = (.50)\sqrt{\frac{25}{2}} = .50\sqrt{12.5} = .50(3.54)$$

$$= 1.77.$$

From Appendix (*power*) we see by interpolation that for $\delta = 1.77$ with a two-tailed test at $\alpha = .05$, power $= .43$. Thus if our experimenter actually ran this experiment with 25 subjects, and if her estimate of δ is correct, then she has a 43% chance of actually rejecting H_0.

We next wish to turn the question around and ask how many subjects would be needed for power $= .80$. From the table we see that this would require $\delta = 2.80$

$$\delta = \gamma\sqrt{\frac{N}{2}}$$

thus

$$N = 2\left(\frac{\delta}{\gamma}\right)^2$$

$$= 2\left(\frac{2.80}{.50}\right)^2 = 2(5.6)^2$$

$$= 62.72.$$

Since N refers to the number of subjects per sample, we would need 63 subjects per sample for a total of 126 subjects if power is to be .80.

Unequal Sample Sizes

In the previous section we dealt with the case where $N_1 = N_2 = N$. However we commonly find experiments where the two sample sizes are unequal. This obviously presents difficulties when we try to solve for δ, since we need one value for N. What value can we use?

With reasonably large and nearly equal samples, a conservative approximation can be obtained by letting N equal the smaller of N_1 and N_2. This is not very satisfactory, however, if the sample sizes are small or if the two Ns are quite different. For those cases we need a more exact solution.

One reasonable, but incorrect, procedure would be to set N equal to the arithmetic mean of N_1 and N_2. This method, however, would weight the two samples equally when in fact we know that the variance of means is proportional not to N, but to $1/N$. The mean which takes this relationship

Harmonic mean   into account is not the arithmetic mean but the harmonic mean. The ***harmonic mean*** of k numbers $(X_1, X_2, \ldots, X_k)$ is defined as

$$\bar{X}_h = \frac{k}{\sum \dfrac{1}{X_i}} \qquad\qquad (8.4)$$

thus for two samples sizes (N_1 and N_2)

$$\bar{N}_h = \frac{2}{\dfrac{1}{N_1} + \dfrac{1}{N_2}} = \frac{2N_1 N_2}{N_1 + N_2}.$$

We can then use $\bar{N}_h$ in our calculation of δ.

As an example consider the situation in which we want to test the hypothesis that, as a result of a change in the textbook, the mean statistics grade for this year's class is different from the mean of the last *two* years' classes. Further assume that the classes have been graded on the same system, so that we have comparable measures for the three years. Finally assume that there have been 20 students in each of the three years and we are interested in an effect size (γ) of .30. We will calculate the effective sample size (the sample size to be used in calculating δ) as

$$\bar{N}_h = \frac{2(40)(20)}{40 + 20} = \frac{1600}{60} = 26.667.$$

From the previous computation we can see that the *effective* sample size is less than the arithmetic mean of the two individual sample sizes. Put another way, this study has the same power as if we had run the same experiment with 26.667 subjects per group for a total of 53.333 subjects, rather than the 60 we actually used.

To continue

$$\delta = \gamma\sqrt{\frac{N}{2}} = .30\sqrt{\frac{26.667}{2}} = .30\sqrt{13.333}$$

$$= 1.10.$$

For $\delta = 1.10$, power = .20.

In this case the power is too low to inspire much confidence in the results of the study. If H_0 is true we stand a 5% chance of rejecting H_0 (a Type I error); and if it is false (to the degree specified) we only stand a 20% chance of rejecting H_0 (a correct decision). It looks almost as if we stand to retain H_0 regardless of its truth or falsity.

If it were possible for us to increase sample sizes in some way (such as including subjects from more years), then it would obviously be desirable to do so. Suppose that we can magically produce an additional 20 subjects and add these to the smaller group, making $N_1 = N_2 = N$. With $N = 40$,

$$\delta = \gamma \sqrt{\frac{N}{2}} = .30 \sqrt{\frac{40}{2}} = 1.34$$

power $\approx .27$.

While this increase in power is not exactly dramatic, it is better than nothing. On the other hand, consider the effect of adding those 20 subjects to the larger group instead. The $N_1 = 20$ and $N_2 = 60$.

$$\bar{N}_h = \frac{2(20)(60)}{20 + 60} = 30$$

$$\delta = .30 \sqrt{\frac{30}{2}} = .30\sqrt{15} = 1.16$$

power $= .21$.

In this case adding 20 subjects increased power by only .01 (as opposed to the increase of .07 when they were added to the smaller group).

The discussion points out the important principle that for a fixed number of subjects power is maximized by setting $N_1 = N_2$. This suggests the general strategy of balancing sample sizes in designing experiments. When unequal sample sizes are unavoidable, the smaller group should be as large as possible relative to the larger group.

8.5 *Power Calculations for Matched-Sample t*

When we move to the situation in which we want to test the difference between two matched samples, the problem becomes a bit more difficult and an additional parameter must be considered. For this reason the analysis of power for this case is frequently impractical. However, the general solution to the problem illustrates an important principle of experimental design, and thus justifies close examination of the matched-sample case.

We are going to define γ as

$$\gamma = \frac{\mu_1 - \mu_2}{\sigma_{X_1 - X_2}}$$

where $\mu_1 - \mu_2$ represents the expected mean difference (the expected mean of the difference scores). The problem arises from the fact that $\sigma_{X_1 - X_2}$ is not the standard deviation of the populations of X_1 and X_2, but rather the standard deviation of difference scores drawn from these populations. While we might be able to make an intelligent guess at σ_{X_1} or σ_{X_2}, we probably have no idea about $\sigma_{X_1 - X_2}$.

All is not lost, however, since it is possible to calculate $\sigma_{X_1 - X_2}$ on the basis of a few assumptions. From our manila folder of "useful statistical goodies" we pull out the variance sum law (discussed in Chapter 7) which gives the variance for a sum or difference of two variables. Specifically

$$\sigma^2_{X_1 - X_2} = \sigma^2_{X_1} + \sigma^2_{X_2} - 2r\sigma_{X_1}\sigma_{X_2}.$$

If we make the general assumption of homogeneity of variance ($\sigma^2_{X_1} = \sigma^2_{X_2} = \sigma^2$)

$$\sigma^2_{X_1 - X_2} = 2\sigma^2 - 2r\sigma^2 = 2\sigma^2(1 - r)$$

$$\sigma_{X_1 - X_2} = \sigma\sqrt{2(1 - r)}$$

where r is the correlation between X_1 and X_2 and can take on values between ± 1, being positive for almost all situations in which we would likely want a matched-sample t.

Assuming for the moment that we can estimate r, from here on the procedure is the same as for the case of the one-sample t. We define

$$\gamma = \frac{\mu_1 - \mu_2}{\sigma_{X_1 - X_2}}$$

and

$$\delta = \gamma\sqrt{N}.$$

We then estimate $\sigma_{X_1 - X_2}$ as $\sigma\sqrt{2(1 - r)}$, and refer the value of δ to the tables.

As an example, assume that we want to see if test performance is better in the morning than at night. Consequently we might want to administer the WAIS (Wechsler Adult Intelligence Scale) to a sample of 30 subjects late one night, send them to bed, and readminister the test the next morning. (A better experiment would have $\frac{1}{2}$ of the subjects tested in the morning first and $\frac{1}{2}$ tested at night first, but this would have no effect on the power *Carry over effect* of the test.) We will make the rather naive assumption that there is no *carry over effect* from one administration to the next. Suppose that we want to evaluate the power for finding a difference as great as 3 IQ points. From any standard text on psychometric measurement we can obtain an estimate of the correlation between the scores on the two sessions. This is nothing but the short term reliability of the test, and a reasonable value for the reliability is .92. Thus

$$\sigma_{X_1 - X_2} = \sigma\sqrt{2(1 - r)} = 15\sqrt{2(1 - .92)} = 15\sqrt{2(.08)}$$

$$= 6.0$$

$$\gamma = \frac{\mu_1 - \mu_2}{\sigma_{X_1 - X_2}} = \frac{3}{6} = .50$$

$$\delta = \gamma\sqrt{N} = .50\sqrt{30} = 2.74$$

power $= .78.$

Suppose, on the other hand, that we had used a less reliable test for which $r = .50$. We will assume that σ remains unchanged. Then

$$\sigma_{X_1 - X_2} = 15\sqrt{2(1 - .50)} = 15\sqrt{2(.5)} = 15\sqrt{1} = 15$$

$$\gamma = \frac{\mu_1 - \mu_2}{\sigma_{X_1 - X_2}} = \frac{3}{15} = .20$$

$$\delta = .20\sqrt{30} = 1.09$$

power $= .20$.

Thus we see that as r drops, so does power. When $r = 0$ our two samples are independent and thus the matched sample case has been reduced to the independent sample case. The very important point to be made here is that for all practical purposes the minimum power for the matched sample case occurs when $r = 0$ and we have independent samples. Thus for all situations in which we are even remotely likely to use matched samples (i.e., when we expect a positive correlation between X_1 and X_2), the matched sample design is more powerful than the corresponding independent groups design. This illustrates one of the main advantages of designs using matched samples.

The previous paragraph needs to be tempered by the fact that we are using an approximation procedure to calculate power. Essentially we are assuming the sample sizes are sufficiently large that the t distribution is closely approximated by z. If this is not the case, then we have to take account of the fact that a matched sample t has only one half as many df as the corresponding independent sample t, and the power of the two designs will not be quite equal when $r = 0$. However, this is generally not a serious problem.

8.6 *Power Calculations for Other Tests of Significance*

While the preceding discussion applies primarily to t tests, similar techniques can be applied to other tests of significance. For most of these the student is referred to Cohen (1969), where they are discussed in detail. One additional case will be discussed here since it involves nothing new, although the statistic (r) will not be considered until the next chapter. The reader may wish to read that chapter before continuing, although that should not be necessary.

Testing the Significance of a Correlation Coefficient

Consider the problem of the individual who wishes to demonstrate the relationship between television violence and aggressive behavior. Let us assume that she has surmounted all of the nearly insurmountable problems associated with this question and has managed to devise a way to obtain a Pearson *product-moment correlation coefficient* **(r)** (to be defined in Chapter 9) between the two variables. She feels that the correlation in the population **(ρ—rho)** is somewhere around .20 (a rather trivial correlation, but statistically significant things are often trivial). She wants to conduct a study to find such a correlation, but wants to know something about the power of her study before she begins. Define

Product-moment correlation coefficient (r)

Rho (ρ)

$$\gamma = \rho_1$$

where ρ_1 is the correlation in the population as defined by H_1—in this case, .20. Further define

$$\delta = \gamma\sqrt{N-1} = \rho_1\sqrt{N-1}.$$

For a sample of size 50,

$$\delta = .20\sqrt{50-1}$$

$$= 1.40$$

power $= .29$.

Power coefficient

A *power coefficient* of .29 is not likely to be very palatable to our crusader, and she must now start casting around for a way to increase power. Suppose that she wants power $= .80$. This will require $\delta = 2.8$. Therefore

$$\delta = \rho_1\sqrt{N-1}$$

$$2.8 = .20\sqrt{N-1}$$

$$\left(\frac{2.8}{.20}\right)^2 + 1 = N$$

$$N = 197.$$

Thus if power is to equal .80 in this situation, it will be necessary to collect data on nearly 200 subjects.

8.7 *Power Considerations in Terms of Sample Size*

The present discussion of power illustrates that reasonably large sample sizes are almost a necessity if one is to run experiments with any decent chance of rejecting H_0 when it is in fact false and the effect is small. As an illustration, a few minutes of calculation will show that if we want to have power $= .80$ and if we accept Cohen's admittedly arbitrary definitions for

Effect Size	γ	t 1 sample	t 2 sample	correlations
Small	.20	196	784	197
Medium	.50	32	126	33
Large	.80	13	49	14

small, medium, and large effects, our samples may not be small. Table 8.1 presents the total *N*s required (at power = .80, $\alpha = .05$) for small, medium, and large effects for the tests we have been discussing. These figures indicate that power (at least a substantial amount of it) is a very expensive commodity, especially for small effects. While one could argue that this is a good thing, since otherwise the literature would contain many more small (trivial?) results than it already does, that will come as little comfort to most experimenters. The general rule is to either look for big effects or use large samples. An interesting article on the power of experiments which are already in the published literature is Cohen (1962).

8.8 Summary

In this chapter we have investigated the concept of power and the variables which affect it. The measure known as *effect size* was developed to represent the degree to which the null hypothesis is false, and we saw how this concept could be used to evaluate the power of a test under specified conditions. Finally, we looked at the procedures for making power calculations for a number of common statistical tests.

Exercises for Chapter 8

8.1 Over the past 10 years a small New England college has been able to hold its mean SAT score (and, by inference, the mean of the population from which it draws) at 520 with a standard deviation of 80. A major competitor would like to demonstrate that standards have slipped and the college is now really drawing from a population of students with a mean of 500. They plan to run a *t* test on the mean SAT of next fall's entering class.

a. What is the effect size in question?
b. What is the value of δ if the size of next fall's class is 100?
c. What is the power of the test?

8.2 Diagram the situation described in Exercise 8.1 along the lines of Figure 8.2.

8.3 In Exercise 8.1, what sample sizes would be needed to raise power to .70, .80, and .90, respectively?

8.4 Unbeknownst to the competition, the college referred to in Exercise 8.1 has started a major campaign to increase the quality of their new students. They are hoping to show a 30 point gain in the mean SAT score for next year. If there are 100 students enrolling next fall, what is the power of a *t* test used to test the significance of any increase?

8.5 Diagram the situation described in Exercise 8.4 along the lines of Figure 8.2.

8.6 A physiological psychology laboratory has been studying avoidance behavior in rabbits for several years and has published numerous papers on the topic. It is clear from this research that the mean response latency for a particular task is 5.8 seconds with a standard deviation of 2 seconds (based on many hundreds of rabbits). Now the investigators wish to lesion certain areas in the amygdala and demonstrate poorer avoidance conditioning in those animals (shorter latencies—i.e., they repeat the punished response sooner). They expect latencies to decrease by about 1 second, and plan to run a one-sample *t* test (of $\mu_0 = 5.8$).

a. How many subjects do they need to have at least a 50:50 chance of success?

b. How many subjects do they need to have at least an 80:20 chance of success?

8.7 Suppose that the laboratory referred to in Exercise 8.6 decided not to run one group and compare it against $\mu_0 = 5.8$, but to run two groups (one with and one without lesions). They still expect the same degree of difference, however.

a. How many subjects do they now need (overall) if they are to have power = .60?

b. How many subjects do they now need (overall) if they are to have power = .90?

8.8 As it turns out, some research assistant has just finished running the experiment described in Exercise 8.7, without having carried out any power calculations. He tried to run 20 subjects in each group, but he accidentally tipped over a rack of cages and had to void 5 subjects in the experimental group. What is the power of this experiment?

8.9 I have just conducted a study comparing cognitive development of low birth weight (premature) and normal babies at one year of age. Using a scale I devised I found that the sample means of the two groups were 25 and 30, respectively, with a pooled standard deviation of 8. There were 20 subjects in each group. *If we assume* that the true means and standard deviations have been estimated exactly, what is the *a priori* probability that this study would in fact find a significant difference?

8.10 We will modify Exercise 8.9 to have means of 25 and 28, with a pooled standard deviation of 8 and sample sizes of 20.

a. What is the *a priori* power of this experiment?
b. Run the *t* test on the data.
c. What, if anything, does the answer to Exercise 8.10*a* have to say about the answer to 8.10*b*?

8.11 Two graduate students have recently completed their dissertations. Each used a *t* test for two independent groups. One found a barely significant *t* using 10 subjects per group. The other found a barely significant *t* using 45 subjects per group. Which result impresses you the most?

8.12 Draw a diagram (analogous to Figure 8.1) to defend your answer to Exercise 8.11.

8.13 An admissions officer at a large university has been accused of incompetence because she uses high school grades as a basis for decisions on admission. The charge has been made that grades do not correlate with college performance. She plans to draw a sample of already admitted students and correlate their present grades with their past performance in high school. Assuming that the true correlation in the population is .40 and she is planning to draw 35 students, what is the probability that she will keep her job (i.e., find a significant correlation)?

8.14 What sample size would the admissions officer referred to in the last exercise need to be 90% sure of keeping her job?

8.15 A poor beleaguered Ph.D. candidate has the impression that he must find significant results if he wants to successfully defend his dissertation. He wants to show a difference in social awareness, as measured by his own scale, between a normal group and a group of ex-delinquents. He has a problem, however. He has data to suggest that the normal group has a true mean = 38 and he has 50 of those subjects. He has access to 100 college students who have been classed as delinquent in the past. Or, he has access to 25 high school dropouts with a history of delinquency. He suspects that the *college group* comes from a population with a mean of approximately 35, while the *dropout group* comes from a population with a mean of approximately 30. If he can only use one of these groups, which should he use?

8.16 I would like to demonstrate a correlation between number of days per year in which a person can go downhill skiing and a rating of mental health. I am only interested in finding such a correlation if the true correlation is .40. What are my chances of finding such a correlation if I use 30 subjects?

8.17 In Exercise 8.16, how many subjects would I need for power = .80?

8.18 Generate a table analogous to Table 8.1 for power = .80, $\alpha = .01$, two-tailed.

8.19   Generate a table analogous to Table 8.1 for power $= .60$, $\alpha = .05$, two-tailed.

8.20   Assume that we want to test a null hypothesis about a single mean at $\alpha = .05$, one-tailed. Further assume that all necessary assumptions are met. Is there ever a case where we are more likely to reject a true H_0 than we are to reject H_0 if it is false? (In other words, can power ever be less than α?)

9 Correlation and Regression

Objective

To introduce the concepts of correlation and regression and to begin to look at ways of representing relationships between variables.

Contents

Relationships
Differences

In Chapter 7 we were concerned with testing hypotheses concerning sample means. In this chapter we will begin examining questions concerning relationships between variables. While one should not make too much of the distinction between **relationships** and **differences** (if treatments have *different* means, then means are *related* to treatments), the distinction is usually a useful one in terms of the interests of the experimenter and the structure of the experiment. When we are concerned with mean differences the experiment usually consists of a few quantitative or qualitative levels of the independent variable (e.g., Treatment *A* and Treatment *B*) and the experimenter is interested in showing that the dependent variable differs from one treatment to another. When we are concerned with relationships, however, the independent variable (X) usually has many quantifiable levels ($X_1, X_2, \ldots, X_k$) and the experimenter is interested in showing that the dependent variable is some *function* of the independent variable.

Correlation
Regression

This chapter will deal with two interwoven topics—**correlation** and **regression**. Statisticians commonly make a distinction between these two techniques, and although the distinction is frequently not followed in practice it is important to consider it briefly. In problems of simple correlation and regression the data consist of two observations from each of N subjects, one observation on each of the variables under consideration. If we were interested in the correlation between running speed in a maze (Y) and number of trials to criterion (X) (both common measures of learning), we would obtain a running speed score and a trials to criterion score from each subject. Similarly if we were interested in regression of running speed (Y) on the number of food pellets per reinforcement (X), each subject would have scores corresponding to his speed and the number of pellets he received. The difference between these two situations is worth noting, since they illustrate the statistical distinction between correlation and regression. In

Random variable

both cases Y is a **random variable**, beyond the control of the experimenter. In the former case X is also a random variable since the number of trials to criterion is beyond our control. Put another way, a replication of the experiment would leave us with different X values. In the latter case,

Fixed variable

however, X is a **fixed variable** and would remain constant across replications, since the values of X are determined by the experimenter.

To most statisticians the word *regression* is reserved for those situations in which the value of X is *fixed* or specified by the experimenter before the data are collected. In these situations there is no sampling error involved in X and repeated replications of the experiment will involve the same X values. The word *correlation*, on the other hand, is used to describe the situation in which both X and Y are random variables. In this case the Xs, as well as the Ys, would vary from one replication to another and thus sampling error would be involved in both variables. This distinction is

Linear regression
Bivariate normal models

basically the distinction between what are called **linear regression** and **bivariate normal models**.

Prediction

As mentioned earlier, the distinction, while perfectly appropriate on statistical grounds, tends to break down in practice. A more pragmatic distinction, and the one adopted here, relies on the interest of the experimenter. If the purpose of the experiment is to allow ***prediction*** of Y on the basis of knowledge about X, we will speak of *regression*. If, on the other hand, the purpose is merely to obtain a statistic expressing the degree of relationship between two variables, we will speak of *correlation*. While it is possible to raise legitimate objections to this distinction, it has the advantage of describing the different ways in which these two procedures are used in practice.

Having differentiated between correlation and regression, we will now proceed to discuss the two techniques together since they are so closely related. The general problem then becomes one of developing an equation to predict one variable from knowledge of the other and of obtaining a measure of the degree or *goodness* of this relationship. The only restriction that we will impose for the moment is that the relationship between X and Y be linear. Curvilinear relationships will not be considered, although we will later see how they can be handled by closely related procedures.

9.1 *Scatter Diagrams*

Scatter diagram

When we collect measures on two variables for the purpose of examining the relationship between these variables, one of the most useful techniques for gaining some insight into this relationship is the preparation of a ***scatter diagram***. Examples of four such diagrams appear in Figure 9.1. In this figure every subject is represented by a point in two-dimensional space, the coordinates of this point (X_i, Y_i) being the individual's scores on variables X and Y respectively.

In preparing a scatter diagram the independent variable is traditionally represented by the abscissa, or X axis, and the dependent variable by the ordinate, or Y axis. If the purpose of the experiment is prediction, the distinction becomes obvious since the dependent variable is that variable to be predicted, while the independent variable is that variable from which the prediction is made. If the problem is one of correlation the distinction may be obvious (incidence of cancer would be dependent upon amount smoked rather than the reverse), or it may not (neither running speed nor number of correct choices is obviously in a dependent position relative to the other). Where the distinction is not obvious it is irrelevant as to which variable is labeled X and which Y.

Consider the four hypothetical scatter diagrams in Figure 9.1. Figure 9.1(a) represents a case in which there is a relatively strong relationship between X and Y. Although the relationship is not perfect, it is generally true that as X increases Y also increases. Figure 9.1(b) illustrates the case

Perfect relationship

of a ***perfect relationship***. Every increase in X is accompanied by an exactly

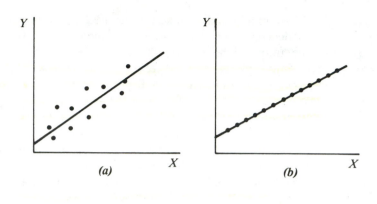

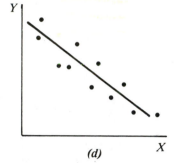

FIGURE 9.1

Scatter diagrams
illustrating various
degrees of relationship

proportional increase in Y, all of the points falling on a straight line. In Figure 9.1(c) we have a situation in which there is **no relationship** between

No relationship

X and Y. There is no systematic tendency for Y to vary with X, and knowing the value of X tells us nothing about the corresponding value of Y. Finally,

Negative relationship

Figure 9.1(d) represents a relatively strong **negative relationship** between X and Y. In fact the degree of relationship, though not its direction, is the same as that shown in Figure 9.1(a) (the scatter diagram has merely been rotated 90°). In this situation an increase in X corresponds to a general decrease in Y.

The lines which have been superimposed upon Figures 9.1(a)–(d) represent those straight lines which best fit the data—the way in which this

Regression lines
Y on X

line is *best* will be defined shortly. These are what we will call the **regression lines** of Y predicted on the basis of X (abbreviated **Y on X**) and represent our best prediction of Y for a given value of X. Given any specified value of X, the corresponding height of the regression line represents our best

Y hat ($\hat{Y}$)

prediction of Y (designated $\hat{Y}$, and read "**Y hat**"). In other words we can draw a vertical line from X_i to the regression line. We can then move horizontally to the Y axis and read off $\hat{Y}_i$.

The degree to which the points cluster about the regression line (in other words the degree to which the actual values of Y agree with the

Correlation r

predicted values) is related to the correlation between X and Y (represented by the symbol *correlation r*). In Figure 9.1(a) the points cluster reasonably closely, and the correlation is high ($r = .81$). In Figure 9.1(b) the points fall exactly on the line and the correlation is perfect ($r = 1.00$). In Figure 9.1(c) the points do not cluster at all round the line and the correlation is .00. And in Figure 9.1(d) the degree of clustering is the same as in Figure 9.1(a), but the relationship is negative, so the correlation is negative ($r = -.81$).

9.2 The Covariance

Covariance

Variance

Before defining the correlation coefficient we must first consider what we mean by the *covariance* of X and Y, since the covariance will play a very important part in what follows. The data in Table 9.1 represent teachers' ratings of the attractiveness of 20 children in 5th grade (X) and 6th grade (Y) respectively. As we already know, the *variance* represents the degree to which the values of one variable vary among themselves (e.g., the differences among the 5th grade ratings). We will define the *covariance* of two variables (X and Y) as the degree to which the corresponding values of the two variables vary together.

$$\text{cov}_{XY} = \frac{\Sigma(X - \bar{X})(Y - \bar{Y})}{N-1} = \frac{\Sigma XY - \dfrac{\Sigma X \Sigma Y}{N}}{N-1}. \tag{9.1}$$

From Equation 9.1 it is apparent that the covariance is very similar in form to the variance. If we change all of the Ys in Equation 9.1 to Xs, we will have s_X^2, and if we change the Xs to Ys we will have s_Y^2. For the data in Table 9.1 the covariance is

$$\text{cov}_{XY} = \frac{\Sigma XY - \dfrac{\Sigma X \Sigma Y}{N}}{N-1} = \frac{756 - \dfrac{(110)(127)}{20}}{19} = 3.026.$$

Some insight into the meaning of the covariance can be gained by considering what we would expect to find in the case of a high positive correlation, such as the data in Table 9.1. In this situation high scores on one variable will in general be matched with high scores on the other. We would expect children rated high in attractiveness by one teacher will be rated high by the other, and those rated low by one teacher will probably be rated low by the other. Thus for an attractive child $(X - \bar{X})$ and $(Y - \bar{Y})$ will both be positive, and their product will be reasonably large. For an unattractive child $(X - \bar{X})$ and $(Y - \bar{Y})$ will both be negative, but their product will be positive and again reasonably large. Thus the sum of the

Cross products

cross products of deviation scores for these individuals will be large and positive, indicating a high positive relationship.

TABLE 9.1

Teachers' Ratings of
Attractiveness of
Children in 5th (X)
and 6th (Y) Grades

Subject	X	Y		
1	3	2	$\Sigma X = 110$	$\bar{X} = 5.5$
2	3	5		
3	4	6	$\Sigma X^2 = 658$	$s_X^2 = 2.789$
4	5	5		
5	6	5		
6	6	8	$\Sigma Y = 127$	$\bar{Y} = 6.35$
7	3	3		
8	4	3	$\Sigma Y^2 = 895$	$s_Y^2 = 4.661$
9	7	9		
10	8	10		
11	7	7	$\Sigma XY = 756$	$\text{cov}_{XY} = 3.026$
12	4	5		
13	8	9		
14	5	7		$N = 20$
15	7	8		
16	6	6		
17	5	8		
18	6	7		
19	5	6		
20	8	8		

Next consider the case of a strong negative relationship. Here large positive values of $(X - \bar{X})$ will most likely be paired with large negative values of $(Y - \bar{Y})$, and vice versa. Thus the sum of deviation cross products will be large and negative, indicating a high negative relationship.

Finally, consider a situation in which there is no relationship between X and Y. In this case a positive value of $(X - \bar{X})$ will sometimes be paired with a positive value of $(Y - \bar{Y})$, and sometimes with a negative value. The result is that the cross products will be positive about half of the time and negative about half of the time, producing a near-zero sum and indicating no relationship between the variables.

For a given set of data, it is possible to show that the cov_{XY} will be at its positive maximum whenever X and Y are perfectly positively correlated ($r = 1.00$), and at its negative maximum whenever they are perfectly negatively correlated ($r = -1.00$). When the two variables are perfectly uncorrelated ($r = .00$) the cov_{XY} will be zero.

9.3   *The Pearson Product-Moment Correlation Coefficient (r)*

What we have just said about the covariance might suggest that we could use the covariance as a measure of the degree of relationship between two variables. An immediate difficulty arises, however, in that the absolute value of cov_{XY} is also a function of the standard deviations of X and Y (or more accurately, of their product). Thus a $\text{cov}_{XY} = 20$, for example, might reflect a high degree of correlation when the standard deviations are small, but a low degree of correlation when the standard deviations are high. To resolve this difficulty we will scale the covariance by the size of the standard deviations, and make this our estimate of correlation. Thus

$$r = \frac{\text{cov}_{XY}}{s_X s_Y}. \tag{9.2}$$

Since it can be shown that the maximum value of cov_{XY} is $\pm s_X s_Y$, it then follows that the limits on r are ± 1.00. One interpretation of r, then, is that it is a measure of the degree to which the covariance approaches its maximum.

An equivalent way of writing Equation 9.2 would be

$$r = \frac{\Sigma(X - \bar{X})(Y - \bar{Y})}{\sqrt{\Sigma(X - \bar{X})^2 \Sigma(Y - \bar{Y})^2}}. \tag{9.3}$$

While this equation would seldom be used for purposes of calculation, it explains why r is referred to as a product-moment correlation. A term of the form $\Sigma(X - \bar{X})^k$ is called the kth *moment* about the mean. We are therefore working with moments and products of moments. There are other correlation coefficients which are not product-moment coefficients, and some of these will be discussed in Chapter 10.

Equations 9.2 and 9.3 are good definitional formulae for r, but a more satisfactory solution exists for purposes of hand calculation. If we replace the variances and covariances by their computational formulae and cancel appropriate terms, we arrive at

$$r = \frac{N\Sigma XY - \Sigma X \Sigma Y}{\sqrt{(N\Sigma X^2 - (\Sigma X)^2)(N\Sigma Y^2 - (\Sigma Y)^2)}}. \tag{9.4}$$

Equation 9.4 is the one we will use for almost all calculations of r.

To take an example, consider the data presented in Table 9.1. Applying Equation 9.4 to our sample data we obtain

$$r = \frac{N\Sigma XY - \Sigma X \Sigma Y}{\sqrt{(N\Sigma X^2 - (\Sigma X)^2)(N\Sigma Y^2 - (\Sigma Y)^2)}}$$

$$= \frac{20(756) - (110)(127)}{\sqrt{(20(658) - 110^2)(20(895) - 127^2)}}$$

$$= \frac{1150}{\sqrt{(1060)(1771)}}$$

$$= .84.$$

Thus the correlation between X and Y (sometimes represented as r_{XY}) is .84.

This coefficient must be interpreted with caution so as not to attribute to it meaning which it does not possess. Specifically, $r = .84$ should not be interpreted to mean that there is 84% of a relationship (whatever that might mean) between X and Y. The correlation coefficient is simply a point on the scale from -1.00 to $+1.00$, and the closer it is to either of those limits the stronger is the relationship between X and Y. For a more specific interpretation we will prefer to speak in terms of r^2, which we will discuss later in this chapter.

9.4   *The Regression Line*

We have just seen that there is a reasonably high degree of relationship between ratings given the same children by two different teachers. However, if our task is one of prediction of one variable (Y) on the basis of the other variable (X), then we must find an appropriate way of expressing Y as some function of X. This book, like most textbooks, will limit itself to the discussion of linear relationships, and therefore we want to solve for Y as some linear function of X.

Linear function   As you learned in high school algebra, a ***linear function*** is an equation of the form $Y = bX + a$. For our purposes this will be expressed as

$$\hat{Y} = bX + a \qquad\qquad\qquad\qquad (9.5)$$

Predicted value   where $\hat{Y}$ is the ***predicted value*** of Y, b is the ***slope*** of our regression line,
Slope   and a is the ***intercept*** (the value of $\hat{Y}$ when $X = 0$). Our task will be to
Intercept   solve for those values of a and b which will produce the best fitting linear function. In other words, we want to solve for the values of a and b such that the regression line (the predicted values of $\hat{Y}$ for different values of X) will come as close as possible to the actual obtained values of Y.

Best fitting   But how are we to define the phrase "***best fitting***"? The most logical
Errors of prediction   way would be in terms of ***errors of prediction***—i.e., in terms of the $Y - \hat{Y}$ deviations. Since the difference $Y - \hat{Y}$ represents an error of prediction, we will define our best fitting line as that which minimizes such errors. However, rather than minimizing the sum of the deviations, which will always be zero, we will solve for the equation of that line which minimizes the sum of the *squared* deviations of Y from $\hat{Y}$—i.e., which minimizes $\Sigma(Y - \hat{Y})^2$. With respect to our discussion of variability in Section 2.4, it might be noted that here we are dealing with the variability of points around the regression line (the predicted values), whereas in Chapter 2 we dealt with variability about the mean. These two concepts have much in common.

To obtain the optimal values of a and b, we will begin with the expression to be minimized $(\Sigma(Y - \hat{Y})^2)$. Substituting $bX + a$ for $\hat{Y}$ we obtain

$$\Sigma(Y - \hat{Y})^2 = \Sigma(Y - (bX + a))^2 = \Sigma(Y - bX - a)^2.$$

As we have already said, we want to find those values of a and b for which $\Sigma(Y - \hat{Y})^2$ is a minimum. Students who have had a course in calculus will recognize at once that if we take the partial derivatives of this expression with respect to a and b separately, set these derivatives equal to zero, and solve, we will obtain the desired values for a and b. Students who have not had a course in calculus can simply take what follows on faith.

$$\Sigma(Y - \hat{Y})^2 = \Sigma(Y - bX - a)^2$$
$$= \Sigma(Y^2 + b^2X^2 + a^2 - 2aY - 2bXY + 2abX).$$

The derivative with respect to a is

$$\frac{d(Y - \hat{Y})^2}{da} = \Sigma(2a - 2Y + 2bX)$$

$$= 2Na - 2\Sigma Y + 2b\Sigma X.$$

Setting this equal to zero

$$2Na - 2\Sigma Y + 2b\Sigma X = 0$$

$$Na + b\Sigma X = \Sigma Y. \tag{9.6}$$

The derivative with respect to b is

$$\frac{d(Y - \hat{Y})^2}{db} = \Sigma(2bX^2 - 2XY + 2aX)$$

$$= 2b\Sigma X^2 - 2\Sigma XY + 2a\Sigma X.$$

Setting this equal to zero

$$2b\Sigma X^2 - 2\Sigma XY + 2a\Sigma X = 0$$

$$b\Sigma X^2 + a\Sigma X = \Sigma XY. \tag{9.7}$$

Normal equations Equations 9.6 and 9.7 are called the ***normal equations*** although they do not have anything to do with the normal distribution. From the normal equations it is a simple matter to solve for a and b. Solving for a we obtain

$$Na + b\Sigma X = \Sigma Y$$

$$a = \frac{\Sigma Y - b\Sigma X}{N}. \tag{9.8}$$

To solve for b we begin with the normal equation

$$b\Sigma X^2 + a\Sigma X = \Sigma XY.$$

Substituting from Equation 9.8 and simplifying, we obtain

$$b = \frac{N\Sigma XY - \Sigma X\Sigma Y}{N\Sigma X^2 - (\Sigma X)^2}. \tag{9.9}$$

We now have solutions for a and b in terms of the original variables. To indicate that our solution was designed to minimize errors in predicting Y from X (rather than the other way around), the constants are sometimes denoted as $a_{Y \cdot X}$ and $b_{Y \cdot X}$. When no confusion would arise, the subscripts are usually omitted.†

Suppose however that we now wanted to predict X from knowledge of Y. The constants $a_{Y \cdot X}$ and $b_{Y \cdot X}$ are not suitable for that purpose, since they minimize error in predicting Y. Although we could begin all over again starting with

$$\hat{X} = bY + a$$

and minimizing $\Sigma(X - \hat{X})^2$, a much simpler solution is to interchange the symbols X and Y in Equations 9.8 and 9.9. Doing this we obtain

$$a_{X \cdot Y} = \frac{\Sigma X - b \Sigma Y}{N} \tag{9.10}$$

and

$$b_{X \cdot Y} = \frac{N \Sigma XY - \Sigma X \Sigma Y}{N \Sigma Y^2 - (\Sigma Y)^2}. \tag{9.11}$$

As an example of the calculation of regression coefficients, consider the data shown in Table 9.2. These are merely the data from Table 9.1, along with the calculations of the regression coefficients for predicting Y on X. The corresponding scatter diagram is presented in Figure 9.2, with the regression lines for both Y on X and X on Y superimposed.

A word is in order about the actual plotting of the regression line. To plot the line Y on X, we can take any two values of X_i, preferably at opposite ends of the scale, and solve for the corresponding values of $\hat{Y}_i$. If we then plot the points specified by these coordinates and connect them with a straight line, we will have our regression line. Thus given the line

$$\hat{Y}_i = 1.058(X_i) + .3821,$$

when $X_i = 0$

$$\hat{Y}_i = 1.058(0) + .3821 = .3821$$

and when $X_i = 10$

$$\hat{Y}_i = 1.058(10) + .3821 = 10.9621.$$

The line, then, passes through the points (0, .3821) and (10, 10.9621), as is shown in Figure 9.2. (Actually an easier procedure is simply to pass a line through $(0, a)$ and $(\bar{X}, \bar{Y})$, assuming that these points are far enough apart to lead to a sufficient degree of accuracy in drawing the line.)

---

† Alternative forms for Equations 9.8 and 9.9 are: $a = \bar{Y} - b\bar{X}$ and $b = \text{cov}_{XY}/s_X^2$.

TABLE 9.2

Calculations of
Correlation and
Regression Coefficients
for Data in
Table 9.1

Subject	X	Y
1	3	2
2	3	5
3	4	6
4	5	5
5	6	5
6	6	8
7	3	3
8	4	3
9	7	9
10	8	10
11	7	7
12	4	5
13	8	9
14	5	7
15	7	8
16	6	6
17	5	8
18	6	7
19	5	6
20	8	8

$\Sigma X = 110$ $\bar{X} = 5.5$

$\Sigma X^2 = 658$ $s_X^2 = 2.789$

$\Sigma Y = 127$ $\bar{Y} = 6.35$

$\Sigma Y^2 = 895$ $s_Y^2 = 4.661$

$\Sigma XY = 756$ $\text{cov}_{XY} = 3.026$

$$N = 20$$

$$b_{Y \cdot X} = \frac{N\Sigma XY - \Sigma X \Sigma Y}{N\Sigma X^2 - (\Sigma X)^2}$$

$$= \frac{20(756) - (110)(127)}{20(658) - 110^2}$$

$$= \frac{15120 - 13970}{13160 - 12100} = \frac{1150}{1060} = 1.085$$

$$a_{Y \cdot X} = \frac{\Sigma Y - b\Sigma X}{N}$$

$$= \frac{127 - (1.085)(110)}{20}$$

$$= \frac{127 - 119.35}{20} = .382$$

From Figure 9.2 it is apparent that the two regression lines are not coincident, and that they intersect at the point $(\bar{X}, \bar{Y})$. The fact that they are different lines reflects the fact that they were designed for different purposes—one minimizes $\Sigma(Y - \hat{Y})^2$ while the other minimizes $\Sigma(X - \hat{X})^2$. They both go through the point $(\bar{X}, \bar{Y})$ because a person who is *average* on one variable would be expected to be *average* on the other. Only when the two variables have the same variance will the two lines be coincident. This follows from the fact that if we were to divide the numerator and denominator of $b_{Y \cdot X}$ by $N(N-1)$ we would have

$$b_{Y \cdot X} = \text{cov}_{XY}/s_X^2$$

and similarly

$$b_{X \cdot Y} = \text{cov}_{XY}/s_Y^2.$$

Since the two equations differ only in their denominators, $b_{Y \cdot X}$ will equal $b_{X \cdot Y}$ when $s_X^2 = s_Y^2$. If the slopes are equal and both lines pass through

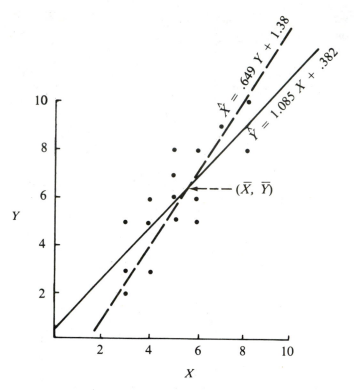

FIGURE 9.2
Scatter diagram
of data from
Table 9.2

$(\bar{X}, \bar{Y})$, then the lines must be coincident. It is useful to keep in mind that if X and Y are both converted to standard score form, the variances of both variables will equal 1, and thus there is only one regression line.

Interpretations of Regression

In certain situations the regression line is useful in its own right. For example a college admissions officer might well be interested in an equation for predicting college performance on the basis of high school grade point average (although he would most likely want to include multiple predictors in ways to be discussed in Chapter 15). Similarly a farmer might be interested in actually predicting crop yield on the basis of number of pounds of fertilizer per acre.

However in most applications of regression in psychology we are not particularly interested in making an actual prediction. While we might be interested in knowing the relationship between family income and educational achievement, it is unlikely that we would take any particular child's family income measure and use that to predict her educational achievement. To a large extent we are interested in general principles, but not in individual predictions. However, a regression equation can in fact tell us something meaningful about these general principles, even though we may never use it to actually form a prediction.

Intercept   We have defined the intercept as that value of $\hat{Y}$ when X equals 0. As such it has meaning in some situations and not in others, primarily as a function of whether or not $X = 0$ is near or within the range of values of X used to derive the estimate of the intercept. If, for example, we took a group of overweight people and looked at the relationship between self-esteem and weight loss (assuming that it is linear), the intercept would tell us what level of self-esteem to expect for an individual who did not lose any weight. Often, however, there is no meaningful interpretation of the intercept (other than a mathematical one). If we were to look at the relationship between height and weight for adults, it is obviously foolish to ask how tall we would expect someone to be if they weighed zero pounds. The intercept would appear to tell us this, but it represents such an extreme extrapolation from available data as to be meaningless. (In this case a non-zero intercept would suggest a lack of linearity over the wider range of weights from 0 to 300 pounds.)

Slope   We have defined the slope as the rate of change in Y for a one-unit change in X. By definition, then, the slope is often a meaningful measure. If we are looking at the regression of income on years of schooling, the slope will tell us how much of a difference in income to expect for each additional year of school. Similarly, if an automobile manufacturer knows that the slope relating fuel economy (in mpg) to weight of the automobile is .01, then he knows that for every pound that he can reduce the weight of a car he will increase its fuel economy by .01 miles per gallon. Thus replacing a 30 pound spare tire with a 20 pound temporary spare will gain him a tenth of a mile per gallon (but an annoyed customer).

People tend to forget that the slope in a regression equation has the meaning just attributed to it, even though that is the definition of the slope. Viewed in this way the slope can really be a very useful statistic, regardless of whether or not one ever computes a prediction on the basis of individual values of X.

Although we rarely work with standardized data (data which have been transformed so as to have a mean of 0 and a standard deviation of 1), it is worth considering what the meaning of b would represent if the data for each variable were standardized separately. In that case a difference of one unit in X or Y represents a difference of one standard deviation. Thus if the slope were .75, for standardized data, we would be able to say that a one standard deviation increase in X will be reflected in three quarters of a standard deviation increase in $\hat{Y}$.

Correlation   What we have just seen with respect to the slope for standardized variables has direct applicability to the correlation coefficient. Recall that r is defined as $cov_{XY}/s_X s_Y$ whereas b is defined as cov_{XY}/s_X^2. If the data are standardized, $s_X = s_Y = s_X^2 = 1$, and the slope and the correlation coefficient will be equal. Thus one interpretation of the correlation coefficient is that it is equal to what the slope would be if the variables were standardized. A derivative interpretation of $r = .80$, for example, is that one standard deviation increase in X would be associated on the average with $\frac{8}{10}$ths of a standard deviation increase in Y. In some situations such an interpretation can be meaningfully applied.

A note of caution   What has just been said about the interpretation of b and r must be tempered with a bit of caution. To say that a one unit increase in family income is associated with .75 units increase in academic achievement is not to be interpreted to mean that raising family income for John Smith will automatically raise his academic achievement. In other words we are not speaking about cause and effect. We can say that people who score higher on income also score higher on achievement without in any way implying causation or suggesting what would happen to a given individual if his/her family income were to increase. Family income is associated (in a correlational sense) with a whole host of other variables (e.g., attitudes toward education, number of books in the home, access to a variety of environments, etc.) and there is no reason to expect all of these to change merely because income changes. Those who argue that eradicating poverty will lead to a wide variety of changes in people's lives often fall into such a cause and effect trap. Eradicating poverty is certainly a worthy goal, but the correlations between income and educational achievement may be totally irrelevant to the issue.

9.5 *The Accuracy of Prediction*

The fact that we can fit a regression line to a set of data does not mean that our problems are solved. On the contrary, they have only begun. The important point is not whether or not a straight line can be drawn through the data (you can always do that) but whether or not that line represents a reasonable fit to the data—in other words whether our effort was worthwhile.

Before discussing errors of prediction, however, it is instructive to consider the situation in which we wish to predict Y without any knowledge of the value of X.

The Standard Deviation as a Measure of Error

As mentioned earlier, the data in Table 9.2 represent teachers' ratings of children's "attractiveness" in 6th grade (Y) as a function of their rated "attractiveness" in 5th grade (X). Assume that you are now given the task of predicting an individual's 6th grade rating without any knowledge of his/her score in 5th grade. Your best prediction in this case would be the mean 6th grade rating $(\bar{Y})$ and the error associated with your prediction would be the standard deviation of $Y(s_Y)$, since your prediction is the mean and s_Y deals with deviations around the mean. Examining s_Y we know that it is defined as

$$s_Y = \sqrt{\frac{\Sigma(Y - \bar{Y})^2}{N-1}}$$

or, in terms of the variance,

$$s_Y^2 = \frac{\Sigma(Y - \bar{Y})^2}{N-1}.$$

The numerator is the sum of squared deviations from $\bar{Y}$ (the point you would have predicted in this particular example), and is commonly referred to as the ***sum of squares*** of Y. The denominator is simply the degrees of freedom. Thus

Sum of squares (SS)

$$s_Y^2 = SS_Y/df.$$

Now suppose that we wish to make a prediction about a 6th grade student who is not part of the original sample of 20 subjects, and are told how he was rated in the 5th grade. What would we now take as our measure of error?

The Standard Error of Estimate

In the situation in which we know the relevant value of X (and the regression equation) the best prediction would be $\hat{Y}$. In line with our previous measure of error (the standard deviation), the error associated with the present prediction would again be a function of the deviations of Y about the predicted point, in this case $\hat{Y}$. Specifically a measure of error can now be taken as

$$s_{Y \cdot X} = \sqrt{\frac{\Sigma(Y - \hat{Y})^2}{N-2}} = \sqrt{\frac{SS_{Y-\hat{Y}}}{df}} = \sqrt{\frac{SS_{error}}{df}} \qquad (9.12)$$

and again the sum of squared deviations are taken about the prediction, in this case $\hat{Y}$. The statistic $s_{Y \cdot X}$ is called the ***standard error of estimate*** and is the most common (though not always the best) measure of the error of prediction. Its square, $s_{Y \cdot X}^2$, is called the ***residual*** or ***error variance*** and it can be shown to be an unbiased estimate of the corresponding parameter $(\sigma_{Y \cdot X}^2)$ in the population. We have $N-2$ df because we lost two degrees of freedom in estimating our regression line. (This becomes apparent when

Standard error of estimate

Residual variance
Error variance

you realize that since two points determine a straight line, given only two points there can be no error.)

One way to calculate the standard error of estimate would be to calculate $\hat{Y}$ for each observation and then to obtain $s_{Y \cdot X}$ directly, as has been done in Table 9.3. Finding the standard error by use of Equation 9.12 is hardly the most enjoyable way of spending a winter evening. Fortunately a much simpler procedure exists which not only represents a way of obtaining the standard error of estimate, but also leads directly into much more important matters.

TABLE 9.3

Direct Calculation of Variance Estimates for Data in Table 9.1

X	Y	$\hat{Y}$	$(Y - \hat{Y})$	$(Y - \hat{Y})^2$
3	2	3.638	−1.638	2.683
3	3	3.638	−.638	.407
3	5	3.638	+1.362	1.855
4	5	4.723	+.277	.077
4	6	4.723	+1.277	1.631
4	3	4.723	−1.723	2.969
5	5	5.808	−.808	.653
5	6	5.808	+.192	.037
5	7	5.808	+1.192	1.421
5	8	5.808	+2.192	4.805
6	5	6.893	−1.893	3.583
6	6	6.893	−.893	.797
6	7	6.893	+.107	.011
6	8	6.893	+1.107	1.225
7	7	7.978	−.978	.956
7	8	7.978	+.022	.000
7	9	7.978	+1.022	1.044
8	8	9.063	−1.063	1.130
8	9	9.063	−.063	.004
8	10	9.063	+.937	.878
Σ 110	127	127.010	0	26.168

$\hat{Y} = 1.085X + .383$

$s_Y^2 = (\Sigma Y^2 - (\Sigma Y)^2/N)/(N-1) = (895 - 127^2/20)/19 = (895 - 806.450)/19 = 4.661$

$s_{Y-\hat{Y}}^2 = s_{Y \cdot X}^2 = (\Sigma(Y - \hat{Y})^2 - (\Sigma(Y - \hat{Y}))^2/N)/(N-2) = (26.168 - 0^2/20)/18$

$\qquad = 26.168/18 = 1.454$

$s_{\hat{Y}}^2 = (\Sigma \hat{Y}^2 - (\Sigma \hat{Y})^2/N)/(N-2) = (868.968 - 127.010^2/20)/18 = 62.391/18 = 3.47$

r^2 and the Standard Error of Estimate

In much of what follows we are going to abandon the term *variance* in favor of sums of squares (SS). As you should recall, a variance is a sum of squared deviations from the mean (generally known as a sum of squares) divided by the degrees of freedom. The problem with variances is that they are not additive unless they are based on the same df. Sums of squares are additive regardless of the degrees of freedom and thus are much easier to work with.

In Equation 9.12 we defined the residual or error variance as

$$s_{Y \cdot X}^2 = \frac{\Sigma(Y - \hat{Y})^2}{N - 2} = \frac{SS_{Y - \hat{Y}}}{N - 2}.$$

Since we are now speaking in terms of sums of squares we can drop the denominator and simply write

$$SS_{error} = \Sigma(Y - \hat{Y})^2.$$

With considerable algebraic manipulation it is possible to express SS_{error} as

$$SS_{error} = SS_Y(1 - r^2). \tag{9.13}$$

Thus we have shown that the sum of squares for residual error is a function of the sum of squares for the original values of Y and the correlation between X and Y.

If we divide Equation 9.13 by $N - 1$, we obtain

$$\frac{SS_{error}}{N - 1} = s_Y^2(1 - r^2)$$

and thus

$$s_{Y \cdot X}^2 = \frac{SS_{error}}{N - 2} = s_Y^2(1 - r^2)\frac{N - 1}{N - 2}.$$

For large samples the fraction $(N - 1)/(N - 2)$ is essentially 1, and we can thus write the equation as it is normally found in most statistics texts

$$s_{Y \cdot X}^2 = s_Y^2(1 - r^2)$$

or

$$s_{Y \cdot X} = s_Y \sqrt{1 - r^2}.$$

Keep in mind, however, that for small samples these equations are only an approximation and $s_{Y \cdot X}^2$ will overestimate the error variance by the fraction $(N - 1)/(N - 2)$. For samples of any size, however, $SS_{error} = SS_Y(1 - r^2)$. This particular formula is going to play a very important role throughout the rest of the book, especially in Chapters 15 and 16.

Error of Prediction as a Function of r

Now that we have obtained an expression for the standard error of estimate in terms of r, it is instructive to consider how this error decreases

TABLE 9.4
The Standard Error
of Estimate as a
Function of *r*

r	$s_{Y \cdot X}$	*r*	$s_{Y \cdot X}$
.00	s_Y	.60	$.800 s_Y$
.10	$.995 s_Y$	.70	$.714 s_Y$
.20	$.980 s_Y$	.80	$.600 s_Y$
.30	$.954 s_Y$	.866	$.500 s_Y$
.40	$.917 s_Y$	.90	$.436 s_Y$
.50	$.866 s_Y$	.95	$.312 s_Y$

as *r* increases. In Table 9.4 we see the magnitude of the standard error relative to the standard deviation of *Y* (the error to be expected when *X* is unknown) for selected values of *r*.

The values in Table 9.4 are somewhat sobering in their implications. Thus with a correlation of .20, the standard error of our estimate is fully 98% of what it would be if *X* were unknown. This means that if the correlation is .20, using $\hat{Y}$ as our prediction rather than $\bar{Y}$ (i.e., taking *X* into account), reduces the standard error by only 2%. Even more discouraging is the fact that if *r* is .50, the standard error of estimate is still 87% of the standard deviation. To reduce our error to one half of what it would be without knowledge of *X* requires a correlation of .866, and even a correlation of .95 reduces the error by only about two thirds. All of this is not to say that there is nothing to be gained by using a regression equation as the basis of prediction, but only that one should interpret the predictions with a certain degree of caution.

r^2 as a Measure of Predictable Variability

From Equation 9.13 it is possible to derive an extremely important interpretation of the correlation coefficient. We have already seen that

$$SS_{error} = SS_Y(1 - r^2).$$

Expanding and rearranging Equation 9.13 we have

$$SS_{error} = SS_Y(1 - r^2)$$
$$= SS_Y - SS_Y r^2$$
$$r^2 = \frac{SS_Y - SS_{error}}{SS_Y}. \qquad (9.14)$$

In Equation 9.14 SS_Y is the sum of squares of *Y* and represents the total of the sum of squares of *Y* which is related to *X* and the sum of squares of *Y* that is independent of *X*. SS_{error} is the sum of squares of *Y* which are independent of *X* and is a measure of the amount of error remaining even after we use *X* to predict *Y*. These concepts require some elaboration.

Suppose that we were interested in studying the relationship between cigarette smoking (X) and age at death (Y). As we watch people die off over time we notice several things. First we see that not all die at precisely the same time—there is variability in age at death and this variability is measured by $SS_Y = \Sigma(Y - \bar{Y})^2$. We also notice the obvious fact that some people smoke more than others. This is variability in smoking and is measured by $SS_X = \Sigma(X - \bar{X})^2$. We further find that cigarette smokers tend to die earlier than nonsmokers, and heavy smokers earlier than light smokers. Thus we write a regression equation to predict Y from X. Since people differ in their smoking behavior they will also differ in their *predicted* life expectancy ($\hat{Y}$) and we will label this variability $SS_{\hat{Y}} = \Sigma(\hat{Y} - \bar{\hat{Y}})^2 = \Sigma(\hat{Y} - \bar{Y})^2$. This last measure is variability in Y which is directly attributable to variability in X, since different values of $\hat{Y}$ arise from different values of X and the same values of $\hat{Y}$ arise from the same value of X—i.e., $\hat{Y}$ does not vary

SS$_{regression}$ unless X varies. (Some textbooks label this term ***SS***$_{regression}$ since it results from the regression of Y on X. We will adopt that notation in Chapter 15 and 16.)

We have one last source of variability, and this is the variability in the life expectancy of those people who smoke exactly the same amount. This is measured by SS_{error} and is variability in Y that can not be explained by variability in X, since these people did not differ in the amount they smoked. These several sources of variability (i.e., sums of squares) are summarized in Table 9.5.

TABLE 9.5
Sources of Variance
in Regression

SS_X = variability in amount smoked

SS_Y = variability in life expectancy

$SS_{\hat{Y}}$ = variability in life expectancy directly attributable to variability in smoking behavior

SS_{error} = variability in life expectancy that cannot be attributable to variability in smoking behavior

If we considered the absurd extreme in which all of the nonsmokers die off at exactly age 72 and all of the smokers smoke precisely the same amount and die off at exactly age 68, then all of the variability in life expectancy is directly attributable to (predictable from) variability in smoking behavior, and $SS_{\hat{Y}} = SS_Y$, while $SS_{error} = 0$.

In a more realistic example, smokers might tend to die off earlier than non-smokers, but within each group there is a certain amount of variability in life expectancy. This is a situation in which some of SS_Y is attributable to smoking ($SS_{\hat{Y}}$) and some is not (SS_{error}). What we want to be able to do is to specify what percentage of the overall variability in life expectancy is attributable to variability in smoking behavior. In other words we want a measure which represents

$$\frac{SS_{\hat{Y}}}{SS_Y} = \frac{SS_Y - SS_{error}}{SS_Y}.$$

r²   That measure is r^2.

This interpretation of r^2 is extremely useful. If, for example, the correlation between amount smoked and life expectancy were an unrealistically high .80, we could say that $.80^2 = 64\%$ of the variability in life expectancy is directly attributable to the variability in smoking behavior. Obviously this is a substantial exaggeration of the real world. If the correlation were a more likely $r = .10$, we would say that $.10^2 = 1\%$ of the variability in life expectancy is related to smoking behavior, while the other 99% is related to other variables.

It is important to note that when we use phrases such as "account for," "attributable to," and "predictable from," these are not to be interpreted as statements of cause and effect. Thus I could say that "pains in my shoulder account for 10% of the variability in the weather" without meaning to imply that sore shoulders cause rain, or even that rain causes sore shoulders.

From the discussion it is apparent that r^2 is a more easily interpretable measure of correlation than r, since it represents the degree to which the variability in one measure is attributable to variability in the other measure. In the remainder of this book we will see r^2 and closely related terms appearing repeatedly to express the percentage of predictable variability.

9.6 Assumptions Underlying Correlation and Regression

You will note that we have derived the standard error of estimate without making any assumptions concerning the population(s) from which the data were drawn. Nor are they required to use $s^2_{Y \cdot X}$ as an unbiased estimator of $\sigma^2_{Y \cdot X}$. However if we are to make use of $s^2_{Y \cdot X}$ in any meaningful way, we will have to begin introducing certain parametric assumptions. To understand why this is so, consider the data plotted in Figure 9.3. Notice the four statistics labeled $s^2_{Y \cdot 1}$, $s^2_{Y \cdot 2}$, $s^2_{Y \cdot 3}$, and $s^2_{Y \cdot 4}$. These represent the variance

Array   of the points around the regression line in each *array* of X. The average of these variances, weighted by the degrees of freedom for each array, would be $s^2_{Y \cdot X}$, the residual or error variance. If $s^2_{Y \cdot X}$ is to have any practical meaning, it must be representative of the various terms of which it is an

Homogeneity of   average. This leads us to the assumption of **homogeneity of variance in**
variance in arrays   **arrays**, which is nothing but the assumption that the variance of Y for each

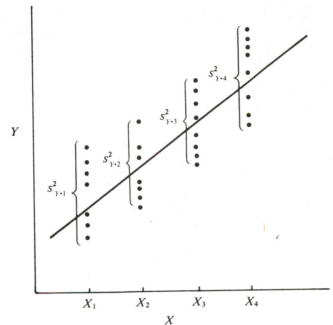

FIGURE 9.3

Scatter diagram illustrating regression assumption

value of X is constant (in the population). This assumption will become important when we come to apply tests of significance using $s^2_{Y \cdot X}$.

Normality in arrays   One further assumption which will prove necessary when we come to testing hypotheses is the assumption of ***normality in arrays***. We are going to assume that in the population the values of Y corresponding to any specified value of X—i.e., the array of Y for X_i—are normally distributed around $\hat{Y}$. This assumption is directly analogous to the normality assumption we made with the t test, where we assumed that each treatment population was normally distributed around its own mean, and is made for similar purposes.

To anticipate what we will discuss in Chapter 11, it can be pointed out here that our assumptions of homogeneity of variance and normality in arrays are equivalent to the assumptions of homogeneity of variance and normality of populations which we will make in discussing the analysis of variance. In Chapter 11 we will assume that the treatment populations from which data were drawn are normally distributed and all have the same variance. If you think of the levels of X in Figure 9.3 as representing different experimental conditions, you can see the relationship between the regression and analysis of variance assumptions.

It might be useful to digress for a moment and point out the relationship between the variance about the regression line and variance about the mean, for any value of X. If the regression of Y on X is in fact linear, and if we had an infinite number of observations at each level of X, then $\hat{Y}_i$ would equal $\bar{Y}_i$ (where i represents the level of X). This means that in the population it is irrelevant whether we speak of the variance around the regression line or variance about the array mean; they will be the same thing.

9.7 *Confidence Limits on $\hat{Y}$*

Although the standard error of estimate is useful as an overall measure of error, it is not a good estimate of the error associated with any single prediction. When we wish to predict $\hat{Y}$ for a given subject, the error in our estimate will be smaller when X is near $\bar{X}$ than when X is far from $\bar{X}$. (For an intuitive understanding of this consider what would happen to the predictions for different values of X if we rotated the regression line slightly.) If we wish to predict Y on the basis of X for a new member of the population (someone who was not included in the original sample), the standard error of our prediction is given by

$$s'_{Y \cdot X} = s_{Y \cdot X} \sqrt{1 + \frac{1}{N} + \frac{(X_i - \bar{X})^2}{(N-1)s_X^2}} \qquad (9.15)$$

where $(X_i - \bar{X})$ is the deviation of the individual's X score from the mean of X. This leads to the following confidence limits on $\hat{Y}$

$$\mathrm{CL}(\hat{Y}) = \hat{Y} \pm (t_{\alpha/2})(s'_{Y \cdot X}). \qquad (9.16)$$

Equation 9.16 will lead to elliptical confidence limits around the regression line, which are narrowest for $X = \bar{X}$, and become wider as $|X - \bar{X}|$ increases.

Example 9.1

A computer example showing grades as a function of IQ

To illustrate a typical computer solution to a correlation and regression problem, consider the data in Table 9.6. These data are a random sample of 30 cases from a study by Howell & Huessy (1980), and represent the relationship between IQ (as assessed by the Otis Lennon Mental Abilities Test administered in grades 5 to 8) and grade point average in 9th grade. The computer printout of this analysis is presented at the bottom of Table 9.6. The analysis was carried out using the MINITAB REGRESSION procedure. Using this procedure (as opposed to CORRELATION) requires that we obtain r by taking the square root of R-SQUARED, but that is not a serious problem. (For these data $r = \sqrt{.492} = .701$.) In addition the test on the significance of r, to be discussed shortly, is given by either the test on the slope or by taking the square root of $\mathrm{MS}_{regression}/\mathrm{MS}_{residual}$. The latter, for these data, is equal to $\sqrt{10.230/.378} = 5.20$.

TABLE 9.6
Data from Howell &
Huessy (1980) and
MINITAB Output

IQ	GPA	IQ	GPA	IQ	GPA
102	2.75	85	2.75	115	4.00
108	4.00	95	2.75	112	3.00
109	2.25	97	2.67	92	2.33
118	3.00	93	2.00	85	1.75
79	1.67	81	2.00	95	3.00
88	2.25	111	3.00	115	3.75
100	2.50	95	1.50	90	2.50
92	3.50	106	3.75	86	1.00
131	3.75	83	.67	106	2.75
83	2.75	81	1.50	85	2.50

```
-- DESCRIBE C1 AND C2
   C1        N = 30     MEAN =    97.267    ST.DEV. =    13.3
   C2        N = 30     MEAN =    2.5863    ST.DEV. =    0.847

-- REGRESSION C2 ON 1 PREDICTOR IN C1

THE REGRESSION EQUATION IS
Y = -  1.76 + .0447 X1

                                   ST.DEV      T-RATIO =
              COLUMN    COEFFICIENT OF COEF.    COEF/S.D.
              --        -1.7639     0.8436      -2.09
   X1   C1    0.04473   0.00860     5.20

THE ST. DEV OF Y ABOUT REGRESSION LINE IS
S =     0.6147
WITH (  30- 2) = 28 DEGREES OF FREEDOM

R-SQUARED = 49.2 PERCENT
R-SQUARED = 47.3 PERCENT, ADJUSTED FOR D.F.

ANALYSIS OF VARIANCE

   DUE TO      DF         SS        MS=SS/DF
REGRESSION     1       10.2295      10.2295
RESIDUAL       28      10.5800      0.3779
TOTAL          29      20.8095
```

9.8 *Hypothesis Testing*

In this chapter we have seen how to calculate r as an estimate of the relationship between two variables, and how to calculate the slope (b) as a measure of the rate of change of Y as a function of X. In addition to estimating r and b, we often wish to perform a significance test on the null hypothesis that the corresponding population parameters equal 0.

Testing the Significance of r

The most common hypothesis which we test for a sample correlation is the hypothesis that the correlation between X and Y in the population
Rho (ρ)   (ρ) is zero. This is a meaningful test because the null hypothesis being tested is really the hypothesis that X and Y are independent. Rejection of

this hypothesis leads to the conclusion that they are not independent and that there is some relationship between the two.

It can be shown that when $\rho = 0$, for large N r will be approximately normally distributed around 0 with a standard error which can be estimated by

$$s_r = \sqrt{\frac{1-r^2}{N-2}}.$$

Since the distribution of r is normal (for $\rho = 0$) and its standard error is estimable, we can set up the ratio

$$t = \frac{r-\rho}{s_r} = \frac{r}{\sqrt{\dfrac{1-r^2}{N-2}}} = \frac{r\sqrt{N-2}}{\sqrt{1-r^2}} \qquad \qquad (9.17)$$

which is distributed as t on $N-2$ df. Returning to our original example in Table 9.1, $r = .839$ and $N = 20$. Thus

$$t = \frac{.839\sqrt{18}}{\sqrt{1-.839^2}} = \frac{.839\sqrt{18}}{\sqrt{.296}}$$

$$= 6.54.$$

This value of t is significant at $\alpha = .05$ (two-tailed), and we can thus conclude that there is a significant relationship between X and Y.

Testing the Significance of b

If you think about the problem for a moment you will realize that a test on b is equivalent to a test on r. If it is true that X and Y are related, then it is also true that Y varies with X—i.e., that the slope is non-zero. This suggests that a test on b will produce the same answer as a test on r, and we could dispense with a test for b altogether. However, since regression coefficients will play an important role when we come to discussing multiple regression, the exact form of the test will be given here.

b^* We will represent the parametric equivalent of b as b^* (the regression coefficient in the population).†

It can be shown that b is normally distributed around b^* with standard error

$$s_b = \frac{s_{Y \cdot X}}{s_x\sqrt{N-1}}.$$

Thus if we wish to test the hypothesis that the true slope of the regression

---

† Many textbooks use β instead of b^* but that would confuse things later.

line in the population is zero, we can simply form the ratio

$$t = \frac{b - b^*}{s_b} = \frac{b}{\dfrac{s_{Y \cdot X}}{s_X \sqrt{N-1}}} = \frac{(b)(s_X)(\sqrt{N-1})}{s_{Y \cdot X}} \qquad (9.18)$$

which is distributed as t on $N-2$ df.

For our sample data, $b = 1.085$, $s_X = 1.67$, and $s_{Y \cdot X} = 1.21$. Thus

$$t = \frac{(1.085)(1.67)(\sqrt{19})}{1.21} = 6.53$$

which is the same answer we obtained when we tested r. Since $t_{\text{obt}} = 6.53$ and $t_{.025}(18) = 2.101$, we will reject H_0 and conclude that our regression line has a non-zero slope.

From what we now know about the sampling distribution of b, it is possible to set up confidence limits on b^*.

$$\text{CI}(b^*) = b + t_{\alpha/2} \left[\frac{s_{Y \cdot X}}{s_X \sqrt{N-1}} \right] \qquad (9.19)$$

where $t_{\alpha/2}$ is the two-tailed critical value of t on $N-2$ df.

For our data the 95% confidence limits are

$$\text{CI}(b^*) = 1.085 \pm \frac{2.101(1.21)}{1.67\sqrt{19}} = 1.085 \pm .349$$

$$= .736 \leq b^* \leq 1.434.$$

Thus the chances are 95 out of 100 that the limits 0.736 and 1.434 encompass the true value of b^*. Note that the confidence limits do not include 0.00. This is in line with the results of our t test, which rejected H_0: $b^* = 0$.

Testing the Difference Between Two Independent bs

Suppose that we have conducted two studies on the relationship between smoking and life expectancy. One study was conducted on females, and the other on males. We have run two separate studies rather than one large one because we did not want our results to be contaminated by normal differences in life expectancy between males and females. Suppose further that we obtained the following data.

	MALES	FEMALES
b	$-.40$	$-.20$
$s_{Y \cdot X}$	2.10	2.30
s_X^2	2.50	2.80
N	101	101

It is apparent that, for our data, the regression line for males is steeper than the regression line for females. If this difference is significant it means that males decrease their life expectancy more than do females for any given increment in the amount smoked. If this were true it would be an important finding, and we are therefore interested in testing the difference between b_1 and b_2.

The t test for differences between two independent regression coefficients is directly analogous to the test of the difference between two independent means. If H_0 is true ($b_1^* = b_2^*$), the sampling distribution of $(b_1 - b_2)$ is normal with a mean of zero and a standard error of

$$s_{b_1-b_2} = \sqrt{s_{b_1}^2 + s_{b_2}^2}.$$

This means that the ratio

$$t = \frac{b_1 - b_2}{\sqrt{s_{b_1}^2 + s_{b_2}^2}}$$

is distributed as t on $N_1 + N_2 - 4$ df. We already know the standard error of b, and therefore can write

$$s_{b_1-b_2} = \sqrt{\frac{s_{Y \cdot X_1}^2}{s_{X_1}^2(N_1 - 1)} + \frac{s_{Y \cdot X_2}^2}{s_{X_2}^2(N_2 - 1)}}$$

where $s_{Y \cdot X_1}^2$ and $s_{Y \cdot X_2}^2$ are the error variances for the two samples. Just as we did with means, if we assume homogeneity of the error variances we can pool these two estimates, weighting each by its degrees of freedom.

$$s_{Y \cdot X}^2 = \frac{(N_1 - 2)(s_{Y \cdot X_1}^2) + (N_2 - 2)(s_{Y \cdot X_2}^2)}{N_1 + N_2 - 4}.$$

For our data

$$s_{Y \cdot X}^2 = \frac{99(2.10^2) + 99(2.30^2)}{101 + 101 - 4} = 4.85.$$

Substituting this pooled estimate into the equation we obtain

$$s_{b_1-b_2} = \sqrt{\frac{s_{Y \cdot X}^2}{s_{X_1}^2(N_1 - 1)} + \frac{s_{Y \cdot X}^2}{s_{X_2}^2(N_2 - 1)}}$$

$$= \sqrt{\frac{4.85}{(2.5)(100)} + \frac{4.85}{(2.8)(100)}}$$

$$= .192.$$

Given $s_{b_1-b_2}$ we can now solve for t

$$t = \frac{b_1 - b_2}{s_{b_1-b_2}} = \frac{(-.40) - (-.20)}{.192} = -1.04$$

on 198 df. Since $t_{.05}(198) = \pm 1.97$, we would fail to reject H_0 and would therefore conclude that we have no reason to doubt that life expectancy decreases as a function of smoking at the same rate for males and females.

It is worth noting that while H_0: $b^* = 0$ is equivalent to H_0: $\rho = 0$, it does not follow that H_0: $b_1^* - b_2^* = 0$ is equivalent to H_0: $\rho_1 - \rho_2 = 0$. With a moment's thought it should be apparent that two scatter diagrams could have the same regression line $(b_1^* = b_2^*)$ but different degrees of scatter around that line, hence $(\rho_1 \neq \rho_2)$. The reverse also holds—two different regression lines could fit their respective sets of data equally well.

A further point should be made that in testing the difference between b_1 and b_2, we are doing something not unlike what we did when we ran a Chi-square test on a contingency table, nor is it unlike what we will be doing when we speak of interaction terms in the analysis of variance. In the present case we have asked whether the change in life expectancy as a function of smoking was the same for males and females. When we ran a Chi-square test on the degree of opinion change as a function of the strength of an opinion, we said that the distribution of responses across categories (*Toward*, *Unchanged*, and *Away*) was different for *Dry* and *Unselected* subjects. What this means is that if we fit a regression line (admittedly nonlinear) to the data for *Drys* it would be different from a line fit to *Unselected* subjects. Aside from the obvious differences between the Chi-square data and the present data, the question is basically the same. This goes to reinforce the point made earlier that the various statistical procedures are highly interrelated and are not as different as they would appear on the surface.

Testing the Difference Between Two Independent *rs*

When it comes to testing the difference between two independent *rs*, a minor difficulty arises. When $\rho \neq 0$, the sampling distribution of r is not normal (becoming more and more skewed as $\rho \to \pm 1.00$), nor is its standard error easily estimated. The same holds for the difference $r_1 - r_2$. This raises an obvious problem, the solution of which is to be attributed to R. A. Fisher.

Fisher (1921) showed that if we transform r to

$$r' = (.5) \log_e \left(\frac{1+r}{1-r} \right) \tag{9.20}$$

r' is approximately normally distributed around ρ' (the transformed value of ρ) with standard error

$$s_{r'} = \frac{1}{\sqrt{N-3}}.$$

(Fisher labeled his statistic z, but r' is used here to avoid confusion with the standard normal deviate.) We can now test the null hypothesis that $\rho_1 - \rho_2 = 0$

by converting each r to r' and solving for

$$z = \frac{r'_1 - r'_2}{\sqrt{\dfrac{1}{N_1 - 3} + \dfrac{1}{N_2 - 3}}}.$$

(9.21)

You should note that our test statistic is z rather than t, since our standard error does not rely on statistics computed from the sample (other than N) and is therefore a parameter.

In Appendix (r') are presented the values of r' for different values of r, thus eliminating the need to solve Equation 9.20.

To take a simple example, assume that for a sample of 53 males the correlation between number of packs of cigarettes smoked per day and life expectancy was .50. For females the correlation was .40. (These are unrealistically high values for r, but they illustrate better the effects of the transformation.) The question of interest is "Are these two coefficients significantly different or are the differences in line with what one would expect when sampling from the same bivariate population of X, Y pairs?"

	MALES	FEMALES
r	.50	.40
r'	.549	.424
N	53	53

$$z = \frac{.549 - .424}{\sqrt{\dfrac{1}{53 - 3} + \dfrac{1}{53 - 3}}} = \frac{.125}{\sqrt{\dfrac{2}{50}}} = \frac{.125}{\dfrac{1}{5}}$$

$$= .625.$$

Since $z_{obt} = .625$ is less than $z_{.05} = \pm 1.96$, we would fail to reject H_0 and would conclude that we have no reason to doubt that the correlation between smoking and life expectancy is the same for males and females.

Testing the Hypothesis that ρ Equals any Specified Value

Now that we have discussed the concept of r', we are in a position to test the null hypothesis that ρ is equal to any value, not just zero. While we seldom wish to test null hypotheses of this type, the ability to do so allows us to establish confidence limits on ρ, a more interesting procedure.

As we have seen, for any value of ρ the sampling distribution of r' is approximately normally distributed around ρ' (the transformed value of ρ)

with a standard error of $1/\sqrt{N-3}$. From this it follows that

$$z = \frac{r'-\rho'}{\sqrt{\dfrac{1}{N-3}}} \tag{9.22}$$

is a standard normal deviate. Thus if we want to test the null hypothesis that a sample r of .30 (with $N = 103$) came from a population where $\rho = .50$, we proceed as follows

$$r = .30 \qquad r' = .310$$

$$\rho = .50 \qquad \rho' = .549$$

$$N = 103 \qquad s_{r'} = 1/\sqrt{N-3} = .10$$

$$z = \frac{.310 - .549}{.10} = \frac{-.239}{.10}$$

$$= -2.39.$$

Since $z_{\text{obt}} = -2.39$ is more extreme than $z_{.05} = \pm 1.96$, we would reject H_0 and conclude that our sample did not come from a population where $\rho = .50$.

Confidence Limits on ρ

We can easily establish confidence limits on ρ by solving Equation 9.22 for ρ instead of z. To do this we first solve for confidence limits on ρ', and then convert ρ' to ρ.

$$z = \frac{r'-\rho'}{\sqrt{\dfrac{1}{N-3}}}$$

therefore

$$\frac{1}{\sqrt{N-3}}(z) + r' = \rho'$$

and thus

$$\text{CI}(\rho') = r' \pm z_{\alpha/2}\frac{1}{\sqrt{N-3}}. \tag{9.23}$$

If $r = .30$ ($r' = .310$) and $N = 103$, then the 95% confidence limits are

$$\text{CI}(\rho') = .310 \pm 1.96\frac{1}{\sqrt{100}}$$

$$= .310 \pm 1.96(.10) = .310 \pm .196$$

$$= .114 \le \rho' \le .506.$$

Converting from ρ' to ρ and rounding,

$$.110 \le \rho \le .465.$$

Thus we are 95% confident that the limits $\rho = .110$ and $\rho = .465$ encompass the true value of ρ. Note that $\rho = 0$ is not included with our limits, thus offering a simultaneous test of H_0: $\rho = 0$, should we be interested in that information.

Testing the Difference Between Two Non-Independent rs

Occasionally we come across a situation in which we wish to test the difference between two correlations which are not independent. For example, the long version of an attitude scale might correlate .70 with some measure of job satisfaction. Since this form takes a long time to administer, a short form is developed and found to correlate .60 with the same criterion. The question then becomes "Is this a significant decrease in the validity of the instrument, or do the two forms predict equally well (i.e., for the whole population is $\rho_{short} = \rho_{long}$)?" When we have two correlations which are not independent—as these are not since the tests contain some of the same items—we must take into account this lack of independence. Specifically we must incorporate a term representing the degree to which the two tests are themselves correlated. This problem was examined by Hotelling (1931) who has shown that

$$t = \frac{(r_{12} - r_{13})\sqrt{(N-3)(1+r_{23})}}{\sqrt{2(1 - r_{12}^2 - r_{13}^2 - r_{23}^2 + 2r_{12}r_{13}r_{23})}}$$

is distributed as t on $N-3$ df. In this equation r_{12} and r_{13} refer to the correlation coefficients whose difference is to be tested, and r_{23} refers to the correlation between the two predictors. To take a specific example, let

r_{12} = correlation between satisfaction and long form = .70

r_{13} = correlation between satisfaction and short form = .60

r_{23} = correlation between long and short form = .80

$N = 50$

then

$$t = \frac{(.70 - .60)\sqrt{(47)(1 + .80)}}{\sqrt{2(1 - .70^2 - .60^2 - .80^2 + 2(.70)(.60)(.80))}}.$$

Squaring both sides to simplify the arithmetic

$$t^2 = \frac{.10^2(47)(1.8)}{2(1-.49-.36-.64+2(.7)(.6)(.8))} = \frac{.846}{.364} = 2.32$$

$$t = \sqrt{2.32} = 1.52.$$

A value of $t_{obt} = 1.52$ on 47 df is not significant, giving support to our intention of replacing the long form with the short form. It is important to keep in mind that our question has put us in the position of hoping to prove the null hypothesis, which is not a very comfortable position in which to be. It is possible that there is no difference between the two forms of the test. It may also be that there is a difference but that our procedure did not have sufficient power to detect this difference. In cases like this the experimenter must be very cautious in interpreting her results.

9.9 Correlation Coefficients as Data

We generally think of raw data as being in the form of traditional measures such as time, distance, and number of items recalled. Occasionally, however, the data are more derived measures such as means, variances, and correlation coefficients. Melzer (1975), for example, asked subjects to estimate IQs on the basis of certain quantitative cues. For each subject she obtained the correlation between the subject's estimates and the true IQs. For one of her analyses she had two groups of 33 subjects, and therefore two sets of 33 correlation coefficients. She wanted to test, by t, the hypothesis that the mean coefficients were different for the two groups. A difficulty arises from the fact that the correlations were in the neighborhood of .80 and .90, and thus the distribution of r about ρ would be very badly skewed. The solution was to convert individual rs to values of r', and to run the t test on r'.

The use of r' instead of r is to be recommended whenever data are in the form of correlations. This ensures an approximately normal sampling distribution of $\overline{r'}$ (and thus $\overline{r'_1} - \overline{r'_2}$), and further ensures homogeneity of variance, something which would not be true if the true values of ρ_1 and ρ_2 were quite different.†

9.10 The Role of Assumptions in Correlation and Regression

There is considerable confusion in the literature concerning the assumptions underlying the use of correlation and regression techniques. Much of the

---

† An improvement can be made in the accuracy of this procedure by incorporating a correction discussed by Fisher (1935, p. 205).

confusion stems from the fact that statisticians tend to make all of their assumptions at the beginning and fail to point out that some of these assumptions are not required for certain purposes.

Linearity of regression

One of the most persistent and unnecessary assumptions is that of *linearity of regression*. Let us dispense with this one immediately and get it out of the way. Correlation and regression are generally used to assess the degree of linearity in the relationship between X and Y. If there is no such linear relationship (although there might be a very definite curvilinear one), both r and b will be zero (except for sampling error), thus reflecting the lack of linearity. Requiring that the relationship be linear before calculating r is in some ways like requiring $\mu_1 = \mu_2$ before calculating t, which is certainly a silly thing to do. Linearity is our null hypothesis; it is not an assumption. As long as we are careful to remember that r is a measure of *linear* relationships, an assumption of linearity is totally unnecessary. (As a matter of fact we might deliberately fit a straight line to data which we know to be nonlinear simply because the fit might be sufficiently accurate for our purposes—though the standard error of a prediction might be poorly estimated.)

As was mentioned earlier, whether or not we make various assumptions is a function of what we wish to do. If our purpose is simply to describe data, no assumptions are necessary. The regression line and r do in fact afford our best description of the data at hand without the necessity of any assumptions about the population from which the data were sampled.

If our purpose is to assess the degree to which variance in Y is linearly attributable to variance in X, we again need no assumptions. This is true because s_Y^2 and $s_{Y \cdot X}^2$ are both unbiased estimators of their corresponding parameters independently of any underlying assumptions, and

$$\frac{SS_Y - SS_{error}}{SS_Y}$$

is algebraically equivalent to r^2.

If we want to set confidence limits on b or $\hat{Y}$, or if we want to test hypotheses about b^*, we will need to make the assumptions of homogeneity of variance and normality in arrays of Y. The assumption of homogeneity of variance is necessary to ensure that $s_{Y \cdot X}^2$ is representative of the variance of each array, and the assumption of normality is necessary since we made use of the standard normal distribution.

Bivariate normal distribution

Lastly, if we want to use r as a (relatively) unbiased estimate of ρ or if we wish to establish confidence limits on ρ we will have to assume that the (X, Y) pairs are a random sample from a *bivariate normal distribution*. For such a distribution we have normality and homogeneity of variance in arrays for both X and Y, and the marginal distributions of X and Y are normal.

9.11   *Factors Which Affect the Correlation*

The correlation coefficient can be importantly affected by characteristics of the sample. Two of these characteristics are the restriction of the range (or variance) of X and/or Y and the use of heterogeneous subsamples.

The Effect of Range Restrictions

Range restrictions   A common problem which arises in many instances concerns restrictions on the range of X and/or Y. The effect of such ***range restrictions*** is to alter the correlation between X and Y from what it would have been if the range had not been so restricted. Depending upon the nature of the data, the correlation may either rise or fall as a result of such restriction, although it is most common that r is reduced.

With the exception of very unusual circumstances, restricting the range of X will increase r only when the restriction results in eliminating some curvilinear relationship. For example, if we correlated height with age, where age ran from 0 to 70, the data would be decidedly curvilinear (rising to about 17 years of age and then leveling off or even declining) and the correlation would be quite low. If however, we restrict the range of ages to 0 to 17, the correlation would be quite high, since we have eliminated those values of Y which were not varying linearly as a function of X.

The more usual effect of restricting the range of X or Y is to reduce the correlation. This problem is especially important in the area of test construction, since here criterion measures (Y) may only be available for the higher values of X. Consider the hypothetical data in Figure 9.4. This figure represents the relation between college grade point average and scores on some standard achievement test (such as the SAT) for a hypothetical sample of students. In the ideal world of the test constructor, all people who took the exam would then be sent on to college and receive a grade point average, and the correlation between test scores and grade point averages would then be computed. As can be seen from Figure 9.4, this correlation would be reasonably high. In the real world, however, not everyone is admitted to college. Colleges only take the better students, whether this be based on achievement test scores, high school performance, or whatever. This means that grade point averages will be available mainly for students having relatively high scores on the standardized test. Suppose that this has the effect of only allowing us to evaluate the relationship between X and Y for those values of $X > 500$. From Figure 9.4 you will note that in this case the correlation will be relatively low, not because the test is worthless, but because the range has been restricted.

The effect of range restrictions must be taken into account whenever we see a validity coefficient based upon a restricted sample. The coefficient

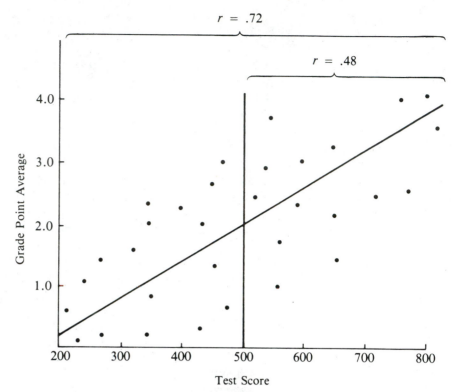

FIGURE 9.4

Hypothetical data
illustrating effect
of restricted range

might be quite inappropriate for the question at hand. Essentially what we have done is to ask how well a standardized test predicts a person's suitability for college, but we have answered that question by reference only to those people who actually are admitted to college.

It is possible to estimate the correlation for an unrestricted sample from a knowledge of the correlation in the restricted sample and the standard deviation which the variable X would have if it were not restricted. Guilford & Fruchter (1973) show that

$$R_{12} = \frac{r_{12}(s_u/s_r)}{\sqrt{1 - r_{12}^2 + r_{12}^2(s_u^2/s_r^2)}} \qquad (9.24)$$

is an estimate of the correlation for the unrestricted sample, where

R_{12} = the correlation in the unrestricted sample

r_{12} = the correlation in the restricted sample

s_u = the standard deviation of X for the unrestricted sample

and

s_r = the standard deviation of X for the restricted sample

The extent to which R_{12} is an estimate of the correlation which would obtain in a sample with an unrestricted range of X depends upon one very important assumption. This is the assumption that the regression line fitted to the restricted data is an adequate estimate of the regression line which would apply to the full sample. This assumption means that we must use a sufficiently large sample to estimate a and b with relatively little error. For this reason, the use of Equation 9.24 is not recommended unless the sample size is quite large (or more precisely, unless s_b is quite small).

The Effect of Heterogeneous Subsamples

Heterogeneous subsamples

Another important consideration in evaluating the results of regression analyses deals with **heterogeneous subsamples**. This point can be illustrated with one simple example. If we go back to our hypothetical study of smoking and life expectancy, you will recall that at one point we analyzed data for males and females separately to eliminate contamination from difference in life expectancy normally found between the two sexes. Assume that the results could be represented as in Figure 9.5, where the data have been

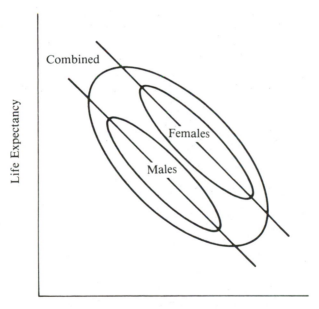

FIGURE 9.5

Illustration of effect of heterogeneous subsamples

exaggerated to better make the point. In this figure the ellipses are being used to represent the clustering of data points. It is apparent that for males there is a high relationship between smoking and life expectancy. This is equally true for females. But if we group the data into one large sample, the relationship deteriorates appreciably. The fact that the correlation is lower for the combined sample has nothing whatsoever to do with the relationship between smoking and life expectancy, but rather with the relationship between sex and life expectancy. This problem will be examined more closely when we discuss partial and semi-partial correlation in Chapter 15. The point to be made here is that experimenters must be very careful when they combine data from several sources, so as not to include variance attributable to irrelevant variables.

9.11 Summary

This chapter has dealt with the twin topics of correlation and regression. We began by plotting our data in two dimensional space, and from there derived the regression line and the correlation coefficient. We saw how the latter can be viewed as a measure of how well the regression line fits the data. We then looked at ways of measuring the accuracy of prediction, and saw that r^2 can be interpreted as the percentage of the variability in the criterion which can be explained by variation in the predictor. We dealt with a number of ways of testing hypotheses involving correlations and regression coefficients, and the role of the underlying assumptions. We then looked at some important ways in which correlations can either be increased or decreased by the general nature of the data (restricted range and hetero-geneous subsamples).

Exercises for Chapter 9

9.1 Plot a scatter diagram for the data in Table 9.6 and superimpose the regression line.

9.2 a. Using the scatter diagram from Exercise 9.1, estimate the predicted value of $\hat{Y}$ for $X = 100$, $X = 110$, $X = 120$, and $X = 130$.

b. Explain why you have less confidence in your prediction when $X = 130$ than when $X = 100$.

9.3 a. Draw scatter diagrams for the following sets of data.

1		2		3	
X	Y	X	Y	X	Y
2	2	2	4	2	8
3	4	3	2	3	6
5	6	5	8	5	4
6	8	6	6	6	2

b. Calculate the covariance for each using the definitional formula.
c. Calculate the covariance for each using the computational formula.

9.4 **a.** Calculate the correlation for each data set in Exercise 9.3.
b. How can the values of Y in Exercise 9.3 be rearranged to produce the smallest possible correlation?

9.5 Prove that Equation 9.4 is algebraically equivalent to Equation 9.2.

9.6 Prove that the equations given in the text for a and b can be derived from what have been labeled as the *normal equations*.

9.7 Using the data from Table 9.6, calculate $a_{X \cdot Y}$ and $b_{X \cdot Y}$.

Regression toward the mean

9.8 In 1885 Francis Galton spoke about "regression toward mediocrity," which we more charitably refer to today as **regression toward the mean**. The basic principle is that those at the ends of any continuum (e.g., height or IQ) tend to have children who are closer toward the mean than they are. Use the concept of r as the regression coefficient with standardized data to explain Galton's idea.

9.9 If Galton was correct and we can speak of regression toward the mean, how is it that evolution has not produced a completely uniform species?

9.10 The following data represent the percentage of voluntary homework problems completed by each of 20 students and their final grade at the end of the course (converted to a 100 point scale).

Problems:	50	60	80	70	90	40	100	85	90	80	50	95	40	80	85	95	70	40	80	30
Grade:	75	75	90	80	85	60	98	95	95	80	75	90	60	50	70	85	75	60	80	55

a. Plot the data points.
b. Compute the correlation between amount of homework completed and final grade.
c. Interpret this correlation.

9.11 **a.** Using the data from Exercise 9.10, calculate the regression line for predicting grade on the basis of homework.
b. Interpret the meaning of the slope and intercept.

9.12 Still using the data from Exercise 9.10.

a. Calculate the standard error of estimate.
b. Calculate the confidence interval on the prediction for a new student who completed 60% of the homework problems.

9.13 In a study of social behavior an investigator was interested in the relationship between the cost of a meal ordered by the person paying the bill and the cost of a meal ordered by the person who was not paying. He observed 15 couples (mixed sexes) and obtained the data below.

Paying: (y)	5.50	6.50	6.25	7.00	4.00	9.00	7.00	8.00	5.00	7.50	11.00	8.00	7.00	5.00	4.00
Not Paying: (x)	6.00	6.00	6.75	8.00	4.50	7.00	9.00	9.00	6.00	6.50	10.50	9.00	8.50	4.50	6.00

a. Plot the data.
b. Calculate the correlation.

c.   Find the equation for the regression line.
d.   Interpret the results.

9.14   Assume that you had the following data on two variables (X and Y).

> X: 2   8   9   10   13   10   8   7   15
> Y: 3   9   8   7   7   9   10   8   18

a.   Obtain the correlation between X and Y.
b.   Interpret the correlation coefficient.
c.   Now plot the data and fit a regression line by eye.
d.   What do you conclude based on the plotting of the data?

9.15   Reanalyze the data in Exercise 9.14 leaving out the first and last data points. What do you conclude?

9.16   *a.*   Using the data in Exercise 9.10, test the hypothesis that $\rho = 0$.
b.   Test the hypothesis that $b^* = 0$.

9.17   *a.*   Using the data in Exercise 9.13, test the hypothesis that $\rho = 0$.
b.   Test the hypothesis that $b^* = 0$.

9.18   At a well known and highly respected university the correlation between salary and years of service is .56, based on the salaries of 200 faculty members. At a small community college in the same city, the correlation (for 100 faculty members) is .75. Are these correlations significantly different? If so, what would the difference indicate?

9.19   Within a group of 200 tenured faculty members who have been at a well known university for less than 15 years (i.e., before the curve levels off) the equation relating salary (in 1000s of dollars) to years of service is $\hat{Y} = .9X + 15$. For 100 administrative staff at this same university the equation is $\hat{Y} = 1.5X + 10$. Assuming that all differences are significant, interpret the meaning of these two equations.

9.20   The following two examples represent the MINITAB and SPSS computer printouts for the data in Exercise 9.10.

a.   What information do you find on the MINITAB output that is not on the SPSS output?
b.   What information is on the SPSS output that is not on the MINITAB output?

```
                                             MINITAB
-- REGRESSION C2 WITH 1 VARIABLE IN C1

THE REGRESSION EQUATION IS
Y =    43.2 + 0.475 X1

                                    ST. DEV.    T-RATIO =
         COLUMN    COEFFICIENT      OF COEF.    COEF/S.D.
           --         43.156         7.531        5.73
X1       C1           0.475          0.102        4.64

THE ST. DEV. OF Y ABOUT REGRESSION LINE IS
S =      9.702
WITH (  20- 2) =  18 DEGREES OF FREEDOM

R-SQUARED = 54.5 PERCENT
R-SQUARED = 52.0 PERCENT, ADJUSTED FOR D.F.

ANALYSIS OF VARIANCE

 DUE TO     DF          SS        MS=SS/DF
REGRESSION   1       2030.33      2030.33
RESIDUAL    18       1694.22        94.12
TOTAL       19       3724.55

            X1          Y       PRED. Y     ST.DEV.
ROW         C1         C2        VALUE      PRED. Y    RESIDUAL    ST.RES.
 14         80       50.00       81.16        2.38      -31.16     -3.31R
 20         30       55.00       57.41        4.68       -2.41     -0.28 X

R DENOTES AN OBS. WITH A LARGE ST. RES.
X DENOTES AN OBS. WHOSE X VALUE GIVES IT LARGE INFLUENCE.


-- STOP
```

```
Correlation coefficients                        SPSS

            PROBLEMS  GRADE

PROBLEMS    1.00000   0.73832
GRADE       0.73832   1.00000


* * * * * * * * * * * * * * * * * *  M U L T I P L E   R E G R E S S I O N  * * * * * * * * * * * * *   Variable list  1
                                                                                                      Regression list  1
Dependent variable:    GRADE

Variable(s) entered on step number  1:     PROBLEMS


Multiple R          0.73832          Analysis of variance   Df    Sum of squares     Mean square        F
R square            0.54512          Regression             1.    2030.32821         2030.32821      21.57091
Adjusted R square   0.51985          Residual              18.    1694.22179           94.12343
Standard error      9.70172


---------------- Variables in the equation -----------------        ------------ Variables not in the equation --------------

Variable       B         Beta    Std error B      F          Variable     Beta in    Partial   Tolerance      F

PROBLEMS    0.4750973D+00  0.73832   0.10229    21.571
(Constant)  0.4315564D+02
```

10 Alternative Correlational Techniques and Measures of Association

Objective

To extend the discussion of correlation and regression to the case of dichotomous variables and ranked data; to present measures of association between categorical variables.

Contents

The Pearson product-moment correlation coefficient (r) is only one of a large number of available correlation coefficients. It is generally thought of as applying to those situations in which the relationship between two variables is basically linear, where both variables are measured on a more-or-less continuous scale, and where some sort of normality and homogeneity of variance assumptions can be made. As this chapter will point out, r can be meaningfully interpreted in other situations as well, although for those cases it is given a different name and most people fail to recognize it for what it actually is.

In this chapter we are going to discuss a variety of coefficients that apply to different kinds of data. For example, the data might represent rankings, one or both of the variables might be dichotomous, or the data might be categorical. Depending upon the assumptions we are willing to make about the underlying nature of our data, different coefficients will be appropriate in different situations. Some of these coefficients will turn out to be calculated as if they were Pearson rs, and some will not. The important point is that they all represent attempts to obtain some measure of the relationship between two variables, and fall under the general heading of *correlation* rather than *regression*.

When we speak of relationship between two variables without any restriction of the nature of these variables, we have to make a distinction

Correlational measures
Measures of association

between **correlational measures** and **measures of association**. When at least some sort of order can be assigned to the levels of each variable, such that higher scores represent more (or less) of some quantity, then it makes sense to speak of correlation. We can speak meaningfully of increases in one variable being correlated with increases in another variable. However there are many times in which different levels of a variable do not represent an orderly increase or decrease in some quantity. Thus we could sort people on the basis of their membership in different campus organizations, and then on the basis of their views on some issue. We might then find that there is in fact an association between people's views and their membership in organizations, and yet neither of these variables represents an ordered continuum. In cases such as this the coefficient which we will compute is not a correlation coefficient. We will instead speak of it as a measure of association.

Most of the measures discussed in this chapter are correlation coefficients of one form or another. The non-correlational measures of association will be discussed at the end of the chapter.

There are three basic reasons why one is interested in calculating any type of coefficient of correlation. The most obvious, but not necessarily the most important, reason is to obtain an estimate of ρ, the correlation in the

Validity

population. Thus someone interested in the *validity* of a test actually cares about the true correlation between his test and some criterion and approaches the calculation of a coefficient with this purpose in mind. This use is the one for which the alternative techniques are least satisfactory, although they can be used for this purpose.

A second use of correlation coefficients is related to such techniques as multiple regression and factor analysis. In this situation the coefficient is not an end product in itself, but rather enters into the calculation of further statistics. For these purposes many of the coefficients to be discussed are perfectly satisfactory.

The final reason for calculating a correlation coefficient is to use its square as a measure of the variation in one variable accountable for by variation in the other variable. Here again, the coefficients to be discussed are in many cases satisfactory for this purpose.

10.1 Point-Biserial Correlation (r_{pb})

Dichotomy   Frequently one of our variables is measured in the form of a **dichotomy**, such as male-female, homeowner-non-homeowner, pass-fail, and so on. Ignoring for the moment that these variables are seldom measured quantitatively (a minor problem), it is quite apparent that they are not measured continuously. There is no way in which we can assume a normal distribution of obtained scores on the dichotomous variable. If we wish to use r as a measure of relationship between variables, we obviously have a problem, since for r to be a good estimate of ρ we need to assume at least an approximation of normality in the joint (bivariate) population of X and Y.

The difficulty over the quantitative measurement of X turns out to be trivial for dichotomous variables. If X represents married vs. unmarried, for example, then we can quite legitimately score married as 0 and unmarried as 1, or vice versa. (In fact *any* two values will do. Thus all married persons could be given a score of 82 on X while all unmarried persons might receive a score of 23, if we were so inclined, without affecting the correlation in the least.) We generally use the numbers 0 and 1 for the simple reason that this makes the arithmetic easier. Given such a system of quantification, it should be apparent that the sign of the correlation will depend solely on the arbitrary way in which we choose to assign 0 and 1, and is therefore meaningless for most purposes.

If we set aside until the end of the chapter the problem of r as an estimate of ρ, things begin to look brighter. For any other purpose we can proceed as usual to calculate the Pearson coefficient (r), although we will
Point-biserial   label it the ***point-biserial coefficient (r_{pb})***. Thus algebraically $r_{pb} = r$ where
coefficient (r_{pb})   one variable is dichotomous while the other is roughly continuous and more or less normal in arrays.

Calculation of r_{pb}

Most textbooks give several special formulae for r_{pb}. (After all, is a statistic any good if it does not have its own, preferably messy, formula?)

All of these formulae, however, are derived from Pearson's original formula and will not be given here. Scoring the dichotomous variable as 0, 1 and calculating a Pearson r (which we now label r_{pb}) is sufficient, and is in fact quite easy with a 0, 1 variable.

An example of the calculation of r_{pb} is given in Table 10.1 where the hypothetical data represent the relationship between marital status ($0 = $ married, $1 = $ unmarried) and income (in thousands of dollars). The scatter diagram for these data is given in Figure 10.1. In this figure coincident points have been plotted as if they were adjacent and the regression line of Y on X has been superimposed. It is important to note that the regression line passes through the mean of each array. Thus when $X = 0$, $\hat{Y}$ is the mean income of the married subjects in the sample (14.64), and when $X = 1$, $\hat{Y}$ is the mean income of the unmarried subjects (12.07). The fact that the regression line passes through the two Y means will assume more relevance when we later consider eta squared (η^2) where the regression line is deliberately drawn so as to pass through several array means.

TABLE 10.1

Calculations of r_{pb} for Hypothetical Data on Marital Status and Income

Marital Status X	Income Y
0	15
0	17
0	14
0	13
0	17
0	11
0	19
0	14
0	15
0	12
0	14
1	11
1	10
1	11
1	12
1	13
1	10
1	14
1	15
1	12
1	13
1	11
1	12
1	12
1	13

$\Sigma X = 14 \qquad \Sigma Y = 3$

$\Sigma X^2 = 14 \qquad \Sigma Y^2 = 4478$

$\bar{X} = .56 \qquad \bar{Y} = 13.2$

$s_X^2 = .257 \qquad s_Y^2 = 5.083$

$\qquad\qquad \bar{Y}_0 = 14.64$

$\qquad\qquad \bar{Y}_1 = 12.07$

$\Sigma XY = 169$

$\text{cov}_{XY} = -.658$

$$r = \frac{N\Sigma XY - \Sigma X \Sigma Y}{\sqrt{(N\Sigma X^2 - (\Sigma X)^2)(N\Sigma Y^2 - (\Sigma Y)^2)}}$$

$$= \frac{25(169) - 14(330)}{\sqrt{(25(14) - 14^2)(25(4478) - 330^2)}}$$

$$= \frac{-395}{\sqrt{(154)(3050)}}$$

$$= -.576$$

$r_{pb} = -.576$

$r_{pb}^2 = .332$

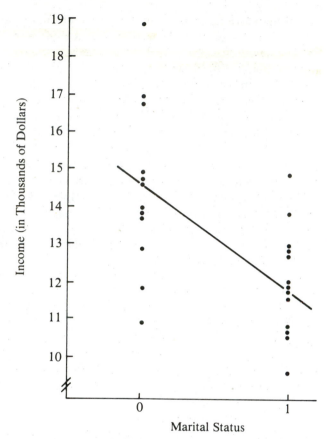

FIGURE 10.1

Scatter diagram for
data from Table 10.1

From Table 10.1 you can see that the correlation between marital status and income is −.576. We can ignore the sign of this correlation, since the decision as to whether married or unmarried subjects should be scored as 1 is an arbitrary one. We can still interpret r^2 as usual, however, and say that 33.2% of the variability in income can be accounted for by marital status. It is important to keep in mind, however, that this does not mean that a change in marital status would automatically lead to a change in income. We are not speaking here of a cause and effect relationship. As a group, married subjects tend to be older, they tend to have more stable jobs, and so on, and it is these other variables which most likely cause the higher income levels. The label "marital status" is really serving as an index of all of these other, more causal, variables.

The Relationship Between r_{pb} and t

One very important relationship involving r_{pb} is the relationship between t and r_{pb}. It can be shown, although the proof will not be given until we discuss the analysis of variance, that

$$r_{pb}^2 = \frac{t^2}{t^2 + df} \tag{10.1}$$

where t is obtained from the t test of the difference between incomes of married and unmarried subjects and df = the degrees of freedom for t, namely $N_1 + N_2 - 2$. For example, if we were to run a t test on the difference in incomes between married and unmarried subjects,

$$s^2 = \frac{(N_1 - 1)s_1^2 + (N_2 - 1)s_2^2}{N_1 + N_2 - 2} = \frac{10(5.454) + 13(2.071)}{23} = 3.5419,$$

and

$$t = \frac{14.64 - 12.07}{\sqrt{\dfrac{3.542}{11} + \dfrac{3.542}{14}}}$$

$$= 3.389.$$

With 23 df, the difference between the two groups is significant. We now calculate

$$r_{pb}^2 = \frac{t^2}{t^2 + df} = \frac{3.389^2}{3.389^2 + 23} = .333$$

$$r_{pb} = \sqrt{.333} = .577$$

which, within rounding error, agrees with the more direct calculation.

What is important about Equation 10.1 is that it first of all demonstrates that the distinction between relationships and differences is not as clear cut as one might at first think. More importantly we can use t and r_{pb}^2 together to obtain a rough estimate of the practical, as well as the statistical, significance of a difference. Thus $t = 3.389$ is evidence in favor of the experimental hypothesis that the two groups differ in mean income. At the same time, r_{pb}^2 (which is a direct function of t) tells us that marital status accounts for 33% of the variation in income.

Testing the Significance of r_{pb}

A test of r_{pb} against the null hypothesis $H_0: \rho = 0$, is quite simple to construct. Since r_{pb} is a Pearson product moment coefficient, it can be tested in exactly the same way as r. Namely

$$t = \frac{r_{pb}\sqrt{N - 2}}{\sqrt{1 - r_{pb}^2}} \tag{10.2}$$

on $N - 2$ df. Furthermore, since Equation 10.2 can be derived directly from

Equation 10.1, the t obtained from Equation 10.2 is exactly the same as a t test between the two levels of the dichotomous variable. This makes sense when you realize that a statement that married and unmarried people differ in income is exactly the same as saying that income varies with (is correlated with or changes as a function of) marital status.

10.2 Biserial Correlation (r_b)

In discussing point-biserial correlation we began to consider dichotomous variables. A dichotomy can be either (1) a discrete or true dichotomy or (2) a continuous or artificial one. Examples of true dichotomies are male vs. female, Group I vs. Group II, alive vs. dead, and so on. In these situations an individual is more or less clearly in one category or another and we generally do not think of an underlying continuum between the two categories. Continuous or artificial dichotomies are dichotomies in which we would assume that there is an underlying continuum, but that individuals are assigned to a particular category on the basis of whether or not they exceed some arbitrary criterion. Thus people are classified as passing or failing a test on the basis of their performance, although everyone would admit that some people fail abysmally, others barely fail, others barely pass, and a few pass brilliantly. Other examples are adult vs. child, tall vs. short, and drunk vs. sober. If we are willing to assume an underlying continuity which is normally distributed, then for some purposes a better estimate of ρ is given by the *biserial correlation coefficient* (r_b), although its calculation is more cumbersome.

Biserial correlation coefficient (r_b)

Calculation of r_b

The two coefficients r_{pb} and r_b computed on the same data will never agree except in the case where $r_b = 0$. However the relationship between them is known, and allows us to obtain r_b from r_{pb} whenever necessary.

$$r_b = \frac{r_{pb}\sqrt{p_1 p_2}}{y}$$

(10.3)

Equation 10.3 contains several terms which need definition. The symbol p_1 refers to the proportion of subjects who fall in category 1 of the dichotomized variable, while p_2 is the proportion falling in category 2. The symbol y represents the ordinate of the normal distribution at the point of the distribution cutting off p_1 percent of the area on one side and p_2 percent on the other.

Although it is difficult to believe that marital status represents a normally distributed continuum, we will assume that it does for the purposes of an example. (Certainly many of the variables which marital status indexes are continuous.)

From Table 10.1 we see that $\frac{11}{25} = 44\%$ of our subjects were married, while 56% were unmarried. From Appendix (z) we see that $z = .15$ divides the normal distribution into two parts with 44% of the area in one and 56% of the area in the other. The ordinate at $z = .15$ is .3945. Knowing these values we can apply Equation 10.3

$$r_b = \frac{r_{pb}\sqrt{p_1 p_2}}{y} = \frac{(.576)\sqrt{(.44)(.56)}}{.3945} = \frac{.2859}{.3945}$$

$$= .725.$$

Thus whereas the point-biserial correlation is .576, the biserial correlation is .725. If we were to calculate the value $\sqrt{p_1 p_2}/y$ for different values of p_1, we would find that as p_1 (and therefore p_2) departs from .50 the difference between r_{pb} and r_b increases. Even at the point where $p_1 = p_2 = .50$, r_{pb} is only equal to about 80% of r_b.

Limits on r_b

One embarrassing difficulty arises with r_b that must be noted. Under certain conditions r_b may exceed 1.0, a very unsatisfactory result. The usual explanation for this phenomenon is that one or the other of the variables, most likely the continuous one (McNemar, 1962), is platykurtic or bimodal. However with the following data, which at least appear to satisfy all reasonable assumptions other than normality in arrays, $r_b = 1.056$

X:	0	0	0	0	0	0	1	1	1	1	1	1
Y:	5	6	6	7	7	7	8	8	8	9	9	10

In the above example r_{pb} equals a more reasonable .843.

A general rule would be to use r_{pb} whenever the data represent a true dichotomy, or whenever the underlying distribution of the dichotomous variable is not fairly certain to be normally distributed, and use r_b only where you are quite sure that a normally distributed underlying dichotomy is present. Whenever there is any doubt, r_{pb} is preferred. In addition, r_{pb} will be the coefficient of choice when computing an intercorrelation matrix for use in a multiple regression or a factor analysis problem. In actual practice the biserial correlation is seldom used.

10.3 The Phi Coefficient (φ)

Occasionally we come across data in which both variables are measured as dichotomies. For example we might be interested in the relationship between sex and employment, where individuals are scored as either employed or unemployed. Similarly we might be interested in the relationship between employment status (employed-unemployed) and whether an individual has been arrested for drunken driving. As a final example we might wish to know the correlation between smoking (smokers vs. nonsmokers) and death by cancer (vs. death by other causes). Unless we are willing to make special assumptions concerning the underlying continuity of our variables, the most appropriate correlation coefficient is the ϕ *(phi) coefficient*.

Phi coefficient (ϕ)

Calculation of ϕ

Consider the relationship between smoking and cancer mentioned above. Table 10.2 contains hypothetical data on this problem, where both variables have been scored as 0, 1 variables—an individual smoked or he did not, and he died of cancer or he did not.

TABLE 10.2

Calculation of ϕ for Hypothetical Data on Smoking and Cancer

X: 0 = smoker
         1 = nonsmoker

Y: 0 = died of cancer
         1 = died of other causes

X: 0 0 0 0 0 0 0 0 0 0 1 1 1 1 1 1 1 1 1 1
Y: 0 1 0 0 1 0 0 0 1 1 0 1 1 1 1 1 0 1 1 1 0

$$\Sigma X = 10 \quad \Sigma X^2 = 10$$
$$\Sigma Y = 11 \quad \Sigma Y^2 = 11$$
$$\Sigma XY = 7$$
$$N = 20$$

$$\phi = r = \frac{N\Sigma XY - \Sigma X \Sigma Y}{\sqrt{(N\Sigma X^2 - (\Sigma X)^2)(N\Sigma Y^2 - (\Sigma Y)^2)}} = \frac{(20)(7) - (10)(11)}{\sqrt{((20)(10) - 10^2)((20)(11) - 11^2)}}$$

$$= \frac{30}{99.50}$$

$$= .302$$

$$\phi^2 = .091$$

The appropriate correlation coefficient for these data would be the ϕ coefficient, which is exactly equivalent to Pearson's r calculated on these data. Again, special formulae exist for those people who can be bothered to remember them, but they will not be considered here. The simplicity of calculating Pearson's r for these data becomes apparent when you realized that ΣX and ΣX^2 are simply the number of individuals who were scored as 1 on variable X. The same holds for ΣY and ΣY^2. Moreover, ΣXY is simply the number of individuals scored as 1 on both variables. It does not really require a desk calculator to obtain these quantities.

Significance of ϕ

The appropriate test of ϕ against H_0: $\rho = 0$ is a Chi-square test, since $N\phi^2$ is distributed as χ^2 on 1 df. For our data

$$\chi^2 = N\phi^2 = 20(.302)^2 = 1.82$$

which, on 1 df, is not significant. We would therefore conclude that we have no evidence to indicate a relationship between smoking and cancer.

The Relationship Between ϕ and χ^2

The data in Table 10.2 could be recast in another form, as in Table 10.3. This table contains the same information as the former, it is merely displayed differently. The student will immediately recognize Table 10.3 as a contingency table, and from it one could compute a value of χ^2 to test the null hypothesis that the variables are independent. In doing so we would obtain a χ^2 of 1.82 which, on 1 df, is not significant.

TABLE 10.3

Calculation of χ^2 for Hypothetical Data on Smoking and Cancer

	Cancer(0)	Other(1)	
Smoker(0)	6 / 4.5	4 / 5.5	10
Nonsmoker(1)	3 / 4.5	7 / 5.5	10
	9	11	20

$$\chi^2 = \frac{(6-4.5)^2}{4.5} + \frac{(4-5.5)^2}{5.5} + \frac{(3-4.5)^2}{4.5} + \frac{(7-5.5)^2}{5.5}$$

$$= 1.818$$

It should be apparent that in calculating ϕ and χ^2 we have been asking the same question in two different ways, and, not surprisingly, we have come to exactly the same conclusion. When we calculated ϕ and tested for significance we were asking whether there was any correlation (relationship) between X and Y. When we ran a Chi-square on Table 10.3 we were also asking whether the variables are related (correlated). Since these are exactly the same question, we would hope that we would come to the same answer, which we did.

It will come as no great surprise that there is a direct linear relationship between ϕ and χ^2. It can be seen from the fact that $\chi^2 = N\phi^2$ that

$$\phi = \sqrt{\frac{\chi^2}{N}}.$$ (10.4)

For our example

$$\phi = \sqrt{\frac{1.82}{20}} = \sqrt{.091} = .302$$

which agrees with our previous calculation.

ϕ^2 as a Measure of the Practical Significance of χ^2

The fact that one can go from χ^2 to ϕ means that we have one way of evaluating the practical significance (importance) of the relationship between two dichotomous variables. Suppose, for example, that in a study based on 1000 subjects we found a χ^2 of 4.5 for the relationship between two dichotomous variables (political party affiliation and attitude towards Europe). Since on 1 df, $\chi^2_{.05} = 3.84$, we would reject H_0 and conclude that the variables were not independent. By use of Equation 10.4 we can convert χ^2 to ϕ^2.

$$\phi^2 = \chi^2/N = 4.5/1000 = .0045$$
$$\phi = \sqrt{\phi^2} = \sqrt{.0045} = .067.$$

It would be tempting to take the squared value of ϕ as a measure of accountable variation. After all, it is a Pearson r and we generally use the square of r for this purpose. Although it would be possible to square ϕ and speak of the percentage of variation in one (0–1) variable accounted for by variation in another (0–1) variable, it is difficult to see what this might mean in the general case. What meaning is to be attached to "variation in party membership", for example? The more common procedure is to simply view ϕ as a measure of association on a scale from 0 to 1.00—much as we viewed r.[†] Thus for the data at hand $\phi = .067$ and indicates a rather weak relationship

---

[†] ϕ can obtain its upper limit of 1.00 only if the marginal totals for both variables are the same. This is not a problem because if the marginal distributions were different the relationship is obviously not perfect.

between the two variables. For a more complete discussion of the issues involved the reader is referred to Hays (1973, pp. 745–749).

One fact must be kept firmly in mind, however, Equation 10.4 applies only to χ^2s calculated from 2×2 tables, and not to χ^2 in general. We will soon discuss the problem of extending the procedure to larger tables.

10.4   *Tetrachoric Correlation* (r_t)

Tetrachoric coefficient (r_t)

Just as we saw with the biserial r, situations may arise in which we are willing to assume an underlying continuity of the dichotomous variables, and to assume that the traits measured by these variables are normally distributed. In this case the ***tetrachoric coefficient*** (r_t) would be appropriate. The difficulty with r_t centers on the fact that its calculation is extremely laborious unless special tables are used. In addition, its standard error is very large relative to the standard error of r. This last point means that r_t is a poor estimator of ρ unless N is very large. In those situations in which it is felt desirable to calculate r_t, the reader is referred to McNemar (1969). Since r_t is only very rarely used in practice, we will not cover its calculation here.

10.5   *Spearman's Correlation Coefficient for Ranked Data* (r_S)

In some experiments the data naturally occur in the form of ranks. Thus, we might ask judges to rank objects in order of preference under two different conditions, and would wish to know the correlation between the two sets of rankings. Usually we are most interested in these correlations when we wish to assess the reliability of some ranking procedure.

A similar procedure which has frequently been recommended in the past is to rank sets of measurement data when there are serious reservations about the nature of the underlying scale of measurement. In this case we are substituting ranks for raw scores. While one could seriously question the necessity of ranking measurement data (for reasons mentioned in the discussion of scales of measurement), this is nonetheless still a fairly common procedure.

Spearman's correlation coefficient for ranked data (r_S)

Spearman's rho

Whether data naturally occur in the form of ranks (as, for example, when a judge orders 20 paintings in terms of preference) or whether ranks have been substituted for raw scores, the appropriate correlation coefficient is ***Spearman's correlation coefficient for ranked data*** (r_S). (This statistic is sometimes referred to as ***Spearman's rho,*** but that name is less commonly used because we do not like to refer to a statistic using a Greek symbol.)

Calculation of r_S

The calculation of r_S is most easily accomplished by applying Pearson's original formula to the ranked data. Alternative formulae do exist although whether they are in fact simpler is a matter for debate. Two of these formulae are given here because the first is extremely common (though I happen to think that it is a nuisance), and because the second offers some real simplification.

$$r_S = 1 - \frac{6\Sigma D^2}{N(N^2 - 1)} \tag{10.5}$$

where D is defined as the difference between the X and Y ranks assigned to each subject. Alternatively, to avoid the necessity of calculating D^2,

$$r_S = \frac{3(4\Sigma XY - N(N+1)^2)}{N(N^2 - 1)}. \tag{10.6}$$

It is important that you understand the origin of these two equations, since the derivation leads to an assumption which is almost never mentioned. It is well known that the sum of the first N integers equals $N(N+1)/2$. (Thus $1+2+3 = 3(4)/2 = 6$.) Similarly, the sum of the squares of the first N integers equals $N(N+1)(2N+1)/6$. If we ask a judge to rank a set of 10 items from 1 to 10, *allowing no ties*, her data will consist of the integers 1 to 10. If another judge ranked the same set of items, again allowing no ties, her data would also consist of the integers 1 to 10. Since this is the case, ΣX and ΣY in Pearson's formula can be replaced by $N(N+1)/2$, and ΣX^2 and ΣY^2 can be replaced by $N(N+1)(2N+1)/6$. In this way we can derive Equations 10.5 and 10.6.

But notice the stipulation in the previous paragraph which requires that there be no tied ranks. If we do have ties, ΣX^2 and ΣY^2 do not equal $N(N+1)(2N+1)/6$, and Equations 10.5 and 10.6 are wrong. This fact is seldom mentioned, although it has not gone completely unnoticed, and a very cumbersome correction procedure has been developed. It seems to me that a much simpler procedure is to calculate Pearson's r in the first place, rather than to calculate r_S and then patch it up to obtain what you would have had if you calculated r to begin with. Since r_S is seldom calculated on huge samples and since the correction procedure itself is far more bothersome than calculating r, the use of Equation 10.5 seems rather silly when ranks are tied, and indeed even when they are not. I will withhold judgment on the value of Equation 10.6, although it would appear to offer a true simplification when there are no ties if you do not mind remembering it or looking it up each time.

The Significance of r_S

There is no generally accepted method for the calculation of the standard error of r_S for small samples. As a result, computation of confidence limits on r_S is not practical. Numerous textbooks contain tables of critical values of r_S, but for $N \geq 8$ these tables are themselves based upon approximations. For $N > 10$, r_S can be tested in the same manner as r (Kendall, 1948). It is important to keep in mind in this connection that a typical judge has difficulty ranking a large number of items, and therefore in practice N is usually small when we are using r_S.

The Ranking of Data

Ranking

Students occasionally experience difficulty in ranking a set of measurement data, and this section is intended to present the method briefly. Assume that we have the following set of data, which have been arranged in increasing order

$$5 \quad 8 \quad 9 \quad 12 \quad 12 \quad 15 \quad 16 \quad 16 \quad 16 \quad 17$$

The lowest value (5) is given the rank of 1. The next two values (8 and 9) are then assigned ranks 2 and 3. We then have two tied values (12) which must be ranked. Since, if they were untied they would be given ranks 4 and 5, we split the difference and rank them both 4.5. The sixth number (15) is now given rank 6. Three values (16) are tied for ranks 7, 8, and 9, the mean of these ranks being 8. Thus all are given ranks of 8. The last value is 17, and has rank 10. The data and their corresponding ranks are given below.

X:	5	8	9	12	12	15	16	16	16	17
Ranks:	1	2	3	4.5	4.5	6	8	8	8	10

10.6 Kendall's Tau Coefficient (τ)

Kendall's τ

A serious competitor to Spearman's r_S is **Kendall's τ**. While Spearman treated the ranks as scores and calculated the correlation between the two sets of ranks, Kendall based his statistic on the number of *inversions* in the rankings. Suppose for a moment that we asked two judges to rank three objects and obtained the following data

		OBJECT	
	A	**B**	**C**
Judge 1:	1	2	3
Judge 2:	1	3	2

You will note that when the objects are listed in the order of rankings given by Judge 1, then there is an inversion of the ranks given by Judge 2 (i.e., rank 3 appears before rank 2). Inversions of this form are the basis for Kendall's statistic.

Calculation of τ

To extend the above example, assume that our judges were asked to rank 10 items and produced the following data

OBJECT

	A	B	D	C	E	H	J	G	F	I
Judge 1:	1	2	3	4	5	6	7	8	9	10
Judge 2:	2	1	5	3	4	6	7	9	8	1∪

Notice that the objects have been ordered by the ranks given by one of the judges, and that lines have been drawn to connect comparable rankings. The easiest way to calculate the number of inversions is to count the number of intersections of the lines. In this example there are four intersections and therefore four inversions.

Kendall defined

$$\tau = 1 - \frac{2(\text{number of inversions})}{\text{number of pairs of objects}}.$$

It is well known that the number of pairs of N objects is given by $N(N-1)/2$. Thus

$$\tau = 1 - \frac{2(\text{number of inversions})}{N(N-1)/2}. \tag{10.7}$$

For the example above, then,

$$\tau = 1 - \frac{2(4)}{(10)(9)/2} = 1 - \frac{8}{45} = 1 - .178$$

$$= .822.$$

The interpretation of τ is far more straightforward than the interpretation of r_S calculated on the same data. If $\tau = .82$, we can state that if a pair of objects are sampled at random, the probability that the two judges will rank these objects in the same order is .82 more than the probability that they will rank them in the reverse order.

When there are tied rankings, the calculation of τ must be modified from that given in Equation 10.7. For the appropriate correction for ties the reader is referred to Hays (1963).

Significance of τ

Unlike r_S, a test on the statistical significance of τ is easily obtained. It can be shown that the standard error of τ is given by

$$s_\tau = \sqrt{\frac{2(2N+5)}{9N(N-1)}}.$$

Thus

$$z = \frac{\tau}{\sqrt{\frac{2(2N+5)}{9N(N-1)}}}$$

is a standard normal deviate and can be referred to the Appendix (z). For our example, $\tau = .822$ and $N = 10$, therefore

$$z = \frac{.822}{\sqrt{\frac{2(25)}{9(10)(9)}}} = \frac{.822}{\sqrt{\frac{50}{810}}}$$

$$= 3.31$$

which is significant at well beyond $\alpha = .05$.

10.7 Estimating ρ and the Choice Among Coefficients

When we have two or more statistics which appear to be measuring the same thing (estimating the same parameter) we usually choose between them on the basis of such things as unbiasedness and efficiency. Thus we chose $SS_X/(N-1)$ rather than SS_X/N as our estimate of σ_X^2 because the former was unbiased while the latter was not. Similarly we chose the standard deviation over the mean absolute deviation partly because the former was more efficient.

When it comes to choosing among correlation coefficients, the issue is not as simple as it might first appear. We first have to decide just what parameter we want to estimate.

To look first at the standard treatment of the problem, consider that two variables (X and Y) represent a bivariate normal distribution in the population. Thus X and Y are both continuous variables. We generally signify the correlation in the population between these two variables as ρ, but to be more specific we will label it ρ_P, since it is a Pearson product moment correlation. Now suppose that we drew a sample from this population. There are a number of different correlation coefficients we could calculate from these data. We could compute the normal Pearson r. Alternatively we could dichotomize one variable and calculate r_b or r_{pb}. Furthermore we could dichotomize both variables and calculate r_t or ϕ. Lastly we could convert our raw data to ranks and calculate r_S or τ. Suppose we calculated all of these coefficients and then repeated the whole procedure an infinite number of times, thus generating the sampling distribution of each statistic around the true value of ρ_P.

The general conclusions from the results of carrying out the above procedure are straightforward. We would find, as expected, r is the best estimate of ρ_P. Among the more derivative coefficients, we would find that τ was the next best (though not an unbiased) estimate of ρ_P. We would also find that r_S is only slightly worse, that r_b is better than r_{pb} and that r_t is better than ϕ.

The preceding paragraph may look as if it has answered our original question, but in fact it has not. It has only answered the question when the variables have in fact a bivariate normal distribution in the population, and when, at least in theory, we could measure these variables on a continuous scale. But suppose that we were interested in correlating group membership (drug-no drug) with speed of learning. If a subject must be a member of one group or the other, there is no way that X can be thought of as a continuous variable, nor can X and Y have a bivariate normal distribution in the population. In this case it becomes meaningless to speak of ρ_P as the parameter; and the value of r_{pb} as an estimate of ρ_P is totally irrelevant. The parameter we really want to estimate is ρ_{pb}, the point-biserial correlation in the population. In this case r_{pb} is a better estimator of the parameter than is r_b. With the appropriate changes in wording, the same kind of statement can be made for ϕ.

An interesting issue arises when we consider r_S and τ. If we think of the population consisting of bivariate pairs of ranks, we have a choice as to what we mean by the relevant parameter. Suppose we define two parameters, ρ_S and ρ_τ, corresponding to the calculation of Spearman's rank order correlation and τ in the population. It turns out that τ is a better estimate of ρ_τ than r_S is of ρ_S. For this reason there is a great deal to recommend a preference for τ over r_S when we want to correlate ranks.

The choice among coefficients also hinges on the interests of the experimenter, and the kinds of decisions he wants to make on the basis of his data. An interesting illustration of this is the fact that Guilford & Fruchter (1973) use pass-fail on a test as an example of a variable for which r_{pb} is appropriate, whereas most books use this as an example for a variable which has an underlying normal distribution. The discussion of Guilford & Fruchter

(1973, p. 298) is instructive in this regard. The following example also illustrates the problem.

Consider two hypothetical experimenters, one theoretically oriented and one applied oriented. The theoretician deals in such questions as "Is the liberalism or conservatism of an individual related to the way in which he will vote in the next election—an election between Smith and Jones?" The basic data for both experimenters will be a dichotomy of *liberal vs. conservative* and the choice *Jones vs. Smith*. The theoretician realizes that there is an obvious continuity between liberal and conservative, and that the continuity is probably normally distributed, with most people piling up in the center. He also realizes that while some people are strongly in favor of Jones, and some are strongly in favor of Smith, the bulk of the votes lie somewhere between these two extremes, and again he assumes an underlying normality. For these reasons he decides that the statistic he needs is r_t, and the parameter he is trying to estimate is ρ_P. In this situation he has made the correct choice, and when he is finished he will be able to say that "the correlation between the liberal-conservative dimension and the Jones–Smith dimension is ___."

Now let us consider our applied experimenter. He is concerned with quite a different problem, namely predicting voting behavior. He does not have the least quarrel with the theoretician's characterization of the scales, he too acknowledges that they represent an underlying normality. But he reasons as follows. "I do not care whether individual X is a radical conservative or just a very moderate conservative, he will still be classified as a conservative in the data. Similarly I do not care if individual Y is a radical liberal or a moderate liberal, in the data he is classified as liberal. Furthermore it is irrelevant whether a person contributed all of his energy toward the Smith campaign, or voted for him because he figured that Smith was slightly the lesser of two evils, the point is that he voted for Smith. If I wish to predict, after the fact, the voting behavior of individuals on the basis of the liberal-conservative dimension, I want ϕ and I want it as an estimate ρ_ϕ." This experimenter is also correct.

Our two experimenters used different statistics on the same data and were both correct. The theoretician was primarily interested in voting tendencies and the underlying nature of the scales, and wanted to say something about the degree of conservatism and the degree of support for Smith. The applied experimenter, while acknowledging the continuity of the scale, was primarily interested in the dichotomous aspects of the situation, and wanted to predict voting behavior. Put another way, the theoretician settled for dichotomous measures because that was the best he could do. The applied individual was happy with dichotomous measures (especially of voting) since that is the nature of the beast.

In most situations where prediction (or percentage of accountable variance) is our primary goal, the coefficients r_{pb} and ϕ are more appropriate in practice, although some exceptions doubtlessly occur. For this reason, when we come to discussing multiple regression we will invariably use r_{pb} and ϕ for dichotomous variables without pausing to consider the underlying nature of these variables.

10.8 Kendall's Coefficient of Concordance (W)

Kendall's Coefficient of Concordance (W)

All of the statistics with which we have been concerned in this chapter have dealt with the relationship between two sets of scores (X and Y). But suppose that instead of having two judges rank a set of objects, we had six judges doing the ranking. What we need is some measure of the degree to which the six judges agree. Such a measure is afforded by **Kendall's Coefficient of Concordance (W)**.

Suppose, as an example, that we asked six judges to rank order the pleasantness of eight colored patches, and obtained the data in Table 10.4. If all of the judges had agreed that Patch B was the most pleasant, they would all have assigned it a rank of 1, and the column total for that patch across six judges would have been 6. Similarly if A had been ranked second by everyone its total would have been 12. Finally if every judge assigned the highest rank to Patch G, its total would have been 48. In other words the column totals would have shown considerable variability.

TABLE 10.4

Judges' Rankings of "Pleasantness" of Colored Patches

Judges		A	B	C	D	E	F	G	H
					COLORED PATCHES				
1		1	2	3	4	5	6	7	8
2		2	1	5	4	3	8	7	6
3		1	3	2	7	5	6	8	4
4		2	1	3	5	4	7	8	6
5		3	1	2	4	6	5	7	8
6		2	1	3	6	5	4	8	7
	Σ	11	9	18	30	28	36	45	39

On the other hand if the judges showed maximal disagreement, each column would have had some high ranks and some low ranks assigned to it and the column totals would have been roughly equal. Thus the variability of the column totals, given disagreement (or random behavior) among judges, would be low.

Kendall made use of the variability of the column totals in deriving his statistic. He defined W as the ratio of the variability among columns to the maximum possible variability.

$$W = \frac{\text{variance of column totals}}{\text{maximum possible variance of column totals}}$$

Since we are dealing with ranks we know what the maximum variance of the totals will be. Thus we can define

$$W = \frac{12\Sigma T_j^2}{k^2 N(N^2-1)} - \frac{3(N+1)}{N-1} \qquad \qquad (10.8)$$

where T_j represents the column totals, N = the number of items to be ranked, and k = the number of judges doing the ranking. For the data in Table 10.4,

$$\Sigma T_j^2 = 11^2 + 9^2 + 18^2 + 30^2 + 28^2 + 36^2 + 45^2 + 39^2 = 7052.$$

$$W = \frac{12\Sigma T_j^2}{k^2 N(N^2-1)} - \frac{3(N+1)}{N-1}$$

$$= \frac{12(7052)}{6^2(8)(63)} - \frac{3(9)}{7} = \frac{84624}{18144} - \frac{27}{7} = 4.6640 - 3.857$$

$$= .807.$$

As you can see from the definition of W, it is not a standard correlation coefficient. It does have an interpretation in terms of a familiar statistic, however, in that W can be viewed as a function of the average Spearman correlation between all possible pairs of rankings. Specifically,

$$\bar{r}_S = \frac{kW-1}{k-1}.$$

For our data

$$\bar{r}_S = \frac{kW-1}{k-1} = \frac{6(.807)-1}{5} = .768.$$

Thus if we took all possible pairs of rankings and computed r_S for each, the average r_S would be .768.

Hays (1973) recommends that W be converted to $\bar{r}_S$ and interpreted that way. Indeed it is hard to disagree with that recommendation since no intuitive meaning attaches to W itself. W does have the advantage of being bounded by 0 and 1, whereas $\bar{r}_S$ does not, but it is difficult to attach much practical meaning to the statement that the variance of column totals is 80.7% of the maximum possible variance. Whatever its faults, $\bar{r}_S$ seems preferable.

A test on the null hypothesis that there is no agreement among judges is possible under certain conditions. If $k \geq 7$, the quantity

$$\chi_{N-1}^2 = k(N-1)W$$

is approximately distributed as χ^2 on $N-1$ degrees of freedom. Such a test is seldom used, however, since W is usually calculated in those situations in which we seek a level of agreement substantially above the minimum level required for significance.

10.9   Measures of Association

Several coefficients exist for dealing with contingency tables of a dimensionality greater than 2×2. These coefficients are generally referred to as **measures of association** rather than correlation coefficients, for reasons discussed at the beginning of the chapter. Here we will deal briefly with two of the most important measures. For a more complete discussion of this issue the reader is referred to Hays (1973, pp. 745–753).

The Contingency Coefficient (C)

When data appear in the form of a contingency table of any dimensionality one of the most commonly employed coefficients is the **Contingency Coefficient (C)**. For all tables, C is defined as

$$C = \sqrt{\frac{\chi^2}{\chi^2 + N}}. \tag{10.9}$$

Several difficulties arise with this coefficient. The first is rather obvious, namely that since N is always greater than 0, C can never equal 1.0. More importantly, however, the maximum value of C is dependent upon the dimensionality of the table from which it is computed. Thus for a 2×2 table, $C_{max} = .707$; for a 3×3, $C_{max} = .816$; and so on. In general

$$C_{max} = \sqrt{\frac{k-1}{k}} \tag{10.10}$$

where k is the smaller of R (the number of rows) or C (the number of columns). This limitation on C_{max} makes interpretation of C quite difficult. Although some people have suggested using C/C_{max} as a measure of association, I know of no statistical justification for this procedure. The Contingency Coefficient has long held an important place in statistical procedures, and it is unlikely that it will be completely replaced in the near future although it does have important, and better, competitors.

Cramér's Phi (ϕ_C)

An alternative to C which is free from the dependence upon the size of the contingency table and which does vary between 0 and 1, is **Cramér's**

Phi (ϕ_C). ϕ_C is defined as

$$\phi_C = \sqrt{\frac{\chi^2}{N(k-1)}} \qquad\qquad (10.11)$$

where N is the sample size and k is defined as in Equation 10.10 (Cramér, 1946).

Cramér's ϕ_C can be seen as an extension of ϕ to the case where $k > 2$. Unlike C, the maximum value of ϕ_C is ± 1.00, regardless of the size of the table. While ϕ_C would appear to be superior to C, it has not seen a great deal of use, most likely from the fact that few working scientists would be likely to have read Cramér's book. Its increased use is to be encouraged, however.

The analysis of contingency tables is not a simple matter, and new techniques are constantly being developed. For an excellent discussion of the problem of measure of association for contingency tables, the reader is referred to Mayo (1959).

10.10   Summary

This chapter has extended the material in Chapter 9 by dealing with alternative measures of correlation and association. We discussed four measures which apply to cases in which one or both variables are measured dichotomously. We then discussed two measures for ranked data, and finally the general problem of estimation of the true correlation in the population. Moving away from standard correlational techniques we considered Kendall's Coefficient of Concordance (W), which is useful as a way of assessing agreement among judges, and then looked at two measures of association. The argument was made that Cramér's Phi (ϕ_C) is a much better measure of association than the more common Contingency Coefficient (C).

Exercises for Chapter 10

10.1   Some people seem to feel that they do their best work in the morning, while others claim that they do their best work at night. We have dichotomized 20 office workers into morning or evening people (0 = morning, 1 = evening) and have obtained independent estimates of the quality of work they produced on some specified morning. The ratings were based on a 100 point scale and appear below.

Peak Time of Day:
0 0 0 0 0 0 0 0 0 0 0 0 0 1 1 1 1 1 1 1

Performance Rating:
65 80 55 60 55 70 60 70 55 70 40 70 50 40 60 50 40 50 40 60

a. Plot these data and fit a regression line.
b. Calculate r_{pb} and test it for significance.
c. Interpret the results.

10.2 Because of a fortunate change in work schedules we were able to re-evaluate the subjects referred to in Exercise 10.1 for performance on the same tasks in the evening. The data are given below.

Peak Time of Day:

0 0 0 0 0 0 0 0 0 0 0 0 0 0 1 1 1 1 1 1 1

Performance Rating:

40 60 40 50 30 40 50 50 20 30 40 50 30 30 50 50 40 50 40 60

a. Plot these data and fit a regression line.
b. Calculate r_{pb} and test it for significance.
c. Interpret the results.

10.3 Compare the results obtained in Exercises 10.1 and 10.2. What might you conclude?

10.4 Why would it not make sense to calculate a biserial correlation on the data in Exercises 10.1 and 10.2?

10.5 Perform a *t* test on the data in Exercise 10.1 and show the relationship between this value of *t* and r_{pb}.

10.6 A graduate school admissions committee is concerned about the relationship between grade point average in college and whether or not the individual eventually completes the requirements for a Ph.D. They first looked at the data on 25 randomly selected students who entered the program seven years ago, assigning a score of 1 to those who completed the Ph.D., and 0 to those who did not. The data are given below.

Ph.D.:

0 0 0   0 0 0   0 0 1 1 1 1   1 1 1 1   1 1 1   1 1   1 1 1 1

GPA:

2.0 3.5 2.75 3.0 3.5 2.75 2.0 2.5 3.0 2.5 3.5 3.25 3.0 3.0 2.75 3.25 3.0 3.33 2.5 2.75 2.0 4.0 3.0 3.25 2.5

a. Plot the data.
b. Calculate r_{pb}.
c. Calculate r_b.
d. Is it reasonable to even look at r_b in this situation?

10.7 Compute the regression equation for the data in Exercise 10.6. Show that the line defined by this equation passes through the means of the two groups.

10.8 Referring back to Exercise 10.7, what do the slope and the intercept represent in terms of the data?

10.9 Referring back to Exercise 10.6, assume that the committee decided that a cutoff of 3.00 would be appropriate. In other words, they classed everyone with a 3.00 average or higher as acceptable and those below 3.00 as unacceptable. They then correlated this with completion of Ph.D.

a. Rescore the data in Exercise 10.6 as indicated.
b. Run the correlation.
c. Test this correlation for significance.

10.10 Visualize the data in Exercise 10.9 as fitting into a contingency table.

a. Compute Chi-square on this table.
b. Show the relationship between Chi-square and ϕ.

10.11 An investigator is interested in the relationship between alcoholism and a childhood history of hyperkinesis. He has collected the following data, where a 1 represents the presence of the relevant problem.

Hyperkinesis:
0 1 0 0 1 1 0 0 0 1 0 0 1 0 0 1 1 1 0 0 0 0 0 0 1 0 0 1 0 0 0
Alcoholism:
0 1 0 0 0 1 0 0 0 1 1 0 0 0 0 1 0 1 0 0 0 0 0 0 1 0 0 1 0 1 0

a. What is the correlation between these two variables?
b. Is the relationship significant?

10.12 In an attempt to develop a scale of language disorder an investigator wants to arrange the items on her scale on the basis of the order in which they appear in development. Not being entirely confident that she has selected the correct ordering, she asks another professional to rank the items from 1 to 15 in terms of the order in which he thinks they should appear. The data are given below

Investigator:	1	2	3	4	5	6	7	8	9	10	11	12	13	14	15
Accomplice:	1	3	2	4	7	5	6	8	10	9	11	12	15	13	14

a. Use Pearson's formula (r) to calculate Spearman's r_S.
b. Rerun the above calculation using the two other formulae given in the text.

10.13 *a.* Compute Kendall's τ on the data in Exercise 10.12.
b. Test τ for significance.

10.14 In a study of diagnostic processes, entering clinical graduate students are shown a 20-min. videotape of behavior and asked to rank-order ten behavioral events on the tape in the order of the importance each has for diagnosis. The data are then averaged to produce an average rank ordering for the entire class. The same thing was then done using experienced clinicians. The data are given below

Experienced Clinicians:	1	3	2	7	5	4	8	6	9	10
New Students:	2	4	1	6	5	3	10	8	7	9

Use Spearman's r_S to measure the agreement between experienced and naive clinicians.

10.15 Rerun the analysis on Exercise 10.14 using Kendall's τ.

10.16   Assume that in Exercise 10.14 there were five entering clinical students. They produced the following data

Student
1	1	4	2	6	5	3	9	10	7	8
2	4	3	2	5	7	1	10	8	6	9
3	1	5	2	6	4	3	8	10	7	9
4	2	5	1	7	4	3	10	8	6	9
5	2	5	1	4	6	3	9	7	8	10

Calculate Kendall's W and $\overline{r}_S$ in these data as a measure of agreement. Interpret your results.

10.17   A psychologist is interested in the relationship between depression and marital status. On the basis of a scale which he has devised he has classified single, divorced, and married males as depressed or non-depressed.

	Single	Divorced	Married
Depressed:	10	10	15
Non-Depressed:	25	10	35

a.   Calculate Cramér's ϕ_C and Cramér's ϕ_C^2.
b.   Interpret the results.

10.18   Calculate the Contingency Coefficient for the data in Exercise 10.17 and interpret it. What is C_{max} for these data?

10.19   The relationship between financial security and income is not always as clear as one might suspect. An experimenter has obtained the following data on reported financial security for four groups of individuals who differ on net income. The cell entries are the number of respondents falling into each category.

		< $5,000	< $10,000	< $20,000	< $30,000
Reported Security:	Secure:	5	10	20	10
	Insecure:	15	10	10	15

a.   Calculate Cramér's ϕ_C on these data.
b.   Calculate the Contingency Coefficient on these data.
c.   Interpret the results.

10.20   Another psychologist argues that it would have been more appropriate to offer a third response alternative in Exercise 10.19. She reran the study adding a *neutral* category and her data look like this

		<$5,000	<$10,000	<$20,000	<$30,000
	Secure:	4	5	5	8
Reported Security:	*Neutral*:	1	5	15	2
	Insecure:	10	10	10	15

a. Calculate Cramér's ϕ_C.

b. Calculate a Contingency Coefficient.

c. Interpret the results.

10.21 Why can we not compare the Contingency Coefficients computed in Exercises 10.19 and 10.20?

10.22 Does it make more sense to speak about ϕ_C^2 in Exercise 10.19 than in Exercise 10.17? Explain your answer.

11 Simple Analysis of Variance

Objective

To introduce the analysis of variance as a procedure for testing differences among two or more means.

Contents

Analysis of variance
(ANOVA)

The ***analysis of variance (ANOVA)*** currently enjoys the status of being probably the most used (some would say abused) statistical technique in psychological research. The popularity and usefulness of this technique can be attributed to two sources. First of all, the analysis of variance, like *t*, deals with differences between or among sample means, and unlike *t*, there is no restriction on the number of means. Instead of asking merely whether two means differ, we can ask whether 3, 4, 5, or *k* means differ. In addition the analysis of variance allows us to deal with two or more independent variables simultaneously, asking not only about the individual effects of each variable separately, but also about the interacting effects of two or more variables.

The present chapter will be concerned with the underlying logic of the analysis of variance (which is really quite simple) and with the analysis of the results of experiments employing only one independent variable. In addition we will deal with a number of related topics which are most easily

One-way analysis
of variance

understood in the context of a one-variable (***one-way***) analysis. Subsequent chapters will deal with comparisons among individual sample means, with the analysis of experiments involving two or more variables, and with designs in which repeated measurements are made on each subject.

11.1   A Hypothetical Sampling Study

Probably the easiest way to understand the analysis of variance is by way of a hypothetical example. To this end consider an experiment in which we wish to determine whether rats learn equally quickly under 10, 20, or 30 hours of food deprivation, the dependent variable being the number of trials required to reach some predetermined criterion. Rather than actually carrying out this experiment, however, we will retreat into the world of fantasy and imagine experiments based upon infinite numbers of subjects.

Suppose that we took an infinite number of rats and ran them in a learning experiment under 10 hours of food deprivation, measuring the number of trials required for each subject to reach a predetermined criterion. The results of this experiment would lead to an infinite number of data points, and to the distribution represented in Figure 11.1(a). This population of numbers will obviously have a mean and variance, and we will designate them as μ_1 and σ_1^2, respectively. Moreover the distribution will very likely be more or less normal in shape.

Now suppose that, being rather patient people, we reran this experiment with a different infinitely large batch of subjects, although this time we ran them under 20 hours of deprivation. Again we would obtain an infinite number of data points which could be plotted as in Figure 11.1(b). This distribution would also be more or less normal, and we will designate its mean and variance as μ_2 and σ_2^2, for the moment saying nothing about the relationships between μ_1 and μ_2 or σ_1^2 and σ_2^2.

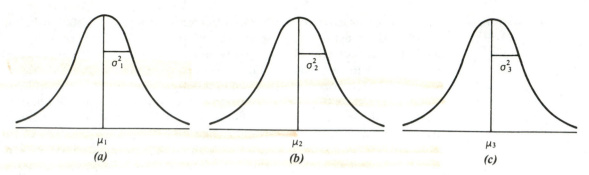

FIGURE 11.1   Results of hypothetical sampling experiment

Lastly, exceeding even Job in patience, we repeat the whole procedure yet a third time with a third infinitely large collection of rats under 30 hours of deprivation and obtain the data displayed in Figure 11.1(c). In this case the mean and variance will be designated μ_3 and σ_3^2, and the distribution would again be expected to be roughly normal.

At this point our life's work is at an end, and we can now state with absolute certainty the relationship between μ_1, μ_2, and μ_3, and thus the relationship between the mean number of trials to criterion under the three conditions of deprivation. The word "certainty" is appropriate in the last sentence because we have *calculated* μ_1, μ_2, and μ_3, and do not have to estimate them. We have merely to look at the means to see if they are different.

It will be obvious that we can not conduct experiments with infinitely large sample sizes, and will thus have to be content with samples of data based on more reasonable numbers of subjects. The main question remains the same, ("what is the relationship between the population means?"), but now we will be required to answer the question using estimates of the μ_j, rather than the true values of the μ_j themselves. Keeping in mind the results of this hypothetical experiment, let us examine the problem in more detail and then impose two assumptions for the purpose of simplification.

The Null Hypothesis

Since we want to know whether the mean number of trials to criterion is the same under the three conditions or treatments, it follows that the null hypothesis can be written as

$$H_0: \mu_1 = \mu_2 = \mu_3 = \mu$$

where the symbol μ without a subscript represents the common value of μ_j. The null hypothesis could be false for several different reasons, for example because $\mu_1 = \mu_2$, but μ_3 is different, but we will for the moment consider only the case in which it is either strictly true or it is false, whatever the reason.

The Population

Population   One of the difficulties that students frequently encounter concerns what we mean by the word *population*. In statistics a population is a collection of *numbers*, not a collection of rats or people or anything else. Thus strictly speaking we are not trying to say that a population of rats trained under one condition performs better or worse than a population of rats trained under another condition, but rather that a population of *scores* obtained under one condition has a mean greater than or less than a population of scores obtained under another condition. This may appear to be a rather trivial point, but consider how silly it would sound to say that the null hypothesis states that rats and children were drawn from the same population. No one would seriously believe this to be true, except possibly parents under extreme duress. However a situation might exist where it made sense to ask if their scores came from the same population of scores. In this context one useful approach is to think of rats and children running around with numbers (learning scores) taped to their noses. We could not care less what the population was that the rats and children were drawn from, but only whether God, when applying the numbers, sampled those numbers from one shopping bag (population) or from two.

The Assumption of Normality

For reasons dealing with our final test of significance we will make the assumption that trials to criterion are normally distributed around μ_j for each population. This is no more than the assumption that Figures 11.1(a–c) are normally distributed. As with *t*, this assumption deals primarily with the sampling distribution of the mean, rather than the distribution of observations. Moreover, even substantial departures from normality may, under certain conditions, have remarkably little influence on the final result.

The Assumption of Homogeneity of Variance

Our second major assumption will be the assumption that each of our populations of scores has the same variance, specifically

$$\sigma_1^2 = \sigma_2^2 = \sigma_3^2 = \sigma_e^2.$$

Here we will use the notation σ_e^2 to indicate the common value held by the three variances. The subscript *e* is an abbreviation for *error*, since this variance is error variance—variance unrelated to any treatment differences. As we will later see, under certain conditions this assumption too can be relaxed without doing too much damage to the final result.

11.2   The Logic of the Analysis of Variance

Consider for a moment the effect of our two major assumptions—normality and homogeneity of variance. By making these assumptions we have said that the three distributions have the same shape and dispersion. As a result, the only way left for them to differ is in terms of their means (recall that the normal distribution is a two-parameter distribution). Now let us make the further assumption that H_0 is true. If $\mu_1 = \mu_2 = \mu_3 = \mu$, then there is no way left for the distributions to differ. They must be identical, and if so nothing would be lost by treating them as one. This is equivalent to saying that all of the trials-to-criterion scores can be thought of as coming from the same bag (population).

We will begin by making no assumption concerning H_0, although we will suppose that due to limited financial resources we were only able to obtain 9 scores under each condition. For any one treatment the variance of the 9 scores would be an estimate of the population variance (σ_e^2). If you prefer you can think of $\sigma_1^2 \doteq s_1^2$, $\sigma_2^2 \doteq s_2^2$, and $\sigma_3^2 \doteq s_3^2$, where $\doteq$ means *is estimated by*. Since we have assumed homogeneity of variance, all of the s_j^2 estimate the common σ_e^2. For the sake of increased reliability we will pool the three estimates by taking their mean (if $n_1 = n_2 = n_3 = n$).

$$\sigma_e^2 \doteq s^2 = \bar{s}_j^2 = \Sigma s_j^2 / k$$

MS$_{within}$
MS$_{error}$

where $k =$ the number of treatments. This gives us one estimate of the population variance, and is what we will later refer to as **MS**$_{within}$ or **MS**$_{error}$ (read "mean square error"). It is important to note that this estimate does not depend upon the truth or falsity of H_0, since s_j^2 is calculated on each sample separately.

Now let us assume that H_0 is true. If this is the case, then our three samples of 9 cases can be thought of as three independent samples from the same population, and we have another possible estimate of σ_e^2. You should recall that the Central Limit Theorem stated that the variance of means drawn from the same population equals the variance of the population divided by the sample size. Under H_0 the sample means have been drawn from the same population (or identical populations, which amounts to the same thing) and therefore

$$\frac{\sigma_e^2}{n} \doteq s_{\bar{X}}^2$$

where n is the size of each sample. Thus we can reverse the usual order of things and calculate the variance of our sample means ($s_{\bar{X}}^2$) to obtain a second estimate of σ_e^2.

$$\sigma_e^2 \doteq n s_{\bar{X}}^2$$

$MS_{treatment}$ This term will shortly be referred to as **$MS_{treatment}$**.

We now have two estimates of the population variance (σ_e^2). One of these estimates (MS_{error}) is independent of the truth or falsity of H_0. The other ($MS_{treatment}$) is an estimate of σ_e^2 only so long as H_0 is true (only so long as the conditions of the Central Limit Theorem are met, namely that the means are drawn from one population). Thus if the two estimates agree we will have support for the truth of H_0, and if they disagree we will have support for the falsity of H_0. But before we consider ways of defining what we mean by *agreement*, let us take two very simple examples, which have been deliberately constructed to represent more or less ideal results under H_0: true and H_0: false. Seldom in practice will data be as neat and tidy as this.

Example 11.1

**The Case of a
True H_0**

In the first example the data from all three groups have been chosen to resemble data which might be drawn from one normally distributed population with a mean of 5 and a variance of 10. The data are presented in Table 11.1. From this table we can see that the average variance with each treatment is 9.250, a respectable estimate of $\sigma_e^2 = 10$. The variance of the group means is 1.000, and, since we know H_0 to be true

$$\frac{\sigma_e^2}{n} \doteq s_{\bar{X}}^2$$

$$\sigma_e^2 \doteq n(s_{\bar{X}}^2) = 9(1) = 9.$$

This value is also reasonably in agreement with σ_e^2 and with our other estimate based upon the variability within treatments. Since these two estimates are in agreement, we would conclude that we have no reason to doubt the truth of H_0.

Example 11.2

**The Case of a
False H_0**

Next we consider an example where we know H_0 to be false. The data in Table 11.2 have been obtained by adding constants to the data in Table 11.1 to produce data which might have come about by sampling Treatment 1 scores from a population which is $N(8, 10)$,[†] Treatment 2 scores from $N(4, 10)$ and Treatment 3 scores from $N(4, 10)$. This represents a substantial departure form H_0.

[†] The notation $N(8, 10)$ represents a distribution which is normally distributed with a mean of 8 and a variance of 10.

TABLE 11.1

Representative Data for Case Where H_0: True

	TREATMENT 1	TREATMENT 2	TREATMENT 3	
	3	1	5	
	6	4	2	
	9	7	8	
	6	4	8	
	3	1	2	
	12	10	8	
	6	4	5	
	3	1	2	
	9	7	8	
$\bar{X}_j =$	6.3333	4.3333	5.3333	Grand Mean $(GM) = 5.333$
$s_j^2 =$	10.0000	10.0000	7.750	average variance $(\bar{s}_j^2) = 9.250$

$$s_{\bar{X}}^2 = \frac{\Sigma(\bar{X}_i - GM)^2}{k-1} = 1.0000$$

$$\bar{s}_i^2 = \frac{10.00 + 10.00 + 7.75}{3} = 9.25$$

$\text{MS}_{\text{error}} = \bar{s}_j^2 = 9.25$

$\text{MS}_{\text{treat}} = ns_{\bar{X}}^2 = 9(1) = 9$

TABLE 11.2

Representative Data for Case Where H_0: False

	TREATMENT 1	TREATMENT 2	TREATMENT 3	
	0	0	5	
	8	3	2	
	11	6	8	
	8	3	8	
	5	0	2	
	14	9	8	
	8	3	5	
	5	0	2	
	11	6	8	
$\bar{X}_j =$	8.333	3.333	5.333	$GM = 5.666$
$s_j^2 =$	10.000	10.000	7.750	$\bar{s}_j^2 = 9.250$

$$s_{\bar{X}}^2 = \frac{\Sigma(\bar{X}_j - GM)^2}{k-1} = 6.333$$

$$\bar{s}_j^2 = \frac{(10.00 + 10.00 + 7.75)}{3} = 9.25$$

$\text{MS}_{\text{error}} = \bar{s}_j^2 = 9.25$

$\text{MS}_{\text{treat}} = ns_{\bar{X}}^2 = 9(6.333) = 57$

From Table 11.2 you will note that the variance within each treatment remains unchanged, since adding or subtracting a constant has no effect on the variance. This illustrates the earlier statement that the variance within groups is independent of the null hypothesis. The variance among the treatment means, however, has increased substantially, reflecting the difference among the population means. In this case the estimate of σ_e^2 based on the sample means is $9(6.333) = 57$, a value which is way out of line with the estimate of 9.25 given by the variance within groups. The most logical conclusion would be that $ns_{\bar{x}}^2$ is not merely estimating population variance (σ_e^2) but is estimating σ_e^2 plus the variance of the population means themselves. In fact we know this to be the case, since the data have been deliberately manufactured for this purpose.

Summary of the Logic of the Analysis of Variance

From the preceding discussion we can state the logic of the analysis of variance very concisely. To test H_0 we calculate two estimates of the population variance, one of which is independent of the truth or falsity of H_0, while the other is dependent upon H_0. If the two agree we have no reason to reject H_0. If they disagree we conclude that underlying treatment differences must have contributed to our second estimate, inflating it and causing it to differ from the first. We therefore reject H_0.

Variance Estimation

We will return later to the theory underlying the analysis of variance, but it might be helpful at this point to state without proof what are the two estimates we are really estimating. We will first define σ_τ^2 as the variance of the true populations' means (μ_1, μ_2, and μ_3).

$$\sigma_\tau^2 = \frac{\Sigma(\mu_j - \mu)^2}{k - 1} = \frac{\Sigma\tau_j^2}{k - 1} \dagger$$

Expected value　In addition you will recall that we defined the ***expected value*** of a statistic

---

† Technically σ_τ^2 is not actually a variance, since, having the actual parameter (μ) we should be dividing by k instead of $k - 1$. Nonetheless, very little is to be lost by thinking of it as a variance, so long as we keep in mind precisely what we have done. This point will reappear when we discuss ways of estimating the magnitude of an experimental effect.

[written $E(\ )$] as its long range average—the average value which that statistic would assume over repeated sampling. With these two concepts we can state

$$E(MS_{error}) = \sigma_e^2 \qquad\qquad\qquad (11.1)$$

$$E(MS_{treat}) = \sigma_e^2 + n\sigma_\tau^2 \qquad\qquad (11.2)$$

where σ_e^2 is the variance of the population(s) and σ_τ^2 is the variance of the μ_j.

Now if H_0 is true and $\mu_1 = \mu_2 = \mu_3 = \mu$, then $\sigma_\tau^2 = 0$ and

$$E(MS_{error}) = \sigma_e^2$$

and

$$E(MS_{treat}) = \sigma_e^2 + n(0) = \sigma_e^2$$

and thus

$$E(MS_{error}) = E(MS_{treat}).$$

Keep in mind that these are expected values, and rarely in practice will the two mean squares be exactly equal.

If H_0 is false, however, the σ_τ^2 will not be zero, but will be some positive number. In this case

$$E(MS_{error}) < E(MS_{treat})$$

since MS_{treat} will contain a nonzero term representing the true differences among the μ_j.

To take an illustration we can return to the example in Table 11.2. In this situation $\sigma_e^2 = 10$ and $\mu_1 = 8, \mu_2 = 4, \mu_3 = 4$. The variance of the $\mu_j = \sigma_\tau^2 = \Sigma(\mu_j - \mu)^2/(k-1) = 5.33$. Thus

$$MS_{error} = 9.25 \qquad E(MS_{error}) = \sigma_e^2 = 10.00$$

$$MS_{treat} = 57.00 \qquad E(MS_{treat}) = \sigma_e^2 + n\sigma_\tau^2 = 10 + 9(5.33) = 58.00$$

Here we can see the way in which MS_{treat} reflects the falsity of H_0.

Sum of Squares

Sums of squares   In the analysis of variance much of our computation deals with **sums of squares**. As we saw in Chapter 9, a sum of squares is merely the sum of the squared deviations about the mean $[\Sigma(X - \bar{X})^2]$ or some multiple of that. Sums of squares have the advantage of being additive, whereas mean squares are additive only if they happen to be based on the same number of df.

When we first defined the sample variance we saw that

$$s_X^2 = \frac{\Sigma(X - \bar{X})^2}{N - 1} = \frac{\Sigma X^2 - (\Sigma X)^2/N}{N - 1}.$$

Here the numerator is a *sum of squares* of X and the denominator is the degrees of freedom. If we want to write a very general expression for a sum of squares (call it SS_Q), we could write

$$SS_Q = \frac{\Sigma Q^2}{a} - \frac{(\Sigma Q)^2}{N}$$

where the divisor "a" may be equal to 1 in some cases, as in calculating the sample variance. This general form applies to all sums of squares which we shall consider, with one very minor exception.

Totals

While we have been speaking in terms of treatment means, we will actually carry out our calculations in terms of treatment totals. This distinction is one of convenience rather than substance, since totals are linearly related to means. If two groups of the same size have different means, they obviously have different totals.

The only important change in what has already been said, when we go from using means to using totals, is in terms of the calculation of SS_{treat} or MS_{treat}. It was shown earlier that

$$\sigma_e^2 \doteq n s_{\bar{X}}^2.$$

In other words we multiply the variance of means by n to produce an estimate of σ_e^2. If we are to work with totals, we will not have $s_{\bar{X}}^2$, but rather s_T^2, where the subscript T refers to *totals*. It is not difficult to show that

$$\sigma_e^2 \doteq \frac{s_T^2}{n}. \tag{11.3}$$

The proof of this lies in the fact that a total is n times the mean, and when we multiply by a constant we multiply the variance by the square of the constant. Thus

$$s_T^2 = n^2 s_{\bar{X}}^2$$

$$\frac{s_T^2}{n^2} = s_{\bar{X}}^2$$

and therefore

$$n s_{\bar{X}}^2 = \frac{n s_T^2}{n^2} = \frac{s_T^2}{n}.$$

Thus we will divide the variance of totals by n to produce an estimate of σ_e^2.

The fact that n appears in Equation 11.3 as a divisor is a point which must be noted carefully. As will be apparent in the next several chapters, strange looking divisors keep appearing in formulae for sums of squares.

These formulae are readily understood if you keep in mind that the divisors are directly analogous to n in Equation 11.3. In each case we are merely dividing by the number of observations on which the total is based, so as to eventually convert a variance of totals into an estimate of σ_e^2.

[handwritten: $Y_{ij} = \mu + T_j + e_{ij}$]

[handwritten: how mean score varies depending on group]

11.3   Calculations in the Analysis of Variance

[handwritten: $H_0: T_1 = T_2 = T_3 = 0$]

For the sake of consistency we will apply the analysis of variance to the data in Table 11.2. These data, along with the resulting computations, which are discussed in detail below, are presented in Table 11.3.

In Table 11.3(a) we see the observations, the individual treatment

Correction factor   totals (T_j), the grand total $(GT = \Sigma X)$, and what we will call the **correction factor** $[CF = (\Sigma X)^2 / N]$. The use of the notation T_j to represent the total of

TABLE 11.3

Calculations of Analysis of Variance for Data in Table 11.2

(a) Data

TREATMENT 1	TREATMENT 2	TREATMENT 3
5	0	5
8	3	2
11	6	8
8	3	8
5	0	2
14	9	8
8	3	5
5	0	2
11	6	8
$T_j = $ 75	30	48

$GT = 153$
$(\Sigma X)^2 / N = 867.000$

(b) Computations

$$SS_{total} = \Sigma X^2 - \frac{(\Sigma X)^2}{N} = (5^2 + 8^2 + \cdots + 2^2 + 8^2) - \frac{153^2}{27} = 1203 - 867 = 336$$

$$SS_{treat} = \frac{\Sigma T_j^2}{n} - \frac{(\Sigma X)^2}{N} = \frac{(75^2 + 30^2 + 48^2)}{9} - \frac{153^2}{27} = \frac{8829}{9} - 867 = 981 - 867 = 114$$

$$SS_{error} = SS_{total} - SS_{treat} = 336 - 114 = 222$$

(c) Summary table

Source	df	SS	MS *[handwritten: $\frac{SS}{df}$]*	F *[handwritten: $\frac{MS_T}{MS_E}$]*
Treatments *[handwritten: / Between]*	2 *[handwritten: G-1]*	114	57.00	6.162
Error *[handwritten: / Within]*	24 *[handwritten: N-G]*	222	9.25	
Total	26 *[handwritten: N-1]*	336		

the jth treatment will be followed throughout the discussion of the analysis of variance. While it would be more correct to speak of the jth treatment total as $\Sigma_i X_{ij}$, such a notational system can become exceedingly awkward. In later analyses where there is more than one independent variable, T_j can be extended to T_{row_i} and T_{column_j} without confusion and without any loss of generality.

In section (b) of Table 11.3 are shown the calculations required to perform a one-way analysis of variance, and some elaboration is required at this point.

SS_{total}

The *SS_{total}*   The *SS_{total}* (read "Sum of Squares total") represents the sum of squares of all of the observations, regardless of which treatment produced them. It is the sum of all the squared observations, minus the sum of the observations squared over N. Thus $SS_{\text{total}} = \Sigma X^2 - (\Sigma X)^2/N$.

SS_{treat}

The *SS_{treat}*   The *SS_{treat}* term is a measure of differences due to treatments, and is directly related to the variability of treatment totals. To calculate SS_{treat} we simply square and sum each of the treatment totals, divide by the number of observations on which each total is based (in this case n) and subtract $(\Sigma X)^2/N$, the correction factor. To gain a better appreciation of exactly what SS_{treat} represents, the formula for it could be written somewhat differently.

$$SS_{\text{treat}} = \frac{\Sigma T_j^2}{n} - \frac{(\Sigma X)^2}{N} = \frac{\Sigma T_j^2}{n} - \frac{(\Sigma T_j)^2}{nk}$$

$$= \frac{\Sigma T_j^2 - \dfrac{(\Sigma T_j)^2}{k}}{n} = \frac{\Sigma (T_j - \bar{T})^2}{n} \qquad (11.4)$$

From Equation 11.4 we can see that SS_{treat} represents the sum of squared deviations of the treatment totals about the mean of the totals ($\bar{T}$), divided by n. The "n" in this case is exactly the same divisor that we discussed in connection with the Central Limit Theorem. Its purpose is eventually to produce an estimate of σ_e^2 rather than of σ_T^2. In all of the sums of squares we are to discuss in this book, the same general principle applies.

General Rule for the Calculation of any Sum of Squares

In conjunction with this discussion of SS_{treat} it is now possible to lay down a general rule for the calculation of any sum of squares (SS) with the possible exception of those we will later calculate by subtraction:

> *For any SS, square the relevant totals, divide by the number of observations on which each total is based, sum the results, and subtract the correction factor $[(\Sigma X)^2/N]$.*

With only a handful of exceptions dealing with the case of more than one variable with unequal numbers of subjects in the different treatment combinations, this rule will allow you to calculate any SS in any problem, no matter how complex the experimental design. This rule applies in the case of SS_{total} as well, although there the divisor is 1 and is not usually shown.

SS_{error}

SS_{error}   In practice SS_{error} is obtained by subtraction. Since it can easily be shown that

$$SS_{total} = SS_{treat} + SS_{error}$$

then it must also be true that $SS_{error} = SS_{total} - SS_{treat}$. This is the procedure presented in Table 11.3. An alternative approach is available, however. As you will recall from earlier discussions, we seek a term which is not influenced by differences among treatments, and therefore a term which represents the variability within each of the three treatments separately. To this end we could calculate a sum of squares within Treatment 1—$SS_{within\ 1}$, and a similar term for the SS within each of the other treatments.

$$SS_{within\ 1} = \left(5^2 + 8^2 + \cdots + 11^2 - \frac{75^2}{9}\right) = 705 - 625 = 80$$

$$SS_{within\ 2} = \left(0^2 + 3^2 + \cdots + 6^2 - \frac{30^2}{9}\right) = 180 - 100 = 80$$

$$SS_{within\ 3} = \left(5^2 + 2^2 + \cdots + 8^2 - \frac{48^2}{9}\right) = 318 - 256 = 62$$

$$SS_{error} = \overline{222}$$

When we sum these individual terms we obtain 222, which agrees exactly with the answer we obtained in Table 11.3.

The Summary Table

Summary table   In part (c) of Table 11.3 is the **Summary table** for the analysis of variance. It is called a summary table for the rather obvious reason that it summarizes a series of calculations, making it possible to tell at a glance what the data have to offer.

Variation

Sources of variation   The first column of the summary table contains the sources of variation—the word **variation** being synonomous with the phrase "sum of squares." As can be seen from the table there are three sources of variation, the total variation, the variation due to treatments (variation among treatment means), and the variation due to error (variation within treatments). These sources reflect the fact that we have partitioned the total sum of squares into two portions, one portion representing variability within the individual groups and the other representing variability between or among the several groups.

df total

df treat
df error

Degrees of freedom   The degrees of freedom column represents the allocation of the total number of degrees of freedom between the two sources of variation. Thus with 26 df overall (i.e., $N - 1$), 2 of these are associated with differences among treatments and the remaining 24 are associated with variability within the treatment groups. The calculation of df is probably the easiest part of our task. The total degrees of freedom (df_{total}) are always $N - 1$, where N is the total number of observations. The degrees of freedom among treatments (df_{treat}) always equal $k - 1$, where k is the number of treatments. The degrees of freedom for error (df_{error}) are most easily thought of as what is left over, although they can be calculated more directly as the sum of the degrees of freedom within each treatment.

Rather than learning a set of equations for calculating degrees of freedom (a most unsatisfactory undertaking), it is important to understand the rationale underlying the allocation of df. SS_{total} is the sum of N squared deviations around one point—the grand mean. The fact that we have taken deviations around this one (estimated) point has cost us 1 df, thus leaving us with $N - 1$ df. SS_{treat} is the sum of k deviations around 1 point (again the grand mean), and again we have lost 1 df in estimating this point, leaving us with $k - 1$ df. SS_{error} represents N deviations about k points (the k treatment means), losing us k df and leaving $N - k = k(n - 1)$ df.

To put this in a slightly different form, the total variability is based on N scores and therefore has $N - 1$ df. The variability of treatment means is based on k scores (means or totals) and therefore has $k - 1$ df. The variability within any one treatment is based on n scores, and thus $n - 1$ df, but since we sum k of these within-treatment terms we will have k times $n - 1 = k(n - 1)$ df.

There is little to be said about the column labeled SS. It simply contains the sums of squares obtained in section b of the table.

Mean squares   The column of mean squares contains our two estimates of σ_e^2. These values are obtained by dividing the sums of squares by their corresponding df. Thus $114/2 = 57$ and $222/24 = 9.25$. We typically do not calculate a MS_{total}, since we have no use for it. If we were to do so, this term would represent the variance of all N observations. While it is true that mean squares are variances, it is important to keep in mind what these terms are variances of. Thus MS_{error} is the (average) variance of the observations within each tretment. However MS_{treat} is not the variance of treatment means or totals, but rather the variance of those means (or totals) corrected by n to produce an estimate of the population variance (σ_e^2).

The F statistic   The last column, headed F, is the most important one in terms of testing the null hypothesis. **F is obtained by dividing MS_{treat} by MS_{error}.** There is a precise way and a sloppy way to explain why this ratio makes sense, and we will start with the latter. As we said earlier, MS_{error} is an estimate of the population variance (σ_e^2). We also said that MS_{treat} is an estimate of population variance (σ_e^2) *if H_0 is true*, but not if it is false. If H_0 is true, then MS_{error} and MS_{treat} are both estimating the same thing, and as such they should be approximately equal. If this is the case, the ratio of one to the other will be approximately 1, give or take a certain amount for sampling error. Thus all we have to do is to compute our ratio and determine whether or not it is close enough to 1 to indicate support for the null hypothesis.

Expected mean squares

So much for the informal way of looking at F. A more precise approach starts with the ***expected mean squares*** for error and treatments. From Equations 11.1 and 11.2 we know

$$E(MS_{error}) = \sigma_e^2$$

$$E(MS_{treat}) = \sigma_e^2 + n\sigma_\tau^2.$$

If we now form the ratio

$$\frac{E(MS_{treat})}{E(MS_{error})} = \frac{\sigma_e^2 + n\sigma_\tau^2}{\sigma_e^2} \tag{11.5}$$

the only time this ratio would have an expectation of 1 is when $\sigma_\tau^2 = 0$—i.e., when H_0 is true and $\mu_1 = \mu_2 = \mu_3 = \mu$.† When $\sigma_\tau^2 > 0$, the expectation will be greater than 1.

The question that remains, however, is how large a ratio will we accept without rejecting H_0 when we use not *expected* mean squares, but mean squares obtained from data and which are subject to sampling error? The answer to this question lies in the fact that one can show that

$$F = \frac{MS_{treat}}{MS_{error}} \tag{11.6}$$

---

† As an aside, it should be noted that the expected value of F is not precisely 1 under H_0 although the expected value of Equation 11.5 is 1 if $\sigma_\tau^2 = 0$. To be exact, under H_0

$$E(F) = \frac{df_{error}}{df_{error-2}}.$$

For all practical purposes nothing is sacrificed by thinking of F as having an expectation of 1 under H_0 and greater than 1 under H_1 (the alternative hypothesis).

is distributed as F on $k-1$ and $k(n-1)$ df. This is the same F distribution we discussed earlier in conjunction with testing the ratio of two variances (which in fact is what we are doing here). It should be noted that the degrees of freedom represent the df associated with the numerator and denominator, respectively.

For our example, $F = 6.162$. We have 2 df for the numerator and 24 df for the denominator, and can enter the F table (Appendix (F)) with these values. From Appendix (F) we find that the critical values for $\alpha = .05$ and $\alpha = .01$ for 2 and 24 df are $F_{.05}(2, 24) = 3.40$ and $F_{.01}(2, 24) = 5.61$. Thus whether we had chosen to work at $\alpha = .05$ or $\alpha = .01$, we would reject H_0 and conclude that there were significant differences among the treatment means.

Example 11.3

Performance Under Stress

The following worked example is intended to offer you a second opportunity to work through the calculations required in the analysis of variance. It is also intended to demonstrate the various formats by which standard computer programs print out their results.

It has been hypothesized that some mild amount of stress actually facilitates performance but that greater amounts of stress are very disruptive. We have designed a study in which 28 subjects are assigned to 4 conditions, with 7 subjects per condition. All subjects perform a pursuit-rotor task in which they are told to keep a pointer on a moving disk. A clock records the amount of time (in seconds) that the stylus is in contact with the disk. The four conditions are (1) no audience, (2) experimenter as audience, (3) peers as audience, (4) senior faculty as audience. The data (time on target), hand calculations, summary table, and computer printout for MINITAB, SPSS, and BMDP appear in Table 11.4.

TABLE 11.4

Hypothetical Data, Calculations, and Computer Printout for Study of Performance on a Motor Task before Different Audiences

(a) Data

	TREATMENT (AUDIENCE)			
None	*Experimenter*	*Peers*	*Faculty*	
45	50	43	41	
50	52	42	42	
43	50	47	46	
48	48	42	49	
55	57	50	41	
59	59	39	37	
45	50	52	50	
$T_j = 345$	366	315	306	

$GT = 1332$
$(\Sigma X)^2/N = 63365.14$

(*b*) Computations

$$SS_{total} = \Sigma X^2 - \frac{(\Sigma X)^2}{N} = (45^2 + 50^2 + \cdots + 37^2 + 50^2) - \frac{1332^2}{28}$$

$$= 64270 - 63365.14 = 904.86$$

$$SS_{treat} = \frac{\Sigma T_j^2}{n} - \frac{(\Sigma X)^2}{N} = \frac{(345^2 + \cdots + 306^2)}{7} - \frac{1332^2}{28} = 63691.71 - 63365.14$$

$$= 326.57$$

$$SS_{error} = SS_{total} - SS_{treat} = 904.86 - 326.57 = 578.29$$

(*c*) Summary table

Source	df	SS	MS	F
Treatments	3	326.57	108.86	4.52
Error	24	578.29	24.10	
Total	27	904.86		

(*d*) MINITAB output

```
-- AOVONEWAY ON DATA IN C1-C4

ANALYSIS OF VARIANCE

DUE TO          DF          SS      MS=SS/DF      F-RATIO
FACTOR           3        326.6       108.9          4.52
ERROR           24        578.3        24.1
TOTAL           27        904.9


LEVEL           N          MEAN      ST. DEV.
C1              7         49.29         5.85
C2              7         52.29         4.11
C3              7         45.00         4.76
C4              7         43.71         4.75

POOLED ST. DEV. =           4.91

INDIVIDUAL 95 PERCENT C. I. FOR LEVEL MEANS
(BASED ON POOLED STANDARD DEVIATION)
        +---------+---------+---------+---------+---------+---------+
C1                            I***********I***********I
C2                                  I***********I***********I
C3              I***********I***********I
C4         I***********I***********I
        +---------+---------+---------+---------+---------+---------+
        39.0      42.0      45.0      48.0      51.0      54.0      57.0


-- STOP

*** Minitab *** Statistics Dept. * Penn. State Univ. * Release 80.1 ***
    *** University of Vermont * Academic Computing Center ***
```

(e) SPSS output

```
                1 RUN NAME        SPSS RUN ON STRESS DATA
                2 VARIABLE LIST   SCORE,GROUP
                3 INPUT FORMAT    FIXED(F2.0,1X,F1.0)
                4 INPUT MEDIUM    STRESS.DAT
                5 N OF CASES      28
                6 ONEWAY          SCORE BY GROUP(1,4)


- - - - - - - - - - - - - - - - - - - - - O N E W A Y - - - - - - - - - - - - - - - - - - - - - - -


     Variable: SCORE

                                    Analysis of Variance

               Source          D.f.  Sum of squares  Mean squares   F-ratio   F-prob.

       Between groups            3       326.5711       108.8570      4.518    0.0120

       Within groups            24       578.2857        24.0952

       Total                    27       904.8568



- - - - - - - - - - - - - - - - - - - - - - - - - - - - - - - - - - - - - - - - - - - - - - - - - -
```

(f) BMDP output

```
   BMDP2V — ANALYSIS OF VARIANCE AND COVARIANCES WITH REPEATED MEASURES.

      PROGRAM CONTROL INFORMATION

   /PROBLEM        TITLE IS 'BMDP2V RUN ON STRESS DATA'.
   /INPUT          VARIABLES ARE 2.
                   FORMAT IS '(F2.0,1X,F1.0)'.
                   CASES ARE 28.
                   UNIT IS 20.
   /VARIABLE       NAMES ARE SCORE,GROUP.
   /DESIGN         DEPENDENT IS SCORE.
                   LEVEL IS 1.
                   NAME IS SCORE.
                   GROUPS = GROUP.
   /END


    PROBLEM TITLE . . . . . . . BMDP2V RUN ON STRESS DATA

      INPUT FORMAT. . . . .
   (F2.0,1X,F1.0)
   GROUP STRUCTURE

      GROUP       COUNT
    * 1.0000       7.
    * 2.0000       7.
    * 3.0000       7.
    * 4.0000       7.
           CELL MEANS  FOR  1-ST DEPENDENT VARIABLE

                                                      MARGINAL
   GROUP   =  * 1.0000   * 2.0000   * 3.0000   * 4.0000

   SCORE      49.28571   52.28571   45.00000   43.71429   47.57143

   COUNT         7          7          7          7          28

   STANDARD DEVIATIONS  FOR  1-ST DEPENDENT VARIABLE

   GROUP   =  * 1.0000   * 2.0000   * 3.0000   * 4.0000

   SCORE       5.85133    4.11154    4.76095    4.75094

   ANALYSIS OF VARIANCE FOR  1-ST
   DEPENDENT VARIABLE — SCORE

          SOURCE              SUM OF     DEGREES OF     MEAN          F         TAIL
                              SQUARES     FREEDOM      SQUARE               PROBABILITY

          MEAN             63365.14286      1      63365.14286    2629.78     0.0000
          GROUP              326.57143      3        108.85714       4.52     0.0120
     1    ERROR              578.28571     24         24.09524
```

11.4   The Structural Model

Structural model

While we will not develop the statistical theory of the analysis of variance in detail, some insight into the underlying **structural model** on which the analysis is based is essential. For the student who wishes a more complete understanding of the theory, there is no better source than Winer (1962 and 1971).

The model in which we are interested states that

$$X_{ij} = \mu + \tau_j + e_{ij}, \tag{11.7}$$

where

$X_{ij} =$ the observation for the ith subject in Treatment$_j$
$\mu =$ the grand mean
$\tau_j =$ the treatment effect associated with the jth treatment
$\quad (\tau_j = \mu_j - \mu)$

and

$e_{ij} =$ the unit of error associated with the ith subject in Treatment$_j$.

Regardless of the truth or falsity of H_0,

$$\mu = (\mu_1 + \mu_2 + \mu_3 + \cdots + \mu_k)/k$$

and $\tau_j = \mu_j - \mu$.

In Equation 11.7 ==we have a model which states that an observation is based upon three components. One component (μ) is constant over all observations and treatments. A second component (τ_j) is constant *within* a treatment, but not between treatments, and a third (e_{ij}) varies across all observations and treatments.== This model is really no more than a way of expressing a very simple idea. If you are a male, your height can be represented as the mean height of the population (66 inches), plus the difference between the mean height of all males and the mean height of the population (+2 inches), plus the difference in height between you and the "average male" (+1 inch). Letting X designate your height, this can be represented as

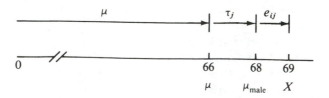

If we add the restriction that the e_{ij} are normally distributed about zero independently of τ_j (which is to say that male heights are normally distributed around μ_{male}), then it is possible, from this simple model, to

$S_x = \sqrt{ms\,error}$

derive the analysis of variance described above. It is important to note, however, just what restrictions we have made. To assume that the e_{ij} are normally distributed is to assume that the populations are normally distributed, since within a treatment the only variable part of the model is e_{ij}. Furthermore to assume that τ_j and e_{ij} are independent is equivalent to the assumption of homogeneity of variance—i.e., variability does not change as a function of treatments. As we examine more complex experimental designs in the analysis of variance, the models will also become more complex. However differences among models are quantitative rather than qualitative, in the sense that we will add more terms, but the basic idea will remain the same.

Our model (i.e., Equation 11.7) leads directly to the statement made earlier that $SS_{total} = SS_{treat} + SS_{error}$, and this in turn produces the analysis of variance. To show this we will start with the basic model

$$X_{ij} = \mu + \tau_j + e_{ij}$$

If we substitute the relevant statistics in place of the parameters we obtain

$$X_{ij} = GM + (\bar{X}_j - GM) + (X_{ij} - \bar{X}_j) \tag{11.8}$$

where GM represents the grand mean. This expression is an identity, as is readily seen by removing the parentheses and collecting terms. Subtracting GM from both sides we have

$$(X_{ij} - GM) = (\bar{X}_j - GM) + (X_{ij} - \bar{X}_j). \tag{11.9}$$

Equation 11.9 states that the deviation of a subject's score from the grand mean is equal to the deviation of his group's mean from the grand mean plus the deviation of his score from the group mean. Equations 11.8 and 11.9 are illustrated geometrically in Figure 11.2. If we square both sides of

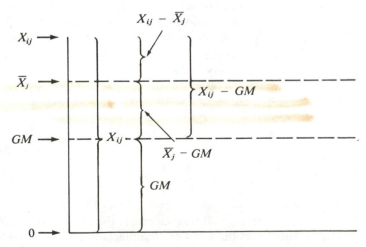

FIGURE 11.2

Geometric representation
of Equations 11.8
and 11.9

Equation 11.9 we obtain

$$(X_{ij} - GM)^2 = (\bar{X}_j - GM)^2 + (X_{ij} - \bar{X}_j)^2 + 2(\bar{X}_j - GM)(X_{ij} - \bar{X}_j).$$

Summing this expression over subjects (i) and treatments (j) produces

$$\Sigma\Sigma_{ij}(X_{ij} - GM)^2 = \Sigma\Sigma_{ij}(\bar{X}_j - GM)^2 + \Sigma\Sigma_{ij}(X_{ij} - \bar{X}_j)^2$$
$$+ 2\Sigma\Sigma_{ij}(\bar{X}_j - GM)(X_{ij} - \bar{X}_j).$$

The term on the far right will be zero, which will thus drop out leaving us with

$$\Sigma\Sigma_{ij}(X_{ij} - GM)^2 = \Sigma\Sigma_{ij}(\bar{X}_j - GM)^2 + \Sigma\Sigma_{ij}(X_{ij} - \bar{X}_j)^2$$

but within any treatment $(\bar{X}_j - GM)$ is a constant, and as a result we have

$$\Sigma\Sigma_{ij}(X_{ij} - GM)^2 = n\Sigma_j(\bar{X}_j - GM)^2 + \Sigma\Sigma_{ij}(X_{ij} - \bar{X}_j)^2$$
$$\text{SS}_{total} \quad = \quad \text{SS}_{treat} \quad + \quad \text{SS}_{error}.$$

Thus we have shown that the total sum of squares is completely partitioned into SS_{treat} and SS_{error}. From here we could proceed to obtain our mean squares and F.

11.5 Unequal Sample Sizes

Most experiments are originally designed with the idea of having the same number of observations in each treatment. Frequently, however, things do not work out that way. Animals often die during an experiment from causes which have nothing to do with the treatment. Subjects fail to arrive for testing, or are eliminated for failure to follow instructions. There is even a case in the literature where an animal was eliminated from the study for repeatedly biting the experimenter. Moreover, studies conducted on intact groups, such as school classes, have to contend with the fact that such groups nearly always vary in size.

If the sample sizes are not equal, the analysis discussed earlier is not appropriate without modification. For the case of one independent variable, however, this modification is relatively minor.

In Equation 11.4 we defined

$$\text{SS}_{treat} = \frac{\Sigma T_j^2}{n} - \frac{(\Sigma X)^2}{N}.$$

We were able to divide each of the T_j^2 (and therefore ΣT_j^2) by n, since n was common to all treatments. If the sample sizes differ, however, and we defined n_j as the number of subjects in the jth treatment ($\Sigma n_j = N$), we can rewrite Equation 11.4 as

$$SS_{treat} = \sum \frac{T_j^2}{n_j} - \frac{(\sum X)^2}{N}$$

(11.10)

which, when all n_j are equal, reduces to Equation 11.4.

To appreciate what this formula is doing, we can speak in terms of means rather than totals, and state that Equation 11.10 is exactly equivalent to

$$SS_{treat} = \sum n_j (\bar{X}_j - GM)^2.$$

(11.11)

(The proof of this expression is not difficult, and it is left to the student.) Equation 11.11 shows us that with unequal *ns* the deviation of each treatment mean from the grand mean is weighted by the sample size. Thus the larger the size of one sample relative to the others, the more it will contribute to $SS_{treat}.$[†]

An example of an analysis with unequal sample sizes is presented in Table 11.5. In this analysis the only important difference from the one presented in Table 11.3 is the calculation of SS_{treat}. From Appendix (F) it can be seen that $F_{.05}(3, 12) = 3.26$. Since $F_{obt} > F_{.05}$, we would reject H_0 and would conclude that we have evidence to support the hypothesis that there are real differences among the treatment means.

TABLE 11.5

Calculation of One-Way Analysis of Variance with Unequal *ns*

(a) Data

	TREATMENTS				
	1	*2*	*3*	*4*	
	8	9	6	8	
	3	10	1	6	
	6	7	3	10	
	2	5		9	
		12			
$T_j =$	19	43	10	33	$GT = 105$
$n_j =$	4	5	3	4	$N = 16$
$\bar{X}_j =$	4.75	8.60	3.33	8.25	$GM = 6.563$

(b) Computations

$$SS_{total} = \sum X^2 - \frac{(\sum X)^2}{N} = 839 - \frac{105^2}{16} = 839 - 689.063 = 149.937$$

$$SS_{treat} = \sum \frac{T_j^2}{n_j} - \frac{(\sum X)^2}{N} = \frac{19^2}{4} + \frac{43^2}{5} + \frac{10^2}{3} + \frac{33^2}{4} - \frac{105^2}{16} = 765.633 - 689.063$$

$$= 76.570$$

$$SS_{error} = SS_{total} - SS_{treat} = 149.937 - 76.570 = 73.367$$

[†] If there is some good reason to weight all groups equally, it is possible to use the harmonic mean of $n(\bar{n}_h)$ in place of n_j in Equation 11.10 (Winer, 1971).

(c) Summary table

Source	df	SS	MS	F
Treatments	3	76.570	25.523	4.174
Error	12	73.367	6.114	
Total	15	149.937		

11.6 Violation of Assumptions

Homoscedasticity

As we have seen, the analysis of variance is based upon the assumptions of normality and homogeneity of variance (sometimes referred to as *homoscedasticity*). In practice, however, the analysis of variance is a very robust statistical procedure, and the assumptions can frequently be violated with relatively minor effects. For studies dealing with this problem, the reader is referred to Box (1953, 1954a, 1954b), Boneau (1960), and Bradley (1964).

In general, if the populations can be assumed to be either symmetric or at least similar in shape (e.g., all negatively skewed), and if the largest variance is no more than 4 or 5 times the smallest, the analysis of variance is most likely to be valid. It is important to note, however, that heterogeneity of variance and unequal sample sizes do not mix. If you have reason to anticipate unequal variances, make every effort to keep your sample sizes as equal as possible.

Given that you are not willing to ignore the heterogeneity or non-normality in your data, there are alternative ways of handling the data. Box (1954a) has shown that with unequal variances the appropriate F distribution against which to compare F_{obt} is a regular F with altered degrees of freedom. If we define the true critical value of F (adjusted for heterogeneity of variance) as F'_α, then Box has shown that

F'_α

$$F_\alpha(1, n-1) \geq F'_\alpha \geq F_\alpha(k-1, k(n-1)).$$

In other words, the true critical value of F lies somewhere between the critical value of F on 1 and $(n-1)$ df, and the critical value of F on $(k-1)$ and $k(n-1)$ df. This latter limit is the critical value we would use if we had normality and homogeneity. If $F_{obt} > F_\alpha(1, n-1)$, the means are significantly different regardless of the heterogeneity of variance. The only difficulty is that this upper limit of F'_α, which is equal to $F_\alpha(1, n-1)$, is extremely conservative. We will have more to say about this problem later in connection with more complex designs.

An alternative method of handling unequal variances and non-normality is by applying some transformation to the data. Some of the most common transformations are the square root ($X' = \sqrt{X}$), logarithmic ($X' =$

log X), inverse $(X' = 1/X)$ and arcsin $(X' = 2 \arcsin \sqrt{X})$. Variants of these particular transformations are sometimes recommended. An excellent discussion of these transformations, and variants of them, is given by Kirk (1968). As a crude rule of thumb, **square root**, **logarithmic**, and **inverse transformations** are useful when the mean and standard deviation (or variance) are proportional, i.e.,

Square root transformation
Logarithmic transformation
Inverse transformation

$$\frac{\bar{X}_1}{s_1} \simeq \frac{\bar{X}_2}{s_2} \simeq \frac{\bar{X}_3}{s_3}$$

Arcsin transformation

while the **arcsin transformation** is useful when the means and variances are proportional and the data are in the form of percentages or proportions.

It might be worthwhile to point out again that heterogeneity of variance might well be viewed as an experimental finding rather than a nuisance. It might be quite useful to know that Treatment 1 produced a marked increase in variance over the other treatments. In this connection a simple test on the largest vs. the smallest of several variances is afforded by

$$F_{\max} = \frac{s^2_{\text{largest}}}{s^2_{\text{smallest}}}. \tag{11.12}$$

F_{max}

The tables of $F_{\max}$ are given in Winer (1971), where the entry points in the table are the number of treatments (k) and the df for any one variance $(n - 1)$.

11.7 Fixed vs. Random Models

In the discussion up to this point we have not said anything about the levels of our independent variable, but have simply spoken of "treatments." In fact if you think about it there are at least two different ways in which we could obtain the levels of the treatment variable; we could deliberately select them or we could sample them at random. The way in which the levels are derived has implications for the generalizations we might draw from our study.

Assume that we were hired as consultants by the Food and Drug Administration and asked to run a study to compare the four most popular pain relievers. In this case we will have four treatment levels (corresponding to the four pain relievers) and those levels were selected by us. In a sense the treatment levels actually used have exhausted the levels of interest, and if we chose to rerun the study we would use the same treatments. The important point here is that the levels are in fact *fixed* in the sense that they do not change randomly from one replication of the study to another. The

Fixed model

analysis of such an experiment is referred to as a ***fixed model*** analysis of variance.

Now assume that we were again hired by the FDA, but they merely told us to compare a number of pain relievers. In this case it would make sense to *randomly* select the pain relievers to be compared from the population of all available pain relievers. Here the treatment levels are the result of a random process and the population of interest with respect to pain relievers is quite large (probably over 100). Moreover if we replicated this study we would again choose the brands randomly, and would probably have a whole new set of brands to compare. Because of the process by which treatment levels are obtained, we speak of treatments as a random variable and of the analysis as a *random model* analysis of variance.

Random model

We will have more to say about fixed and random models as we go on. The important point at this time is that a fixed model refers to a situation in which the treatment levels are deliberately selected and would remain constant from one replication to another, while a random model refers to the situation in which treatment levels are obtained by some random process and would be expected to vary across replications. Within a one-way analysis of variance the distinction is largely irrelevant (except when dealing with the magnitude of an effect), but it becomes quite important in more complex designs.

11.8   *Magnitude of Experimental Effect*

The fact that an analysis of variance has produced a significant F simply tells us that there are differences among the means of treatments which cannot be attributed to error. It says nothing about whether or not these differences are of any practical importance. For this reason we must look beyond the value of F to define an additional measure reflecting the "importance" of the difference. This raises the immediate question of what we mean by *importance* and how it is to be measured. At this point we can only give the general answer that our measure of importance will be a term analogous to r^2. In other words we will measure importance by calculating how much of the overall variability can be attributed to the treatment effect.

Magnitude of the experimental effect

At last count I have found in the literature at least five different measures of the *magnitude of the experimental effect*—all different and most claiming to be less biased than some other measure. In this section we will discuss only the two most common measures (η^2 and ω^2), since they have the strongest claim to our attention.

Eta-squared (η^2)

Eta-squared (η^2)

This is probably the oldest measure of the strength of an experimental effect. While one could easily argue that it is certainly not the best, it has several points to recommend it. As you will see, *eta-squared* has a certain intuitive appeal. Moreover, it forms a strong link between the traditional analysis of variance and multiple regression, as we will see in Chapter 16.

Curvilinear
regression

In many textbooks η is defined as the correlation coefficient associated with **curvilinear regression**—i.e., regression where the best fitting line is not a straight line. Suppose that we were to propose calculating the correlation between treatment levels 1, 2, 3, and 4 and the dependent variable for the example in Table 11.5. The first criticism that would be raised is that the numbers 1 to 4 are merely labels for the treatments, and bear no relationship to anything. True enough, but no big deal. The next argument raised might be that the treatments do not represent any particular ordering on some underlying scale and therefore we do not know in what order to place the treatments if we were to plot the data. Again, true enough, and again no big deal. You might even argue that the regression might not be linear. True again, but we can get around this problem by calling the coefficient η instead of r. Having cavalierly brushed aside all of the objections, we set about plotting the data as shown in Figure 11.3. As you may recall from high school (but probably don't), a kth order polynomial will exactly fit $k + 1$ points, which means that if we did try to fit a third order polynomial to the four points represented by the treatment means, it would fit perfectly. We

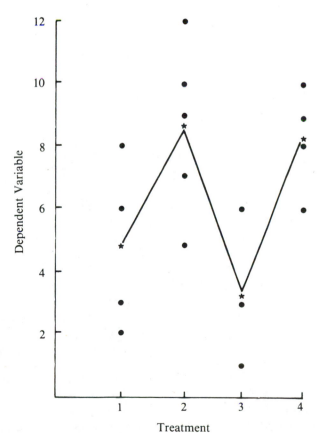

FIGURE 11.3

Scatter diagram
of data in
Table 11.5

do not particularly care what the equation would look like, but we can draw the line (as in Figure 11.3) simply by connecting the array means.

You should recall from Chapter 9 that there is more than one way to calculate r. One definition, in terms of parameters, is

$$\rho^2 = \frac{\sigma_Y^2 - \sigma_{Y \cdot X}^2}{\sigma_Y^2}$$

where $\sigma_Y^2 = \Sigma(Y_{ij} - \mu_Y)^2/N$ and $\sigma_{Y \cdot X}^2 = \Sigma(Y_{ij} - \hat{Y}_j)^2/N$. If we are concerned solely with our data, rather than with generalizing to the population, then the data represent the population of interest and $\bar{Y} = \mu_Y$. Furthermore, since the regression line passes through the array means, for each array $\hat{Y}_j = \bar{Y}_j$. These simplifications leave us with

$$\eta^2 = \frac{\Sigma(Y_{ij} - \bar{Y})^2 - \Sigma(Y_{ij} - \bar{Y}_j)^2}{\Sigma(Y_{ij} - \bar{Y})^2}$$

$$= \frac{SS_{total} - SS_{error}}{SS_{total}}$$

$$\eta^2 = \frac{SS_{treat}}{SS_{total}}. \hspace{3cm} (11.13)$$

We have now defined η^2 in terms of the sums of squares of our analysis of variance. Applying η^2 to Table 11.3 (instead of to Table 11.5)

$$\eta^2 = \frac{SS_{treat}}{SS_{total}} = \frac{114}{336} = .339.$$

Equation 11.13 provides a simple way to estimate the maximum squared correlation between the independent variable and the dependent variable. Its derivation also points out the fact that it can be treated as any other squared correlation coefficient, indicating the proportion of variation accounted for by the independent variable. For our data, 33.9% of the variation in the dependent variable can be attributable to the treatment effect. The student should also note that when there are only two treatments, η^2 is reduced to r_{pb}^2, the index used in relation to t.

It is important to realize that η^2 assumes that the regression line passes through the individual treatment means. When the data are treated as a population, the assumption is correct. When the data are treated as a sample from some larger population, bias is introduced. Since these means are really sample means, they are subject to sampling error, and η^2 will be biased upward—whatever the *true* regression line through the population means, it will probably not pass exactly through each sample mean, and thus we have underestimated $\sigma_{Y \cdot X}^2$. While all measures we discuss will be biased, η^2 is probably the most biased. Thus though it has the advantage of simplicity and is intuitively appealing, we will generally prefer to use a less biased estimate when our interest is in making general statements about our variables. If we are only interested in making statements about our particular set of data, or if we just want a rough idea of the magnitude of effect, then η^2 is a perfectly good measure.

Omega-squared (ω^2)

An alternative, and for most purposes better, method of assessing the magnitude of the experimental effect is **omega-squared (ω^2)**. This statistic has been discussed by Hays (1963) and developed more extensively by Fleiss (1969), Vaughan & Corballis (1969), and Dodd & Schultz (1973). The approach essentially relies on the underlying structural model.

Our estimate of ω^2 (designated $\hat{\omega}^2$) will depend upon whether we are using a random or fixed model, as previously defined, and we will first consider the solution from the point of view of a random model, since this is somewhat easier to see.

Random model   Assume that we start from the following random model

$$X_{ij} = \mu + \tau_j + e_{ij}.$$

We have already seen in Equations 11.1 and 11.2 that in this case

$$E(\text{MS}_{\text{error}}) = \sigma_e^2$$

$$E(\text{MS}_{\text{treat}}) = \sigma_e^2 + n\sigma_\tau^2.$$

We will define

$$\omega^2 = \frac{\sigma_\tau^2}{\sigma_\tau^2 + \sigma_e^2}. \tag{11.14}$$

In other words ω^2 is defined as the ratio of the treatment variance to the sum of the treatment and error variance. While we cannot measure σ_τ^2 and σ_e^2 directly, it is easy to estimate them (the estimates being represented by $\hat{\sigma}_\tau^2$ and $\hat{\sigma}_e^2$). Based on Equations 11.1 and 11.2

$$\hat{\sigma}_e^2 = \text{MS}_{\text{error}}$$

$$\hat{\sigma}_\tau^2 = \frac{\text{MS}_{\text{treat}} - \text{MS}_{\text{error}}}{n}.$$

If we let $\hat{\omega}^2$ represent an estimate of ω^2,

$$\hat{\omega}^2 = \frac{\hat{\sigma}_\tau^2}{\hat{\sigma}_\tau^2 + \hat{\sigma}_e^2} = \frac{\dfrac{\text{MS}_{\text{treat}} - \text{MS}_{\text{error}}}{n}}{\dfrac{\text{MS}_{\text{treat}} - \text{MS}_{\text{error}}}{n} + \text{MS}_{\text{error}}}$$

$$\hat{\omega}^2 = \frac{\text{MS}_{\text{treat}} - \text{MS}_{\text{error}}}{\text{MS}_{\text{treat}} + (n-1)\text{MS}_{\text{error}}}.$$

For the data in Table 11.3, assuming that treatment levels were sampled at random

$$\hat{\omega}^2 = \frac{MS_{treat} - MS_{error}}{MS_{treat} + (n-1)MS_{error}} = \frac{57 - 9.25}{57 + 8(9.25)}$$

$$\hat{\omega}^2 = .364.$$

We can now say that 36.4% of the variance in this study can be attributable to treatment effects.

Fixed model   When we move to the fixed model the situation becomes slightly more complicated. We will still define ω^2 as $\hat{\sigma}_\tau^2/(\hat{\sigma}_\tau^2 + \hat{\sigma}_e^2)$, but our estimate of σ_τ^2 is going to be somewhat different. When we discussed expected mean squares earlier we said that

$$E(MS_{treat}) = \sigma_e^2 + \frac{n\Sigma\tau_j^2}{k-1} = \sigma_e^2 + n\sigma_\tau^2$$

where $\tau_j = \mu_j - \mu$. In fact, with a fixed model we have exhausted our treatment populations and $\Sigma\tau_j^2/k$, not $\Sigma\tau_j^2/(k-1)$, is equal to σ_τ^2. In other words, $\Sigma\tau_j^2/(k-1)$ should not really be denoted as σ_τ^2, although we do so by convention. If we really want an estimate of $\sigma_\tau^2 = \Sigma\tau_j^2/k$, we are going to have to manipulate our $E(MS_{treat})$ to accomplish this.
   Define

$$\theta_\tau^2 = \frac{\Sigma\tau_j^2}{k-1}$$

and

$$\sigma_\tau^2 = \frac{\Sigma\tau_j^2}{k} = \frac{k-1}{k}(\theta_\tau^2).$$

Now σ_τ^2 is our measure of variance among treatment means.

$$E(MS_{treat}) = \sigma_e^2 + \frac{n\Sigma\tau^2}{k-1} = \sigma_e^2 + n\theta_\tau^2 = \sigma_e^2 + n\left(\frac{k}{k-1}\right)\sigma_\tau^2$$

We can then arrive at an estimate of σ_τ^2.

$$\hat{\sigma}_\tau^2 = \frac{(k-1)(MS_{treat} - \sigma_e^2)}{nk}$$

Since $E(MS_{error}) = \sigma_e^2$,

$$\hat{\sigma}_\tau^2 = \frac{(k-1)(MS_{treat} - MS_{error})}{nk}.$$

Since $\hat{\sigma}_\tau^2$ is our estimate of treatment variance, we again define

$$\omega^2 = \frac{\sigma_\tau^2}{\sigma_\tau^2 + \sigma_e^2}.$$

Replacing σ_τ^2 and σ_e^2 by their estimates we obtain

$$\hat{\omega}^2 = \frac{\hat{\sigma}_\tau^2}{\hat{\sigma}_\tau^2 + \hat{\sigma}_e^2}$$

$$= \frac{\dfrac{(k-1)(MS_{treat} - MS_{error})}{nk}}{\dfrac{(k-1)(MS_{treat} - MS_{error})}{nk} + MS_{error}}$$

$$= \frac{(k-1)(MS_{treat} - MS_{error})}{(k-1)MS_{treat} - (k-1)MS_{error} + nkMS_{error}}$$

$$= \frac{SS_{treat} - (k-1)MS_{error}}{SS_{treat} + (k(n-1)+1)MS_{error}}$$

$$= \frac{SS_{treat} - (k-1)MS_{error}}{SS_{treat} + k(n-1)MS_{error} + MS_{error}}$$

$$\hat{\omega}^2 = \frac{SS_{treat} - (k-1)MS_{error}}{SS_{total} + MS_{error}}. \qquad (11.15)$$

Applying Equation 11.15 to our data from Table 11.3 we have

$$\hat{\omega}^2 = \frac{114 - 2(9.25)}{336 + 9.25} = \frac{95.5}{345.25} = .277.$$

The value of $\hat{\omega}^2$ in this case (.277) is not much different from the value of .364 we obtained for the random model. This will usually be the case, especially for high levels of accountable variance. Since it is generally the case that when we have only one independent variable we will usually have a fixed model, Equation 11.15 is the more commonly used. When we investigate more complex designs, however, random variables will become more common.

We have discussed two measures of the degree of association between the dependent and independent variables, with $\hat{\omega}^2$ having two forms depending upon the underlying structural model. These are only three of many that have been put forth. In general, $\hat{\omega}^2$ is probably the best measure. Its derivation is relatively straightforward and it is amenable to the treatment of both fixed and random variables. Although all of these measures are biased, η^2 is more biased than the others. If you apply a partial correction for bias to η^2, you come out with something which is very closely related to what is called the **squared intraclass correlation**, which has been put *Squared intraclass* forward as yet another measure of the magnitude of effect. In fact the *correlation* intraclass correlation is nothing but ω^2 for the random model, thus providing some sort of link between the traditional η^2 and the newer, more appropriate ω^2. For all practical purposes, the choice among measures is generally not very important. For our data, for example, the estimates ranged from .277

to .364, a rather small difference in terms of deciding whether an effect is important in terms of accountable variation.

11.9 Power

Estimation of power in the analysis of variance is more or less a straight-forward extension of power analysis for t, although the notation is somewhat different. We will define a statistic (ϕ') estimating the expected differences among the μ_j, derive a second statistic (ϕ) which is a function of n and ϕ',

Noncentral F   and then calculate power from tables of the **noncentral F** distribution. A more complete treatment of power can be found in Cohen (1969).

We already know that

$$\frac{E(\text{MS}_{\text{treat}})}{E(\text{MS}_{\text{error}})} = \frac{\sigma_e^2 + n\Sigma\tau_j^2/(k-1)}{\sigma_e^2}.$$

If H_0 is true, $\Sigma\tau_j^2 = 0$ and the ratio $F = \text{MS}_{\text{treat}}/\text{MS}_{\text{error}}$ will be distributed as the usual (central) F distribution. If H_0 is false, this ratio will depart from the central F distribution by a factor of

$$\frac{n\Sigma\tau_j^2}{\sigma_e^2(k-1)}.$$

In other words, the $E(F)$ will be approximately equal to

$$1 + \frac{n\Sigma\tau_j^2}{\sigma_e^2(k-1)}$$

Noncentrality parameter (λ)   rather than 1. One common approach is to define a **noncentrality parameter**, lambda (λ):

$$\lambda = \frac{n\Sigma\tau_j^2}{\sigma_e^2}.$$

It is then possible to develop tables of the noncentral F distribution in terms of λ as our noncentrality parameter. However most tables are set up somewhat differently, based upon

Phi (ϕ)
$$\phi = \sqrt{\frac{\lambda}{k}} = \sqrt{\frac{n\Sigma\tau_j^2}{k\sigma_e^2}}$$

as the noncentrality parameter. The difficulty with either approach is that it makes it difficult to separate n from the rest, thereby making it more difficult to calculate required sample sizes. To circumvent this difficulty we will define

(ϕ')
$$\phi' = \sqrt{\frac{\Sigma\tau_j^2}{k\sigma_e^2}}$$

and then define

$$\phi = \phi'\sqrt{n}.$$

The first problem concerns the estimate of ϕ'. Since $\tau_j = \mu_j - \mu$, we will have to estimate the various values of μ_j, or at least the differences $(\mu_j - \mu)$. This can be done either on the basis of past research or on the basis of deciding what minimum differences would be considered important.

Suppose that we wished to investigate differences in IQ among different types of students. We plan to take 15 students classified by their teachers as currently unmanageable, 15 classified as potentially unmanageable, and 15 classified as normal. We have some reason to expect (or hope for) mean IQs of 95, 100, and 105 for the three groups, respectively. Then

$$\mu = \frac{\Sigma\mu_j}{k} = \frac{(95 + 100 + 105)}{3} = 100$$

and

$$\Sigma\tau_j^2 = (95 - 100)^2 + (100 - 100)^2 + (105 - 100)^2 = 50.$$

In this particular case we will have no trouble estimating σ_e^2, since we know that the variance of IQ scores $= 15^2 = 225$. In other cases we might have to go back to previous data or to the literature for our estimate. We now are in a position to estimate ϕ'.

$$\phi' = \sqrt{\frac{\Sigma\tau_j^2}{k\sigma_e^2}} = \sqrt{\frac{50}{3(225)}} = .272.$$

Each of our samples contains 15 students, so $n = 15$.

$$\phi = \phi'\sqrt{n} = .272\sqrt{15} = 1.053.$$

In order to use the table of the noncentral F distribution we must enter it with ϕ, f_t, and f_e, where f_t is the df for treatments and f_e is the df for error. For our example, $f_t = 2$ and $f_e = 3(15 - 1) = 42$. Thus we enter the table with $\phi = 1.05$, $f_t = 2$, and $f_e = 42$. Since this table (Appendix (ncF)) does not contain all possible values of ϕ, f_t, and f_e, we will either have to interpolate or else round off to the nearest value. For purposes of illustration we will round everything off in the conservative direction. Thus we will take $\phi = 1.0$, $f_t = 2$, and $f_e = 30$. The tabled entry for $F(2, 30; 1.0)$ is .71 for $\alpha = .05$. This entry is β, the probability of a Type II error. Since power $= 1 - \beta$, the power for our proposed experiment is $1 - .71 = .29$.

If we wish a greater degree of power, the most obvious approach is to increase our sample size. To calculate the required sample sizes we simply need to work the problem backwards. Suppose that we desire power $= .80$. Then $\beta = .20$, and we simply need to find that value of ϕ for which $\beta = .20$. A minor complication arises since we cannot enter Appendix (ncF) without f_e, and we can not calculate f_e without knowing n. This is not really a serious problem, however, because whether f_e is 30, 50, 180, or whatever will not make any really important difference in the tables. We will therefore make the arbitrary decision that $f_e = \infty$, since we already know that it will have to be greater than 30. With $f_t = 2$, $f_e = \infty$, and $\beta = .20$, we find from the table that ϕ will have to be 1.8.

Since

$$\phi = \phi'\sqrt{n}$$

then

$$n = \phi^2/\phi'^2$$
$$= 1.8^2/.272^2$$
$$= 44.$$

Thus we would need 44 students per group to have an 80% chance of rejecting H_0 if it is false to the extent that we believe it to be.

For those who were a little disturbed by arbitrarily setting $f_e = \infty$, it might be instructive to calculate the power if $n = 44$.

$$\phi = .272\sqrt{44} = 1.8$$
$$f_t = 2$$
$$f_e = 3(43) = 129$$

From Appendix (ncF) for $F(2, 129; 1.80)$ we see that β is between .24 (for $f_e = 30$) and .20 (for $f_e = \infty$). Thus our power is between .76 and .80, which is close enough for our purposes. Alternatively, Winer (1971) provides charts for the calculation of n given ϕ, but for these charts the visual interpolation required will lead to no greater accuracy than the recommendations given above. After all, considering the guesswork which has gone into estimating ϕ', who are we to get all worked up over whether power is really .78 or .79?

Cohen (1969) has made several interesting proposals for estimating ϕ without having to specify $(\mu_j - \mu)$. For a thorough discussion of these techniques the reader is referred to Cohen's book. However, one very simple technique can be discussed here. If we let η^2 represent the percentage of variance accounted for by the treatment effect, Cohen shows that

$$\phi' = \sqrt{\frac{\eta^2}{1 - \eta^2}}.$$

Thus if we have 15 subjects in each of three treatments and expect (or hope that) the treatments to account for 25% of the variance,

$$\phi' = \sqrt{\frac{.25}{1 - .25}} = .577$$

$$\phi = \phi'\sqrt{n} = .577\sqrt{15} = 2.235.$$

With $f_t = 2$, $f_e = 42$, and $\phi = 2.24$, at $\alpha = .05$, power is somewhere around .92.

As an additional aid, but one to be used with reluctance, Cohen has defined a small effect as $\phi' = .10$, a medium effect as $\phi' = .25$, and a large effect as $\phi' = .40$. These are only crude and rather arbitrary guidelines, although they should be useful when all else fails.

11.10 Summary

The analysis of variance is one of our most powerful tools. In this chapter we began by elaborating the logic behind the analysis, and only then turned to the calculations. The logic is far more important than the calculations. After developing the structural model assumed to lie behind the data, we considered the analysis of experiments having unequal sample sizes, and the effects of violations of the assumptions on which the analysis of variance is based. Fixed and random models were briefly discussed, and these will become more important in later chapters. The magnitude of effect is an important concept, and we saw alternative ways by which it could be assessed. Finally, we extended the discussion of power begun in Chapter 8 by considering power calculations for the analysis of variance.

Exercises for Chapter 11

11.1 To investigate maternal behavior of laboratory rats we separate the rat pup from the mother and record the time required for the mother to retrieve the pup. We run the study with 5, 20, and 35 day old pups, move the pups a fixed distance from the mother, and record the retrieval time in seconds. The data are given below, where there are six pups per group.

5 days:	15	10	25	15	20	18
20 days:	30	15	20	25	23	20
35 days:	40	35	50	43	45	40

Run a one-way analysis of variance with $\alpha = .05$.

11.2 It has been hypothesized that the person paying the bill orders a less expensive meal than his/her partner. To avoid confusing the issue we chose only same sex pairs and record the price of the meal for only one of the people in each pair. Subjects are assigned to groups on the basis of whether or not the subject eventually picks up the tab. The dependent variable is the cost of the entrée.

Payee:	9.50	8.75	10.25	9.00	9.25
Nonpayee:	10.75	9.50	8.50	10.50	12.25

a. Run the analysis of variance on these two groups.

b.   Run an independent *t* test on the same data and compare the results.

c.   Why was it necessary to insure that we only had data on one member of each pair? (Answer with respect to what you know about *t*.)

11.3   It might be predicted that consumer buying behavior would vary with the location of the product in the store, even if the product in question has a high degree of brand loyalty. We therefore look at the purchases of well known and unknown brands of cigarettes when they are in their usual place behind the counter and when they are prominently displayed next to the cash register. The dependent variable is the number of packs of each brand sold per day. (We will ignore the fact that this design might better be analyzed by techniques to be discussed in Chapter 13.)

Known/Usual:	15	23	18	16	25	29	17
Known/Prominent:	24	14	15	19	30	26	18
Unknown/Usual:	10	5	8	12	13	6	10
Unknown/Prominent:	15	13	10	17	18	11	15

a.   Run one-way analysis of variance.

b.   Now run a one-way on Groups 1 and 3 combined vs. Groups 2 and 4 combined. What question does this test ask?

11.4   Refer to Exercise 11.1. Assume that for reasons beyond our control the data for the last pup in the 5 day group could not be used, nor could the data for the last two pups in the 35 day group. Rerun the analysis of variance using the remaining data.

11.5   Refer to Exercise 11.2. Suppose that we collected two additional data points for the payee group. The data now look like

Payee:	9.50	8.75	10.25	9.00	9.25	11.75	9.00
Nonpayee:	10.75	9.50	8.50	10.50	12.25		

a.   Rerun the analysis of variance.

b.   Run an independent *t* without pooling the variance.

c.   Run a dependent *t* after pooling the variance.

d.   Which of these values of *t* corresponds (after squaring) to the *F* in part *a*?

11.6   Calculate η^2 and $\hat{\omega}^2$ for the data in Exercise 11.2. Would you assume a fixed or a random model to obtain $\hat{\omega}^2$?

11.7   Would you assume that the experimental design in Exercise 11.1 represents a fixed or a random model?

11.8   Some words in a prose passage are particularly important for the meaning of the passage while other words are of no real importance. If it is hypothesized that good readers read primarily the important words, then if these words were capitalized, while the other words were not, it might be expected that the passage could be read more rapidly. We define three groups. Group 1 is asked to read the standard passage with no capitalization. Group 2 reads the same passage in which a random set of words is capitalized. Group 3 has a passage in which the key words are capitalized. The dependent variable is the time to read the passage (in seconds).

	n	*Mean*	*Standard Deviation*
Group 1	10	30.2	6.21
Group 2	10	38.3	7.55
Group 3	10	25.6	5.75

a. Run the analysis and draw whatever conclusions seem warranted.

b. Point out at least one major failing in the design of this experiment as it relates to the hypothesis that *good* readers look for key words.

c. What does rejection of H_0 mean in this case?

11.9 Suppose that the data in Exercise 11.8 had shown a standard deviation of 20.75 for Group 3. What could we conclude and why?

11.10 What would we conclude if we had the same means and standard deviations in Exercise 11.8, but if the *n*s had each been 5 instead of 10?

11.11 Assuming that Exercise 11.10 still produced a significant difference, do you have more or less faith in the effect? Why?

11.12 The computer output on page 273 is from a BMDP analysis of the data in Exercise 11.1.

a. Compare these results with the ones that you obtained in Exercise 11.1.

b. What does the sum of squares labeled MEAN represent? (*Hint*: You found the same numerical value when you solved the problem by hand.)

11.13 Obtain a computer solution to Exercise 11.2 and compare it with your answer. (Obtain solutions for both *F* and *t*.)

11.14 The computer output on page 273 is from an SPSS analysis of the data in Exercise 11.3.

a. Compare these results with the ones that you obtained in Exercise 11.3*a*.

b. How do you interpret the column labeled *F*-prob.?

11.15 Write an appropriate statistical model for Exercise 11.1.

11.16 Write an appropriate statistical model for Exercise 11.2.

11.17 Write an appropriate statistical model for Exercise 11.3. Save this model for later use in Chapter 13.

11.18 When *F* is less than 1.00 we usually write <1 rather than the actual value. What meaning can be attached to an *F* appreciably less than 1. Can we speak intelligibly about an F "significantly" less than 1? Include the $E(MS)$ in your answer.

11.19   Howell and Huessy (1980) classified children as exhibiting (or not exhibiting) hyperkinetic-type behaviors in 2nd, 4th, and 5th grade. The subjects were then sorted on the basis of year(s) in which the individual was classed as hyperkinetic. We then looked at grade point average when these people were seniors in high school. The data are given below in terms of mean grade point average per group.

	Never Hyper.	2nd Only	4th Only	2 & 4	5th Only	2 & 5	4 & 5	2, 4, & 5
$\bar{X}_i$	2.6774	1.6123	1.9975	2.0287	1.7000	1.9000	1.8986	1.4225
s_i	.9721	1.0097	.7642	.5461	.8788	1.0318	.3045	.5884
n_i	201	13	12	8	14	9	7	8

Run the analysis of variance and draw the appropriate conclusion.

11.20   Rerun the analysis in Exercise 11.19 leaving out the *never identified as hyper.* group. In what way does this analysis clarify the interpretation of the data?

EXERCISE 11.12

```
BMDP2V - ANALYSIS OF VARIANCE AND COVARIANCES WITH REPEATED MEASURES.

   PROGRAM CONTROL INFORMATION

/PROBLEM       TITLE IS 'BMDP2V ANALYSIS OF DATA IN EXERCISE 11.1'.
/INPUT         VARIABLES ARE 2.
               FORMAT IS '(F2.0,F3.0)'.
               CASES ARE 18.
               UNIT IS 20.
/VARIABLES     NAMES ARE GROUP,SCORE.
/DESIGN        DEPENDENT IS SCORE.
               GROUPS ARE GROUP.
/END


   PROBLEM TITLE . . . . . . . BMDP2V ANALYSIS OF DATA IN EXERCISE 11.1


GROUP STRUCTURE

  GROUP         COUNT
  * 1.0000       6.
  * 2.0000       6.
  * 3.0000       6.

        CELL MEANS   FOR 1-ST DEPENDENT VARIABLE

                                          MARGINAL
GROUP   =  * 1.0000    * 2.0000    * 3.0000

SCORE      17.16667   22.16667   42.16667   27.16667

COUNT          6          6          6        18

STANDARD DEVIATIONS  FOR  1-ST DEPENDENT VARIABLE

GROUP   =  * 1.0000    * 2.0000    * 3.0000

SCORE       5.11534    5.11534    5.11534

ANALYSIS OF VARIANCE FOR  1-ST
DEPENDENT VARIABLE - SCORE
```

SOURCE	SUM OF SQUARES	DEGREES OF FREEDOM	MEAN SQUARE	F	TAIL PROBABILITY
MEAN	13284.50000	1	13284.50000	507.69	0.0000
GROUP	2100.00000	2	1050.00000	40.13	0.0000
1 ERROR	392.50000	15	26.16667		

EXERCISE 11.14

```
            1 RUN NAME       ANALYSIS OF DATA IN QUESTION 11.3
            2 VARIABLE LIST  GROUP,SCORE
            3 INPUT FORMAT   FIXED(F2.0,F3.0)
            4 INPUT MEDIUM   EX1114.DAT
            5 N OF CASES     28
            6 ONEWAY         SCORE BY GROUP(1,4)

- - - - - - - - - - - - - - - - - - - - - O N E W A Y - - - - - - - - - - - - - - - - - - - - - - -


     Variable: SCORE

                           Analysis of Variance
```

Source	D.f.	Sum of squares	Mean squares	F-ratio	F-prob.
Between groups	3	655.1429	218.3810	10.778	0.0001
Within groups	24	486.2857	20.2619		
Total	27	1141.4286			

```
- - - - - - - - - - - - - - - - - - - - - - - - - - - - - - - - - - - - - - - - - - - - - - - - - -
```

12

Multiple Comparisons Among Treatment Means

Objective

To extend the discussion of the analysis of variance by examining ways of making comparisons within a set of means.

Contents

When an analysis produces a significant value of F, we conclude that the population means are not all equal. We do not know, however, just which means are different from which other means. As a result, the overall analysis of variance may raise more questions than it answers. The problem which now faces us is one of examining differences among individual means for the purpose of isolating significant differences or testing particular hypotheses. (It might be, for example, that $\mu_1 = \mu_2$, $\mu_3 = \mu_4$, but μ_1 and $\mu_2 \neq \mu_3$ and μ_4.)

There are a very large number of techniques for making comparisons (contrasts) among means, and all that we can do here is to discuss the most common ones. For a thorough discussion of this topic the reader is referred to Miller (1966).

12.1 The General Problem

Consider a situation in which we ran an experiment with five treatments. For the sake of the generality of the example we will not specify further the

TABLE 12.1
Numerical Example

(a) Data

	1	2	3	4	5	
	18	20	6	15	12	
	20	25	9	10	11	
	21	23	8	9	8	
	16	27	6	12	13	
	15	25	11	14	11	
T_j	90	120	40	60	55	$GT = 365$
$\bar{X}_j$	18	24	8	12	11	$GM = 14.60$
						$\Sigma X^2 = 6257$

(b) Computations

$$SS_{total} = \Sigma X^2 - \frac{(\Sigma X)^2}{N} = 6257 - \frac{365^2}{25} = 6257 - 5329 = 928$$

$$SS_{treat} = \frac{\Sigma T_j^2}{n} - \frac{(\Sigma X)^2}{N} = \frac{(90^2 + 120^2 + \cdots + 55^2)}{5} - 5329 = 6145 - 5329 = 816$$

$$SS_{error} = SS_{total} - SS_{treat} = 928 - 816 = 112$$

(c) Summary table

Source	df	SS	MS	F
Treatments	4	816	204.00	36.43*
Error	20	112	5.60	
Total	24	928		

*$p < .05$

nature of the experiment. The data from this experiment are presented in Table 12.1. From this analysis it is obvious that there are significant differences among the treatment means, since $F_{.05}$ (4, 20) = 2.87, whereas F_{obt} = 36.43. This does not tell us, however, which means are different from which other means. For that we will have to look more closely at the data.

12.2   A Priori vs. Post Hoc Analyses

A priori comparisons

Post hoc comparisons

A posteriori comparisons

A distinction must be drawn between *a priori comparisons* which are decided upon before the data have been collected, and *post hoc* (or *a posteriori*) *comparisons* which are formulated after the data have been examined and differences noted. In general, *a priori* comparisons are to be preferred, since they tend to have greater power (sometimes substantially so) for any given level of α. This last point can be illustrated with a simple example. Consider an experiment with three treatments in which H_0 is known to be true. If it is decided *a priori* to test the difference between two specified means at the 5% level of confidence, then the probability of a Type I error is .05. If, however, the experimenter decides to wait to see the results before testing the largest difference at the 5% level, then the true probability of a Type I error is approximately .15. The reason for this is that he is implicitly testing $\bar{X}_1$ vs. $\bar{X}_2$, $\bar{X}_1$ vs. $\bar{X}_3$, and $\bar{X}_2$ vs. $\bar{X}_3$ when he looks at the data, even though he only actually runs the test on the largest difference. To put this another way, assume that H_0 is true but that one of the differences would lead to rejection of H_0 (a Type I error). Our "*post-hoc* experimenter" is certain to find it, since he tests the largest difference. On the other hand our "*a priori* experimenter" who has to specify which means he will test before he sees the data has only a one out of three chance of settling on that particular comparison which would produce a difference.

Since *post hoc* tests if left unchanged would produce high rates of Type I errors, they are usually modified to keep α at some low level. At the same time this modification leads to a corresponding loss in power. For this reason *a priori* tests are to be preferred where applicable whenever the experimenter is interested in something less than the full set of possible comparisons. If he wishes to make all possible comparisons, it is immaterial whether he decides that *a priori* or *post hoc*; the results will be the same.

12.3   Error Rates

Before we can consider any system of making multiple comparisons among treatment means, we must first consider the problem of specifying error rates.

We can distinguish three basic ways of specifying error rates, or the probability of Type I errors.[†] In doing so we shall use the terminology which has become more or less standard (cf. Ryan, 1959a; O'Neil & Wetherill, 1971).

Error Rate Per Comparison (PC)

This is the error rate we have used in the past and refers simply to the probability that any given comparison will produce a Type I error.

Error Rate Per Experiment (PE)

This is the *number* of erroneous statements that we expect to make in any given experiment. For example assume that we gave a group of males and a group of females 50 words and asked them to give as many associations to these words as possible in one minute. For each word we then test (at $\alpha = .05$) whether there is a difference in the number of associations given by male and female subjects. Assume that H_0 is always true. Since we have run 50 more or less independent t tests, each at $\alpha = .05$ we would expect that an average of $50(.05) = 2.5$ tests would be *significant* by chance. Thus the error rate for this experiment would be 2.5, while the **error rate per comparison** is .05. Note that unlike the other two types of error rates that we will consider, the **error rate per experiment** is a frequency, not a probability.

Error rate per comparison (PC)

Error rate per experiment (PE)

Error Rate Experimentwise (EW)

This abominable semantic construction refers to the probability that the results of our experiment will contain one or more erroneous conclusions. In other words, if we treat the complete set of conclusions we draw from an experiment (e.g., $\mu_1 > \mu_2$, $\mu_3 < \mu_4$, $\mu_1 < \mu_4$, and so on) as a unit, the probability that we will make a Type I error someplace is the **error rate experimentwise**.

Error rate experimentwise (EW)

To take an example from Ryan (1959a), suppose that we ran 1000 experiments on the same variables, with each experiment producing 10 comparisons among means. Suppose further than $\alpha = .01$ for each comparison, and that out of the total of 10,000 statements of significance 90

Error rates on families of comparisons

[†] While other types of error rates can be defined (Tukey prefers **error rates on families of comparisons**, for example), the three discussed here illustrate the general approach and are the most commonly used. For a good discussion of error rates for families of comparisons, the reader is referred to Myers (1979).

were actually Type I errors and these 90 errors occur in 70 of the 1,000 experiments. Then

$$\text{error rate per comparison} = \frac{\text{No. of errors}}{\text{No. of comparisons}}$$

$$= \frac{90}{10,000} = .009 \approx .01 = \alpha$$

$$\text{error rate per experiment} = \frac{\text{No. of errors}}{\text{No. of experiments}} = \frac{90}{1000} = .09$$

$$\text{error rate experimentwise} = \frac{\text{No. of experiments with 1 or more errors}}{\text{No. of experiments}} = \frac{70}{1000} = .07$$

While on a *per comparison* basis we would say that the probability of a Type I error is approximately .01 (actually .009), the fact remains that 7% of our experiments contained at least one Type I error. What this means is that if a given volume of a journal contained only papers which made ten comparisons at $\alpha = .01$ (and H_0 was true for all), then 7% of those experimental reports would draw at least one erroneous conclusion. Furthermore, the average *number* of erroneous conclusions per experiment would be .09.

In an experiment where only one comparison is made, all three error rates will be the same. But as the number of comparisons increase, the three rates diverge. If we let α represent the true error rate, α' represent the error rate for any one comparison, and c represent the number of comparisons, then

error rate per comparison (PC): $\alpha = \alpha'$

error rate per experiment (PE): $\alpha = c\alpha'$

error rate experimentwise (EW): $\alpha = 1 - (1 - \alpha')^c$
(if comparisons are independent)

If comparisons are not independent, the first two error rates remain unchanged, but the experimentwise rate is affected. In most situations, $1 - (1 - \alpha')^c$ still represents a reasonable approximation to α. It is worth noting that the limits on EW are $PC \le EW \le PE$, and in most reasonable cases EW is in the general vicinity of PE.

The Null Hypothesis and Error Rates

Complete null hypothesis

We have been speaking as if the null hypothesis in question were what Ryan (1959a) calls the ***complete null hypothesis*** ($\mu_1 = \mu_2 = \cdots = \mu_k$). In fact this is the null hypothesis tested by the overall analysis of variance. However in most experiments nobody is seriously interested in the complete null hypothesis, but in a few more restricted null hypotheses, such as ($\mu_1 = \mu_2 = \mu_3$, $\mu_4 = \mu_5$, $\mu_6 = \mu_7$), with differences between the various subsets. If this is the case the problem becomes more complex, and we will wish to take this into account in designating the error rates for the different tests we shall discuss.

12.4 Comparisons When the Overall F is Not Significant

The question of whether it is legitimate to compare individual treatment means when the overall treatment difference is not significant is one on which there is no universal agreement. Gaito (1959), Hays (1963), and Guilford & Fruchter (1973) either state or suggest that the overall F must be significant before further tests can be conducted. Ryan (1959b), Edwards (1968) and I would maintain that this is not the case, and that such a procedure could in fact severely limit the testing of some very important hypotheses. Ignoring the statistical arguments (which in fact permit the use of multiple comparisons regardless of the overall F) the matter can be easily understood by considering the situation in which an extremely conscientious experimenter runs two experimental groups and four control groups. She doesn't expect to find any differences among the control groups, but has included them just to be safe. When she runs her analysis of variance she obtains an insignificant F. Rather than arguing against the experimental hypotheses, this F may primarily argue for the fact that all control groups performed as expected. Since

$$\text{SS}_{\text{treat}} = n\Sigma(\bar{X}_j - GM)^2 = \frac{n\Sigma(\bar{X}_i - \bar{X}_j)^2}{k} \qquad \hat{ji} < j$$

the more *nondifferences* that are built into a study, the smaller the MS_{treat} becomes.

The important consideration is not whether F is or is not significant, but whether a given comparison is meaningful in light of the experimental hypotheses. If it is meaningful it should be tested, regardless of the overall F.

12.5 A Priori Comparisons

As we have already seen, *a priori* comparisons are comparisons (contrasts) which were planned before the data were collected. There are several different kinds of *a priori* comparison procedures, and these will be discussed in turn.

Multiple t Tests

One common approach to the pre-planned testing of differences among means, not to be recommended except in very special cases, is the use of individual t tests between pairs of treatment groups. The disadvantage (although occasionally the advantage) of this procedure, quite aside from any considerations of error rates, is the fact that it employs numerically different error terms for every comparison. This reduces the power of the individual tests by reducing the degrees of freedom for error.

Fisher's Least Significant Difference (LSD) procedure A closely related technique (known as **Fisher's Least Significant Difference (LSD) procedure**) which overcomes this problem uses the error term from the overall analysis of variance, thus pooling the within-treatment variances and degrees of freedom. The difficulty with both of these procedures, however, is that their indiscriminate use frequently produces very large per experiment and experimentwise error rates.

Linear Contrasts

Linear contrasts In making comparisons between two means (or two sets of means) we make use of what are called **linear contrasts**. The idea is really very simple—we want some way of measuring the difference between two means (or two sets of means) and a linear contrast supplies us with a simple way of obtaining this measure. The use of the word *contrast* instead of *comparison* is purely a matter of convention. To compare A with B is merely to contrast A with B. The two words are used interchangeably.

Linear combination A **linear combination** of means takes the form

$$L = a_1\bar{X}_1 + a_2\bar{X}_2 + a_3\bar{X}_3 + \cdots + a_k\bar{X}_k = \Sigma a_i\bar{X}_i. \qquad (12.1)$$

Equation 12.1 simply states that a linear combination is a weighted sum of the treatment means. When we impose the restriction that $\Sigma a_i = 0$, a linear combination becomes a linear *contrast* or a linear *comparison*. With the proper selection of the a_i, a linear contrast may be very useful indeed. As an example, consider the means $\bar{X}_1$, $\bar{X}_2$, and $\bar{X}_3$. Letting $a_1 = 1$, $a_2 = -1$, and $a_3 = 0$, $\Sigma a_i = 0$ and

$$L = (1)(\bar{X}_1) + (-1)(\bar{X}_2) + (0)(\bar{X}_3)$$

$$= \bar{X}_1 - \bar{X}_2.$$

In this case L is simply the difference between the means of Group 1 and Group 2. If, on the other hand, we let $a_1 = \frac{1}{2}$, $a_2 = \frac{1}{2}$, and $a_3 = -1$

$$L = (\tfrac{1}{2})(\bar{X}_1) + (\tfrac{1}{2})(\bar{X}_2) + (-1)(\bar{X}_3)$$

$$= \frac{\bar{X}_1 + \bar{X}_2}{2} - \bar{X}_3$$

in which case L represents the difference between the average of the first two treatments and the third treatment.

Sums of squares for contrasts   One of the advantages of linear contrasts is that they can be very easily converted to sums of squares, and represent the sum of squared differences between the means of sets of treatments. If we follow standard practice in the analysis of variance and work with totals (T_i) rather than means, and if $\Sigma a_i = 0$, then letting

$$L = a_1 T_1 + a_2 T_2 + a_3 T_3 + \cdots + a_k T_k = \Sigma a_i T_i$$

it can be shown that

$$SS_{contrast} = \frac{L^2}{n \Sigma a_i^2} \qquad\qquad (12.2)$$

is a component of the SS_{treat} on 1df, where n represents the number of scores per treatment. (Notice that we have switched to working with totals rather than means. Equation 12.2 would be incorrect if the a_i were applied to the means.)

Let us first consider an extremely simple example of a study in which we have only two treatments. Assume that there were ten observations per treatment and that the treatment totals were 25 and 30. Then to calculate SS_{treat} as in a traditional analysis of variance,

$$SS_{treat} = \frac{\Sigma T_j^2}{n} - \frac{(\Sigma X)^2}{N}$$

$$= \frac{25^2 + 30^2}{10} - \frac{(55)^2}{20}$$

$$= 1.25.$$

If we were now to calculate the linear contrast between the two treatment totals we would let $a_1 = 1$, $a_2 = -1$. Then

$$L = \Sigma a_i T_i = (1)(25) + (-1)(30) = -5$$

$$SS_{contrast} = \frac{L^2}{n \Sigma a_i^2} = \frac{(-5)^2}{10(1^2 + (-1)^2)} = \frac{25}{10(2)} = \frac{25}{20}$$

$$= 1.25$$

which is the same answer we obtained previously. This example illustrates that $SS_{contrast}$ is a component of the treatment sum of squares (in this case all of the treatment sum of squares). This particular example is an extreme one, and in practice there would be no point in obtaining the contrast when there are only two means.

However, suppose that we have three treatments such that

$$n = 10, \; T_1 = 15, \; T_2 = 20, \text{ and } T_3 = 30.$$

In the overall analysis of variance

$$SS_{treat} = \frac{15^2 + 20^2 + 30^2}{10} - \frac{65^2}{30} = 11.67.$$

Let $a_1 = 1$, $a_2 = 1$, $a_3 = -2$. Then

$$L = \Sigma a_i T_i = (1)(15) + (1)(20) + (-2)(30) = -25$$

$$SS_{contrast} = \frac{L^2}{n\Sigma a_i^2} = \frac{(-25)^2}{10(6)} = \frac{625}{60}$$

$$= 10.42.$$

This sum of squares is a component of the overall SS_{treat} on 1 df. We have 1 df because we are really comparing two means (the mean of the first two treatments with the mean of the third treatment). Now suppose that we obtained an additional linear contrast

Let $a_1 = 1$, $a_2 = -1$, and $a_3 = 0$. Then

$$L = \Sigma a_i T_i = (1)(15) + (-1)(20) + (0)(30) = -5$$

$$SS_{contrast} = \frac{L^2}{n\Sigma a_i^2} = \frac{(-5)^2}{10(2)} = \frac{25}{20}$$

$$= 1.25.$$

This $SS_{contrast}$ is also a component of SS_{treat} on 1 df. In addition, because of the way in which these particular coefficients were obtained

$$SS_{treat} = SS_{contrast_1} + SS_{contrast_2}$$

$$11.67 =   10.42 +   1.25$$

and thus the two contrasts account for all of the sum of squares (and all of the df) attributable to treatments.

It is important to recognize that most of the procedures we will discuss are based on the concept of linear contrasts described above. More specifically the sum of squares for a contrast will always be defined as

$$SS_{contrast} = \frac{(\Sigma a_i T_i)^2}{n\Sigma a_i^2} = \frac{L^2}{n\Sigma a_i^2}.$$

The alternative methods for comparing treatment means will differ primarily in terms of the way in which the set of contrasts is selected, the coefficients which are used, and/or the way in which error rates are controlled. In each case the actual numerical calculations will remain the same.

Orthogonal Contrasts

Orthogonal contrasts   One common method of obtaining a set of comparisons or contrasts between treatments is referred to as the method of ***orthogonal contrasts***. What sets this method apart from others is the fact that within a set of orthogonal contrasts each contrast is orthogonal to (independent of) the other contrasts.

The fact that one contrast shows a significant difference between two groups (or sets of groups) says nothing about whether or not another contrast will be significant—they are asking independent questions. The second feature of these contrasts is that because they are orthogonal the sum of the sums of squares for the set of contrasts is equal to SS_{treat} and thus these contrasts account for all of the variation among treatment means.

From a calculational point of view, what sets orthogonal contrasts apart from other types of contrasts we might choose is the selection of the coefficients. More precisely, it is the relationship between the coefficients for one contrast and the coefficients for other contrasts in the set.

Orthogonal coefficients   In the example just given there are other comparisons between means that could have been made instead of the two that were actually carried out. However, not all of these would have been orthogonal and sum to the SS_{treat}. Given that there are equal sample sizes, the coefficients must meet the following three criteria for comparisons to sum to SS_{treat}.

1. $\Sigma a_i = 0$
2.   Number of comparisons = number of df for treatments
3. $\Sigma a_i b_i = 0$

where a_i and b_i are the sets of coefficients for different contrasts.

The first restriction has already been discussed. This is the restriction that results in the contrast being a sum of squares. The second restriction says nothing more than that if you want the parts to sum to the whole, you had better have all of the parts. The last restriction ($\Sigma a_i b_i = 0$) ensures that the contrasts are independent of (or orthogonal to) one another, and thus that we are summing non-overlapping components.

At first glance it would appear that finding sets of coefficients satisfying the requirement $\Sigma a_i b_i = 0$ would require either a frustrating process of trial and error or else solving a set of simultaneous equations. In fact a very simple rule exists for finding orthogonal sets of coefficients, and although the rule will not find all possible sets, it will lead to most of them. The rule for forming the coefficients visualizes the process of breaking down SS_{treat} in terms of a tree diagram. The overall F for five treatments treats all five treatment means simultaneously. If we then compare the combination of Treatments 1 and 2 with the combination of Treatments 3, 4, and 5, we have formed two branches of our tree, one representing Treatments 1 and 2 and the other representing Treatments 3, 4, and 5. Thus

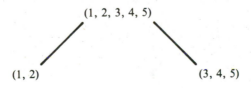

The value of a_i for the treatment means on the left will be equal to the number of treatments on the right, and vice versa, with one of the sets being negative. Thus the coefficients are $(3, 3, -2, -2, -2)$ for the five treatments, respectively.

Now that we have formed two limbs or branches of our tree, we can never compare treatments on one limb with treatments on another limb, although we can compare treatments on the same limb. Thus

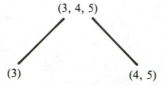

is an example of a legitimate comparison. The coefficients in this case would be $(0, 0, 2, -1, -1)$. Treatments 1 and 2 have coefficients of 0 because they are not part of this comparison. Treatment 3 has a coefficient of 2 since it is compared with two other treatments. Treatments 4 and 5 receive coefficients of -1 since they are compared with one other treatment. The negative signs can be arbitrarily assigned to either side of the comparison.

The previous procedure could be carried on until all comparisons are exhausted, at which point will be reached when we have made as many comparisons as there are df for treatments.

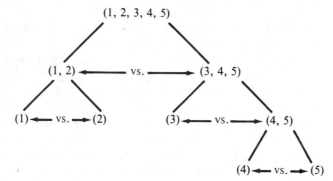

FIGURE 12.1

Tree diagram illustrating orthogonal partitions of SS_{treat}

As a result of this procedure we might arrive at the comparisons shown in Figure 12.1. The coefficients for these comparisons are then

	TREATMENTS				
	1	*2*	*3*	*4*	*5*
a_i:	3	3	-2	-2	-2
b_i:	0	0	2	-1	-1
c_i:	0	0	0	1	-1
d_i:	1	-1	0	0	0

To show that these coefficients are orthogonal we need only to show that all pair-wise products of the coefficients sum to 0. For example

$$\Sigma a_i b_i = (3)(0) + (3)(0) + (-2)(2) + (-2)(-1) + (-2)(-1) = 0$$

and

$$\Sigma a_i c_i = (3)(0) + (3)(0) + (-2)(0) + (-2)(1) + (-2)(-1) = 0.$$

Thus we see that the first and second and the first and third contrasts are both independent. Similar calculations will show that all of the other contrasts are also independent of one another.

It is important to note that the above coefficients will lead to only one of many possible sets of orthogonal contrasts. If we had begun by comparing Treatment 1 with the combination of Treatments 2, 3, 4, and 5, the resulting set of contrasts would have been entirely different. It is important for the experimenter to decide what contrasts she considers important, and to plan accordingly.

Example 12.1

Learning as a Function of Deprivation

Let us now examine the data in Table 12.1 with the intention of testing differences among individual means. Assume that the data represent the effects of food and/or water deprivation on behavior in a learning task. Treatments 1 and 2 represent control conditions in which the animal received *ad lib* food and water (1) or else food and water twice a day (2). In Treatment 3 animals were food-deprived, in Treatment 4 they were water-deprived, and in Treatment 5 they were deprived of both food and water. Assume that before running our experiment we decided that we wanted to compare the combined control groups (Treatments 1 and 2) with the combined experimental groups, the control groups with each other, the singly deprived treatments with the doubly deprived treatment, and the singly deprived treatments with each other. This leads to the following comparisons:

1.   (1, 2) vs. (3, 4, 5)
2.   (1) vs. (2)
3.   (3, 4) vs. (5)
4.   (3) vs. (4)

We further have decided to run our tests at $\alpha = .05$ per comparison.

For your convenience the raw data and the summary table from Table 12.1 are reproduced in Table 12.2. To test the difference between control

TABLE 12.2

Data and Analysis
for Hypothetical
Study of
Performance Under
Food &/or Water
Deprivation

(a) Data

	ad lib control	*2/day* control	*food* deprived	*water* deprived	*f&w* deprived
	18	20	6	15	12
	20	25	9	10	11
	21	23	8	9	8
	16	27	6	12	13
	15	25	11	14	11
T_i	90	120	40	60	55

TREATMENTS

$GT = 365$

(b) Summary table

Source	df	SS	MS	F
Treatments	4	816	204.00	36.43
Error	20	112	5.60	
Total	24	928		

and experimental conditions:

T_i	90	120	40	60	55
a_i	3	3	−2	−2	−2
a_iT_i	270	360	−80	−120	−110

$L = \Sigma a_i T_i = 320$

$$SS_{1, 2 \text{ vs. } 3, 4, 5} = \frac{L^2}{n\Sigma a_i^2} = \frac{320^2}{5(30)} = 682.67.$$

To test the difference between the two control conditions:

T_i	90	120	40	60	55
b_i	1	−1	0	0	0
b_iT_i	90	−120	0	0	0

$L = \Sigma b_i T_i = -30$

$$SS_{1 \text{ vs. } 2} = \frac{L^2}{n\Sigma b_i^2} = \frac{(-30)^2}{5(2)} = 90.00.$$

To compare Treatment 5 with the combined mean of Treatments 3 and 4:

T_i	90	120	40	60	55
c_i	0	0	1	1	−2
c_iT_i	0	0	40	60	−110

$L = \Sigma c_i T_i = -10$

$$SS_{3, 4 \text{ vs. } 5} = \frac{L^2}{n\Sigma c_i^2} = \frac{(-10)^2}{5(6)} = 3.33.$$

Finally, to compare Treatments 3 and 4:

T_i	90	120	40	60	55
d_i	0	0	1	−1	0
$d_i T_i$	0	0	40	−60	0

$L = \Sigma d_i T_i = -20$

$$SS_{3 \text{ vs. } 4} = \frac{L^2}{n \Sigma d_i^2} = \frac{(-20)^2}{5(2)} = 40.00.$$

We now have computed four sums of squares and have accounted for all of the df for treatments. If we sum these four values for $SS_{contrast}$ we obtain

$$682.67 + 90.00 + 3.33 + 40.00 = 816.00$$

which is exactly equal to SS_{treat}. Thus we have partitioned our SS_{treat} into four independent components.

Although we have calculated the individual sums of squares for the contrasts, the problem of testing them remains. This is in fact no problem at all, since they can be tested as any other sums of squares between treatments. There is only 1 df for each contrast, and as a result these terms are also mean squares, and can be converted to F on 1 and $k(n-1)$ df by division by MS_{error}. The results for our data are presented in Table 12.3.

TABLE 12.3

Summary Table of Contrasts on Data in Table 12.2

Source	df	SS	MS	F
Treatments	4	816.00	204.00	36.429*
1, 2 vs. 3, 4, 5	1	682.67	682.67	121.905**
1 vs. 2	1	90.00	90.00	16.071**
3, 4 vs. 5	1	3.33	3.33	<1
3 vs. 4	1	40.00	40.00	7.143*
Error	20	112.00	5.60	
Total	24	928.00		

$\left.\begin{array}{l} {}^*p < .05 \\ {}^{**}p < .01 \end{array}\right\}$ See explanation in text.

From Table 12.3 we can obtain a reasonably good picture of what the data have to offer. We already knew that there were significant differences overall. In addition we now know that there is a significant difference between the control groups and the experimental groups ($F = 121.905$). Moreover there is a difference between the two control groups ($F = 16.071$) and between the *food only* and *water only* deprived conditions ($F = 7.143$). There is no difference between the mean of the two "singly deprived" conditions and the "doubly deprived" condition ($F < 1$), due to the fact that the two singly-deprived conditions balance each other off.

Levels of significance   In Table 12.3 each F was tested for significance at $\alpha = .05$, and we thus have an error rate per comparison of .05. While this is probably the most common procedure, there are very strong arguments why it might be better to work at a more stringent level of significance. If in the course of an experiment we make five independent tests at $\alpha = .05$, the experimentwise error rate is $1 - .95^5$ against the complete null hypothesis. With five independent tests, $1 - .95^5 = .23$.† Thus we stand about one chance in four of reporting at least one significant difference when H_0 is in fact true, even though each individual test is run at $\alpha = .05$. This level of error is uncomfortably high, and a strong case can be made for reducing the overall experimentwise error rate by reducing the error rate per comparison. If we had tested at $\alpha = .01$, then the experimentwise error rate would be approximately $1 - .99^5 = .05$, a much more acceptable level. My own particular preference would be to test the overall F at whatever level of α seems appropriate, but to test the individual comparisons at a level of α' (the error rate per comparison) which will produce an experimentwise error rate of approximately .05. For most practical situations, α' will be approximately α/c, where c is the number of comparisons. For the present example this would mean that MS_{treat} would be tested at $\alpha = .05$, but that the individual contrasts would be tested at $\alpha' = \alpha/c = .05/4 = .0125 \approx .01$. The effect of this change on our example would be to eliminate differences within the experimental treatments, while retaining all other differences, as is indicated by the pattern of (**) in Table 12.3.

As a further precaution to reduce the experimentwise and per experiment error rates, tests which are not of interest should be omitted. It is silly to run five comparisons when you are only interested in four of them. In fact the number of contrasts is generally more important than their orthogonality as far as the experimentwise error rate is concerned.

Nonorthogonal comparisons   Orthogonal comparisons have the advantage of completely partitioning the SS_{treat}, accounting for all of the variability among treatments. However many instances exist where the particular comparisons of interest are not orthogonal to one another. In the past most textbooks have left the impression that comparisons must, or at least should, be orthogonal. In fact orthogonality is relatively unimportant in comparison to the total number of contrasts, and it is generally better to run two contrasts

---

† While the contrasts are orthogonal in the above example, the Fs themselves are not, since we used the same error term for all tests. However, while the Fs are not strictly independent, the estimate of the experimentwise error rate is not likely to be seriously affected.

which are not orthogonal than three which are. In addition, the error rate per comparison and the error rate per experiment are totally unaffected by orthogonality, while the error rate experimentwise is usually only moderately affected. For example, for five comparisons (at $\alpha = .05$ per comparison) which are non-independent, the maximum value for the experimentwise error rate would be .25, as opposed to .23 for independent contrasts, not a very crucial difference.

The only practical difference produced by using nonorthogonal comparisons is the fact that the contrast sums of squares will not sum to SS_{treat}. This is not a serious problem. We will have more to say about nonorthogonal comparisons when we come to Dunn's test.

Unequal sample sizes   In the case of equal sample sizes we made two restrictions on the coefficients. We said that to have a linear contrast which was part of the SS_{treat} the a_i must sum to zero, and for two contrasts to be orthogonal the sum of cross products of the coefficients must sum to zero. In the case of unequal sample sizes these restrictions are modified to

$$\Sigma n_i a_i = 0$$

and

$$\Sigma n_i a_i b_i = 0$$

where the coefficients are to be applied directly to the treatment totals, as we have done in the previous paragraph. Then $F = L^2 / \Sigma n_i a_i^2 \, (MS_{error})$.

It can be shown (Howell & Stacey, 1972) that these restrictions are met if we apply the tree diagram rule, but set a_i = the number of *observations* on the other side of the contrast, rather than the number of treatments. An example of an orthogonal set of contrasts is presented in Table 12.4 for four treatments with *n*s of 9, 10, 8, and 10, respectively.

TABLE 12.4
Orthogonal Contrasts with Unequal Sample Sizes

			TREATMENTS			
			I	II	III	IV
		n_i	9	10	8	10
Contrasts	*Coefficients*					
II and II vs. III and IV	a_i		18	18	−19	−19
I vs. II	b_i		10	−9	0	0
III vs. IV	c_i		0	0	10	−8

Dunn's Test (Bonferroni t)

When we have several means there are an infinite number of linear combinations of the form

$$L = \Sigma a_i T_i$$

Dunn's test

corresponding to an infinite number of possible values for the a_i. Even if we restrict ourselves to linear contrasts (i.e., adding the restriction that $\Sigma a_i = 0$), there are still an infinite number of them. Even if we look only at potentially meaningful contrasts, the possible number is still quite large. If our interest centers on only a few of the possible number of comparisons, **Dunn's test** is an appropriate technique. While this test has been known for a long time, Dunn (1961) was the first to formalize it and to present tables for its use.

Bonferroni Inequality

The Bonferroni Inequality   The test is based on the **Bonferroni Inequality**, which, for our purposes, states nothing more than that the experimentwise error rate is less than or equal to $c\alpha'$, where c = the number of comparisons and α' = the level of significance at which any single comparison is run. Thus the Bonferroni Inequality merely states that the error rate experimentwise (EW) is less than or equal to the error rate per experiment (PE). From this it follows that if α' is set at α/c where α is the desired *maximum EW*, then $EW \le \alpha$, i.e.,

$$c\alpha' = c\left(\frac{\alpha}{c}\right) = \alpha.$$

Furthermore the error rate per experiment will be exactly equal to α. Dunn made use of this inequality to design a test in which each comparison is run at α', leaving the EW for the set of comparisons $\le \alpha$. This can be accomplished with a minor modification to the standard t test.

t'

Suppose we first consider pairwise comparisons. Let t' represent both the result of applying Dunn's test and the critical value of t at α/c. (The distribution of t' is given in Appendix (t').) In other words for five comparisons at a maximum $\alpha = .05$ experimentwise, $\alpha' = \alpha/c = .05/5 = .01$, and t' is merely the critical value of t at the .01 level. A difference between two means will be significant if the ratio

$$\frac{\bar{X}_1 - \bar{X}_2}{\sqrt{\dfrac{s^2}{n} + \dfrac{s^2}{n}}} = \frac{\bar{X}_1 - \bar{X}_2}{\sqrt{\dfrac{2s^2}{n}}} = \frac{\bar{X}_1 - \bar{X}_2}{\sqrt{\dfrac{2\text{MS}_{\text{error}}}{n}}} \qquad (12.3)$$

exceeds t'. Equation 12.3 makes use of the fact that MS_{error} in the analysis of variance is equivalent to the pooled variance in t. (Moreover, it is not just a coincidence that the "2" in the denominator is equal to the Σa_i^2 which we would have if we used coefficients of 1 and -1 to make a comparison between the two means by the procedure discussed earlier.)

In terms of totals, Equation 12.3 becomes

$$t' = \frac{T_i - T_j}{\sqrt{2n\,\text{MS}_{\text{error}}}}. \qquad (12.4)$$

Equation 12.4 applies to underlined differences between *pairs* of totals, because the denominator is actually $\sqrt{n\Sigma a_i^2 \mathrm{MS}_{\mathrm{error}}}$, where, when we deal only with pairs,

$$\Sigma a_i^2 = 1^2 + (-1)^2 = 2.$$

If we want to write a general expression which allows us to test any comparison of means or totals† pairwise or not, then let

$$L = \Sigma a_i T_i$$

and

$$t' = \frac{L}{\sqrt{n\Sigma a_i^2 \mathrm{MS}_{\mathrm{error}}}}. \qquad\qquad (12.5)$$

Equation 12.5 represents the most general form for Dunn's test, and it can be shown (Dunn, 1961) that if L is *any* linear combination (not necessarily even a linear contrast (requiring $\Sigma a_i = 0$)) then the error rate experimentwise with c comparisons is at most α. To put it most simply, Dunn runs a regular t test, but evaluates the result against a modified critical value of t (t') which has been chosen so as to limit EW. However, as we will see in the following example, an alternative form of the test calls for the substitution of the tabled value of t' in Equation 12.5 and then the solution for the smallest value of L which could be declared significant.

Example 12.2

Further Consideration of Learning as a Function of Deprivation

As an example we will use the data we considered earlier on the effects of food and water deprivation. These data are to be found in Table 12.2 on page 286. In that table we had totals of 90, 120, 40, 60, and 55, with $n = 5$ and $\mathrm{MS}_{\mathrm{error}} = 5.60$. Suppose that we had *a priori* reasons for wanting to test the following null hypotheses:

A. $\mu_1 - \mu_2 = 0$

B. $\mu_3 - \mu_4 = 0$

C. $\mu_5 - \mu_3 = 0$

D. $\mu_5 - \mu_4 = 0$

E. $\dfrac{\mu_3 + \mu_4}{2} - \mu_5 = 0 = \mu_3 + \mu_4 - 2\mu_5$

---

† In this test and future ones it is important to keep in mind whether you are comparing totals or means. When you are comparing totals the denominator will be of the general form $\sqrt{n\Sigma a_i^2 \mathrm{MS}_{\mathrm{error}}}$, whereas in comparing means it will be of the form $\sqrt{\Sigma a_i^2 \mathrm{MS}_{\mathrm{error}}/n}$. This is the only real difference, allowing us to hop back and forth from means to totals, depending upon which is more convenient at the moment.

The first four of these represent pairwise comparisons while the last is a comparison of the average of two means vs. a third. Comparisons **A**, **B**, and **E** are equivalent to those we made with orthogonal contrasts, and are orthogonal among themselves. Comparisons **C** and **D**, on the other hand, are not orthogonal to the other three nor to each other.

Given that $c = 5$, $df_{error} = 20$, and $\alpha = .05$, we find from Appendix (t') that $t' = 2.85$. (Notice that this is nothing but $t_{.01}$ on 20 df, since $\alpha/c = .05/5 = .01$.)

For all pairwise comparisons, $\Sigma a_i^2 = 2$. Thus $t' = (T_i - T_j)/\sqrt{2n MS_{error}}$ or alternatively $T_i - T_j = t'\sqrt{2n MS_{error}}$ where $T_i - T_j$ (the critical difference) is the smallest difference which will lead to rejection of H_0.

$$T_i - T_j = 2.85\sqrt{2(5)(5.6)} = 2.85(7.483) = 21.33$$

Thus any pairwise difference greater than ± 21.33 will be judged significant. Four of our planned comparisons are pairwise. Thus

$\mu_1 - \mu_2 = 0$ is tested by $T_1 - T_2 = 90 - 120 = -30$

$\mu_3 - \mu_4 = 0$ is tested by $T_3 - T_4 = 40 - 60 = -20$

$\mu_5 - \mu_3 = 0$ is tested by $T_5 - T_3 = 55 - 40 = 15$

$\mu_5 - \mu_4 = 0$ is tested by $T_5 - T_4 = 55 - 60 = -5$

Since we want a two-tailed test the sign of the difference is irrelevant. The only difference between totals which is greater than 21.33 is the difference $T_1 - T_2$, and we will thus conclude that $\mu_1 \neq \mu_2$. We will not reject H_0 for the other three comparisons.

To test the hypothesis that $\dfrac{\mu_3 + \mu_4}{2} - \mu_5 = 0$ we can avoid fractions by testing the exactly equivalent null hypothesis $\mu_3 + \mu_4 - 2\mu_5 = 0$. For this contrast we have $(1)T_3 + (1)T_4 + (-2)T_5 = 60 + 40 - 2(55) = -10$. In this case $\Sigma a_i^2 = (0^2 + 0^2 + 1^2 + 1^2 + (-2)^2) = 6$ and

critical difference $= t'\sqrt{n\Sigma a_i^2 MS_{error}} = 2.85\sqrt{5(6)(5.6)} = 36.94$.

Since the obtained difference of (-10) is less than the critical difference of 36.94, we will not reject H_0.

Dunn's test vs. orthogonal comparisons   On the surface Dunn's test would seem to differ in many ways from the orthogonal contrast procedure discussed earlier. However, considerable insight into the general nature of multiple comparison techniques results from examining the apparent differences more closely.

The first difference is that Dunn's test uses t whereas orthogonal comparisons use F. This difference is trivial because it can readily be shown that when there is 1 df due to treatments, $t = \sqrt{F}$. In other words, if we took two independent groups and computed t, and then took the same data and computed F, $t_{obt} = \sqrt{F_{obt}}$. Moreover, the student can easily verify by glancing at the tables, that $t_{.05}$ on v df $= \sqrt{F_{.05}}$ on 1, v df.

The second difference concerns the fact that with orthogonal comparisons we solve for F whereas with Dunn's test we solve for the critical value of $T_i - T_j$ (or L). Here again the difference is trivial. All that Dunn is doing is saving us the labor of computing t'_{obt} by saying that if L is not greater than the critical value $(T_i - T_j)$, then t'_{obt} will be less than t'_α.

The next difference to be considered concerns the fact that Dunn does not require the comparisons to be orthogonal. There are two ways to approach this problem. When contrasts are orthogonal, then $EW = 1 - (1 - \alpha)^c$, and thus we can specify the experimentwise error rate precisely. Dunn, by allowing nonorthogonal contrasts, has lost the ability to specify EW precisely, and can only use the inequality $EW \leq c\alpha'$. While this is a real difference, it turns out to be rather trivial. Five orthogonal comparisons at $\alpha = .01$ have an EW of $1 - .99^5 = .049$. Five nonorthogonal comparisons have a maximum EW of $5(.01) = .050$. It is difficult to see that Dunn has sacrificed a great deal. In addition, it has already been stated that if the experimenter has a reason to run comparisons which are meaningful but not orthogonal she should go ahead and do so, and thus the earlier recommendation agrees with Dunn's procedure.

The final difference between the two tests concerns the error rates. Traditionally nonorthogonal contrasts are tested at an error rate per comparison of α, whereas Dunn sets an error rate per experiment at α (or $EW \leq \alpha$). Thus for a given level of α Dunn's test is more conservative. Here again the difference is not as important as it might seem. There is no reason why we could not set an error rate per experiment rather than per comparison for orthogonal comparisons, or an error rate per comparison for Dunn's test. In fact $\alpha' = \alpha/c$ is the error rate per comparison for Dunn. Thus the difference in error rates is really a difference in philosophy. Those who stress orthogonal comparisons are really arguing for holding the error rate per comparison constant, while Dunn's supporters are really arguing for making the experiment the basic unit for error.

Confidence limits on L   While most psychologists and other social scientists tend to think in terms of tests of significance, most statisticians prefer to think in terms of confidence limits. My prediction is that the confidence limit approach is likely to win more and more advocates in the future, and for this reason it is worth considering how confidence limits would be formed for the differences we just tested. In fact it should be self-evident to most of you, since the approach is the same as that taken for other confidence intervals.

With confidence intervals it makes more sense to work with means than with totals, and thus

$$t' = \frac{L_m}{\sqrt{\dfrac{\Sigma a_i^2 \, MS_{error}}{n}}} \qquad \qquad (12.6)$$

where L_m is a linear combination of means.[†] The confidence limits for differences between means then become

$$CI = L_m + t' \sqrt{\frac{\Sigma a_i^2 \, MS_{error}}{n}} . \qquad \qquad (12.7)$$

For pairs of means $\Sigma a_i^2 = 2$, and for our data

$$CI = L_m \pm 2.85 \sqrt{\frac{2(5.6)}{5}} = L_m \pm 2.85 \sqrt{2.24} = L_m \pm 4.265.$$

To set confidence limits on $\mu_1 - \mu_2$, $L_m = \bar{X}_1 - \bar{X}_2 = 18 - 24 = -6$

$$CI_{\mu_1 - \mu_2} = -6 \pm 4.265.$$

Since we have $\alpha = .05$ and are going to be concerned with five mean differences, we know that $\alpha' = \alpha/c = .01$. Thus, with probability $1 - \alpha' = .99$

$$-10.265 \le (\mu_1 - \mu_2) \le -1.735.$$

Similarly, for the other pairwise comparisons:

$$-8.265 \le (\mu_3 - \mu_4) \le +.265$$

$$-1.265 \le (\mu_5 - \mu_3) \le +7.265$$

$$-5.265 \le (\mu_5 - \mu_4) \le +3.265$$

and for the last comparison

$$\left(\frac{\mu_3 + \mu_4}{2} - \mu_5 \right)$$

$$CI = L_m \pm t' \sqrt{\frac{\Sigma a_i^2 \, MS_{error}}{n}}$$

$$L_m = (\tfrac{1}{2})(\bar{X}_3) + (\tfrac{1}{2})(\bar{X}_4) + (-1)(\bar{X}_5) = -1$$

$$CI = -1 \pm 2.85 \sqrt{\frac{1.5(5.6)}{5}} = -1 \pm 3.69$$

$$-4.69 \le \frac{\mu_3 + \mu_4}{2} - \mu_5 \le 2.69.$$

[†] We use $\Sigma a_i^2/n$ rather than $n\Sigma a_i^2$ because we are now working with means instead of totals.

Since $\alpha' = .01$, each of these confidence intervals taken individually has a probability of .99 of enclosing the relevant parameter. Taken as a set, these five statements have a probability of $1 - \alpha = .95$ of *simultaneously* enclosing the relevant parameters.

12.6 A Posteriori Tests

There is much to recommend the use of orthogonal contrasts and Dunn's test when comparisons can be specified *a priori*, especially if the desired number of comparisons is small. However, many experiments involve hypotheses which are only arrived at after the data have been examined. In this situation a number of *a posteriori* or *post hoc* techniques are available.

Many of the *a posteriori* tests are based upon the Studentized Range Statistic or special variants of it, and thus we will need to consider this statistic further before proceeding.

The Studentized Range Statistic

Studentized Range Statistic (q)

The ***Studentized Range Statistic* (q)** is defined as

$$q_r = \frac{T_l - T_s}{\sqrt{n\mathrm{MS}_{\mathrm{error}}}} \qquad\qquad (12.8)$$

where T_l and T_s represent the largest and smallest treatment totals and r is the number of treatments in the experiment. To appreciate just what this statistic represents, consider the case where we have only two treatments and run a t test on the difference between their means. If $n_1 = n_2 = n$ and if we let $\mathrm{MS}_{\mathrm{error}}$ represent the pooled within-treatment variances ($\mathrm{MS}_{\mathrm{error}} = s^2$), then

$$t = \frac{\bar{X}_1 - \bar{X}_2}{\sqrt{\dfrac{2\mathrm{MS}_{\mathrm{error}}}{n}}} = \frac{T_1 - T_2}{\sqrt{2n\mathrm{MS}_{\mathrm{error}}}}.$$

If we now multiply both sides of the equation by $\sqrt{2}$, we have

$$\frac{T_1 - T_2}{\sqrt{n\mathrm{MS}_{\mathrm{error}}}} = \frac{T_l - T_s}{\sqrt{n\mathrm{MS}_{\mathrm{error}}}} = q.$$

We thus see that in this case q is merely a linear function of t. Do not ask why q is defined as $t\sqrt{2}$ rather than as t. I haven't the slightest idea, although I'm sure that there is a reason. Nonetheless, when there are only two treatments, $q = t\sqrt{2}$, and whether we solve for t or q is irrelevant.

When we have only two means or when we wish to compare two means chosen *at random* from the set of available means, there is no difficulty—t is a perfectly appropriate test. But suppose that we looked at a set of means and deliberately selected the largest and smallest means for testing. It is apparent that we have drastically altered the probability of a Type I error. Given that H_0 is true, the largest and smallest means certainly have a greater chance of being called "significantly" different than do means which are adjacent in an ordered series of means. This is the point at which the Studentized Range Statistic comes to the rescue. It was designed for just this purpose.

To use q we first rank the means from smallest to largest. We then take into account the number of steps between the means to be compared. For adjacent means, no change is made and $q_{.05} = t_{.05}\sqrt{2}$. For means which are not adjacent, however, the critical value of q increases, growing in magnitude as the number of intervening steps between means increases.

As an example of the use of q, consider the data used earlier (page 286). The totals were

T_1	T_2	T_3	T_4	T_5
90	120	40	60	55

with $n = 5$, $df_{error} = 20$, and $MS_{error} = 5.6$. The largest total is 120 and the smallest is 40, and there are a total (r) of 5 means in the set (in the terminology of most tables we say that these means are $r = 5$ steps apart).

$$q = \frac{T_l - T_s}{\sqrt{nMS_{error}}} = \frac{120 - 40}{\sqrt{5(5.6)}} = \frac{80}{5.292}$$

$$= 15.12.$$

Notice that r is not involved in the calculation. It is involved, however, when we go to the tables. From Appendix (q) we find that for $r = 5$ and $df_{error} = 20$, $q_{.05} = 4.23$. Since $15.12 > 4.23$, we will reject H_0 and conclude that there is a significant difference between the largest and smallest means.

An alternative to solving for q_{obt} and referring q_{obt} to the sampling distribution of q, would be to solve for the smallest difference which would be significant, and then to compare our actual difference with the minimum significant difference, as we did with Dunn's test. If

$$q_r = \frac{T_l - T_s}{\sqrt{nMS_{error}}}$$

then

$$T_l - T_s = q_r\sqrt{nMS_{error}} \qquad\qquad (12.9)$$

where $T_l - T_s$ is the minimum difference between two totals which will be considered to be significant.

We know that with five means, $q_{.05} = 4.23$. Then, for our data

$$T_l - T_s = 4.23 \sqrt{5(5.6)}$$

$$= 22.38.$$

Thus a difference in totals equal to or greater than 22.38 would be judged significant, while a smaller difference would not. Since the difference between the largest and smallest totals in the example is 80, we would reject H_0. (It might be instructive for you to imagine two totals which were just over 22.38 units apart and test their difference using Equation 12.8.)

Although q could be used in place of an overall F (i.e., instead of running the traditional analysis of variance we would test the difference between the two extreme means), there is rarely an occasion to do so. In most cases F is more powerful than q. However where you expect several control group means to be equal to each other, but different from an experimental treatment mean (e.g., $\mu_1 = \mu_2 = \mu_3 = \mu_4 \neq \mu_5$), q might well be the more appropriate statistic.

Although q is seldom a reasonable substitute for the overall F for Treatments it is a very important statistic when it comes to making multiple comparisons among individual treatment means. In this case we will be testing the difference between the largest and smallest means in a *subset* of means, and r will represent the number of means in that subset.

The Newman-Keuls Test

Newman-Keuls test

The basic purpose of the **Newman-Keuls test** is to sort all of the treatment means into subsets of treatments. These subsets will be homogeneous in the sense that they do not differ within themselves, but do differ from other subsets.

We will again use the data from Table 12.2. We will start out by arranging the treatment totals in ascending order, from smallest to largest. We will designate these totals as $T_1 \ldots T_5$, *where the subscript now refers to the position of that total in the ordered series.* For the data in our example

		TREATMENT		
food deprived	f & w deprived	water deprived	ad lib control	2/day control
T_1	T_2	T_3	T_4	T_5
40	55	60	90	120

We will define the *range* of totals as the number of steps in an ordered series between those totals. Adjacent totals will be defined as being 2 steps apart, totals which have one other total intervening between them will have a range of 3, and so on. In general the range between T_i and $T_j = i - j + 1$ (for $i > j$).

If we wished to test the difference $T_5 - T_1$, the range would be $5 - 1 + 1 = 5 = r$. For this example we have 20 df for error, and thus (from Appendix (q)) would require $q_{\text{obt}} \geq 4.23$ if the difference is to be significant. Given this information we could now solve for the smallest difference which would be judged significant. As we saw previously, this critical difference would be 22.38. Thus when the totals are 5 steps apart, a difference of at least 22.38 is required for significance.

If we were only concerned with totals that are four steps apart (e.g., $T_4 - T_1$ or $T_5 - T_2$), then $r = 4$, df $= 20$, and $q_{.05}(4, 20) = 3.96$. Thus the minimum difference which would be significant is

$$T_i - T_j = q\sqrt{n\text{Ms}_{\text{error}}} = 3.96\sqrt{5(5.60)} = 3.96(5.29) = 20.95.$$

Thus the four-step differences of greater than 20.95 will be classified as significant.[†]

This procedure could be repeated for all ranges possible with our data. If we define W_r as the smallest width or difference between totals r steps apart which will be significant, then

$$W_r = q_{.05}(r, \text{df})\sqrt{n\text{MS}_{\text{error}}}. \qquad\qquad \textbf{\textit{(12.10)}}$$

For our example

$$W_2 = q_{.05}(2, 20)\sqrt{n\text{MS}_{\text{error}}} = 2.95(5.29) = 15.61$$

$$W_3 = q_{.05}(3, 20)\sqrt{n\text{MS}_{\text{error}}} = 3.58(5.29) = 18.94$$

$$W_4 = q_{.05}(4, 20)\sqrt{n\text{MS}_{\text{error}}} = 3.96(5.29) = 20.95$$

$$W_5 = q_{.05}(5, 20)\sqrt{n\text{MS}_{\text{error}}} = 4.23(5.29) = 22.38.$$

The Newman-Keuls test employs the values of W along with a set of rules designed to control the experimentwise error rate and to prevent inconsistent conclusions. The problem is that if we do not adopt a set of rules governing what tests will be made and the order of the testing, we will lose control of the experimentwise error rate and, in addition, we may find ourselves making contradictory statements. For example, if three totals are ordered T_1, T_2, and T_3, it would be embarrassing if we found that T_1 was different from T_2, but not from T_3 (since T_3 is larger than T_2).

To systematize the procedure we will adopt an approach similar to the one used by Winer (1962). We will form a matrix with treatment totals on

Layered test   [†] The Newman-Keuls is sometimes referred to as a *"layered"* test because it adjusts the critical difference as a function of the number of means contained within a subset of means. This is in contrast to the Tukey HSD and Scheffé tests which essentially use a constant critical difference for all contrasts.

the rows and columns, and differences between totals as the cell entries. Such a matrix is presented in Table 12.5(a) for the data in Table 12.2. The dashed lines in this table connect differences between totals r steps apart with values of r and W_r. Thus any values along a dashed line which are greater than the corresponding value of W_r are *potentially* significant.

We now start in the upper right hand corner, and test along the first row until we reach a difference which is not significant. The upper right hand entry is 80, which represents a five step difference. Since $80 > 22.38$, this difference is significant, and an asterisk is placed in the corresponding cell of Table 12.5(b). Moving to the left we find an entry of 50 which represents a difference of four steps. We thus compare 50 against $W_4 = 20.95$, and again reject H_0. Once again we place an asterisk in the corresponding cell of Table 12.5(b). Moving further to the left we find the entry of 20 which represents a three step difference and is significant since $W_3 < 20$.

TABLE 12.5

Newman-Keuls Test Applied to Data in Table 12.2

(a)

Treatment			food deprived T_1 40	f & w deprived T_2 55	water deprived T_3 60	ad lib control T_4 90	2/day control T_5 120	r	W_r
food deprived	T_1	40	—	15	20	50	80	5	−22.38
f & w deprived	T_2	55		—	5	35	65	4	−20.95
water deprived	T_3	60			—	30	60	3	−18.94
ad lib control	T_4	90				—	30	2	−15.61
2/day control	T_5	120					—		

(b)

Treatment		food deprived T_1	f & w deprived T_2	water deprived T_3	ad lib control T_4	2/day control T_5
food deprived	T_1			*	*	*
f & w deprived	T_2				*	*
water deprived	T_3				*	*
ad lib control	T_4					*
2/day control	T_5					

Again we place an asterisk in Table 12.5(b). When we come to the far left we find that a two step difference of 15 is not significant ($15 < 15.61$), and thus no asterisk is entered in the matrix.

When we either reach a point where a difference is not significant, or else exhaust a row, we move to the next row. We now start working across the row, but stop under one of three conditions. (1) We exhaust the row, (2) we reach an insignificant difference, or (3) we reach a column at which an insignificant difference was found in an earlier row.

In row two, $65 > 20.95$, $35 > 18.94$, but $5 < 15.61$. Thus we place two asterisks in Table 12.5(b) and continue to the next row. In row three both differences are significant, since $60 > 18.94$ and $30 > 15.61$. Going to row four we also find our one difference to be significant.

The resulting pattern of significant differences is given in Table 12.5(b). Here we can see that the two control groups are different from each other and from all other groups, the water deprived group differs from all groups except the doubly-deprived condition, and the food deprived and the food and water deprived conditions do not differ. These results could be represented graphically by writing down the treatments and underlining homogeneous subsets. Thus

food deprived	f & w deprived	water deprived	ad lib control	2/day control

Treatments that are not underlined by a common line differ significantly from each other.

It is important to note that if a difference in one row is not significant, the tests on that or subsequent rows do not proceed at or beyond that point. The contrived data in Table 12.6 illustrate the difficulty that arises if this rule is ignored. In Table 12.6(a) are the totals and differences. In part (b) are the differences that would be significant if we imposed no restrictions whatsoever, but only asked if $T_i - T_j > W_r$. Here we would be led to conclude that T_3 is greater than T_1, but T_4 (which is numerically larger than T_3) is not different from T_1 (a very curious result). We would also be forced to conclude that T_4 is greater than T_2, but that T_4 is not greater than T_1, even though T_1 is less than T_2.

In Table 12.6(c) are the results that would be obtained if, in any given row, we tested at or beyond a point (column) of non-significance in a *previous* row. When we found that T_4 vs. T_1 was not significant, we should have refrained from any further tests of T_4 or anything to its left. By testing T_2 vs. T_4 we have placed ourselves in the position of saying that T_4 is not different from T_1, but that it is different from T_2. Instead, what we should have concluded, had we followed the rules, is merely that T_5 differs from all other totals, which themselves form a homogeneous set.

TABLE 12.6

Illustration of Effect of Violating Newman-Keuls Sequential Procedures

(a)

	T_1	T_2	T_3	T_4	T_5	r	Wr
	40	**41**	**59**	**60**	**120**		
40	—	1	19	20	80	5	22.38
41		—	18	19	79	4	20.95
59			—	1	61	3	18.94
60				—	60	2	15.61

(b)

	T_1	T_2	T_3	T_4	T_5
T_1			*		*
T_2			*	*	*
T_3					*
T_4					*
T_5					

(c)

	T_1	T_2	T_3	T_4	T_5
T_1					*
T_2			*	*	*
T_3					*
T_4					*
T_5					

By using the Studentized Range Statistic in the way that it does, the Newman-Keuls test holds the experimentwise error rate constant at α, but only against the complete null hypothesis. This is to say that if H_0 is completely true ($\mu_1 = \mu_2 = \cdots = \mu_k$), the probability that at least one of the conclusions is a Type I error $= \alpha$. If the complete null hypothesis is false, but a more limited set of null hypotheses is true (e.g., $(\mu_1 = \mu_2) \neq (\mu_3 = \mu_4) \neq (\mu_5 = \mu_6)$), then the error rate experimentwise will rise from α to a maximum of approximately $\alpha(k/2)$ (Ryan, 1959a). The reason for this is the fact that for each true null hypothesis we have a probability (α) of making a Type I error, and the maximum number of null hypotheses out of k means is $k/2$. If each has a probability α of being falsely rejected, then the probability of one or more false rejections $= 1 - (1 - \alpha)^{k/2}$ which (for any reasonable k) is approximately $\alpha k/2$. (Note that if $\mu_1 = \mu_2 = \mu_3$ but $\bar{X}_1 < \bar{X}_2 < \bar{X}_3$ we do not have to take into account the probability of committing an error on μ_1 vs. μ_2 since the rules preclude our ever running that test unless we have rejected (and therefore committed our first error on) μ_1 vs. μ_3. This is an important feature of the way in which the test controls error rates.)

Unequal sample sizes   The Newman-Keuls procedure (and the Tukey procedures which follow) were primarily designed for the case of equal sample sizes $(n_i = n_j = n)$. Frequently, however, we find ourselves with samples containing unequal numbers of observations and want to carry out a Newman-Keuls or related test on the means. There has not been a great deal of work on this topic, but Keselman, Murray, & Rogan (1976) investigated two alternative solutions. One of their solutions was to replace n by the harmonic mean (n') of *all* sample ns. The other was to replace n by the harmonic mean (n'') of the sample sizes for the two means being compared. Their conclusion was that the use of n'' led to less bias than did the use of n'.

Keselman & Rogan (1977) extended this work and in fact concluded that there was an even better solution. This solution utilizes what was referred to as the Behrens-Fisher approach in Chapter 7. Basically the suggestion amounts to replacing totals with means and then using

$$q = \frac{\bar{X}_i - \bar{X}_j}{\sqrt{\left(\dfrac{s_i^2}{n_i} + \dfrac{s_j^2}{n_j}\right)\Big/ 2}}.$$

The obtained q is compared against $q.05(r, df')$, where $q.05$ is taken from the tables of the Studentized Range Statistic and

$$df' = \frac{\left(\dfrac{s_i^2}{n_i} + \dfrac{s_j^2}{n_j}\right)^2}{\left(\dfrac{s_i^2}{n_i}\right)^2 \Big/ (n_i - 1) + \left(\dfrac{s_j^2}{n_j}\right)^2 \Big/ (n_j - 1)}$$

is substituted for df_{error}.

Duncan's New Multiple Range Test

Duncan's New Multiple Range Test

Duncan (1955) has developed a test which, like the Newman-Keuls, is used for making pairwise comparisons among means. In fact it resembles the Newman-Keuls in every way except for the values of q, which have been adjusted by Duncan. For **Duncan's New Multiple Range Test** we need special tables of q, since this test controls the error rate in a different manner. In effect, Duncan controls the error rate per degree of freedom, rather than per comparison or per experiment. This means that the error rate per experiment is set as high as $(k-1)\alpha$. This value is uncomfortably high, and as a result the Newman-Keuls is recommended over the Duncan.

Duncan's procedures have been challenged by Scheffé (1959, p. 78), and this has led many writers to recommend against using Duncan's test. Since Scheffé's criticisms have not been spelled out specifically, they do not represent an adequate basis for rejecting Duncan's test—even admitting Scheffé's stature as a statistician. However the high error rate per experiment does argue strongly against its use.

Tukey's Tests

Tukey$_a$ test
Honestly Significant
Difference (HSD) test

Much of the work on multiple comparisons has been based on the original work of Tukey, and two important tests bear his name. The ***Tukey$_a$*** ***test*** (sometimes called the **HSD (*Honestly Significant Difference*) *test***) is similar to the Newman-Keuls, except that q_{HSD} is always taken as the maximum value of q_r. In other words, if there are five means, all differences are tested as if they were five steps apart. The effect is to fix the experiment-wise error rate at α against all possible null hypotheses, not just the complete null hypothesis, although with an often substantial loss of power.

Tukey$_b$ test
Wholly Significant
Difference (WSD) test

An alternative test, called the ***Tukey$_b$*** or the ***WSD (Wholly Significant Difference) test*** is a compromise, not being as conservative as the HSD test. In this procedure q_{WSD} is taken as the mean of the value of q_r for the Newman-Keuls and the value of q_{HSD} for the HSD tests. In other words if there are k means and we want to test two means which are r steps apart

$$q_{WSD} = \frac{q_k + q_r}{2}.$$
(12.11)

With this modification, the Tukey WSD proceeds in the same manner as the Newman-Keuls. For a more complete discussion of the test, the student is referred to Ryan (1959a).

Scheffé's Method

Scheffé's test

The *post-hoc* tests we have considered up to now all primarily involve pairwise comparisons of means, although they can be extended to more complex contrasts. ***Scheffé***, using the F distribution, has developed a test which sets the experimentwise error rate at α against all possible linear contrasts, not just pairwise contrasts. If we let

$$L = \Sigma a_i T_i$$

and

$$SS_{contrast} = \frac{L^2}{n \Sigma a_i^2}$$

then

$$F = \frac{L^2}{n \Sigma a_i^2 MS_{error}}.$$

This is precisely the approach we adopted in speaking of linear comparisons. Scheffé then shows that if F_{obt} is evaluated against $(k-1)F_\alpha(k-1, df_{error})$, rather than against $F_\alpha(1, df_{error})$, the experimentwise error is at most α. While this test has the advantage of holding constant the experimentwise error rate for all possible linear contrasts, not just pairwise ones, it has the least power of all of the tests we have discussed. Partly to overcome this objection, Scheffé recommends running his test at $\alpha = .10$. Scheffé further shows that the test is much less sensitive than the Tukey$_a$ to pairwise differences, but more sensitive than the Tukey$_a$ to complex comparisons. In general the Scheffé should never be used to make a set of solely pairwise comparisons, nor should it normally be used for *a priori* comparisons. The test was specifically designed as a *post hoc* test (as were the Newman-Keuls and Tukey's tests), and its use on a limited set of comparisons which were planned before the data were collected would generally be foolish.

Dunnett's Test for Comparing All Treatments with a Control

In some experiments the important comparisons are between one control treatment and each of several experimental treatments. In this case

Dunnett's test   the most appropriate test is **Dunnett's test**. This test will be more powerful (in this situation) than any of the other tests we have discussed which seek to hold the experimentwise error rate at or below α.

We will let t_d represent the critical value of a modified t statistic. This statistic is found in tables supplied by Dunnett (1955, 1964) and reproduced in Appendix (t_d). For a difference between totals T_c and T_j (where T_c represents the total of the control group) to be significant, the difference must exceed

$$\text{critical value } (T_c - T_j) = t_d \sqrt{2n\text{MS}_{\text{error}}}. \qquad (12.12)$$

Applying this test to our data, letting Treatment 1 from Table 12.2 be the control treatment,

$$\text{critical value } (T_c - T_j) = t_d \sqrt{2(5)(5.6)}.$$

We enter Appendix (t_d) with $k = 5$ means and $\text{df}_{\text{error}} = 20$. The resulting value of $t_d = 2.65$.

$$\text{critical value } (T_c - T_j) = 2.65\sqrt{2(5)(5.6)} = 2.65(7.483) = 19.831.$$

Thus whenever the difference between the control treatment (Treatment 1) total and one of the other treatment totals exceeds ± 19.831, that difference will be significant. The $k - 1$ statements we will make concerning this difference will have an experimentwise error rate of $\alpha = .05$.

$$1 \text{ vs. } 2 = 90 - 120 = -30$$

$$1 \text{ vs. } 3 = 90 - 40 = 50$$

$$1 \text{ vs. } 4 = 90 - 60 = 30$$

$$1 \text{ vs. } 5 = 90 - 55 = 35$$

Since we have a two-tailed test (t_d was taken from two-tailed tables), the sign of the difference is irrelevant. All of the differences exceed 19.831 and are therefore declared to be significant.

Unequal sample sizes   In the case where the treatments have unequal sample sizes, a test on the difference in treatment *means* (rather than totals) is given by

$$t_d = \frac{\bar{X}_c - \bar{X}_j}{\sqrt{MS_{error}\left(\dfrac{1}{n_c} + \dfrac{1}{n_j}\right)}},$$

or alternatively

$$\text{crit. diff. } (\bar{X}_c - \bar{X}_j) = t_d \sqrt{MS_{error}\left(\frac{1}{n_c} + \frac{1}{n_j}\right)}.$$

Confidence intervals   To establish confidence intervals on the difference between control and treatment means, the intervals are given by

$$CI(\mu_c - \mu_j) = (\bar{X}_c - \bar{X}_j) \pm t_d \sqrt{\frac{2MS_{error}}{n}}.$$

For our data, again treating Treatment 1 as the control treatment,

$$CI(\mu_c - \mu_2) = (18 - 24) \pm 2.65 \sqrt{\frac{2(5.6)}{5}} = -6 \pm 3.966$$

$$CI(\mu_c - \mu_3) = 10 \pm 3.966$$

$$CI(\mu_c - \mu_4) = 6 \pm 3.966$$

$$CI(\mu_c - \mu_5) = 7 \pm 3.966.$$

Notice that none of the confidence intervals includes zero, which is in line with our previous tests of significance.

Comparison of Dunnett's and Dunn's Tests

Since Dunn's test allows the experimenter to make any *a priori* test, it is reasonable to ask what would happen if we decided *a priori* to apply Dunn's test to the differences between the control mean and the experimental treatment means. If we did this for our data we would find that the required critical difference would be 20.579 instead of 19.831, and thus we would have a less powerful test since a larger difference is needed for rejection of H_0. Both Dunn and Dunnett have based their tests on inequalities of the form $EW \le \alpha$, but Dunnett's is a sharper inequality (Miller, 1966). To put this rather crudely, in Dunnett's case there is more of the *equal to* and less of the *less than* involved in the relationship between *EW* and α. For this reason it is a more powerful test whenever you want to simply compare one treatment (it does not really have to be called a control treatment) with each of the others.

12.7 Comparison of the Alternative Procedures

Since each of the multiple comparison techniques which we have been discussing has been designed for different purposes, there is no truly fair basis on which they can be compared. There is something to be gained, however, from summarizing their particular features and comparing the critical differences they require for the same set of data. In Table 12.7 are listed the tests, the error rate most commonly associated with them, the kinds of comparisons they are primarily designed to test, and the type of test (range test, *F* test, or *t*—modified or not in each case).

TABLE 12.7

Comparison of Alternative Multiple Comparison Procedures

TEST	ERROR RATE*	COMPARISON	TYPE	A PRIORI/ POST HOC
1. Individual *t* tests	*PC*	pairwise	*t*	*a priori*
2. Orthogonal contrasts	*PC*	orthogonal contrasts	*F*	*a priori*
3. Dunn's test	*PE* or *EW*	any contrasts	*t*§	*a priori*
4. Newman-Keuls	*EW*†	pairwise	range	*post hoc*
5. Tukey$_a$ (HSD)	*EW*	pairwise‡	range§	*post hoc*
6. Tukey$_b$ (WSD)	*EW*?	pairwise‡	range§	*post hoc*
7. Scheffé	*EW*	any contrasts	*F*§	*post hoc*

* *PC* = per comparison
  PE = per experiment
  EW = experimentwise

† Against complete H_0.
‡ Tukey$_a$ and Tukey$_b$ can be used for all contrasts, but are poor in this case.
§ Modified.

If we compare the tests in terms of the critical values they require, we are being somewhat unfair to the *a priori* tests. To say that Dunn's test, for example, requires a large critical value when making all possible pairwise comparisons is not really doing the test justice, since it was designed to make relatively few individual comparisons and not to be limited to only pairwise contrasts. However, with this word of caution, Table 12.8 has been constructed to compare the critical differences (W_r) for each test. Orthogonal comparisons have been omitted from this table because they are not appropriate to the structure of the table, and the critical values for pairwise comparisons would be the same as for the individual *t* tests. Dunnett's test has also been omitted because it does not fit with the structure of the table.

TABLE 12.8

Comparison of
Critical Differences
for Alternative
Multiple Comparison
Procedures

	W_2	W_3	W_4	W_5
Individual *t* tests	15.61	15.61	15.61	15.61
Dunn	23.65	23.65	23.65	23.65
Dunn*	20.58	20.58	20.58	20.58
Newman-Keuls	15.61	18.94	20.95	22.38
Tukey$_a$	22.38	22.38	22.38	22.38
Tukey$_b$	19.00	20.66	21.66	22.38
Scheffé	24.64	24.64	24.64	24.64

* Assuming only four pairwise comparisons were desired.

Each of the tests described previously has its proper place in statistical analyses. When complex *a priori* comparisons are called for, Dunn's test is likely to be the most appropriate. In general, however, the Newman-Keuls probably strikes the best balance when *post hoc* comparisons are desired. This test holds the error rate per experiment, and hence the experimentwise error rate, to acceptable levels (for 5 groups *EW* could not exceed .10), while in most cases having considerably more power than the Scheffé and somewhat more power than the Tukey$_a$.

In selecting among the various alternative tests, it is perfectly proper and appropriate to compare the critical differences required by each test for the conditions imposed by the experimental design, and then to choose the test with the smallest critical difference. The choice is independent of the data actually observed, and is therefore both theoretically sound and desirable (Keselman, 1974).

12.8 Summary

In the previous chapter we dealt with the *F* test on the overall null hypothesis. In this chapter we extended this by investigating ways of deriving more information about differences among individual groups or subsets of groups. We spent considerable time on the importance of error rates and the different types of error rates. We then looked at alternative methods for making *a priori* comparisons (of which Dunn's is probably the best) and then at alternative ways of making *post hoc* comparisons (where the Newman-Keuls was considered to be the best choice for the general case). Finally, we compared the alternative procedures in terms of their general characteristics and the size of the critical difference.

Exercises for Chapter 12

12.1   Using the data from Exercise 11.1, compute the linear contrasts for 5 vs. (20 & 35) days and 20 vs. 35 days, using $\alpha = .05$ for each contrast.

12.2   What would be the per comparison, per experiment, and experiment-wise error rates in Exercise 12.1? (*Hint*: Are the contrasts orthogonal?)

12.3   Compute the F for the linear contrast on the two groups in Exercise 11.2. Why was this a waste of time?

12.4   Compute the Studentized Range Statistic for the two groups in Exercise 11.2 and show that it is equal to $t\sqrt{2}$ (where t is taken from Exercise 11.2*b*).

12.5   Compute the Fs for the following linear contrasts in Exercise 11.3. Save the results for use in Chapter 13.
a.   1 & 2 vs. 3 & 4
b.   1 & 3 vs. 2 & 4
c.   1 & 4 vs. 2 & 3
d.   What questions do these contrasts answer?

12.6   Run Dunn's test on the data for Exercise 11.1 using the contrasts supplied in Exercise 12.1. Set the maximum experimentwise error rate at .05.

12.7   Run a Newman-Keuls test on the example given in Table 11.3(a) and interpret the results.

12.8   Calculate the two Tukey tests on the data in the example in Table 11.3(a) and compare those results to the results in the previous question.

12.9   Consider the following data for five groups:

Group	1	2	3	4	5
$\bar{X}_j$	10	18	19	21	29
n_j	8	5	8	7	9
s_j^2	7.4	8.9	8.6	7.2	9.3

Run a Newman-Keuls test on these data.

12.10   Run a Tukey WSD procedure on the data in the preceding question.

12.11   Use the Scheffé procedure on the data in Exercise 12.9 to compare groups 1, 2, & 3 (combined) with groups 4 & 5 (combined). Then compare group 1 with groups 2–4 (combined). (*Hint*: You will need to go back to the section on unequal sample sizes under the heading of orthogonal contrasts.)

12.12   Use an SPSS ONEWAY procedure to confirm your answers to Exercises 12.7 and 12.8.

12.13   How could MINITAB (for example) be used to run Dunn's test on the data in Exercise 12.6?

13

Factorial Analysis of Variance

Objective

To further extend the discussion of the analysis of variance to the case in which we have two or more independent variables.

Contents

In the last two chapters we dealt with a one-way analysis of variance in which we had only one independent variable. In this chapter we are going to extend the analysis of variance to the treatment of experimental designs involving two or more independent variables. For purposes of simplicity, we will be concerned primarily with experiments involving two or three variables, although the extension to more complex designs should be immediately obvious.

For an example, we might wish to compare the number of stress ulcers for shocked, yoked-shock, and control subjects after six hours of stress.† Taken by itself this would be a traditional one-way design. At the same time we might think that stress duration is an important variable and would want to compare our three shock conditions under each of four different stress durations (e.g., 2, 4, 6, or 8 hours of stress). This study would now contain two independent variables (Shock Condition and Stress Duration) and would *Two-way factorial* be an instance of what is called a ***two-way factorial design***.
design

Our experiment on stress could be extended to include three variables if we consider the fact that some studies have shown that female rats show more ulceration than male rats. Thus we might employ all combinations of two levels of Sex, three levels of Shock Condition, and four levels of Duration *Three-way factorial* into one study. This would produce a ***three-way factorial design***.
design

When we have an experimental design in which every level of every variable is paired with every level of every other variable, we have what is *Factorial design* called a ***factorial design***. In other words a factorial design is one in which we include all *combinations* of the levels of the independent variables. The phrase "factorial design" is *usually* applied only to those designs in which separate groups of subjects receive the different treatment combinations. When the research plan calls for the same subject to be included under more *Repeated measures* than one treatment combination we will speak of ***repeated measures designs***, *designs* even if the arrangement of treatment combinations does in fact form a factorial pattern. The discussion of repeated measures designs will be left until the next chapter, and in this chapter we will consider only those designs involving independent groups of subjects.

Factorial designs have several very important advantages over one-way designs. First of all they allow greater generalizability of the results. Consider the study involving Shock Condition and Stress Duration mentioned previously. If we were to run an experiment using only the three shock conditions, we would most likely use only one duration, and thus our results would apply only to that duration. When we use a factorial design with the three shock conditions and four stress durations, our results on Shock Condition are averaged across the four Durations, very likely resulting in a much broader interpretation of the data on the effects of the different

advantages over 1way

---

† A shocked animal is one who receives shock contingent in some way on his behavior. A yoked-shock animal is one who receives the same shocks as another animal with whom he is yoked, independent of his own behavior.

Interaction

conditions. At the same time we retain the ability to examine the data for each individual duration if we so desire.

The second important feature of factorial designs is that they allow us to look at the *interaction* of variables. We can ask if the effect of Shock Condition is independent of the Duration of the stress, or if there is some interaction of effects between Condition and Duration. We might find, for example, that the Shock group showed ulceration after only two hours of stress and that prolonging the stress led to no further increment in ulceration. For the yoked-shock animals, on the other hand, we might find no ulceration at first, but an increase in ulceration with longer durations. The control group would most likely show no ulceration under any duration. Thus we would conclude that differences between Conditions are dependent upon the Duration used.

A third advantage of a factorial design is its economy in terms of subjects. Since we will be averaging the effects of one variable across all levels of the other variable, a two variable factorial will require fewer subjects than two one-ways for the same degree of power. Essentially we are getting something for nothing.

Factorial designs are labeled by the number of variables involved. Thus a factorial design with two independent variables or factors is called a two-way factorial, and one with three factors is called a three-way. An alternative method of labeling designs is in terms of the number of levels of each variable. Our hypothetical stress study had three levels of the Shock Condition and four levels of Stress Duration. As such, it might be referred to as a *3 × 4 factorial design*. A study with three variables, two of them having three levels and one having four levels might be called a $3 \times 3 \times 4$ factorial. The use of such terms as "two-way" and "2×3" are both common ways of designating designs, and both will be used in this book.

3×4 factorial design

13.1   Two-way Factorial Analysis of Variance

In much of what follows we will concern ourselves primarily with the two-way analysis. Higher order analyses follow almost automatically once you understand the two-way, and many of the related problems we will discuss are most simply explained in terms of two variables. For the moment we will also limit our discussion to fixed, as opposed to random, models as these were defined in Chapter 11.

Notation

Consider a hypothetical experiment with two variables, *A* and *B*. A design of this type is illustrated in Table 13.1. The number of levels of *A*

TABLE 13.1

Representation of
Factorial Design

	B_1	B_2	$\cdots$	B_b	
A_1	X_{111} X_{112} $\cdots$ $\underline{X_{11n}}$ T_{11}	X_{121} X_{122} $\cdots$ $\underline{X_{12n}}$ T_{12}		X_{1b1} X_{1b2} $\cdots$ $\underline{X_{1bn}}$ T_{1b}	T_{A_1}
A_2	X_{211} X_{212} $\cdots$ $\underline{X_{21n}}$ T_{21}	X_{221} X_{222} $\cdots$ $\underline{X_{22n}}$ T_{22}		X_{2b1} X_{2b2} $\cdots$ $\underline{X_{2bn}}$ T_{2b}	T_{A_2}
$\cdots$					$\cdots$
A_a	X_{a11} X_{a12} $\cdots$ $\underline{X_{a1n}}$ T_{a1}	X_{a21} X_{a22} $\cdots$ $\underline{X_{a2n}}$ T_{a2}		X_{ab1} X_{ab2} $\cdots$ $\underline{X_{abn}}$ T_{ab}	T_{A_a}
	T_{B1}	T_{B2}	$\cdots$	T_{B_b}	GT

will be designated by "a", and the number of levels of B will be designated by "b". Any given combination of one level of A and one level of B is called a *cell*, and the number of observations per cell is denoted "n", or, more precisely, n_{ij}. The total number of observations is $N = \Sigma n_{ij} = abn$. When any confusion might arise an individual observation (X) can be designated by three subscripts, i.e., X_{ijk}, where the subscript i refers to the number of the row (level of A), the subscript j refers to the number of the column (level of B), and the subscript k refers to the kth observation in the ijth cell. Thus X_{234} is the 4th subject in the cell corresponding to the 2nd row and 3rd column. Totals for the individual levels of A will be denoted T_{A_i}, and for the levels of B will be denoted T_{B_j}. The cell totals will be designated T_{ij}. The Grand Total is symbolized by GT or ΣX. Needless subscripts serve only as a source of confusion, and whenever possible they will be omitted. The notation outlined above will be used throughout the discussion of the analysis of variance, and it is important that you thoroughly understand it before proceeding. The advantage of the present system is that it is easily generalized to more complex designs. Thus if we had a third variable (C), there should be no question as to what T_{C_2} refers.

Example 13.1

**Hypothetical Data
for a 2 × 3
Factorial Design**

We will begin our discussion by proceeding immediately to the calculation of a completed summary table for the analysis of a 2 × 3 factorial.

Following that we will discuss the various aspects of the analysis in more detail. As an illustration of a two-way analysis of variance consider the data presented in Table 13.2(a). Here we have two levels of A, three levels of B, and five scores per cell. Thus $a = 2$, $b = 3$, $n = 5$, and $N = abn = 30$. Before we consider any calculations, look only at the totals. From the totals it would appear that there are differences between the two levels of A and among the three levels of B. We can also see that the increase from B_1 to B_3 is more rapid under A_1 than under A_2. This is what we mean by an interaction between A and B—the effect of B appears to be dependent upon the level of A. Whether these differences which we have mentioned turn out to be significant remains to be seen, but at least we have some vague idea of what to expect from the analysis.

The calculations for the sums of squares appear in Table 13.2(b). Many of these calculations should be familiar, since they resemble the procedures used with a one-way. For example, SS_{total} is computed in exactly the same way that it was computed in Chapter 11, and in exactly the same way in which it is always computed. We sum all of the squared observations and subtract $(\Sigma X)^2/N$, the *Correction Factor* (*CF*).

The sum of squares for variable A (SS_A) is nothing but the SS_{treat} we would obtain if this were a one-way analysis of variance without variable B. In other words we simply sum the squared A totals, divide by the number of observations on which each A total is based, and subtract the correction factor. The same thing can be said for SS_B, except that here we ignore the presence of variable A.

You will note that ΣT_A^2 is divided by nb and ΣT_B^2 is divided by na. If you try to remember these denominators as formulae, you will only succeed in accumulating unnecessary, and easily forgotten, information. The denominators represent the number of scores per total, and nothing more. They are exactly analogous to the denominator (n) we used in the one-way when we wanted to turn a variance of totals into an estimate of σ_e^2. The only difference is that in a one-way n represented the number of observations per treatment and here it represents the number of observations per cell—since b cells receive Treatment A_i, there must be nb observations for T_{Ai}.

After more than ten years of teaching this material I have concluded that confusion about denominators in the analysis of variance is innate—you were born confused. In fact there is no good reason for such confusion. ***Whenever you square any total, divide that square by the number of observations on which the total was based.*** Above all, never try to memorize formulae for denominators. They exist only so that textbook writers have a way of writing equations precisely. I have heard of one instructor who rewrites all

TABLE 13.2		B_1	B_2	B_3	T_{Ai}
Hypothetical Data					
and Calculations		2	8	10	
for 2×3		4	9	15	
Factorial Design	A_1	6	4	12	
(a) Data		1	7	16	
		7	12	17	
		20	40	70	130
		10	7	13	
		8	12	16	
	A_2	12	10	18	
		5	17	17	
		15	14	11	
		50	60	75	185
	T_{Bj}	70	100	145	$315 = \Sigma X$

(b) Computations

$$\Sigma X^2 = 3969 \qquad (\Sigma X)^2/N = CF = \frac{315^2}{30} = 3307.50$$

$$SS_{total} = \Sigma X^2 - (\Sigma X)^2/N = 3969 - 3307.50 = 661.50$$

$$SS_A = \frac{\Sigma T_{A_i}^2}{nb} - \frac{(\Sigma X)^2}{N} = \frac{130^2 + 185^2}{15} - CF$$

$$= 3408.333 - 3307.50 = 100.833$$

$$SS_B = \frac{\Sigma T_{B_j}^2}{na} - \frac{(\Sigma X)^2}{N} = \frac{70^2 + 100^2 + 145^2}{10} - CF$$

$$= 3592.50 - 3307.50 = 285.00$$

$$SS_{cells} = \frac{\Sigma T_{ij}^2}{n} - \frac{(\Sigma X)^2}{N} = \frac{20^2 + 40^2 + \cdots + 75^2}{5} - CF$$

$$= 3725 - 3307.50 = 417.40$$

$$SS_{AB} = SS_{cells} - SS_A - SS_B$$

$$= 417.50 - 100.833 - 285.00 = 31.667$$

$$SS_{error} = SS_{total} - SS_{cells} = 661.50 - 417.50 = 244$$

(c) Summary table

Source	df	SS	MS	F
A row	1	100.833	100.833	9.918*
B column	2	285.000	142.500	14.016*
AB interaction	2	31.667	15.833	1.557
Error	24	244.000	10.167	
Total	29	661.500		

* $p < .05$.

$$Y_{ijk} = \mu + \alpha_j + \beta_k + \alpha\beta_{jk} + e_{ijk}$$

denominators as "fln" which translates to "funny little numbers." If I weren't afraid of not being taken seriously, I would follow his lead in this book.

Having obtained SS_{total}, SS_A, and SS_B, we come to an unfamiliar term (SS_{cells}). This term represents the variability of the individual cell totals, and is in fact only a dummy term which will not appear in the summary table. It is calculated just like any other sum of squares. We take the *cell* totals, square and sum them, divide by the number of observations per total, and subtract the correction factor. While it might not be readily apparent why we want this term, its usefulness becomes clear when we come to calculating a sum of squares for the interaction of A and B.

The SS_{cells} is a measure of how much the cell totals (and thus means) differ. Two cell totals may differ for any of three reasons. They may differ because they come from different levels of A. They may also differ because they come from different levels of B. Thirdly, they may differ because of an interaction between A and B. We already have a measure of how much the cells differ, since we know SS_{cells}. SS_A tells us how much of this difference can be attributed to differences in A, and SS_B tells us how much can be attributed to differences in B. Whatever can not be attributed to A or B, must be attributable to the interaction of A and B (SS_{AB}). Thus to obtain SS_{AB} we simply subtract SS_A and SS_B from SS_{cells}. Whatever is left over is SS_{AB}. In our example

$$SS_{AB} = SS_{cells} - SS_A - SS_B$$

$$31.667 = 417.500 - 100.833 - 285.000.$$

All that we have left to calculate is the sum of squares due to error. Just as in the one-way analysis we will obtain this by subtraction. The total variation is represented by SS_{total}. Of this total we know how much can be attributed to A, B, and AB. What is left over represents unaccountable variation, or error. Thus

$$SS_{error} = SS_{total} - (SS_A + SS_B + SS_{AB}).$$

But since $SS_A + SS_B + SS_{AB} = SS_{cells}$, it is simpler to write

$$SS_{error} = SS_{total} - SS_{cells}.$$

This provides us with our sum of squares for error, and we now have all of the necessary sums of squares for our analysis.

A more direct, but tiresome, method of obtaining SS_{error} exists, and it makes explicit just what the error sum of squares is measuring. SS_{error} represents the variation within each cell, and as such can be calculated by obtaining the sum of squares for each cell separately. For example,

$$SS_{cell\ 11} = 2^2 + 4^2 + 6^2 + 1^2 + 7^2 - \frac{20^2}{5} = 26.$$

We could perform a similar operation on each of the remaining cells obtaining

$$SS_{cell\ 11} = 26$$
$$SS_{cell\ 12} = 34$$
$$SS_{cell\ 13} = 34$$
$$SS_{cell\ 21} = 58$$
$$SS_{cell\ 22} = 58$$
$$SS_{cell\ 23} = 34$$
$$\overline{244.}$$

The sum of squares within each cell are then summed over the six cells to produce SS_{error}. While this is the hard way of going about computing an error term, it demonstrates that SS_{error} is in fact the sum of the within-cell variation.

In part (c) of Table 13.2 is the summary table for the analysis of variance. The source column and the sum of squares column are fairly obvious from what has already been said. It is instructive to note, however, that we could organize the summary table somewhat differently, although we would seldom do so in practice. Thus we could have

Source	df	SS	
Among cells	5	417.500	
A ~~rows −1~~	1		100.833
B ~~col −1~~	2		285.000
AB ~~(row −1)(col−1)~~	2		31.667
Within cells (Error) ~~N − row(col)~~	24	244.000	
Total ~~N−1~~	29	661.500	

This alternative summary table makes it clear that we have partitioned the total variation into variation among the cell totals and variation within the cells. The former is then further partitioned into *A*, *B*, and *AB*.

Returning to Table 13.2(c) we come to the degrees of freedom. The calculation of df is straightforward. The total degrees of freedom (df_{total}) are always equal to $N-1$. The df for *A* and *B* are the number of levels of the variable minus 1. Thus $df_A = a-1$ and $df_B = b-1$. The number of degrees of freedom for any interaction is simply the product of the degrees of freedom for the components of that interaction.[†] Thus $df_{AB} = df_A \times df_B = (a-1)(b-1)$. The degrees of freedom for error can either be obtained by subtraction ($df_{total} - df_A - df_B - df_{AB}$), or by realizing that the error term represents variability within each cell, that the cells have $n-1$ each, and that there are *ab* cells. Therefore $df_{error} = ab(n-1) = 2 \times 3 \times 4 = 24$.

[†] These three rules apply to *any* analysis of variance, no matter how complex.

Just as with the one-way analysis of variance the mean squares are again obtained by dividing the sums of squares by the corresponding degrees of freedom. This is the same procedure we will use in any analysis of variance.

Finally, to calculate F, we divide each MS by MS_{error}. Thus for A, $F_A = MS_A/MS_{error}$; for B, $F_B = MS_B/MS_{error}$; and for AB, $F_{AB} = MS_{AB}/MS_{error}$. To appreciate why MS_{error} is the appropriate divisor in each case, we must make a brief digression and consider the underlying structural model and the expected mean squares.

Structural Model and Expected Mean Squares

You should recall that in discussing a one-way analysis of variance we employed the structural model

$$X_{ij} = \mu + \tau_j + e_{ij}$$

where $\tau_j = \mu_j - \mu$ represented the effect of the jth treatment. In a two-way we have two "treatment" variables (A and B) and their interaction. These can be represented in the model by the symbols α, β, and $\alpha\beta$, producing a slightly more complex model. This model can be written

$$X_{ijk} = \mu + \alpha_i + \beta_j + \alpha\beta_{ij} + e_{ijk}$$

where

X_{ijk} = any observation
μ = the grand mean
α_i = the effect of Treatment $A_i = \mu_{A_i} - \mu$; $\Sigma\alpha_i = 0$
β_j = the effect of Treatment $B_j = \mu_{B_j} - \mu$; $\Sigma\beta_j = 0$
$\alpha\beta_{ij}$ = the interaction effect of Treatment A_i and B_j
       = $\mu - \mu_{A_i} - \mu_{B_j} + \mu_{ij}$; $\Sigma_i\alpha\beta_{ij} = \Sigma_j\alpha\beta_{ij} = 0$
e_{ijk} = the unit of error associated with observation X_{ijk};
$e_{ijk} = N(0, \sigma_e^2)$.

From this model it can be shown that, with fixed variables, the expected mean squares are those given in Table 13.3. From the table it is apparent that the error term is the proper denominator for each F ratio, since the $E(MS)$ for any effect contains only one term other than σ_e^2. Consider for a moment the test of the effect of variable A.

$$\frac{E(MS_A)}{E(MS_{error})} = \frac{\sigma_e^2 + nb\sigma_\alpha^2}{\sigma_e^2}.$$

If H_0 is true, then $\mu_{A_1} = \mu_{A_2} = \mu$, and σ_α^2 will be zero. In this case F would have an expectation of approximately 1 and would be distributed as the standard F distribution (actually the expectation for F under H_0 is $df_{error}/(df_{error} - 2)$). If H_0 is false, however, then σ_α^2 will not be zero and F will have an expectation greater than 1 and will not follow the central

TABLE 13.3

Expected Mean
Squares for
2-way Analysis
of Variance

Source	E(MS)
A	$\sigma_e^2 + nb\sigma_\alpha^2$
B	$\sigma_e^2 + na\sigma_\beta^2$
AB	$\sigma_e^2 + n\sigma_{\alpha\beta}^2$
Error	σ_e^2

F distribution. The same type of logic applies to tests on the effects of B and AB.

Interpretation

From Table 13.2(c) we find that the effects of A and B are significant, while the AB interaction is not significant. Thus we can conclude that there are differences in performance due to variable A ($A_1 < A_2$), and differences in performance due to variable B. Due to the fact that the AB interaction is not significant, we can conclude that we have no evidence against the hypothesis that the effect of A is the same for each level of B, and conversely, the effect of B is the same for each level of A. This is most easily seen when the data are plotted as in Figure 13.1. In this figure the ordinate represents the dependent variable, the abscissa represents the levels of one of the variables (in this case B), and the two lines represent the two levels of the other independent variable (A).

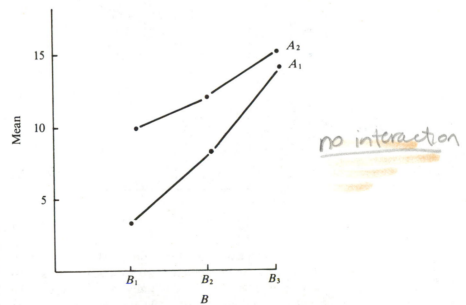

FIGURE 13.1

Cell means for
data in
Table 13.2

From Figure 13.1 we can see that the two lines are more or less parallel, meaning that the differences between the levels of A are approximately the same whether we look at B_1, B_2, or B_3. Had the lines been perfectly parallel, the SS_{AB} would have been exactly zero. On the other hand, had the lines been running at right angles to one another, SS_{AB} would have been at its maximum and the effect of A would have been dependent upon the level of B.

Interactions

Main effects

One of the major benefits of factorial designs is the fact that they allow us to examine the interaction of variables. Indeed in many cases the interaction term may well be of greater interest than the ***main effects*** (the effects of variables taken individually). Consider, for example, a study in which we endeavor to change opinions concerning some issue. It might be reasonable to assume that if we took subjects who have no particular opinion on the issue, the more extreme the communication (within limits), the more the shift in the direction of the communication. On the other hand, if subjects are strongly opposed to the position we advocate, stronger and stronger communications might well result in more and more of a shift *away* from our position. Data from such a hypothetical study are illustrated in Figure 13.2.

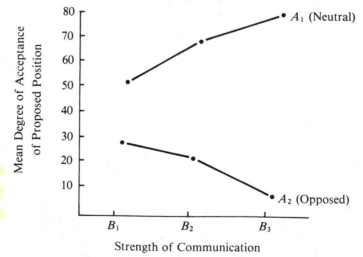

FIGURE 13.2

Hypothetical data illustrating interaction between two variables

In this experiment it is obviously of very little interest to ask if there are differences between the two groups. Of course there are, since we selected our groups on that basis initially, and our theory hardly predicts that they will come closer together. At the same time we probably have very little interest in the main effect of the *strength of communication* variable. Since we expect that one set of scores will increase and the other will decrease, it might not be of any interest how these diverging curves average out in the end. It is the interaction term which is of primary interest. We have predicted that the two groups will behave in different ways to different levels of the communication variable, and that is precisely what a significant interaction would tell us is happening. This is not to say that if we obtain a significant interaction we are finished; we still have to ask if the variables interact in the way we predict, but we will postpone that problem for a while.

There are many people who will argue that if you find a significant interaction, the main effects should be ignored. Some readers may see the previous example as an illustration of this principle. However, I can not accept the validity of this rule as a firm *caveat* against looking beyond a significant interaction. As an illustration of the problem, consider Figure 13.3 as representing alternative data we might have obtained from our communication experiment. These data are purely hypothetical, and probably could not be obtained in practice, but they illustrate the point nicely.

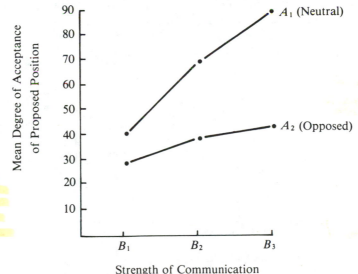

FIGURE 13.3

Hypothetical data illustrating interaction and interpretable main effects

Here we see that the two variables interact, since one curve has a much steeper slope than the other. However both groups rise to some extent, and if this effect is significant it may be worth knowing about. In this case we would have data to suggest that if you can not select your audience you should make your message strong rather than weak (at least within the limits established by this study). For both groups a strong message will have more effect than a weak one, although the effect is not as noticeable for the Opposed Group.

The important point to be gained from this discussion is that when an interaction is significant the experimenter should look even more carefully than usual at the data before making any statements about the main effects. These statements may be justified or they may not, depending on the nature of the data. No rules will substitute for common sense.

Simple Effects

Simple effects

A very important technique for analyzing data which contain significant interactions is the examination and testing of what are called *simple effects*. A simple effect is defined as the effect of one variable at *one* level of the other variable. In our example the effect of the communication variable for the Neutral Group would be a simple effect. The effect of the communication variable for the Opposed Group would be another simple effect. A third simple effect might be the difference between groups for the weakest level of the communication variable.

As an illustration, assume that the data in Table 13.4 represent those data plotted in Figure 13.3. The data in this table are cell totals, the individual observations having been omitted. An analysis of variance can be computed, however, if we define ΣX^2 to be 212850 and n to be 10.

TABLE 13.4

Illustration of Calculation of Simple Effects

(*a*) Data (cell totals)

			COMMUNICATION				
			Weak	*Moderate*	*Strong*		
			B_1	B_2	B_3		
GROUP	*Neutral*	A_1	400	700	900	2000	
	Opposed	A_2	300	400	450	1150	$\Sigma X^2 = 212850$
			700	1100	1350	3150	$CF = \dfrac{3150^2}{60} = 165375.0$

(*b*) Computations

(1*b*) Overall analysis

$$SS_{total} = \Sigma X^2 - \frac{(\Sigma X)^2}{N} = 212850 - 165375 = 47475$$

$$SS_A = \frac{\Sigma T_A^2}{nb} - CF = \frac{2000^2 + 1150^2}{30} - 165375 = 12041.67$$

$$SS_B = \frac{\Sigma T_B^2}{na} - CF = \frac{700^2 + 1100^2 + 1350^2}{20} - 165375 = 10750$$

$$SS_{cells} = \frac{\Sigma T_{cell}^2}{n} - CF = \frac{400^2 + 700^2 + \cdots + 450^2}{10} - 165375 = 25875$$

$$SS_{AB} = SS_{cells} - SS_A - SS_B = 25875 - 12041.67 - 10750 = 3083.33$$

$$SS_{error} = SS_{total} - SS_{cells} = 21600$$

(2b) Simple effects

$$SS_{B \text{ at } A_1} = \frac{400^2 + 700^2 + 900^2}{10} - \frac{2000^2}{30} = 12666.67$$

$$SS_{B \text{ at } A_2} = \frac{300^2 + 400^2 + 450^2}{10} - \frac{1150^2}{30} = 1166.67$$

$$SS_{A \text{ at } B_1} = \frac{400^2 + 300^2}{10} - \frac{700^2}{20} = 500$$

$$SS_{A \text{ at } B_2} = \frac{700^2 + 400^2}{10} - \frac{1100^2}{20} = 4500$$

$$SS_{A \text{ at } B_3} = \frac{900^2 + 450^2}{10} - \frac{1350^2}{20} = 10125$$

(c) Summary tables   **(1c)** Overall analysis

Source	df	SS	MS	F
A (Group)	1	12041.67	12041.67	30.10*
B (Communication)	2	10750.00	5375.00	13.44*
AB	2	3083.33	1541.67	3.85*
Error	54	21600.00	400.00	
Total	59	47475.00		

* $p < .05$.

(2c) Simple effects

Source	df	SS	MS	F
A (Group)				
A at B_1	1	500.00	500.00	1.25
A at B_2	1	4500.00	4500.00	11.25*
A at B_3	1	10125.00	10125.00	25.31*
B (Communication)				
B at A_1	2	12666.67	6333.33	15.83*
B at A_2	2	1166.67	583.33	1.46
Error	54	21600.00	400.00	

* $p < .05$.

The analysis as presented in parts **(1b)** and **(1c)** of Table 13.4 is a straightforward two-way analysis of variance. It reveals that both main effects and the interaction are significant at $p < .05$. The main effect of A (Group) indicates that in general the group which was initially opposed to the position advocated by the communication (A_1) is still more opposed to it than the Neutral Group (A_2) after the communication has been presented, a result which is not expected to surprise very many people. The fact that the main effect of the communications variable (B) is significant means that *on the average* the stronger the communication the greater its effect in changing reported opinions. (As a matter of fact it is an article of faith (but a reasonable one) to suggest a trend in the data. All we can really say is that at least one mean is different from the others.)

The significant interaction reveals that the two groups respond differently to the different levels of the communications variable. Inspection of the data suggests that the Opposed Groups change very little while the Neutral Groups increase rapidly across the levels of Communication. In response to these results we might do well to ask whether there are significant differences among the three Opposed Groups, since that line is relatively flat. Even if the three Opposed means were identical, the marked differences among the Neutral groups could produce a significant main effect. At the same time we might wish to ask if the two groups were really different at the weakest form of the communication. The analyses of these simple effects are presented in parts **(2b)** and **(2c)** of Table 13.4. In fact all of the simple effects are analyzed for the sake of completeness, although in general we would only look at those simple effects in which we have some particular interest.

In Table 13.4**(2b)** it can be seen that $SS_{A \text{ at } B_1}$ is calculated in the same way as any sum of squares. We simply calculate SS_A for the data from B_1 only. If we consider only the B_1 data, the totals for A are 400 and 300. Thus the sum of squares will be

$$SS_{A \text{ at } B_1} = \frac{\Sigma T_A^2 \text{ at } B_1}{n} - \frac{(\Sigma X)^2}{N}$$

where N is now 20 rather than 60, ΣX is 700 rather than 3150, and the totals for A are the totals at level B_1. Thus

$$SS_{A \text{ at } B_1} = \frac{400^2 + 300^2}{10} - \frac{700^2}{20} = 500.00.$$

The other simple effects are calculated in the same way, by ignoring all data in which you are not at the moment interested.

The degrees of freedom for the simple effects are the same as for the corresponding main effects. This is as it should be, since the number of means being compared remains constant.

To test the simple effects we use the error term from the overall analysis (MS_{error}). The expected mean squares presented in Table 13.5 make it clear why this should be so. The expected mean squares for each simple effect contain only one effect other than error (e.g., $n\sigma_{\alpha \text{ at } B_1}^2$), while MS_{error} is an estimate of error variance (σ_e^2).

From the column of F in Table 13.4**(2c)** it is evident that two of our simple effects are not significant. First of all, there are no differences among

TABLE 13.5

Expected Mean Squares for Simple Effects

Source	E(MS)
Simple effects of A	
A at B_1	$\sigma_e^2 + n\sigma_{\alpha \text{ at } B_1}^2$
A at B_2	$\sigma_e^2 + n\sigma_{\alpha \text{ at } B_2}^2$
A at B_3	$\sigma_e^2 + n\sigma_{\alpha \text{ at } B_3}^2$
Simple effects of B	
B at A_1	$\sigma_e^2 + n\sigma_{\beta \text{ at } A_1}^2$
B at A_2	$\sigma_e^2 + n\sigma_{\beta \text{ at } A_2}^2$
Error	σ_e^2

the three levels of the communications variable for the Opposed Group (B at A_2). Thus in this experiment increasing the strength of the communication had no reliable effect for this group, although it does for the Neutral Group. We can also see that the two groups do not differ at the weakest level of the communication (A at B_1), but only begin to differ as the communication becomes stronger.

The present example has shown that we can employ tests on simple effects to clarify significant main effects and interactions. It is also important to note that simple effects can make important contributions to the interpretation of nonsignificant main effects. Examine the data illustrated in Figure 13.4. In this figure the main effects of both A and B will be nonsignificant, and yet these variables obviously play an important role in the data (in fact both SS_A and SS_B will be zero). This does not mean that A and B are not important, however. If we calculate the simple effects we could easily find that they all are significant.

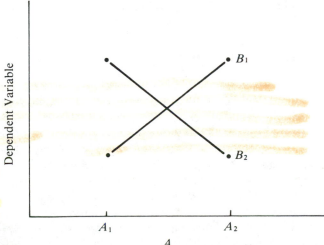

FIGURE 13.4

Illustration of significant simple effects with no main effects

interaction diagram

In general, we would seldom look at simple effects unless there is a significant interaction. However, like all rules this one must be interpreted in the light of common sense. It is not difficult to imagine data for which an analysis of simple effects would be warranted even in the face of a non-significant interaction, or imagine studies in which the simple effects are the prime focus of interest.

Among the important points to be drawn from the discussion of simple effects, one of the most important is the fact that the experimenter must examine her data carefully. Plotting the data and considering what they mean is an important, if not the *most* important, part of an appropriate analysis of variance.

Additivity of simple effects   All sums of squares in the analysis of variance (other than SS_{total}) represent a partitioning of some larger sum of squares, and the simple effects are no exception. The simple effects of A at each level of B represent a partitioning of SS_A and SS_{AB}, while the effects of B at each level of A partition SS_B and SS_{AB}. Thus

$$\Sigma(SS_{A \text{ at } B_j}) = 500 + 4500 + 10125 = 15125$$

$$SS_A + SS_{AB} = 12401.67 + 3083.33 = 15125$$

$$\Sigma(SS_{B \text{ at } A_i}) = 12666.67 + 1166.67 = 13833.34$$

$$SS_B + SS_{AB} = 10750.00 + 3083.33 = 13833.33.$$

A similar additive relationship holds for the degrees of freedom. The fact that the sums of squares for simple effects sum to the combined sums of squares for the corresponding main effect and interaction affords us a quick and simple check on our calculations.

Error Rates

In testing simple effects it is important to keep in mind that we are generally working with an error rate per comparison of α. In the present example we have calculated eight Fs, each at $\alpha = .05$. This means that we have an error rate per experiment of $8(\alpha) = .40$, and an error rate experiment-wise which probably approaches .40. This is an uncomfortably high error rate, and not one to be recommended without careful consideration. As a general rule, the experimenter must carefully balance the gain to be expected from testing all simple effects against the danger to be incurred from an unpleasantly high error rate. In practice one usually finds that only a very few of the possible simple effects are of *a priori* interest, and only these few should be tested.

Example 13.2

A Computer Example: a Reinstatement of a Conditioned Response

As a final example of a two-way factorial, and to illustrate the output of several computer programs, consider the following learning experiment. An interesting phenomenon in the learning literature is called *reinstatement*, and refers to the fact that if we pair a tone and a shock until the tone comes to elicit a (conditioned) response, and then we extinguish that response by presenting the tone alone, a single presentation of the (unpaired) shock will serve to "reinstate" the tone as a stimulus which will produce the conditioned response. In the following experiment we examine reinstatement when the animal is presented with either one, two, or three trials of either a shock or a loud buzzer (which is aversive but has never been paired with the tone). The dependent variable is the magnitude of the (reinstated) response.

		NUMBER OF REINSTATEMENT TRIALS		
		1	**2**	**3**
REINSTATING STIMULUS	*Shock*	10	9	8
		8	11	9
		12	16	7
		15	13	9
	Buzzer	10	10	5
		7	8	7
		6	9	7
		8	5	8

The results of the analysis using MINITAB, SPSS, and BMDP2V are presented in Table 13.6(a), (b), and (c). As you can see, each program produces slightly different printout, but the essential features are the same.

MINITAB presents the analysis of variance summary table (leaving the calculation of the F statistic to the user), the cell and marginal means, and a schematic presentation of row and column means. SPSS merely shows the summary table for the analysis of variance, although the cell means could be generated with the SSPS-BREAKDOWN procedure. The unique feature of SPSS is that it shows the total variation explained by main effects, the total variation explained by interaction effects, and the total explained variation. BMDP2V presents the most complete output. The one unique feature of the BMDP2V summary table is the line labeled MEAN. The sum of squares for this term (SS_{mean}) is merely the correction factor ($(\Sigma X)^2/N$), and the corresponding F tests the null hypothesis that $\mu = 0$. In most cases the result of this test is a foregone conclusion and we have no interest in it.

From each of these analyses we see that there is a significant effect of the stimulus used (with the shock producing more reinstatement than the buzzer) and also a significant effect due to the number of reinstatement trials. Contrary to what we might expect, reinstatement does not monotonically increase with trials. Rather it increases at first and then decreases. This could be explained by arguing that with three unpaired trials the animal is learning that the aversive stimulus and the tone are not correlated.

TABLE 13.6

Results of Analysis of Variance on Reinstatement Data

(*a*) MINITAB output

```
-- TWOWAY ANOVA WITH DATA IN C1, STIMULUS IN C2, AND  REINSTATEMENTS IN C3

ANALYSIS OF VARIANCE

DUE TO            DF        SS       MS=SS/DF
C2                 1      57.04        57.04
C3                 2      30.08        15.04
C2    * C3         2       8.08         4.04
ERROR             18      83.75         4.65
TOTAL             23     178.96

CELL MEANS
ROWS ARE LEVELS OF C2     COLS ARE LEVELS OF C3
                                              ROW
              1         2         3         MEANS
      1     11.25     12.25      8.25       10.58
      2      7.75      8.00      6.75        7.50
COL.
MEANS       9.50     10.13      7.50        9.04

POOLED ST. DEV. =      2.16

INDIVIDUAL 95 PERCENT C. I. FOR LEVEL MEANS OF C2
(BASED ON POOLED STANDARD DEVIATION)
       +---------+---------+---------+---------+---------+---------+
1                                      I*************I*************I
2          I*************I*************I
       +---------+---------+---------+---------+---------+---------+
       6.0       7.0       8.0       9.0      10.0      11.0      12.0

1

INDIVIDUAL 95 PERCENT C. I. FOR LEVEL MEANS OF C3
(BASED ON POOLED STANDARD DEVIATION)
       +---------+---------+---------+---------+---------+---------+
1                         I************I***********I
2                            I************I***********I
3          I***********I************I
       +---------+---------+---------+---------+---------+---------+
       5.5       6.8       8.1       9.4      10.7      12.0      13.3


*** Minitab *** Statistics Dept. * Penn. State Univ. * Release 80.1 ***
 *** University of Vermont * Academic Computing Center ***
STORAGE AVAILABLE   10000
```

TABLE 13.6 (Cont.)
(*b*) SPSS output

```
1 RUN NAME        TWOWAY ANALYSIS OF VARIANCE ON REINSTATEMENT DATA
2 VARIABLE LIST   STIM,TRIALS,SCORE
3 INPUT FORMAT    FIXED(2F2.0,F3.0)
4 INPUT MEDIUM    T1333.DAT
5 N OF CASES      24
6 ANOVA           SCORE BY STIM(1,2) TRIALS(1,3)
```

```
* * * * * * * * * * A N A L Y S I S   O F   V A R I A N C E * * * * * * * * * *
                SCORE
        by STIM
           TRIALS
* * * * * * * * * * * * * * * * * * * * * * * * * * * * * * * * * * * * * * * * *
```

Source of variation	Sum of Squares	df	Mean Square	F	Signif of F
Main effects	87.125	3	29.042	6.242	0.004
STIM	57.042	1	57.042	12.260	0.003
TRIALS	30.083	2	15.042	3.233	0.063
2-way interactions	8.083	2	4.042	0.869	0.436
STIM TRIALS	8.083	2	4.042	0.869	0.436
Explained	95.208	5	19.042	4.093	0.012
Residual	83.750	18	4.653		
Total	178.958	23	7.781		

```
24 Cases were processed.
 0 Cases (  0.0 %) were missing.
```

(*c*) BMDP2V output

```
BMDP2V - ANALYSIS OF VARIANCE AND COVARIANCES WITH REPEATED MEASURES.

   PROGRAM CONTROL INFORMATION

/PROBLEM        TITLE IS 'BMDP2V ANALYSIS OF REINSTATEMENT DATA'.
/INPUT          VARIABLES ARE 3.
                FORMAT IS '(2F2.0,F3.0)'.
                CASES ARE 24.
                UNIT IS 20.
/VARIABLE       NAMES ARE STIM,TRIALS,SCORE.
/DESIGN         DEPENDENT IS SCORE.
                GROUPS ARE STIM,TRIALS.
/END
```

```
   PROBLEM TITLE . . . . . . . BMDP2V ANALYSIS OF REINSTATEMENT DATA

GROUP STRUCTURE

   STIM       TRIALS     COUNT
 * 1.0000   * 1.0000      4.
 * 1.0000   * 2.0000      4.
 * 1.0000   * 3.0000      4.
 * 2.0000   * 1.0000      4.
 * 2.0000   * 2.0000      4.
 * 2.0000   * 3.0000      4.
```

```
        CELL MEANS   FOR  1-ST DEPENDENT VARIABLE
```

							MARGINAL
STIM =	* 1.0000	* 1.0000	* 1.0000	* 2.0000	* 2.0000	* 2.0000	
TRIALS =	* 1.0000	* 2.0000	* 3.0000	* 1.0000	* 2.0000	* 3.0000	
SCORE	11.25000	12.25000	8.25000	7.75000	8.00000	6.75000	9.04167
COUNT	4	4	4	4	4	4	24

```
STANDARD DEVIATIONS   FOR  1-ST DEPENDENT VARIABLE
```

STIM =	* 1.0000	* 1.0000	* 1.0000	* 2.0000	* 2.0000	* 2.0000
TRIALS =	* 1.0000	* 2.0000	* 3.0000	* 1.0000	* 2.0000	* 3.0000
SCORE	2.98608	2.98608	0.95743	1.70783	2.16025	1.25831

```
ANALYSIS OF VARIANCE FOR  1-ST
DEPENDENT VARIABLE - SCORE
```

SOURCE	SUM OF SQUARES	DEGREES OF FREEDOM	MEAN SQUARE	F	TAIL PROBABILITY
MEAN	1962.04167	1	1962.04167	421.69	0.0000
STIM	57.04167	1	57.04167	12.26	0.0025
TRIALS	30.08333	2	15.04167	3.23	0.0632
ST	8.08333	2	4.04167	0.87	0.4364
1 ERROR	83.75000	18	4.65278		

Multiple Comparisons

All of the multiple comparison procedures discussed in Chapter 12 are applicable to the analysis of factorial designs.† Thus we can test the differences among the three means for variable B by use of Dunn's test, Newman-Keul's test, and so on. On rare occasions it is relevant to compare the individual cell means, rather than the means attributable to the main effects. Thus we might wish to compare AB_{11} with AB_{23}. For this purpose we could consider the experiment as consisting of six treatments, rather than as a 2×3 factorial, and then run our tests just as we would for a one-way design. But again it is important to consider the number of tests we wish to run, and to be careful not to produce totally unacceptable error rates.

Power Analysis for Factorial Experiments

The calculation of power for fixed variable factorial designs is basically the same as it was for one-way designs. In the one-way design we defined

$$\phi' = \sqrt{\frac{\Sigma \tau_j^2}{k \sigma_e^2}}$$

and

$$\phi = \phi' \sqrt{n}$$

where $\Sigma \tau_j^2 = \Sigma(\mu_j - \mu)^2$,

$\quad k =$ number of treatments,

and

$\quad n =$ the number of observations in each treatment.

In the two-way and higher order designed we have more than one "treatment," but this does not alter the procedure in any important way. If we let $\alpha_i = \mu_i - \mu$, and $\beta_j = \mu_j - \mu$, where μ_i represents the parametric mean of Treatment A_i (across all levels of B) and μ_j represents the parametric mean of Treatment B_j (across all levels of A), then we can define the following terms

$$\phi'_\alpha = \sqrt{\frac{\Sigma \alpha_i^2}{a \sigma_e^2}}$$

$$\phi_\alpha = \phi'_\alpha \sqrt{nb}$$

---

† For a much more complete discussion of the use of multiple comparison techniques with factorial designs the reader is referred to Keppel (1973).

and

$$\phi'_\beta = \sqrt{\frac{\Sigma \beta_j^2}{b\sigma_e^2}}$$

$$\phi_\beta = \phi'_\beta \sqrt{na}.$$

Examination of these formulae will reveal that to calculate the power against a null hypothesis concerning A, we act as if variable B did not exist. To calculate the power of the test against a null hypothesis concerning B, we similarly act as if variable A did not exist.

Calculation of the power against the null hypothesis concerning the interaction follows the same logic. We define

$$\phi'_{\alpha\beta} = \sqrt{\frac{\Sigma \alpha\beta_{ij}^2}{ab\sigma_e^2}}$$

and then

$$\phi_{\alpha\beta} = \phi'_{\alpha\beta} \sqrt{n}$$

where $\alpha\beta_{ij}$ is defined as for the underlying structural model ($\alpha\beta_{ij} = \mu - \mu_i - \mu_j + \mu_{ij}$). Given ϕ we can simply obtain the power of the test just as we did for the one-way design.

Calculation of power for the random model is somewhat more complicated, and for the mixed model (to be discussed shortly) requires a set of rather unrealistic assumptions. To obtain estimates of power with these models the reader is referred to Winer (1971, p. 334).

In certain situations the two-way factorial will be more powerful than two separate one-way designs, in addition to the other advantages which accrue to factorial designs. Consider two hypothetical experimental studies, where the number of subjects per teaching method are held constant across different designs.

In Experiment I an investigator wishes to examine the efficacy of three different teaching methods. She has introduced all three methods in each of four schools. Our experimenter is faced with two choices. She can run a one-way analysis on the three teaching methods, ignoring the *Schools* variable entirely or she can run a 3×4 two-way factorial analysis on the three methods and four schools. In this case the two-way has more power than the one-way. In the one-way we would ignore any differences among schools and the interaction of Schools with Methods and these would go toward increasing the error term. In the two-way we take into account differences which can be attributed to Schools and to the interaction between Methods and Schools, thus removing them from the error term. The error term for the two-way would thus be smaller than for the one-way, giving us greater power.

On the other hand consider the experimenter who had originally planned to apply her three methods in only one school. Her error term would not be inflated by differences among Schools and the interaction of Schools with Methods, since she has used only one school. If she now *expanded* her study to include several schools, SS_{total} would increase to account for additional effects due to Schools and the interaction of Methods with Schools, but the error term would remain constant because the extra variation is accounted for by the extra terms. Since the error term will remain constant, she will have no increase in power in this situation over the power she would have had in her first study.

As a general rule a factorial design is more powerful than a one-way design only when the extra factors can be thought of as refining or purifying the error term. In other words when extra factors or variables account for variance which would normally be incorporated into the error term, the factorial design is more powerful. Otherwise, all other things equal, it is not, although it still possesses the advantage of allowing us to examine interaction terms and simple effects.

Expected Mean Squares for Fixed, Random, and Mixed Models

While fixed and random models led to the same F test when we were discussing the one-way analysis of variance, the same is not the case in more complex designs. Since the denominator in an F ratio is a function of the type of model we are considering, when we come to the factorial designs we find that MS_{error} is not always the appropriate denominator for F.

As you should recall, a variable is defined as a *fixed* variable if we *select* the levels of that variable, and as a *random* variable if the levels are obtained by random sampling. Designs which consist of one or more fixed variables and one or more random variables are referred to as **mixed model** designs. The difference between a fixed and a random term in any design becomes somewhat clearer if we first define a **sampling fraction**. The sampling fraction for a variable will be defined as the ratio of the number of levels of a given variable which are *actually* used to the potential number of levels that *could have* been used. We will use lower case letters to represent the number of levels used, and upper case letters to represent the potential number of levels available.

Mixed model

Sampling fraction

As was pointed out in the previous chapter, for a *fixed* variable the population of levels is limited to the levels actually used. This means that if variable A is fixed, $a = A$ and $a/A = 1$. For a fixed variable the sampling fraction is always 1. For a random variable, however, this is not the case, for the number of potential levels is generally very large indeed, and a would be very much smaller than A, meaning that $a/A = 0$ for all practical purposes. From the above discussion we can write:

VARIABLE	SAMPLING FRACTION
A (fixed)	$a/A = 1$
A (random)	$a/A = 0$
B (fixed)	$b/B = 1$
B (random)	$b/B = 0$
Subjects (random)	$n/N = 0$

We will always treat *subjects* as if they were sampled at random from a large population.

While it is possible to have sampling fractions between 0 and 1, as, for example, when the variable is a high school class, which has only four possible levels, these rarely occur in practice. When there are a small number of potential levels, that variable is almost always treated as a fixed variable anyway. When peculiar sampling fractions do arise, the investigator will have to work out the E(MS) for herself, and is usually advised to design her experiment so that the factor is fixed.

Given the concept of a sampling fraction, it is possible to define the expected mean squares for all models. These are given in Table 13.7 for a two-way factorial.

TABLE 13.7
Expected Mean
Squares for
All Models

Source	E(MS)
A	$(1 - n/N)\sigma_e^2 + n(1 - b/B)\sigma_{\alpha\beta}^2 + nb\sigma_{\alpha}^2$
B	$(1 - n/N)\sigma_e^2 + n(1 - a/A)\sigma_{\alpha\beta}^2 + na\sigma_{\beta}^2$
AB	$(1 - n/N)\sigma_e^2 + n\sigma_{\alpha\beta}^2$
Error	$(1 - n/N)\sigma_e^2$

Each E(MS) in this table contains the term

$$\left(1 - \frac{n}{N}\right)\sigma_e^2.$$

Since subjects are almost always assumed to be chosen at random (at least we look around innocently and pretend that they are), and since the population of potential subjects is huge, n/N vanishes and we are left with σ_e^2. Similar reasoning applies to the other terms in Table 13.7, where, for example, $1 - \frac{a}{A}$ is 0 for fixed effects and 1 for random effects. If we substitute values of 0 and 1 for fixed and random effects we arrive at the results presented in Table 13.8.

It is clear from Table 13.8 that the expected mean squares are heavily dependent upon the underlying structural model. This in turn means that the denominators for our F ratios will also depend upon the model we adopt.

	FIXED	RANDOM	MIXED	
Source	**A fixed** **B fixed**	**A random** **B random**	**A random** **B fixed**	**A fixed** **B random**
A	$\sigma_e^2 + nb\sigma_\alpha^2$	$\sigma_e^2 + n\sigma_{\alpha\beta}^2 + nb\sigma_\alpha^2$	$\sigma_e^2 + nb\sigma_\alpha^2$	$\sigma_e^2 + n\sigma_{\alpha\beta}^2 + nb\sigma_\alpha^2$
B	$\sigma_e^2 + na\sigma_\beta^2$	$\sigma_e^2 + n\sigma_{\alpha\beta}^2 + na\sigma_\beta^2$	$\sigma_e^2 + n\sigma_{\alpha\beta}^2 + na\sigma_\beta^2$	$\sigma_e^2 + na\sigma_\beta^2$
AB	$\sigma_e^2 + n\sigma_{\alpha\beta}^2$	$\sigma_e^2 + n\sigma_{\alpha\beta}^2$	$\sigma_e^2 + n\sigma_{\alpha\beta}^2$	$\sigma_e^2 + n\sigma_{\alpha\beta}^2$
Error	σ_e^2	σ_e^2	σ_e^2	σ_e^2

TABLE 13.8
Expected Mean
Squares for Fixed,
Random, and
Mixed Models

Consider first the usual fixed model. From Table 13.8 we can see that MS_{error} will always form a suitable test term, since the other $E(MS)$s differ from $E(MS_{error})$ only by the parameter in question. Thus, for example,

$$\frac{E(MS_A)}{E(MS_{error})} = \frac{\sigma_e^2 + nb\sigma_\alpha^2}{\sigma_e^2}$$

will have an expectation appreciably greater than 1 only if $\sigma_\alpha^2 \neq 0$.

For the random model it is apparent from the expected mean squares that MS_{error} is not appropriate for testing the main effects. For example, consider

$$\frac{E(MS_A)}{E(MS_{error})} = \frac{\sigma_e^2 + n\sigma_{\alpha\beta}^2 + nb\sigma_\alpha^2}{\sigma_e^2}.$$

This ratio would have an expectancy appreciably greater than 1 if either σ_α^2 or $\sigma_{\alpha\beta}^2$ were greater than zero, and a significant F would not indicate which H_0 should be rejected. However the interaction term does provide us with a proper test, since

$$\frac{E(MS_A)}{E(MS_{AB})} = \frac{\sigma_e^2 + n\sigma_{\alpha\beta}^2 + nb\sigma_\alpha^2}{\sigma_e^2 + n\sigma_{\alpha\beta}^2}$$

would have an expectation of approximately 1 unless σ_α^2 were greater than zero. In this case a significant F would have an unequivocal interpretation. Thus to test the two main effects we would use MS_{AB} as our denominator.

Even with the random model MS_{error} does serve as the test term against the null hypothesis concerning the interaction, however, as is obvious from the ratio

$$\frac{E(MS_{AB})}{E(MS_{error})} = \frac{\sigma_e^2 + n\sigma_{\alpha\beta}^2}{\sigma_e^2}$$

where a significant F can only be attributed to $\sigma_{\alpha\beta}^2$ greater than zero.

For the mixed models the situation is more complex, since one main effect will be tested against MS_{error} and the other will be tested against MS_{AB}. The interaction will again be tested against MS_{error}. These tests can be illustrated for the case where A is random and B is fixed.

$$\frac{E(MS_A)}{E(MS_{error})} = \frac{\sigma_e^2 + nb\sigma_\alpha^2}{\sigma_e^2}$$

$$\frac{E(MS_B)}{E(MS_{AB})} = \frac{\sigma_e^2 + n\sigma_{\alpha\beta}^2 + na\sigma_\beta^2}{\sigma_e^2 + n\sigma_{\alpha\beta}^2}$$

$$\frac{E(MS_{AB})}{E(MS_{error})} = \frac{\sigma_e^2 + n\sigma_{\alpha\beta}^2}{\sigma_e^2}.$$

It is interesting to note that in a mixed model it is the *fixed* term that is tested against MS interaction and the *random* term that is tested against MS_{error}. While this looks backward, it follows from what we have said about the role of the sampling fraction.

Pooling of Error Terms

In both the random and mixed models we often find that an important variable is tested against MS interaction. Since interactions usually have relatively few degrees of freedom as compared with MS_{error}, this may result in a substantial loss in power, turning what might otherwise be a significant result into a nonsignificant one.

One way out of this difficulty lies in first showing that there is no evidence to cause us to doubt that $\sigma_{\alpha\beta}^2 = 0$, and then dropping the interaction term from the model. If this is possible we may now pool MS_{AB} and MS_{error}, forming a new error term, and use this to test the main effects.

We started out with the model

$$X_{ijk} = \mu + \alpha_i + \beta_j + \alpha\beta_{ij} + e_{ijk}.$$

If there is no interaction between A and B, the model is unnecessarily complicated by the inclusion of $\alpha\beta_{ij}$. We might therefore begin by testing the null hypothesis $H_0: \sigma_{\alpha\beta}^2 = 0$. To reduce the risk of a Type II error, this test should be run at a relatively high level of α—e.g., $\alpha = .25$. If we can not reject H_0 at this level, we can then have a reasonable degree of confidence in deleting $\alpha\beta_{ij}$ from our model, leaving

$$X_{ijk} = \mu + \alpha_i + \beta_j + e_{ijk}.$$

The effect of deleting $\alpha\beta_{ij}$ from the model is to delete all terms of the form $n\sigma_{\alpha\beta}^2$ from the table of expected mean squares (Table 13.8), with the result that both MS_{AB} and MS_{error} will now be estimates of σ_e^2. We can then form a new test by combining the error and interaction mean squares as $MS_{residual}$

$$MS_{residual} = \frac{SS_{AB} + SS_{error}}{df_{AB} + df_{error}}.$$

This new term, on $(df_{AB} + df_{error})$ degrees of freedom, is now used to test the main effects.

Although we may make a preliminary test on the interaction at $\alpha = .25$, we would not declare the interaction to be significant (in terms of our final conclusions about the data) unless we can also reject H_0 at $\alpha = .05$. In other words our two tests represent two different strategies (i.e., "accepting" vs. "rejecting" H_0), and our levels of α must reflect these differing strategies.

The entire procedure of pooling mean squares is usually relevant only for the random and mixed models. For fixed models the MS_{error} is always an appropriate error term. As a matter of fact Winer (1971) suggests that if a denominator for F has at least 20 df, there is probably nothing to be gained by pooling in any case.

Magnitude of Experimental Effects

As with the one-way design, it is both possible and desirable to calculate the magnitude of effect associated with each of our independent variables. The easiest, but also the most biased, way to do this is to calculate η^2. Here we would simply take the relevant sum of squares and divide by the SS_{total}. Thus the magnitude of effect for variable A is SS_A/SS_{total} and for variable B is SS_B/SS_{total}, while for the interaction it is SS_{AB}/SS_{total}.

The main difficulty with η^2 is that it is a biased estimate of the true magnitude of effect in the population. To put this somewhat differently, η^2 is a very good descriptive statistic, but a poor inferential statistic.

While $\hat{\omega}^2$ is also biased, the bias is much less than for η^2. In addition, the statistical theory underlying $\hat{\omega}^2$ allows us to differentiate between fixed and random variables, and to act accordingly.

The development of $\hat{\omega}^2$ for two-way and higher order designs is basically an extension of what we have already seen with the one-way. We begin with the set of expected mean squares, derive estimates of σ_α^2, σ_β^2, $\sigma_{\alpha\beta}^2$, and σ_e^2, and then form ratios of each of these components to the total variance. We will begin with the purely random model because of its greater simplicity.

Random model   From Table 13.8 we know that for the completely random model

$$E(\mathrm{MS}_{error}) = \sigma_e^2$$

and thus

$$\hat{\sigma}_e^2 = \mathrm{MS}_{error}.$$

Further,

$$E(\mathrm{MS}_{AB}) = \sigma_e^2 + n\sigma_{\alpha\beta}^2$$
$$n\sigma_{\alpha\beta}^2 = E(\mathrm{MS}_{AB}) - \sigma_e^2.$$

Substituting estimates for parameters

$$n\hat{\sigma}^2_{\alpha\beta} = MS_{AB} - \hat{\sigma}^2_e$$

and substituting our estimate of $\hat{\sigma}^2_e$ we arrive at

$$\hat{\sigma}^2_{\alpha\beta} = \frac{MS_{AB} - MS_{error}}{n}.$$

For variance estimates on main effects we have

$$E(MS_A) = \sigma^2_e + n\sigma^2_{\alpha\beta} + nb\sigma^2_\alpha$$

$$nb\hat{\sigma}^2_\alpha = MS_A - \hat{\sigma}^2_e - n\hat{\sigma}^2_{\alpha\beta}.$$

Substituting from the results obtained above we have

$$nb\hat{\sigma}^2_\alpha = MS_A - MS_{error} - MS_{AB} + MS_{error}$$

and therefore

$$\hat{\sigma}^2_\alpha = \frac{MS_A - MS_{AB}}{nb}.$$

Similarly

$$\hat{\sigma}^2_\beta = \frac{MS_B - MS_{AB}}{na}.$$

To summarize these terms and illustrating them with the results from Table 13.4† we have

$$\hat{\sigma}^2_\alpha = (MS_A - MS_{AB})/nb = (12041.67 - 1541.67)/(10)(3) = 350.00$$

$$\hat{\sigma}^2_\beta = (MS_B - MS_{AB})/na = (5375.00 - 1541.67)/(10)(2) = 191.67$$

$$\hat{\sigma}^2_{\alpha\beta} = (MS_{AB} - MS_{error})/n = (1541.67 - 400)/10 = 114.17$$

$$\hat{\sigma}^2_e = MS_{error} = 400.00$$

$$\overline{ 1055.84}$$

We will now define our estimate of the magnitude of the effect of A as

$$\hat{\omega}^2_A = \frac{\hat{\sigma}^2_\alpha}{\sigma^2_{total}} = \frac{\hat{\sigma}^2_\alpha}{\hat{\sigma}^2_\alpha + \hat{\sigma}^2_\beta + \hat{\sigma}^2_{\alpha\beta} + \hat{\sigma}^2_e} = \frac{350.00}{1055.84} = .33.$$

Similarly

$$\hat{\omega}^2_\beta = \frac{\hat{\sigma}^2_\beta}{\hat{\sigma}^2_\alpha + \hat{\sigma}^2_\beta + \hat{\sigma}^2_{\alpha\beta} + \hat{\sigma}^2_e} = \frac{191.67}{1055.84} = .18$$

† While no one would seriously consider the data in Table 13.4 to really represent a random model, we will consider Group and Communication as random variables simply for the purpose of illustration.

and

$$\hat{\omega}_{\alpha\beta}^2 = \frac{\hat{\sigma}_{\alpha\beta}^2}{\hat{\sigma}_\alpha^2 + \hat{\sigma}_\beta^2 + \hat{\sigma}_{\alpha\beta}^2 + \hat{\sigma}_e^2} = \frac{114.17}{1055.84} = .11.$$

While these equations could be expressed in many different ways by substituting the actual estimators, there is little point in doing so. Once the four estimates are obtained, the calculation of ω^2 is straightforward.

Fixed model   Next we will consider the completely fixed model, where we run across the same difficulty we encountered in the one-way—namely that the quantity

$$\frac{\Sigma \alpha_i^2}{a-1}$$

is neither a population variance nor an unbiased estimate of one when we have measured the entire population of treatment levels, as we have with a fixed variable.

As before, we will let the terms

$$\theta_\alpha^2 = \Sigma \alpha_i^2 / (a-1)$$

$$\theta_\beta^2 = \Sigma \beta_j^2 / (b-1)$$

$$\theta_{\alpha\beta}^2 = \Sigma \alpha\beta_{ij}^2 / (a-1)(b-1)$$

while reserving σ_α^2, σ_β^2, and $\sigma_{\alpha\beta}^2$ as variances with denominators a, b, and ab respectively (e.g., $\sigma_\alpha^2 = \Sigma \alpha_i^2 / a$).

Modifying the $E(\text{MS})$ from Table 13.8 to reflect our new, and more exact, terminology, the expected means squares for the fixed model become

$$E(\text{MS}_A) = \sigma_e^2 + nb\theta_\alpha^2 = \sigma_e^2 + \frac{nb\,\Sigma \alpha_i^2}{a-1}$$

$$= \sigma_e^2 + \frac{nba}{a-1}\left(\frac{\Sigma \alpha_i^2}{a}\right) = \sigma_e^2 + \frac{nba}{a-1}\,\sigma_\alpha^2$$

$$E(\text{MS}_B) = \sigma_e^2 + na\theta_\beta^2 = \sigma_e^2 + \frac{nab}{b-1}\,\sigma_\beta^2$$

$$E(\text{MS}_{AB}) = \sigma_e^2 + n\theta_{\alpha\beta}^2 = \sigma_e^2 + \frac{nab}{(a-1)(b-1)}\,\sigma_{\alpha\beta}^2$$

$$E(\text{MS}_{\text{error}}) = \sigma_e^2 .$$

As before,

$$\hat{\sigma}_e^2 = \text{MS}_{\text{error}}.$$

Since

$$E(\text{MS}_A) = \sigma_e^2 + \frac{nba\sigma_\alpha^2}{a-1}$$

then

$$\hat{\sigma}_\alpha^2 = \frac{(MS_A - MS_{error})(a-1)}{nab}.$$

By a similar line of reasoning we obtain

$$\hat{\sigma}_\beta^2 = \frac{(MS_B - MS_{error})(b-1)}{nab}.$$

and

$$\hat{\sigma}_{\alpha\beta}^2 = \frac{(MS_{AB} - MS_{error})(a-1)(b-1)}{nab}.$$

Once again we will define

$$\hat{\omega}_A^2 = \frac{\hat{\sigma}_\alpha^2}{\hat{\sigma}_{total}^2} = \frac{\hat{\sigma}_\alpha^2}{\hat{\sigma}_\alpha^2 + \hat{\sigma}_\beta^2 + \hat{\sigma}_{\alpha\beta}^2 + \hat{\sigma}_e^2}.$$

The other terms ($\hat{\omega}_B^2$ and $\hat{\omega}_{AB}^2$) are defined in a similar fashion. A little algebraic manipulation will show that the denominator in the above expression is exactly equivalent to $\frac{SS_{total} + MS_{error}}{nab}$, and that the numerators for the variance effects are

EFFECT	NUMERATOR
A	$(SS_A - (a-1)MS_{error})/nab$
B	$(SS_B - (b-1)MS_{error})/nab$
AB	$(SS_{AB} - (a-1)(b-1)MS_{error})/nab$

Thus the calculations become quite simple. As an example we will use the data which appear in Table 13.4, this time legitimately treating the two variables as fixed. The summary table has been reproduced in Table 13.9.

TABLE 13.9
Summary Table for Data in Table 13.4

Source	df	SS	MS	F	$\hat{\omega}^2$
A	1	12041.67	12041.67	30.10	.243
B	2	10750.00	5375.00	13.44	.208
AB	2	3083.33	1541.67	3.85	.048
Error	54	21600.00	400.00		
Total	59	47475.00			

For the main effect of A

$$\hat{\omega}_A^2 = \frac{SS_A - (a-1)MS_{error}}{SS_{total} + MS_{error}} = \frac{12041.67 - 1(400)}{47475.00 + 400} = .243.$$

Similarly for B and AB

$$\hat{\omega}_B^2 = \frac{SS_B - (b-1)MS_{error}}{SS_{total} + MS_{error}} = \frac{10750 - 2(400)}{47475.00 + 400} = .208$$

$$\hat{\omega}_{AB}^2 = \frac{SS_{AB} - (a-1)(b-1)MS_{error}}{SS_{total} + MS_{error}} = \frac{3083.33 - 1(2)(400)}{47475.00 + 400} = .048.$$

We can now conclude that for our example 24% of the total variance is attributable to the main effect of variable A, 21% is attributable to the main effect of variable B, and 5% is attributable to the interaction of A and B. Thus we can say that a total of 49.9% of the variance is attributable to treatment effects while the remaining 50.1% is error variance. When we treated the variables as random, the effects for A, B, and AB accounted for 33%, 18%, 11% of the variance, respectively. Thus you can see that correct choice of a model is important.

Following the principles involved in obtaining variance components for the fixed and random models, it is not difficult to work out the terms for a mixed model. The actual derivation of these is left to the student, although Table 13.10 contains the final results. This table is modified from

TABLE 13.10

Estimates of Variance Components in One-way, Two-way, and Three-way Designs

MODEL	VARIANCE COMPONENT
A_f	$\sigma_\alpha^2 = (a-1)(MS_A - MS_e)/na$
	$\sigma_e^2 = MS_e$
Ar	$\sigma_\alpha^2 = (MS_A - MS_e)/n$
	$\sigma_e^2 = MS_e$
$A_f B_f$	$\sigma_\alpha^2 = (a-1)(MS_A - MS_e)/nab$
	$\sigma_\beta^2 = (b-1)(MS_B - MS_e)/nab$
	$\sigma_{\alpha\beta}^2 = (a-1)(b-1)(MS_{AB} - MS_e)/nab$
	$\sigma_e^2 = MS_e$
A, B_f	$\sigma_\alpha^2 = (MS_A - MS_e)/nb$
	$\sigma_\beta^2 = (b-1)(MS_B - MS_{AB})/nab$
	$\sigma_{\alpha\beta}^2 = (MS_{AB} - MS_e)/n$
	$\sigma_e^2 = MS_e$
A, B_r	$\sigma_\alpha^2 = (MS_A - MS_{AB})/nb$
	$\sigma_\beta^2 = (MS_B - MS_{AB})/na$
	$\sigma_{\alpha\beta}^2 = (MS_{AB} - MS_e)/n$
	$\sigma_e^2 = MS_e$

MODEL	VARIANCE COMPONENT
$A_f B_f C_f$	$\sigma_\alpha^2 = (a-1)(\mathrm{MS}_A - \mathrm{MS}_e)/nabc$
	$\sigma_\beta^2 = (b-1)(\mathrm{MS}_B - \mathrm{MS}_e)/nabc$
	$\sigma_\gamma^2 = (c-1)(\mathrm{MS}_C - \mathrm{MS}_e)/nabc$
	$\sigma_{\alpha\beta}^2 = (a-1)(b-1)(\mathrm{MS}_{AB} - \mathrm{MS}_e)/nabc$
	$\sigma_{\alpha\gamma}^2 = (a-1)(c-1)(\mathrm{MS}_{AC} - \mathrm{MS}_e)/nabc$
	$\sigma_{\beta\gamma}^2 = (b-1)(c-1)(\mathrm{MS}_{BC} - \mathrm{MS}_e)/nabc$
	$\sigma_{\alpha\beta\gamma}^2 = (a-1)(b-1)(c-1)(\mathrm{MS}_{ABC} - \mathrm{MS}_e)/nabc$
	$\sigma_e^2 = \mathrm{MS}_e$
$A_r B_f C_f$	$\sigma_\alpha^2 = (\mathrm{MS}_A - \mathrm{MS}_e)/nbc$
	$\sigma_\beta^2 = (b-1)(\mathrm{MS}_B - \mathrm{MS}_{AB})/nabc$
	$\sigma_\gamma^2 = (c-1)(\mathrm{MS}_C - \mathrm{MS}_{AC})/nabc$
	$\sigma_{\alpha\beta}^2 = (\mathrm{MS}_{AB} - \mathrm{MS}_e)/nc$
	$\sigma_{\alpha\gamma}^2 = (\mathrm{MS}_{AC} - \mathrm{MS}_e)/nb$
	$\sigma_{\beta\gamma}^2 = (b-1)(c-1)(\mathrm{MS}_{BC} - \mathrm{MS}_{ABC})/nabc$
	$\sigma_{\alpha\beta\gamma}^2 = (\mathrm{MS}_{ABC} - \mathrm{MS}_e)n$
	$\sigma_e^2 = \mathrm{MS}_e$
$A_r B_r C_f$	$\sigma_\alpha^2 = (\mathrm{MS}_A - \mathrm{MS}_{AB})/nbc$
	$\sigma_\beta^2 = (\mathrm{MS}_B - \mathrm{MS}_{AB})/nac$
	$\sigma_\gamma^2 = (c-1)(\mathrm{MS}_C - \mathrm{MS}_{AC} - \mathrm{MS}_{BC} + \mathrm{MS}_{ABC})/nabc$
	$\sigma_{\alpha\beta}^2 = (\mathrm{MS}_{AB} - \mathrm{MS}_e)/nc$
	$\sigma_{\alpha\gamma}^2 = (\mathrm{MS}_{AC} - \mathrm{MS}_{ABC})/nb$
	$\sigma_{\beta\gamma}^2 = (\mathrm{MS}_{BC} - \mathrm{MS}_{ABC})/na$
	$\sigma_{\alpha\beta\gamma}^2 = (\mathrm{MS}_{ABC} - \mathrm{MS}_e)/n$
	$\sigma_e^2 = \mathrm{MS}_e$
$A_r B_r C_r$	$\sigma_\alpha^2 = (\mathrm{MS}_A - \mathrm{MS}_{AB} - \mathrm{MS}_{AC} + \mathrm{MS}_{ABC})/nbc$
	$\sigma_\beta^2 = (\mathrm{MS}_B - \mathrm{MS}_{AB} - \mathrm{MS}_{BC} + \mathrm{MS}_{ABC})/nac$
	$\sigma_\gamma^2 = (\mathrm{MS}_C - \mathrm{MS}_{AC} - \mathrm{MS}_{BC} + \mathrm{MS}_{ABC})/nab$
	$\sigma_{\alpha\beta}^2 = (\mathrm{MS}_{AB} - \mathrm{MS}_{ABC})/nc$
	$\sigma_{\alpha\gamma}^2 = (\mathrm{MS}_{AC} - \mathrm{MS}_{ABC})/nb$
	$\sigma_{\beta\gamma}^2 = (\mathrm{MS}_{BC} - \mathrm{MS}_{ABC})/na$
	$\sigma_{\alpha\beta\gamma}^2 = (\mathrm{MS}_{ABC} - \mathrm{MS}_e)/n$
	$\sigma_e^2 = \mathrm{MS}_e$

Tables 1 and 2 of Vaughan & Corballis (1969). In the left hand column of this table the designations A_f, B_f, and C_f represent fixed terms, while the designations A_r, B_r, and C_r represent random variables. As usual, the lower case letters represent the number of levels of that variable. Variance components for the three-way factorial (which we shall discuss shortly) have been included for the sake of completeness. On the basis of the variance components given in Table 13.10, the student should be able to derive the variance components for any factorial design, given the expected mean squares.

For most calculations of $\hat{\omega}^2$ the numerator is the variance component for the term in question, while the denominator is the sum of all components. Depending upon the interests of the experimenter, however, other denominators are possible. In this context a paper by Cohen (1973) is highly recommended. Although that paper deals with $\hat{\eta}^2$ instead of $\hat{\omega}^2$, the generalization is straightforward. The overriding consideration in determining the appropriate denominator is that the experimenter must think about what he is doing, and not simply apply a formula he finds in this or any other book.

Unequal Sample Sizes

While most experiments are designed with the intention of having equal numbers of observations in each cell, the cruel hand of fate frequently intervenes to upset even the most carefully laid plans. Subjects fail to arrive for testing, animals die, data are lost, apparatus fails, and so on. When such problems arise, we are faced with several alternative solutions, the choice of a solution being dependent upon the nature of the data and the reasons why data are missing.

The difficulty that we face when we have unequal sample sizes is the fact that in this case the row, column, and interaction effects are no longer independent. The lack of independence produces some difficulty in interpretation.

Most textbooks have been concerned with three general types of solutions, viz., the solution for proportional sample sizes, the unweighted means solution, and the least squares solution. We will postpone the last of these until Chapter 16, and deal in this chapter with only the proportional and unweighted means solution. Unfortunately, it is not possible to draw a clear distinction between these procedures. The ***unweighted means solution*** is generally applicable to all situations, whereas the ***proportional solution*** can only be used where the sample sizes meet certain conditions. But even when those conditions are met, the choice between the two solutions depends importantly on the way in which we visualize the role of the sample sizes themselves. This last point will be elaborated in some detail after we examine the computations associated with the proportional solution.

Unweighted means solution

Proportional solution

Proportional cell frequencies   Suppose that we selected two different class-rooms, and for reasons related to the particular experiment administered Treatment B_1 to one half of the students in each classroom, Treatment B_2 to one quarter of them, and Treatment B_3 to the remaining quarter. Further assume that there were 20 students in Classroom A_1 and 32 students in Classroom A_2. The resulting sample sizes would be

	B_1	B_2	B_3	n_i
A_1	10	5	5	20
A_2	16	8	8	32
n_j	26	13	13	$52 = N$

You will note from this table that there is a certain proportionality among the cell frequencies. For example, $10:16::5:8$, $10:5::16:8$, and so on. In general,

$$n_{ij} = \frac{n_i n_j}{N}$$

where n_i represents the number of subjects in row i, n_j represents the number of observations in column j, and n_{ij} represents the number of subjects in cell$_{ij}$ (e.g., $n_{12} = 20(13)/52 = 5$). When this type of proportionality holds, and the experimenter decides it is appropriate to let the sample sizes play a role in the analysis, the analysis of the data is straightforward. We will simply return to the procedure discussed in Chapter 11 of dividing each squared term by its appropriate denominator *before* summing. Thus, letting T_{Ai} and T_{Bj} refer to the totals for row i and column j respectively,

$$SS_A = \Sigma \left(\frac{T_{Ai}^2}{n_i} \right) - CF$$

$$SS_B = \Sigma \left(\frac{T_{Bj}^2}{n_j} \right) - CF$$

$$SS_{cells} = \Sigma \left(\frac{T_{ij}^2}{n_{ij}} \right) - CF$$

$$SS_{AB} = SS_{cells} - SS_A - SS_B$$

$$SS_{error} = SS_{total} - SS_{cells}.$$

A simple example of this approach is presented in Table 13.11, where the entries are the cell totals. The individual observations have been omitted, but $SS_{total} = 1000$. The cell means are presented simply for the purpose of clarifying the meaning of the data.

TABLE 13.11

Illustration of
Calculations for
Proportional Sample
Sizes

(a) Data

	CELL TOTALS						CELL NS			
	B_1	B_2	B_3	Total			B_1	B_2	B_3	Total
A_1	25	40	50	115		A_1	10	5	5	20
A_2	30	30	20	80		A_2	20	10	10	40
	55	70	70	195			30	15	15	60

	CELL MEANS		
	B_1	B_2	B_3
A_1	2.5	8.0	10.0
A_2	1.5	3.0	2.0

(b) Computations

$SS_{total} = 1000$ (given)

$$SS_A = \Sigma \left(\frac{T_{Aj}^2}{n_i} \right) - \frac{GT^2}{N} = \frac{115^2}{20} + \frac{80^2}{40} - \frac{195^2}{60} = 821.25 - 633.75 = 187.50$$

$$SS_B = \Sigma \left(\frac{T_{Bi}^2}{n_j} \right) - CF = \frac{55^2}{30} + \frac{70^2}{15} + \frac{70^2}{15} - 633.75 = 745.1667 - 633.75$$

$$= 120.417$$

$$SS_{cells} = \Sigma \left(\frac{T_{ij}^2}{n_{ij}} \right) - CF = \frac{25^2}{10} + \frac{40^2}{5} + \cdots + \frac{20^2}{10} - 633.75 = 1057.5$$

$$- 633.75 = 423.75$$

$$SS_{AB} = SS_{cells} - SS_A - SS_B = 423.75 - 187.50 - 120.417 = 115.833$$

$$SS_{error} = SS_{total} - SS_{cells} = 1000 - 423.75 = 576.25$$

(c) Summary table

Source	df	SS	MS	F
A	1	187.50	187.50	17.571*
B	2	120.417	60.208	5.642*
AB	2	115.833	57.916	5.427*
Error	54	576.250	10.671	
Total	59	1000.000		

*$p < .05$.

It has generally been assumed in the past that if our sample sizes exhibit the property of proportionality, as defined previously, the solution is straightforward. Unfortunately, this is not the case. While it is often stated (Winer, 1971, p. 404) that with proportionality row, column, and interaction effects are independent, this is not correct. The row and column effects are independent of each other, but they are not independent of the interaction effects.

What this means in practical terms is that with this procedure the sample sizes play an active role in the result, and in fact we are really analyzing a set of weighted means. As just noted, the sample sizes are treated as part of the treatment effect in that larger samples carry more weight in the analysis.

The issue of *weighted* vs. *unweighted* means frequently causes confusion. Consider the following set of data from two schools broken down by sex. The dependent variable could be anything but suppose that it is weight (as a measure of nutrition). Further assume that School I was found in a middle class suburb (Junk-Food Heights) while School II came from a very economically depressed urban neighborhood.

	MALES		FEMALES		Mean of Scores	Mean of Means
	$\bar{X}$	n	$\bar{X}$	n		
School I	155	10	110	20	125	132.5
School II	135	20	120	40	125	127.5

The traditional method of obtaining mean weights for each school (and the method employed by the solution in Table 13.11) is to add up the scores within each school and divide by the number of students in that school. But notice what this entails.

$$\bar{X}_{\text{School I}} = \frac{T_{\text{males}} + T_{\text{females}}}{N} = \frac{n_{\text{males}}\bar{X}_{\text{males}} + n_{\text{females}}\bar{X}_{\text{females}}}{N}$$

Weighted means

Here we see that the contribution made by the male and female means is a function of the sample sizes, and thus our value of 125 is a **weighted** combination of means. Using this system, we find that there is no difference between the two schools, and SS_{schools} obtained by the *proportional* approach to the analysis of variance would be exactly zero.

An alternative approach would be to give equal weight to male and female means, arguing that since males and females are equally represented in the general population, they should each make the same contribution to the school's mean, especially if that mean is going to be used to assess the students' nutrition. This can be accomplished by simply taking the mean of the means—e.g., $(155 + 110)/2 = 132.5$. This represents a case of equally

Unweighted means

weighted (or **unweighted**) means. By this approach we see that the mean weights of the two schools differ by about five pounds. (In fact with nonproportional data it is very easy to have $\text{School}_\text{I} < \text{School}_\text{II}$ for each sex, and yet have a greater overall mean for School_I.)

As has been said, the *proportional* approach to the analysis of variance compares weighted means (e.g., 125 vs. 125). The method to be discussed in the next section (the *unweighted means solution*) can be thought of as an approximation to the comparison of unweighted means (e.g., 132.5 vs. 127.5). (A more exact solution will be discussed in Chapter 16.)

Whether it is more appropriate to compare weighted means or unweighted means depends primarily on the nature of the experiment. If we were mainly interested in studying these two particular schools, and if males and females are really distributed (in the schools) in this peculiar way, then 125 pounds is our best estimate of each school's mean. But if we are using these schools just because they are a convenient source of warm bodies, and if we assume that males and females are distributed about 50:50 in each community, then the unweighted means of 132.5 and 127.5 pounds are our best guesses as to the mean weights of those communities (at least within the age-range covered by our study). (In fact with data such as these the interaction is probably of more interest than the main effects.)

The decision as to which approach is more relevant is an important one, since using the *unweighted means* method leads to tests of the form $H_0: \mu_1 = \mu_2$ whereas using the *proportional* approach leads to tests of the form $H_0: (n_1/N)\mu_1 = (n_2/N)\mu_2$. By and large, it generally makes much more sense to ignore the proportional nature of the frequencies and use an unweighted means solution instead.

Unweighted means solution   When cell frequencies are not proportional, one appropriate method of analysis is the *unweighted means solution*. The term "unweighted means" is actually a misnomer, since what we really have are "equally weighted means." As we saw in the last section, dividing each squared term by its own sample size as we go along (i.e., $\Sigma(T_i^2/n_i)$) amounts to weighting each mean in proportion to its sample size. In this section we will weight all means equally by using a form of average sample size (the harmonic mean of the n_{ij}).

We will take as an example the sample data shown in Table 13.12. In part (1a) of the table are the raw data, the individual cell frequencies, the individual cell means, and the harmonic mean of the n_{ij} ($\bar{n}_h$). The harmonic mean of k observations ($X_1, X_2, X_3, \ldots, X_k$) is defined as

$$\bar{X}_h = \frac{k}{\dfrac{1}{X_1} + \dfrac{1}{X_2} + \dfrac{1}{X_3} + \cdots + \dfrac{1}{X_k}}.$$

From this point on we are going to act as if every cell contained $\bar{n}_h$ observations. Thus the number of subjects per row will equal $\bar{n}_h$ times the number of cells in that row, and similarly for the number of observations per column and the overall sample size. The new values are tabled in part (2a) of Table 13.12. The last section of part (2a) contains what we will call *corrected* or *adjusted* totals. If the mean of cell$_{11}$ is 7.25 and if we are going to act as if cell$_{11}$ contained 4.44 observations, then the adjusted total must be $(\bar{X}_{ij})(\bar{n}_h) = (7.25)(4.44) = 32.190$. The same line of reasoning holds for all other totals in this table.

TABLE 13.12

Illustration of
Unweighted Means
Analysis

(1a) Raw Data

(a) Data

RAW DATA

	B_1	B_2	B_3	B_4
A_1	5, 7, 9, 8	2, 5, 7, 3, 9	8, 11, 12, 14	11, 15, 16, 10, 9
A_2	7, 9, 10, 9	3, 8, 9, 11	9, 12, 14, 8, 7	11, 14, 10, 12, 13

CELL MEANS

	B_1	B_2	B_3	B_4
A_1	7.25	5.20	11.25	12.20
A_2	8.75	7.75	10.00	12.00

n_{ij}

	B_1	B_2	B_3	B_4
A_1	4	5	4	5
A_2	4	4	5	5

$$\bar{n}_h = \frac{8}{\frac{1}{4}+\frac{1}{5}+\frac{1}{4}+\frac{1}{5}+\frac{1}{4}+\frac{1}{4}+\frac{1}{5}+\frac{1}{5}} = \frac{8}{1.80} = 4.44$$

(2a) Adjusted Data

ADJUSTED n_{ij}

	B_1	B_2	B_3	B_4	
A_1	4.44	4.44	4.44	4.44	17.76
A_2	4.44	4.44	4.44	4.44	17.76
	8.88	8.88	8.88	8.88	35.52

ADJUSTED TOTALS

	B_1	B_2	B_3	B_4	T_i
A_1	32.190	23.088	49.950	54.168	159.396
A_2	38.850	34.410	44.400	53.280	170.940
T_j	71.040	57.498	94.350	107.448	330.336

(b) Computations

Correction Factor $(CF) = \dfrac{(\Sigma X)^2}{ab\bar{n}_h} = \dfrac{330.336^2}{(2)(4)(4.44)} = 3072.1248$

$SS_A = \dfrac{\Sigma T_{Ai}^2}{b\bar{n}_h} - CF = \dfrac{159.396^2 + 170.940^2}{(4)(4.44)} - CF$

$\quad = 3075.8766 - 3072.1248 = 3.7518$

$SS_B = \dfrac{\Sigma T_{Bj}^2}{a\bar{n}_h} - CF = \dfrac{71.040^2 + \cdots + 107.448^2}{(2)(4.44)} - CF$

$\quad = 3243.2091 - 3072.1248 = 171.0843$

$SS_{\text{cells}} = \dfrac{\Sigma T_{ij}^2}{\bar{n}_h} - CF = \dfrac{32.190^2 + \cdots + 53.280^2}{4.44} - CF$

$\quad = 3266.1972 - 3072.1248 = 194.0724$

$SS_{AB} = SS_{\text{cells}} - SS_A - SS_B = 194.0724 - 3.7518 - 171.0843$

$\quad = 19.2363$

TABLE 13.12 (Cont.) SS_{error}

		B_1	B_2	B_3	B_4
A_1	n_{ij}	4	5	4	5
	ΣX_{ij}	29	26	45	61
	ΣX_{ij}^2	219	168	525	783
	SS_{ij}	8.75	32.80	18.75	38.80

		B_1	B_2	B_3	B_4
A_2	n_{ij}	4	4	5	5
	ΣX_{ij}	35	31	50	60
	ΣX_{ij}^2	311	275	534	730
	SS_{ij}	4.75	34.75	34.00	10.00

$$SS_{error} = \Sigma SS_{ij} = 8.75 + 32.80 + \cdots + 34.00 + 10.00 = 182.60$$

(c) Summary table

Source	df	SS	MS	F
A	1	3.752	3.752	<1
B	3	171.084	57.028	8.745*
AB	3	19.236	6.412	<1
Error	28	182.600	6.521	
Total	35			

*$p < .05$

From here on the calculation of main effects and the interaction proceeds just as in the equal-n case, with the substitution of the adjusted totals for the actual totals, and of $\bar{n}_h$ for n. The calculations are shown in part (b) of the table. Note that the error term (SS_{error}) is not obtained by subtraction; instead we calculate $SS_{within\ cell}$ for *each* cell of the design, and then sum these terms to obtain the sum of squares due to error. For cell$_{11}$, for example, $SS_{within\ cell} = SS_{11} = 219 - \dfrac{29^2}{4} = 8.75$. These $SS_{within\ cell}$ terms are obtained in a similar fashion for the other cells.

The summary table appears in part (c), where it is apparent that the main effect of B is significant, while the other two effects are not. Had the interaction been significant we would have had to interpret main effects (significant or not) with caution, and might have wished to calculate the simple effects of B at each level of A. In such a case simple effects would be calculated in the normal way, using the adjusted totals and the $\bar{n}_h$ based on all eight cells.

You will note that in the summary table the SS_{total} has been omitted. The separate sums of squares will not sum to SS_{total} in the case of unequal sample sizes (unless the n_{ij} are proportional as defined above). In the case of equal sample sizes the individual sums of squares are independent, and thus account for non-overlapping portions of the overall variation. With unequal sample sizes, however, the sums of squares lose this property and to a certain extent begin to account for similar portions of the overall variation. This is why they will not sum to SS_{total} and why we can not obtain SS_{error} by subtraction.

13.2 *Higher Order Factorial Designs*

All of the principles concerning a two-way factorial design apply equally well to a three-way or higher order design. With one additional piece of information the student should have no difficulty running an analysis of variance on any factorial design imaginable, although the arithmetic becomes increasingly more tedious as variables are added.

We will take a simple three-way factorial as an example, since it is the easiest to work with. The only major way in which a three-way differs from the two-way is in the presence of more than one interaction term. To see this we must first look at the underlying structural model for a factorial design with three variables.

$$X_{ijkl} = \mu + \alpha_i + \beta_j + \gamma_k + \alpha\beta_{ij} + \alpha\gamma_{ik} + \beta\gamma_{jk} + \alpha\beta\gamma_{ijk} + \varepsilon_{ijkl}.$$

You will note that in this model we not only have main effects, symbolized by α_i, β_j, and γ_k, but we also have two kinds of interaction terms. The two-variable or ***first order interactions*** are $\alpha\beta_{ij}$, $\alpha\gamma_{ik}$, and $\beta\gamma_{jk}$, which refer to the interaction of variables A and B, A and C, and B and C, respectively. We also have a ***second order interaction*** term $\alpha\beta\gamma_{ijk}$, which refers to the joint effect of all three variables. The first order interactions we have already examined in discussing the two-way. The second order interaction can be viewed in several ways. Probably the easiest way to think of the ABC interaction is to think of the AB interaction itself interacting with variable C. Suppose that we had two levels of each variable, and plotted the AB interaction separately for each level of C? We might have the following result.

First order interactions

Second order interactions

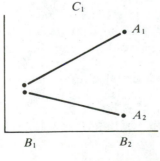
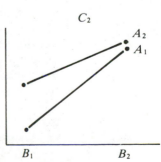

ABC interaction

You will note for the C_1 we have one AB interaction, while for C_2 we have a quite different one. Thus AB depends upon C, producing an ABC interaction. This same kind of reasoning could be invoked using the AC interaction at different levels of B, or the BC interaction at different levels of A. The result would be the same.

As has already been said, the three-way factorial is merely an extension of the two-way, with a slight twist. The twist comes about in obtaining the interaction sums of squares. In the two-way we took an $A \times B$ table of cell totals, calculated SS_{cells}, subtracted the main effects, and were left with SS_{AB}. In the three-way we have several interactions, but we will calculate them in ways analogous to those employed earlier. Thus to obtain SS_{BC} we will take a $B \times C$ table of cell totals (summing over A), obtain $SS_{cells\ BC}$, subtract the main effects of B and C, and end up with SS_{BC}. The same applies to SS_{AB} and SS_{AC}. We also follow the same procedure to obtain SS_{ABC}, but here we need to begin with an $A \times B \times C$ table of cell totals obtain $SS_{cells\ ABC}$, and then subtract the main effects *and* the lower order interactions to arrive at SS_{ABC}. In other words, for each interaction we start with a different table of cell totals, summing over the variable(s) in which we are not at the moment interested. We then obtain a SS_{cells} for that table and subtract from it any main effects and lower order interactions which involve terms included in that interaction.

Example 13.3

Variables Which Affect the Performance of Drivers

For an example consider an experiment concerning the driving ability of two different types of drivers—inexperienced (A_1) or experienced (A_2). These drivers will drive on one of three types of roads—first class (B_1), second class (B_2), or dirt (B_3) under one of two different driving conditions—Day (C_1) and Night (C_2). Thus we have a $2 \times 3 \times 2$ factorial. The experiment will include four subjects per condition (for a total of 48 subjects) and the dependent variable will be the number of steering corrections in a one mile section of roadway. The raw data are presented in Table 13.13(a).

The lower half of part (a) of Table 13.13 contains all of the necessary matrices of cell totals for the subsequent calculation of the interaction sums of squares. These matrices are obtained simply by summing across the levels of the irrelevant variable. Thus the upper left hand cell of the AB summary table contains the sum of all scores obtained under the treatment combination AB_{11}, regardless of the level of C.

In part (b) of the table are to be found the calculations of the sums of squares. For the main effects, the sums of squares are obtained exactly as they would be for a one-way. For the first order interactions the calculations are just as they would be for a two-way, taking two variables at a time. The only new calculation is for the second order interaction, and the difference is only a matter of degree. Here we first obtain the SS_{cells} for the three dimensional matrix. This sum of squares represents all of the variation among the cell totals in the full factorial design. From this we must subtract out all of the variation that can be accounted for by the main effects *and* by the first order interactions. What remains is the variation which can only be accounted for by the joint effect of all three variables, namely SS_{ABC}.

The final sum of squares is SS_{error}. This is most easily obtained by subtracting $SS_{cells\ ABC}$ from SS_{total}. Since $SS_{cells\ ABC}$ represents all of the variation which can be attributable to differences among cells (recall that $SS_{cells\ ABC} = SS_A + SS_B + SS_C + SS_{AB} + SS_{AC} + SS_{BC} + SS_{ABC}$), subtracting it from SS_{total} will leave us with only that variation within the cells themselves.

The summary table for the analysis of variance is presented in Table 13.13(c). From this we can see that the three main effects and the $A \times C$ interaction are significant. None of the other interactions is significant.

TABLE 13.13
Illustration of Calculations for $2 \times 3 \times 2$ Factorial Design

(1a) Raw Data

(a) Data

		C_1			C_2		
		B_1	B_2	B_3	B_1	B_2	B_3
A_1		4	20	16	21	28	32
		18	12	27	14	36	42
		8	18	23	19	33	46
		10	10	14	26	23	40
A_2		6	5	20	11	20	17
		4	9	15	7	11	16
		13	11	8	6	10	25
		7	15	17	16	9	12

(2a) Tables of Cell Totals

			ABC				
		C_1			C_2		
	B_1	B_2	B_3	B_1	B_2	B_3	Total
A_1	40	60	80	80	120	160	540
A_2	30	40	60	40	50	70	290
Total	70	100	140	120	170	230	830

TABLE 13.13 (Cont.)

| | | **AB** | | | | | **AC** | | |
	B_1	B_2	B_3	*Total*		C_1	C_2	*Total*
A_1	120	180	240	540	A_1	180	360	540
A_2	70	90	130	290	A_2	130	160	290
Total	190	270	370	830	*Total*	310	520	830

| | | **BC** | | |
	B_1	B_2	B_3	*Total*
C_1	70	100	140	310
C_2	120	170	230	520
Total	190	270	370	830

(b) Computations

$$SS_{total} = \Sigma X^2 - \frac{(\Sigma X)^2}{N} = 19236 - \frac{830^2}{48} = 19236 - 14352.08 = 4883.92$$

$$SS_A = \frac{\Sigma T_{A_i}^2}{nbc} - CF = \frac{540^2 + 290^2}{24} - CF = 15654.17 - 14352.08 = 1302.09$$

$$SS_B = \frac{\Sigma T_{B_j}^2}{nac} - CF = \frac{190^2 + 270^2 + 370^2}{16} - CF = 15368.75 - 14352.08 = 1016.67$$

$$SS_C = \frac{\Sigma T_{C_k}^2}{nab} - CF = \frac{310^2 + 520^2}{24} - CF = 15270.83 - 14352.08 = 918.75$$

$$SS_{cells\ AB} = \frac{\Sigma T_{AB_{ij}}^2}{nc} - CF = \frac{120^2 + 180^2 + \cdots + 130^2}{8} - CF = 16787.50$$
$$-14352.08 = 2435.42$$

$$SS_{AB} = SS_{cells\ AB} - SS_A - SS_B = 2435.42 - 1302.09 - 1016.67 = 116.66$$

$$SS_{cells\ AC} = \frac{\Sigma T_{AC_{ik}}^2}{nb} - CF = \frac{180^2 + \cdots + 160^2}{12} - CF = 17041.67 - 14352.08$$
$$= 2689.59$$

$$SS_{AC} = SS_{cells\ AC} - SS_A - SS_C = 2689.59 - 1302.09 - 918.75 = 468.75$$

$$SS_{cells\ BC} = \frac{\Sigma T_{BC_{jk}}^2}{na} - CF = \frac{70^2 + \cdots + 230^2}{8} - CF = 16337.50 - 14352.08$$
$$= 1985.42$$

$$SS_{BC} = SS_{cells\ BC} - SS_B - SS_C = 1985.42 - 1016.67 - 918.75 = 50.00$$

$$SS_{cells\ ABC} = \frac{\Sigma T_{ABC_{ijk}}^2}{n} - CF = \frac{40^2 + \cdots + 70^2}{4} - CF = 18275.00 - 14352.08$$
$$= 3922.92$$

$$SS_{ABC} = SS_{cells\ ABC} - SS_A - SS_B - SS_C - SS_{AB} - SS_{AC} - SS_{BC} = 3922.92$$
$$-1302.09 - 1016.67 - 918.75 - 116.66 - 468.75 - 50.00 = 50.00$$

$$SS_{error} = SS_{total} - SS_{cells\ ABC} = 4883.92 - 3922.92 = 961.00$$

TABLE 13.13 (Cont.)
(c) Summary table

Source	df	SS	MS	F
A (exp.)	1	1302.09	1302.09	48.79*
B (road)	2	1016.67	508.34	19.05*
C (cond.)	1	918.75	918.75	34.42*
AB	2	116.66	58.33	2.18
AC	1	468.75	468.75	17.56*
BC	2	50.00	25.00	<1
ABC	2	50.00	25.00	<1
Error	36	961.00	26.69	
Total	47	4883.92		

$* p < .05.$

Simple Effects

Since we have a significant interaction, the main effects of A and C should be interpreted with caution. To this end the AC interaction has been plotted in Figure 13.5. The data when plotted show that for the inexperienced driver night conditions produce considerably more steering corrections than do day conditions, while for the experienced driver the differences in the number of corrections made under the two conditions is relatively slight. While the data do give us confidence in reporting a significant effect for A (the difference between experienced and inexperienced drivers), they should

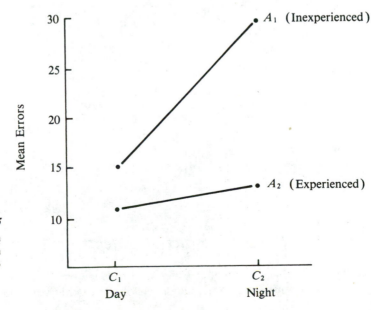

FIGURE 13.5
AC interaction
for data in
Table 13.13

leave us a bit suspicious about differences due to Variable C. At a quick glance it would appear that there is a significant C effect for the inexperienced drivers, but not for the experienced drivers. To examine this question more closely we must consider the simple effects of C under A_1 and A_2 separately. This analysis is presented in Table 13.14, from which we can see that there is a significant effect between day and night conditions for the inexperienced drivers, but not for the experienced drivers. (Note that we can again check the accuracy of our calculations due to the fact that the simple effects should sum to $SS_C + SS_{AC}$.)

From this hypothetical experiment we would conclude that there are significant differences among the three types of roadway, and between experienced and inexperienced drivers. We would also conclude that there is a significant difference between day and night conditions, but only for the inexperienced driver.

TABLE 13.14
Simple Effects
for Data in
Table 13.13

(**a**) Data

	C_1	C_2	
A_1	180	360	540
A_2	130	160	290

(**b**) Computations

$$SS_{C\ at\ A_1} = \frac{180^2 + 360^2}{12} - \frac{540^2}{24} = 13500 - 12150 = 1350.00$$

$$SS_{C\ at\ A_2} = \frac{130^2 + 160^2}{12} - \frac{290^2}{24} = 3541.66 - 3504.16 = 37.50$$

(**c**) Summary table

Source	df	SS	MS	F
C at A_1	1	1350.00	1350.00	50.58*
C at A_2	1	37.50	37.50	1.40
Error	36	961.00	26.69	

* $p < .05$.

(**d**) Decomposition
of Sums of Squares

$$SS_{C\ at\ A_1} + SS_{C\ at\ A2} = SS_C + SS_{AC}$$
$$1350.00 + 37.50 = 918.75 + 468.75$$
$$1387.50 = 1387.50$$

Simple Interaction Effects

With the higher order factorials we can not only look at the effects of one variable at individual levels of some other variable (what we have called simple effects but which should more accurately be called *simple main effects*), but we can also look at the interaction of two variables at individual levels of some third variable. This we will refer to as a *simple interaction effect.*

Although in our example the second order interaction (ABC) was not significant ($F < 1$), we will pretend for the moment that it was, and break it down accordingly. This interaction is plotted in Figure 13.6, where the AB

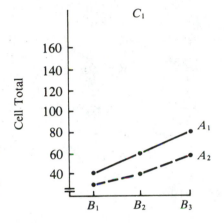
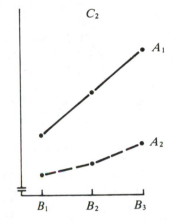

FIGURE 13.6

ABC interaction
for data in
Table 13.13

interaction has been plotted separately for each level of C. Although we already know better, with a little imagination you might claim that the two lines were parallel under C_1, but were diverging under C_2. This would suggest that there is no AB interaction at C_1, but that there is one at C_2. This hypothesis is open to test by calculating the AB interaction at each level of C, in a manner logically equivalent to that used for the simple main effects. Essentially all that we need to do is to treat the C_1 and C_2 data separately, calculating SS_{AB} for the C_1 data and then for the C_2 data. These simple interaction effects are then tested using MS_{error} from the overall analysis. This has been done in Table 13.15.

From the analysis of the simple interaction effects it is apparent that the AB interaction is not significant under either level of C, nor did we expect it to be since neither AB nor ABC was significant. Thus we have no reason to conclude that the joint effect of A and B, whatever it might be, is itself a function of some third variable (C).

While there is nothing to prevent someone from examining simple interaction effects in the absence of a significant higher order interaction, there are seldom cases where this would make any logical sense. If, however, the experimenter has a particular reason for looking at, for example, the AB interaction at each level of C, he is perfectly free to do so. On the other hand, if a higher order interaction is significant, the experimenter should cast a wary eye on all lower order effects and consider testing the important simple effects. However, to steal a line from Winer (1971, p. 442): "Statistical elegance does not necessarily imply scientifically meaningful inferences." Common sense is at least as important as statistical manipulations.

TABLE 13.15

Simple Interaction Effects for Data in Table 13.13

(a) Data and computations for $SS_{AB \text{ at } C_1}$

C_1 Totals

	B_1	B_2	B_3	**Total**
A_1	40	60	80	180
A_2	30	40	60	130
	70	100	140	310

$$SS_{A \text{ at } C_1} = \frac{180^2 + 130^2}{12} - \frac{310^2}{24} = 4108.33 - 4004.17 = 104.16$$

$$SS_{B \text{ at } C_1} = \frac{70^2 + 100^2 + 140^2}{8} - \frac{310^2}{24} = 4312.50 - 4004.17 = 308.33$$

$$SS_{\text{cells } AB \text{ at } C_1} = \frac{40^2 + \cdots + 60^2}{4} - \frac{310^2}{24} = 4425.00 - 4004.17 = 420.83$$

$$SS_{AB \text{ at } C_1} = SS_{\text{cells } AB \text{ at } C_1} - SS_{A \text{ at } C_1} - SS_{B \text{ at } C_1}$$
$$= 420.83 - 104.16 - 308.33 = 8.34$$

(b) Data and computations for $SS_{AB \text{ at } C_2}$

C_2 Totals

	B_1	B_2	B_3	**Total**
A_1	80	120	160	360
A_2	40	50	70	160
	120	170	230	520

$$SS_{A \text{ at } C_2} = \frac{360^2 + 160^2}{12} - \frac{520^2}{24} = 12933.33 - 11266.67 = 1666.66$$

$$SS_{B \text{ at } C_2} = \frac{120^2 + 170^2 + 230^2}{8} - \frac{520^2}{24} = 12025.00 - 11266.67 = 758.33$$

$$SS_{\text{cells } AB \text{ at } C_2} = \frac{80^2 + \cdots + 70^2}{4} - \frac{520^2}{24} = 13850.00 - 11266.67 = 2583.33$$

$$SS_{B \text{ at } C_2} = SS_{\text{cells } AB \text{ at } C_2} - SS_{A \text{ at } C_2} - SS_{B \text{ at } C_2}$$
$$= 2583.33 - 1666.66 - 758.33 = 158.34$$

(c) Summary table

Source	df	SS	MS	F
AB at C_1	2	8.34	4.17	<1
AB at C_2	2	158.34	79.17	2.97
Error	36	961.00	26.69	

13.3 Summary

This chapter continued to extend the discussion of the analysis of variance, here to include designs in which more than one independent variable is manipulated. In all of the designs discussed in this chapter we have assumed that different subjects were assigned to each treatment combination. With factorial designs we have the additional effect of a possible interaction between variables, in which the effect of one variable may depend upon the level of the other variable. We also have the problem of unequal sample sizes, where there are alternative solutions depending upon the question we wish to ask. Toward the end of the chapter we extended the analysis from two variables to three, and found that more complex designs involve the same general principles as simpler designs.

Exercises for Chapter 13

13.1 In a more complete study of restaurant behavior than we had in Chapter 11 (Exercise 11.2) we observe restaurant patrons who sit as same-sex couples. We record the price of the entrée ordered by one person in each pair, and categorize subjects on the basis of the subject's sex and whether or not he/she pays the bill. The data are given below.

	PAYEE		*NON-PAYEE*	
Male	*Female*		*Male*	*Female*
8.00	8.25		9.75	8.75
7.00	8.75		10.25	9.00
8.25	9.75		9.50	9.25
9.00	8.00		9.00	8.50
8.25	9.25		10.50	8.75

a. Run a two-way analysis of variance.
b. Write the underlying structural model for the data in this experiment.

13.2 In a study of mother-infant interaction, mothers are rated by trained observers on the quality of their interactions with their infants. Mothers were classified on the basis of whether or not this was their first child (primiparous vs. multiparous) and on the basis of whether this was a low birth weight (LBW) infant or a full-term infant. Low birth weight mothers were further classified on the basis of whether they were under 18 years old or not. The data represent a score on a 12-point scale, where a high score represents better interaction.

PRIMIPAROUS			MULTIPAROUS		
LBW < 18	LBW ≥ 18	Full Term	LBW < 18	LBW ≥ 18	Full Term
4	6	8	3	7	9
6	5	7	4	8	8
5	5	7	3	8	9
3	4	6	3	9	9
3	9	7	6	8	3
7	6	2	7	2	10
4	2	5	1	1	9
5	6	8	4	9	8
4	5	7	4	9	7
4	5	7	4	8	10

a.   Run the appropriate analysis of variance.

b.   Interpret the results in a meaningful fashion.

13.3   In Exercise 13.2 the design may have a major weakness from a practical point of view. Notice the group of multiparous mother under 18. Without regard to the data, would you expect this group to lie on the same continua as the others?

13.4   Referring back to Exercise 13.2, it seems obvious that the sample sizes do not reflect the relative frequency of these characteristics in the population. Under what conditions would this be a relevant consideration and when would it not?

13.5   In a study of memory processes animals were presented with a one-trial avoidance task. As soon as they stepped across a line down the center of their cage they were shocked. Three groups of animals differed in the area in which they had electrode implants in their brains (neutral site, Area *A*, or Area *B*). Each group was further divided and given electrical stimulation either 50, 100, or 150 msec. after crossing the line and receiving foot shock. If the brain area is involved in memory, stimulation would be expected to interfere with consolidation and retard learning of the avoidance response. The dependent variable was the number of seconds it took the animal to cross the line on the second trial.

	STIMULATION AREA								
	Neutral Site			Area A			Area B		
Delay of Stimulation	*50*	*100*	*150*	*50*	*100*	*150*	*50*	*100*	*150*
	25	30	28	11	31	23	23	18	28
	30	25	31	18	20	28	30	24	21
	28	27	26	26	22	35	18	9	30
	40	35	20	15	23	27	28	16	30
	20	23	35	14	19	21	23	13	23

a. Run the analysis of variance.

b. Write the specific model for the third subject at Area A, 100 msec.

13.6 *a.* In Exercise 13.5, what is $\hat{\alpha}_1$ (if A is used to represent areas)?

b. What is $\hat{\beta}_3$, $\widehat{\alpha\beta}_{11}$, and $\widehat{\alpha\beta}_{23}$?

13.7 *a.* Use simple effects to clarify the findings in Exercise 13.5.

b. Show that these simple effects sum to what they should.

13.8 *a.* Calculate the simple effect of three birthweight groups for primiparous mothers in Exercise 13.2.

b. Do the same for multiparous mothers.

c. Show that the simple effects sum correctly.

13.9 As discussed in Exercise 11.19, Howell & Huessy (1980) classified children as to whether or not they exhibited hyperkinetic-like behavior when they were in elementary school and then looked at subsequent performance in high school. In this example the dependent variable is grade point average in high school. Run the analysis of variance using an unweighted means solution.

Male	Never Hyper.	2nd	4th	2 & 4	5th	2 & 5	4 & 5	2, 4, & 5	All Ss
$\bar{X}_j$	2.4066	2.2092	1.6660	1.8000	1.9583	2.0000	1.3111	1.1675	2.1648
s_j	.7578	.8384	1.2606	.8257	.9413	.4677	.6351	.5764	.8476
n_j	77	12	5	8	6	5	9	4	126

Female	Never Hyper.	2nd	4th	2 & 4	5th	2 & 5	4 & 5	2, 4, & 5	All Ss
$\bar{X}_j$	2.9486	2.6144	2.4340	2.0467	2.3500	2.1050	2.7500	1.4020	2.6899
s_j	.6652	.6448	.4351	.7397	.8216	.6370	.3536	.7679	.7724
n_j	70	9	5	9	5	4	2	5	109

13.10 The last problem is an interesting one because the sample sizes are so very unequal. Is it legitimate to assume that sample sizes are independent of treatment effects?

13.11 Assume that in Exercise 13.2 the last three subjects in cell$_{12}$ and the last two subjects in cell$_{23}$ refused to give consent for the data to be analyzed. Rerun the analysis.

13.12 If you go back to Exercise 11.3 you will discover that it really represents a 2×2 factorial. Rerun the analysis and compare the sums of squares and the Fs to the answers you found there.

13.13 Now go to Exercise 12.5 and compare the answers there to the answers you just found for Exercise 13.12.

13.14   An experimenter was interested in hospital patients' responses to two different forms of physical therapy. For his own reasons he felt it important to have greater precision in estimates of means for treatment B (we need not be concerned with why) and thus allocated $\frac{2}{3}$ of the subjects to treatment B and $\frac{1}{3}$ to treatment A. He ran the study at two different hospitals, one of which had more patients available. The data are given below in terms of recovery ratings.

		TREATMENT	
		A	B
		5	10
	1	8	12
		6	14
			12
			10
HOSPITAL			8
		10	15
	2	12	28
			32
			34

Run the analysis for proportional data.

13.15   *a.*   Go back to Exercise 13.14 and run the unweighted means analysis.

b.   Compare the results with those obtained in Exercise 13.14.

13.16   Given the experiment described in Exercise 13.14, does it make sense to allow the sample sizes to influence the results? Under what conditions might you give the opposite answer?

13.17   Calculate η^2 and $\hat{\omega}^2$ for the data in Exercise 13.1.

13.18   Calculate η^2 and $\hat{\omega}^2$ for the data in Exercise 13.2.

13.19   In an effort to study the effects of early experience on conditioning, an experimenter raised four groups of rats in the presence of (1) no special stimuli, (2) a tone stimulus, (3) a vibratory stimulus, and (4) both a tone and a vibratory stimulus. The rats were later classically conditioned using either a tone or a vibratory stimulus as the conditioned stimulus and one of three levels of foot shock as the unconditioned stimulus. This is a $4 \times 2 \times 3$ factorial design. The cell totals, rather than the raw data, are given here. The $SS_{total} = 1646.00$ and $n_{ijk} = 5$. The dependent variable was the number of trials to a predetermined criterion.

	Shock Intensity	CONDITIONED STIMULUS					
		Tone			*Vibration*		
		High	*Med.*	*Low*	*High*	*Med.*	*Low*
Early Experience	Control	11	16	21	19	24	29
	Tone	24	29	34	21	26	31
	Vib.	8	13	18	42	47	52
	T & V	22	27	32	33	38	43

Analyze the data and interpret the results.

13.20 Why are simple effect analyses not a useful way of clarifying the significant interaction in Exercise 13.19?

13.21 Rerun the analysis in Exercise 13.2 using MINITAB, SPSS, or BMDP.

13.22 Rerun the analysis in Exercise 13.5 using MINITAB, SPSS, or BMDP.

13.23 The computer printout which follows is from an SPSS analysis of the data described in Exercise 13.11, using SPSS option 9.

```
        1 RUN NAME        SPSS FOR EXERCISE 13.11 --USING OPTION 9
        2 VARIABLE LIST   PARITY,SIZE,SCORE
        3 INPUT FORMAT    FIXED (2F2.0,F2.0)
        4 INPUT MEDIUM    EX1324.DAT
        5 N OF CASES      55
        6 ANOVA           SCORE BY PARITY(1,2) SIZE(1,3)
        7 OPTION          9

    * * * * * * * * * *A N A L Y S I S   O F   V A R I A N C E* * * * * * * * * *
              SCORE
          by PARITY
             SIZE
    * * * * * * * * * * * * * * * * * * * * * * * * * * * * * * * * * * * * * * *

                                  Sum of              Mean           Signif
    Source of variation          Squares      df     Square      F    of F

    Main effects                 100.269       3     33.423   7.989  0.000
       PARITY                     11.235       1     11.235   2.686  0.108
       SIZE                       90.612       2     45.306  10.829  0.000

    2-way interactions            16.317       2      8.158   1.950  0.153
       PARITY   SIZE              16.317       2      8.158   1.950  0.153

    Explained                    113.796       5     22.759   5.440  0.000

    Residual                     205.004      49      4.184

    Total                        318.800      54      5.904


       55 Cases were processed.
        0 Cases (  0.0 %) were missing.
```

a. Compare the values in the printout with the answers you obtained in Exercise 13.11.

b. How would you interpret the Sums of Squares labeled Main Effects and Explained?

14 *Repeated Measures Designs*

Objective

To conclude the discussion of the analysis of variance by considering experimental designs in which the same subject is measured under all levels of one or more independent variables.

Contents

In our discussion of the analysis of variance we have concerned ourselves with experimental designs with different subjects in the different cells. More precisely, we have been concerned with designs in which the cells are independent or, if you prefer, uncorrelated. (Under the assumptions of the analysis of variance, *independent* and *uncorrelated* are synonymous.) Thus if you think of a typical one-way analysis of variance, as diagrammed here, you would probably be willing to concede that the correlations between Treatments 1 and 2, 1 and 3, and 2 and 3 have an expectancy of zero.

TREATMENT 1	TREATMENT 2	TREATMENT 3
X_{11}	X_{21}	X_{31}
X_{12}	X_{22}	X_{32}
X_{13}	X_{23}	X_{33}
...	...	...
X_{1n}	X_{2n}	X_{3n}

However, suppose that in the design diagrammed here the same subjects were used in all three treatments. Thus instead of $3n$ subjects measured once, we had n subjects measured three times. In this case we would be hard put to expect that the intercorrelations of the three treatments would have expectancies of zero. On the contrary, the better subjects under Treatment 1 would probably also perform well under Treatments 2 and 3, and the poorer subjects under Treatment 1 would probably perform poorly under the other conditions.

Partition

Repeated measures designs

This lack of independence among the treatments would cause a very serious problem if it were not for the fact that we can separate out (*partition*) and remove the dependence imposed by repeated measurements on the same subjects. In fact one of the main advantages of *repeated measures designs* is that they allow us to reduce overall variability by using a common subject pool for all treatments, and at the same time allow us to remove subject differences from our error term, leaving the error components independent from treatment to treatment or cell to cell.

As an illustration consider the highly exaggerated set of data on four subjects over three treatments which are presented in Table 14.1. Here the dependent variable is the number of trials-to-criterion on some task. If we look first at the treatment totals we will see that there are some slight differences, but nothing to write home to mother about. There is so much variability within each of the treatments that it would at first appear that the totals differ only by chance. But next look at the subject totals. It is apparent that Subject 1 learns quickly under all conditions, and that Subjects 3 and 4 learn remarkably slowly. These differences among the subjects are producing most of the differences within the treatments, and yet have nothing to do with the treatment effect. If we could remove these subject differences we would have a better (and smaller) estimate of error. At the same time,

TABLE 14.1

Hypothetical Data
for Simple Repeated
Measures Design

	TREATMENT			
Subject	*1*	*2*	*3*	*Total*
1	2	4	7	13
2	10	12	13	35
3	23	29	30	82
4	30	31	34	95
Total	65	76	84	225

it is the subject differences which are creating the high positive intercorrelations among the treatments, and this too we could partial out by forming a separate error term for subjects.

One very laborious way to do this would be to put each subject's contribution on a common footing by equating subject means, without altering the relationships among the scores obtained by that particular subject. Thus we could set $X'_{ij} = X_{ij} - \bar{X}_i$, where $\bar{X}_i$ is the mean of the ith subject. Now subjects would all have the same means ($\bar{X}'_i = 0$) and any remaining differences among the scores could only be attributable to error or to treatments. While this approach is perfectly correct, it is certainly not practical. An alternative, and easier, approach is to calculate a sum of squares

SS_S between subjects (denoted as either $SS_{\text{between subj}}$ or SS_S) and remove this from SS_{total} before we begin. This can be shown to be algebraically equivalent to the first procedure, and is essentially the approach we will adopt.

Partition of Sums of Squares

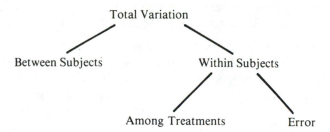

Partition of Degrees of Freedom

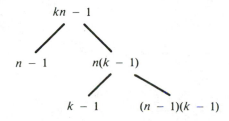

FIGURE 14.1

We can represent the problem diagramatically as in Figure 14.1. Here we partition the overall variation into variation between subjects and variation within subjects. Some of the variation within a subject is attributable to the fact that his scores come from different treatments, and some is to be attributable to error. We will always think of a repeated measures analysis as *first* partitioning the SS_{total} into $SS_{between\ subj}$ and $SS_{within\ subj}$. Depending upon the complexity of the design one or both of these partitions will then be further partitioned.

$SS_{between\ subj}$

$SS_{within\ subj}$

The following discussion of repeated measures designs can only begin to explore the problem. For historical reasons the statistical literature has tended to underemphasize the importance of these designs. As a result much of the important development has been in the area of the social sciences. By far the most complete coverage of these designs is to be found in Winer (1971). His treatment of the problem is excellent and extensive, and much of this chapter shows the influence of his work.

14.1 *The Structural Model*

There are actually two possible structural models which could underlie the analysis of data like those shown in Table 14.1. The simplest model is

$$X_{ij} = \mu + \pi_i + \tau_j + e_{ij} \tag{14.1}$$

[handwritten: $Y_{ij} = \mu + T_j + \rho_i + e_i$, subject variation]

where μ = the grand mean,

π_i = a constant associated with the *i*th person or subject,
τ_j = a constant associated with the *j*th treatment, and
e_{ij} = the experimental error associated with the *i*th subject under the *j*th treatment.

The variables π_i and e_{ij} are assumed to be independently and normally distributed around zero within each treatment. In addition, σ_π^2 and σ_e^2 are assumed to be homogeneous across treatments. With these assumptions it is possible to derive the expected mean squares shown on the left of Table 14.2.

TABLE 14.2

Expected Mean Squares for Simple Repeated Measures Designs

Model I $X_{ij} = \mu + \pi_i + \tau_j + e_{ij}$		Model II $X_{ij} = \mu + \pi_i + \tau_j + \pi\tau_{ij} + e_{ij}$	
Source	**E(MS)**	**Source**	**E(MS)**
Subjects	$\sigma_e^2 + k\sigma_\pi^2$	Subjects	$\sigma_e^2 + k\sigma_\pi^2$
Treatments	$\sigma_e^2 + n\sigma_\tau^2$	Treatments	$\sigma_e^2 + \sigma_{\pi\tau}^2 + n\sigma_\tau^2$
Error	σ_e^2	Error	$\sigma_e^2 + \sigma_{\pi\tau}^2$

An alternative, and probably more realistic model is given by

$$X_{ij} = \mu + \pi_i + \tau_j + \pi\tau_{ij} + e_{ij}.$$ *(14.2)*

Here we have added a subject × treatments interaction term to the model. The assumptions of the first model (Equation 14.1) will continue to hold, and we will also assume the $\pi\tau_{ij}$ to be distributed around zero independently of the other elements of the model. This second model gives rise to the expected mean squares shown on the right of Table 14.2.

14.2 F Ratios

The expected mean squares indicate that the model we adopt influences the F ratios we employ. If we are willing to assume that there is no subject × treatment interaction, we can form the following ratios:

$$\frac{E(\text{MS}_{\text{between subj}})}{E(\text{MS}_{\text{error}})} = \frac{\sigma_e^2 + k\sigma_\pi^2}{\sigma_e^2}$$

and

$$\frac{E(\text{MS}_{\text{treat}})}{E(\text{MS}_{\text{error}})} = \frac{\sigma_e^2 + n\sigma_\tau^2}{\sigma_e^2}.$$

Both of these lead to respectable F ratios, given an additional assumption discussed below, which can be used to test the relevant null hypothesis.

Usually one is quite cautious about assuming that there is no subject × treatment interaction. As a result we usually prefer to work with the more complete model (Equation 14.2). Tukey (1949) has developed a test for additivity of effects which is useful in choosing between the two models. This test is discussed in Kirk (1968) and Winer (1962, 1971).

The full model (including the interaction term) leads to the following ratios:

$$\frac{E(\text{MS}_{\text{between subj}})}{E(\text{MS}_{\text{error}})} = \frac{\sigma_e^2 + k\sigma_\pi^2}{\sigma_e^2 + \sigma_{\pi\tau}^2}$$

and

$$\frac{E(\text{MS}_{\text{treat}})}{E(\text{MS}_{\text{error}})} = \frac{\sigma_e^2 + \sigma_{\pi\tau}^2 + n\sigma_\tau^2}{\sigma_e^2 + \sigma_{\pi\tau}^2}.$$

While the resulting F for treatments is perfectly appropriate, the F for subjects is seen to be biased. If we did form this latter ratio and obtained a significant F, we would be fairly confident that there really were subject differences. However if the F were not significant, the interpretation would be ambiguous. A nonsignificant F would either mean that $k\sigma_\pi^2 = 0$, or that $k\sigma_\pi^2 > 0$ but $\leq \sigma_{\pi\tau}^2$. For this reason we seldom test the effect due to subjects.

This represents no great loss, however, since we have very little to gain by testing the subject effect. The main reason for obtaining $SS_{between\ subj}$ in the first place is to absorb the correlations between treatments and thereby remove subject differences from the error term. A test on the subject effect, if it were significant, would merely indicate that people are different—hardly a momentous finding.

14.3   *The Covariance Matrix*

One of the necessary assumptions required for any *F* ratio to be distributed as the central (tabled) *F* is the assumption of compound symmetry of the covariance matrix.† To understand what is meant by this, consider a matrix ($\hat{\Sigma}$) representing the covariances among the three treatments for the data given in Table 14.1.

[handwritten annotations: sum of cross products gp1 to gp2; sums of squares about the mean of Gp1]

$$
\hat{\Sigma} = \begin{array}{c} A_1 \\ A_2 \\ A_3 \end{array}
\begin{array}{ccc}
A_1 & A_2 & A_3 \\
\left[\begin{array}{ccc} 158.92 & 163.33 & 163.00 \\ 163.33 & 172.67 & 170.67 \\ 163.00 & 170.67 & 170.00 \end{array}\right]
\end{array}
$$

Main diagonal

Off-diagonal elements

On the ***main diagonal*** of this matrix are the variances within each treatment ($\sigma^2_{A_j}$). You will note that they are all more or less equal, indicating that we have met the assumption of homogeneity of variance. The ***off-diagonal elements*** represent the covariances among the treatments (cov_{12}, cov_{13}, and cov_{23}). You will note that these are also more or less equal. The fact that they are also of the same magnitude as the variances is irrelevant, reflecting merely the very high intercorrelations among treatments. When we have a pattern of constant variances on the diagonal and constant covariances off the diagonal we have what is referred to as ***compound symmetry***. (Again, the relationship between the variances and covariances is irrelevant.) The assumption of compound symmetry of the (*population*) ***covariance matrix*** (Σ), of which $\hat{\Sigma}$ is an estimate, is one of the assumptions underlying the analysis of variance. Without this assumption the *F* ratios will not have a distribution given by the tabled distribution of *F*. While this assumption applies to any analysis of variance design, when the cells are independent the covariances are always zero, and there is no problem—we merely need to assume homogeneity of variance. With repeated measures designs, however, the covariances will not be zero and we need to make the assumption that they are all equal. This has led some people (e.g., Hays, 1963) to refuse to consider repeated measures designs—as if no one ever

Compound symmetry

Covariance matrix

---

† This assumption is overly stringent, and will shortly be relaxed somewhat. It is none-the-less a sufficient assumption, and a common one to make.

tested the same subject twice. However when we do have compound symmetry the Fs are valid, and when we do not we can either use very good approximation procedures (to be discussed later in this chapter), or else we can use alternative methods which do not depend upon assumptions about Σ.†

Example 14.1

Verbal Retention Over Time

As an illustration of a simple repeated measures design, consider an experiment on the recall of a list of 15 paralogs (pseudowords) after three different time intervals (10 sec., 1 min., or 2 min.). Suppose that we asked six subjects to listen to and recall these lists, with the order of testing with the different time delays randomized separately for each subject. The dependent variable is the number of items recalled correctly, and the data and analysis are presented in Table 14.3.

From the arrangement of the data in part (a) of this table, and the calculations of the sums of squares in part (b), it is apparent that the analysis is basically the same as for a two-way factorial with one score per cell. Since there is only one score per cell, there is no within-cell term. However, as we have already seen from the tables of expected mean squares, $MS_{error}(= MS_{A \times S})$ is a perfectly legitimate test term for treatments, regardless of the underlying model.

In the summary table in part (c) there is included an additional term not directly calculated in part (b). This is the within-subjects term. As we saw in the diagram in Figure 14.1, the total sum of squares can be partitioned into $SS_{between\,subj}$ and $SS_{within\,subj}$, and the latter can be further partitioned into SS_{treat} and SS_{error} (or $SS_{A \times S}$). The most general method of calculation of $SS_{within\,subj}$ is to make use of the relation

$$SS_{total} = SS_{between\,subj} + SS_{within\,subj}$$

and to obtain $SS_{within\,subj}$ by subtraction. While there is no particular need for the inclusion of $SS_{within\,subj}$ in the present summary table, it serves to illustrate exactly what we are doing. In more complex designs this term will in fact play a very useful role in the calculation of the error term.

From the summary table it is apparent that the main effect of Retention Interval (A) is significant $(F_{obt} = 30.23; F_{.05}(2, 10) = 4.10)$. Thus we would reject $H_0: \mu_1 = \mu_2 = \mu_3$ and conclude that the number

Hotelling's T^2
Multivariate techniques

† One alternative procedure which does not require any assumptions about the covariance matrix is ***Hotelling's T^2***. This is a ***multivariate technique*** and is covered in Winer (1971). While multivariate techniques are coming into greater use, they are conceptually more difficult and are unlikely to be in everyday use for a considerable time. The interested reader is referred to Bock (1963), Bock & Haggard (1968) and Davidson (1972).

TABLE 14.3

Illustration of
Calculations for
Simple Repeated
Measures Design

(*a*) Data

		RETENTION INTERVAL (A)			
Subject	2 min.	1 min.	10 sec.		T_{S_i}
1	7	8	11		26
2	1	3	5		9
3	3	5	6		14
4	9	12	11		32
5	11	14	14		39
6	5	7	8		20
T_{treat_j}	36	49	55		140

(*b*) Computations

$$SS_{\text{total}} = \Sigma X^2 - \frac{(\Sigma X)^2}{N} = 7^2 + 1^2 + \cdots + 8^2 - \frac{140^2}{18} = 1336 - 1088.89 = 247.11$$

$$SS_S = \frac{\Sigma T_{S_i}^2}{a} - CF = \frac{26^2 + 9^2 + \cdots + 20^2}{3} - CF = 1299.33 - 1088.89 = 210.44$$

$$SS_A = \frac{\Sigma T_{A_j}^2}{n} - CF = \frac{36^2 + 49^2 + 55^2}{6} - CF = 1120.33 - 1088.89 = 31.44$$

$$SS_{\text{error}} = SS_{A \times S} = SS_{\text{total}} - SS_A - SS_S = 247.11 - 31.44 - 210.44 = 5.23$$

(*c*) Summary table

Source	df	SS	MS	F
Between Subj	5	210.44		
Within Subj	12	36.67		
A	2	31.44	15.72	30.23*
$A \times S$ (Error)	10	5.23	.52	
Total	17	247.11		

* $p < .05$.

of items recalled is a function of the length of the retention interval.
If we had any desire to do so, we could form contrasts among the
means or apply one of the other multiple comparison procedures such
as Dunn's test or the Newman-Keuls test. This would entail the straightforward application of the methods discussed in Chapter 12.

In performing an analysis of variance on these data and, more
specifically, in evaluating F_{obt} against the tabled distribution of F, we
have implicitly assumed compound symmetry of Σ. For our data

$$\hat{\Sigma} = \begin{bmatrix} 14.00 & 15.40 & 12.60 \\ 15.40 & 17.37 & 13.57 \\ 12.60 & 13.57 & 11.77 \end{bmatrix}.$$

Visual inspection of this matrix would suggest that the assumption of compound symmetry of Σ is a reasonable one. A statistical test of this assumption is given by Winer (1971, p. 596) and would in fact show that we have no basis for rejecting the symmetry hypothesis. Box (1954b) has shown, however, that regardless of the form of Σ, a conservative test on null hypotheses in the analysis of variance is given by comparing F_{obt} against $F_{.05}(1, n-1)$—i.e., by assuming 1 df for treatments. This test is exceedingly conservative, however, and for most situations we may be better advised to evaluate F in the usual way. We will return to this problem later when we consider Greenhouse & Geisser's (1959) extension of Box's work.

As has already been noted, one of the major advantages of the repeated measures design is the fact that it allows us to reduce our error term by using the same subject for all treatments. Suppose for a moment that the data illustrated had actually been produced by three independent groups of subjects. In this case we would not be able to pull out a subject term ($SS_{between\ subj}$ would be synonymous with SS_{total} in this case). As a result, differences among subjects would be inseparable from error, and in fact SS_{error} would be the sum of what we have labeled SS_{error} and $SS_{between\ subj} = 5.23 + 210.44 = 215.67$ on $10 + 5 = 15$ df. This would lead to

$$F = \frac{MS_{treat}}{MS_{error}} = \frac{15.72}{14.38} = 1.09$$

which is far from significant.

To put it briefly, subjects differ. When subjects are observed only once, these subject differences contribute to SS_{error}. When subjects are observed repeatedly, we can obtain an estimate of the degree of subject differences and partial these differences out of the error term. In general, the greater the differences among subjects, the higher the correlations between pairs of treatments. The higher the correlations among treatments, the greater the relative power of repeated measures designs.

14.4 Two-Variable Repeated Measures Designs

We have been speaking of the simple case where we have one independent variable (other than subjects) and test each subject on every level of that variable. In actual practice there are many different ways in which we could design a study using repeated measures. For example we could set up an experiment using two independent variables and test each subject under all combinations of both variables. Alternatively each subject might serve under only one level of one of the variables, but under all levels of the other. If we had three variables the possibilities are even greater. In this chapter we are going to deal with only a few of the possible designs. If you understand the designs to be discussed here, you should have no difficulty generalizing to even the most complex problems.

One Between-Subjects Variable and One Within-Subject Variable

Consider the data presented in Table 14.4. Variable A will be taken to represent groups of drivers who have been classified as poor risks (A_1) or good risks (A_2) by their insurance company. (The word "group" in this connection is generally taken to imply separate groups of people (or things), and, as such, always involves comparisons between (or among) different sets of subjects.) Variable B represents three driving conditions—open road (B_1), city streets (B_2) and a specially arranged driving track (B_3). We will assume that all drivers were asked to drive each of the three courses at what they considered to be a reasonable speed, and that the number of steering errors was recorded as the dependent variable.

This design can be represented diagrammatically as:

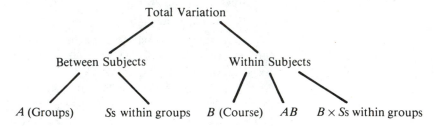

Here we have distinguished those effects which represent differences between subjects from those representing differences within subjects. When we consider the between-subjects term we can partition it into differences between groups of subjects (A) and differences between subjects in the same group (Ss within groups). The within-subject term can similarly be subdivided into three components—the main effect of B and its interactions with the two partitions of the between-subject variation.

Partitioning of Between-Subjects Effects

Let us first consider the partition of the between-subjects term in more detail. From the design of the experiment we know that this term can be

TABLE 14.4

Illustration of Calculations for One Between- and One Within- Subject Variable

(a) Data

		COURSE			
RISK GROUPS	Subject	B_1	B_2	B_3	T_{S_k}
A_1	1	4	9	14	27
	2	8	12	19	39
	3	6	10	13	29
	4	3	6	11	20
A_2	5	5	6	9	20
	6	3	3	3	9
	7	8	10	9	27
	8	4	3	3	10

AB	CELL TOTALS			
	B_1	B_2	B_3	T_{A_i}
A_1	21	37	57	115
A_2	20	22	24	66
T_{B_j}	41	59	81	181

(b) Computations

$$SS_{total} = \Sigma X^2 - \frac{(\Sigma X)^2}{N} = 4^2 + 8^2 + \cdots + 9^2 + 3^2 - \frac{181^2}{24} = 1781 - 1365.04 = 415.96$$

$$SS_S = \frac{\Sigma T_{S_k}^2}{b} - CF = \frac{27^2 + \cdots + 10^2}{3} - CF = 1600.33 - 1365.04 = 235.29$$

$$SS_A = \frac{\Sigma T_{A_i}^2}{nb} - CF = \frac{115^2 + 66^2}{12} - CF = 1465.08 - 1365.04 = 100.04$$

$$SS_B = \frac{\Sigma T_{B_j}^2}{na} - CF = \frac{41^2 + 59^2 + 81^2}{8} - CF = 1465.38 - 1365.04 = 100.34$$

$$SS_{cells\ AB} = \frac{\Sigma T_{AB_{ij}}^2}{n} - CF = \frac{21^2 + \cdots + 24^2}{4} - CF = 1629.75 - 1365.04 = 264.71$$

$$SS_{AB} = SS_{cells\ AB} - SS_A - SS_B = 264.71 - 100.04 - 100.34 = 64.33$$

(c) Summary table

Source	df	SS	MS	F
Between Subj	7	235.29		
$\quad A$ (Groups)	1		100.04	4.44
$\quad S$s within groups	6		22.54	
Within Subj	16	180.67		
$\quad B$ (Course)	2		50.17	37.72*
$\quad AB$	2		32.16	24.18*
$\quad B \times S$s Within Groups	12		1.33	
Total	23	415.96		

* $p < .05$.

partitioned into two parts. One of these partitions is the main effect of A (groups), since A_1 and A_2 involve different groups of subjects. This is not the only source of differences between subjects, however. We have four different subjects within A_1, and differences among them are certainly between-subject differences. The same holds for the four subjects within A_2. Here we are speaking of differences between subjects in the same group—i.e., Ss within groups.

If we ignore B entirely we can think of the study as producing the following data.

A_1	A_2
27	20
39	9
29	27
20	10
115	66

where the raw scores are the subject totals from Table 14.4. An analysis of this form is directly analogous to the analysis we will in fact apply to the between-subjects components of variance. Indeed, except for a constant representing the number of scores per subject (which cancels out in the end), the sums of squares for the simple one-way above would be the same as those in the actual analysis. The F which tests the main effect of A for the above data would be exactly equal to the one which we will obtain from the full analysis. Thus the between-subjects partition of the total variation can be seen as essentially a separate analysis of variance, with its own error term *Error*~between~ (sometimes referred to as ***error***~between~) independent of the within-subject effects.

Partitioning of Within-Subjects Effects

We will next consider the within-subjects partition of SS_{total}. As we have already seen, this is itself partitioned into three terms. A comparison of B_1, B_2, and B_3 involves comparison of scores from the same subject, and thus B is a within-subjects term—it depends upon differences within each subject. Since B is a within-subject term, the interaction of B with A is also a within-subject effect. The third term ($B \times S$s within groups) is *Error*~within~ sometimes referred to as ***error***~within~, since it is the error term for the within-subject effects. This term is actually the sum of the $B \times S$ interactions calculated separately for each group. Thus it can be seen as logically equivalent to the error term ($A \times S$) employed in the previous design.

The Analysis

Before considering the analysis in detail, it will be instructive to consider the general pattern of the results. From the marginal totals we can make a few tentative statements about what the data seem to show. There appears to be a slight tendency for the poor risk drivers (A_1) to make more errors than the good risk drivers (A_2). There is also a noticeable effect of B, with errors increasing as driving conditions deteriorate. Equally noticeable is what appears to be an interaction between A and B, with the poor risk drivers showing marked changes across B, while the performance of the good risk drivers remains more or less constant. This suggests that we might later wish to look at the simple effects of B for A_1 and the simple effect of A for B_3. While these tentative conclusions must await confirmation by the analysis of variance, they at least show us roughly what to expect.

An important point to notice is that we need not say anything about the calculations in part (b) of Table 14.4, since they are no different from the usual calculations of main effects and interactions, although you should examine them carefully to verify this fact. Instead we will go directly to consideration of the summary table in part (c). Here we can see that the source column reflects the design of the experiment, with SS_{total} first partitioned into $SS_{between\ subj}$ and $SS_{within\ subj}$. Each of these sums of squares is then further subdivided. We can also see that we calculate three of the terms ($SS_{within\ subj}$, $SS_{Ss\ within\ groups}$, and $SS_{B \times Ss\ within\ groups}$) by subtraction, simplifying our work considerably. Thus

$$SS_{within\ subj} = SS_{total} - SS_{between\ subj}$$

$$SS_{Ss\ within\ groups} = SS_{between\ subj} - SS_A$$

$$SS_{B \times Ss\ within\ groups} = SS_{within\ subj} - SS_B - SS_{AB}.$$

These last two terms will become error terms for the analysis.

The degrees of freedom are obtained in a relatively straightforward manner. For each of the main effects, the degrees of freedom are equal to the number of levels of the variable minus one. Thus for Subjects there are $8 - 1 = 7$ df, for A there are $2 - 1 = 1$ df, and for B there are $3 - 1 = 2$ df. As for all interactions, the df for AB are equal to the product of the df for the component terms. Thus $df_{AB} = (2 - 1)(3 - 1) = 2$. The easiest way to obtain the remaining degrees of freedom is by subtraction.

$$df_{within\ subj} = df_{total} - df_{between\ subj}$$

$$df_{Ss\ within\ groups} = df_{between\ subj} - df_A$$

$$df_{B \times Ss\ within\ groups} = df_{within\ subj} - df_B - df_{AB}$$

These df can also be obtained directly by considering what these terms represent. Within each subject we have $3 - 1 = 2$ df. With eight subjects this amounts to $(8)(2) = 16\ df_{within\ subj}$. Within each level of A (groups) we have

$4 - 1 = 3$ df between subjects, and with two levels of A we have $(2)(3) = 6$ df $_{Ss\ within\ groups}$. $B \times Ss$ within groups is really an interaction term, and its df represent the product of df$_B$ and df$_{Ss\ within\ groups} = (2)(6) = 12$. Alternatively, within each level of A the $B \times S$ interaction is based on 6 df, which gives us 12 df over the two levels of A.

Skipping over the mean squares, which are merely the sums of squares divided by their degrees of freedom, we come to F. From the column of F it is apparent that, as we had anticipated, B and AB are significant. The main effect of A fails to reach significance ($F_{.05}(1, 6) = 5.99$).

To see why these Fs are appropriate we must examine the expected mean squares presented in Table 14.5.

TABLE 14.5

Expected Mean Squares for Analysis in Table 14.4

Source	df	E(MS)
Between Subj	$an - 1$	
A	$a - 1$	$\sigma_e^2 + b\sigma_\pi^2 + nb\sigma_\alpha^2$
Ss within groups	$a(n - 1)$	$\sigma_e^2 + b\sigma_\pi^2$
Within Subj	$an(b - 1)$	
B	$b - 1$	$\sigma_e^2 + \sigma_{\beta\pi}^2 + na\sigma_\beta^2$
AB	$(a - 1)(b - 1)$	$\sigma_e^2 + \sigma_{\beta\pi}^2 + n\sigma_{\alpha\beta}^2$
$B \times Ss$ within groups	$a(n - 1)(b - 1)$	$\sigma_e^2 + \sigma_{\beta\pi}^2$
Total	$N - 1$	

Based upon these expectations the F ratios have the following form:

$$\frac{E(MS_A)}{E(MS_{Ss\ within\ groups})} = \frac{\sigma_e^2 + b\sigma_\pi^2 + nb\sigma_\alpha^2}{\sigma_e^2 + b\sigma_\pi^2}$$

$$\frac{E(MS_B)}{E(MS_{B \times Ss\ within\ groups})} = \frac{\sigma_e^2 + \sigma_{\beta\pi}^2 + na\sigma_\beta^2}{\sigma_e^2 + \sigma_{\beta\pi}^2}$$

$$\frac{E(MS_{AB})}{E(MS_{B \times Ss\ within\ groups})} = \frac{\sigma_e^2 + \sigma_{\beta\pi}^2 + n\sigma_{\alpha\beta}^2}{\sigma_e^2 + \sigma_{\beta\pi}^2}.$$

In each case the numerator differs from the denominator by only the term in question, thus providing an appropriate test of the relevant null hypothesis.

Assumptions

For the F ratios to actually follow the F distribution we must invoke the usual assumptions of normality, homogeneity of variance, and compound symmetry of Σ. For the *between-subjects* term(s) this means that we must assume that the variance of subjects within any one level of A is the same as the variance of subjects within every other level of A. If necessary this assumption can be tested by calculating each of the variances and testing the two extreme variances with $F_{\max}$ on $(a, n-1)$ df. In practice, however, the analysis of variance is relatively robust against reasonable violations of this assumption (see references cited earlier; Collier, Baker, & Mandeville, 1967; and Collier, Baker, Mandeville, & Hayes, 1967). Since the groups are independent, compound symmetry of the covariance matrix is assured if we have homogeneity of variance, since all off-diagonal elements will be zero.

For the *within-subjects* terms we must also consider the usual assumptions of homogeneity of variance and normality. The homogeneity of variance assumption in this case is the assumption that the $B \times S$ interactions are constant across the levels of A, and here again this can be tested against $F_{\max_\alpha}$ $(a, (n-1)(b-1))$. For the within-subjects effects we must also make assumptions concerning the covariance matrix.

There are two assumptions on the covariance matrix or matrices. Again we will let $\hat{\Sigma}$ represent the matrix of variances and covariances among the levels of B. Thus

$$\hat{\Sigma} = \begin{array}{c} \phantom{\hat{\Sigma}=} \begin{array}{ccc} B_1 & B_2 & B_3 \end{array} \\ \begin{bmatrix} \hat{\sigma}_{11} & \hat{\sigma}_{12} & \hat{\sigma}_{13} \\ \hat{\sigma}_{21} & \hat{\sigma}_{22} & \hat{\sigma}_{23} \\ \hat{\sigma}_{31} & \hat{\sigma}_{32} & \hat{\sigma}_{33} \end{bmatrix} \end{array}$$

For each level of A we could have a variance-covariance matrix Σ_{A_i}. (Σ and Σ_{A_i} are estimated by $\hat{\Sigma}$ and $\hat{\Sigma}_{A_i}$, respectively.) For $B \times Ss$ within groups to be an appropriate error term we must first assume that the Σ_{A_i} are the same for all levels of A. This can be thought of as an extension (to covariances) of the common assumption of homogeneity of variance.

The second assumption concerning covariances deals with the overall matrix Σ, where Σ is the pooled average of the Σ_{A_i}. A sufficient, but not necessary, assumption is that the matrix exhibits compound symmetry, meaning, as we have said, that all of the variances on the main diagonal are equal, and all of the covariances off the main diagonal are equal. Again, the variances do not have to equal the covariances, and usually will not. This assumption is in fact more stringent than necessary. All that we really need to assume is that the standard errors of the differences between pairs of means of B are constant—in other words that $\sigma^2_{\bar{B}_i - \bar{B}_j}$ is constant for all i and j $(i \neq j)$. This requirement is automatically met if Σ exhibits compound symmetry, but other patterns of Σ will also have this property. For a more extensive discussion of the covariance assumptions, the reader is referred to Winer (1971) and Huynh & Feldt (1970).

Greenhouse & Geisser (1959) have investigated the effects of departure from this assumption on Σ. They have shown that regardless of the form of Σ the F ratio will be approximately distributed as F on

$$(b-1)e, a(n-1)(b-1)e \text{ df } \text{ for } F_B$$

and

$$(a-1)(b-1)e, \; a(n-1)(b-1)e \; \text{df} \quad \text{for } F_{AB}$$

where e is estimated by

$$\hat{e} = \frac{b^2(\bar{s}_{ii} - \bar{s})^2}{(b-1)(\Sigma s_{ij}^2 - 2b\Sigma \bar{s}_i^2 + b^2(\bar{s})^2)} \qquad\qquad (14.3)$$

and where $\bar{s}_{ii}$ is the mean of the entries on the main diagonal of $\hat{\Sigma}$, $\bar{s}$ is the mean of all entries in $\hat{\Sigma}$, s_{ij} is the ijth entry in $\hat{\Sigma}$, and $\bar{s}_i$ is the mean of all entries in the ith row of $\hat{\Sigma}$.

Greenhouse and Geisser go on to show that when all assumptions are met, $e = 1$, and as we depart more and more from compound symmetry e approaches $1/(b-1)$ as a minimum. They therefore suggest that a conservative test can be made by setting $\hat{e} = 1/(b-1)$, which reduces to setting

$$\text{df}_B = 1, \; a(n-1)$$

and

$$\text{df}_{AB} = (a-1), \; a(n-1).$$

There is evidence to suggest that Greenhouse & Geisser's (1959) suggested correction is far too conservative. Collier, Baker, Mandeville, & Hayes (1967) ran a **Monte Carlo** sampling study which showed rather minor effects for values of e greater than approximately .70. In general, if the data suggest only moderate violations of the covariance assumptions the experimenter will probably introduce less bias by running the usual F test than by adopting the convention of automatically setting $\hat{e} = 1/(b-1)$. Probably the best procedure would be to estimate e and calculate the required degrees of freedom directly. For tests on Σ the reader is referred to Winer (1971).

For our data the Fs are such that the results would be unchanged by any legitimate value of e. However for purposes of demonstration $\hat{\Sigma}_{A_i}$ and $\hat{\Sigma}$ are given in Table 14.6, along with the calculation of $\hat{e}$, df_B and df_{AB}. In this table the elements of $\hat{\Sigma}$ are the means of the corresponding elements of $\hat{\Sigma}_{A_1}$ and $\hat{\Sigma}_{A_2}$. From the results of the calculations we can see that the corrected df round off to (2, 10) for both Fs, as opposed to the uncorrected df of (2, 12). This change makes no difference in the interpretation of the results. Since A is a between-subjects factor, its df are unaffected.

Simple Effects

The most important result obtained from the sample data is the presence of the *AB* interaction. This interaction is plotted in Figure 14.2, where it is obvious that considerable suspicion is cast on the interpretation of the main effects. Figure 14.2 suggests that under good road conditions the two

TABLE 14.6

Illustrative Calculation of Greenhouse and Geisser's $\hat{e}$

$$\hat{\Sigma}_{A_1} = \begin{bmatrix} 4.92 & 5.25 & 6.58 \\ 5.25 & 6.25 & 7.58 \\ 6.58 & 7.58 & 11.58 \end{bmatrix}$$

$$\hat{\Sigma}_{A_2} = \begin{bmatrix} 4.67 & 7.00 & 6.00 \\ 7.00 & 11.00 & 10.00 \\ 6.00 & 10.00 & 12.00 \end{bmatrix}$$

$$\hat{\Sigma} = \begin{bmatrix} 4.80 & 6.12 & 6.29 \\ 6.12 & 8.62 & 8.79 \\ 6.29 & 8.79 & 11.79 \end{bmatrix} \quad \begin{matrix} \bar{s}_i \\ 5.74 \\ 7.84 \\ 8.96 \end{matrix}$$

$$\bar{s}_{ii} = \frac{4.80 + 8.62 + 11.79}{3} = 8.40$$

$$\bar{s} = \frac{4.80 + 6.12 + \cdots + 8.79 + 11.79}{9} = 7.51$$

$$\Sigma s_{ii}^2 = 4.80^2 + 6.12^2 + \cdots + 8.79^2 + 11.79^2 = 544.91$$

$$\Sigma(\bar{s}_i)^2 = 5.74^2 + 7.84^2 + 8.96^2 = 174.69$$

$$\hat{e} = \frac{b^2(\bar{s}_{ii} - \bar{s})^2}{(b-1)(\Sigma s_{ij}^2 - 2b\Sigma(\bar{s}_i^2) + b^2(\bar{s})^2)} = \frac{3^2(8.40 - 7.51)^2}{2(544.91 - 6(174.69) + 9(7.51^2))}$$

$$= \frac{9(.792)}{2(4.37)} = .82$$

$$\text{df}_B = ((b-1)\hat{e}, a(n-1)(b-1)\hat{e}) = (1.62, 9.84) = (2, 10)$$

$$\text{df}_{AB} = ((a-1)(b-1)\hat{e}, a(n-1)(b-1)\hat{e}) = (1.62, 9.84) = (2, 10)$$

$$F_{.05}(2, 10) = 4.10$$

groups do not differ, but as conditions deteriorate so does the performance of the poor risk groups. At the same time the good risk drivers maintain their performance under all conditions. This suggests that we might wish to examine the simple effects of A at each level of B. We might also wish to examine the effects of B for each level of A, especially to see if there is any evidence that the good risk drivers deteriorate at all across conditions. For the data from Table 14.4 (page 373), the calculation of the sums of squares for these effects is presented in Table 14.7.

Testing the simple effects requires special considerations in the case of a repeated measures design. As far as the within-subject terms are concerned, there is no difficulty, since $\text{MS}_{B \times Ss \text{ within } A}$ is an appropriate error term. Thus

$$F_{B \text{ within } A_1} = \frac{\text{MS}_{B \text{ within } A_1}}{\text{MS}_{B \times Ss \text{ within } A}} = \frac{162.67/2}{1.33} = \frac{81.335}{1.33} = 61.154$$

$$F_{B \text{ within } A_2} = \frac{\text{MS}_{B \text{ within } A_2}}{\text{MS}_{B \times Ss \text{ within } A}} = \frac{2.00/2}{1.33} = \frac{1.00}{1.33} < 1.$$

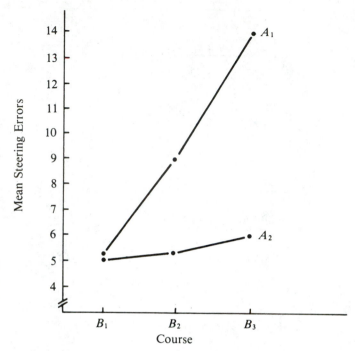

FIGURE 14.2

AB interaction
for data in
Table 14.4

When we come to testing the simple effects of between-subject terms, however, things become a little trickier. Consider for a moment the simple effect of A at B_1. This is essentially a one-way analysis of variance with no repeated measures, since the A_i totals now represent individual observations on subjects, rather than the sum of repeated observations on subjects. Thus subject differences are confounded with experimental error. In this case the appropriate error sum of squares is $SS_{within\ cell}$ where

$$SS_{within\ cell} = SS_{Ss\ within\ A} + SS_{B \times Ss\ within\ A} \qquad (14.4)$$

$$= 135.25 + 16.00 = 151.25$$

and

$$MS_{within\ cell} = \frac{SS_{within\ cell}}{df_{Ss\ within\ A} + df_{B \times Ss\ within\ A}} \qquad (14.5)$$

$$= \frac{151.25}{6 + 12} = \frac{151.25}{18} = 8.403$$

It might be easier to understand why we need this special $MS_{within\ cell}$ error term if you think about what it really represents. If you were presented with only the data in Column B_1 of Table 14.4 and wished to test the differences between the A_1 and A_2 groups, the MS_{error} would be the average of the variances within each of the two groups. Similarly, if you had only

TABLE 14.7
Simple Effects

	CELL TOTALS			
	B_1	B_2	B_3	*Total*
A_1	21	37	57	115
A_2	20	22	24	66
	41	59	81	181

Simple Effects of A at B_i

$$SS_{A \text{ at } B_1} = \frac{21^2 + 20^2}{4} - \frac{41^2}{8} = 210.25 - 210.125 = \quad .125$$

$$SS_{A \text{ at } B_2} = \frac{37^2 + 22^2}{4} - \frac{59^2}{8} = 463.25 - 435.125 = \quad 28.125$$

$$SS_{A \text{ at } B_3} = \frac{57^2 + 24^2}{4} - \frac{81^2}{8} = 956.25 - 820.125 = 136.125$$

$$SS_A + SS_{AB} = 100.04 + 64.33 = \qquad \overline{164.375}$$

Simple Effects of B at A_i

$$SS_{B \text{ at } A_1} = \frac{21^2 + 37^2 + 57^2}{4} - \frac{115^2}{12} = 1264.75 - 1102.08 = 162.67$$

$$SS_{B \text{ at } A_2} = \frac{20^2 + 22^2 + 24^2}{4} - \frac{66^2}{12} = 365.00 - 363.00 = \quad 2.00$$

$$SS_B + SS_{AB} = 100.34 + 64.33 = \qquad \overline{164.67}$$

the data from Column B_2 or B_3 you would average the variances within the A_1 and A_2 groups. The $MS_{\text{within cell}}$ which we have just finished calculating is in reality the average of the error terms for these three hypothetical comparisons. As such, it is the average of the variances within each of the six cells.

We can now proceed to form our F ratios

$$F_{A \text{ at } B_1} = \frac{MS_{A \text{ at } B_1}}{MS_{\text{within cell}}} = \frac{.125}{8.403} < 1$$

$$F_{A \text{ at } B_2} = \frac{MS_{A \text{ at } B_2}}{MS_{\text{within cell}}} = \frac{28.125}{8.403} = 3.347$$

$$F_{A \text{ at } B_3} = \frac{MS_{A \text{ at } B_3}}{MS_{\text{within cell}}} = \frac{136.125}{8.403} = 16.20.$$

A further difficulty arises in the evaluation of F. Since $MS_{\text{within cell}}$ also represents the sum of two *heterogeneous* sources of error (as can be seen by examination of the $E(MS)$ for Ss within A and $B \times Ss$ within A), our F will not be distributed on 1 and 18 df. We will get ourselves out of this difficulty the same way we did when we faced a similar problem concerning t in Chapter 7. We will simply calculate the relevant df against which to evaluate F—more precisely we will calculate a statistic denoted as (**f**) and evaluate F_{obt} against $F_{.05}(a-1, f)$. In this case the value of (f) is defined by Satterthwaite (1946) as

$$f = \frac{(u+v)^2}{\dfrac{u^2}{df_u} + \dfrac{v^2}{df_v}} \tag{14.6}$$

where

$$u = SS_{Ss \text{ within } A}$$
$$v = SS_{B \times Ss \text{ within } A}$$
$$df_u = df_{Ss \text{ within } A}$$
$$df_v = df_{B \times Ss \text{ within } A}.$$

For our example

$$u = 135.25$$
$$v = 16.00$$
$$df_u = 6$$
$$df_v = 12$$

$$f = \frac{(135.25 + 16.00)^2}{\dfrac{135.25^2}{6} + \dfrac{16.00^2}{12}} = \frac{22876.5625}{3070.094} = 7.451.$$

Rounding to the nearest integer, $f = 7$. Thus our Fs are distributed on $a-1$, $f = 1, 7$ df under H_0. For 1 and 7 df, $F_{.05} = 5.59$. Thus only the simple effect of A at B_3 reaches significance.

From the simple effects we can conclude that there are significant differences due to driving conditions for the poor risk drivers, and that the two groups differ for the worst driving conditions. We have insufficient evidence to reject other simple effect hypotheses. It is worth noting that the conclusions we have drawn on the basis of the simple effects are quite different from the ones we would have drawn had we only considered the main effects. This illustrates the importance of being extremely cautious concerning main effects in the presence of a significant interaction.

Example 14.2

A Computer Analysis of Increasing Social Interaction in Geriatric Patients

Winkler (1977) wrote a dissertation comparing Reality Orientation (RO) and Behavior Therapy (BT) as treatment for increasing levels of social interaction in geriatric patients. He assigned 21 subjects at a state mental hospital to one of three groups (RO, BT, or untreated control) and then recorded the percentage of time in which each patient was observed engaging in the relevant social interaction. The data on patient-staff interaction are given in Table 14.8 for four time periods. The BMDP2V printout follows in Table 14.9. SPSS and MINITAB do not handle repeated measures designs, and thus do not appear.

TABLE 14.8
Data from
Winkler (1977)

		Baseline	Treatment	Withdrawn	Follow-up
BT		1.5%	9.0%	5.0%	4.0%
		5.0	14.0	4.5	7.0
		1.0	8.0	4.5	2.5
		5.0	14.0	8.0	5.0
		3.0	8.0	4.0	4.0
		0.5	3.5	1.3	1.0
		0.5	3.0	1.0	0.0
RT		2.0	5.0	5.0	1.5
		1.5	1.9	1.5	1.0
		3.5	7.0	8.0	4.0
		1.5	4.2	2.0	1.5
		1.5	3.6	2.0	1.0
		1.5	2.5	2.8	4.0
		1.5	2.4	0.5	0.0
Control		3.0	3.1	0.5	2.0
		5.0	4.3	3.5	4.0
		1.5	0.8	1.3	3.0
		2.0	2.6	1.5	2.0
		6.0	3.5	4.0	3.0
		1.0	1.0	0.3	0.0
		0.0	0.3	0.3	1.0

Two Within-Subject Variables

Occasionally one runs across a study containing two variables, in which every subject serves under all combinations of both variables. In this design there will be no between-subject variables. Since this design is merely a simplified version of the final design considered in this chapter (three within-subject effects and no between-subject effects), it will not be discussed here. the interested reader can simply refer to the more complex analysis, ignoring all references there to variable C and its interactions.

TABLE 14.9   BMDP2V Analysis of Winkler's Data

```
BMDP2V - ANALYSIS OF VARIANCE AND COVARIANCES WITH REPEATED MEASURES.

    PROGRAM CONTROL INFORMATION

PROBLEM       TITLE IS 'ANALYSIS OF WINKLER  PATIENT TO STAFF DATA'./
INPUT         VARIABLES ARE 5.
              FORMAT IS '(F1.0,4F4.3)'.
              CASES ARE 21.
              UNIT IS 21./
VARIABLE      NAMES ARE GROUP,BASE,TREA,WITH,FOLL./
DESIGN        DEPENDENT ARE 2,3,4,5.
              LEVELS ARE 4.
              NAME IS PERIOD.
              GROUPS = 1./
END/


    VARIABLES TO BE USED
       1 GROUP       2 BASE       3 TREA       4 WITH       5 FOLL

GROUP STRUCTURE

    GROUP       COUNT
  * 1.0000        7.
  * 2.0000        7.
  * 3.0000        7.

          CELL MEANS  FOR   1-ST DEPENDENT VARIABLE

                                                        MARGINAL
        GROUP   =  * 1.0000    * 2.0000    * 3.0000
              PERI
BASE          1     0.02357     0.01857     0.02643      0.02286
TREA          2     0.08500     0.03800     0.02229      0.04843
WITH          3     0.04043     0.03114     0.01629      0.02929
FOLL          4     0.03357     0.01286     0.02143      0.02262

        MARGINAL     0.04564     0.02514     0.02161      0.03080

        COUNT            7           7           7           21

STANDARD DEVIATIONS  FOR  1-ST DEPENDENT VARIABLE

        GROUP   =  * 1.0000    * 2.0000    * 3.0000
              PERI
BASE          1     0.01994     0.00748     0.02174
TREA          2     0.04406     0.01786     0.01532
WITH          3     0.02373     0.02564     0.01530
FOLL          4     0.02393     0.01350     0.01345

ANALYSIS OF VARIANCE FOR  1-ST
DEPENDENT VARIABLE - BASE    TREA     WITH     FOLL

         SOURCE                SUM OF    DEGREES OF    MEAN         F       TAIL
                               SQUARES    FREEDOM     SQUARE             PROBABILITY

          MEAN                 0.07967        1       0.07967      50.68    0.0000
          GROUP                0.00943        2       0.00472       3.00    0.0751
   1      ERROR                0.02830       18       0.00157

          PERI                 0.00930        3       0.00310      25.48    0.0000
          PG                   0.00929        6       0.00155      12.72    0.0000
   2      ERROR                0.00657       54       0.00012
```

14.5 *Three Variable Designs*

The basic theory of repeated measures analysis of variance has already been laid out in the discussion of the previous designs. However since it is quite common for experimenters to plan experiments with three variables (some or all of which represent repeated measurements on the same subjects), we will next briefly discuss the analysis of these designs. The calculations are basically very simple, since the sums of squares for main effects and interactions are obtained in the usual way and the error terms are obtained by subtraction.

Due to space considerations we will not consider the theory behind these designs at any length. Essentially it amounts to the extrapolation of what has already been said about the two-variable case. For an excellent discussion of the underlying statistical theory the reader is again referred to Winer (1971).

Two Between-Subjects Variables and One Within-Subject Variable

In keeping with our example of automobile driving, assume that we wanted to examine driving behavior as a function of two times of day—Day (A_1) and Night (A_2); three types of course—special serpentine track (B_1), city streets (B_2) and open highway (B_3); and three sizes of cars—small (C_1), medium (C_2), and large (C_3). For this first design let us assume that we will have independent groups of drivers for the Time (A) and Course (B) variables. This design is diagrammed below, where G_i represents the ith group of drivers.

	A_1			A_2		
	C_1	C_2	C_3	C_1	C_2	C_3
B_1	G_1	G_1	G_1	G_4	G_4	G_4
B_2	G_2	G_2	G_2	G_5	G_5	G_5
B_3	G_3	G_3	G_3	G_6	G_6	G_6

We will further assume that there are three subjects per group and that the dependent variable is again the number of steering errors.

The raw data and the necessary summary tables of cell totals are presented in Table 14.10(a). In part (b) of the table are the calculations for the main effects and interactions. Here, as elsewhere, the calculations are carried out exactly as they are for any main effects and interactions.

The summary table for the analysis of variance is presented in part (c). In this table the double ** indicate terms which were obtained by subtraction. Thus

$$SS_{\text{within subj}} = SS_{\text{total}} - SS_{\text{between subj}}$$

$$SS_{S \text{ within group}} = SS_{\text{between subj}} - SS_A - SS_B - SS_{AB}$$

$$SS_{C \times Ss \text{ within groups}} = SS_{\text{within subj}} - SS_C - SS_{AC} - SS_{BC} - SS_{ABC}.$$

TABLE 14.10

Illustration of Calculations for Two Between- and One Within-Subject Variables

(a) Data

		A_1 (NIGHT)				A_2 (DAY)			
		C_1	C_2	C_3	T_{S_i}	C_1	C_2	C_3	T_{S_i}
		Small	Med	Large		Small	Med	Large	
B_1 (Track)		10	8	6	24	5	4	3	12
		9	8	5	22	4	3	3	10
		8	7	4	19	4	1	2	7
Total		27	23	15	65	13	8	8	29
B_2 (City)		9	7	5	21	4	3	3	10
		10	6	4	20	4	2	2	8
		7	4	3	14	3	3	2	8
Total		26	17	12	55	11	8	7	26
B_3 (Highway)		7	6	3	16	2	2	1	5
		4	5	2	11	2	3	2	7
		3	4	2	9	1	0	1	2
Total		14	15	7	36	5	5	4	14

AB CELL TOTALS

	A_1	A_2	Total
B_1	65	29	94
B_2	55	26	81
B_3	36	14	50
Total	156	69	225

AC CELL TOTALS

	A_1	A_2	Total
C_1	67	29	96
C_2	55	21	76
C_3	34	19	53
Total	156	69	225

BC CELL TOTALS

	C_1	C_2	C_3	Total
B_1	40	31	23	94
B_2	37	25	19	81
B_3	19	20	11	50
Total	96	76	53	225

(b) Computations

$$SS_{total} = \Sigma X^2 - \frac{(\Sigma X)^2}{N} = 1261 - 937.50 = 323.50$$

$$SS_S = \frac{\Sigma T_{S_i}^2}{c} - CF = \frac{24^2 + 22^2 + \cdots + 7^2 + 2^2}{3} - CF = 1171.67 - 937.50 = 234.17$$

$$SS_A = \frac{\Sigma T_{A_i}^2}{nbc} - CF = 1077.67 - 937.50 = 140.17$$

$$SS_B = \frac{\Sigma T_{B_j}^2}{nac} - CF = 994.28 - 937.50 = 56.78$$

$$SS_C = \frac{\Sigma T^2_{C_k}}{nab} - CF = 988.94 - 937.50 = 51.44$$

$$SS_{\text{cells } AB} = \frac{\Sigma T^2_{AB_{ij}}}{nc} - CF = 1139.89 - 937.50 = 202.39$$

$$SS_{AB} = SS_{\text{cells } AB} - SS_A - SS_B = 202.39 - 140.17 - 56.78 = 5.44$$

$$SS_{\text{cells } AC} = \frac{\Sigma T^2_{AC_{ik}}}{nb} - CF = 1145.89 - 937.50 = 208.39$$

$$SS_{AC} = SS_{\text{cells } AC} - SS_A - SS_C = 208.39 - 140.17 - 51.44 = 16.78$$

$$SS_{\text{cells } BC} = \frac{\Sigma T^2_{BC_{jk}}}{na} - CF = 1054.50 - 937.50 = 117.00$$

$$SS_{BC} = SS_{\text{cells } BC} - SS_B - SS_C = 117.00 - 56.78 - 51.44 = 8.78$$

$$SS_{\text{cells } ABC} = \frac{\Sigma T^2_{ABC_{ijk}}}{n} - CF = 1219.67 - 937.50 = 282.17$$

$$SS_{ABC} = SS_{\text{cells } ABC} - SS_A - SS_B - SS_C - SS_{AB} - SS_{AC} - SS_{BC}$$
$$= 282.17 - 140.17 - 56.78 - 51.44 - 5.44 - 16.78 - 8.78 = 2.78$$

(c) Summary table

Source	df	SS		MS	F
Between Subj	17	234.17			
A	1		140.17	140.17	52.89*
B	2		56.78	28.39	10.71*
AB	2		5.44	2.72	1.03
Ss within groups	12		31.78**	2.65	
Within Subj	36	89.33**			
C	2	51.44		25.72	64.30*
AC	2		16.78	8.39	20.98*
BC	4		8.78	2.20	5.50*
ABC	4		2.78	.70	1.75
C × Ss within groups	24		9.55**	.40	
Total	53		323.50		

handwritten annotations in left margin:
error { subjects — subjects, subjects×A, subjects×C, subjects×AB, error }

* $p < .05$.
** Term obtained by subtraction.

These last two terms are the error terms for between-subject and within-subject effects, respectively. That these are appropriate error terms is shown by examination of the expected mean squares presented in Table 14.11. For the expected mean squares of random and mixed models, the reader is referred to Kirk (1968, p. 293) or Winer (1971, p. 558).

From the column of F in the summary table we see that all three main effects as well as the AC and BC interactions are significant. The presence of the two significant interactions suggests caution in interpreting the main

TABLE 14.11

Expected Mean Squares with A, B, and C Fixed

Source	df	E(MS)
Between Subj	$abn-1$	
A	$a-1$	$\sigma_e^2 + c\sigma_\pi^2 + nbc\sigma_\alpha^2$
B	$b-1$	$\sigma_e^2 + c\sigma_\pi^2 + nac\sigma_\beta^2$
AB	$(a-1)(b-1)$	$\sigma_e^2 + c\sigma_\pi^2 + nc\sigma_{\alpha\beta}^2$
Ss within groups	$ab(n-1)$	$\sigma_e^2 + c\sigma_\pi^2$
Within Subj	$nab(c-1)$	
C	$c-1$	$\sigma_e^2 + \sigma_{\gamma\pi}^2 + nab\sigma_\gamma^2$
AC	$(a-1)(c-1)$	$\sigma_e^2 + \sigma_{\gamma\pi}^2 + nb\sigma_{\alpha\gamma}^2$
BC	$(b-1)(c-1)$	$\sigma_e^2 + \sigma_{\gamma\pi}^2 + na\sigma_{\beta\gamma}^2$
ABC	$(a-1)(b-1)(c-1)$	$\sigma_e^2 + \sigma_{\gamma\pi}^2 + n\sigma_{\alpha\beta\gamma}^2$
$C \times Ss$ with groups	$ab(n-1)(c-1)$	$\sigma_e^2 + \sigma_{\gamma\pi}^2$
Total	$N-1$	

effects. Examination of the data suggests that nighttime conditions produced more errors than daytime conditions (A_1 vs. A_2), but that this difference decreases as the cars beome larger and more stable (AC). There are still substantial differences even for large cars, and thus the main effect of A has meaning in spite of (or in addition to) the AC interaction. The main effect of B is of questionable importance in light of the pattern of the BC interaction. Here the analysis of simple effects will be instructive. The main effect of C is also thrown into question by the BC interaction, and again the analysis of simple effects would be profitable.

Simple Effects for Complex Repeated Measures Designs

There is no particular difficulty involved in the calculation of the mean squares for simple effects since these calculations are carried out just as they would be for factorial designs. The problem arises, however, when we come to finding an appropriate error term for testing some of these effects. We ran into similar problems testing simple effects with the two-variable design. In the present case there are a greater variety of simple effects which could be tested, and our explanation will have to be more complete and generalizable.

You will recall from earlier discussions that the simple effects represent a partitioning of the combined sums of squares for a main effect and an interaction. Thus if we take the simple effect of B at C_k for example,

$$\text{(simple effects of } B \text{ at } C_k) = \text{SS}_B + \text{SS}_{BC}.$$

In the original analysis, the effects of B and BC were themselves tested by different error terms, because they contained different sources of error.

When it comes to the simple effects, the denominator for the F ratio must reflect these two sources of error. Using subscripts to identify error terms, for the simple effects of B at C_k we will define

$$\text{SS}_{\text{error}_{B \text{ at } C_k}} = SS_{\text{error}_B} + SS_{\text{error}_{BC}}$$

where error_B and error_{BC} represent the SS_{error} terms used to test the effects of B and BC, respectively. Thus for this particular example

$$\text{SS}_{\text{error}_B} = \text{SS}_{S\text{s within groups}}$$

and

$$\text{SS}_{\text{error}_{BC}} = \text{SS}_{C \times S\text{s within groups}}.$$

Therefore

$$\text{SS}_{\text{error}_{B \text{ at } C_k}} = \text{SS}_{S\text{s within groups}} + \text{SS}_{C \times S\text{s within groups}}.$$

This sum of squares will have degrees of freedom $= \text{df}_{\text{error}_B} + \text{df}_{\text{error}_{BC}}$. Thus

$$\text{MS}_{\text{error}_{B \text{ at } C_k}} = \frac{\text{SS}_{S\text{s within groups}} + \text{SS}_{C \times S\text{s within groups}}}{\text{df}_{S\text{s within groups}} + \text{df}_{C \times S\text{s within groups}}}.$$

For our example

$$\text{MS}_{\text{error}_{B \text{ at } C_k}} = \frac{31.78 + 9.55}{12 + 24} = 1.15.$$

It should be noted that this MS_{error} is nothing but a weighted average of the two error mean squares, where the weights are the corresponding degrees of freedom.

The general rule can be stated quite easily, and applies to all of the repeated measures designs we will discuss. *When a simple effect partitions a main effect and an interaction that were themselves tested by different error terms, the appropriate MS_{error} equals the sum of the relevant error sums of squares, divided by the sum of the corresponding degrees of freedom.* When the main effect and interaction were themselves tested by the same error term, then that error term is also the error term for the simple effects.

We are not quite out of the woods yet. Since our new error term represents a pooling of two heterogeneous sources of error, the obtained F will not follow the usual F distribution. To get around this problem we will adopt the approach used earlier of obtaining an estimate (f) of the degrees of freedom for error, and then evaluating F_{obt} against $F_{.05}(\text{df}_{\text{simple effect}}, f)$. As we did earlier we will define

$$f = \frac{(u + v)^2}{\dfrac{u^2}{\text{df}_u} + \dfrac{v^2}{df_v}}$$

where u and df_u represent the sum of squares and degrees of freedom for one of the component error terms and v and df_v represent the sum of squares and df for the other component error term. For the example of the simple effects of B at C_k,

$$u = \mathrm{SS}_{Ss \text{ within groups}} = 31.78 \qquad \mathrm{df}_u = 12$$

$$v = \mathrm{SS}_{C \times Ss \text{ within groups}} = 9.55 \qquad \mathrm{df}_v = 24$$

$$f = \frac{(31.78 + 9.55)^2}{\dfrac{31.78^2}{12} + \dfrac{9.55^2}{24}} = 19.42.$$

Thus F_{obt} for the simple effects of B at C_k would be evaluated against $F_{.05}(2, 19)$. The relevant tests on the simple effects are presented in Table 14.12. Note that for the simple effect of C at B_j there is no need to adjust the error term, since both C and BC were originally tested against $\mathrm{MS}_{C \times Ss \text{ within groups}}$.

The pattern of simple effects in Table 14.12 makes it plain that the effect of B is significant at each level of C, and the effect of C is significant at each level of B. Tests not presented here show that the simple effects of A at C_k and C at A_i are also significant. Thus from the results we can conclude that there are more errors at night than during the day for all levels of Course and Size, that there are significant effects due to the size of the car for all levels of Time and Course, and that the type of course has a significant effect for all levels of Time and Size. We have also shown an interaction of A and C indicating that differences among car sizes are more

TABLE 14.12

Simple Effects for Data in Table 14.8

Source	SIMPLE EFFECTS OF B AT C_k			
	SS	df	MS	F
B at C_1	$\dfrac{40^2 + 37^2 + 19^2}{6} - \dfrac{96^2}{18} = 43.00$	2	21.50	18.70*
B at C_2	$\dfrac{31^2 + 25^2 + 20^2}{6} - \dfrac{76^2}{18} = 10.11$	2	5.06	4.40*
B at C_3	$\dfrac{23^2 + 19^2 + 11^2}{6} - \dfrac{53^2}{18} = 12.44$	2	6.22	5.41*
Error B at C_k		19	1.15	

$$\mathrm{MS}_{\text{error } B \text{ at } C_k} = \frac{31.78 + 9.55}{12 + 24} = 1.15$$

$$f = \frac{(31.78 + 9.55)^2}{\dfrac{31.78^2}{12} + \dfrac{9.55^2}{24}} = 19.42 = 19$$

$$F_{.05}(2, 19) = 3.52$$

TABLE 14.12 (Cont.)

Source	SS	df	MS	F
	SIMPLE EFFECTS OF C AT B_j			
C at B_1	$\dfrac{40^2+31^2+23^2}{6} - \dfrac{94^2}{18} = 24.11$	2	12.06	30.15*
C at B_2	$\dfrac{37^2+25^2+19^2}{6} - \dfrac{81^2}{18} = 28.00$	2	14.00	35.00*
C at B_3	$\dfrac{19^2+20^2+11^2}{6} - \dfrac{50^2}{18} = 8.11$	2	4.06	10.15*
Error C at B_j		24	.40	

$$MS_{\text{error } C \text{ at } B_j} = MS_{C \times Ss \text{ within groups}}$$

$$F_{.05}(2, 24) = 3.40$$

* $p < .05$.

pronounced at night than during the day, and an interaction between B and C, with Size apparently making a greater difference on a serpentine track and city streets than on the highway.

Two Within-Subjects Variables and One Between-Subject Variable

The design which we have just considered can be seen as a straightforward extension of the case of one between- and one within-subject variable. All that we needed to add to the summary table was another main effect and the corresponding interactions. However when we come to a design with two within-subject main effects, the problem becomes slightly more complicated due to the presence of additional error terms.

Suppose that as a modification of the previous study we continued to use different subjects for the two levels of variable A (Time), but ran each subject under all combinations of variables B and C. This design can be diagrammed as:

	A_1			A_2		
	C_1	C_2	C_3	C_1	C_2	C_3
B_1	G_1	G_1	G_1	G_2	G_2	G_2
B_2	G_1	G_1	G_1	G_2	G_2	G_2
B_3	G_1	G_1	G_1	G_2	G_2	G_2

Before we consider an example we will examine the expected mean squares for this design. These are presented in Table 14.13 for the case of

TABLE 14.13
Expected Mean Squares

Source	df		E(MS)
Between Subj	$an-1$		
A		$a-1$	$\sigma_e^2 + bc\sigma_\pi^2 + nbc\sigma_\alpha^2$
Ss within groups		$a(n-1)$	$\sigma_e^2 + bc\sigma_\pi^2$
Within Subj	$na(bc-1)$		
B		$b-1$	$\sigma_e^2 + c\sigma_{\beta\pi}^2 + nac\sigma_\beta^2$
AB		$(a-1)(b-1)$	$\sigma_e^2 + c\sigma_{\beta\pi}^2 + nc\sigma_{\alpha\beta}^2$
$B \times Ss$ within groups		$a(b-1)(n-1)$	$\sigma_e^2 + c\sigma_{\beta\pi}^2$
C		$c-1$	$\sigma_e^2 + b\sigma_{\gamma\pi}^2 + nab\sigma_\gamma^2$
AC		$(a-1)(c-1)$	$\sigma_e^2 + b\sigma_{\gamma\pi}^2 + nb\sigma_{\alpha\gamma}^2$
$C \times Ss$ within groups		$a(c-1)(n-1)$	$\sigma_e^2 + b\sigma_{\gamma\pi}^2$
BC		$(b-1)(c-1)$	$\sigma_e^2 + \sigma_{\beta\gamma\pi}^2 + na\sigma_{\beta\gamma}^2$
ABC		$(a-1)(b-1)(c-1)$	$\sigma_e^2 + \sigma_{\beta\gamma\pi}^2 + n\sigma_{\alpha\beta\gamma}^2$
$BC \times Ss$ within groups		$a(b-1)(c-1)(n-1)$	$\sigma_e^2 + \sigma_{\beta\gamma\pi}^2$
Total	$N-1$		

the fixed model. From the expected mean squares it is evident that we will have four error terms for this design. As before, the $\text{MS}_{Ss \text{ within groups}}$ is used to test the between-subjects effect. When it comes to the within-subject terms, however, B and the interaction of B with A are tested by $B \times Ss$ within groups; C and its interaction with A are tested by $C \times Ss$ within groups; and BC and its interaction with A are tested by $BC \times Ss$ within

TABLE 14.14
Alternative Partition of Total Variation

Source	df		
Between Subj	$an-1$		
A (groups)		$a-1$	
Ss within groups		$a(n-1)$	
Within Subj	$na(bc-1)$		
B		$b-1$	
$B \times S$		$(b-1)(an-1)$	
AB			$(a-1)(b-1)$
$B \times Ss$ within groups			$a(b-1)(n-1)$
C		$c-1$	
$C \times S$		$(c-1)(an-1)$	
AC			$(a-1)(c-1)$
$C \times Ss$ within groups			$a(c-1)(n-1)$
BC		$(b-1)(c-1)$	
$BC \times S$		$(b-1)(c-1)$ $\times (an-1)$	
ABC			$(a-1)(b-1)(c-1)$
$BC \times Ss$ within groups			$a(b-1)(c-1)$ $\times (n-1)$
Total	$N-1$		

groups. Why this is necessary is apparent from the expected mean squares. It might be easier to appreciate what is happening, however, if we rewrite the source column of the summary table as in Table 14.14. Here we can see that each within-subject effect is considered as interacting with the between-subjects term, and consequently with the partitions of the between-subjects variation. (These new terms are often called *dummy* terms since they play no real role in the analysis.) A similar kind of table could have been drawn up for the previous design, but there was no necessity of doing so. Here we must consider the form of Table 14.14 because it gives us a hint as to how we will compute our within-subject error terms.

Direct computation of error terms in this design would be a most unpleasant undertaking. However the calculation of the (dummy) terms $SS_{B \times S}$ and $SS_{C \times S}$ is relatively straightforward, since they are calculated just as is any interaction term. Because we know from Table 14.14 that $SS_{B \times S}$ is partitioned into SS_{AB} and $SS_{B \times Ss \text{ within groups}}$, then

$$SS_{B \times Ss \text{ within groups}} = SS_{B \times S} - SS_{AB}.$$

The same reasoning holds for $SS_{C \times Ss \text{ within groups}}$ and $SS_{BC \times Ss \text{ within groups}}$. We do not need to calculate $SS_{BC \times S}$ directly, however, since it is readily obtained by subtraction.

$$SS_{BC \times S} = SS_{\text{within subj}} - SS_B - SS_{B \times S} - SS_C - SS_{C \times S} - SS_{BC}$$

A common convention is to label the separate error terms as error_a, error_b, error_c, and error_d, starting from the top of the table. While this would certainly win friends among typists and typesetters, I have not adopted that convention here because it tends to obscure what these terms represent.

For an example we will use the same data employed for the preceding design (Table 14.10), except that we will redefine B to be a within-subject variable. While this approach wreaks havoc with the assumptions concerning Σ (variables which should be correlated probably will not be), it has the advantage of pointing out the similarities and differences between the two designs. The raw data and the necessary tables of cell totals are presented in Table 14.15.

The sums of squares are presented in Table 14.15(b). The calculations have been omitted for those terms which are exactly the same as those found in Table 14.10(b). It should be noted that aside from the error terms, the only sum of squares that differs from those found in Table 14.10(b) is SS_S. This term is obviously different since the number of subjects, and therefore the scores attributable to each subject, has changed. The fact that the vast majority of the values remain unaltered once again points up the limited knowledge that numbers possess concerning the way in which they were obtained.

In part (c) of Table 14.15 we find the summary table for the analysis of variance. The same terms are again significant and the interpretation would be the same as for the results in the previous example. Once again

	A_1 (NIGHT)				A_2 (DAY)			
	C_1	C_2	C_3	Total	C_1	C_2	C_3	Total
	Small	Med	Large		Small	Med	Large	
B_1 (Track)	10	8	6	24	5	4	3	12
	9	8	5	22	4	3	3	10
	8	7	4	19	4	1	2	7
Total	27	23	15	65	13	8	8	29
B_2 (City)	9	7	5	21	4	3	3	10
	10	6	4	20	4	2	2	8
	7	4	3	14	3	3	2	8
Total	26	17	12	55	11	8	7	26
B_3 (Highway)	7	6	3	16	2	2	1	5
	4	5	2	11	2	3	2	7
	3	4	2	9	1	0	1	2
Total	14	15	7	36	5	5	4	14

AB CELL TOTALS

	A_1	A_2	Total
B_1	65	29	94
B_2	55	26	81
B_3	36	14	50
Total	156	69	225

AC CELL TOTALS

	A_1	A_2	Total
C_1	67	29	96
C_2	55	21	76
C_3	34	19	53
Total	156	69	225

BC CELL TOTALS

	C_1	C_2	C_3	Total
B_1	40	31	23	94
B_2	37	25	19	81
B_3	19	20	11	50
Total	96	76	53	225

$B \times S$ CELL TOTALS

	S_1	S_2	S_3	S_4	S_5	S_6	Total
B_1	24	22	19	12	10	7	94
B_2	21	20	14	10	8	8	81
B_3	16	11	9	5	7	2	50
Total	61	53	42	27	25	17	225

$C \times S$ CELL TOTALS

	S_1	S_2	S_3	S_4	S_5	S_6	Total
C_1	26	23	18	11	10	8	96
C_2	21	19	15	9	8	4	76
C_3	14	11	9	7	7	5	53
Total	61	53	42	27	25	17	225

TABLE 14.15 (Cont.)

(b) Computations (Calculations are omitted for those terms which are identical to those given in Table 14.8.)

$$CF = (\Sigma X)^2 / N = 225^2 / 54 = 937.50$$

$$SS_{total} = 323.50$$

$$SS_S = \frac{\Sigma T_{S_i}^2}{bc} - CF = \frac{61^2 + 53^2 + \cdots + 17^2}{9} - CF = 1104.11 - 937.50 = 166.61$$

$SS_A = 140.17$	$SS_{AB} = 5.44$	$SS_{ABC} = 2.78$
$SS_B = 56.78$	$SS_{AC} = 16.78$	
$SS_C = 51.44$	$SS_{BC} = 8.78$	

$$SS_{cells\ B \times S} = \frac{\Sigma T_{BSjl}^2}{c} - CF = 1171.67 - 937.50 = 234.17$$

$$SS_{B \times S} = SS_{cells\ B \times S} - SS_B - SS_S = 234.17 - 56.78 - 166.61 = 10.78$$

$$SS_{cells\ C \times S} = \frac{\Sigma T_{CSkl}^2}{b} - CF = 1174.33 - 937.50 = 236.83$$

$$SS_{C \times S} = SS_{cells\ C \times S} - SS_C - SS_S = 236.83 - 51.44 - 166.61 = 18.78$$

$$SS_{within\ subj} = SS_{total} - SS_S = 323.50 - 166.61 = 156.89$$

$$SS_{BC \times S} = SS_{within\ subj} - SS_B - SS_{B \times S} - SS_C - SS_{C \times S} - SS_{BC}$$

$$= 156.89 - 56.78 - 10.78 - 51.44 - 18.78 - 8.78 = 10.33$$

$$SS_{Ss\ within\ groups} = SS_S - SS_A = 166.61 - 140.17 = 26.44$$

$$SS_{B \times Ss\ within\ groups} = SS_{B \times S} - SS_{AB} = 10.78 - 5.44 = 5.34$$

$$SS_{C \times Ss\ within\ groups} = SS_{C \times S} - SS_{AC} = 18.78 - 16.78 = 2.00$$

$$SS_{BC \times Ss\ within\ groups} = SS_{BC \times S} - SS_{ABC} = 10.33 - 2.78 = 7.55$$

(c) Summary table

Source	df	SS	MS	F
Between Subj	5	166.61		
A	1		140.17	21.20*
*S*s within groups	4		26.44	
Within Subj	48	156.89		
B	2		56.78	42.37*
AB	2		5.44	4.06
$B \times Ss$ within groups	8		5.34	
C	2		51.44	102.88*
AC	2		16.78	33.56*
$C \times Ss$ within groups	8		2.00	
BC	4		8.78	4.68*
ABC	4		2.78	1.49
$BC \times Ss$ within groups	16		7.55	
Total	53	323.50		

* $p < .05$.

an intelligent interpretation of the data would require the analysis of simple effects, but this is left to the reader. The appropriate error terms and the error df are obtained following the same logic which applied for the last design.

Three Within-Subject Variables

A design which is seldom discussed in the statistical literature but which occurs fairly frequently in practice is one in which every subject serves in every cell. Such designs seem to be particularly prevalent in research areas, such as perception, where subjects are hard to find but once found are particularly dedicated (often they are the experimenter's children and co-authors).

This type of design can be conceptualized in two different ways. We can think of it as a repeated measures design in which all variables are within-subject variables. Alternatively, we can think of it as a factorial design in which "Subjects" is a variable—i.e., $S \times A \times B \times C$—with one score per cell. We can conceptualize the design as a factorial because every subject is paired with every combination of every other variable. We assume subjects to be a random variable, although in some cases this involves a major strain on the imagination (especially when the subjects are the experimenter's children).

There are two major possible models lying behind this design, and the choice of a model will determine the error terms for the various F ratios. The simplest, but least realistic, model is

$$X_{ijkl} = \mu + \alpha_i + \beta_j + \gamma_k + \alpha\beta_{ij} + \alpha\gamma_{ik} + \beta\gamma_{jk} + \alpha\beta\gamma_{ijk} + \pi_l + e_{ijkl}$$

In this model the experimental variables (A, B, and C) and their interactions are all represented, as is the main effect of Subjects (π_l), but we assume that there are no interactions of the Subject variable with any of the other variables. If these interactions are present, they are confounded with error. If we are willing to adopt this model, which admittedly requires a strong element of faith, the expected mean squares are as given in Table 14.16 (variables A, B, and C are assumed to be fixed).

A more reasonable model, but one which makes life somewhat more difficult, is given by

$$x_{ijkl} = \mu + \alpha_i + \beta_j + \gamma_k + \alpha\beta_{ij} + \alpha\gamma_{ik} + \beta\gamma_{jk} + \alpha\beta\gamma_{ijk}$$

$$+ \pi_l + \alpha\pi_{il} + \beta\pi_{jl} + \gamma\pi_{kl} + \alpha\beta\pi_{ijl} + \alpha\gamma\pi_{ikl}$$

$$+ \beta\gamma\pi_{jkl} + \alpha\beta\gamma\pi_{ijkl} + e_{ijkl}.$$

This model presents us with a minor problem, in that while it contains an error component, there is no way to obtain an independent estimate of that component. If *Subjects* is to be considered a variable, we have only one

TABLE 14.16

Expected Mean Squares

Source	df	E(MS)
S	$n-1$	$\sigma_e^2 + abc\sigma_\pi^2$
A	$a-1$	$\sigma_e^2 + nbc\sigma_\alpha^2$
B	$b-1$	$\sigma_e^2 + nac\sigma_\beta^2$
C	$c-1$	$\sigma_e^2 + nab\sigma_\gamma^2$
AB	$(a-1)(b-1)$	$\sigma_e^2 + nc\sigma_{\alpha\beta}^2$
AC	$(a-1)(c-1)$	$\sigma_e^2 + nb\sigma_{\alpha\gamma}^2$
BC	$(b-1)(c-1)$	$\sigma_e^2 + na\sigma_{\beta\gamma}^2$
ABC	$(a-1)(b-1)(c-1)$	$\sigma_e^2 + n\sigma_{\alpha\beta\gamma}^2$
Residual (Error)	$(n-1)(abc-1)$	σ_e^2

score per cell, and therefore no within-cell variance. The previous model assumed no interactions with *Subjects*, and could thus use a residual term (that portion of SS_{total} not accounted for by the other terms in the model) as an estimate of error. This amounts to assuming that $\alpha\pi_{il}$, for example $= 0$ and therefore $MS_{A\times S}$ can be taken as an estimate of experimental error (actually the residual would be the sum of *all* interactions with Subjects). In the present model there will not be any residual for estimating error. All is not lost, however, as each of the interactions with Subjects can be shown to serve as a denominator for an *F* ratio. This can be seen from the expected mean squares for this model given in Table 14.17.

It is evident from the expected mean squares that each effect to be tested has its own error term. Thus every effect is tested by the interaction of that effect with the Subject effect. MS_S can not be tested under this model, but this is seldom a problem.

TABLE 14.17

Expected Mean Squares for Full Model

Source	df	E(MS)
S	$n-1$	
A	$a-1$	$\sigma_e^2 + bc\sigma_{\alpha\pi}^2 + nbc\sigma_\alpha^2$
$A \times S$	$(a-1)(n-1)$	$\sigma_e^2 + bc\sigma_{\alpha\pi}^2$
B	$b-1$	$\sigma_e^2 + ac\sigma_{\beta\pi}^2 + nac\sigma_\beta^2$
$B \times S$	$(b-1)(n-1)$	$\sigma_e^2 + ac\sigma_{\beta\pi}^2$
C	$c-1$	$\sigma_e^2 + ab\sigma_{\gamma\pi}^2 + nab\sigma_\gamma^2$
$C \times S$	$(c-1)(n-1)$	$\sigma_e^2 + ab\sigma_{\gamma\pi}^2$
AB	$(a-1)(b-1)$	$\sigma_e^2 + c\sigma_{\alpha\beta\pi}^2 + nc\sigma_{\alpha\beta}^2$
$AB \times S$	$(a-1)(b-1)(n-1)$	$\sigma_e^2 + c\sigma_{\alpha\beta\pi}^2$
AC	$(a-1)(c-1)$	$\sigma_e^2 + b\sigma_{\alpha\gamma\pi}^2 + nb\sigma_{\alpha\gamma}^2$
$AC \times S$	$(a-1)(c-1)(n-1)$	$\sigma_e^2 + b\sigma_{\alpha\gamma\pi}^2$
BC	$(b-1)(c-1)$	$\sigma_e^2 + a\sigma_{\beta\gamma\pi}^2 + na\sigma_{\beta\gamma}^2$
$BC \times S$	$(b-1)(c-1)(n-1)$	$\sigma_e^2 + a\sigma_{\beta\gamma\pi}^2$
ABC	$(a-1)(b-1)(c-1)$	$\sigma_e^2 + \sigma_{\alpha\beta\gamma\pi}^2 + n\sigma_{\alpha\beta\gamma}^2$
$ABC \times S$	$(a-1)(b-1)(c-1)(n-1)$	$\sigma_e^2 + \sigma_{\alpha\beta\gamma\pi}^2$

The relationship between the two models becomes clearer when we see that $SS_{residual}$ in the first model can be seen as

$$SS_{residual} = SS_{A \times S} + SS_{B \times S} + SS_{C \times S} + SS_{AB \times S}$$
$$+ SS_{AC \times S} + SS_{BC \times S} + SS_{ABC \times S},$$

and thus represents a pooling of the several sources of error variance. If the assumptions behind the first model are reasonable (i.e., that the Subject variable does not interact with any of the other varibles), then the residual or pooled error term in the appropriate denominator for all Fs. If the assumption is not reasonable, then use of the residual term would provide a negatively biased (conservative) test. In general the full model is to be preferred to the reduced model, although in some cases this leads to Fs on relatively few degrees of freedom. (Tukey (1949) has developed a test for additivity for testing whether the reduced model is appropriate. The reader is referred to Winer (1971, p. 394) or Kirk (1968, p. 137).)

As an example of a study involving repeated measures on all variables we will again make use of the driving data, this time by assuming that there were only three subjects, each subject serving in all ABC cells. Since most of the calculations are the same as in the last example, only the calculation of the $SS_{A \times S}$ term will be shown as an illustration. The reader should by this time be able to carry out the rest of the calculations on his or her own.

From the raw data in Table 14.15 we find the following $A \times S$ table of cell totals for our revised design.

	A_1	A_2	*Total*
S_1	61	27	88
S_2	53	25	78
S_3	42	17	59
Total	156	69	225

We already know that $SS_A = 140.17$

$$SS_S = \frac{\Sigma T_{S_i}^2}{abc} - CF = 961.61 - 937.50 = 24.11$$

$$SS_{cells\ A \times S} = \frac{\Sigma T_{AS_{il}}^2}{bc} - CF = 1104.11 - 937.50 = 166.61$$

$$SS_{A \times S} = SS_{cells\ A \times S} - SS_A - SS_S = 166.61 - 140.17 - 24.11 = 2.33$$

The calculation of $SS_{A \times S}$ illustrates that the error terms in this design are calculated just as is any other interaction. The resulting summary table for the analysis is given in Table 14.18. From the summary table we see that the three main effects (A, B, and C) are significant, as is the AC

TABLE 14.18
Summary Table
for Design
with Repeated
Measures on
All Variables

Source	df	SS	MS	F
S	2	24.11		
A	1	140.17	140.17	119.80*
$A \times S$	2	2.33	1.17	
B	2	56.78	28.39	946.33*
$B \times S$	4	.11	.03	
C	2	51.44	25.72	91.86*
$C \times S$	4	1.11	.28	
AB	2	5.44	2.72	2.08
$AB \times S$	4	5.22	1.31	
AC	2	16.78	8.39	38.14*
$AC \times S$	4	.89	.22	
BC	4	8.78	2.20	3.79
$BC \times S$	8	4.67	.58	
ABC	4	2.78	.70	1.94
$ABC \times S$	8	2.89	.36	
Total	53	323.50		

* $p < .05$.

interaction. We would thus wish to examine the simple effects of C at each level of A, since the data suggest that there is a substantial effect for C at A_1, but that C at A_2 is questionable. The latter is tested below. Once again tests on the simple effects employ a denominator for F which is a weighted average of the MS_{error} for the relevant main effect and interaction. Thus to test the simple effect of C at A_2,

$$SS_{C \text{ at } A_2} = \frac{29^2 + 21^2 + 19^2}{9} - \frac{69^2}{27} = 6.22$$

$$MS_{C \text{ at } A_2} = \frac{SS_{C \text{ at } A_2}}{c - 1} = \frac{6.22}{2} = 3.11$$

$$MS_{pooled \; error} = \frac{SS_{C \times S} + SS_{AC \times S}}{df_{C \times S} + df_{AC \times S}} = \frac{1.11 + .89}{4 + 4} = .25$$

$$F_{C \text{ at } A_2} = \frac{MS_{C \text{ at } A_2}}{MS_{pooled \; error}} = \frac{3.11}{.25} = 12.44$$

$$f = \frac{(SS_{C \times S} + SS_{AC \times S})^2}{\frac{SS_{C \times S}^2}{df_{C \times S}} + \frac{SS_{AC \times S}^2}{df_{AC \times S}}} = \frac{(1.11 + .89)^2}{\frac{1.11^2}{4} + \frac{.89^2}{4}} = 7.904 \approx 8$$

$F_{.05}(2, 8) = 4.46$.

The effect of C at A_2 is significant at $p < .05$, since $12.44 > 4.46$. The calculation of the other effects is left to the reader.

14.6 *Other Considerations*

Sequence Effects

Sequence effects
Carry-over effects

Repeated measures designs are notoriously susceptible to ***sequence effects*** and ***carry-over*** (practice) ***effects***. Whenever the possibility exists that exposure to one treatment will have an influence on the effect of another treatment, the experimenter should consider very seriously before deciding to use a repeated measures design. In certain studies carry-over effects are desirable. In learning studies, for example, the basic data represent what is carried over from one trial to another. In most situations, however, carry-over effects (and especially differential carry-over effects) are considered as a nuisance, and something to be avoided.

The statistical theory of repeated measures designs assumes that the order of administration is randomized separately for each subject. In some situations, however, it makes more sense to assign testing sequences by *Latin square* means of a ***latin square*** or some other device. While this violates the assumption of randomization, in some situations the gains very likely outweigh the losses. What is important, however, is that random assignment, latin squares, and so on do not in themselves eliminate sequence effects. Ignoring analyses in which the data are *analyzed* by means of a latin square, or a related statistical procedure, any system of assignment simply distributes sequence and carry-over effects across the cells of the design, with luck lumping them into the error term(s). The phrase "with luck" was used in the above sentence, because if this does not happen the carry-over effects are compounded with treatment effects and the results will be very difficult, if not impossible, to interpret. For those particularly interested in examining sequence effects, Winer (1971), Kirk (1968) and Cochran & Cox (1957) present excellent coverages of latin square and related designs.

Unequal Group Sizes

One of the pleasant features of repeated measures designs is that when a subject fails to arrive for an experiment it usually means that that subject is missing from every cell in which he was to serve. This has the effect of keeping the cell sizes proportional, even if unequal. From this it follows that the solution for proportionally unequal sample sizes is possible, if the experimenter feels that the solution's treatment of sample sizes is appropriate. Otherwise the unweighted means solution is available, and probably preferable, for most cases. If you are so unlucky as to have a subject for whom you have partial data, the best procedure would probably be to eliminate that subject from the analysis. If, however, only one or two scores are missing, it is possible to replace them with estimates, and in many cases this is a satisfactory approach. For a thorough discussion of this topic an excellent reference is Federer (1955, pp. 125–126, 133ff).

Matched Samples and Related Problems

In discussing repeated measures designs we have spoken in terms of repeated measurements on the same subject. While this represents the most common instance of the use of these designs, it is not the only one. The specific fact that a subject is tested several times really has nothing to do with the matter. Technically, what distinguishes repeated measures designs from the common factorial designs with equal *n*s is the fact that for repeated measures designs the off-diagonal elements of Σ do not have an expectancy of zero—i.e., the treatments are correlated. Repeated use of the same subject *Matched samples* leads to such correlations, but so does use of *matched samples* of subjects. Thus if we formed 10 sets of three subjects each, where the subjects are matched on driving experience, for example, and then set up an experiment where the first subject, for example, under each treatment came from the same matched triad, we would have correlations among treatments and would thus have a repeated measures design. Any other data collection procedure leading to non-zero correlations (or covariances) could also be treated as a repeated measures design.

14.7 Summary

In this chapter we developed the analysis of variance further to include those designs in which subjects serve at all levels of one or more variables. We started the chapter by seeing how the variability can be partitioned into those effects which involve comparisons between different subjects and those effects which require comparisons within the same subject. We saw that the feature which complicates this analysis is the fact that the scores obtained by repeated measurements on the same subjects are correlated, and this correlation must be taken into account. We also saw that the removal of the effects of this correlation led to a more powerful test on the null hypothesis than we would have had if the observations had been independent. After considering the design in which we have one between-subjects variable and one within-subject variable, we examined three-variable designs with either two between-subjects, two within-subject, or three within-subject variables. Each of these designs presents its own particular problems and has its own particular strengths.

Exercises for Chapter 14

14.1 It is at least part of the folklore that repeated experience with the Graduate Record Examination (GRE) leads to better scores, even without any intervening study. We obtain eight subjects and give them the GRE verbal exam every Saturday morning for three weeks. The data are given:

| | | TEST SESSION | |
S	*1st*	*2nd*	*3rd*
1	550	575	580
2	440	440	470
3	610	630	610
4	650	670	670
5	400	460	450
6	700	680	710
7	490	510	515
8	580	550	590

a. Write the statistical model for these data.

b. Run the analysis of variance.

c. What, if anything, would you conclude about practice effects on the GRE?

14.2   Using the data from Exercise 14.1:

a. Delete the data for the third session and run a (matched sample) *t* test between sessions 1 and 2.

b. Now run a repeated measures analysis of variance on those same two columns and compare this *F* with the preceding *t*.

14.3   In an attempt to demonstrate the practical uses of basic learning principles, a psychologist with an interest in behavior modification has collected data on a study designed to teach self-care skills to severely retarded children. One group was an experimental group and received reinforcement for activities related to self-care. A second group received an equivalent amount of attention, but no reinforcement. The children were scored (blind) by a rater who rated them on a 10-point scale of self-sufficiency. The ratings were done in a baseline session and at the end of training. The data are given below.

| EXPERIMENTAL GROUP | | CONTROL GROUP | |
Baseline	*Training*	*Baseline*	*Training*
8	9	3	5
5	7	5	5
3	2	8	10
5	7	2	5
2	9	5	3
6	7	6	10
5	8	6	9
6	5	4	5
4	7	3	7
4	9	5	5

4.8   7   4.7   6.4

Run the appropriate analysis and state your conclusions.

14.4 An experimenter with only a modicum of statistical training took the data in Exercise 14.3 and ran an independent groups *t* test instead, using the difference scores (Training − Baseline) as the raw data.

a. Run that analysis.
b. Square the value of *t* and compare it to the *F*s obtained in the preceding analysis.
c. Explain why t^2 is not equal to *F* for Groups.

14.5 In an effort to understand just what happened in the experiment involving the training of severely retarded children (Exercise 14.3) our experimenter looked at a third group who wcrc cvaluated at the same times as our first two groups, but who were otherwise treated just like all other residents of the training school. In other words they did not receive reinforcement or even the extra attention that the control group did. Their data are:

Baseline	3	5	8	5	5	6	6	6	3	4
Training	4	5	6	6	4	7	7	3	2	2

a. Add these data to the data in Exercise 14.3 and rerun the analysis.
b. Plot the results.
c. What would you conclude from these results?

14.6 For two years I have carried on a running argument with my daughter concerning hand calculators. She wants one. I maintain that children who use calculators never learn to do arithmetic correctly, whereas she maintains that they do. To settle the argument we take five of her classmates who have calculators and five who don't, and make a totally unwarranted assumption that the presence or absence of calculators is all that distinguishes these children. We then give each child three 10-point tests (addition, subtraction, and multiplication) which they are required to do in a very short time in their heads. The scores are given below.

	ADDITION	SUBTRACTION	MULTIPLICATION
	8	5	3
	7	5	2
CALCULATOR OWNERS	9	7	3
	6	3	1
	8	5	1
	10	7	6
	7	6	5
NON-CALCULATOR OWNERS	6	5	5
	9	7	8
	9	6	9

a.   Run the analysis of variance.

b.   Would the data suggest that I should give in and buy her a calculator?

14.7   *a.* Calculate the variance-covariance matrices for the data in Exercise 14.6.

b.   Calculate $\hat{e}$ using the answers to part *a*.

14.8   From the results in Exercise 14.7 do we appear to have reason to believe that we have met the assumptions required for the analysis of repeated measures?

14.9   *a.* Calculate all possible simple effects for the data in Exercise 14.6, after first plotting the results.

b.   Test the simple effects, calculating test terms and adjusted degrees of freedom where necessary.

14.10   In a study of the way children and adults summarize stories, we select 10 fifth graders and 10 adults. These are further subdivided into equal groups of good and poor readers (on the hypothesis that good and poor readers may store or retrieve story information differently). All subjects read 10 short stories, and were asked to summarize the story in their own words immediately after reading it. All summaries were content analyzed, and the numbers of statements related to settings, goals, and inferred dispositions were recorded. The data are given below, collapsed across the 10 stories.

Age:	*Adults*			*Children*		
Items:	*Setting*	*Goal*	*Disp.*	*Setting*	*Goal*	*Disp.*
	8	7	6	5	5	2
	5	6	4	7	8	4
Good Readers	5	5	5	7	7	4
	7	8	6	6	4	3
	6	4	4	4	4	2
	7	6	3	2	2	2
	5	3	1	2	0	1
Poor Readers	6	6	2	5	4	1
	4	4	1	4	4	2
	5	5	3	2	2	0

a.   Run the appropriate analysis.

14.11   Referring back to Exercise 14.10.

a.   Calculate the simple effect of reading ability for children.

b.   Calculate the simple effect of items for adult good readers.

14.12 Calculate the within-groups covariance matrices for the data in Exercise 14.10.

14.13 Suppose that we instructed our subjects to limit their summaries to ten words. What effect might that have on the data in Exercise 14.10?

14.14 In an investigation of cigarette smoking an experimenter decided to compare three different procedures for quitting smoking (tapering off, immediate stopping, and aversion therapy). She took five subjects in each group and asked them to rate (on a 10-point scale) their desire to smoke "right now" in two different environments (home vs. work) both before and after quitting. Thus we have one between-subject variable (treatment group) and two within-subject variables (environment and pre/post).

| | Pre | | Post | |
	Home	Work	Home	Work
	7	6	6	4
	5	4	5	2
Taper	8	7	7	4
	8	8	6	5
	6	5	5	3
	8	7	7	6
	5	5	5	4
Immediate	7	6	6	5
	8	7	6	5
	7	6	5	4
	9	8	5	4
	4	4	3	2
Aversion	7	7	5	3
	7	5	5	0
	8	7	6	3

a. Run the appropriate analysis of variance.
b. Interpret the results.

14.15 Plot the results in Exercise 14.14.

14.16 Run simple effects on the data in Exercise 14.14 to clarify the results.

14.17 The following abbreviated BMDP printout represents the analysis of the data in Exercise 14.5.

```
BMDP2V - ANALYSIS OF VARIANCE AND COVARIANCES WITH REPEATED MEASURES.

    PROGRAM CONTROL INFORMATION

/PROBLEM          TITLE IS 'BMDP2V ANALYSIS OF EXERCISE 14.5'.
/INPUT            VARIABLES ARE 3.
                  FORMAT IS '(3F2.0)'.
                  CASES ARE 30.
                  UNIT IS 21.
/VARIABLE         NAMES ARE GROUP,PRE,POST.
/DESIGN           DEPENDENT ARE 2,3.
                  LEVELS ARE 2.
                  NAMES IS TIME.
                  GROUP = 1.
/END

GROUP STRUCTURE

  GROUP         COUNT
* 1.0000        10.
* 2.0000        10.
* 3.0000        10.

       CELL MEANS   FOR  1-ST DEPENDENT VARIABLE

                                               MARGINAL
       GROUP   =  * 1.0000     * 2.0000    * 3.0000
          TIME
PRE       1       4.80000      4.70000      5.10000     4.86667
POST      2       7.00000      6.40000      4.60000     6.00000

       MARGINAL    5.90000     5.55000      4.85000     5.43333

       COUNT         10          10           10          30

STANDARD DEVIATIONS  FOR  1-ST DEPENDENT VARIABLE

       GROUP   =  * 1.0000     * 2.0000    * 3.0000
          TIME
PRE       1       1.68655      1.76698      1.52388
POST      2       2.16025      2.45855      1.89737

ANALYSIS OF VARIANCE FOR  1-ST
DEPENDENT VARIABLE - PRE      POST

         SOURCE              SUM OF      DEGREES OF     MEAN          F        TAIL
                             SQUARES      FREEDOM      SQUARE               PROBABILITY

       MEAN               1771.26667        1      1771.26667    322.48     0.0000
       GROUP                11.43333        2         5.71667      1.04     0.3669
  1    ERROR               148.30000       27         5.49259

       TIME                 19.26667        1        19.26667      9.44     0.0048
       TG                   20.63333        2        10.31667      5.06     0.0137
  2    ERROR                55.10000       27         2.04074
BMDP2V - ANALYSIS OF VARIANCE AND COVARIANCES WITH REPEATED MEASURES.
HEALTH SCIENCES COMPUTING FACILITY
UNIVERSITY OF CALIFORNIA, LOS ANGELES 90024
```

a. Compare this printout with the results you obtained from Exercise 14.5.

b. What does a significant F for MEAN tell us?

c. Relate $MS_{\text{within cell}}$ to the table of cell standard deviations.

14.18   Use BMDP2V to analyze the data in Exercise 14.10.

14.19   The following SPSS printout was obtained by treating the data in Exercise 14.10 *as if* all variables were between subjects variables (i.e. as if the data represented a standard three-way factorial).

```
                         1 RUN NAME        ANALYSIS OF DATA FOR EX14.10 AS IF FACTORIAL
                         2 VARIABLE LIST   READ, AGE, PART, SCORE
                         3 INPUT FORMAT    FIXED(4F2.0)
                         4 INPUT MEDIUM    EX1410.DAT
                         5 N OF CASES      60
                         6 ANOVA           SCORE BY READ,AGE(1,2),PART(1,3)

 * * * * * * * * * * A N A L Y S I S   O F   V A R I A N C E * * * * * * * * * *
                    SCORE
            by READ
               AGE
               PART
 * * * * * * * * * * * * * * * * * * * * * * * * * * * * * * * * * * * * * * * *


                                    Sum of                 Mean              Signif
 Source of variation                Squares     df        Square      F       of F

 Main effects                       158.067      4        39.517    22.908   0.000
        READ                         68.267      1        68.267    39.575   0.000
        AGE                          29.400      1        29.400    17.043   0.000
        PART                         60.400      2        30.200    17.507   0.000

 2-way interactions                   4.200      5         0.840     0.487   0.784
        READ      AGE                 3.267      1         3.267     1.894   0.175
        READ      PART                0.933      2         0.467     0.271   0.764
        AGE       PART                0.000      2         0.000     0.000   1.000

 3-way interactions                   8.533      2         4.267     2.473   0.095
        READ      AGE      PART       8.533      2         4.267     2.473   0.095

 Explained                          170.800     11        15.527     9.001   0.000

 Residual                            82.800     48         1.725

 Total                              253.600     59         4.298


     60 Cases were processed.
      0 Cases (  0.0 %) were missing.

 - - - - - - - - - - - - - - - - - - - - - - - - - - - - - - - - - - - - - - -
```

Show that the error terms for the correct analysis represent a partition of the error term for the factorial analysis.

14.20 Outline the summary table for an $A \times B \times C \times D$ design with repeated measures on A and B and independent measures on C and D.

15

Multiple Regression

Objective

To show how we can predict a criterion variable on the basis of several predictor variables simultaneously; to point out the problems inherent in such a procedure.

Contents

In Chapter 9 we considered the situation in which we have one criterion (Y) and one predictor (X) and wish to predict Y on the basis of X. In this chapter we will consider the case where we still have one criterion (Y) but have multiple predictors ($X_1, X_2, X_3, \ldots, X_p$), and want to predict Y on the basis of simultaneous knowledge of all p predictors. In a very real sense Chapter 9 can be viewed as a special case of the material discussed in this chapter, or, alternatively, this chapter can be viewed as an extension of Chapter 9. We will continue to make use of many familiar concepts, such as the correlation coefficient, the slope, the standard error of estimate, and $SS_{regression}$.

Scalar algebra   The standard approach to multiple regression in a book of this type involves the use of the usual **scalar algebra** taught in high school. The main problem with that approach is that when there are more than two predictors the arithmetic becomes appallingly laborious. Even with two predictors the equations themselves lead to very little insight into what is actually going on when we solve a multiple regression problem.

Matrix algebra   An alternative and much better approach taken by more advanced texts is to cast the problem in terms of **matrix algebra**, and to sneak in a "quickie" chapter on matrices. Unfortunately even the brightest and most diligent students come away from such a chapter with only the vaguest of ideas of matrix theory.

The third approach, and the one to be adopted here, is to bow to reality and recognize that almost all multiple regression problems are solved by use of canned computer programs. Thus what we need to concentrate on is not so much how the solution is actually obtained, but what the potential problems are and what interpretation can be assigned to the wealth of statistics printed out by any good computer program.

Rather than simplifying the problem, the approach taken here actually complicates the issue. Formulae tend to be generally agreed-upon facts over which there can be very little argument. On the other hand questions concerning the optimal number of predictors, the relative importance of various predictors, and the selection of predictors do not have universally accepted answers. You should be forewarned that the opinions expressed in this chapter are only opinions, and are open to dispute by others—but then that is what makes statistics interesting. Excellent supplementary sources for the study of multiple regression are Cohen & Cohen (1975), Kleinbaum & Kupper (1978), and Younger (1979).

We can not avoid matrix algebra altogether, however. There are certain principles that must be discussed for any intelligent understanding of multiple regression. These include the definitions of a matrix and a vector, the concept of an inverse of a matrix, and what is meant by a *singular* matrix. These concepts are briefly discussed in what follows. The student who would like to pursue the topic further would do well to first read Overall & Klett (1972, Chapter 2) and then go on to a more traditional text in matrix algebra (Graybill, 1961, and Green & Carroll, 1976, are excellent books).

15.1 *Important Matrix Concepts*

Matrices

Matrix Elements   A *matrix* consists of a collection of numbers (*elements*) in an orderly rectangular array. Thus

$$A = \begin{bmatrix} 2 & 8 & 12 & 10 \\ 3 & 6 & 1 & 3 \\ 8 & 2 & 4 & 7 \end{bmatrix}$$

is a 3×4 matrix, designated by the boldface letter A, with three rows and four columns.

Although in general there is no restriction on what the elements of a matrix represent, we will deal almost exclusively with two kinds of matrices— a data matrix and an intercorrelation matrix.

Data matrix   **Data matrix**   A *data matrix* is an $N \times (p+1)$ matrix where the N individuals are represented on the rows and the criterion and p predictors are represented on the columns. Suppose, for example, that we have data on 300 individuals and want to predict income (Y) (in 1000s of dollars) on the basis of years of education (X_1), IQ (X_2), and socio-economic status of parents measured on a 9-point scale (X_3). Then our data matrix might look like

$$X = \begin{matrix} Individual & Y & X_1 & X_2 & X_3 \\ 1 & \begin{bmatrix} 15.5 & 20 & 125 & 6 \\ 2 & 20.0 & 12 & 115 & 5 \\ 3 & 8.6 & 8 & 93 & 8 \\ 4 & 9.7 & 16 & 110 & 5 \\ \ldots & \ldots & \ldots & \ldots & \ldots \\ 300 & 5.3 & 7 & 85 & 3 \end{bmatrix} \end{matrix}$$

In this matrix the first person earns \$15,500, has had 20 years of education, has an IQ of 125, and his parents had an SES rating of 6. The 300th person earns \$5,300, has only 7 years of formal education, has an IQ of 85, and his parents had a SES score of 3. In most data matrices the

Criterion   dependent variable (*criterion*) is placed in the first column, but this is simply a convention, and one which is frequently ignored.

Intercorrelation matrix (R)   **Intercorrelation matrix**   An *intercorrelation matrix* (usually designated R) is one which contains the correlations between pairs of variables. As such it is always a square matrix. The intercorrelation matrix for our previous example might look like

$$
\begin{array}{cccc}
 & Y & X_1 & X_2 & X_3 \\
\end{array}
$$

$$
R = \begin{array}{c} Y \\ X_1 \\ X_2 \\ X_3 \end{array}
\begin{bmatrix}
1.00 & .55 & .40 & .43 \\
.55 & 1.00 & .65 & .30 \\
.40 & .65 & 1.00 & .25 \\
.43 & .30 & .25 & 1.00
\end{bmatrix}
$$

This matrix tells us that income (Y) correlates .55 with years of education (X_1), .40 with IQ (X_2), and .43 with SES (X_3). Years of education correlates .65 with IQ and .30 with SES, and IQ and SES have a correlation
Diagonal elements of .25. Notice that the **diagonal elements** are all 1.00 since a variable is assumed to correlate perfectly with itself. Notice also that the matrix is a
Symmetric matrix **symmetric matrix** in that the elements below the **main diagonal** are a mirror
Main diagonal image of the elements above the diagonal. This is so because the correlation of income with SES is the same as the correlation of SES with income.

Occasionally only the upper triangular part of an intercorrelation matrix is presented in print, while the lower half is left blank. This is usually done to make it easier to read the matrix, and nothing is lost because of the symmetry.

Vector   **Vectors**   A **vector** is nothing but a one-dimensional matrix. Thus

$$
a = \begin{bmatrix} 5 \\ 4 \\ 2 \end{bmatrix}
$$

and

$$
a' = \begin{bmatrix} 2 & 1 & 6 \end{bmatrix}
$$

Column vector are both vectors—the first being a **column vector** and the second a **row**
Row vector **vector**. Vectors are denoted here by boldface, lower case letters, with a "prime" added to signify row vectors.

In multiple regression we will come across a number of different kinds of vectors. Thus we might have one vector contain the variable means, another containing variances, and a third containing individual regression coefficients. Thus

$$
b' = \begin{bmatrix} 1.83 & .265 & .036 & .370 \end{bmatrix}
$$

might represent the intercept and the regression coefficients for each of the three predictors in the previous example.

Matrix Operations

Without going into the actual details, it should be noted that, within certain constraints, matrices and vectors can be added, subtracted, multiplied, and can enter into equations. In this sense matrix procedures resemble procedures used in ordinary scalar algebra. Thus, for example, the equation

$$\hat{y} = bX$$

is no different in form from

$$\hat{Y}_i = bX_i + a$$

found in Chapter 9. (In the former equation the intercept is incorporated into the vector **b**.) The only difference between the two equations is that the elements of the first are vectors and a matrix, whereas in the second they are individual numbers.

The Inverse

No mention was made in the preceding section of matrix division for the simple reason that we cannot divide matrices—at least in the way that we usually think of division. The way out of this particular difficulty makes use of what is called the *inverse of a matrix.*

Inverse of a matrix

The concept of an inverse is basically very simple. Everyone would agree without a great deal of thought that if

$$8Y = 7$$

then

$$Y = \tfrac{7}{8}.$$

However consider carefully how this problem is actually solved. As you were originally taught by your high school algebra teacher the solution really involves multiplying both sides of the equation by $\frac{1}{8}$. Thus

$$8Y = 7$$
$$(\tfrac{1}{8})8Y = (\tfrac{1}{8})7$$
$$1Y = \tfrac{7}{8}.$$
$$Y = \tfrac{7}{8}.$$

In other words we really do not divide by 8 so much as we multiply by the reciprocal (inverse) of 8. Since the product of a number and its reciprocal (inverse) is equal to 1, that clears the left side of the equation, leaving 7 times the reciprocal (inverse) of 8 on the other. This may look like a rather trivial elaboration of the obvious, but the logic is important when we come to matrices.

In scalar algebra the inverse or reciprocal of a number (n) is merely $1/n$, or, that number which when multiplied by n leaves a product of 1.

Identity matrix (I)

This last definition is really the one in which we are interested. In matrix algebra the *identity matrix* (*I*) has 1s on the main diagonal and 0s off the diagonal and is the logical equivalent of the number 1 in scalar algebra.

A^{-1}

Thus what we need to find is some matrix (A^{-1}) such that

$$A^{-1}A = I.$$

If A^{-1} exists it is called the inverse of A.

We need inverses because given matrices A, B, and C, the equation

$$AB = C$$

can be solved for B using A^{-1}

$$AB = C$$

$$A^{-1}AB = A^{-1}C$$

$$IB = A^{-1}C$$

$$B = A^{-1}C.$$

Such a procedure is required to solve a multiple regression problem, whether the solution is being attempted by hand or by a computer.

Singularity

Generalized inverse
Singular matrix

The problem is that not all matrices have an inverse. (While there are *generalized inverses* (g-inverses), they are not unique and will not be discussed here.) If a matrix does not have an inverse, it is called a *singular matrix*. In multiple regression we want to avoid singular intercorrelation matrices at all costs, since their existence brings everything to a halt before the problem is solved.

This leads to the main reason for discussing inverses in the first place. We want to avoid generating an intercorrelation matrix which has no inverse—i.e., which is singular. There are several ways of producing singular matrices, and once these are known they can easily be avoided.

The simplest way of generating a singular intercorrelation matrix is to have more variables than subjects. Thus the experimenter who tries to run a multiple regression problem using 75 variables and only 50 subjects is doomed to failure before he even begins. This is not as uncommon a procedure as it might appear, especially in "shotgun" research in which experimenters collect data on every variable in sight, hoping that something may turn out to be useful. As long as the number of subjects (N) exceeds the

Nonsingular

number of predictors (p) the matrix is likely to be *nonsingular* unless some other error is committed. Serious statistical problems do arise as p approaches N, but discussion of these will be postponed until later.

The second method of producing singular matrices is to use a variable which is a linear function of other variables. Thus the matrix

$$
X = \begin{array}{cccc}
Y & X_1 & X_2 & X_3 \\
\begin{bmatrix}
10 & 9 & 2 & 3 \\
15 & 12 & 1 & 5 \\
8 & 8 & 3 & 2 \\
17 & 7 & 2 & 2 \\
23 & 13 & 6 & 3 \\
15 & 16 & 3 & 6
\end{bmatrix}
\end{array}
$$

is singular because $X_1 = X_2 + 2X_3 + 1$. Again this is actually a common type of problem in some areas of research. For example if the predictors in some problem were the Verbal and Performance subscores of the Wechsler Adult Intelligence Scale, and the researcher also threw in the Full Scale score, the resulting matrix would be singular and the problem would have no solution.

A related way of producing a singular matrix is to have all of the predictors sum to a constant. If, for example, we were observing children and recording the time spent in five mutually exclusive and exhaustive categories of behavior ($X_1 - X_5$), the five scores would sum to the total observation time. Thus $X_5 = \text{total} - X_1 - X_2 - X_3 - X_4$, which is a linear combination.

It is important to keep these cases firmly in mind, since they represent the most common errors in attempts to use multiple regression. If you avoid allowing (1) $p \geq N$, (2) a predictor to be a linear combination of other predictors, or (3) the predictors to sum to a constant, you are unlikely to end up with a singular matrix.

15.2 *Multiple Linear Regression*

The problem of multiple regression is that of finding a regression equation to predict Y (sometimes denoted X_0) on the basis of p predictors ($X_1, X_2, X_3, \ldots, X_p$). Thus we might wish to predict success in graduate school (Y) on the basis of undergraduate grade point average (X_1), Graduate Record Exam scores (X_2), number of courses taken in the major discipline (X_3), and some rating of "favorableness" of letters of recommendation (X_4). Similarly we might wish to predict the time it takes to go from one point in a city to another on the basis a number of traffic lights (X_1), posted speed limit (X_2), presence or absence of "right turn on red" (X_3), and traffic density (X_4). The answers to both of these examples are obtained in the same way, although in the first we presumably care about predictions for individual applicants whereas in the second we might be more interested in the role played by each of the predictors.

multiple $Y_j = \beta_0 + \beta_1 x_{i1} + \beta_2 x_{i2} + \cdots + e_i$

$Y_j = \beta_0 + \beta_1 x_i + e_i$ simple

The Regression Equation

In Chapter 9 we started with the equation of a straight line ($\hat{Y} = bX + a$) and solved for the two unknowns (a and b) subject to the constraint that $\Sigma(Y - \hat{Y})^2$ is a minimum. In multiple regression we are going to do the same thing, although in this case we will solve the equation $\hat{Y} = b_0 + b_1X_1 + b_2X_2 + \cdots + b_pX_p$ where b_0 represents the intercept and $b_1, b_2, \ldots, b_p$ are the regression coefficients for the predictors $X_1, X_2, \ldots, X_p$, respectively.† We will retain the restriction that $\Sigma(Y - \hat{Y})^2$ is to be minimized, since it still makes sense to find predicted values which come as close as possible to the obtained values of Y. As was mentioned earlier, the calculations required to estimate the b_i become more and more cumbersome as the number of predictors increases, and we will not discuss these calculations here. Instead we will begin with a simple example and assume that the solution was obtained by any available computer program, such as MINITAB, SPSS, or BMDP.

A number of years ago the Student Association of a large university published an evaluation of over 100 courses taught during the preceding semester. Students in each course had completed a questionnaire in which they rated a number of different aspects of the course on a 5-point scale (1 = failure, very bad . . . 5 = excellent, exceptional). The data in Table 15.1 represent mean scores on six variables for a random sample of 50 courses. These variables were: (1) overall quality of lectures (OVERALL), (2) teaching skills of the instructor (TEACH), (3) quality of the tests and exams (EXAM), (4) instructor's perceived knowledge of the subject matter (KNOWLEDGE), (5) the student's expected grade in the course (GRADE— $F = 1$, $A = 5$), and (6) the enrollment of the course (ENROLL). On the assumption that the best available overall rating of the course is the overall rating of the lectures (OVERALL), we will use that as the dependent variable (Y) and derive a regression equation predicting Y on the basis of the other five variables. The regression solution (as supplied by SPSS) is given in Table 15.2.

From the means shown in the table we can see that the average rating for each category was greater than the midpoint of the scale, which had been labeled *average*. Thus there is an upward bias to the responses. Also note that the standard deviation of ENROLL is large, indicating a wide dispersion of class sizes.

The first row of the intercorrelation matrix contains the correlations of each of the predictors with the criterion. (These correlations are often

---

† Although in this chapter we will always write our regression equation in this form, it is important to recognize that it could be written in matrix notation. In that case the equation would be $\hat{y} = bX$ or $y = bX + e$ where $e = y - \hat{y}$. In this form X is a matrix of predictors and y, $\hat{y}$, and e are vectors of criterion values, predicted values, or errors. The more concise matrix terminology will frequently be used in the next chapter.

TABLE 15.1

Course Evaluation Data

OVERALL	TEACH	EXAM	KNOWLEDGE	GRADE	ENROLL
3.4	3.8	3.8	4.5	3.5	2.1
2.9	2.8	3.2	3.8	3.2	50
2.6	2.2	1.9	3.9	2.8	800
3.8	3.5	3.5	4.1	3.3	221
3.0	3.2	2.8	3.5	3.2	7
2.5	2.7	3.8	4.2	3.2	108
3.9	4.1	3.8	4.5	3.6	54
4.3	4.2	4.1	4.7	4.0	99
3.8	3.7	3.6	4.1	3.0	51
3.4	3.7	3.6	4.1	3.1	47
2.8	3.3	3.5	3.9	3.0	73
2.9	3.3	3.3	3.9	3.3	25
4.1	4.1	3.6	4.0	3.2	37
2.7	3.1	3.8	4.1	3.4	83
3.9	2.9	3.8	4.5	3.7	70
4.1	4.5	4.2	4.5	3.8	16
4.2	4.3	4.1	4.5	3.8	14
3.1	3.7	4.0	4.5	3.7	12
4.1	4.2	4.3	4.7	4.2	20
3.6	4.0	4.2	4.0	3.8	18
4.3	3.7	4.0	4.5	3.3	260
4.0	4.0	4.1	4.6	3.2	100
2.1	2.9	2.7	3.7	3.1	118
3.8	4.0	4.4	4.1	3.9	35
2.7	3.3	4.4	3.6	4.3	32
4.4	4.4	4.3	4.4	2.9	25
3.1	3.4	3.6	3.3	3.2	55
3.6	3.8	4.1	3.8	3.5	28
3.9	3.7	4.2	4.2	3.3	28
2.9	3.1	3.6	3.8	3.2	27
3.7	3.8	4.4	4.0	4.1	25
2.8	3.2	3.4	3.1	3.5	50
3.3	3.5	3.2	4.4	3.6	76
3.7	3.8	3.7	4.3	3.7	28
4.2	4.4	4.3	5.0	3.3	85
2.9	3.7	4.1	4.2	3.6	75
3.9	4.0	3.7	4.5	3.5	90
3.5	3.4	4.0	4.5	3.4	94
3.8	3.2	3.6	4.7	3.0	65
4.0	3.8	4.0	4.3	3.4	100
3.1	3.7	3.7	4.0	3.7	105
4.2	4.3	4.2	4.2	3.8	70
3.0	3.4	4.2	3.8	3.7	49
4.8	4.0	4.1	4.9	3.7	64
3.0	3.1	3.2	3.7	3.3	700
4.4	4.5	4.5	4.6	4.0	27
4.4	4.8	4.3	4.3	3.6	15
3.4	3.4	3.6	3.5	3.3	40
4.0	4.2	4.0	4.4	4.1	18
3.5	3.4	3.9	4.4	3.3	90

TABLE 15.2 SPSS REGRESSION Analysis of Course Evaluation Data

```
      1 RUN NAME       ANALYSIS OF FIRST SET OF DATA ON COURSE RATINGS
      2 PRINT BACK     CONTROL
      3 VARIABLE LIST  OVERALL,TEACH,EXAM,KNOWLEDGE,GRADE,ENROLL
      4 INPUT FORMAT   FIXED(F2.1,4F3.1,F3.0)
      5 INPUT MEDIUM   ALBAT.DAT
      6 N OF CASES     50
      7 REGRESSION     VARIABLES = OVERALL TO ENROLL/
      8                REGRESSION = OVERALL WITH TEACH TO ENROLL(2)/
      9 STATISTICS     ALL
     10 OPTION         7
```
- -

Variable	Mean	Standard dev	Cases
OVERALL	3.5500	0.6135	50
TEACH	3.6640	0.5321	50
EXAM	3.8080	0.4932	50
KNOWLEDG	4.1760	0.4079	50
GRADE	3.4860	0.3511	50
ENROLL	88.0000	145.0595	50

- -

Correlation coefficients

A value of 99.00000 is printed
if a coefficient cannot be computed.

	OVERALL	TEACH	EXAM	KNOWLEDG	GRADE	ENROLL
OVERALL	1.00000	0.80386	0.59558	0.68180	0.30080	-0.23960
TEACH	0.80386	1.00000	0.71970	0.52627	0.46913	-0.45112
EXAM	0.59558	0.71970	1.00000	0.45147	0.61004	-0.55807
KNOWLEDG	0.68180	0.52627	0.45147	1.00000	0.22421	-0.12787
GRADE	0.30080	0.46913	0.61004	0.22421	1.00000	-0.33708
ENROLL	-0.23960	-0.45112	-0.55807	-0.12787	-0.33708	1.00000

* M U L T I P L E   R E G R E S S I O N * * * * * * * * * * * * * * Variable list 1
Regression List 1

Dependent variable: OVERALL

Variable(s) entered on step number 1:   ENROLL
                                          TEACH
                                          EXAM
                                          KNOWLEDG
                                          GRADE

Multiple R	0.86917		Analysis of variance	Df	Sum of squares	Mean square	F
R square	0.75545		Regression	5.	13.93426	2.78685	27.18433
Adjusted R square	0.72766		Residual	44.	4.51074	0.10252	
Standard error	0.32018						

----------------- Variables in the equation ------------------   ------------- Variables not in the equation -------------

Variable	B	Beta	Std error B	F		Variable	Beta in	Partial	Tolerance	F
ENROLL	0.5254911D-03	0.12424	0.00039	1.815						
TEACH	0.7632367D+00	0.66197	0.13292	32.971						
EXAM	0.1319805D+00	0.10608	0.16280	0.657						
KNOWLEDG	0.4889843D+00	0.32506	0.13654	12.826						
GRADE	-0.1843075D+00	-0.10547	0.16550	1.240						
(Constant)	-0.1194827D+01									

└ standardized regression coefficients

All variables are in the equation

Statistics which cannot be computed are printed as all nines.

- -

Validities referred to as *validities*.) From the matrix it is apparent that teaching skills (TEACH) has the highest correlation with the rated quality of the lectures (.804). The instructor's apparent knowledge of the material and the quality of the exams come next in order of correlations with the criterion (.682 and .596, respectively), while the student's expected grade and the size of the class have relatively low correlations with the criterion (.301 and −.240, respectively). These last two correlations run counter to traditional folklore among faculty, who often assume that those instructors who teach large classes and/or grade strictly will suffer in their teaching evaluations. At least in terms of rating the quality of the lectures, these variables play a minor role.

From the intercorrelations we also see that some of our variables have reasonably high intercorrelations with each other. Thus the perceived quality of the exams seems to be related to the instructor's teaching skills ($r = .720$), to the student's expected grade ($r = .610$) and to the enrollment ($r = −.558$). This would suggest that EXAM has much in common with several other variables, and may have very little information which is unique to it.

When we solve for the regression equations we find the following *Regression coefficients* *regression coefficients*

$$b_0 = -1.195$$

$$b_1 = .763$$

$$b_2 = .132$$

$$b_3 = .489$$

$$b_4 = -.184$$

$$b_5 = .0005$$

or, in matrix notation

$$b' = [-1.195 \quad .763 \quad .132 \quad .489 \quad -.184 \quad .0005].$$

Thus we can write

$$\hat{Y} = -1.195 + .763\text{TEACH} + .132\text{EXAM} + .489\text{KNOWLEDGE}$$
$$- .184\text{GRADE} + .0005\text{ENROLL}.$$

For course 1, then, using the data in Table 15.1,

$$\hat{Y} = -1.195 + .763(3.8) + .132(3.8) + .489(4.5) - .184(3.5) + .0005(21)$$
$$= 3.773.$$

Since course 1 actually obtained a mean lecture rating of 3.4, our error for that particular course is $e = Y - \hat{Y} = 3.4 - 3.773 = -.373$.

From our regression equation we can see that a one-unit difference in teaching skills will produce a difference of .763 in our predicted overall rating, while a one-unit difference in enrollment will lead to a .0005 unit difference in the predicted rating. One mistake which is commonly made is to treat the relative magnitudes of the b_i as an index of the relative importance of the individual predictors. By this (mistaken) logic we might be tempted to conclude that TEACH is a more important predictor than ENROLL. While this might actually be the case, we can not draw such a conclusion based on the b_i. The relative magnitudes of the b_i are in part a function of the standard deviations of the corresponding variables. Since the standard deviation of ENROLL is very large relative to the standard deviation of the other variables, its regression coefficient (b_5) is almost certain to be small regardless of the importance of that variable.

This last point can easily be seen by looking at the problem somewhat differently. For one instructor to have a 1 point higher TEACH rating than another would be a major accomplishment, whereas having one additional student is a trivial matter. We would hardly expect on *a priori* grounds that those two 1-point differences will lead to equal differences in $\hat{Y}$.

Standardized Regression Coefficients

Importance

As we shall see later, the question of relative importance of variables has several different answers depending upon what we mean by "importance." One measure of **importance** should be mentioned here, however, since it is a legitimate statistic in its own right. Suppose that before we obtained our multiple regression equation we had standardized each of our variables. As you should recall, standardizing a variable reduces its mean to zero and its standard deviation to 1.00. Now all of our variables would have equal standard deviations and a 1-unit difference between two courses in one variable would be comparable to a 1-unit difference in any other variable. If we now solved for our regression coefficients using the standardized variables we would obtain

$$\hat{Y}_z = .662Z_1 + .106Z_2 + .325Z_3 - .105Z_4 + .124Z_5$$

Standardized regression coefficients (β_i)

where the letter Z is used to denote standardized variables. In this case the regression coefficients are called **standardized regression coefficients** and denoted β_i. Thus

$$\beta_1 = .662$$

$$\beta_2 = .106$$

$$\beta_3 = .325$$

$$\beta_4 = -.105$$

$$\beta_5 = .124.$$

When variables have been standardized the intercept (β_0) = 0, and is never shown.

From the values of β_i given above we can conclude that a one standard deviation increase in X_1 will increase $\hat{Y}$ by .662 standard deviations, while comparable increases in X_2 and X_3 will increase $\hat{Y}$ by .106 and .325 standard deviations, respectively. While the relative magnitude of the β_i are not necessarily the best indicators of "importance", they have a simple interpretation, are printed by most regression programs, and generally give at least a rough estimate of the relative contributions of the variables in the equation.

Lest the reader think that she will be required to standardize the raw data in order to calculate the β_i, should the computer program not print them (MINITAB does not, for example), it should be noted that there is an easier way. It can be shown quite easily that

$$\beta_i = \frac{b_i s_i}{s_0}$$

and, vice versa,

$$b_i = \beta_i s_0 / s_i$$

(In fact most computer programs calculate the β_i first and then obtain the b_i.) For our data

$$\beta_1 = \frac{.763(.5321)}{.6135} = .662$$

$$\beta_2 = \frac{.132(.4932)}{.6135} = .106.$$

15.3 *The Multiple Correlation Coefficient*

Multiple correlation coefficient ($R_{0.123\ldots p}$)

Before considering errors of prediction, which is logically the next topic, we will first consider the *multiple correlation coefficient ($R_{0.123\ldots p}$)*. The notation denotes the fact that the criterion (Y or X_0) is predicted from predictors $1, 2, 3 \ldots p$ simultaneously. When there is no confusion as to which predictors are involved, we generally drop the subscript and use plain old R.

We will define R as the correlation between the criterion (Y) and the best linear combination of the predictors. As such, R is really nothing but $r_{Y\hat{Y}}$, where

$$\hat{Y} = b_0 + b_1 X_1 + b_2 X_2 + \cdots + b_p X_p$$

Thus if we wished we could use the regression equation to generate $\hat{Y}$, and then correlate Y and $\hat{Y}$. While no one would seriously propose calculating R in this way, it is important to realize that this is what the multiple correlation actually represents. In actual practice R is printed out by every multiple regression computer program. For our data the multiple correlation between the criterion and the five predictors, taken simultaneously, is .869.

The coefficient R is a regular correlation coefficient and can be treated just like any other Pearson product-moment correlation. (This is obviously true since $R = r_{Y\hat{Y}}$.) However in multiple correlation (as should also be the case with simple correlation) we are more interested in R^2 than R, because it can be directly interpreted in terms of percentage of accountable variation. Thus $R^2 = .869^2 = .755$, and we can say that 75.5% of the variance in the overall quality of the lectures can be predicted on the basis of the five predictors. This is about 11 percentage points more than could be predicted on the basis of TEACH, our best single predictor.

$R_{0.123\ldots p}^{*2}$

Unfortunately, R^2 is not an unbiased estimate of the corresponding parameter in the population ($R_{0.123\ldots p}^{*2}$). The extent of this bias depends upon the relative size of N and p. When $N = p + 1$ prediction is perfect and $R = 1$ regardless of the true relationship between Y and $X_1, X_2, \ldots, X_p$ in the population. (A straight line will perfectly fit any two points, a plane will perfectly fit any three points, and so on.) A relatively unbiased estimate of R^{*2} is given by

$$\text{est. } R^{*2} = 1 - \frac{(1 - R^2)(N - 1)}{N - p - 1}$$

Correction for shrinkage

This estimate is sometimes referred to as a ***correction for shrinkage***, and reflects the fact that the sample R^2 is partly a function of the relative magnitudes of p and N. The correction also reflects the fact that the prediction of $\hat{Y}$ is tailored for the particular set of data, and will probably not be the best prediction in a new sample of data, causing R^2 to shrink on cross-validation.

For our data

$$\text{est. } R^{*2} = 1 - \frac{(1 - .75545)(49)}{44} = .72766$$

This value agrees with the "Adjusted R square" printed by SPSS in Table 15.2.

It should be apparent from the definition of R that it can only take on values between 0 and 1. This follows both from the fact that it is defined as the positive square root of R^2, and from the fact that it can be viewed as $r_{Y\hat{Y}}$ and we would hardly expect $\hat{Y}$ to be negatively correlated with Y.

Distribution Assumptions

Up to this point we have made no assumptions about the nature of the distributions of our variables. β_i, b_i, R, and R^2 are perfectly legitimate measures independent of any distribution assumptions. Having said that, however, it is necessary to point out that certain assumptions will be necessary if we are to use these measures in several important ways.

In order to provide tests on these statistics which we have been discussing, we will need to make one of two different kinds of assumptions, depending upon the nature of our variables. If $Y, X_1, X_2, \ldots, X_p$ are thought of as random variables, as they are in this example since we measure the predictors as we find them rather than fixing them in advance, we will make the general assumption that the joint distribution of $Y, X_1, X_2, \ldots, X_p$ is

Multivariate-normal   ***multivariate-normal***. While in theory this assumption is necessary for many of our tests, it is likely that rather substantial departures from a multivariate-normal distribution are tolerable. First of all our tests are reasonably robust. Secondly, in actual practice we are not so much concerned about whether or not R is significantly different from zero as we are concerned over whether R is large or small. In other words, with X_i random we are not as interested in hypothesis testing as we were in the analysis of variance kinds of problems (whether $R = .20$ is significant or not is largely irrelevant, since it only accounts for 4% of the variance).

If the variables $X_1, X_2, \ldots, X_p$ are fixed variables, we will simply make the assumption that the $e_i = Y_i - \hat{Y}_i$ are normally and independently distributed. Here again moderate departures from normality are tolerable.

In general the fixed model and the corresponding assumption of normality in e will be considered in Chapter 16. In this chapter we will generally be concerned with random variables. The multivariate-normal assumption is more stringent than necessary for much of what follows, but it is a sufficient assumption. For example the standard error of β_i does not require an assumption of multivariate normality. However one seldom wishes to find the standard error of β_i unless he or she wishes to test (or form confidence limits on) β_i, and this test requires the normality assumption. We will therefore impose this assumption on what follows.

Standard Error of Estimate

In any multiple regression problem we have several estimates that are subject to sampling error. Thus β_i, b_i, and $R_{0.123 \ldots p}$ are all estimates of their corresponding parameters (β_i^*, b_i^*, and $R_{0.123 \ldots p}^*$), and as such will differ from sample to sample. In addition we have the variance of $\hat{Y}$ about Y (the residual variance), which is a measure of the accuracy of prediction.

Standard error   Probably the most common measure of error is the ***standard error of***
of estimate   ***estimate*** and derivatives of it. This is the measure of the agreement between Y and $\hat{Y}$, and is denoted as $s_{0.123 \ldots p}$.

$$s_{0.123 \ldots p}^2 = \text{MS}_{\text{residual}} = \frac{\Sigma(Y - \hat{Y})^2}{N - p - 1} = \frac{\text{SS}_{Y - \hat{Y}}}{N - p - 1}$$

$$= \frac{\text{SS}_Y(1 - R_{0.123 \ldots p}^2)}{N - p - 1}$$

$$s_{0.123 \ldots p} = \sqrt{s_{0.123 \ldots p}^2}$$

You will note that the definition of $s_{0.123...p}$ is merely an extension of the definition for the one predictor case, and thus the derivation is not given here. Note also that the degrees of freedom (the denominator), and hence the standard error of estimate, depend upon the number of predictors. We will have more to say about this later, but it should be pointed out here that if we added a predictor which contributed absolutely nothing, $\Sigma(Y-\hat{Y})^2$ would remain unchanged while the denominator would decrease, thus increasing the standard error of estimate.

The sum of squares of Y which is predicted from the X_i (the sum of squares due to regression) is $SS_{\hat{Y}}$. Since, as we saw in Chapter 9,

$$SS_Y = SS_{\hat{Y}} + SS_{Y-\hat{Y}}$$

or, with a different notation,

$$SS_Y = SS_{\text{regression}} + SS_{\text{residual}}$$

then a little algebra will show that

$$SS_Y = SS_{\hat{Y}} + SS_Y(1-R^2)$$

$$SS_{\hat{Y}} = SS_Y R^2.$$

Given the sum of squares due to regression ($SS_{\hat{Y}} = SS_{\text{regression}}$) and the sum of squares not due to regression ($SS_{Y-\hat{Y}} = SS_{\text{residual}}$), we are in a position to test whether our regression equation allows us to predict at better than chance levels. This test is equivalent to the test that $R^* = 0$, since if we can predict Y at better than chance levels, $R = r_{Y\hat{Y}}$ will be significant.

It has already been stated that

$$SS_Y = SS_{\hat{Y}} + SS_{Y-\hat{Y}}$$

$$SS_Y = SS_{\text{regression}} + SS_{\text{residual}}.$$

This expression can be derived in a manner exactly analogous to

$$SS_{\text{total}} = SS_{\text{treat}} + SS_{\text{error}}$$

in the analysis of variance, and, as we shall see, the two expressions are more similar than might at first appear. If we set up a summary table we have:

		SUMMARY TABLE		
Source	**df**	**SS**	**MS**	**F**
Regression	p	$SS_Y R^2$	$\dfrac{SS_Y R^2}{p}$	$\dfrac{(N-p-1)R^2}{p(1-R^2)}$
Residual	$N-p-1$	$SS_Y(1-R^2)$	$\dfrac{SS_Y(1-R^2)}{N-p-1}$	
Total	$N-1$	SS_Y		

Thus

$$F = \frac{(N-p-1)R^2}{p(1-R^2)}$$

is distributed as F on p and $N-p-1$ df. For the data in Table 15.1 we have $N = 50$, $p = 5$, and $R^2 = .755$. Thus

$$F = \frac{(50-5-1)(.755)}{5(.245)} = \frac{44(.755)}{5(.245)} = 27.184.$$

This is the same value of F given in the summary table shown in Table 15.2. An F of 27.184 on 5 and 44 df is significant beyond $p = .05$, and we can therefore reject $H_0: R^* = 0$ and conclude that we can predict at better than chance levels.

15.4   Standard Errors and Tests of Regression Coefficients

Standard error of β_i and b_i

Two more terms are of particular interest to us. They are the ***standard errors of β_i and b_i.*** One or the other of these standard errors are printed by most computer programs and can be used to form tests of $H_0: \beta_i^* = 0$ or $H_0: b_i^* = 0$. Thus

$$t = \frac{\beta_i}{s_{\beta_i}} \quad \text{on } N-p-1 \text{ df}$$

or equivalently

$$F(1, N-p-1) = \frac{\beta_i^2}{s_{\beta_i}^2}$$

and

$$t = \frac{b_i}{s_{b_i}} \quad \text{on } N-p-1 \text{ df}$$

or

$$F(1, N-p-1) = \frac{b_i^2}{s_{b_i}^2}.$$

Since b_i is a linear function of β_i these tests are all equivalent. As an illustration consider the example given in Table 15.2. Here $b_i = .763$ and $s_{b_i} = .133$. Then

$$F(1, 44) = \left(\frac{.763}{.133}\right)^2 = 32.9.$$

Thus we can reject the hypothesis that $b_i = 0$, and would conclude that X_1 contributes significantly to the prediction of Y.

The corresponding test on b_2 would take the form

$$F(1,44) = \left(\frac{.132}{.163}\right)^2 = .657$$

This result is not significant, meaning that, *given the other four predictors*, EXAM does not contribute significantly to the prediction of Y.

We might then consider dropping this predictor, but we will have more to say about this problem later. It is important to recognize that a test on a variable is done in the context of all other variables in the equation. A variable might have a very high individual correlation with the criterion, but have nothing useful to contribute once several other variables are included. This is in fact the case with EXAM.

15.5 *Geometric Representation of Multiple Regression*

Hyperspace
Regression surface

Any linear multiple regression problem involving p predictors can be represented graphically in $p + 1$ dimensions. Thus with one predictor we can readily draw a two-dimensional scatter diagram and fit a regression line through the points. With two predictors we can represent the data in three-dimensional space with a plane passing through the points. With more than three predictors we would have to begin to think in terms of multi-dimensional space (**hyperspace**) with the **regression surface** (the analog of the regression line or plane) fitted through the points. Being rather dimwitted, I have a great deal of trouble conceptualizing five-dimensional space, and as a result we will consider only a two-predictor example. In Figure 15.1 is a three-dimensional plot of the data given below. Each piece of data is represented as the ball on top of a flagpole. The base of the flagpole is located at the point (X_1, X_2), and the height of the flagpole is Y.

Y	1	2	1	3	3	3	3	4	6	5	7
X_1	3	3	3	3	4	4	5	5	5	7	7
X_2	0	1	2	4	1	4	4	6	7	5	7

In Figure 15.1 you can see that as you move from the lower left to the upper right, the heights of the flagpoles (and therefore the values of Y) increase. If you had the three dimensional model represented by this figure you could actually pass a plane through (or near) the points so as to give the best possible fit. Some of the flagpoles would actually stick up through the plane and some would not reach it. The vertical distance of the points from the plane would be the distance $Y - \hat{Y}$.

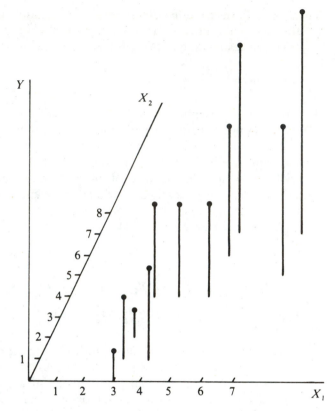

FIGURE 15.1

Three dimensional
representation of
Y as a function
of X_1 and X_2

We can derive one additional bit of insight from this three-dimensional model. The plane we have been discussing forms some angle (in this case positive) with the axis X_1. The slope of that plane relative to X_1 would be b_1. Similarly the slope of the plane with respect to X_2 would be b_2. The height of the plane at the point $(X_1, X_2) = (0, 0)$ would be b_0.

Further Interpretation of Regression Coefficients

Partial regression coefficients

The regression coefficients we have been discussing (both β and b) are in fact called **partial regression coefficients**. That is to say that b_1 is the coefficient for the regression of Y on X_1 when we partial out (remove, hold constant) the effect of $X_2, X_3, \ldots, X_p$. As such it should actually be denoted as $b_{01.23\ldots p}$, although we employ the shorter notation except in places where confusion might otherwise result. Perhaps the easiest way to see what we mean by the partialling out of X_2 is to consider Figure 15.1. If we look only at the data for $X_2 = 1$ (for example) we see that we could fit a straight line to the regression of Y on X_1. We do not need to consider X_2 because we are only considering those cases where $X_2 = 1 = $ a constant. Similarly we could look at only those cases where $X_2 = 4$, and so on. For any one value of X_2 we have a regression for Y on X_1. The average of these is $b_{01.2}$. Now consider the values of Y and X_2 for only the cases where $X_1 = 3$ (or 4 or 5, etc.). Here we have the regression of Y on X_2, with X_1 partialled out. The average of these coefficients would be $b_{02.1}$.

One common mistake is to equate $b_{01.2}$ with $b_{Y \cdot X_1}$—i.e., with the simple regression coefficient we would obtain if we regressed Y on X_1 *without regard to* X_2. That these coefficients can not be equated can be seen in a simple extreme example shown in Figure 15.2. The raw data from which this figure was obtained are:

Y	2	1	4	3	6	5
X_1	1	2	3	4	5	6
X_2	2	2	4	4	6	6

Figure 15.2(*a*) represents the three-dimensional projection of Y on X_1 and X_2. You will note that for any single values of X_2, the slope of the regression

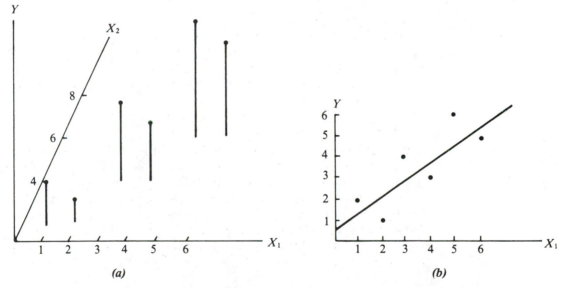

(a)   (b)

FIGURE 15.2   (*a*) Y as a function of X_1 and X_2. (*b*) Y plotted as a function of X_1 only

line of Y on X_1 is decidedly negative (in fact $b_{01.2} = -1$). But if you look at Figure 15.2(*b*) where Y is plotted against X_1, *ignoring* X_2, the slope is positive ($b_{Y \cdot X_1} = .829$). Thus there is quite a difference between partialling out a variable and ignoring it. While this is a deliberately extreme example, it is merely an exaggeration of more typical cases. Only when X_1 and X_2 are independent ($r_{12} = 0$) will $b_{01.2}$ be equal to $b_{Y \cdot X_1}$.

There is an alternative way of viewing partial regression coefficients which is of no practical use in calculations, but it is very useful in understanding the process of partialling. Consider the partial regression coefficient $b_{01.2}$

for the data in Figure 15.2. As mentioned earlier, $b_{01.2} = -1$. Suppose that we regress Y on X_2 and obtain the values of $Y - \hat{Y}$ for this regression. These residual values would represent that part of Y that can not be predicted by (i.e., is independent of) X_2. We will represent these residuals by the symbol Y_r. Now we regress X_1 on X_2 and generate the residuals $X_{1_i} - \hat{X}_{1_i}$. These represent that part of X_1 which is independent of X_2 and will be symbolized as X_{1r}. We now have two sets of residuals—that part of Y which is independent of X_2 and that part of X_1 which is independent of X_2. We have partialled X_2 out of Y and out of X_1. If we now regress Y_r on X_{1r}, the slope will be $b_{01.2}$. Moreover the correlation between Y_r and X_{1r} is called the *partial correlation* of Y and X_1, with X_2 partialled out ($r_{01.2}$). Table 15.3 contains a simple illustration of what we have been discussing using the data from Figure 15.2(*a*).

TABLE 15.3

Illustrative Calculation of Partial Regression Coefficient

DATA		
Y	X₁	X₂
Y	X_1	X_2
2	1	2
1	2	2
4	3	4
3	4	4
6	5	6
5	6	6

Y on X₂ $\hat{Y} = 1.0X_2 - .50$			X₁ on X₂ $\hat{X}_1 = 1.0X_2 - .50$			Y_r on X₁_r	
Y	$\hat{Y}$	Y_r	X_1	$\hat{X}_1$	X_{1r}	Y_r	X_{1r}
2	1.5	.5	1	1.5	-.5	.5	-.5
1	1.5	-.5	2	1.5	.5	-.5	.5
4	3.5	.5	3	3.5	-.5	.5	-.5
3	3.5	-.5	4	3.5	.5	-.5	.5
6	5.5	.5	5	5.5	-.5	.5	-.5
5	5.5	-.5	6	5.5	.5	-.5	.5

$$b_{Y_r X_{1r}} = \frac{N\Sigma Y_r X_{1r} - \Sigma Y_r \Sigma X_{1r}}{N\Sigma X_{1r}^2 - (\Sigma X_{1r})^2}$$

$$= \frac{6(-1.5) - (0)(0)}{6(1.5) - 0^2}$$

$$= -1 = b_{01.2}$$

15.6 *Partial Correlation*

Partial correlation

We have just indicated that a ***partial correlation*** is the correlation between two variables with one or more variables partialled out. More specifically it is the correlation between the two sets of residuals formed from the prediction of the original variables by one or more other variables.

Consider an experimenter who wanted to investigate the relationship between earned income and success in college. He obtained measures for each variable and ran his correlation, which turned out to be significant. Elated with the results he harangues his students with the admonition that if they do not do well in college they are not likely to earn large salaries. In the back of the class, however, is a bright student who realizes that both variables are (presumably) related to IQ. He argues that people with high IQs tend to do well in college and also earn good salaries, and that the correlation between income and college success is an artifact of this relationship.

The simple way to settle this argument is to calculate the partial correlation between income and college success with IQ partialled out of both variables. Thus we regress Income on IQ and obtain the residuals. These residuals represent the variance in Income that can not be attributed to IQ. We next regress Success on IQ and again obtain the residuals, which here represent the variance in Success which is not to be attributable to IQ. We can now answer the important question: "Can the variance in Income not explained by (independent of) IQ, be predicted by the variance in Success which is also not explained by IQ?" The correlation between these two variables is the partial correlation of Income and Success, partialling out IQ.

$r_{01.23...p}$

The partial correlation coefficient is represented by $r_{01.23...p}$. The two subscripts to the left of the dot represent the variables being correlated, and the subscript(s) to the right of the dot represent those variables partialled out.

A simple example illustrating the principle of partial correlation is presented in Table 15.4. Here you can see the calculation of all of the residuals and the correlation between the two sets of residuals. The partial correlation ($r_{01.2} = .738$) represents the independent contribution of variable X_1 toward the prediction of Y, partialling out X_2.

Hand calculation of partial correlation coefficients is exceedingly tedious, especially when you think of the potential number of partials we could have for any reasonably large value of p. It is not uncommon, however, to desire the partial correlation between two variables with only one other partialled out. This can be calculated quite readily from the simple rs.

$$r_{01.2} = \frac{r_{01} - r_{02}r_{12}}{\sqrt{(1 - r_{02}^2)(1 - r_{12}^2)}}.$$

TABLE 15.4

Illustrative Calculation of
Partial Correlation
Coefficient

DATA		
Y	X_1	X_2
4	2	4
3	4	1
6	6	5
1	1	2
5	3	3

Y on X_2			X₁ on X_2		
$\hat{Y} = .90X_2 + 1.1$			$\hat{X}_1 = .50X_2 + 1.7$		
Y	$\hat{Y}$	$Y_r = Y - \hat{Y}$	X_1	$\hat{X}_1$	$X_{1r} = X_1 - \hat{X}_1$
4	4.7	−.7	2	3.7	−1.7
3	2.0	1.0	4	2.2	1.8
6	5.6	0.4	6	4.2	1.8
1	2.9	−1.9	1	2.7	−1.7
5	3.8	1.2	3	3.2	−.2
$\Sigma Y_r = 0$		$\Sigma Y_r^2 = 6.70$	$\Sigma X_{1r} = 0$		$\Sigma X_{1r}^2 = 12.30$
					$\Sigma Y_r X_{1r} = 6.70$

$$r_{01.2} = r_{Y_r X_{1r}} = \frac{5(6.70) - 0}{\sqrt{(5(6.70) - 0)(5(12.30) - 0)}}$$

$$= .738$$

For our example, $r_{01} = .757$; $r_{02} = .740$; and $r_{12} = .411$. Thus

$$r_{01.2} = \frac{.757 - (.740)(.411)}{\sqrt{(1 - .740^2)(1 - .411^2)}} = .739$$

which agrees, within rounding error, with our previous calculation. For similar special formulae for the hand calculation of simple partial regression problems, the interested reader is referred to McNemar (1962) and Nunnally (1967).

15.7 *Semi-Partial Correlation*

Semi-partial correlation

A type of correlation which will prove to be exceedingly useful in the next chapter is the *semi-partial correlation* (sometimes called *part* correlation). As the name suggests, in the simplest case a semi-partial correlation is the correlation between the criterion and a partialled predictor variable. In other words, whereas the partial correlation ($r_{01.2}$) has variable 2 partialled out of

$r_{0(1.2)}$ both the criterion and predictor 1, the semi-partial correlation $r_{0(1.2)}$ has variable 2 only partialled out of predictor 1. In this case the semi-partial correlation is simply the correlation between Y and the residual $(X_1 - \hat{X}_1 = X_{1r})$ of X_1 predicted on X_2. As such it is the correlation of Y with that part of X_1 which is independent of X_2. As an illustration, the computation of $r_{0(1.2)}$ by way of the residuals is presented in Table 15.5 for the data given

TABLE 15.5

Illustrative Calculation of Semi-Partial Correlation Coefficient $(\hat{X}_1 = .50X_2 + 1.7)$

Y	X_1	X_2	X_{1r}
4	2	4	−1.7
3	4	1	1.8
6	6	5	1.8
1	1	2	−1.7
5	3	3	−.2

$\Sigma Y = 19 \qquad \Sigma X_{1r} = 0.0$

$\Sigma Y^2 = 87 \qquad \Sigma X_{1r}^2 = 12.3$

$\Sigma Y X_{1r} = 6.7$

$$r_{YX_{1r}} = \frac{5(6.7) - 19(0)}{\sqrt{(5(87) - 19^2)(5(12.3) - 0^2)}}$$

$$= .497 = r_{0(1.2)}$$

in Table 15.4. A much simpler method of computation exists, however. It can be shown that

$$r_{0(1.2)}^2 = R_{0.12}^2 - r_{02}^2.$$

Using this formula we can verify the calculation in Table 15.5. For those data, $R_{0.12}^2 = .79389$, and $r_{02}^2 = .54729$. Thus

$$r_{0(1.2)}^2 = .79389 - .54729 = .24660$$

$$r_{0(1.2)} = \sqrt{r_{0(1.2)}^2} = \sqrt{.24660} = .497$$

which agrees with the result in Table 15.5.

The above formula for $r_{0(1.2)}$ affords an opportunity to explore further just what multiple regression equations and correlations represent. Rearranging the formula we have

$$R_{0.12}^2 = r_{02}^2 + r_{0(1.2)}^2.$$

This formula illustrates that the squared multiple correlation is the sum of the squared correlation between the criterion and one of the variables plus the squared correlation between the criterion and that part of the other variable which is independent of the first. Thus we can think of R as being based on as much information as possible from one variable, any *additional*, *nonredundant* information from a second, and so on. In general

$$R_{0.123...p}^2 = r_{01}^2 + r_{0(2.1)}^2 + r_{0(3.12)}^2 + \cdots + r_{0(p.123...p-1)}^2$$

where $r_{0(3.12)}^2$ is the squared correlation between the criterion and variable 3, with variables 1 and 2 partialled out of 3. This way of looking at multiple regression will be particularly helpful when we consider the role of individual variables in predicting the criterion, and when we consider the least squares approach to the analysis of variance. As an aside, it should be mentioned that when the predictors are independent of one another, the above formula reduces to

$$R_{0.123...p}^2 = r_{01}^2 + r_{02}^2 + r_{03}^2 + \cdots + r_{0p}^2$$

since, if the variables are independent, there is no variance in common to be partialled out.

15.8   *Alternative Interpretation of Partial and Semi-Partial Correlation*

Venn diagrams

There is an alternative way of viewing the meaning of partial and semipartial correlation which can be very instructive. This method is best presented in terms of what are called ***Venn diagrams***.

Suppose that the following box is taken to represent all of the variability of the criterion in a regression problem. We will set the area of the box equal to 100%—the percentage of the sum of squares of Y to be explained. The circle labeled X_1 is taken to represent the percentage of the sum of squares of Y which is explained by X_1. In other words the area of the circle = $r_{YX_1}^2$. Similarly the area of the circle labeled X_2 is the percentage of the sum of squares of Y explained by X_2. Finally the overlap between the two circles represents that portion of Y which both X_1 and X_2 have in common.

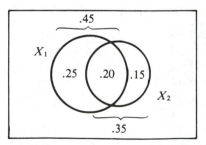

In this example you can see that 45% of the variance in Y can be explained by X_1 alone, 35% can be explained by X_2 alone and 20% is shared in common by both X_1 and X_2.

The two predictors in our example account for 60% of the variance of Y, i.e., $25 + 20 + 15$. The *squared semi-partial correlation* between X_1 and Y, with X_2 partialled out of X_1 is that portion of the variance of Y which X_1 accounts for *over-and-above* that portion accounted for by X_2. As such it is .25. Thus $r_{0(1.2)} = \sqrt{.25} = .50$. This is in line with our earlier definition.

$$r_{0(1.2)}^2 = R_{0.12}^2 - r_{02}^2 = .60 - .35 = .25$$

The *squared partial correlation* has a similar interpretation. However, instead of being the percentage of Y that X_1 explains but which X_2 did not, it is the additional amount that X_1 explains *relative* to the amount which X_2 left to be explained. For example $r_{02}^2 = .35$ and $1 - r_{02}^2 = .65$,

$$r_{01.2}^2 = .25/.65 = .385$$

$$r_{01.2} = \sqrt{.385} = .620$$

To put this even more schematically:

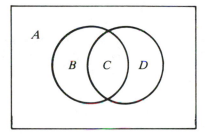

$$r_{0(1.2)}^2 = B = \text{semi-partial correlation squared}$$

$$r_{01.2}^2 = B/(A + B) = \text{partial correlation squared}$$

15.9 Suppressor Variables

Suppose that we have a multiple regression problem in which all variables are scored so as to correlate positively with the criterion. Since the scoring of variables is relatively arbitrary anyway, this presents no difficulty (if X is negatively related to Y, $C - X$ will be positively related to Y, where C is any constant). In such a situation one would expect all of the regression coefficients (β_i or b_i) to be positive. Occasionally, however, a regression coefficient in this situation will come out to be (significantly) negative. In *Suppressor variable* such a case that variable is called a *suppressor variable*.

Supressor variables seem, at first glance, to be unreasonable. We know that the simple correlation between the criterion and the variable is positive (by our definition), yet in the resulting regression equation an increment on this variable produces a decrement in $\hat{Y}$. Moreover, it can be shown that

$R^2 = \Sigma \beta_i r_{0i}$. If r_{0i} is positive and β_i is negative, the product $\beta_i r_{0i}$ will be negative. Thus by assigning β_i a negative value, the regression solution (whose task it is to minimize error) would *appear* to be reducing R^2. This does not seem to fit with our preconceived ideas of what should be happening, and yet obviously there must be some logical explanation.

Space considerations do not allow an extensive discussion of the theory of suppressor variables, but it is important to illustrate one intuitively sensible explanation. For a more extensive discussion of suppressor variables the reader is referred to Darlington (1968). Here we will merely take an example from Darlington's paper. Suppose that a speeded history examination (a long exam with a short time in which to complete it) is used as a measure of some external criterion of knowledge of history. While knowledge of history is presumably independent of reading speed, performance on the speeded test will not be. Thus some of the variance in test scores will reflect differences in reading speed, rather than differences in the actual knowledge of the student. What we would really like to do is to penalize students who did well *only* because they read quickly, and help students who did poorly *only* because they read slowly. This is precisely what is accomplished by having reading speed serve as a suppressor variable.

As Darlington points out, a variable will serve as a suppressor variable when it correlates more highly with Y_r than with Y (where Y_r represents the residual when predicting history knowledge from history score), and will not serve as a suppressor variable when it correlates more highly with Y than Y_r.

15.10   *Constructing a Regression Equation*

A major problem for anyone who has ever attempted to write a regression equation to predict some criterion concerns the choice of the variables to be included in the model. We usually suffer from having too many potential variables, rather than too few. While it would be possible to toss in all of the variables, this solution is neither practical nor statistically justifiable. Given that we are going to use some of the potential variables, then, how are we to select the ones that we will use?

Several alternative selection methods have been proposed, and these have been debated extensively in the literature. No one solution receives universal, or even majority, support, and the argument will go on for some time. In this chapter we will only consider two of the most common methods. These are the step-up and step-down methods, and are usually lumped *Stepwise regression* together under the title ***stepwise regression***. For an excellent and readable discussion of a number of alternative methods of deriving the optimum regression equation the reader is referred to Younger (1979) and to Hocking (1976).

Stepwise Regression

The two methods of stepwise regression (step-up and step-down) differ primarily in the order in which variables are added or deleted from the model. The ***step-up method*** begins by selecting that variable with the highest validity (correlation with the criterion), and then adds successive variables to the model until there is no appreciable improvement in R. The step-down method starts with the full set of predictors and begins deleting variables until there is some appreciable decrement in R.

The step-up method relies on the fact that

$$R^2_{0.123...p} = r^2_{01} + r^2_{0(2.1)} + r^2_{0(3.12)} + \cdots .$$

If we define variable 1 as that variable with the highest validity, then the first step in the process involves only variable 1. We then calculate all semi-partials of the form $r_{0(1.i)}$, $i = 2 \ldots p$. That variable (assume it is X_2) with the highest (first order) semi-partial correlation with the criterion is the one which will produce the greatest increment in R^2. This variable is then entered and we obtain the regression of the criterion on X_1 and X_2. We now test to see if the increment in R^2 is significant (or at least exceeds some preselected criterion). Such a test is afforded by

$$F(f - r, N - f - 1) = \frac{(N - f - 1)(R^2_f - R^2_r)}{(f - r)(1 - R^2_f)}$$

where R^2_f is the R^2 for the full model $= R^2_{0.12}$, R^2_r is the R^2 for the reduced model $= R^2_{0.1}$, f is the number of predictors in the full model $= 2$, r is the number of predictors in the reduced model $= 1$.

This process is repeated until the addition of further variables produces no significant (by whatever criterion we use) increment in R^2. An example of the use of the step-up procedure is shown in Table 15.6 for the data in Table 15.1. The solution was obtained using SPSS, substituting a "*1*" in place of the "*2*" on the "REGRESSION = " card.

This technique has several advantages, the most important of which is that variables are only brought into the equation if they have something to add. It does, however, suffer from the disadvantage that it need not have the best regression equation at every stage. Thus it is possible that $r_{03} < r_{01}$, but that $R_{0.23} > R_{0.12}$. This step-up procedure will leave us at the second stage with $R_{0.12}$, however, due to the nature of the selection procedure. (This kind of problem is partially circumvented in some computer programs for stepwise multiple regression (e.g., BMDP2R, Dixon & Brown, 1977) by checking whether a variable which was included at one stage should be deleted at another.)

The ***step-down method*** is just the reverse of the step-up method. Here we start with the full model and delete that variable which contributes the least to R^2—in other words we delete that variable for which $R^2_f - R^2_r$ is a

TABLE 15.6   Stepwise Multiple Regression of Course Evaluation Data Using SPSS REGRESSION

```
         1 RUN NAME        ANALYSIS OF FIRST SET OF DATA ON COURSE RATINGS
         2 PRINT BACK      CONTROL
         3 VARIABLE LIST   OVERALL,TEACH,EXAM,KNOWLEDGE,GRADE,ENROLL
         4 INPUT FORMAT    FIXED(F2.1,4F3.1,F3.0)
         5 INPUT MEDIUM    ALBAT.DAT
         6 N OF CASES      50
         7 REGRESSION      VARIABLES = OVERALL TO ENROLL/
         8                 REGRESSION = OVERALL WITH TEACH TO ENROLL(1)/
         9 STATISTICS      ALL
        10 OPTION          7
```

- -

Variable	Mean	Standard dev	Cases
OVERALL	3.5500	0.6135	50
TEACH	3.6640	0.5321	50
EXAM	3.8080	0.4932	50
KNOWLEDG	4.1760	0.4079	50
GRADE	3.4860	0.3511	50
ENROLL	88.0000	145.0595	50

- -

Correlation coefficients

A value of 99.00000 is printed
if a coefficient cannot be computed.

	OVERALL	TEACH	EXAM	KNOWLEDG	GRADE	ENROLL
OVERALL	1.00000	0.80386	0.59558	0.68180	0.30080	-0.23960
TEACH	0.80386	1.00000	0.71970	0.52627	0.46913	-0.45112
EXAM	0.59558	0.71970	1.00000	0.45147	0.61004	-0.55807
KNOWLEDG	0.68180	0.52627	0.45147	1.00000	0.22421	-0.12787
GRADE	0.30080	0.46913	0.61004	0.22421	1.00000	-0.33708
ENROLL	-0.23960	-0.45112	-0.55807	-0.12787	-0.33708	1.00000

* M U L T I P L E   R E G R E S S I O N * * * * * * * * * * * * *   Variable list 1
                                                                                                         Regression List 1
Dependent variable: OVERALL

Variable(s) entered on step number 1:   TEACH

Multiple R	0.80386		Analysis of variance	Df	Sum of squares	Mean square	F
R square	0.64620		Regression	1.	11.91908	11.91908	87.66820
Adjusted R square	0.63882		Residual	48.	6.52592	0.13596	
Standard error	0.36872						

---------------- Variables in the equation ------------------   ------------ Variables not in the equation -------------

Variable	B	Beta	Std error B	F	Variable	Beta in	Partial	Tolerance	F
TEACH	0.9268335D+00	0.80386	0.09899	87.668	EXAM	0.03536	0.04127	0.48204	0.080
(Constant)	0.1540821D+00				KNOWLEDG	0.35786	0.51158	0.72304	16.661
					GRADE	-0.09786	-0.14529	0.77991	1.014
					ENROLL	0.15447	0.23177	0.79649	2.668

* *

TABLE 15.6   (Continued)

```
* * * * * * * * * * * * * * * * * * * * * * * * * * * * * * * * * * * * * * * * * * * * * * * * * * * * * * * * * * * *

Variable(s) entered on step number  2:     KNOWLEDG


Multiple R         0.85953            Analysis of variance    Df    Sum of squares    Mean square        F
R square           0.73879            Regression              2.      13.62703           6.81351       66.46675
Adjusted R square  0.72768            Residual               47.       4.81797           0.10251
Standard error     0.32017


---------------- Variables in the equation ------------------       ------------ Variables not in the equation -------------

Variable       B          Beta     Std error B       F            Variable    Beta in    Partial    Tolerance      F

TEACH     0.7096903D+00   0.61553    0.10108       49.292          EXAM       -0.01891   -0.02549    0.47473      0.030
KNOWLEDG  0.5383263D+00   0.35786    0.13188       16.661          GRADE      -0.08753   -0.15117    0.77920      1.076
(Constant) -0.1298356D+01                                         ENROLL      0.10750    0.18574    0.77990      1.644


* * * * * * * * * * * * * * * * * * * * * * * * * * * * * * * * * * * * * * * * * * * * * * * * * * * * * * * * * * * *

Variable(s) entered on step number  3:     ENROLL


Multiple R         0.86476            Analysis of variance    Df    Sum of squares    Mean square        F
R square           0.74780            Regression              3.      13.79325           4.59775       45.46600
Adjusted R square  0.73136            Residual               46.       4.65175           0.10113
Standard error     0.31800


---------------- Variables in the equation ------------------       ------------ Variables not in the equation -------------

Variable       B          Beta     Std error B       F            Variable    Beta in    Partial    Tolerance      F

TEACH     0.7754835D+00   0.67259    0.11275       47.302          EXAM       0.04345    0.05459     0.39812      0.134
KNOWLEDG  0.5138281D+00   0.34158    0.13238       15.067          GRADE     -0.07247   -0.12582     0.76011      0.724
ENROLL    0.4546574D-03   0.10750    0.00035        1.644
(Constant) -0.1477128D+01


* * * * * * * * * * * * * * * * * * * * * * * * * * * * * * * * * * * * * * * * * * * * * * * * * * * * * * * * * * * *

Variable(s) entered on step number  4:     GRADE


Multiple R         0.86706            Analysis of variance    Df    Sum of squares    Mean square        F
R square           0.75180            Regression              4.      13.86688           3.46672       34.07569
Adjusted R square  0.72973            Residual               45.       4.57812           0.10174
Standard error     0.31896


---------------- Variables in the equation ------------------       ------------ Variables not in the equation -------------

Variable       B          Beta     Std error B       F            Variable    Beta in    Partial    Tolerance      F

TEACH     0.8091238D+00   0.70177    0.11981       45.611          EXAM       0.10608    0.12131     0.32457      0.657
KNOWLEDG  0.5129913D+00   0.34102    0.13278       14.927
ENROLL    0.4067064D-03   0.09616    0.00036        1.275
GRADE    -0.1266417D+00  -0.07247    0.14886        0.724
(Constant) -0.1151198D+01


* * * * * * * * * * * * * * * * * * * * * * * * * * * * * * * * * * * * * * * * * * * * * * * * * * * * * * * * * * * *

Variable(s) entered on step number  5:     EXAM


Multiple R         0.86917            Analysis of variance    Df    Sum of squares    Mean square        F
R square           0.75545            Regression              5.      13.93426           2.78685       27.18433
Adjusted R square  0.72766            Residual               44.       4.51074           0.10252
Standard error     0.32018
```

TABLE 15.6   (Continued)

```
---------------- Variables in the equation ------------------          ------------ Variables not in the equation -----------

Variable        B          Beta      Std error B       F            Variable      Beta in     Partial    Tolerance         F

TEACH       0.7632367D+00    0.66197    0.13292      32.971
KNOWLEDG    0.4889843D+00    0.32506    0.13654      12.826
ENROLL      0.5254911D-03    0.12424    0.00039       1.815
GRADE      -0.1843075D+00   -0.10547    0.16550       1.240
EXAM        0.1319805D+00    0.10608    0.16280       0.657
(Constant) -0.1194827D+01


Maximum step reached

Statistics which cannot be computed are printed as all nines.

- - - - - - - - - - - - - - - - - - - - - - - - - - - - - - - - - - - - - - - - -
```

minimum. As we shall soon see, this will be that variable for which the F test on b_i produces the smallest value of F. By the definition of a semi-partial correlation,

$$R_f^2 - R_r^2 = r_{0(m.123...p)}^2$$

where m is the variable under consideration. In other words, the difference between R_f^2 and R_r^2 is a squared semi-partial correlation, and we delete that variable with the smallest squared semi-partial correlation with the criterion.

The step-down procedure has at least one advantage over the step-up procedure, in that it is less likely to commit the error previously attributed to the step-up procedure. However it is not free from error by any means, since a predictor which is relatively useless when included with several other variables might be quite useful in conjunction with only one or two other variables. For the data in Table 15.1 the step-down procedure happens to lead to the same solution as the step-up procedure.

How Many Variables?

The question of how many variables to include, ignoring which variables they are, can in part be treated as a separate issue. We have already said that the stepwise procedure stops adding (or subtracting) when the increment (or decrement) in R fails to reach some predetermined criterion. However something else must be considered. We have previously defined

$$\text{MS}_{\text{error}} = \frac{\text{SS}_Y(1 - R^2)}{N - p - 1}$$

and

$$\text{est } R^{*2} = 1 - \frac{(1 - R^2)(N - 1)}{N - p - 1}.$$

In general, increasing R^2 will decrease MS_{error} and increase est R^{*2}. But at the same time we are increasing R^2 we will be increasing p, and there must come a point at which the change in p overshadows the change in R^2, and MS_{error} begins to increase and est R^{*2} begins to decrease. Thus if $SS_Y = 100$, $R^2 = .50$, $N = 20$, and $p = 4$,

$$MS_{error} = \frac{100(1-.5)}{20-4-1} = 3.33.$$

Suppose that adding a fifth predictor yields $R^2 = .52$ (a reasonable assumption in practice). Then

$$MS_{error} = \frac{100(1-.52)}{20-5-1} = 3.42$$

Although we have increased R^2, we have also increased MS_{error}, leaving us worse off than we were before. This would suggest that one stopping rule might depend upon the relative magnitude of MS_{error}. By this rule we would continue adding variables until MS_{error} began to increase. A more exact treatment of this problem is suggested by Darlington (1968). For the data in Table 15.1, such a procedure would result in stopping the step-up procedure after the third step (i.e., using TEACH, KNOWLEDGE, and ENROLL as predictors), since adding GRADE causes $MS_{residual}$ to increase from .10113 to .10174.

Beta weights

An alternative procedure employed by many people is to start with the full model and to begin dropping the variables with the lowest β coefficients (often called *beta weights*), rather than the lowest semi-partial correlations. Darlington has presented a strong case against this approach, and anyone who has had experience with β weights oscillating wildly from sample to sample would be likely to side with him. These weights are probably the least satisfactory indices for adding or deleting variables. For further support for this position the reader is referred to the rather sobering comments by Cooley & Lohnes (1971, pp. 54–57) and to the interesting paper by Dawes & Corrigan (1974).

Cross-Validation

Cross-validation

The stumbling block for most multiple regression studies is the concept of *cross-validation* of the regression equation against an independent data set. Thus we might obtain data on 1000 subjects and then break the sample into two subsamples of 500 subjects each. For each sample we obtain a regression equation. We then apply the regression coefficients obtained from one sample against the data in the other sample, to obtain predicted values of Y on a cross-validation sample ($\hat{Y}_{cv}$). The question of interest then becomes the question of the relationship between Y and $\hat{Y}_{cv}$ in the new subsample. If the regression equations have any reasonable level of validity, then the cross validation correlation (R_{cv}—the correlation between Y and $\hat{Y}_{cv}$ predicted on the other sample's regression equation) should be high. If they are not, our solution does not amount to much. R_{cv}^2 will in almost all cases be less than R^2, since R^2 depends upon a regression equation tailor-made for that set of data. Essentially we have an equation which does its best to account for every bump and wiggle (including sampling error) in the data. We should not be surprised when it does not do as well in accounting for different bumps and wiggles in a different set of data. However, substantial differences between R^2 and R_{cv}^2 are an indication that our solution lacks appreciable validity. When our regression equation for the data from Table 15.1 (using TEACH, KNOWLEDGE, and ENROLL as predictors) was applied to a new set of 50 courses, the correlation of Y and the $\hat{Y}$ derived from the equation in Table 15.2 was 0.8181, representing a very acceptable level of cross-validation.

As Darlington has pointed out (1968), our correction for shrinkage

$$\text{est } R^{*2} = 1 - \frac{(1 - R^2)(N - 1)}{N - p - 1}$$

is an estimate of the correlation in the population between Y and a *population* regression equation for $\hat{Y}$. It is not (and in fact it is an overestimation of) the expected correlation in a cross-validation sample.

15.11   The "Importance" of Individual Variables

When an investigator derives a regression equation to predict some criterion on the basis of several variables, it is logical for her to ask "Which of these variables is most important in predicting Y?" Unfortunately there is no simple answer to the question except in the unusual case in which the predictors are mutually independent. As we have seen, β_i (or more appropriately β_i^2) is sometimes taken as a measure of importance. This is done on the grounds that β^2 can be interpreted as the *unique* contribution of each variable to the prediction of Y. Thus X_1 has some variance in common with Y which is not shared by any of the other variables, and this variance is represented by β_1^2. The difficulty with this measure is that it has nothing to say about that portion of the variance of Y which X_1 shares with the other variables, but which is in some sense part of the contribution of X_1 to the prediction of Y. For an attempt to circumvent this problem (not necessarily successfully) see Chase (1960).

A second measure based on beta weights was proposed by Hoffman (1960, 1962). Hoffman reasoned that since

$$R^2 = \Sigma \beta_i r_{0i}$$

then for variable i, $\beta_i r_{0i}/R^2$ was a measure of the independent contribution of this variable to the variance of $\hat{Y}$. In fact there is very little to recommend this measure, as I realized to my chagrin the first time I tried to use it. What does it mean when $\beta_i r_{0i}$ is negative? In fact what does it mean to speak of the independent contribution to the variance when the predictors are not independent? Hoffman's defense of the measure (Hoffman, 1962) only served to obscure the issue further.

Multicollinearity

Basing a measure of importance on the beta weights has the further serious drawback that when variables are highly intercorrelated (a condition known as *multicollinearity*), the values of β are very unstable from sample to sample, although R^2 may change very little. Given two sets of data it would not be particularly unusual to find

$$\hat{Y} = .50Z_1 + .25Z_2$$

in one case and

$$\hat{Y} = .25Z_1 + .50Z_2$$

in the other, with reasonably equal values of R^2 associated with the two equations. If we now seek for a measure of the contribution of each of the predictors in accounting for Y (as opposed to simply predicting Y for a given set of data), we could come to quite different conclusions for the two data sets. Darlington (1968) presents an interesting discussion of this issue and concludes that β_i has only limited utility as a measure of "importance." An even stronger stand is taken by Cooley & Lohnes (1971), who point out that our estimate of β ultimately relies on our estimates of the elements of the intercorrelation matrix. Since this matrix contains $p + p(p-1)/2$ intercorrelations which are all subject to sampling error, Cooley and Lohnes suggest that we must be exceedingly careful about attaching practical significance to the regression coefficients.

As an illustration of the variability of the regression coefficients, a second set of 50 courses was drawn from the same source as the data in Table 15.1. In this case R^2 was more or less the same as it had been for the first example ($R^2 = .70983$) but the regression equation looked quite different. In terms of standardized variables,

$$Z_{\hat{Y}} = .371\text{TEACH} + .113\text{EXAM} + .567\text{KNOWLEDGE}$$

$$- .027\text{GRADE} + .184\text{ENROLL}$$

If you compare this equation with the one found from Table 15.2 it is clear that there are substantial differences in some of the values of β_i.

Another measure of importance, which has much to recommend it, is the squared semi-partial correlation between predictor i and the criterion (with all other predictors partialled out)—i.e., $r_{0(i.1,2,...,p)}^2$. Darlington (1968) refers to this measure as the "usefulness" of a predictor. As we have already seen, this semi-partial correlation squared represents the decrement in R^2

which would result from the elimination of the ith predictor from the model. When the main goal is that of prediction rather than explanation, this is probably the best measure of "importance." Fortunately it is easy to obtain from most computer printouts, since

$$r^2_{0(i.123...p)} = \frac{F_i(1 - R^2_{0.123...p})}{N - p - 1}$$

where F_i is the F test on the individual β_i (or b_i) coefficients. Since all terms but F_i are constant for $i = 1 \ldots p$, the F_is order the variables in the same way as do the squared semi-partials, and thus can be used to rank order the variables in terms of their usefulness.

One final, and intriguing, proposal has been offered by Cooley & Lohnes (1971). They have proposed

$$\frac{r_{0i}}{R_{0.123...p}}$$

as a measure of the importance of the ith variable. It can be shown that this measure represents the correlation between X_i and $\hat{Y}$. As such this measure has a certain intuitive appeal in that it is a direct measure of the degree to which variable i is related to the values actually predicted by the regression equation. The advantages and disadvantages of this measure have not been fully investigated, but it is certainly worthy of serious consideration.

A considerable amount of work in Psychology has been devoted to regression models of decision making and to the general problem of clinical versus actuarial prediction. An excellent, though somewhat dated, review of this literature is to be found in Slovik & Lichtenstein (1971). This work represents a good example of the application of multiple regression to applied and theoretical problems in Psychology.

15.12   The Use of Approximate Regression Coefficients

I have pointed out that regression coefficients frequently show substantial fluctuations from sample to sample, yet without producing drastic changes in R. This might lead someone to suggest that we might use rather crude approximations of these coefficients as a substitute for the more precise estimates obtained from the data. For example, suppose that a five predictor problem produced the following regression equation.

$$\hat{Y} = 9.2 + .85X_1 + 2.1X_2 - .74X_3 + 3.6X_4 - 2.4X_5$$

We might ask how much loss we would suffer if we rounded these values off to

$$\hat{Y} = 10 + 1X_1 + 2X_2 - 1X_3 + 4X_4 - 2X_5.$$

The answer is that we will probably lose very little. An excellent discussion of this problem is given by Guilford & Fruchter (1973) and especially by Dawes & Corrigan (1974) and Wainer (1976, 1978).

This method of rounding off regression coefficients is more common than one might suppose. For example, the college admissions officer who quantifies the various predictors he has available and then weights grade point average twice as highly as the letter of recommendation is really using crude estimates of what he thinks would be the actual regression coefficients. Similarly there are a great many scoring systems for the MMPI which are in fact based upon the reduction of coefficients to convenient integers. Whether the use of these *diagnostic signs* produces results which are better than, worse than, or equivalent to the use of the usual linear regression equations is still a matter of debate. A dated but very comprehensive study of this question is to be found in Goldberg (1965).

15.13   *Curvilinear and Configural Variables*

We tend to think of multiple regression as being concerned solely with linear variables, although that is not necessarily the case. When we speak of *linear* multiple regression we are not referring to the fact that X_1 must be linear, but to the fact that the regression surface must be linear. Thus in the one predictor case if we can draw a straight line representing the relationship between Y and X^2, we have a linear regression problem (although here the relationship between Y and X would be curvilinear). The same holds for the case of multiple regression. Thus there is nothing to prevent us from writing a model of the form

$$\hat{Y} = b_0 + b_1X_1 + b_2X_2^2 + b_3X_3^4 + b_4X_4^{1/2}$$

The only requirement is that our raw data matrix must contain the values of X_1, X_2^2, X_3^4, and $X_4^{1/2}$, and not X_1, X_2, X_3, and X_4.

A related problem is that presented by configural relationships among predictors. Thus if we thought that X_1 and X_2 interacted with one another to produce a joint result, we might conceivably want a model of the form

$$\hat{Y} = b_0 + b_1X_1X_2 + b_2X_3$$

Nonlinear predictors
Configural predictors

Here again the raw data would consist of a column whose entries were the products X_1X_2 and a column whose entries were X_3. For examples of problems involving **nonlinear predictors** and **configural predictors** the reader is referred to Slovic & Lichtenstein (1971) and Goldberg (1971).

15.14   Summary

We began this chapter by examining several matrix concepts which are important for the general understanding of the procedures of multiple regression. We then considered the multiple linear regression equation and its interpretation. Discussion of the regression equation led directly to the multiple correlation coefficient as a measure of the degree to which a regression surface fits the data. We then considered partial and semi-partial correlations and their interpretation, and used these principles to develop methods for a logical approach to the construction of an optimal regression equation. Next, we considered what was meant by the "importance" of a variable and saw a number of measures that could be used, with varying success, as an index of "importance". Finally, we saw that approximate regression coefficients will often do just about as well as the more exact values, and touched on the use of curvilinear and configural variables.

Exercises for Chapter 15

NOTE: Each of the problems below is based on a very small data set for reasons of economy of space. For actual applications of multiple regression sample sizes should be appreciably larger than those used here.

15.1   A psychologist studying the perceived "quality of life" in a large number of cities ($N = 150$) came up with the following equation using mean temperature (TEMP), median income in $1000 (INCOME), per capita expenditure on social services (SOCSER), and population density (POPUL) as predictors.

$$\hat{Y} = 5.37 - .01\text{TEMP} + .05\text{INCOME} + .003\text{SOCSER} - .01\text{POPUL}$$

a.   Interpret the regression equation in terms of the coefficients.
b.   Assume a city with a mean temperature of 55 degrees, a median income of $12,000, which spends $500 per capita on social services, and has a population density of 200 people per block. What is its predicted "quality of life" score?
c.   What would we predict in a different city which was identical in every way except that it spent $100 per capita on social services?

15.2   Referring to Exercise 15.1, assume that

$$\boldsymbol{\beta}' = [-.438 \quad .762 \quad .081 \quad -.132]$$

Interpret the results.

15.3   For the values of $\boldsymbol{\beta}'$ in Exercise 15.2, the corresponding standard errors are [.397   .252   .052   .025]. Which, if any, predictor would you be most likely to drop if you wanted to refine your regression equation?

15.4 A large corporation is interested in predicting a measure of job satisfaction among its employees. They have collected data on each of 15 employees who each supplied information on job satisfaction, level of responsibility, number of people supervised, rating of work environment, and years of service. The data are:

Satisfaction	2 2 3 3 5 5 5 6 6 6 7 8 8 8 9 9
Responsibility	4 2 3 6 2 8 4 5 8 8 9 6 3 7 9
No. Supervised	5 3 4 7 4 8 6 5 9 8 9 3 6 9 9
Environment	1 1 7 3 5 8 5 5 6 4 7 2 8 7 9
Years of Service	5 7 5 3 3 6 3 2 7 3 5 5 8 8 1

The following is an abbreviated form of the printout from BMDP1R.

```
      DEPENDENT VARIABLE. . . . . . . . . . . . . . .     1 SATIF
      TOLERANCE . . . . . . . . . . . . . . . . . . . 0.0100
 ALL DATA CONSIDERED AS A SINGLE GROUP
 MULTIPLE R              0.6974          STD. ERROR OF EST.        2.0572
 MULTIPLE R-SQUARE       0.4864

 ANALYSIS OF VARIANCE
                     SUM OF SQUARES    DF    MEAN SQUARE    F RATIO    P(TAIL)
         REGRESSION        40.078       4       10.020       2.367    0.12267
         RESIDUAL          42.322      10        4.232

                                                STD. REG
     VARIABLE       COEFFICIENT   STD. ERROR      COEFF       T    P(2 TAIL) TOLERANCE

 INTERCEPT            1.66926
 RESPON      2        0.60516       0.428         0.624     1.414    0.188    0.263940
 NUMSUP      3       -0.33399       0.537        -0.311    -0.622    0.548    0.205947
 ENVIR       4        0.48552       0.276         0.514     1.758    0.109    0.600837
 YRS         5        0.07023       0.262         0.063     0.268    0.794    0.919492
 BMDP1R - MULTIPLE LINEAR REGRESSION
 HEALTH SCIENCES COMPUTING FACILITY
 UNIVERSITY OF CALIFORNIA, LOS ANGELES 90024
 PROGRAM REVISED NOVEMBER 1979
```

a. What is the regression equation using all 5 predictors?
b. What is the vector of β_is?

15.5 *a.* Referring to Exercise 15.4, which variable has the largest semi-partial correlation with the criterion, partialling out the other variables?

b. The overall F in Exercise 15.4 is not significant, but yet ENVIR correlates significantly ($r = .58$) with Y. How can this be?

15.6 Calculate the adjusted R^2 for the data in Exercise 15.4.

15.7 All other things equal, the ability of two variables to predict a third will increase as the correlation between them decreases. Explain this in terms of semi-partial correlation.

15.8 All other things equal, the stability of any given regression coefficient across different samples of data is partly a function of how that variable correlates with other predictors. Explain this.

15.9   Using the following (random) data, demonstrate what happens to the multiple correlation when you drop out *cases* from the data set (e.g., use 15 cases, then 10, 6, 5, and 4 cases).

Y	5	0	5	9	4	8	3	7	0	4	7	1	4	7	9
X_1	3	8	1	5	8	2	4	7	9	1	3	5	6	8	9
X_2	7	6	4	3	1	9	7	5	3	1	8	6	0	3	7
X_3	1	7	4	1	8	8	6	8	3	6	1	9	7	7	7
X_4	3	6	0	5	1	3	5	9	1	1	7	4	2	0	9

15.10   Using the data in Exercise 15.4, generate $\hat{Y}$ and show that $R_{0.12345} = r_{Y\hat{Y}}$.

15.11   Use Y and $\hat{Y}$ from the previous exercise to show that $MS_{residual}$ is $\Sigma(Y-\hat{Y})^2/(N-p-1)$.

15.12   Calculate the adjusted R^2 for the 15 cases in Exercise 15.9.

15.13   *a.*   Taking the first three variables from Exercise 15.4, use any computer program to calculate the squared semi-partial correlation and the squared partial correlation for Satisfaction as the criterion and No. Supervised as the predictor, partialling out Responsibility.
b.   Draw a Venn diagram to illustrate these two coefficients.

15.14   *a.*   Draw a figure comparable to Figure 15.1 for the first three variables in Exercise 15.4.
b.   Obtain the regression solution for these same data and relate the solution to the figure.

15.15   The State of Vermont is divided into ten Health Planning Districts—corresponding roughly to counties. The following data represent the percentage of live births under 2500 grams (Y), the fertility rate for females ≤ 17 (X_1), total high risk fertility rate for females ≤ 17 or ≥ 35 (X_2), percentage of mothers with fewer than 12 years of education (X_3), percentage illegitimate births (X_4), and percentage of mothers not seeking medical care until the third trimester (X_5).

Y	X_1	X_2	X_3	X_4	X_5
6.1	22.8	43.0	23.8	9.2	6
7.1	28.7	55.3	24.8	12.0	10
7.4	29.7	48.5	23.9	10.4	5
6.3	18.3	38.8	16.6	9.8	4
6.5	21.1	46.2	19.6	9.8	5
5.7	21.2	39.9	21.4	7.7	6
6.6	22.2	43.1	20.7	10.9	7
8.1	22.3	48.5	21.8	9.5	5
6.3	21.8	40.0	20.6	11.6	7
6.9	31.2	56.7	25.2	11.6	9

A stepwise regression using BMDP2R follows. (Only the first three steps are shown to conserve space. For purposes of an example we will not let the lack of statistical significance worry us.)

```
STEP NO. 1
VARIABLE ENTERED     3  X2
MULTIPLE R            0.6215
MULTIPLE R-SQUARE     0.3862
ADJUSTED R-SQUARE     0.3095
STD. ERROR OF EST.    0.5797

ANALYSIS OF VARIANCE
                 SUM OF SQUARES    DF    MEAN SQUARE    F RATIO
REGRESSION       1.6917006          1    1.6917006       5.03
RESIDUAL         2.6882995          8    0.3360374

                          VARIABLES IN EQUATION
                          STD. ERROR   STD REG               F TO
VARIABLE    COEFFICIENT   OF COEFF     COEFF     TOLERANCE   REMOVE   LEVEL
(Y-INTERCEPT  -3.529 )
X2       3     0.069       0.031        0.621    1.00000     5.03      1

                          VARIABLES NOT IN EQUATION
                          PARTIAL                    F TO
VARIABLE   LEVEL          CORR.     TOLERANCE   ENTER    LEVEL
X1    2 .  1 .           -0.19730   0.25831     0.28      1
X3    4 .               -0.25039   0.43280     0.47      1
X4    5 .                0.00688   0.69838     0.00      1
X5    6 .               -0.59063   0.58000     3.75      1


STEP NO. 2
VARIABLE ENTERED     6  X5
MULTIPLE R            0.7748
MULTIPLE R-SQUARE     0.6003
ADJUSTED R-SQUARE     0.4862
STD. ERROR OF EST.    0.5001

ANALYSIS OF VARIANCE
                 SUM OF SQUARES    DF    MEAN SQUARE    F RATIO
REGRESSION       2.6294919          2    1.314746        5.26
RESIDUAL         1.7505082          7    0.2500726

                          VARIABLES IN EQUATION
                          STD. ERROR   STD REG               F TO
VARIABLE    COEFFICIENT   OF COEFF     COEFF     TOLERANCE   REMOVE   LEVEL
(Y-INTERCEPT   2.949 )
X2       3     0.113       0.035        1.015    0.58000     10.47     1
X5       6    -0.223       0.115       -0.608    0.58000      3.75     1

                          VARIABLES NOT IN EQUATION
                          PARTIAL                    F TO
VARIABLE   LEVEL          CORR.     TOLERANCE   ENTER    LEVEL
X1    2 .  1 .           -0.09613   0.24739     0.06      1
X3    4 .               -0.05399   0.37826     0.02      1
X4    5 .                0.41559   0.53416     1.25      1


STEP NO. 3
VARIABLE ENTERED     5  X4
MULTIPLE R            0.8181
MULTIPLE R-SQUARE     0.6694
ADJUSTED R-SQUARE     0.5041
STD. ERROR OF EST.    0.4913

ANALYSIS OF VARIANCE
                 SUM OF SQUARES    DF    MEAN SQUARE    F RATIO
REGRESSION       2.9318295          3    0.9772765       4.05
RESIDUAL         1.4481706          6    0.2413618

                          VARIABLES IN EQUATION
                          STD. ERROR   STD REG               F TO
VARIABLE    COEFFICIENT   OF COEFF     COEFF     TOLERANCE   REMOVE   LEVEL
(Y-INTERCEPT   1.830 )
X2       3     0.104       0.035        0.942    0.55484     8.93      1
X4       5     0.190       0.170        0.359    0.53416     1.25      1
X5       6    -0.294       0.130       -0.799    0.44362     5.14      1

                          VARIABLES NOT IN EQUATION
                          PARTIAL                    F TO
VARIABLE   LEVEL          CORR.     TOLERANCE   ENTER    LEVEL
X1    2 .  1 .           -0.14937   0.24520     0.11      1
X3    4 .                0.14753   0.31072     0.11      1
```

a. What are the values of R for the successive steps?

b. From the definition of a partial correlation (in terms of Venn Diagrams) show that the R^2 at step 2 is a function of R^2 at step 1 and the partial correlation listed under step 1-VARIABLES NOT IN EQUATION.

15.16   In Exercise 15.15, what meaning attaches to R^* as far as the Vermont Department of Health is concerned?

15.17   In Exercise 15.15 the adjusted R^2 would actually be lower for five predictors than it is for three predictors. Why?

15.18   In Exercise 15.15 the 5th predictor has a very low correlation with the criterion ($r = .05$), and yet plays a significant role in the regression. Why?

15.19   For the data in Exercise 15.15, compute $\hat{Y} = 1X_2 + 1X_4 - 3X_5$. How well does this equation fit compared with the optimal equation? Why should this be?

15.20   For the data in Exercise 15.15, would it be safe to conclude that decreasing the number of mothers who fail to seek medical care before the third trimester is a good way to decrease the incidence of low-birth-weight infants?

16

Least Squares Analysis of Variance and Covariance

Objective

To show how the analysis of variance can be viewed as a special case of multiple regression; to present procedures for the treatment of unequal sample sizes; to present the analysis of covariance.

Contents

Most people tend to think of multiple regression and the analysis of variance as two totally separate statistical techniques answering two entirely different sets of questions. In fact this is not at all the case. In the first place they ask the same kind of questions, and in the second place, they return the same kind of answers, although the answers may be phrased somewhat differently. The analysis of variance tells us that three treatments (X_1, X_2, and X_3) have different means ($\bar{X}_i$). Multiple regression tells us that means ($\bar{Y}_i$) are related to treatments (X_1, X_2, and X_3), which really amounts to the same thing. Furthermore the analysis of variance produces a statistic (F) on the differences among means. The analysis of regression produces a statistic (F) on the significance of R. As we shall shortly see, these Fs are exactly equivalent.

16.1   *The General Linear Hypothesis*

General linear hypothesis

Just as the two procedures can be seen to be concerned with the same general type of question, so also are they basically the same technique. In fact the analysis of variance is a special case of multiple linear regression, which in turn is a special case of what is commonly referred to as the **general linear hypothesis**. The fact that the analysis of variance has its own formal set of equations can primarily be set down to good fortune. It happens that when certain conditions are met (as they are in the analysis of variance), the somewhat cumbersome multiple regression calculations are reduced to a few relatively simple equations. If it were not for this there might not even be a separate set of procedures called the analysis of variance.

For the student interested solely in the application of statistical techniques, a word is in order in defense of even including a chapter on this topic. Why, you may ask, should you study what amounts to a cumbersome way of doing what you already know how to do in a simple way? Ignoring the cry of "intellectual curiosity," which is something that most people are loath to *admit* that they do not possess in abundance, there are several practical (i.e., applied) answers to such a question. First of all this approach represents a relatively straightforward way of handling particular cases of unequal sample sizes. Secondly it provides us with a simple, and intuitively appealing, way of running, and especially of understanding, an analysis of covariance—which is a very clumsy technique when viewed from the more traditional approach. Lastly, and most importantly, it represents a glimpse at the direction in which statistical techniques are moving. With the greatly extended use of larger and faster computers, many of the traditional statistical techniques are giving way to what were previously impractical procedures. The increase in the popularity of multivariate analysis of variance (with all of its attendant strengths and weaknesses) is a case in point. Other examples are such techniques as discriminant analysis, cluster analysis, and that old and much abused standby, factor analysis. Unless you understand the relationship between the analysis of variance and the general linear hypothesis (as represented by multiple linear regression), and unless you understand how the data for simple analysis of variance problems can be cast in a multiple regression framework, you will find yourself in the near future using more and more techniques about which you know less and less. This is not to say that t, χ^2, F, and so on are likely to diappear, but only that other techniques will be added, opening up entirely new ways of looking at data.

In the past 15 years there have been several excellent and very readable papers on this general topic. The clearest presentation is Cohen (1968), although a paper by Overall & Spiegel (1969) is also worth seeing. Both of these papers appeared in the *Psychological Bulletin*, and are therefore readily available. Other good discussions can be found in Overall (1972), Overall & Klett (1972), Overall, Spiegel, & Cohen (1975), and Carlson & Timm (1974). Appelbaum & Cramer (1974), Cramer & Appelbaum (1980) and Howell & McConaughy (1982) provide contrasting views on the choice of the underlying model and the procedures to be followed.

The Linear Model

Consider first the traditional multiple regression problem with a criterion (Y) and three predictors (X_1, X_2, and X_3). We can write the usual model

$$Y_i = b_0 + b_1 X_{1i} + b_2 X_{2i} + b_3 X_{3i} + e_i \qquad (16.1)$$

or, in terms of *vector* notation

$$y = b_0 + b_1 x_1 + b_2 x_2 + b_3 x_3 + e \qquad (16.2)$$

where y, x_1, x_2, and x_3 are ($n \times 1$) vectors of data, e is a ($n \times 1$) vector of errors, and b_0 is a ($n \times 1$) vector whose elements are the intercept. This equation can be further reduced to

$$y = Xb + e \qquad (16.3)$$

where X is a $n \times (p + 1)$ matrix of predictors, the first column of which is 1s, and b is a $(p + 1) \times 1$ vector of regression coefficients.

Now consider the traditional model for a one-way analysis of variance.

$$Y_{ij} = \mu + \tau_j + e_{ij}. \qquad (16.4)$$

Here the symbol τ_j is simply a shorthand way of writing $\tau_1, \tau_2, \tau_3, \ldots, \tau_p$, where for any given subject we are only interested in that value of τ_j which pertains to the particular treatment in question. To see the relationship between this model and the traditional regression model (Equation 16.3), it is necessary to introduce the concept of a design matrix.

Design Matrices

Design matrix   A ***design matrix*** is a matrix of *coded*, or *dummy*, or *counter* variables representing group membership. The *complete* form the design matrix (X) will have $p+1$ columns, representing the mean (μ) and the p treatment effects. A subject is always scored 1 for μ, since μ is part of all observations. In all other columns she is scored 1 if she is a member of the treatment associated with that column, and zero otherwise. Thus for three treatments with two subjects per treatment the complete design matrix would be

$$
X = \begin{array}{c} S \\ 1 \\ 2 \\ 3 \\ 4 \\ 5 \\ 6 \end{array}
\begin{array}{cccc} \mu & A_1 & A_2 & A_3 \\ \left[\begin{array}{cccc} 1 & 1 & 0 & 0 \\ 1 & 1 & 0 & 0 \\ 1 & 0 & 1 & 0 \\ 1 & 0 & 1 & 0 \\ 1 & 0 & 0 & 1 \\ 1 & 0 & 0 & 1 \end{array}\right] \end{array}.
$$

Notice that subjects 1 and 2 (who received Treatment A_1) are scored 1 on μ and A_1, and zero on A_2 and A_3, since they did not receive those treatments. Similarly, subjects 3 and 4 are scored 1 on μ and A_2, and zero on A_1 and A_3.

We will now define the vector τ' as $[\mu \quad \tau_1 \quad \tau_2 \quad \tau_3]$. Taking X as the design matrix, Equation 16.4 (the analysis of variance model) can be written in matrix terms as

$$y = X\tau + e \tag{16.5}$$

which can be seen as being of the same form as Equation 16.3 (the traditional regression equation). Expanding Equation 16.5 we would obtain

$$
y = \begin{bmatrix} 1 & 1 & 0 & 0 \\ 1 & 1 & 0 & 0 \\ 1 & 0 & 1 & 0 \\ 1 & 0 & 1 & 0 \\ 1 & 0 & 0 & 1 \\ 1 & 0 & 0 & 1 \end{bmatrix} \times \begin{bmatrix} \mu \\ \tau_1 \\ \tau_2 \\ \tau_3 \end{bmatrix} + \begin{bmatrix} e_{11} \\ e_{21} \\ e_{12} \\ e_{22} \\ e_{13} \\ e_{23} \end{bmatrix}
$$

$$y = \qquad\qquad X \qquad\qquad \times \quad \tau \quad + \quad e$$

which produces

$$Y_{11} = \mu + \tau_1 + e_{11}$$

$$Y_{21} = \mu + \tau_1 + e_{21}$$

$$Y_{12} = \mu + \tau_2 + e_{12}$$

$$Y_{22} = \mu + \tau_2 + e_{22}$$

$$Y_{13} = \mu + \tau_3 + e_{13}$$

$$Y_{23} = \mu + \tau_3 + e_{23}.$$

For each subject we now have the model associated with her response. Thus for the second subject in Treatment 2, $Y_{22} = \mu + \tau_2 + e_{22}$, and for the ith subject in Treatment j we have $Y_{ij} = \mu + \tau_j + e_{ij}$, which is the usual analysis of variance model.

The point is that the design matrix allows us to view the analysis of variance in a multiple regression framework, in that it permits us to go from

$$Y_{ij} = \mu + \tau_j + e_{ij}$$

to

$$y = Xb + e.$$

Moreover, the elements of b are the values of $\mu, \tau_1, \tau_2, \ldots, \tau_k$. In other words these are the actual treatment effects in which we are interested.

The design matrix with which we have been working has certain technical difficulties which must be circumvented. First of all it is redundant in the sense that if we are told that a subject is not in A_1 or A_2, we know without being told that she must be in A_3. This is another way of saying that there are only 2 df for treatments. For this reason we will eliminate the column headed A_3, leaving only $a-1$ columns for the treatment effects. A second change is necessary if we want to use any computer program which obtains a multiple regression equation by way of first calculating the intercorrelation matrix. The column headed μ has no variance, and therefore can not enter into a standard multiple regression program—it would cause us to attempt division by zero. Thus it too must be eliminated. This is no real loss, since our ultimate solution will not be affected.

One further change will be made simply for the sake of allowing us to test the correct null hypotheses using the method to be later advocated for factorial designs. Since we have omitted a column dealing with the third (or ath) level of treatments, solutions given our modified design matrix would produce estimates of treatment effects in relation to $\bar{X}_3$, rather than in relation to μ. In other words, b_1 would turn out to be $(\bar{X}_1 - \bar{X}_3)$ rather than $(\bar{X}_1 - \mu)$. This problem can be eliminated, however, by a modification of the design matrix to make the mean $(\bar{X}_i)$ of each column of X equal to zero. Under this new system a subject is scored 1 in column A_i if she is a member of treatment A_i; she is scored -1 if she is a member of the ath treatment; and she is scored zero if neither of these conditions apply. (This restriction corresponds to the fixed-model analysis of variance requirement that $\Sigma\tau_i = 0$.)

These modifications have led us from

$$X = \begin{bmatrix} 1 & 1 & 0 & 0 \\ 1 & 1 & 0 & 0 \\ 1 & 0 & 1 & 0 \\ 1 & 0 & 1 & 0 \\ 1 & 0 & 0 & 1 \\ 1 & 0 & 0 & 1 \end{bmatrix} \quad \text{to} \quad \begin{bmatrix} 1 & 1 & 0 \\ 1 & 1 & 0 \\ 1 & 0 & 1 \\ 1 & 0 & 1 \\ 1 & 0 & 0 \\ 1 & 0 & 0 \end{bmatrix} \quad \text{to} \quad \begin{bmatrix} 1 & 0 \\ 1 & 0 \\ 0 & 1 \\ 0 & 1 \\ 0 & 0 \\ 0 & 0 \end{bmatrix}$$

$$\text{to} \quad \begin{bmatrix} 1 & 0 \\ 1 & 0 \\ 0 & 1 \\ 0 & 1 \\ -1 & -1 \\ -1 & -1 \end{bmatrix}.$$

While these look like major changes, in that the last form of X appears to be far removed from where we started, it actually carries all of the necessary information. We have merely eliminated redundant information, removed a constant term, and then caused the treatment effects to be given as deviations from μ.

16.2 *One-Way Analysis of Variance*

At this point a simple example is in order. Table 16.1 contains data for three subjects in each of four treatments. In part (b) of the table is the summary table for the corresponding analysis of variance, along with the value of η^2 (discussed in Chapter 11). In part (c) are the estimated treatment effects $(\hat{\tau}_i)$ where $\hat{\tau}_i = \hat{\mu}_i - \hat{\mu}$. Since the fixed model analysis of variance imposes the restriction that $\Sigma \tau_i = 0$, τ_4 is automatically defined by τ_1, τ_2, and τ_3.

Now let us approach the statistical treatment of these data by means of least squares multiple linear regression. We will take as our criterion (Y) the raw data in Table 16.1. For the predictors we will use a design matrix of the form

$$X = \begin{array}{c} \\ \textit{Treatment 1} \\ \textit{Treatment 2} \\ \textit{Treatment 3} \\ \textit{Treatment 4} \end{array} \begin{array}{ccc} \mathbf{A_1} & \mathbf{A_2} & \mathbf{A_3} \\ \begin{bmatrix} 1 & 0 & 0 \\ 0 & 1 & 0 \\ 0 & 0 & 1 \\ -1 & -1 & -1 \end{bmatrix} \end{array}$$

Here the elements of any one row are taken to apply to all of the subjects in

TABLE 16.1

Illustrative Calculations
for Simple
One-Way Design
with Equal *n*s

(*a*) Data

	TREATMENT 1	TREATMENT 2	TREATMENT 3	TREATMENT 4
	8	5	3	6
	9	7	4	4
	7	3	1	9
Means	8	5	2.667	6.333
				GM = 5.5

(*b*) Summary table

Source	df	SS	MS	F	η^2
Treatments	3	45.6667	15.222	4.46	.626
Error	8	27.3333	3.417		
Total	11	73.0000			

(*c*) Estimated
treatment effects

$$\hat{\tau}_1 = \bar{X}_1 - GM = 8.0 - 5.5 = 2.5$$

$$\hat{\tau}_2 = \bar{X}_2 - GM = 5.0 - 5.5 = -.5$$

$$\hat{\tau}_3 = \bar{X}_3 - GM = 2.67 - 5.5 = -2.83$$

that treatment. The multiple regression solution using the design matrix X as the matrix of predictors is presented in Table 16.2.

Notice the pattern of correlations in the intercorrelation matrix in Table 16.2. This type of pattern (constant off-diagonal correlations) will occur whenever there are equal numbers of subjects in the various treatments.

When we come to the vector of regression coefficients, notice that b_1 (2.50) is exactly equal to the estimated treatment effect of Treatment 1 shown in Table 16.1. In other words, $b_1 = \hat{\tau}_1$. Similarly for b_2 and b_3. This fact necessarily follows from our definition of X and τ. Moreover, if we were to test the significance of b_i, we would simultaneously have a test on the hypothesis (H_0: $\tau_i = \mu_i - \mu = 0$). Notice further than the intercept is equal to the grand mean ($\bar{Y}$). This follows directly from the fact that we scored the ath treatment as -1 on all coded variables. Using the (-1) coding, the mean of every column of $X(\bar{X}_i)$ is equal to zero, and as a result, $\Sigma b_i \bar{X}_i = 0$ and therefore $b_0 = \bar{Y} - \Sigma b_i \bar{X}_i = \bar{Y}$. This situation holds only in the case of equal ns, since otherwise $\bar{X}_i$ will not be zero for all i. However in all cases b_0 is our best estimate of μ in a least squares sense.

The value of $R^2 = .626$ is exactly equivalent to η^2, since they both estimate the percentage of variation in the dependent variable accounted for by variation among treatments. Furthermore, if we correct R^2 for shrinkage, the resulting value would be the squared ***intra-class correlation coefficient***, occasionally used as a measure of accountable variation, especially for random models where it is equivalent to $\hat{\omega}^2$.

Intra-class correlation coefficient

TABLE 16.2

Regression
Solution for Data
in Table 16.1

(a) Data

$$y = \begin{bmatrix} 8 \\ 9 \\ 7 \\ 5 \\ 7 \\ 3 \\ 3 \\ 4 \\ 1 \\ 6 \\ 4 \\ 9 \end{bmatrix} \quad X = \begin{bmatrix} 1 & 0 & 0 \\ 1 & 0 & 0 \\ 1 & 0 & 0 \\ 0 & 1 & 0 \\ 0 & 1 & 0 \\ 0 & 1 & 0 \\ 0 & 0 & 1 \\ 0 & 0 & 1 \\ 0 & 0 & 1 \\ -1 & -1 & -1 \\ -1 & -1 & -1 \\ -1 & -1 & -1 \end{bmatrix}$$

(b) Intercorrelation matrix

$$\begin{bmatrix} 1.0 & .5 & .5 \\ .5 & 1.0 & .5 \\ .5 & .5 & 1.0 \end{bmatrix}$$

(c) Regression and
correlation coefficients

$$b = \begin{bmatrix} 2.50 \\ -.50 \\ -2.833 \end{bmatrix}$$

$$b_0 = \bar{Y} - \Sigma b_i \bar{X}_i = 5.5 - 0 = 5.5$$

$$R^2 = .626$$

$$R = .791$$

If we test R for significance we have

$$F(p, N - p - 1) = \frac{R^2(N - p - 1)}{(1 - R^2)p}$$

$$F(3, 8) = \frac{.626(8)}{.374(3)} = 4.46$$

which is the same value of F we obtained in the analysis of variance.

Finally, the sum of squares for regression equals

$$SS_{regression} = SS_Y R^2 = 73(.626) = 45.6667$$

where $SS_Y = (N - 1)s_Y^2 = SS_{total}$ from the analysis of variance, and the residual sum of squares (deviation from regression) equals

$$SS_{residual} = SS_Y(1 - R^2) = 73(.374) = 27.333.$$

Notice that $SS_{regression}$ and $SS_{residual}$ are SS_{treat} and SS_{error} in the analysis of variance.

The foregoing analysis has shown the marked similarity between the analysis of variance and multiple linear regression. This is primarily an illustration of the fact that there is no important difference between asking if different treatments produce different means, and asking if means are a function of treatments. We are simply looking at two sides of the same coin.

Contrast Coding

Contrast coding

We have discussed only the most common way of forming a design matrix. There are a number of other very useful forms that this matrix could take, and for these the reader is referred to Cohen (1968). We will, however, briefly consider one important alternative coding system—**contrast coding**. If we set up the following design matrix

$$X = \begin{bmatrix} 1 & 1 & 0 \\ 1 & -1 & 0 \\ -1 & 0 & 1 \\ -1 & 0 & -1 \end{bmatrix},$$

where each row of the matrix relates to all subjects in that particular treatment group, then Column 1 would carry information on (produce the treatment effect for) the contrast between Treatments 1 and 2 and Treatments 3 and 4. Column 2 would carry information on the contrast of Treatment 1 versus Treatment 2, and Column 3 would carry information on the contrast of Treatment 3 versus Treatment 4. If we have equal sample sizes, the tests on the b_i will be equivalent to the tests on the corresponding orthogonal contrasts. Thus to say that b_1 is significantly different from 0 is to say that Treatments 1 and 2 differ from Treatments 3 and 4. Whether or not we have equal ns, the overall test on R^2 is equivalent to the overall F in the analysis of variance. Students who have computer facilities available are encouraged to apply this design matrix to the sample data in Table 16.1.

16.3 *Factorial Designs*

We can readily extend the analysis of regression to two-way and higher order factorial designs, and doing so illustrates some important features of both the analysis of variance and the analysis of regression. We will consider first a two-way analysis of variance with equal ns.

The Full Model

The most common model for a two-way analysis of variance is

$$Y_{ijk} = \mu + \alpha_i + \beta_j + \alpha\beta_{ij} + e_{ijk}$$

As we did before we can expand the α_i and β_i terms by use of a design matrix, but the question then arises as to how the interaction term is to be handled. The answer quite simply relies on the fact that an interaction represents a multiplicative effect of the component variables. Suppose we consider the simplest case of a 2×2 factorial design. Letting the entries in each row represent the coefficients for all subjects in the corresponding cell of the design, we can write our design matrix as

$$
X = \begin{array}{c} \\ a_1b_1 \\ a_1b_2 \\ a_2b_1 \\ a_2b_2 \end{array}
\begin{array}{ccc} A_1 & B_1 & AB_{11} \\ \left[\begin{array}{ccc} 1 & 1 & 1 \\ 1 & -1 & -1 \\ -1 & 1 & -1 \\ -1 & -1 & 1 \end{array}\right] \end{array}
$$

The first column represents the main effect of A, and distinguishes between those subjects who received A_1 and those who received A_2. The next column represents the main effect of B, separating B_1 subjects from B_2 subjects. The third column is the interaction of A and B. Its elements are obtained by multiplying corresponding elements of Columns 1 and 2. Thus $1 = 1 \times 1$, $-1 = 1 \times -1$, $-1 = -1 \times 1$, and $1 = -1 \times -1$. Once again we have as many columns per effect as we have degrees of freedom for that effect. We have no entries of zero simply because with only two levels of each variable a subject must either be in the first or last level.

Now consider the case of a 2×3 factorial. With two levels of A and three levels of B, we will have $\mathrm{df}_A = 1$, $\mathrm{df}_B = 2$, and $\mathrm{df}_{AB} = 2$. This means that our design matrix will require one column for A and two columns each for B and AB. This leads to the following matrix.

$$
X = \begin{array}{c} \\ a_1b_1 \\ a_1b_2 \\ a_1b_3 \\ a_2b_1 \\ a_2b_2 \\ a_2b_3 \end{array}
\begin{array}{ccccc} A_1 & B_1 & B_2 & AB_{11} & AB_{12} \\ \left[\begin{array}{ccccc} 1 & 1 & 0 & 1 & 0 \\ 1 & 0 & 1 & 0 & 1 \\ 1 & -1 & -1 & -1 & -1 \\ -1 & 1 & 0 & -1 & 0 \\ -1 & 0 & 1 & 0 & -1 \\ -1 & -1 & -1 & 1 & 1 \end{array}\right] \end{array}.
$$

Column A_1 distinguishes between those subjects who are in treatment level A_1 and those in treatment level A_2. Column 2 distinguishes level B_1 subjects from those who are not in B_1, while Column 3 does the same for level B_2. Once again subjects in the first $a - 1$ and first $b - 1$ treatment levels are scored 1 or 0 depending upon whether or not they served in the treatment level in question. Subjects in the ath or bth treatment level are scored -1 for each column related to that treatment effect. The column labelled AB_{11} is simply the product of columns A_1 and B_1, while AB_{12} is the product of A_1 and B_2.

The analysis for a factorial design is somewhat more cumbersome than for a simple one-way design, since we wish to test two or more main effects and one or more interaction effects. However if we consider the relatively simple case of a two-way factorial, the reader should have no difficulty in generalizing to more complex factorial designs. The basic principles are the same—only the arithmetic is messier.

As an illustration we will consider the case of a 2×4 factorial with four subjects per cell. Such a design is analyzed by the conventional analysis of variance in Table 16.3, which also includes means, estimated effects, and values of η^2. From the summary table it is apparent that the main effect of B is significant, but that the effects of A and AB are not.

TABLE 16.3
Sample Data and Summary Table for 2×4 Factorial Design

(a) Data

		B_1	B_2	B_3	B_4	*Means*
A_1		5	2	8	11	
		7	5	11	15	
		9	7	12	16	
		8	3	14	10	8.93750
A_2		7	3	9	11	
		9	8	12	14	
		10	9	14	10	
		9	11	8	12	9.75000
Means		8.000	6.000	11.000	12.375	9.34375

(b) Summary table

Source	df	SS	MS	*F*	η^2
A	1	5.282	5.282	<1	.014
B	3	199.344	66.448	11.452*	.536
AB	3	27.343	9.114	1.571	.074
Error	24	139.250	5.802		
Total	31	371.219			

* $p < .05$.

(c) Estimated treatment effects

$\hat{\mu} = GM = 9.34375$

$\hat{\alpha}_1 = \bar{A}_1 - GM = 8.9375 - 9.34375 = -.40625$

$\hat{\beta}_1 = \bar{B}_1 - GM = 8.0000 - 9.34375 = -1.34375$

$\hat{\beta}_2 = \bar{B}_2 - GM = 6.0000 - 9.34375 = -3.34375$

$\hat{\beta}_3 = \bar{B}_3 - GM = 11.0000 - 9.34375 = 1.65625$

$\widehat{\alpha\beta}_{11} = \overline{AB}_{11} - \bar{A}_1 - \bar{B}_1 + GM = 7.25 - 8.9375 - 8.0000 + 9.34375 = -.34375$

$\widehat{\alpha\beta}_{12} = \overline{AB}_{12} - \bar{A}_1 - \bar{B}_2 + GM = 4.25 - 8.9375 - 6.000 + 9.34375 = -1.34375$

$\widehat{\alpha\beta}_{13} = \overline{AB}_{13} - \bar{A}_1 - \bar{B}_3 + GM = 11.25 - 8.9365 - 11.0000 + 9.34375 = .65625$

To analyze these data from the point of view of multiple regression we begin with the following design matrix, where once again the elements of each row apply to all subjects in the corresponding treatment combination.

$$
X = \begin{array}{c}
 \\
a_1b_1 \\
a_1b_2 \\
a_1b_3 \\
a_1b_4 \\
a_2b_1 \\
a_2b_2 \\
a_2b_3 \\
a_2b_4
\end{array}
\begin{array}{ccccccc}
A_1 & B_1 & B_2 & B_3 & AB_{11} & AB_{12} & AB_{13} \\
\left[\begin{array}{ccccccc}
1 & 1 & 0 & 0 & 1 & 0 & 0 \\
1 & 0 & 1 & 0 & 0 & 1 & 0 \\
1 & 0 & 0 & 1 & 0 & 0 & 1 \\
1 & -1 & -1 & -1 & -1 & -1 & -1 \\
-1 & 1 & 0 & 0 & -1 & 0 & 0 \\
-1 & 0 & 1 & 0 & 0 & -1 & 0 \\
-1 & 0 & 0 & 1 & 0 & 0 & -1 \\
-1 & -1 & -1 & -1 & 1 & 1 & 1
\end{array}\right]
\end{array}
$$

The first step in a multiple regression analysis is presented in Table 16.4 using all seven predictors (A_1 to AB_{13}). The results have been reported to two or three decimal places, although the calculations were carried to eight significant digits. (This is true of all tables and equations in this chapter.)

TABLE 16.4

Regression Solution Using All Predictors for Data in Table 16.3

(a) Intercorrelation matrix (**R**)

	A_1	B_1	B_2	B_3	AB_{11}	AB_{12}	AB_{13}
A_1	1.00	0	0	0	0	0	0
B_1	0	1.00	.50	.50	0	0	0
B_2	0	.50	1.00	.50	0	0	0
B_3	0	.50	.50	1.00	0	0	0
AB_{11}	0	0	0	0	1.00	.50	.50
AB_{12}	0	0	0	0	.50	1.00	.50
AB_{13}	0	0	0	0	.50	.50	1.00

(b) Regression results

$b' = [9.34 \quad -.41 \quad -1.34 \quad -3.34 \quad 1.66 \quad -.34 \quad -1.34 \quad .66]$

$R^2 = .625$

$R = .790$

$SS_{regression} = SS_Y(R^2) = (371.219)(.625) = 231.969$

$SS_{residual} = SS_Y(1 - R^2) = (371.219)(.375) = 139.250$

(c) Summary table for the analysis of variance for regression

Source	df	SS	MS	F
Regression	7	231.969	33.138	5.711*
Residual	24	139.250	5.802	
Total	31	371.219		

* $p < .05$.

There are several important features of Table 16.4. First of all consider the matrix $\boldsymbol{R}$. Suppose that we simplify this matrix by defining the following sets of predictors: $A' = [A_1]$, $B' = [B_1, B_2, B_3]$ and $AB' = [AB_{11}, AB_{12}, \text{ and } AB_{13}]$. If we then rewrite the intercorrelation matrix we have

$$
\begin{array}{c c c c}
 & A' & B' & AB' \\
A' & \begin{bmatrix} 1.00 & .00 & .00 \\ B' & .00 & 1.00 & .00 \\ AB' & .00 & .00 & 1.00 \end{bmatrix}
\end{array}.
$$

Notice that each of the effects is independent of the others. Such a pattern occurs only if there are equal numbers of subjects in each cell, and is what makes simplified formulae for the analysis of variance possible. The fact that this structure disappears in the case of unequal ns is what makes our life more difficult when we have missing subjects.

Next notice the vector $\boldsymbol{b}'$. The first entry (b_0) is the grand mean, and the subsequent entries ($b_1, \dots, b_7$) are the estimates of the corresponding treatment effects. Thus $b_1 = \hat{\alpha}_1$, $b_2 = \hat{\beta}_1$, and so on. Tests on these regression coefficients, which are not shown, would represent tests on the corresponding treatment effects. The fact that we have only the $(a-1)(b-1) = 3$ interaction effects presents no problem, due to the restriction that these effects must sum to zero across rows and down columns. Thus if $\alpha\beta_{12} = -1.34$, then $\alpha\beta_{22}$ must be $+1.34$. Similarly, $\alpha\beta_{14} = 0 - \Sigma\alpha\beta_{1j} = -\Sigma\alpha\beta_{1j} = 1.03125$.

The value of $R^2 = .625$ represents the percentage of variation which can be accounted for by all of the variables simultaneously. With equal ns, and therefore independent effects, it is equivalent to $\eta_A^2 + \eta_B^2 + \eta_{AB}^2$. The test on R^2 produces an F of 5.711 on 7 and 24 df, which, since it is significant ($p < .05$), shows that there is a non-chance relationship between the treatment variables and the dependent variable (Y).

Two more parallels can be drawn between Tables 16.3 and 16.4. First of all notice that $SS_{\text{regression}} = SS_Y(R^2) = 231.969$. This is the variation which can be predicted by a linear combination of the predictors. This value is equal to $SS_A + SS_B + SS_{AB}$, although from Table 16.4 we can not yet partition the variation among the separate sources. Finally notice that $SS_{\text{residual}} = SS_Y(1 - R^2) = 139.250$, which is the error sum of squares in the analysis of variance. This makes sense when you recall that error is the variation which can not be attributed to the separate or joint effects of the treatment variables.

Reduced Models

At this point we know only the amount of variation which can be accounted for by all of the predictors simultaneously. What we wish to know is how this variation can be partitioned among A, B, and AB. This information can be readily obtained by the computation of several reduced regression equations.

Since in the subsequent course of the analysis we must compute several multiple correlation coefficients relating to the different effects, we will change our notational system and use the ***effect labels*** (α, β, and $\alpha\beta$) as subscripts. For the multiple regression just computed, the model contained variables to account for α, β, and $\alpha\beta$. Thus we will designate the correlation coefficient (squared) as $R^2_{\alpha,\beta,\alpha\beta}$. If we dropped the last three predictors (AB_{11}, AB_{12}, and AB_{13}) we would be deleting those predictors carrying information concerning the interaction, but would retain those predictors concerned with α and β. Thus we would use the designation $R^2_{\alpha,\beta}$. If we used only A, AB_{11}, AB_{12}, and AB_{13} as predictors, the model would only account for α and $\alpha\beta$, and the resulting R^2 would be denoted $R^2_{\alpha,\alpha\beta}$.

Effect labels (α, β, $\alpha\beta$)

For our particular example,

$$R^2_{\alpha,\beta,\alpha\beta} = R^2_{0.1234567}$$

$$R^2_{\alpha,\beta} = R^2_{0.1234}$$

$$R^2_{\alpha,\alpha\beta} = R^2_{0.1567}$$

$$R^2_{\beta,\alpha\beta} = R^2_{0.234567}.$$

The left-hand side of these equations represents a conventional notational system for the least squares analysis of variance.

If the interaction term accounts for any of the variation, then removing the interaction predictors from the model should lead to a decrease in accountable variation. This decrease will be equal to that variation which can be attributable to the interaction. By this reasoning,

$$SS_{AB} = SS_{reg_{\alpha,\beta,\alpha\beta}} - SS_{reg_{\alpha,\beta}} = SS_Y(R^2_{\alpha,\beta,\alpha\beta}) - SS_Y(R^2_{\alpha,\beta})$$

where $SS_{reg_{\alpha,\beta,\alpha\beta}}$ represents the sum of squares for regression using all predictors. A similar line of reasoning holds for SS_A and SS_B. Thus

$$SS_A = SS_{reg_{\alpha,\beta,\alpha\beta}} - SS_{reg_{\beta,\alpha\beta}} = SS_Y(R^2_{\alpha,\beta,\alpha\beta}) - SS_Y(R^2_{\beta,\alpha\beta})$$

$$SS_B = SS_{reg_{\alpha,\beta,\alpha\beta}} - SS_{reg_{\alpha,\alpha\beta}} = SS_Y(R^2_{\alpha,\beta,\alpha\beta}) - SS_Y(R^2_{\alpha,\alpha\beta}).$$

The relevant calculations are presented in Table 16.5, although the calculations of the individual R^2s have been omitted. Students with access to a computer are urged to reproduce these results starting with the raw data.

Looking first at the AB interactions we see from Table 16.5 that when the interaction terms were deleted from the model the proportion of accountable variation dropped from .625 to .551. This is a decrease of .074, which equals η^2_{AB} in Table 16.3. In terms of accountable variation, omitting the interaction terms produced a decrement of

$$SS_Y(R^2_{\alpha,\beta,\alpha\beta}) - SS_Y(R^2_{\alpha,\beta}) = 231.969 - 204.625 = 27.343$$

units of variation. This decrement can only be attributable to the predictive

TABLE 16.5

Regression Solution
for Data in
Table 16.3

$R^2_{\alpha,\beta,\alpha\beta} = .625$

$SS_{reg_{\alpha,\beta,\alpha\beta}} = SS_Y(R^2_{\alpha,\beta,\alpha\beta}) = 231.969$

$SS_{residual} = SS_Y(1 - R^2) = 139.250$

$R^2_{\alpha,\beta} = .551$

$SS_{reg_{\alpha,\beta}} = SS_Y(R^2_{\alpha,\beta}) = 204.625$

$R^2_{\beta,\alpha\beta} = .611$

$SS_{reg_{\beta,\alpha\beta}} = SS_Y(R^2_{\beta,\alpha\beta}) = 226.687$

$R^2_{\alpha,\alpha\beta} = .088$

$SS_{reg_{\alpha,\alpha\beta}} = SS_Y(R^2_{\alpha,\alpha\beta}) = 32.625$

SUMMARY TABLE

Source	df	SS	MS	F
A	1	5.282	5.282	<1
B	3	199.344	66.448	11.452*
AB	3	27.343	9.114	1.571
Error	24	139.250	5.802	
Total	31	371.219		

* $p < .05.$

value of the interaction terms, and therefore

$$SS_{AB} = 27.343.$$

By a similar line of reasoning we can find the other sums of squares given in the summary table. Thus

$$SS_A = 231.969 - 226.687 = 5.282$$

$$SS_B = 231.969 - 32.625 = 199.344.$$

Notice that these values agree exactly with those obtained by the more traditional procedures. Notice also that the corresponding decrements in R^2 agree with the computed values of η^2.

Completely equivalent tests on the main effects and interaction can be made by testing the decrement in R^2 (rather than SS_{reg}) resulting from the deletion of a set of predictors. Thus using the test statistic

$$F(f - r, N - f - 1) = \frac{(R^2_f - R^2_r)(N - f - 1)}{(1 - R^2_f)(f - r)}$$

where f and r are the number of predictors in the full and reduced models, respectively, we obtain

$$F_A(1, 24) = \frac{(.625 - .611)(24)}{(.375)(1)} = .911$$

$$F_B(3, 24) = \frac{(.625 - .088)(24)}{(.375)(3)} = 11.452$$

$$F_{AB}(3, 24) = \frac{(.625 - .551)(24)}{(.375)(3)} = 1.571.$$

These are the same values of F obtained by the more traditional procedures.

As Overall & Spiegel (1969) point out, the approach which we have taken in testing the effects of A, B, and AB is not the only one we could have chosen. They present two alternative models which might have been considered in place of this one. Fortunately, however, the different models all lead to the same conclusions in the case of equal sample sizes, since in this situation effects are independent of one another and therefore additive. When we come to the case of unequal sample sizes, however, the choice of an underlying model will require careful consideration.

16.4 *Analysis of Variance with Unequal Sample Sizes*

The least squares approach to the analysis of variance is particularly useful for the case of factorial experiments with unequal sample sizes. However special care must be used in selecting the particular restricted models which are employed in generating the various sums of squares.

There are several different models which could underlie an analysis of variance. In the case of equal sample sizes these models all lead to exactly the same results, but in the unequal n case they do not. This stems from the fact that with unequal ns the row, column, and interaction effects are no longer orthogonal, and thus account for overlapping portions of the variance. Consider the following Venn diagram. The area enclosed by the surrounding square will be taken to represent SS_{total}. Each of the circles represents the variation attributable to (or accounted for by) one of the effects. The area outside of the circles but within the square represents SS_{error}. Finally, the total area enclosed by the circles represents $SS_Y(R^2_{\alpha,\beta,\alpha\beta})$—i.e., the sum of squares for regression when all of the terms are included in the model. If we have equal sample sizes none of the circles would overlap, and each effect would be accounting for a separate, independent, portion of the variation. In that case the decrease in $SS_{regression}$ resulting from deletion of an effect from the model has a clear interpretation—it is

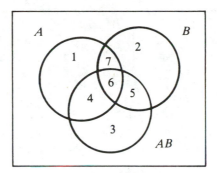

the area enclosed by the omitted circle and is thus the sum of squares for the corresponding effect.

But what do we do when the circles overlap? If we were to take a model which included terms for A, B, and AB and compared it to a model containing only A and B terms, the decrement would not represent the area of the AB circle, since some of that area is still accounted for by A and/or B. Thus SS_{AB}, which we calculate as $SS_Y(R^2_{\alpha,\beta,\alpha\beta}) - SS_Y(R^2_{\alpha,\beta})$, represents only that portion of the enclosed area which is *unique* to AB—the area labelled with a "*3*". So far, all of the models which have seriously been proposed are in agreement. SS_{AB} is that portion of the AB circle remaining after adjusting for A and B.

But now things begin to get a little sticky. Two major approaches have been put forth which differ in the way the remainder of the pie is allotted to A and B. These are Methods I and II of Overall & Spiegel (1969) and have generated a voluminous literature debating their proper use and interpretation. Basically the choice between them hinges on how we see the relationship between the sample size and the treatments themselves, or, more specifically, how we want to weight the various cell means to produce row and column means. Before exploring that issue, however, we must first examine the competing methods.

Method I   ***Method I*** is the method we have already used in the preceding section. In this case each effect is adjusted for all other effects. Thus we obtain SS_{AB} as $SS_Y(R^2_{\alpha,\beta,\alpha\beta} - R^2_{\alpha,\beta})$, SS_A as $SS_Y(R^2_{\alpha,\beta,\alpha\beta} - R^2_{\beta,\alpha\beta})$ and SS_B as $SS_Y(R^2_{\alpha,\beta,\alpha\beta} - R^2_{\alpha,\alpha\beta})$. In terms of the previous diagram, each effect is defined as that part of the area which is unique to that effect. Thus SS_A is represented by area "1," SS_B by area "2," and SS_{AB} by area "3."

Method II   ***Method II***, on the other hand, breaks the pie up differently. We continue to define SS_{AB} as area "3." But now that we have taken care of the interaction, we still have areas "1," "2," "4," "5," "6," and "7" which can be accounted for by the effects of A and/or B. Method II essentially redefines the full model as $R^2_{\alpha,\beta}$ and obtains $SS_A = SS_Y(R^2_{\alpha,\beta} - R^2_\beta)$ and $SS_B = SS_Y(R^2_{\alpha,\beta} - R^2_\alpha)$. Thus A is allotted areas "1" and "4" while B is allotted areas "2" and "5." Methods I and II are summarized in Table 16.6.

TABLE 16.6
Alternative Models
for Solution of
Nonorthogonal
Designs

METHOD I

$Y_{ijk} = \mu + \alpha_i + \beta_j + \alpha\beta_{ij} + e_{ijk}$

Source	df	SS
A	$a-1$	$SS_Y(R^2_{\alpha,\beta,\alpha\beta} - R^2_{\beta,\alpha\beta})$
B	$b-1$	$SS_Y(R^2_{\alpha,\beta,\alpha\beta} - R^2_{\alpha,\alpha\beta})$
AB	$(a-1)(b-1)$	$SS_Y(R^2_{\alpha,\beta,\alpha\beta} - R^2_{\alpha,\beta})$
Error	$N-ab$	$SS_Y(1 - R^2_{\alpha,\beta,\alpha\beta})$
Total	$N-1$	SS_Y

METHOD II

$Y_{ijk} = \mu + \alpha_i + \beta_j + \alpha\beta_{ij} + e_{ijk}$ and $Y_{ijk} = \mu + \alpha_i + \beta_j + e_{ijk}$

Source	df	SS
A	$a-1$	$SS_Y(R^2_{\alpha,\beta} - R^2_{\beta})$
B	$b-1$	$SS_Y(R^2_{\alpha,\beta} - R^2_{\alpha})$
AB	$(a-1)(b-1)$	$SS_Y(R^2_{\alpha,\beta,\alpha\beta} - R^2_{\alpha,\beta})$
Error	$N-ab$	$SS_Y(1 - R^2_{\alpha,\beta,\alpha\beta})$
Total	$N-1$	SS_Y

Both of these methods make a certain amount of sense when viewed from the point of view of the Venn diagram. However the diagram is only a crude approximation and we have pushed it about as far as we can go.†

As Carlson & Timm (1974) have shown, a more appropriate way to compare the models is to examine the hypotheses they test. They point out that Method I represents an estimation of treatment effects when cell means are weighted equally, and is particularly appropriate whenever we consider sample size to be independent of treatment conditions. A convincing demonstration of this is found in Overall, Spiegel, & Cohen (1975). Carlson and Timm have also shown that Method II produces estimates of treatment effects when row and column means are weighted by the sample sizes, but only when there is no interaction present. When an interaction is present, simple estimates of row and column effects can not be made, and, in fact, the null hypotheses actually tested are very bizarre indeed (cf. Carlson & Timm, 1974, for a statement of H_0). In that event, Winer (1971) who seems to prefer Method II, falls back upon Method I, although in fact that method represents an equal weighting of cell means. An excellent discussion of the hypotheses tested by different approaches can be found in Blair & Higgins (1978) and Blair (1978). As Cochran & Cox (1957) have suggested, "the only complete solution of the 'missing data' problem is not to have them" (p. 82).

† From this dicsussion you could easily get the impression that Method II will always account for more of the variation than Method I. This is not necessarily the case, since the degree of overlap represents the correlation between effects and suppressor relationships might appear as "black holes," cancelling out accountable variation.

Howell & McConaughy (1982) have argued that there are very few instances in which one would desire to test the peculiar null hypothesis tested by Method II. The debate over the "correct" model will probably continue for some time, mainly because no one model is universally "correct," and because there are philosophical differences in the approaches to model specification (cf. Howell & McConaughy (1982) and Lewis & Keren (1977) vs. Appelbaum & Cramer (1974) and O'Brien (1976)). However the conclusion to be drawn from the literature at present is that for the most common situations Method I is appropriate. This is the method employed by BMDP2V and by SPSS-option 9. It is also the method which is approximated by the *unweighted means solution* discussed in Chapter 13.

We will take as an illustration the data used in the previous example, but with the addition of four scores to produce unequal cell sizes. These are the same data analyzed by way of the unweighted means solution in Table 13.12. The data are given in Table 16.7, along with the unweighted and weighted row and column means and the values resulting from the various

TABLE 16.7

Illustrative Calculations for Nonorthogonal Factorial Design

	B_1	B_2	B_3	B_4	Unweighted mean	Weighted mean
A_1	5	2	8	11		
	7	5	11	15		
	9	7	12	16	8.975	8.944
	8	3	14	10		
		9		9		
A_2	7	3	9	11		
	9	8	12	14		
	10	9	14	10	9.625	9.778
	9	11	8	12		
			7	13		
Unweighted mean	8.00	6.475	10.625	12.1		
Weighted mean	8.00	6.333	10.556	12.1		

FULL MODEL: $R^2_{\alpha,\beta,\alpha\beta} = .532$

$$SS_{\text{regression}} = SS_Y(R^2_{\alpha,\beta,\alpha\beta}) = 390.30559(.532) = 207.7055$$

$$SS_{\text{residual}} = SS_Y(1 - R^2_{\alpha,\beta,\alpha\beta}) = 390.30559(1 - .532) = 182.600$$

REDUCED MODEL: $R^2_{\alpha,\beta} = .483$

$$SS_{\text{regression}} = SS_Y(R^2_{\alpha,\beta}) = 390.30559(.483) = 188.430$$

$$R^2_{\beta,\alpha\beta} = .523$$

$$SS_{\text{regression}} = SS_Y(R^2_{\beta,\alpha\beta}) = 203.9500$$

$$R^2_{\alpha,\alpha\beta} = .076$$

$$SS_{\text{regression}} = SS_Y(R^2_{\alpha,\alpha\beta}) = 29.7499$$

regression solutions. The unweighted means are the mean of means (e.g., the mean of row_1 is the mean of the four cell means in that row). The weighted mean of row_1, for example, is really just the sum of the scores in row_1 divided by the number of scores in row_1.

An SPSS regression program might help to summarize the computations required to run this analysis and illustrate the ease with which the analysis can be carried out. Such a program is given below.

```
RUN NAME          ANALYSIS OF DATA IN TABLE 16.7
VARIABLE LIST     Y,A1,B1,B2,B3,AB11,AB12,AB13
INPUT FORMAT      FIXED(8F3.0)
INPUT MEDIUM      DATA.DAT
N OF CASES        36
REGRESSION        VARIABLES = Y TO AB13/
                  REGRESSION = Y WITH A1 TO AB13(2)/
                  REGRESSION = Y WITH A1 TO B3(2)/
                  REGRESSION = Y WITH B1 TO AB13(2)/
                  REGRESSION = Y WITH A1,AB11 TO AB13(2)/
FINISH
```

From Table 16.7 we see that $R^2_{\alpha,\beta,\alpha\beta} = .532$, indicating that approximately 53% of the variation can be accounted for by a linear combination of the predictor variables. We do not know, however, how this variation is to be distributed among A, B, and AB. For that we need to form and calculate the reduced models.

Testing the Interaction Effects

First of all we delete the predictors associated with the interaction term, and calculate $R^2_{\alpha,\beta}$. For these data $R^2_{\alpha,\beta} = .483$, representing a drop in R^2 of about .05. If we examine the predictable sum of squares ($SS_{\text{regression}}$) we see that eliminating the interaction terms has produced a decrement in $SS_{\text{regression}}$ of

$$SS_Y(R^2_{\alpha,\beta,\alpha\beta}) = 207.7055$$
$$-SS_Y(R^2_{\alpha,\beta}) = 188.4301$$
$$SS_{AB} = \overline{19.2754}$$

This decrement is the sum of squares attributable to the AB interaction (SS_{AB}).

In the case of unequal ns it is particularly important to understand what this term represents.

$$SS_{AB} = SS_Y(R^2_{\alpha,\beta,\alpha\beta}) - SS_Y(R^2_{\alpha,\beta})$$
$$= SS_Y(R^2_{\alpha,\beta,\alpha\beta} - R^2_{\alpha,\beta})$$
$$= SS_Y(R^2_{0(\alpha\beta.\alpha,\beta)}) \tag{16.6}$$

The term in parentheses in Equation 16.6 is the squared semi-partial correlation between the criterion and the interaction effects, partialling out (adjusting for) the effects of A and B. In other words it is the squared correlation between the criterion and that part of the AB interaction which is orthogonal to A and B. Thus we can think of SS_{AB} as really being $SS_{AB(adj)}$, where the adjustment is for the effects of A and B. (In the equal n case the issue does not arise because A, B, and AB are independent, and therefore there is no overlapping variation to partial out.)†

Testing the Main Effects

Since we are using Overall and Spiegel's Method I, we will calculate the main effects of A and B in a way which is directly comparable to our estimation of the interaction effect. Here each main effect represents the sum of squares attributable to that variable after partialling out the other main effect and the interaction.

To obtain SS_A we will delete the predictor associated with the main effect of A and calculate $R^2_{\beta,\alpha\beta}$. For these data $R^2_{\beta,\alpha\beta} = .523$, producing a drop in R^2 of $.532 - .523 = .009$. In terms of the predictable sum of squares ($SS_{regression}$), the elimination of α from the model produces a decrement in $SS_{regression}$ of

$$
\begin{aligned}
SS_Y(R^2_{\alpha,\beta,\alpha\beta}) &= 207.7055 \\
-SS_Y(R^2_{\beta,\alpha\beta}) &= \underline{203.9500} \\
SS_A &= 3.7555
\end{aligned}
$$

This decrement is the sum of squares attributable to the main effect of A.

By the same reasoning we can obtain SS_B by comparing $SS_{regression}$ for the full model and for a model omitting β.

---

† Some people have trouble with concept of non-independent treatment effects, and perhaps an extreme example will help point out how a row effect could cause an *apparent* column effect, or vice versa. Consider the following two-way table. Are we looking at a difference due to A, B, or AB?

	B_1	B_2	*Means*
A_1	$\bar{X} = 10$, $n = 20$	$n = 0$	10
A_2	$n = 0$	$\bar{X} = 30$, $n = 20$	30
Means	10	30	

$$SS_Y(R^2_{\alpha,\beta,\alpha\beta}) = 207.7055$$
$$-SS_Y(R^2_{\alpha,\alpha\beta}) = \underline{29.7499}$$
$$SS_B = 177.9556$$

These results are summarized in Table 16.8 along with the method by which they were obtained. You will note that the sums of squares do not sum to SS_{total}. This is as it should be since the overlapping portions of accountable variation (i.e., segments "4," "5," "6," and "7" of our Venn diagram) are not represented anywhere. You will also note that SS_{error} is taken as the $SS_{residual}$ from the full model, just as in the case of equal sample sizes. Here again we define SS_{error} as that portion of the total variation which can not be explained by any one or more of the independent variables.

TABLE 16.8

Calculation of Sums of Squares Using Model I

	MODEL I	
Source	**df**	**SS**
A	$a-1$	$SS_Y(R^2_{\alpha,\beta,\alpha\beta} - R^2_{\beta,\alpha\beta})$
B	$b-1$	$SS_Y(R^2_{\alpha,\beta,\alpha\beta} - R^2_{\alpha,\alpha\beta})$
AB	$(a-1)(b-1)$	$SS_Y(R^2_{\alpha,\beta,\alpha\beta} - R^2_{\alpha,\beta})$
Error	$N-ab$	$SS_Y(1 - R^2_{\alpha,\beta,\alpha\beta})$
Total	$N-1$	SS_Y

SUMMARY TABLE FOR ANALYSIS OF VARIANCE				
Source	**df**	**SS**	**MS**	**F**
A	1	3.7555	3.7555	<1
B	3	177.9556	59.3185	9.10
AB	3	19.2754	6.4251	<1
Error	28	182.6001	6.5214	
Total	35	(390.3056)		

You should compare the results in Table 16.8 with those in Table 13.12 (the unweighted means solution). The differences are relatively small, since the results in Table 13.12 are intended to estimate the more accurate results given in Table 16.8.

16.5   The One-Way Analysis of Covariance

Analysis of covariance

An extremely useful tool in the analysis of experimental data is the ***analysis of covariance***. As normally presented within the context of the analysis of variance, the analysis of covariance appears to be unpleasantly cumbersome, especially so when there is more than one covariate. Within the framework of multiple regression, however, it is remarkably simple, requiring little, if any, more work than the analysis of variance.

Suppose that we wish to compare driving proficiency on three different sizes of cars to test the experimental hypothesis that small cars are easier to handle. We have available three different groups of drivers, but we are not able to match individual subjects on driving experience, which varies considerably within each group. Let us make the simplifying assumption, which will be discussed in more detail later, that the mean level of driving experience is equal across groups. Suppose further that using the number of steering errors as our dependent variable, we obtain the somewhat exaggerated data plotted in Figure 16.1. In this figure the data have been plotted separately for each group (size of car), as a function of driving *Covariate* experience (**the covariate**), and the separate regression lines have been superimposed.

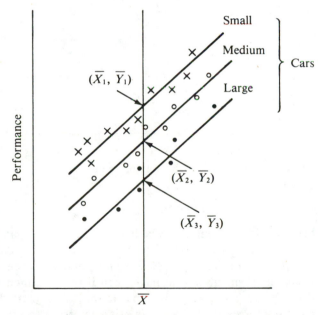

FIGURE 16.1

Hypothetical data illustrating error-reduction in analysis of covariance

One of the most striking things about Figure 16.1 is the very large variability in both performance and experience within each treatment. This variability is so great that an analysis of variance on performance scores would almost certainly fail to produce a significant effect. However most of the variability in performance is directly attributable to differences in driving experience, which has nothing to do with what we wish to study. If we could somehow remove (partial out) that variance which can be attributable to experience (the covariate), we would have a clearer test of our original hypothesis. This is exactly what the analysis of covariance is designed to do, and this is precisely the situation in which it does its job best—its job in this case being to reduce the error term.

A somewhat more controversial use of the analysis of covariance concerns situations in which the treatment groups have different covariate (driving experience) means. Such a situation (using the same hypothetical experiment) is depicted in Figure 16.2, where two of the treatments have

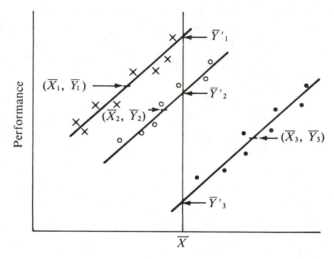

FIGURE 16.2

Hypothetical data illustrating mean-adjustment in analysis of covariance

been displaced along the X axis. At the point at which the three regression lines intersect the vertical line $X = \bar{X}$, can be seen the values $\bar{Y}'_1$, $\bar{Y}'_2$, and

Adjusted Y means $\bar{Y}'_3$. These are the ***adjusted Y means***, and represent our best guess as to what the Y means would have been if the treatments had not differed on the covariate. The analysis of covariance then tests whether these adjusted means differ significantly, again using an error term from which the variance attributable to the covariate has been partialled out.

Although the structure and procedures of the analysis of covariance are the same regardless of whether or not the treatment groups differ on the covariate means, the different ways of visualizing the problem as represented in Figures 16.1 and 16.2 are instructive. In the first case we are simply reducing the error term. In the second case we are both reducing the error term *and* adjusting the means on the dependent variable. We will have more to say on this problem later in the chapter.

Assumptions of the Analysis of Covariance

Homogeneity of regression

Aside from the usual analysis of variance assumptions of normality and homogeneity of variance, we must add two more assumptions. We will assume that whatever the relationship between Y and the covariate (C), this relationship is linear.[†] Secondly we will assume *homogeneity of regression* (i.e. that the regression coefficients are equal across treatments—$b_1^* = b_2^* = b_3^* = \cdots = b^*$). This is merely the assumption that the three lines in Figure 16.1 or 16.2 are parallel. This assumption is necessary to justify our substitution of one regression line (the pooled within-groups regression line) for the separate regression lines. As we shall shortly see, this assumption is testable. Note that no assumption has been made about the nature of the covariate; it may be either a fixed or a random variable.

[handwritten: covariate]

[handwritten: $Y_{ij} = \beta_0 + \beta_1 X_{ij} + T_j + e_{ij}$]

Calculation of the Analysis of Covariance

When viewed within the framework of multiple regression, the analysis of covariance is basically no different from the analysis of variance, except that we wish to partial out the effects of the covariate. As Cohen (1968) has put it, "A covariate is, after all, nothing but an independent variable which, because of the logic dictated by the substantive issues of the research, assumes priority among the set of independent variables as a basis for accounting for Y variance." (p.439)

If we want to ask about the variation in Y after the covariate (C) has been partialled out, and if variation in Y can only be associated with C, the treatment effect (α), and error, then $R_{c,\alpha}^2$ represents the total percentage of accountable variation. If we now compare $R_{c,\alpha}^2$ with R_c^2, the difference will be the variation attributable to treatment effects *over and above* that attributable to the covariate.

We will take as an example one given by Winer (1971, pp. 776 ff.), since this offers the student the opportunity to compare the present approach with the more traditional method of calculation which Winer follows. The data and the design matrix are presented in Table 16.9. In the design matrix only the first and last subject in each group is represented. Columns 4 and 5 of X represent the interaction of C with A. The presence of these two columns affords a test on the hypothesis of constant regression coefficients across groups (H_0: $b_1^* = b_2^* = b_3^*$).

The full model states that $Y_{ijk} = \mu + \alpha_i + c_j + \alpha c_{ij} + e_{ijk}$. The regression analysis on this model produces

$$R_{\alpha,c,\alpha c}^2 = .8490.$$

[†] Methods for handling nonlinear relationships are available, but will not be discussed here.

TABLE 16.9

Raw Data on
Independent
Variable (Y)
and Covariate (C)

TREATMENT 1		TREATMENT 2		TREATMENT 3	
Y	C	Y	C	Y	C
6	3	8	4	6	3
4	1	9	5	7	2
5	3	7	5	7	2
3	1	9	4	7	3
4	2	8	3	8	4
3	1	5	1	5	1
6	4	7	2	7	4

DESIGN MATRIX

$$
\underset{21\times5}{X} =
\begin{bmatrix}
C & A_1 & A_2 & CA_1 & CA_2 \\
3 & 1 & 0 & 3 & 0 \\
\cdots & \cdots & \cdots & \cdots & \cdots \\
4 & 1 & 0 & 4 & 0 \\
4 & 0 & 1 & 0 & 4 \\
\cdots & \cdots & \cdots & \cdots & \cdots \\
2 & 0 & 1 & 0 & 2 \\
3 & -1 & -1 & -3 & -3 \\
\cdots & \cdots & \cdots & \cdots & \cdots \\
4 & -1 & -1 & -4 & -4
\end{bmatrix}
\qquad
\underset{21\times1}{y} =
\begin{bmatrix}
6 \\
\cdots \\
6 \\
8 \\
\cdots \\
7 \\
6 \\
\cdots \\
7
\end{bmatrix}
$$

If there is no significant difference in within-treatment regressions, the deletion of the interaction term should produce only a trivial decrement in the percentage of accountable variance. When we delete the AC terms we have

$$R_{\alpha,c}^2 = .8385.$$

The F test on this decrement is the usual F test on the difference between two models.

$$
F(f-r, N-f-1) = \frac{(R_{\alpha,c,\alpha c}^2 - R_{\alpha,c}^2)(N-f-1)}{(1-R_{\alpha,c,\alpha c}^2)(f-r)}
$$

$$
= \frac{(.8490 - .8385)(15)}{(.1510)(2)} = .522
$$

Given this value of F we have no basis on which to reject the assumption of common regression coefficients within the three treatments. Thus we can proceed with the analysis on the basis of the revised full model $Y_{ijk} = \mu + \alpha_i + c_j + e_{ijk}$.

We have just seen that using a model containing both the covariate and the treatment terms we can account for approximately 84% of the variation ($R^2_{\alpha,c} = .8385$). Since $SS_Y = 63.80955$,

$$SS_{regression} = SS_Y R^2_{\alpha,c} = (63.80955)(.8385) = 53.50752$$

and

$$SS_{residual} = SS_Y(1 - R^2_{\alpha,c}) = (63.80955)(.1615) = 10.30203.$$

If we delete the treatment term from our model, the decrement in R^2 will be the percentage of variation attributable to treatments after partialling out the covariate. Similarly, the decrement in $SS_{regression}$ will be the variation attributable to treatments with the covariate partialled out—i.e., $SS_A(adj)$.

Deleting the treatment effects we find

$$R^2_c = .57319$$

$$SS_{regression} = (63.80955)(.57319) = 36.57533.$$

Therefore

$$SS_A(adj) = SS_Y(R^2_{\alpha,c} - R^2_c)$$

$$= SS_Y(R^2_{\alpha,c}) - SS_Y(R^2_c)$$

$$= 53.50752 - 36.57533$$

$$= 16.93219.$$

We now have all of the information necessary to construct the analysis of covariance summary table. This is presented in Table 16.10. Notice that an extra term is included in the model to account for the sum of squares due to the covariate, which is defined as $SS_Y(R^2_c)$. Alternative approaches delete this term and reduce SS_{total} accordingly, with the result that SS_{total} represents that portion of the variation of Y which is not directly attributable to the covariate. The system used here has the advantage of making it clear how all of the variation is to be distributed.

Notice also in Table 16.10 that we lose 1 df from the error term for the covariate. With c covariates we would lose c df from error (one for each covariate).

Adjusted Means

Since $F_{.05}(2,17) = 3.59 < F_{obs} = 13.96$ we would reject H_0: $\mu_1(adj) = \mu_2(adj) = \mu_3(adj)$, and conclude that there were significant differences among the treatment means after the effect of the covariate has been partialled out of the analysis. In order to interpret these differences it would be useful to obtain the treatment means adjusted for the effects of the covariate. What we are essentially asking for is an estimate of what the treatment means

GENERAL SUMMARY TABLE FOR ONE-WAY ANALYSIS OF COVARIANCE

Source	df	SS
Treat (adj)	$a-1$	$SS_Y(R^2_{c,\alpha} - R^2_c)$
Error	$N-a-c$	$SS_Y(1 - R^2_{c,\alpha})$
Covariate	c	$SS_Y(R^2_c)$
Total	$N-1$	SS_Y

SUMMARY TABLE FOR DATA IN TABLE 16.9

Source	df	SS	MS	F
Treat (adj)	2	16.93219	8.466	13.96
Error	17	10.30203	.606	
Covariate	1	36.57553		
Total	20	63.80955		

FULL MODEL

$$\hat{Y} = 4.18639 + .74285C - 1.34966A_1 + .83809A_2$$

would have been had the groups not differed on the covariate. The adjusted means are readily obtainable from the regression solution using the covariate and treatments as predictors.

From the analysis of the revised full model we obtain

$$Y_{ij} = 4.18639 + .74285C - 1.34966A_1 + .83809A_2.$$

Writing this in terms of means, and representing adjusted means as $\bar{Y}'_j$, we have

$$\bar{Y}'_j = 4.18639 + .74285\bar{C} - 1.34966A_1 + .83809A_2$$

where $\bar{C} = 2.76190$ and A_1 and A_2 are $(0, 1, -1)$ variables. (We substitute $\bar{C}$ for C because we are interested in the means for Y if all subjects received the mean score on the covariate). For our data, the adjusted means of Treatments 1, 2, and 3 are (rounding to three decimal places):

$$\bar{Y}'_1 = 4.186 + (.743)(2.762) - 1.350(1) + .838(0)$$

$$= 4.888$$

$$\bar{Y}'_2 = 4.186 + (.743)(2.762) - 1.350(0) + .838(1)$$

$$= 7.076$$

$$\bar{Y}'_3 = 4.186 + (.743)(2.762) - 1.350(-1) + .838(-1)$$

$$= 6.750.$$

The grand mean is

$$\bar{Y}' = 4.186 + (.743)(2.762) - 1.350(0) + .838(0)$$

$$= 6.238 = \bar{Y}$$

Any individual comparisons among treatments would now be made using these adjusted means. In this case, however, we must modify our error term from that of the overall analysis of covariance. If we let $SS_{e(c)}$ represent the error sum of squares in an analysis of variance on the *covariate*, then Winer (1971) gives

$$F(1, N-a-1) = \frac{(\bar{Y}'_j - \bar{Y}'_k)^2}{MS'_{error}\left[\frac{2}{n} + \frac{(\bar{C}_j - \bar{C}_k)^2}{SS_{e(c)}}\right]}$$

MS'_{error}   (where MS'_{error} is the error term from the analysis of covariance) as a test of the difference between two adjusted means. For a more complete treatment of effective error terms the reader is referred to Winer (1971, p. 771f).

As an example suppose that we wish to compare $\bar{Y}'_2$ and $\bar{Y}'_3$. From the preceding analysis we either know or can compute

$$MS'_{error} = .606$$

$$SS_{e(c)} = 30.00$$

$$n = 7$$

$$\bar{c}_j = [2.143 \quad 3.429 \quad 2.714]$$

$$\bar{y}'_i = [4.888 \quad 7.076 \quad 6.750]$$

$$F(1, 17) = \frac{(7.076 - 6.750)^2}{.606\left[\frac{2}{7} + \frac{(3.429 - 2.714)^2}{30.00}\right]}$$

$$= \frac{.1063}{.1835} = .579.$$

The critical value $(F_{.05}[1, 17]) = 4.45$. We would thus not reject the null hypothesis that $\mu_{2(adj)} - \mu_{3(adj)} = 0$.

Interpreting an Analysis of Covariance

The interpretation of an analysis of covariance can present certain problems, depending upon the nature of the data. A thorough discussion of some of these problems can be found in Anderson (1963), Evans & Anastasio (1968), Lord (1967, 1969), Smith (1957), Winer (1971), Maxwell & Cramer (1975), and Weisberg (1979). It is possible here to present only a cursory examination of the difficulties which may arise.

When the treatment groups (or cells in a factorial design) all have approximately the *same means on the covariate*, no particular problem arises and the interpretation is straightforward. In this case the analysis of covariance serves primarily to reduce the error term by partialling out error variance which can be attributed to the covariate.

When the treatments have *different covariate means*, but when the treatment has no effect on the covariate (for example if the covariate is measured before the treatments are applied), the interpretation becomes a bit more difficult. Assuming that all necessary assumptions have been met, covariance analysis is a perfectly proper statistical procedure. However it can be questioned whether the results of this procedure apply to any real world phenomenon. The whole problem is best summed up by Anderson (1963) who stated "One may well wonder exactly what it means to ask what the data would be like if they were not what they are." (p.170) All of this is not to say that the analysis of covariance has no place in the analysis of data in which the treatments differ on the covariate. It is to say, however, that anyone using covariance analysis must think carefully about his data and the practical validity of the conclusions he draws.

A third situation exists in which the *treatment directly influences the covariate*. The classic and most common example comes from the partial reinforcement literature. Suppose that we want to ask if animals trained under continuous reinforcement extinguish more quickly than animals trained under partial reinforcement. Noticing, however, that there are performance differences between the groups at the end of acquisition, we decide to use final level of acquisition as the covariate. But since the final level of acquisition is a function of reinforcement, the treatment (reinforcement) affects the covariate. In this case the covariate and the treatment effects are confounded, and the process of adjustment may remove part of the treatment effect.

This result can be seen quite easily from the point of view of multiple regression. Suppose that the treatment affects the covariate. Then there is a non-chance correlation between C and α_1. We have defined

$$SS_A(\text{adj}) = SS_Y(R^2_{\alpha,c} - R^2_c)$$

$$= SS_Y(R^2_{0(\alpha.c)}).$$

This last term in parentheses is the squared semi-partial correlation between Y and that part of A which is independent of C. If C is correlated with A, R^2_c will contain part of the treatment effect and, for high values of r_{0c}, $R^2_{0(\alpha.c)}$ will be relatively small.[†] However, if A and C are independent (in the population), then in the sample $R^2_{0(\alpha.c)}$ will approximate $r^2_{0.\alpha}$ and C will not remove any appreciable part of the treatment effect.

[†] This same relationship holds when covariate means differ across treatments, but there the interpretation is more straightforward.

Evans & Anastasio (1968) argue that a correlation (in the population) between the treatment effects and the covariate invalidates the analysis of covariance. Winer (1971) argues that the analysis is still valid but that the interpretation of the data is clouded. Everyone is in agreement that this correlation leads to difficulties in interpretation. When the treatment affects the covariate you should think very seriously about the meaning of the analysis and consider treating the covariate as a separate dependent variable.

A problem related to the last two situations concerns the analysis of covariance on data from intact groups. Suppose, for example, that I wanted to compare the reading levels of people in noisy active environments and people in quiet peaceful environments. I therefore select subjects from a nursery school and from a retirement village. Being particularly perceptive I note that these groups differ in age, and decide to treat age as a covariate. By the use of the analysis of covariance I can compare the two groups while statistically equating for age. Whatever differences I can attribute to noisy environments (nursery schools) versus quiet environments (retirement villages) might be very useful to someone planning to set up nursery schools for octogenarians, but certainly any fool should recognize that I am a bigger one. What kind of an idiot would say "If the occupants of nursery schools and retirement villages were the same age, then. . . ?" And what about the 83 year old grandmother who is surrounded with wooden blocks? Would she read at the level my test said she should? I would maintain that the answer we have obtained from this particular analysis of covariance does not apply to any meaningful situation in the real world, and is for all practical purposes useless.

16.6   *The Factorial Analysis of Covariance*

The analysis of covariance applies to factorial designs just as well as to single variable designs. Once again the covariate may be treated as a variable which, because of methodological considerations, assumes priority in the analysis. In this chapter we will deal only with the case of equal cell sizes, but the generalization to unequal ns is immediate.

The logic of the analysis is straightforward, and follows that used in the previous examples. The coefficient $R^2_{c,\alpha,\beta,\alpha\beta}$ is the percentage of variance attributable to a linear combination of the covariate, the main effects of A and B, and the AB interaction. Similarly, $R^2_{c,\alpha,\beta}$ is the percentage of variation attributable to a linear combination of the covariate and the main effects of A and B. The difference

$$R^2_{c,\alpha,\beta,\alpha\beta} - R^2_{c,\alpha,\beta}$$

is the percentage of variation attributable to the AB interaction, with the covariate and the main effects partialled out. Since, with equal cell sizes, the two main effects and the interaction are all orthogonal, all that is *actually* partialled out is the covariate.

By the same line of reasoning,

$$R^2_{c,\alpha,\beta,\alpha\beta} - R^2_{c,\alpha,\alpha\beta}$$

represents the percentage of variation attributable to B, partialling out the covariate, and

$$R^2_{c,\alpha,\beta,\alpha\beta} - R^2_{c,\beta,\alpha\beta}$$

represents the percentage of variation attributable to the main effect of A, again partialling out the covariate.

The error term represents the variation remaining after controlling for A, B, AB, and the covariate. As such it is given by

$$\text{SS}_{\text{error}} = \text{SS}_Y(1 - R^2_{c,\alpha,\beta,\alpha\beta}).$$

The general structure of the analysis is presented in Table 16.11. Notice that once again the error term loses a degree of freedom to each covariate. Since the independent variables and the covariate account for overlapping portions of the variance, their sums of squares will not add to SS_{total}. (It should be noted that some programs (e.g., BMDP2V) calculate $\text{SS}_{\text{covariate}}$ by also adjusting the *covariate* for all other terms in the model. That is not done here, in line with the earlier statement that the covariate is treated as a variable which assumes priority in the analysis. This assignment of priority to the covariate implies that it is not adjusted. Whether or not we adjust the covariate, however, the other terms are unaffected.)

TABLE 16.11
Structure of the Analysis of Covariance

Source	df	SS
A(adj)	$a - 1$	$\text{SS}_Y(R^2_{c,\alpha,\beta,\alpha\beta} - R^2_{c,\beta,\alpha\beta})$
B(adj)	$b - 1$	$\text{SS}_Y(R^2_{c,\alpha,\beta,\alpha\beta} - R^2_{c,\alpha,\alpha\beta})$
AB(adj)	$(a-1)(b-1)$	$\text{SS}_Y(R^2_{c,\alpha,\beta,\alpha\beta} - R^2_{c,\alpha,\beta})$
Error	$N - ab - c$	$\text{SS}_Y(1 - R^2_{c,\alpha,\beta,\alpha\beta})$
Covariate	c	$\text{SS}_Y(R^2_c)$
Total	$N - 1$	

Example 16.1

How Shall We Teach Map Reading?

As an example consider a hypothetical study in which we wished to examine three methods of teaching map reading. For Method I all teaching is done in the classroom, with no field experience at all. For Method II half of the teaching takes place in the classroom and half of it takes place in the field. For Method III all of the teaching takes place in the field. Suppose further that we feel that it is important to consider where the people we are teaching grew up. We assume that people who were raised in the country have more experience with walking in the woods, climbing hills, and so on than do people who have lived all of their lives in the city, and this experience might prove useful in a course in map reading. Since we have a large number of subjects from which to select, we choose to draw equal numbers of subjects from rural and urban populations, and make this a second variable in our study. Lastly, assume that in looking over our subjects we notice that there appears to be substantial variability in terms of years of formal schooling. It seems a reasonable assumption that the more formal education to which a person has been exposed, the better he or she might be expected to do in our course. Thus in turn will introduce substantial amounts of within-cell variance. In an attempt to remove the effects of this unwanted variance, we have chosen to use years of formal education as a covariate.

TABLE 16.12

Data for the Analysis of Covariance

Place of residence		Teaching Methods						Row means	
		B_1		B_2		B_3			
		Y	C	Y	C	Y	C	Y	C
Urban	A_1	5	8	15	10	28	11		
		12	10	10	13	26	8		
		16	12	26	15	13	6		
		28	15	23	17	12	5		
	Means	15.25	11.25	18.50	13.75	19.75	7.50	17.833	10.833
Rural	A_2	8	8	7	7	32	11		
		16	10	23	10	30	7		
		18	13	25	12	17	5		
		27	16	36	14	17	4		
	Means	17.25	11.75	22.75	10.75	24.00	6.75	21.33	9.75
Column means		16.250	11.500	20.625	12.250	21.875	7.125	19.583	10.292

The data are presented in Table 16.12. The dependent variable (Y) is the final score on a 40-point map reading exam, while the covariate (C) is the number of years of formal education. The data represent a 2×3 analysis of covariance with one covariate and four scores per cell.

In Table 16.13 is an abbreviated form of the design matrix, showing only the entries for the first subject in every cell. Notice that the matrix

TABLE 16.13

Design Matrix
for the Analysis
of Covariance

$$
X = \begin{bmatrix}
C & A_1 & B_1 & B_2 & AB_{11} & AB_{12} & CA_1 & CB_1 & CB_2 & CAB_{11} & CAB_{12} \\
8 & 1 & 1 & 0 & 1 & 0 & 8 & 8 & 0 & 8 & 0 \\
\cdots & \cdots & \cdots & \cdots & \cdots & \cdots & \cdots & \cdots & \cdots & \cdots & \cdots \\
10 & 1 & 0 & 1 & 0 & 1 & 10 & 0 & 10 & 0 & 10 \\
\cdots & \cdots & \cdots & \cdots & \cdots & \cdots & \cdots & \cdots & \cdots & \cdots & \cdots \\
11 & 1 & -1 & -1 & -1 & -1 & 11 & -11 & -11 & -11 & -11 \\
\cdots & \cdots & \cdots & \cdots & \cdots & \cdots & \cdots & \cdots & \cdots & \cdots & \cdots \\
8 & -1 & 1 & 0 & -1 & 0 & -8 & 8 & 0 & -8 & 0 \\
\cdots & \cdots & \cdots & \cdots & \cdots & \cdots & \cdots & \cdots & \cdots & \cdots & \cdots \\
7 & -1 & 0 & 1 & 0 & -1 & -7 & 0 & 7 & 0 & -7 \\
\cdots & \cdots & \cdots & \cdots & \cdots & \cdots & \cdots & \cdots & \cdots & \cdots & \cdots \\
11 & -1 & -1 & -1 & 1 & 1 & -11 & -11 & -11 & 11 & 11 \\
\cdots & \cdots & \cdots & \cdots & \cdots & \cdots & \cdots & \cdots & \cdots & \cdots & \cdots
\end{bmatrix}
\quad
y = \begin{bmatrix} 5 \\ \cdots \\ 15 \\ \cdots \\ 28 \\ \cdots \\ 8 \\ \cdots \\ 7 \\ \cdots \\ 32 \\ \cdots \end{bmatrix}
$$

contains a column for the covariate, the usual design matrix elements for the main effects of A and B and the AB interaction, and the interaction of the covariate with each of the treatment effects. The latter will be used to test the hypothesis H_0: $b_i^* = b_j^*$ (for all i, j), since the assumption of homogeneity of regression applies to any analysis of covariance.

It is important to consider just what the interactions involving the covariate represent. Terms such as CA_1 carry information concerning the question of whether the regression lines for Y on C have the same slope for Treatment A_1 as for Treatment A_2. The terms CB_1 and CB_2 carry information on whether the slope of the regression line of Y on C within B_1 is the same as it is within B_2 and B_3. Finally, the terms CAB_{11} and CAB_{12} deal specifically with the within-cells regression lines—the regression line for the data in each cell of the design. Since our hypothesis concerns homogeneity of within-cells regression, we will ignore columns CA_1, CB_1, and CB_2 in favour of CAB_{11} and CAB_{12}. While a good case might be made for considering all of these columns, we do not do so here because to do so would require sacrificing much-needed degrees of freedom for error. For a larger problem the experimenter might consider the other columns, as they offer a test on the homogeneity of within-treatment (as opposed to within-cell) regression.

The first regression analysis is based on all predictors in X, except for the three we have just ruled out. From this analysis we obtain

$$R^2_{c,\alpha,\beta,\alpha\beta,c\alpha\beta} = .88031.$$

Thus 88% of the variation in this study can be accounted for by a model which includes the covariate, the main and interaction effects of A and B, and the CAB interaction. The first question concerns this CAB interaction. If we can delete these predictors from the model without any significant decrease in our ability to account for variation, then we can be satisfied that we have met the assumption of homogeneity of regression.

Rerunning the analysis using only the first six predictors, we obtain

$$R^2_{c,\alpha,\beta,\alpha\beta} = .82654.$$

This decrement in R^2 is tested in the usual way.

$$F(f-r, N-f-1) = \frac{(R^2_f - R^2_r)(N-f-1)}{(1-R^2_f)(f-r)}$$

$$F(2, 15) = \frac{(.88031 - .82654)(15)}{(.11969)(2)}$$

$$= 3.369.$$

For 2 and 15 degrees of freedom the critical value of $F_{.05}(2, 15) = 3.68$. Therefore we will fail to reject H_0, and conclude that we have no basis for assuming that there is not homogeneity of regression.

At this point we can define our model as

$$\hat{Y} = b_0 + b_1C + b_2A_1 + b_3B_1 + b_4B_2 + b_5AB_{11} + b_6AB_{12}$$

or, in more traditional analysis of variance terms

$$Y_{ijk} = \mu + c^k + \alpha_i + \beta_j + \alpha\beta_{ij} + e_{ijk}.$$

This is our full model, against which we will evaluate the effects of deleting individual terms. For this model

$$R^2_f = R^2_{c,\alpha,\beta,\alpha\beta} = .82654$$

$$SS_Y = 1681.833$$

$$SS_{reg(c,\alpha,\beta,\alpha\beta)} = SS_Y(R^2_{c,\alpha,\beta,\alpha\beta}) = 1390.107$$

$$SS_{residual} = SS_Y(1 - R^2_{c,\alpha,\beta,\alpha\beta}) = 291.727.$$

To obtain an adjusted estimate of the variation attributable to the AB interaction, partialling out (or adjusting for) the covariate, we solve a reduced model which does not contain the interaction effects. This produces

$$R^2_{c,\alpha,\beta} = .75300$$

$$SS_{reg(c,\alpha,\beta)} = 1266.423.$$

Since

$$SS_{AB}(\text{adj}) = SS_Y(R^2_{c,\alpha,\beta,\alpha\beta} - R^2_{c,\alpha,\beta})$$

$$= SS_{reg(c,\alpha,\beta,\alpha\beta)} - SS_{reg(c,\alpha,\beta)}$$

the adjusted variation attributable to the AB interaction is

$$SS_{AB}(\text{adj}) = 1390.107 - 1266.423$$

$$= 123.684.$$

We can estimate the adjusted sums of squares for the main effects of A and B in a similar fashion. For $SS_B(adj)$ we delete the B_j terms from the full model, producing

$$R^2_{c,\alpha,\alpha\beta} = .32570$$

$$SS_{reg(c,\alpha,\alpha\beta)} = 547.776.$$

The adjusted sum of squares for B is then given by

$$SS_B(adj) = SS_{reg(c,\alpha,\beta,\alpha\beta)} - SS_{reg(c,\alpha,\alpha\beta)}$$

$$= 1390.107 - 547.776$$

$$= 842.331.$$

To solve for the adjusted sum of squares for A we delete the A_1 term from the design matrix. This produces

$$R^2_{c,\beta,\alpha\beta} = .68765$$

$$SS_{reg(c,\beta,\alpha\beta)} = 1156.514$$

Then

$$SS_A(adj) = SS_{reg(c,\alpha,\beta,\alpha\beta)} - SS_{reg(c,\beta,\alpha\beta)}$$

$$= 1390.107 - 1156.514$$

$$= 233.593.$$

Finally, $SS_{covariate}$ represents all of the variation accountable for by $C = SS_{reg(c)=369.589}.$

Based on the above calculations we can now form the analysis of covariance summary table. This table is presented in Table 16.14 along with the regression equation derived from the full model. From this table it is

TABLE 16.14
Summary Table
for the Analysis
of Covariance

Source	df	SS	MS	F
A_{adj}	1	233.593	233.593	13.613*
B_{adj}	2	842.331	421.165	24.543*
AB_{adj}	2	123.684	61.842	3.604*
Error	17	291.727	17.160	
Covariate	1	369.589		
Total	23	1681.833		

FULL MODEL
$$\hat{Y} = -7.681 + 2.649C - 3.185A_1 - 6.534B_1 - 4.146B_2$$
$$+ 2.847AB_{11} - 2.914AB_{12}$$

apparent that all three effects are significant, although the interaction effect is borderline ($F_{.05}(2, 17) = 3.59$). Given the presence of a significant interaction it would be especially prudent to plot the adjusted means and look at the simple effects.

Adjusted Means

The method of obtaining adjusted means is simply an extension of the method employed in our previous example. We want to know what the cell means would have been if the treatment combinations had not differed on the covariate.

From the full model we have

$$\hat{Y} = -7.681 + 2.649C - 3.185A_1 - 6.534B_1$$
$$- 4.146B_2 + 2.847AB_{11} - 2.914AB_{12}.$$

Since we want to know what the Y means would be if the treatments did not differ on the covariate, we will set $C = \bar{C} = 10.292$ for all treatments.

For all observations in cell$_{11}$, the appropriate row of the design matrix, with $C = \bar{C}$, is

$$10.292 \quad 1 \quad 1 \quad 0 \quad 1 \quad 0.$$

Applying the regression weights and taking into account the intercept we have

$$\hat{\bar{Y}}_{11} = -7.681 + 2.649(10.292) - 3.185(1) - 6.534(1)$$
$$- 4.146(0) + 2.847(1) - 2.914(0)$$
$$= -7.681 + 27.264 - 3.185 - 6.534 + 2.847$$
$$= 12.711.$$

Applying this procedure to all of the cells we obtain the following adjusted means

		B_1	B_2	B_3	Row means
	A_1	12.711	9.338	27.145	16.398
	A_2	13.387	21.536	33.382	22.768
Column means		13.049	15.437	30.264	19.583

The row and column means can be found as the mean of means. Thus, for example,

$$\bar{A}_1' = \frac{\overline{\Sigma AB_{1j}}}{b}.$$

Alternatively, since the regression coefficient for predictor A_1 (-3.185) is equal to the treatment effect $(\alpha_1 = \mu_{A_1} - \mu)$, we can find $\bar{A}_1$ directly as

$$GM + \hat{\alpha}_1 = 19.583 - 3.185 = 16.398$$

Testing Adjusted Means

The adjusted means are plotted in Figure 16.3, and illustrate the interaction and also the meaning which may be attached to the main effects. Further analyses of these data depend upon the interests of the experimenter. The experimenter who is mainly interested in whether there are differences in effectiveness among the three training methods could stop right here. The main effect of methods (even considering the presence of an interaction), together with the adjusted means plotted in Figure 16.3 makes it clear that

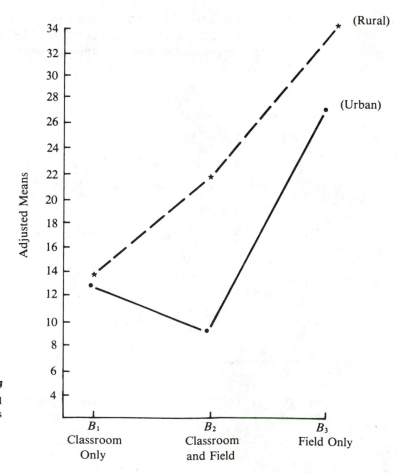

FIGURE 16.3

Adjusted cell means

different methods do produce different degrees of learning. If, however, our experimenter wishes to show that (averaged across place of residence) Method III is better than the other two methods, he should then consider the comparison of $\bar{B}'_3$ with $\bar{B}'_1$ and $\bar{B}'_2$. This comparison requires some modification of the error term, to account for differences in the covariate. This adjustment is given by Winer (1971) as

$$MS''_{error} = MS'_{error}\left[1 + \frac{\dfrac{SS_{b(c)}}{b-1}}{SS_{e(c)}}\right]$$

where $SS_{b(c)}$ and $SS_{e(c)}$ represent the sum of squares attributable to B and error (respectively) in an analysis of variance performed on the *covariate*, and MS'_{error} is the error term from the overall analysis of covariance.

For our data

$$MS'_{error} = 17.16$$

$$SS_{b(c)} = 122.583$$

$$SS_{e(c)} = 166.750.$$

Thus

$$MS''_{error} = 17.16\left[1 + \frac{122.583/2}{166.750}\right] = 23.468.$$

To compare the combination of $\bar{B}'_1$ and $\bar{B}'_2$ with $\bar{B}'_3$ we will first convert to adjusted totals, in line with the way similar comparisons were treated in Chapter 11.

$$T'_{B_1} = (\bar{B}'_1)(an) = 13.049(8) = 104.392$$

$$T'_{B_2} = (\bar{B}'_2)(an) = 15.437(8) = 123.496$$

$$T'_{B_3} = (\bar{B}'_3)(an) = 30.264(8) = 242.112$$

Then

$$L = 1(104.392) + 1(123.496) - 2(242.112) = -256.336$$

$$F(1,\ 17) = \frac{L^2}{n\Sigma a_i^2 MS''_{error}} = \frac{(-256.336)^2}{8(6)(23.468)} = 58.331.$$

There can be no question that this difference is significant.

On the basis of this last result, our experimenter would conclude that Method II is better than the average of the other two methods, and would most likely recommend adoption of that method in the future teaching of map reading.

Another experimenter might be interested in examining the simple effects of teaching methods at each level of the residence variable. This would be especially true if one method appeared to be superior for the urban students and a second measure appeared to be superior for the rural students. If only one teaching method could be employed in the future (for example if urban and rural students must be taught all in one class), we would most likely choose that method which was higher *on the average*, which we have just shown to be Method III. But if we can separate the students into two classes we will wish to know which method is best for each group. If we want to examine these simple effects, we will again need to modify our error term in some way. This is necessary because we will be looking at the $\bar{B}_i$ at level A_1 only (for example), and the A_1 means on the covariate will most likely differ from the overall covariate mean. Probably the safest course in this case is to run separate analyses of covariance at each level of A. While this method has the disadvantage of costing us degrees of freedom for error, it has the advantage of simplicity and the elimination of the need to make discomforting assumptions in the adjustment of our error term.

If we were to run these separate analyses of covariance, we would find a significant effect of B at both levels of A. Thus for B at A_1, $F(2, 8) = 8.444$, and for B at A_2, $F(2, 8) = 16.984$. Both of these Fs are significant at $p < .05$.

To complete the coverage of the tests we might wish to conduct, consider the experimenter who wishes to compare two particular adjusted cell means (whether or not they are in the same row or column). The adjusted error term for this comparison is given by Winer (1971) as

$$MS''_{error} = \frac{2MS'_{error}}{n}\left[1 + \frac{SS_{cells(c)}/(ab-1)}{SS_{\dot{e}(c)}}\right]$$

where $SS_{cells(c)}$ is the sum of squares cells from an analysis of variance on the covariate.

You may wonder why we continually worry about adjusting the error term in making comparisons. The general nature of the answer is apparent when you recall what the confidence limits around the regression line looked like in Chapter 9. For $X = \bar{X}$ we were relatively confident about $\hat{Y}$. However as X departed more and more from $\bar{X}$ we became less and less confident of our prediction, and consequently the confidence limits widened. If you now go back to Figure 16.2 you will see that the problem applies directly to the case of adjusted means. In that figure $\bar{Y}'_1$ is a long way from $\bar{Y}_1$, and we would probably have relatively little confidence that we have estimated it correctly. On the other hand we can probably have a reasonable degree of confidence in our estimate of $\bar{Y}'_2$. It is just this type of consideration which causes us constantly to adjust our error term.

The particular example we have used points up an important feature of the analysis of covariance—the fact that the covariate is simply just another variable that happens to receive priority. In designing the study we were primarily concerned with evaluating three different teaching methods.

However we had two variables which we considered it necessary to control; place of residence and years of schooling. The first one (place of residence) we controlled by incorporating it into our design as an independent variable. The second (years of schooling) we controlled by treating it as a covariate. In many respects these are two ways of treating the same problem. Although there are obvious differences in the way these two variables are treated, there are also important similarities. In obtaining $SS_{methods}$ we are actually partialling out *both* Place of Residence and the covariate. It is true that in the case of equal ns Place of Residence is orthogonal to Methods, leaving nothing to partial out, but that is merely a technicality. In the case of unequal ns, the partialling out of both variables is a very real procedure. While it is important not to lose sight of the fact that the analysis of covariance is a unique technique with its own additional assumptions, it is equally important to keep in mind the fact that a covariate is just another variable. An experimenter with a different subject pool might easily find himself with Teaching Methods and Years of Schooling as variables and Place of Residence as a covariate. One person's variable may be another person's covariate.

16.7   The Analysis of Covariance Versus the Analysis of Variance

It will be instructive to compare the analysis of covariance with an analysis of variance on the same data. In Table 16.15 are the results of the analysis of variance on the data presented in Table 16.12. This analysis contrasts sharply with the analysis of covariance presented in Table 16.14. First of all the main effects and interaction sum of squares are markedly reduced. Second, the error term is substantially larger. The analysis of covariance has a considerably smaller error term because it has partialled out that portion of the within-cell variance which can be attributed to the covariate (years of schooling). In addition, the analysis of covariance has larger treatment effects because it has adjusted the means to account for mean differences on the covariate, which can be seen in the comparison of the unadjusted

TABLE 16.15

Summary Table for the Analysis of Variance

Source	df	SS	MS	F
A	1	73.500	73.500	<1
B	2	139.583	69.792	<1
AB	2	6.750	3.375	<1
Error	18	1461.998	81.222	
Total	23	1681.831		

and adjusted means. While this is an extreme example, it serves to illustrate the two different influences an analysis of covariance has on our perception of the data.

The Use of Multiple Covariates

Until now we have been concerned with the use of a single covariate. There is no theoretical or practical reason, however, why we must restrict ourselves in this way. For example a study on the effectiveness of several different teaching methods might wish to treat IQ, Age, and Type of School (progressive or conservative) as covariates. When viewed from the point of view of multiple regression, this presents no particular problem, whereas when viewed within the traditional framework of the analysis of variance the computational complexities for only a very few covariates would be overwhelming.

In the expression $R^2_{c,\alpha,\beta,\alpha\beta}$, β is really only a shorthand way of representing a set of predictors (e.g., B_1, B_2, ... B_b). By the same token, c can be used to stand for a set of covariates (C_1, C_2, ... C_k). Thus in terms of the more specific notation, $R^2_{c,\alpha,\beta,\alpha\beta}$ might really represent

$$R^2_{0.IQ, \text{ Age, School, } A_1, B_1, B_2, AB_{11}, AB_{12}}.$$

When seen in this light the use of multiple covariates is no different from the use of single covariates. If C represents the covariates IQ, Age, and School, then $SS_{AB}(\text{adj})$ remains

$$SS_Y(R^2_{c,\alpha,\beta,\alpha\beta} - R^2_{c,\alpha,\beta}) = SS_{\text{reg(IQ, Age, School, } A_1, B_1, B_2, AB_{11}, AB_{12})}$$
$$- SS_{\text{reg(IQ, Age, School, } A_1, B_1, B_2}).$$

It should be apparent from the previous example that no restriction is placed upon the nature of the covariate, other than that it is assumed to be linearly related to the criterion. It can be a continuous variable, as in the case of IQ and Age, or a discrete variable, as in the dichotomizing of schools into progressive and conservative.

A word of warning is in order at this point. Just because it is possible (and in fact easy) to use multiple covariates, that is not a recommendation for adopting this procedure. Interpretation of an analysis of covariance may be difficult enough (if not impossible) with only one covariate. The problems increase rapidly with the addition of multiple covariates. Thus it might be easy to *say*, in evaluating several methods of teaching English, that such and such a method is better if groups are equated for age, IQ, type of school, parents' occupation, and so on. But the experimenter must then ask himself if such equated groups actually exist in the population. If they do not, he has just answered a question as to what would happen in groups that could never exist, and it is unlikely that he will receive much applause for his answer. Moreover, even if it is possible to form such groups, will they behave in the expected manner? The very fact that the students are now in homogeneous classes may itself have an effect upon the dependent variable which could not have been predicted.

Alternative Experimental Designs

Stratification

The analysis of covariance is not the only way to handle data in which a covariate is important. Two common alternative procedures are also available, namely *stratification* (matched samples) and difference scores.

If we have available measures on the covariate and are free to assign subjects to treatment groups, then we can form subsets of subjects who are homogeneous with respect to the covariate, and then assign one member of each subset to a different treatment group. In the analysis of variance we can then pull out an effect due to blocks (subsets) from the error term.

The use of matched samples and the analysis of covariance are almost equally effective when the regression of Y on C is linear. If ρ equals the correlation in the population between Y and C, and σ_e^2 represents the error variance in a straight analysis of variance on Y, then the use of matched samples reduces the error variance to

$$\sigma_e^2(1-\rho^2).$$

The reduction due to the analysis of covariance in this situation is given by Winer (1971) as

$$\sigma_e^2(1-\rho^2)\frac{(f_e)}{(f_e-1)}$$

where f_e is the degrees of freedom for the error variance. Obviously for any reasonable value of f_e, the two procedures are almost equally effective, assuming linearity of regression. If the relationship between Y and C is not linear, however, matching will be more effective than covariance analysis.

A second alternative to the analysis of covariance concerns the use of difference scores. If the covariate (C) represents a test score before the treatment is administered and Y a score on the same test after the administration of the treatment, the variable $C-Y$ is sometimes used as the dependent variable in an analysis of variance to control for initial differences on C. Obviously this approach will only work if C and Y are comparable measures. We could hardly justify subtracting a test score (Y) from an IQ score (C). If the relationship between C and Y is linear and if $b_{CY}=1.00$, the analysis of difference scores and the analysis of covariance will give the same estimates of the treatment effects. When b_{CY} is not equal to one, the two methods will produce different results, and in this case it is difficult to justify the use of difference scores. For a more complete treatment of this entire problem the reader is referred to Harris (1963).

16.8 *Summary*

This chapter brings together material from multiple regression and the analysis of variance and shows the relationship between those two apparently distinct topics. The least squares approach to the analysis of variance is put forth not as a computational device so much as it is as an explanatory device. We saw how one can develop design matrices which allow the prediction of the dependent variable on the basis of predictors that carry the information on group membership. After considering the treatment of factorial designs, we saw how the least squares approach handles the problem of unequal sample sizes with respect to the weighting or unweighting of sample means. We then saw how the least squares approach can be extended to the analysis of covariance, and that a covariate is basically just like any independent variable except that it assumes some kind of priority in the analysis. We also saw that the use of multiple covariates is really no different from the use of single covariates.

Exercises for Chapter 16

16.1 The following hypothetical data were obtained from poor, average, and good readers on the number of eye fixations per line of text.

POOR	*AVERAGE*	*GOOD*
10	5	3
7	8	5
8	4	2
11	6	3
5	5	4

a. Construct the design matrix for these data.
b. Use any standard regression program to calculate a least squares analysis of variance.
c. Run the analysis of variance in the traditional manner and compare your answers.

16.2   **a.** For the data in the previous question calculate treatment effects and show that the regression model reproduces these treatment effects.
b. Demonstrate that R^2 for the regression model is equal to η^2 for the analysis of variance.

16.3 Taking the data from Exercise 16.1, add the scores 5 and 8 to the *Average* group and the scores 2, 3, 3, and 5 to the *Good* group. Rerun the analysis for Exercise 16.1 using the more complete data.

16.4 Rerun the analysis of Exercise 16.2 for the amended data from Exercise 16.3.

16.5 Apply the design matrix for contrast coding given in the text to the data of Table 16.1, and demonstrate that the discussion in the text is correct.

16.6 A psychologist was concerned with the relationship between sex, socio-economic status (SES), and perceived locus of control. She took eight adults (age = 25–30) in each sex-SES combination and administered a scale dealing with locus of control (a high score indicates that the individual feels in control of his everyday life).

	SES		
	Low	*Average*	*High*
Male	10	16	18
	12	12	14
	8	19	17
	14	17	13
	10	15	19
	16	11	15
	15	14	22
	13	10	20
Female	8	14	12
	10	10	18
	7	13	14
	9	9	21
	12	17	19
	5	15	17
	8	12	13
	7	8	16

a. Run a traditional analysis of variance on these data.
b. The following sums of squares have been computed on the data using the appropriate design matrix (α = sex, β = SES).

$$SS_Y = 777.6667 \quad SS_{reg(\alpha,\beta,\alpha\beta)} = 422.6667$$

$$SS_{reg(\alpha,\beta)} = 404.0000 \quad SS_{reg(\beta,\alpha\beta)} = 357.3333 \quad SS_{reg(\alpha,\alpha\beta)} = 84.000$$

Compute the summary table for the analysis of variance using these sums of squares.

16.7 Using only the SES portion of the design matrix as our predictor, we find that $SS_{reg(\beta)} = 338.6667$.

a. Why is this value the same as SS_{SES} in the answer to Exercise 16.6?
b. Will this be the case in all analyses of variance?

16.8   When we take the data in Exercise 16.6 and delete the last two low SES males, the last three average SES males, and the last two high SES females, we obtain the following sums of squares.

$$SS_Y = 750.1951 \quad SS_{reg(\alpha,\beta,\alpha\beta)} = 458.7285 \quad SS_{reg(\alpha,\beta)} = 437.6338$$
$$SS_{reg(\beta,\alpha\beta)} = 398.7135 \quad SS_{reg(\alpha,\alpha\beta)} = 112.3392$$

Compute the analysis of variance using these sums of squares.

16.9   Using only the SES predictors for the data in Exercise 16.8, we find $SS_{reg(\beta)} = 379.3325$. How does this compare to SS_{SES} in Exercise 16.8?

16.10   For the data in Exercise 16.6 the complete model is:

$$1.1667A_1 - 3.1667B_1 - .1667B_2 + .8333AB_{11} - .1667AB_{12} + 13.4167$$

Show that this model reproduces the treatment and interaction effects calculated as in Table 16.3.

16.11   For the data in Exercise 16.8 the complete model is:

$$1.2306A_1 - 3.7167B_1 + .3500B_2 + .4778AB_{11} + .5444AB_{12} + 13.6750$$

Show that this model reproduces the treatment and interaction effects calculated as in Table 16.3.

16.12   Using the following data demonstrate that Method I (the method advocated in this chapter) really deals with unweighted means.

	B_1	B_2
A_1	5	11
	3	9
		14
		6
		11
		9
A_2	10	6
	11	2
	12	
	7	

16.13   Draw a Venn diagram representing the sums of squares in Exercise 16.6.

16.14   Draw a Venn diagram representing the sums of squares in Exercise 16.8.

16.15 Use the data in Exercise 16.8 (and your answer to the question) to compare options 7, 8, and 9 on SPSS-ANOVA.

16.16 In studying the energy consumption of families, we have broken them into three groups—group I consists of those who have enrolled in a time-of-day electrical rate system (the charge per kilowatt hour of electricity is higher during peak demand times of the day). Group II is made up of those who inquired into such a system but did not use it, and Group III represents those who have shown no interest in the system. We record the amount of the electrical bill per month for each household as our dependent variable (Y). As a covariate we take the electrical bill for that household for the same month last year (C). The data follows.

GROUP 1		GROUP 2		GROUP 3	
Y	C	Y	C	Y	C
58	75	60	70	75	80
25	40	30	25	60	55
50	68	55	65	70	73
40	62	50	50	65	61
55	67	45	55	55	65

a. Set up the design matrix.
b. Run the analysis of covariance.

16.17 Use BMDP to run the analysis of covariance for the data in Exercise 16.16.

16.18 In an attempt to refine the experiment described in Exercise 16.16, a psychologist added an additional set of households to each group in which a special meter was installed to show the occupants exactly how fast their electric bill was increasing. (The amount to-date was displayed on the meter.) The data follow, where the non-metered data are the same as those in Exercise 16.16.

	Y	C	Y	C	Y	C
	58	75	60	70	75	80
	25	40	30	25	60	55
Non-metered	50	68	55	65	70	73
	40	62	50	50	65	61
	55	67	45	55	55	65
	25	42	40	55	55	56
	38	64	47	52	62	74
Metered	46	70	56	68	57	60
	50	67	28	30	50	68
	55	75	55	72	70	76

a. Run the analysis of covariance on these data—after first checking the assumption of homogeneity of regression.

b. Draw the appropriate conclusions.

16.19   Run BMDP (or SPSS-option 9) on the data in Exercise 16.18. Why do they not agree with you on $SS_{covariance}$?

16.20   Compute the adjusted means for the data in Exercise 16.18.

16.21   Compute the energy *savings* per household for the data in Exercise 16.18 by subtracting this year's bill from last year's bill. Then run an analysis of variance on the savings scores and compare that to the analysis of covariance.

17

Nonparametric and Distribution-Free Statistical Tests

Objective

To present nonparametric (distribution-free) procedures which can be used for testing hypotheses about group differences but which rely on less restrictive assumptions about populations than do previously discussed tests.

Contents

Most of the statistical procedures which we have discussed in the preceding chapters have involved both the estimation of one or more parameters of the distribution of scores in the population(s) from which the data were sampled and assumptions concerning the shape of that distribution. To cite a specific example, the t-test makes use of the sample variance (s^2) as an estimate of the population variance (σ^2) and also requires the assumption that the population from which we sampled is normal (or at least that the sampling distribution of the mean is normal). Tests, such as the t-test, which involve either assumptions about specific parameters, or else their estimation, *Parametric tests*   are referred to as ***parametric tests***.

There is a class of tests, however, which do not rely on parameter estimation and/or distribution assumptions. Such tests are usually referred *Nonparametric tests*   to as ***nonparametric tests*** or ***distribution-free tests***. By and large, if a test is *Distribution-free*   a nonparametric test it is also distribution-free, and in fact it is the distribu-*tests*   tion-free nature of the test which is most valuable to us. While the two names are often used interchangeably, the tests will be referred to here as "distribution-free" tests.

The argument over the value of distribution-free tests has gone on for many years, and it certainly can not be resolved in this chapter. There are many who feel that, for the vast majority of cases, parametric tests are sufficiently robust to make distribution-free tests unnecessary. There are others, however, who believe just as strongly in the unsuitability of parametric tests and the overwhelming superiority of the distribution-free approach. (Bradley, 1968, is a forceful and articulate spokesman for the latter group.) Regardless of the position one takes on this issue, it is important that the student be familiar with the most common distribution-free procedures and with their underlying rationale. These tests are too prevalent in the experimental literature to simply be ignored.

While it is relatively easy to list the major advantages and disadvantages normally attributed to distribution-free methods, it is equally easy to find someone eager to argue the other side of the issue. This state of affairs merely reflects the continued debate in the literature.

The major advantage generally attributed to distribution-free tests is also the most obvious—they do not rely on any very seriously restrictive assumptions concerning the shape of the sampled population(s). This is not to say that distribution-free tests do not make *any* distribution assumptions, but only that the assumptions are far more general than for the parametric tests. The exact null hypothesis being tested may depend, for example, on whether or not two populations are symmetric or have a similar shape. None of these tests, however, makes an assumption about the specific shape of the distribution. A parametric test, on the other hand, usually includes some type of normality assumption.

Those who argue in favor of using parametric tests in every case do not deny the fact that the distribution-free tests are more liberal in the assumptions which they require. They argue, however, that the assumptions normally cited as being required of parametric tests are overly restrictive in practice, and that the parametric tests are remarkably unaffected by violations of distribution assumptions.

The major disadvantage generally attributed to distribution-free tests is their lower power relative to the corresponding parametric test. In general, when the assumptions of the parametric test are met, the distribution-free test requires more observations than the comparable parametric test for the same level of power. Thus for a given set of data the parametric test is more likely to lead to rejection of a false null hypothesis than is the corresponding distribution-free test. Moreover, when the distribution assumptions are violated to a moderate degree the parametric tests are thought to maintain their advantage. (However an important paper by Blair & Higgins (1980) contains results which seriously challenge this last statement.)

It is often claimed that the distribution-free procedures are particularly useful because of the simplicity of their calculations. However, for an experimenter who has just invested six months in collecting her data, a difference of five minutes in computation time hardly justifies the use of a less desirable test.

This chapter will be concerned with four of the most important distribution-free methods. The first two to be discussed are analogues of the *t*-test—one for independent samples and one for matched samples. The next two tests to be discussed are distribution-free analogues of the analysis of variance—the first for k independent groups and the second for k repeated

Rank-randomization tests

measures. All of these tests are members of a class known as **rank-randomization tests** because they deal with ranked data and take as their null distribution the theoretical distribution of randomly distributed ranks.

17.1 *Wilcoxon's Rank-Sum Test*

Wilcoxon Rank-Sum Test

One of the most common and best known distribution-free tests is the **Wilcoxon Rank-Sum Test** for two independent samples. This test is often thought of as the distribution-free analogue of the *t*-test for two independent samples, although it tests a slightly different, and broader, null hypothesis. Its null hypothesis is the hypothesis that the two samples were drawn at random from identical populations, and it is especially sensitive to population differences in central tendency.

The logical basis of Wilcoxon's Rank-Sum Test is particularly easy to understand. Assume that we have two independent treatment groups, with n_1 observations in Group 1 and n_2 observations in Group 2. Further assume that the null hypothesis is *false* to a very substantial degree, such that the population from which Group 1 scores have been sampled contains values generally lower than the population from which Group 2 scores were drawn. Then if we were to rank all $n_1 + n_2 = N$ scores from lowest to highest without regard to group membership, we would expect that the lower ranks would generally fall in Group 1 and the higher ranks in Group 2. Going one step further, if we were to sum the ranks assigned to each group, the sum of the ranks in Group 1 would be expected to be appreciably smaller than the sum of the ranks in Group 2.

Now consider the opposite case in which the null hypothesis is *true* and the scores for the two groups were sampled from identical populations. In this situation if we were to rank all N scores without regard to group membership we would expect some low ranks and some high ranks in each group, and the sum of the ranks assigned to Group 1 would be roughly equal to the sum of the ranks assigned to Group 2. These situations are illustrated in Table 17.1.

TABLE 17.1

Illustration of Typical Results to be Expected Under H_0 False and H_0 True

| | | | | | H_0 FALSE | | | | | | | |
			Group 1						Group 2			
Raw Data	10	12	17	13	19	20		30	26	25	33	18	27
Ranks	1	2	4	3	6	7		11	9	8	12	5	10
ΣR_i			23							55		

| | | | | | H_0 TRUE | | | | | | | |
			Group 1						Group 2			
Raw Data	22	28	32	19	24	33		18	25	29	20	23	34
Ranks	4	8	10	2	6	11		1	7	9	3	5	12
ΣR_i			41							37		

Wilcoxon based his test on the logic just described, using the sum of the ranks in one of the groups as his test statistic. If that sum is too small relative to the other sum, the null hypothesis will be rejected. More specifically, we will take as our test statistic the sum of the ranks assigned to the *smaller* group, or, if $n_1 = n_2$, the *smaller* of the two sums. Given this W_s value we can use tables of the Wilcoxon statistic (W_s) to test the null hypothesis.

To take a specific example, consider the following hypothetical data on the number of recent stressful life events reported by a group of cardiac patients in a local hospital and a control group of orthopedic patients in the same hospital.

	CARDIAC PATIENTS						ORTHOPEDIC PATIENTS				
Raw data	12	8	7	9	5	0	1	2	2	3	6
Ranks	11	9	8	10	6	1	2	3.5	3.5	5	7

We first rank all 11 scores from lowest to highest, assigning tied ranks to tied scores (see the discussion on ranking in Chapter 10). If orthopedic patients have generally had fewer recent stressful life events, then the sum of the ranks assigned to that group should be relatively low. Letting W_s stand for the sum of the ranks in the smaller group (the orthopedic group), we find

$$W_s = 2 + 3.5 + 3.5 + 5 + 7 = 21$$

We can evaluate our obtained value of W_s by use of Wilcoxon's table (Appendix W_s) which gives the smallest value of W_s that we would expect to obtain by chance if the null hypothesis were true. From Appendix (W_s) we find that for $n_1 = 5$ subjects in the smaller group and $n_2 = 6$ subjects in the larger group the entry for $\alpha = .025$ (one-tailed) is 18. This means that for a difference between groups to be significant at the one-tailed .025 level, or the two-tailed .05 level, W_s must be less than or equal to 18. Since we found $W_s = 21$, we can not reject H_0.

The entries in Appendix (W_s) are for a one-tailed test, and will lead to rejection of the null hypothesis only if the sum of the ranks for the smaller group is sufficiently *small*. It is possible, however, that the larger ranks could be congregated in the smaller group, in which case the sum of the ranks would be larger than chance expectation rather than smaller. One rather awkward way around this problem would be to rank the data all over again, this time ranking from high to low. If we did this then the smaller ranks would now appear in the smaller group and we could proceed as before. We do not have to go through the process of reranking data, however. We can make use of the symmetric properties of the distribution of the rank-sum W'_s and calculate W'_s, which is the sum of the ranks for the smaller group that we would have found if we had reversed our ranking and ranked from highest to lowest.

$$W'_s = 2\bar{W} - W_s$$

where $2\bar{W} = n_1(n_1 + n_2 + 1)$ and is tabled in Appendix (W_s). We could then evaluate W'_s against the tabled value, and have a one-tailed test on the upper tail of the distribution. For a two-tailed test of H_0 (which is what we normally want), we calculate W_s and W'_s, enter the table with whichever is smaller, and double the listed value of α.

To illustrate W_s and W'_s, consider the following two sets of data

		GROUP 1				GROUP 2						
Set 1	X	10	15	16	19	18	23	25	26	29	$W_s = 11$	$W'_s = 29$
	Ranks	1	2	3	5	4	6	7	8	9		
Set 2	X	30	26	24	21	23	18	15	14	13	$W_s = 29$	$W'_s = 11$
	Ranks	9	8	7	5	6	4	3	2	1		

Notice that the two data sets exhibit the same degree of *extremeness*. In the first set four of the five lowest ranks are in Group 1, and in the second set four of the five highest ranks are in Group 1. Moreover, W_s for Set 1 is equal to W'_s for Set 2, and vice versa. Thus if we establish the rule that we will calculate both W_s and W'_s for the smaller group and refer the smaller of W_s and W'_s to the tables, we will come to the same conclusion with respect to the two data sets.

The Normal Approximation

Appendix (W_s) is suitable for all cases in which n_1 and n_2 are less than or equal to 25. For larger values of n_1 and/or n_2 we can make use of the fact that the distribution of W_s approaches a normal distribution as sample sizes increase. This distribution has a mean $= n_1(n_1 + n_2 + 1)/2$ and a standard deviation $= \sqrt{n_1 n_2(n_1 + n_2 + 1)/12}$. Thus we can calculate

$$z = \frac{W_s - n_1(n_1 + n_2 + 1)/2}{\sqrt{n_1 n_2(n_1 + n_2 + 1)/12}}$$

and obtain from the tables of the normal distribution an approximation of the true probability of a value of W_s (or W'_s if appropriate) at least as low as the one obtained.

To illustrate the computations for the case in which the larger ranks fall in the smaller groups, and to illustrate the use of the normal approximation, consider the data in Table 17.2. These are purely hypothetical data on the birthweight (in grams) of children born to mothers who did not seek prenatal care until the third trimester and mothers who received prenatal care starting in the first trimester.

For the data in Table 17.2 the sum of the ranks in the smaller group = 100. From Appendix (W_s) we find $2\bar{W} = 152$, and thus $W'_s = 2\bar{W} - W_s = 52$. Since 52 is smaller than 100 we enter Appendix (W_s) with $W'_s = 52$, $n_1 = 8$, and $n_2 = 10$. (n_1 is defined as the smaller sample size.) Since we want a two-tailed test we will double the tabled value of α. The critical value of W_s (or W'_s) for a two-tailed test at $\alpha = .05$ is 53, meaning that only 5% of the time would we expect a value of W_s or $W'_s \leq 53$ if H_0 is true. Since our obtained value of W'_s is 52, this falls in the rejection region and we will reject H_0, concluding that mothers who do not receive prenatal care until the third trimester are more likely to give birth to smaller babies.

The use of the normal approximation for evaluating W_s is illustrated in the bottom part of Table 17.2. Here we find that $z = -2.13$. From Appendix (z) we find that the probability of a value as large as $+2.13 = .0166$, and thus for a two-tailed test the probability of W_s or W'_s as small as 52 is $2(.0166) = .033$. Since this is smaller than our traditional cutoff of $\alpha = .05$, we will reject H_0 and again conclude that there is sufficient evidence to say

	BEGINNING OF CARE			
TABLE 17.2	***Third Trimester***		***First Trimester***	
Hypothetical Data	*Weight*	*Rank*	*Weight*	*Rank*
on Birthweight				
of Infants Born	2480	2	2940	10
to Mothers	3400	17	3380	16
with Different	3110	14	3830	18
Levels of	2760	5	2810	9
Prenatal Care	2530	3	2800	8
	2790	7	3210	15
	3050	12	3080	13
	2660	4	2950	11
	2110	1		
	2775	6		

$W_s = \Sigma$ ranks in group $2 = 100$

$W'_s = 2\bar{W} - W_s = 152 - 100 = 52$

$$z = \frac{W'_s - n_1(n_1+n_2+1)/2}{\sqrt{n_1 n_2(n_1+n_2+1)/12}} = \frac{52 - 8(8+10+1)/2}{\sqrt{8(10)(8+10+1)/12}}$$

$$= \frac{52-76}{\sqrt{126.6667}} = -2.13$$

that failing to seek early prenatal care is related to lower birthweight. Note that both the exact solution and the normal approximation lead to the same conclusion with respect to H_0.

The Treatment of Ties

When the data contain tied scores, any test which ranks the data is likely to be somewhat distorted. This is especially true when using a normal approximation, since the formula for the standard error of W_s assumes consecutive integers. The most common approach to tied scores is to assign them tied ranks and then continue as if there were no problem. This approach is certainly valid with the present test if all of the ties occur in the same group, since W_s would not be affected by any method of breaking ties. If two or more tied scores occur in different groups, the method of assigning tied ranks could lead to different conclusions with respect to H_0 in borderline cases. The conservative approach in this case is to assign ranks in such a way as to work against rejection of H_0. If the result is still significant, then you know that you are safe. For a complete discussion of the problem of tied scores the reader is referred to Bradley (1968).

The Null Hypothesis

Wilcoxon's Rank-Sum Test evaluates the null hypothesis that the two sets of scores were sampled from identical populations. This is broader than the null hypothesis tested by the corresponding *t*-test, which dealt specifically with means (primarily as a result of the underlying assumptions which ruled out other sources of difference). If the two populations are assumed to have the same shape and dispersion, then the null hypothesis tested by the Rank-Sum Test would actually deal with the central tendency of the two populations, and if the populations are also symmetric the test will be a test of means. In any event the Rank-Sum Test is particularly sensitive to differences in central tendency.

The Mann-Whitney U Statistic

Mann-Whitney U Test

A common competitor to the Wilcoxon Rank-Sum Test is the ***Mann-Whitney U Test***. We do not need to discuss the Mann-Whitney test at any length, however, because the two tests are exactly equivalent tests, and there is a perfect linear relationship between W_s and U.

$$U = \frac{n_1(n_1 + 2n_2 + 1)}{2} - W_s$$

From this formula we can see that for any given set of sample sizes U and W_s differ only by a constant (as do their critical values). Since we have this relationship between the two statistics, we can always convert U to W_s and evaluate W_s using Appendix (W_s). The only reason for including any discussion of U here is the fact that it is frequently mentioned in published research.

17.2 Wilcoxon's Matched-Pairs Signed-Ranks Test

Wilcoxon is not only credited with developing the most popular distribution-free test for independent groups, but he also deserves credit for developing the most popular test for matched groups (or paired scores). This test is the distribution-free analogue of the *t*-test for matched scores, and tests the null hypothesis that two matched samples were drawn from identical populations or else from symmetric populations with the same mean. More specifically, it tests the null hypothesis that the distribution of difference scores (in the population) is symmetric about zero. This is the same hypothesis tested by the corresponding *t*-test when that test's normality assumption is met.

Wilcoxon Matched-
Pairs Signed-Ranks
Test

The development of the logic behind the **Wilcoxon Matched-Pairs Signed-Ranks Test** is as straightforward as it was for his Rank-Sum Test, and can be illustrated with a simple example. Assume that we want to test the often stated hypothesis that a long-range program of running will reduce blood pressure. To test this hypothesis we measure the blood pressure of a number of subjects, ask them to engage in a systematic program of running for six weeks, and again test their blood pressure at the end of that period. Our dependent variable will be the change in blood pressure over the six-week interval. If the running does reduce blood pressure we would expect that most of the subjects would show a lower reading the second time, and thus a positive pre-post difference. We would also expect that those whose blood pressure actually went up (and thus have a negative pre-post difference) would be only *slightly* higher. On the other hand, if running is worthless as a method of controlling blood pressure, then about half of the difference scores will be positive and half will be negative, and the positive differences will be about as large as the negative ones. In other words, if H_0 is really true we would no longer expect most changes to be in the predicted direction with only small changes in the unpredicted direction.

As is illustrated in the following numerical example, in carrying out the Wilcoxon Matched-Pairs Signed-Ranks Test we first calculate the difference score for each pair of measurements. We then rank all difference scores *without* regard to the sign of the difference, then assign the algebraic sign of the differences to the ranks themselves, and finally sum the positive and negative ranks separately. The test statistic (T) is taken as the smaller of the absolute values (i.e., ignoring sign) of the two sums, and is evaluated against the tabled entries in Appendix (T). (It is important to note that we only attach algebraic signs to the ranks for convenience. We could just as easily, for example, circle those ranks which went with improvement and underline those which went with deterioration. We are merely trying to differentiate between the two cases.)

T

Assume that the study previously described produced the following data on systolic blood pressure before and after the six-week training session.

Before	130	170	125	160	143	130	145	160
After	120	163	120	135	130	136	144	120
Change $(B-A)$	10	7	5	25	13	−6	1	40
Rank of Change	5	4	2	7	6	3	1	8
Signed Rank	5	4	2	7	6	−3	1	8

$T_+ = \Sigma(\text{positive ranks}) = 33$ $T_- = \Sigma(\text{negative ranks}) = -3$

The first two rows contain the subjects' blood pressure as measured before and after a six-week program of running. In the third row you see the change scores obtained by subtracting the "after" score from the "before". Notice that only one subject showed a negative change—i.e., increased his blood pressure. In the fourth row all of the change scores are ranked without regard to the direction of the change, and in the fifth row the appropriate sign has been appended to the ranks to discriminate those whose blood pressure decreased from those whose blood pressure increased. At the bottom of the table we see the sum of the positive and negative ranks (T_+ and T_-). Since T is defined as the smaller absolute value of T_+ and T_-, $T = 3$.

To evaluate T we refer to Appendix (T), but this table has a somewhat different format from the other tables we have seen. The easiest way to understand what the entries in the table represent is by way of an analogy. Suppose that to test the fairness of a coin you were going to flip it eight times and reject the null hypothesis, at $\alpha = .05$ (one-tailed), if there were too few heads. Out of eight flips of a coin there is no set of outcomes which has a probability of *exactly* .05 under H_0. The binomial distribution tells us that the probability of 1 or fewer heads is .0352 and the probability of two or fewer heads is .1445. Thus if we want to work at $\alpha = .05$, we can either reject for 1 or fewer heads, in which case the probability of a Type I error is .0352 (less than .05), or we can reject for two or fewer heads, in which case the probability of a Type I error is .1445 (very much greater than .05). The same kind of problem arises with T because it, like the binomial, is a discrete distribution.

In Appendix (T) we find that for a one-tailed test at $\alpha = .025$ (or a two-tailed test at $\alpha = .05$) with $n = 8$ the entries are 3(.0195) and 4(.0273). This tells us that if we want to work at a (one-tailed) $\alpha = .025$ we can either reject H_0 for $T \le 3$ (in which case α actually equals .0195) or we can reject for $T \le 4$ (in which case the true value of α is .0273). Since we want a two-tailed test the probabilities should be doubled to 3(.0390) and 4(.0546). Since we obtained a T value of 3, we will reject H_0 at a "nominal" $\alpha = .05$, but an actual $\alpha = .0390$. We will therefore conclude that blood pressure was generally reduced following the training program.

Ties

Ties can occur in our data in two different ways. A given subject could have the same before and after scores, leading to a different score of zero, which has no sign. In this case we normally eliminate that subject from consideration and reduce the sample size accordingly.

In addition, we could have tied difference scores which lead to tied rankings. If the tied scores are both of the same sign, we can break the ties in any way we wish (or assign tied ranks) without affecting the final outcome. If the scores are of opposite sign we normally assign tied ranks and proceed as usual (although Bradley (1968) argues for alternative procedures for actually breaking the tie).

The Normal Approximation

When the sample size is larger than 50, which is the limit for Appendix (T), a normal approximation is available to evaluate T. For large sample sizes we know that the sampling distribution is approximately normally distributed with mean $= n(n+1)/4$ and standard error $= \sqrt{n(n+1)(2n+1)/24}$. Thus we can calculate

$$z = \frac{T - n(n+1)/4}{\sqrt{n(n+1)(2n+1)/24}}$$

and evaluate z using Appendix (z). The procedure is directly analogous to that used with the Rank-Sum Test and will not be repeated here.

17.3 *Kruskal-Wallis One-Way Analysis of Variance*

Kruskal-Wallis One-Way Analysis of Variance

The ***Kruskal-Wallis One-Way Analysis of Variance*** is a direct generalization of the Wilcoxon Rank-Sum test to the case where we have three or more independent groups. As such it is the distribution-free analogue of the one-way analysis of variance discussed in Chapter 11. It tests the hypothesis that all samples were drawn from identical populations, and is particularly sensitive to differences in central tendency.

To perform the Kruskal-Wallis test we simply rank all scores without regard to group membership, and then compute the sum of the ranks for each group. The sums are denoted by R_i. If the null hypothesis is true we would expect the R_is to be more-or-less equal (aside from differences due to the size of the samples). A measure of the degree to which the R_i differ is provided by

$$H = \frac{12}{N(N+1)} \sum_{i=1}^{k} \frac{R_i^2}{n_i} - 3(N+1)$$

where $k =$ the number of groups, $n_i =$ the number of observations in Group$_i$, $R_i =$ the sum of the ranks in Group$_i$, and, $N = \Sigma n_i =$ total sample size. H is then evaluated against the χ^2 distribution on $k - 1$ df.

As an example assume that the data in Table 17.3 represent the number of simple arithmetic problems solved (correctly or incorrectly) in one hour by subjects given a depressant drug, a stimulant, or a placebo. The calculations are shown in the lower part of the table. The obtained value of $H = 10.10$, which can be treated as a χ^2 on $3 - 1 = 2$ df. The critical value of χ_2^2 for $\alpha = .05$ is found in Appendix (χ^2) to be 5.99. Since $10.10 > 5.99$, we can reject H_0 and conclude that the three drugs lead to different rates of performance.

TABLE 17.3
Kruskal-Wallis
Test Applied
to Data on
Problem-Solving

	DEPRESSANT		STIMULANT		PLACEBO	
	Score	*Rank*	*Score*	*Rank*	*Score*	*Rank*
	55	9	73	15	61	11
	23	2	82	18	54	8
	40	3	51	7	80	17
	17	1	63	12	47	5
	50	6	74	16		
	60	10	85	19		
	44	4	66	13		
			69	14		
R_i		35		114		41

$$H = \frac{12}{N(N+1)} \sum_{i=1}^{k} \frac{R_i^2}{n_i} - 3(N+1)$$

$$= \frac{12}{19(20)} \left(\frac{35^2}{7} + \frac{114^2}{8} + \frac{41^2}{4} \right) - 3(20)$$

$$= \frac{12}{380}(2219.75) - 60$$

$$= 70.10 - 60 = 10.10$$

$$\chi_2^2(.05) = 5.99$$

Ties

Here again we run into problems with tied scores. If the ties are among scores in the same group, any method of breaking ties leads to the same answer. If the ties are among scores in different groups, you can assign tied ranks and proceed as usual, or you can assign tied ranks and apply a correction procedure for ties (cf. Siegel, 1956), or you can adopt one of the approaches discussed by Bradley (1968). Bradley recommends using some sort of random process such as flipping a coin, although very few people actually adopt this approach.

17.4 Friedman's Rank Test for k Correlated Samples

Friedman's Rank Test for k Correlated Samples

The last test to be discussed in this chapter is the distribution-free analogue of the one-way repeated measures analysis of variance, ***Friedman's Rank Test for k Correlated Samples***. This test is closely related to a standard repeated measures analysis of variance applied to ranks instead of raw scores.

It is a test on the null hypothesis that the scores for each treatment were drawn from identical populations, and is especially sensitive to population differences in central tendency.

Assume that we want to test the hypothesis that the judged quality of a lecture is related to the number of visual aids used. The experimenter obtains 17 people who are willing to give lectures to local groups on a variety of topics. Each lecturer delivers the same lecture to three different, but equivalent, audiences, once with no visual aids, once with a few transparencies to illustrate major points, and once with transparencies and flip charts to illustrate every point to be made. At the end of each lecture the audience is asked to rate the lecture on a 75 point scale, and the mean rating across all members of the audience is taken as the dependent variable. Hypothetical data are presented in Table 17.4, where a high score represents a more

TABLE 17.4

Hypothetical Data on Rated Quality of Lectures

		NUMBER OF VISUAL AIDS		
Lecturer		None	Few	Many
1		50 (1)	55 (3)	54 (2)
2		32 (2)	37 (3)	25 (1)
3		60 (1)	70 (3)	63 (2)
4		58 (2)	60 (3)	55 (1)
5		41 (1)	66 (3)	59 (2)
6		36 (2)	40 (3)	28 (1)
7		26 (3)	25 (2)	20 (1)
8		49 (1)	60 (3)	50 (2)
9		72 (1)	73 (2)	75 (3)
10		49 (2)	54 (3)	42 (1)
11		52 (2)	57 (3)	47 (1)
12		36 (2)	42 (3)	29 (1)
13		37 (3)	34 (2)	31 (1)
14		58 (3)	50 (1)	56 (2)
15		39 (1)	48 (3)	44 (2)
16		25 (2)	29 (3)	18 (1)
17		51 (1)	63 (2)	68 (3)
		30	45	27

$$\chi_F^2 = \frac{12}{Nk(k+1)}\Sigma R_i^2 - 3N(k+1)$$

$$= \frac{12}{17(3)(4)}(30^2 + 45^2 + 27^2) - 3(17)(4)$$

$$= \frac{12}{204}(3654) - 204$$

$$= 214.94 - 204 = 10.94$$

favorable rating. The ranking of the raw scores within each subject are shown in parentheses.

If the null hypothesis is true we would expect the rankings to be randomly distributed within each lecturer, and the sum of the rankings in each condition (column) would be approximately equal. On the other hand, if a few visual aids were to lead to the most popular lecture, then most lecturers would have their highest rating under that condition, and the sum of the rankings for the three conditions would be decidedly unequal.

To apply Friedman's test we rank the raw scores for each lecturer separately, and then sum the rankings for each condition. We then evaluate the variability of the sums by computing

$$\chi_F^2 = \frac{12}{Nk(k+1)} \sum_{i=1}^{k} (R_i)^2 - 3N(k+1)$$

where R_i = the sum of the ranks for the ith condition, N = the number of subjects (lecturers), k = the number of conditions. This value of χ_F^2 can be referred to the χ^2 distribution on $k-1$ df.[†]

For the data in Table 17.4, $\chi_F^2 = 10.94$ on 2 df. Since $\chi_2^2(.05) = 5.99$, we will reject H_0 and conclude that the judged quality of a lecture differs as a function of the degree to which visual aids are included. (Note that the null hypothesis that we have just tested says nothing about differences among subjects, and in fact subject differences are completely eliminated by the ranking procedure.)

There is an interesting relationship between Friedman's test statistic (χ_F^2) and Kendall's Coefficient of Concordance (W). Although the two statistics were developed for different purposes, it is easy to demonstrate that

$$W = \frac{\chi_F^2}{N(k-1)}.$$

(In fact this is the basis for the test on W given in Chapter 10.) Knowing this relationship between the two statistics, we can readily convert a test of significance to a measure of the degree to which subjects agree (in this example) on the relative quality of the lectures. Once again we see that our statistical procedures (and the questions they address) are highly interrelated.

17.5 Summary

This chapter has briefly summarized a set of procedures which require far less restrictive assumptions concerning the populations from which our data

---

[†] The Chi-square approximation used with Friedman's test is not particularly satisfactory with small sample sizes. Bradley (1968) includes exact tables for $k = 3$, $N \leq 15$ and for $k = 4$, $N \leq 8$. Siegel (1956) presents similar, though less complete, tables.

have been sampled. We first discussed Wilcoxon's Rank-Sum test, which is the distribution-free analogue of the independent-sample *t* test. To perform the test we simply ranked the data and asked if the distribution of ranks resembled the distribution that we would expect if the null hypothesis were true. The same general logic applies to the Wilcoxon Matched-Pairs Signed-Ranks test, which is the distribution-free analogue of the matched-sample *t* test. We then discussed two distribution-free tests which are analogous to an analysis of variance on independent measures (the Kruskal-Wallis) and repeated measures (the Friedman). Although it is important to be familiar with these four tests simply because they are commonly used, it was argued at the beginning of the chapter that the advantages we gain by limiting our assumptions may not be worth the loss in power which often accompanies the use of distribution-free tests. Whatever one's stand on this question, the general principle remains that the overriding concern in the use and interpretation of any statistical procedure is not statistical sophistication, but common sense.

Exercises for Chapter 17

17.1 One of the methods advocated by Bradley (1968) for breaking ties is to randomly assign to tied scores the ranks they would have had if they had not been exactly tied. What advantages and disadvantages can you find for such a procedure?

17.2 What is the difference between the null hypothesis tested by Wilcoxon's Rank-Sum Test and the corresponding *t* test?

17.3 What is the difference between the null hypothesis tested by Wilcoxon's Signed-Ranks Test and the corresponding *t* test?

17.4 One of the arguments put forth in favor of distribution-free tests is that they are more appropriate for ordinal scale data. This issue was addressed earlier in the book. Give two reasons why this argument is not a good one.

17.5 Why is rejection of the null hypothesis using a *t* test a more specific statement than rejection of the null using the appropriate distribution-free test?

17.6 McConaughy (1980) has argued that younger children organize stories in terms of simple descriptive ("and then . . .") models, whereas older children incorporate causal and social inferences. Suppose that we asked two groups of children differing in age to summarize a story they just read. We then counted the number of statements in the summary that can be classed as inferences. The data are:

> *Younger*: 0 1 0 3 2 5 2
> *Older*:   4 7 6 4 8 7

a. Analyze these data using the two-tailed Rank-Sum Test.
b. What would you conclude?

17.7 Kapp, Frysinger, Gallagher, & Hazelton (1979) have demonstrated that lesions in the amygdala can reduce certain responses commonly associated with fear (e.g., decreases in heart rate). If fear is really reduced, then it should be more difficult to train an avoidance response in lesioned animals since the aversiveness of the stimulus will be reduced. Assume two groups of rabbits: Group I has lesions in the amygdala, while Group II does not. The following data represent number of trails to learn an avoidance response for each animal.

> *Lesions*: 15 14 15   8   7 22 36 19 14 18 17
> *Control*:   9   4   9 10   6   6   4   5   9

a. Analyze the data using the Wilcoxon Rank-Sum Test (two-tailed).
b. What would you conclude?

17.8 Repeat the analysis in Exercise 17.7 using the normal approximation.

17.9 Repeat the analysis in Exercise 17.7 using the appropriate one-tailed test.

17.10 Nurcombe & Fitzhenry-Coor (1979) have argued that training in diagnostic techniques should lead a clinician to generate (and test) more hypotheses in coming to a decision about a case. Suppose that we take 10 psychiatric residents who are just beginning their residency and ask them to watch a video-tape of an interview and record their thoughts on the case every few minutes. We then count the number of hypotheses each resident includes in his written remarks. The experiment is repeated at the end of the residency with a comparable video tape. The data are:

Subject	**1**	**2**	**3**	**4**	**5**	**6**	**7**	**8**	**9**	**10**
Before	8	4	2	2	4	8	3	1	3	9
After	7	9	3	6	3	10	6	7	8	7

a. Analyze the data using Wilcoxon's Signed-Ranks Test.
b. What would you conclude?

17.11 a. Repeat the analysis for Exercise 17.10 using the normal approximation.
b. How well do the two answers agree? Why don't they agree exactly?

17.12   It has been argued that first-born children tend to be more independent than later-born children. Suppose that we develop a 20-point scale of
independence and rate each of 20 second-born children and their first-born
sibling using our scale. We do this when both siblings are adults, thus
eliminating obvious age effects. The data are:

Sibling Pair:	1	2	3	4	5	6	7	8	9	10	11	12	13	14	15	16	17	18	19	20
1st Born:	12	18	13	17	8	15	16	5	8	12	13	5	14	20	19	17	2	5	15	18
2nd Born:	10	12	15	13	9	12	13	8	10	8	8	9	8	10	14	11	7	7	13	12

a.   Analyze the data using Wilcoxon's Matched-pairs Signed-Ranks Test.
b.   What would you conclude?

17.13   The results in Exercise 17.12 are not quite as clear-cut as we might
like. Plot the differences as a function of the first born's score. What does
this figure suggest?

17.14   Rerun the analysis in Exercise 17.12 using the normal approximation.

17.15   Three rival Professors teaching English I all claim the honor of
having the dumbest students. To settle the issue eight students are randomly
drawn from each class and given the same exam, which is graded by a neutral
professor who does not know from which class the students came. The data
are:

Prof. A:	82	71	56	58	63	64	62	53
Prof. B:	55	88	85	83	71	70	68	72
Prof. C:	65	54	66	68	72	78	65	73

Run the appropriate test and draw the appropriate conclusions.

17.16   A group of psychologists operating a group home for delinquent
adolescents needs to show that it is successful. They sample ten adolescents
living at home who have been identified by the police as having problems,
ten similar adolescents living in foster homes, and ten adolescents living in
the group home. As an indicator variable they use truancy (number of days
truant in the past semester), which is readily obtained from school records.
On the basis of the following data, draw the appropriate conclusions.

Natural Home:	15	18	19	14	5	8	12	13	7
Foster Home:	16	14	20	22	19	5	17	18	12
Group Home:	10	13	14	11	7	3	4	18	2

17.17   As an alternative method of evaluating a Group Home, suppose that
we take 12 adolescents who have been declared delinquent. We take the
number of days truant 1) during the month before they are placed in the
home, 2) during the month they live in the home, and 3) during the month

after they leave the home. The data are:

Time	ADOLESCENT											
	1	*2*	*3*	*4*	*5*	*6*	*7*	*8*	*9*	*10*	*11*	*12*
Before	10	12	12	19	5	13	20	8	12	10	8	18
During	5	8	13	10	10	8	16	4	14	3	3	16
After	8	7	10	12	8	7	12	5	9	5	3	2

Apply Friedman's test. What do you conclude?

17.18   It would be possible to apply Friedman's test to the data in Exercise 17.10. What would we lose if we did so?

17.19   For the data in Exercise 17.10 we could say that three out of ten residents used fewer hypotheses the second time and seven used more. We could test this with χ^2. How would this differ from Friedman's test?

17.20   The history of statistical hypothesis testing really began with a tea tasting experiment (Fisher, 1935), so it seems fitting for this book to end with one. The owner of a small tearoom doesn't really think that people can tell the difference between the first cup made with a given tea bag and the second and third cups made with the same bag (that is why it is still a *small* tearoom). He chooses eight different brands of tea bags, makes three cups of tea with each, and then has a group of customers rate each cup on a 20-point scale (without knowing which cup is which). The data are shown here:

Tea Brands	CUP		
	First	Second	Third
1	8	3	2
2	15	14	4
3	16	17	12
4	7	5	4
5	9	3	6
6	8	9	4
7	10	3	4
8	12	10	2

Using Friedman's test, draw the appropriate conclusions.

Appendices

APPENDIX (z)   The Normal Distribution

z	Mean to z	Larger portion	Smaller portion	y	z	Mean to z	Larger portion	Smaller portion	y
.00	0.0000	0.5000	0.5000	0.3989	.45	0.1736	0.6736	0.3264	0.3605
.01	0.0040	0.5040	0.4960	0.3989	.46	0.1772	0.6772	0.3228	0.3589
.02	0.0080	0.5080	0.4920	0.3989	.47	0.1808	0.6808	0.3192	0.3572
.03	0.0120	0.5120	0.4880	0.3988	.48	0.1844	0.6844	0.3156	0.3555
.04	0.0160	0.5160	0.4840	0.3986	.49	0.1879	0.6879	0.3121	0.3538
.05	0.0199	0.5199	0.4801	0.3984	.50	0.1915	0.6915	0.3085	0.3521
.06	0.0239	0.5239	0.4761	0.3982	.51	0.1950	0.6950	0.3050	0.3503
.07	0.0279	0.5279	0.4721	0.3980	.52	0.1985	0.6985	0.3015	0.3485
.08	0.0319	0.5319	0.4681	0.3977	.53	0.2019	0.7019	0.2981	0.3467
.09	0.0359	0.5359	0.4641	0.3973	.54	0.2054	0.7054	0.2946	0.3448
.10	0.0398	0.5398	0.4602	0.3970	.55	0.2088	0.7088	0.2912	0.3429
.11	0.0438	0.5438	0.4562	0.3965	.56	0.2123	0.7123	0.2877	0.3410
.12	0.0478	0.5478	0.4522	0.3961	.57	0.2157	0.7157	0.2843	0.3391
.13	0.0517	0.5517	0.4483	0.3956	.58	0.2190	0.7190	0.2810	0.3372
.14	0.0557	0.5557	0.4443	0.3951	.59	0.2224	0.7224	0.2776	0.3352
.15	0.0596	0.5596	0.4404	0.3945	.60	0.2257	0.7257	0.2743	0.3332
.16	0.0636	0.5636	0.4364	0.3939	.61	0.2291	0.7291	0.2709	0.3312
.17	0.0675	0.5675	0.4325	0.3932	.62	0.2324	0.7324	0.2676	0.3292
.18	0.0714	0.5714	0.4286	0.3925	.63	0.2357	0.7357	0.2643	0.3271
.19	0.0753	0.5753	0.4247	0.3918	.64	0.2389	0.7389	0.2611	0.3251
.20	0.0793	0.5793	0.4207	0.3910	.65	0.2422	0.7422	0.2578	0.3230
.21	0.0832	0.5832	0.4168	0.3902	.66	0.2454	0.7454	0.2546	0.3209
.22	0.0871	0.5871	0.4129	0.3894	.67	0.2486	0.7486	0.2514	0.3187
.23	0.0910	0.5910	0.4090	0.3885	.68	0.2517	0.7517	0.2483	0.3166
.24	0.0948	0.5948	0.4052	0.3876	.69	0.2549	0.7549	0.2451	0.3144
.25	0.0987	0.5987	0.4013	0.3867	.70	0.2580	0.7580	0.2420	0.3123
.26	0.1026	0.6026	0.3974	0.3857	.71	0.2611	0.7611	0.2389	0.3101
.27	0.1064	0.6064	0.3936	0.3847	.72	0.2642	0.7642	0.2358	0.3079
.28	0.1103	0.6103	0.3897	0.3836	.73	0.2673	0.7673	0.2327	0.3056
.29	0.1141	0.6141	0.3859	0.3825	.74	0.2704	0.7704	0.2296	0.3034
.30	0.1179	0.6179	0.3821	0.3814	.75	0.2734	0.7734	0.2266	0.3011
.31	0.1217	0.6217	0.3783	0.3802	.76	0.2764	0.7764	0.2236	0.2989
.32	0.1255	0.6255	0.3745	0.3790	.77	0.2794	0.7794	0.2206	0.2966
.33	0.1293	0.6293	0.3707	0.3778	.78	0.2823	0.7823	0.2177	0.2943
.34	0.1331	0.6331	0.3669	0.3765	.79	0.2852	0.7852	0.2148	0.2920
.35	0.1368	0.6368	0.3632	0.3752	.80	0.2881	0.7881	0.2119	0.2897
.36	0.1406	0.6406	0.3594	0.3739	.81	0.2910	0.7910	0.2090	0.2874
.37	0.1443	0.6443	0.3557	0.3725	.82	0.2939	0.7939	0.2061	0.2850
.38	0.1480	0.6480	0.3520	0.3712	.83	0.2967	0.7967	0.2033	0.2827
.39	0.1517	0.6517	0.3483	0.3697	.84	0.2995	0.7995	0.2005	0.2803
.40	0.1554	0.6554	0.3446	0.3683	.85	0.3023	0.8023	0.1977	0.2780
.41	0.1591	0.6591	0.3409	0.3668	.86	0.3051	0.8051	0.1949	0.2756
.42	0.1628	0.6628	0.3372	0.3653	.87	0.3078	0.8078	0.1922	0.2732
.43	0.1664	0.6664	0.3336	0.3637	.88	0.3106	0.8106	0.1894	0.2709
.44	0.1700	0.6700	0.3300	0.3621	.89	0.3133	0.8133	0.1867	0.2685

APPENDIX (z)   (Cont.)

z	Mean to z	Larger portion	Smaller portion	y	z	Mean to z	Larger portion	Smaller portion	y
.90	0.3159	0.8159	0.1841	0.2661	1.35	0.4115	0.9115	0.0885	0.1604
.91	0.3186	0.8186	0.1814	0.2637	1.36	0.4131	0.9131	0.0869	0.1582
.92	0.3212	0.8212	0.1788	0.2613	1.37	0.4147	0.9147	0.0853	0.1561
.93	0.3238	0.8238	0.1762	0.2589	1.38	0.4162	0.9162	0.0838	0.1539
.94	0.3264	0.8264	0.1736	0.2565	1.39	0.4177	0.9177	0.0823	0.1518
.95	0.3289	0.8289	0.1711	0.2541	1.40	0.4192	0.9192	0.0808	0.1497
.96	0.3315	0.8315	0.1685	0.2516	1.41	0.4207	0.9207	0.0793	0.1476
.97	0.3340	0.8340	0.1660	0.2492	1.42	0.4222	0.9222	0.0778	0.1456
.98	0.3365	0.8365	0.1635	0.2468	1.43	0.4236	0.9236	0.0764	0.1435
.99	0.3389	0.8389	0.1611	0.2444	1.44	0.4251	0.9251	0.0749	0.1415
1.00	0.3413	0.8413	0.1587	0.2420	1.45	0.4265	0.9265	0.0735	0.1394
1.01	0.3438	0.8438	0.1562	0.2396	1.46	0.4279	0.9279	0.0721	0.1374
1.02	0.3461	0.8461	0.1539	0.2371	1.47	0.4292	0.9292	0.0708	0.1354
1.03	0.3485	0.8485	0.1515	0.2347	1.48	0.4306	0.9306	0.0694	0.1334
1.04	0.3508	0.8508	0.1492	0.2323	1.49	0.4319	0.9319	0.0681	0.1315
1.05	0.3531	0.8531	0.1469	0.2299	1.50	0.4332	0.9332	0.0668	0.1295
1.06	0.3554	0.8554	0.1446	0.2275	1.51	0.4345	0.9345	0.0655	0.1276
1.07	0.3577	0.8577	0.1423	0.2251	1.52	0.4357	0.9357	0.0643	0.1257
1.08	0.3599	0.8599	0.1401	0.2227	1.53	0.4370	0.9370	0.0630	0.1238
1.09	0.3621	0.8621	0.1379	0.2203	1.54	0.4382	0.9382	0.0618	0.1219
1.10	0.3643	0.8643	0.1357	0.2179	1.55	0.4394	0.9394	0.0606	0.1200
1.11	0.3665	0.8665	0.1335	0.2155	1.56	0.4406	0.9406	0.0594	0.1182
1.12	0.3686	0.8686	0.1314	0.2131	1.57	0.4418	0.9418	0.0582	0.1163
1.13	0.3708	0.8708	0.1292	0.2107	1.58	0.4429	0.9429	0.0571	0.1145
1.14	0.3729	0.8729	0.1271	0.2083	1.59	0.4441	0.9441	0.0559	0.1127
1.15	0.3749	0.8749	0.1251	0.2059	1.60	0.4452	0.9452	0.0548	0.1109
1.16	0.3770	0.8770	0.1230	0.2036	1.61	0.4463	0.9463	0.0537	0.1092
1.17	0.3790	0.8790	0.1210	0.2012	1.62	0.4474	0.9474	0.0526	0.1074
1.18	0.3810	0.8810	0.1190	0.1989	1.63	0.4484	0.9484	0.0516	0.1057
1.19	0.3830	0.8830	0.1170	0.1965	1.64	0.4495	0.9495	0.0505	0.1040
1.20	0.3849	0.8849	0.1151	0.1942	1.65	0.4505	0.9505	0.0495	0.1023
1.21	0.3869	0.8869	0.1131	0.1919	1.66	0.4515	0.9515	0.0485	0.1006
1.22	0.3888	0.8888	0.1112	0.1895	1.67	0.4525	0.9525	0.0475	0.0989
1.23	0.3907	0.8907	0.1093	0.1872	1.68	0.4535	0.9535	0.0465	0.0973
1.24	0.3925	0.8925	0.1075	0.1849	1.69	0.4545	0.9545	0.0455	0.0957
1.25	0.3944	0.8944	0.1056	0.1826	1.70	0.4554	0.9554	0.0446	0.0940
1.26	0.3962	0.8962	0.1038	0.1804	1.71	0.4564	0.9564	0.0436	0.0925
1.27	0.3980	0.8980	0.1020	0.1781	1.72	0.4573	0.9573	0.0427	0.0909
1.28	0.3997	0.8997	0.1003	0.1758	1.73	0.4582	0.9582	0.0418	0.0893
1.29	0.4015	0.9015	0.0985	0.1736	1.74	0.4591	0.9591	0.0409	0.0878
1.30	0.4032	0.9032	0.0968	0.1714	1.75	0.4599	0.9599	0.0401	0.0863
1.31	0.4049	0.9049	0.0951	0.1691	1.76	0.4608	0.9608	0.0392	0.0848
1.32	0.4066	0.9066	0.0934	0.1669	1.77	0.4616	0.9616	0.0384	0.0833
1.33	0.4082	0.9082	0.0918	0.1647	1.78	0.4625	0.9625	0.0375	0.0818
1.34	0.4099	0.9099	0.0901	0.1626	1.79	0.4633	0.9633	0.0367	0.0804

APPENDIX **(z)**   **(Cont.)**

z	Mean to z	Larger portion	Smaller portion	y	z	Mean to z	Larger portion	Smaller portion	y
1.80	0.4641	0.9641	0.0359	0.0790	2.25	0.4878	0.9878	0.0122	0.0317
1.81	0.4649	0.9649	0.0351	0.0775	2.26	0.4881	0.9881	0.0119	0.0310
1.82	0.4656	0.9656	0.0344	0.0761	2.27	0.4884	0.9884	0.0116	0.0303
1.83	0.4664	0.9664	0.0336	0.0748	2.28	0.4887	0.9887	0.0113	0.0297
1.84	0.4671	0.9671	0.0329	0.0734	2.29	0.4890	0.9890	0.0110	0.0290
1.85	0.4678	0.9678	0.0322	0.0721	2.30	0.4893	0.9893	0.0107	0.0283
1.86	0.4686	0.9686	0.0314	0.0707	2.31	0.4896	0.9896	0.0104	0.0277
1.87	0.4693	0.9693	0.0307	0.0694	2.32	0.4898	0.9898	0.0102	0.0270
1.88	0.4699	0.9699	0.0301	0.0681	2.33	0.4901	0.9901	0.0099	0.0264
1.89	0.4706	0.9706	0.0294	0.0669	2.34	0.4904	0.9904	0.0096	0.0258
1.90	0.4713	0.9713	0.0287	0.0656	2.35	0.4906	0.9906	0.0094	0.0252
1.91	0.4719	0.9719	0.0281	0.0644	2.36	0.4909	0.9909	0.0091	0.0246
1.92	0.4726	0.9726	0.0274	0.0632	2.37	0.4911	0.9911	0.0089	0.0241
1.93	0.4732	0.9732	0.0268	0.0620	2.38	0.4913	0.9913	0.0087	0.0235
1.94	0.4738	0.9738	0.0262	0.0608	2.39	0.4916	0.9916	0.0084	0.0229
1.95	0.4744	0.9744	0.0256	0.0596	2.40	0.4918	0.9918	0.0082	0.0224
1.96	0.4750	0.9750	0.0250	0.0584	2.41	0.4920	0.9920	0.0080	0.0219
1.97	0.4756	0.9756	0.0244	0.0573	2.42	0.4922	0.9922	0.0078	0.0213
1.98	0.4761	0.9761	0.0239	0.0562	2.43	0.4925	0.9925	0.0075	0.0208
1.99	0.4767	0.9767	0.0233	0.0551	2.44	0.4927	0.9927	0.0073	0.0203
2.00	0.4772	0.9772	0.0228	0.0540	2.45	0.4929	0.9929	0.0071	0.0198
2.01	0.4778	0.9778	0.0222	0.0529	2.46	0.4931	0.9931	0.0069	0.0194
2.02	0.4783	0.9783	0.0217	0.0519	2.47	0.4932	0.9932	0.0068	0.0189
2.03	0.4788	0.9788	0.0212	0.0508	2.48	0.4934	0.9934	0.0066	0.0184
2.04	0.4793	0.9793	0.0207	0.0498	2.49	0.4936	0.9936	0.0064	0.0180
2.05	0.4798	0.9798	0.0202	0.0488	2.50	0.4938	0.9938	0.0062	0.0175
2.06	0.4803	0.9803	0.0197	0.0478	2.51	0.4940	0.9940	0.0060	0.0171
2.07	0.4808	0.9808	0.0192	0.0468	2.52	0.4941	0.9941	0.0059	0.0167
2.08	0.4812	0.9812	0.0188	0.0459	2.53	0.4943	0.9943	0.0057	0.0163
2.09	0.4817	0.9817	0.0183	0.0449	2.54	0.4945	0.9945	0.0055	0.0158
2.10	0.4821	0.9821	0.0179	0.0440	2.55	0.4946	0.9946	0.0054	0.0154
2.11	0.4826	0.9826	0.0174	0.0431	2.56	0.4948	0.9948	0.0052	0.0151
2.12	0.4830	0.9830	0.0170	0.0422	2.57	0.4949	0.9949	0.0051	0.0147
2.13	0.4834	0.9834	0.0166	0.0413	2.58	0.4951	0.9951	0.0049	0.0143
2.14	0.4838	0.9838	0.0162	0.0404	2.59	0.4952	0.9952	0.0048	0.0139
2.15	0.4842	0.9842	0.0158	0.0396	2.60	0.4953	0.9953	0.0047	0.0136
2.16	0.4846	0.9846	0.0154	0.0387	2.61	0.4955	0.9955	0.0045	0.0132
2.17	0.4850	0.9850	0.0150	0.0379	2.62	0.4956	0.9956	0.0044	0.0129
2.18	0.4854	0.9854	0.0146	0.0371	2.63	0.4957	0.9957	0.0043	0.0126
2.19	0.4857	0.9857	0.0143	0.0363	2.64	0.4959	0.9959	0.0041	0.0122
2.20	0.4861	0.9861	0.0139	0.0355	2.65	0.4960	0.9960	0.0040	0.0119
2.21	0.4864	0.9864	0.0136	0.0347	2.66	0.4961	0.9961	0.0039	0.0116
2.22	0.4868	0.9868	0.0132	0.0339	2.67	0.4962	0.9962	0.0038	0.0113
2.23	0.4871	0.9871	0.0129	0.0332	2.68	0.4963	0.9963	0.0037	0.0110
2.24	0.4875	0.9875	0.0125	0.0325	2.69	0.4964	0.9964	0.0036	0.0107

two tailed

APPENDIX (z)   (Cont.)

z	Mean to z	Larger portion	Smaller portion	y	z	Mean to z	Larger portion	Smaller portion	y
2.70	0.4965	0.9965	0.0035	0.0104	2.90	0.4981	0.9981	0.0019	0.0060
2.71	0.4966	0.9966	0.0034	0.0101	2.91	0.4982	0.9982	0.0018	0.0058
2.72	0.4967	0.9967	0.0033	0.0099	2.92	0.4982	0.9982	0.0018	0.0056
2.73	0.4968	0.9968	0.0032	0.0096	2.93	0.4983	0.9983	0.0017	0.0055
2.74	0.4969	0.9969	0.0031	0.0093	2.94	0.4984	0.9984	0.0016	0.0053
2.75	0.4970	0.9970	0.0030	0.0091	2.95	0.4984	0.9984	0.0016	0.0051
2.76	0.4971	0.9971	0.0029	0.0088	2.96	0.4985	0.9985	0.0015	0.0050
2.77	0.4972	0.9972	0.0028	0.0086	2.97	0.4985	0.9985	0.0015	0.0048
2.78	0.4973	0.9973	0.0027	0.0084	2.98	0.4986	0.9986	0.0014	0.0047
2.79	0.4974	0.9974	0.0026	0.0081	2.99	0.4986	0.9986	0.0014	0.0046
2.80	0.4974	0.9974	0.0026	0.0079	3.00	0.4987	0.9987	0.0013	0.0044
2.81	0.4975	0.9975	0.0025	0.0077	. . .	. . .	. . .	. . .	. . .
2.82	0.4976	0.9976	0.0024	0.0075	3.25	0.4994	0.9994	0.0006	0.0020
2.83	0.4977	0.9977	0.0023	0.0073	. . .	. . .	. . .	. . .	. . .
2.84	0.4977	0.9977	0.0023	0.0071	3.50	0.4998	0.9998	0.0002	0.0009
2.85	0.4978	0.9978	0.0022	0.0069	. . .	. . .	. . .	. . .	. . .
2.86	0.4979	0.9979	0.0021	0.0067	3.75	0.4999	0.9999	0.0001	0.0004
2.87	0.4979	0.9979	0.0021	0.0065	. . .	. . .	. . .	. . .	. . .
2.88	0.4980	0.9980	0.0020	0.0063	4.00	0.5000	1.0000	0.0000	0.0001
2.89	0.4981	0.9981	0.0019	0.0061					

cannonical = extension of regression. many Y's + many x's.

Source: The entries in this table were computed by the author.

R=corr btwn Y (criterion) & best linear combo of predictors
use F to asses sig of R.

R² = % of accountable variation

b = slope

β² = used in F to assess standard error. F = b²/Sb²
does β contribe significantly to Y Ho = β = 0

increment of b = see if increase of b significantly more
variance explained. like stepwise.

APPENDIX (χ²) Upper Percentage Points of the χ^2 Distribution

df	.995	.990	.975	.950	.900	.750	.500	.250	.100	.050	.025	.010	.005
1	0.00	0.00	0.00	0.00	0.02	0.10	0.45	1.32	2.71	3.84	5.02	6.63	7.88
2	0.01	0.02	0.05	0.10	0.21	0.58	1.39	2.77	4.61	5.99	7.38	9.21	10.60
3	0.07	0.11	0.22	0.35	0.58	1.21	2.37	4.11	6.25	7.82	9.35	11.35	12.84
4	0.21	0.30	0.48	0.71	1.06	1.92	3.36	5.39	7.78	9.49	11.14	13.28	14.86
5	0.41	0.55	0.83	1.15	1.61	2.67	4.35	6.63	9.24	11.07	12.83	15.09	16.75
6	0.68	0.87	1.24	1.64	2.20	3.45	5.35	7.84	10.64	12.59	14.45	16.81	18.55
7	0.99	1.24	1.69	2.17	2.83	4.25	6.35	9.04	12.02	14.07	16.01	18.48	20.28
8	1.34	1.65	2.18	2.73	3.49	5.07	7.34	10.22	13.36	15.51	17.54	20.09	21.96
9	1.73	2.09	2.70	3.33	4.17	5.90	8.34	11.39	14.68	16.92	19.02	21.66	23.59
10	2.15	2.56	3.25	3.94	4.87	6.74	9.34	12.55	15.99	18.31	20.48	23.21	25.19
11	2.60	3.05	3.82	4.57	5.58	7.58	10.34	13.70	17.28	19.68	21.92	24.72	26.75
12	3.07	3.57	4.40	5.23	6.30	8.44	11.34	14.85	18.55	21.03	23.34	26.21	28.30
13	3.56	4.11	5.01	5.89	7.04	9.30	12.34	15.98	19.81	22.36	24.74	27.69	29.82
14	4.07	4.66	5.63	6.57	7.79	10.17	13.34	17.12	21.06	23.69	26.12	29.14	31.31
15	4.60	5.23	6.26	7.26	8.55	11.04	14.34	18.25	22.31	25.00	27.49	30.58	32.80
16	5.14	5.81	6.91	7.96	9.31	11.91	15.34	19.37	23.54	26.30	28.85	32.00	34.27
17	5.70	6.41	7.56	8.67	10.09	12.79	16.34	20.49	24.77	27.59	30.19	33.41	35.72
18	6.26	7.01	8.23	9.39	10.86	13.68	17.34	21.60	25.99	28.87	31.53	34.81	37.15
19	6.84	7.63	8.91	10.12	11.65	14.56	18.34	22.72	27.20	30.14	32.85	36.19	38.58
20	7.43	8.26	9.59	10.85	12.44	15.45	19.34	23.83	28.41	31.41	34.17	37.56	40.00
21	8.03	8.90	10.28	11.59	13.24	16.34	20.34	24.93	29.62	32.67	35.48	38.93	41.40
22	8.64	9.54	10.98	12.34	14.04	17.24	21.34	26.04	30.81	33.93	36.78	40.29	42.80
23	9.26	10.19	11.69	13.09	14.85	18.14	22.34	27.14	32.01	35.17	38.08	41.64	44.18
24	9.88	10.86	12.40	13.85	15.66	19.04	23.34	28.24	33.20	36.42	39.37	42.98	45.56
25	10.52	11.52	13.12	14.61	16.47	19.94	24.34	29.34	34.38	37.65	40.65	44.32	46.93
26	11.16	12.20	13.84	15.38	17.29	20.84	25.34	30.43	35.56	38.89	41.92	45.64	48.29
27	11.80	12.88	14.57	16.15	18.11	21.75	26.34	31.53	36.74	40.11	43.20	46.96	49.64
28	12.46	13.56	15.31	16.93	18.94	22.66	27.34	32.62	37.92	41.34	44.46	48.28	50.99
29	13.12	14.26	16.05	17.71	19.77	23.57	28.34	33.71	39.09	42.56	45.72	49.59	52.34
30	13.78	14.95	16.79	18.49	20.60	24.48	29.34	34.80	40.26	43.77	46.98	50.89	53.67
40	20.67	22.14	24.42	26.51	29.06	33.67	39.34	45.61	51.80	55.75	59.34	63.71	66.80
50	27.96	29.68	32.35	34.76	37.69	42.95	49.34	56.33	63.16	67.50	71.42	76.17	79.52
60	35.50	37.46	40.47	43.19	46.46	52.30	59.34	66.98	74.39	79.08	83.30	88.40	91.98
70	43.25	45.42	48.75	51.74	55.33	61.70	69.34	77.57	85.52	90.53	95.03	100.44	104.24
80	51.14	53.52	57.15	60.39	64.28	71.15	79.34	88.13	96.57	101.88	106.63	112.34	116.35
90	59.17	61.74	65.64	69.13	73.29	80.63	89.33	98.65	107.56	113.14	118.14	124.13	128.32
100	67.30	70.05	74.22	77.93	82.36	90.14	99.33	109.14	118.49	124.34	129.56	135.82	140.19

Source: The entries in this table were computed by the author.

1 tail

2 tail

df	.25	.20	.15	.10	.05	.025	.01	.005	.0005
1	1.000	1.376	1.963	3.078	6.314	12.706	31.821	63.657	636.62
2	0.816	1.061	1.386	1.886	2.920	4.303	6.965	9.925	31.599
3	0.765	0.978	1.250	1.638	2.353	3.182	4.541	5.841	12.924
4	0.741	0.941	1.190	1.533	2.132	2.776	3.747	4.604	8.610
5	0.727	0.920	1.156	1.476	2.015	2.571	3.365	4.032	6.869
6	0.718	0.906	1.134	1.440	1.943	2.447	3.143	3.707	5.959
7	0.711	0.896	1.119	1.415	1.895	2.365	2.998	3.499	5.408
8	0.706	0.889	1.108	1.397	1.860	2.306	2.896	3.355	5.041
9	0.703	0.883	1.100	1.383	1.833	2.262	2.821	3.250	4.781
10	0.700	0.879	1.093	1.372	1.812	2.228	2.764	3.169	4.587
11	0.697	0.876	1.088	1.363	1.796	2.201	2.718	3.106	4.437
12	0.695	0.873	1.083	1.356	1.782	2.179	2.681	3.055	4.318
13	0.694	0.870	1.079	1.350	1.771	2.160	2.650	3.012	4.221
14	0.692	0.868	1.076	1.345	1.761	2.145	2.624	2.977	4.140
15	0.691	0.866	1.074	1.341	1.753	2.131	2.602	2.947	4.073
16	0.690	0.865	1.071	1.337	1.746	2.120	2.583	2.921	4.015
17	0.689	0.863	1.069	1.333	1.740	2.110	2.567	2.898	3.965
18	0.688	0.862	1.067	1.330	1.734	2.101	2.552	2.878	3.922
19	0.688	0.861	1.066	1.328	1.729	2.093	2.539	2.861	3.883
20	0.687	0.860	1.064	1.325	1.725	2.086	2.528	2.845	3.850
21	0.686	0.859	1.063	1.323	1.721	2.080	2.518	2.831	3.819
22	0.686	0.858	1.061	1.321	1.717	2.074	2.508	2.819	3.792
23	0.685	0.858	1.060	1.319	1.714	2.069	2.500	2.807	3.768
24	0.685	0.857	1.059	1.318	1.711	2.064	2.492	2.797	3.745
25	0.684	0.856	1.058	1.316	1.708	2.060	2.485	2.787	3.725
26	0.684	0.856	1.058	1.315	1.706	2.056	2.479	2.779	3.707
27	0.684	0.855	1.057	1.314	1.703	2.052	2.473	2.771	3.690
28	0.683	0.855	1.056	1.313	1.701	2.048	2.467	2.763	3.674
29	0.683	0.854	1.055	1.311	1.699	2.045	2.462	2.756	3.659
30	0.683	0.854	1.055	1.310	1.697	2.042	2.457	2.750	3.646
40	0.681	0.851	1.050	1.303	1.684	2.021	2.423	2.704	3.551
50	0.679	0.849	1.047	1.299	1.676	2.009	2.403	2.678	3.496
100	0.677	0.845	1.042	1.290	1.660	1.984	2.364	2.626	3.390
∞	0.674	0.842	1.036	1.282	1.645	1.960	2.326	2.576	3.291

Source: The entries in this table were computed by the author.

APPENDIX (Power)

Power as a
Function of δ
and Significance
Level (α)

δ	ALPHA FOR TWO-TAILED TEST			
	.10	**.05**	**.02**	**.01**
1.00	0.26	0.17	0.09	0.06
1.10	0.29	0.20	0.11	0.07
1.20	0.33	0.22	0.13	0.08
1.30	0.37	0.26	0.15	0.10
1.40	0.40	0.29	0.18	0.12
1.50	0.44	0.32	0.20	0.14
1.60	0.48	0.36	0.23	0.17
1.70	0.52	0.40	0.27	0.19
1.80	0.56	0.44	0.30	0.22
1.90	0.60	0.48	0.34	0.25
2.00	0.64	0.52	0.37	0.28
2.10	0.68	0.56	0.41	0.32
2.20	0.71	0.60	0.45	0.35
2.30	0.74	0.63	0.49	0.39
2.40	0.78	0.67	0.53	0.43
2.50	0.80	0.71	0.57	0.47
2.60	0.83	0.74	0.61	0.51
2.70	0.85	0.77	0.65	0.55
2.80	0.88	0.80	0.68	0.59
2.90	0.90	0.83	0.72	0.63
3.00	0.91	0.85	0.75	0.66
3.10	0.93	0.87	0.78	0.70
3.20	0.94	0.89	0.81	0.73
3.30	0.95	0.91	0.84	0.77
3.40	0.96	0.93	0.86	0.80
3.50	0.97	0.94	0.88	0.82
3.60	0.98	0.95	0.90	0.85
3.70	0.98	0.96	0.92	0.87
3.80	0.98	0.97	0.93	0.89
3.90	0.99	0.97	0.94	0.91
4.00	0.99	0.98	0.95	0.92
4.10	0.99	0.98	0.96	0.94
4.20	—	0.99	0.97	0.95
4.30	—	0.99	0.98	0.96
4.40	—	0.99	0.98	0.97
4.50	—	0.99	0.99	0.97
4.60	—	—	0.99	0.98
4.70	—	—	0.99	0.98
4.80	—	—	0.99	0.99
4.90	—	—	—	0.99
5.00	—	—	—	0.99

Source: The entries in this table were computed by the author.

APPENDIX (r')   Table of Fisher's Transformation of r to r'

r	r'	r	r'	r	r'	r	r'	r	r'
0.000	0.000	0.200	0.203	0.400	0.424	0.600	0.693	0.800	1.099
0.005	0.005	0.205	0.208	0.405	0.430	0.605	0.701	0.805	1.113
0.010	0.010	0.210	0.213	0.410	0.436	0.610	0.709	0.810	1.127
0.015	0.015	0.215	0.218	0.415	0.442	0.615	0.717	0.815	1.142
0.020	0.020	0.220	0.224	0.420	0.448	0.620	0.725	0.820	1.157
0.025	0.025	0.225	0.229	0.425	0.454	0.625	0.733	0.825	1.172
0.030	0.030	0.230	0.234	0.430	0.460	0.630	0.741	0.830	1.188
0.035	0.035	0.235	0.239	0.435	0.466	0.635	0.750	0.835	1.204
0.040	0.040	0.240	0.245	0.440	0.472	0.640	0.758	0.840	1.221
0.045	0.045	0.245	0.250	0.445	0.478	0.645	0.767	0.845	1.238
0.050	0.050	0.250	0.255	0.450	0.485	0.650	0.775	0.850	1.256
0.055	0.055	0.255	0.261	0.455	0.491	0.655	0.784	0.855	1.274
0.060	0.060	0.260	0.266	0.460	0.497	0.660	0.793	0.860	1.293
0.065	0.065	0.265	0.271	0.465	0.504	0.665	0.802	0.865	1.313
0.070	0.070	0.270	0.277	0.470	0.510	0.670	0.811	0.870	1.333
0.075	0.075	0.275	0.282	0.475	0.517	0.675	0.820	0.875	1.354
0.080	0.080	0.280	0.288	0.480	0.523	0.680	0.829	0.880	1.376
0.085	0.085	0.285	0.293	0.485	0.530	0.685	0.838	0.885	1.398
0.090	0.090	0.290	0.299	0.490	0.536	0.690	0.848	0.890	1.422
0.095	0.095	0.295	0.304	0.495	0.543	0.695	0.858	0.895	1.447
0.100	0.100	0.300	0.310	0.500	0.549	0.700	0.867	0.900	1.472
0.105	0.105	0.305	0.315	0.505	0.556	0.705	0.877	0.905	1.499
0.110	0.110	0.310	0.321	0.510	0.563	0.710	0.887	0.910	1.528
0.115	0.116	0.315	0.326	0.515	0.570	0.715	0.897	0.915	1.557
0.120	0.121	0.320	0.332	0.520	0.576	0.720	0.908	0.920	1.589
0.125	0.126	0.325	0.337	0.525	0.583	0.725	0.918	0.925	1.623
0.130	0.131	0.330	0.343	0.530	0.590	0.730	0.929	0.930	1.658
0.135	0.136	0.335	0.348	0.535	0.597	0.735	0.940	0.935	1.697
0.140	0.141	0.340	0.354	0.540	0.604	0.740	0.950	0.940	1.738
0.145	0.146	0.345	0.360	0.545	0.611	0.745	0.962	0.945	1.783
0.150	0.151	0.350	0.365	0.550	0.618	0.750	0.973	0.950	1.832
0.155	0.156	0.355	0.371	0.555	0.626	0.755	0.984	0.955	1.886
0.160	0.161	0.360	0.377	0.560	0.633	0.760	0.996	0.960	1.946
0.165	0.167	0.365	0.383	0.565	0.640	0.765	1.008	0.965	2.014
0.170	0.172	0.370	0.388	0.570	0.648	0.770	1.020	0.970	2.092
0.175	0.177	0.375	0.394	0.575	0.655	0.775	1.033	0.975	2.185
0.180	0.182	0.380	0.400	0.580	0.662	0.780	1.045	0.980	2.298
0.185	0.187	0.385	0.406	0.585	0.670	0.785	1.058	0.985	2.443
0.190	0.192	0.390	0.412	0.590	0.678	0.790	1.071	0.990	2.647
0.195	0.198	0.395	0.418	0.595	0.685	0.795	1.085	0.995	2.994

Source: The entries in this table were computed by the author.

APPENDIX (F) Critical Values of the *F* Distribution Alpha = .05

DEGREES OF FREEDOM FOR NUMERATOR

	1	2	3	4	5	6	7	8	9	10	15	20	25	30	40	50
1	161.4	199.5	215.8	224.8	230.0	233.8	236.5	238.6	240.1	242.1	245.2	248.4	248.9	250.5	250.8	252.6
2	18.51	19.00	19.16	19.25	19.30	19.33	19.35	19.37	19.38	19.40	19.43	19.44	19.46	19.47	19.48	19.48
3	10.13	9.55	9.28	9.12	9.01	8.94	8.89	8.85	8.81	8.79	8.70	8.66	8.63	8.62	8.59	8.58
4	7.71	6.94	6.59	6.39	6.26	6.16	6.09	6.04	6.00	5.96	5.86	5.80	5.77	5.75	5.72	5.70
5	6.61	5.79	5.41	5.19	5.05	4.95	4.88	4.82	4.77	4.74	4.62	4.56	4.52	4.50	4.46	4.44
6	5.99	5.14	4.76	4.53	4.39	4.28	4.21	4.15	4.10	4.06	3.94	3.87	3.83	3.81	3.77	3.75
7	5.59	4.74	4.35	4.12	3.97	3.87	3.79	3.73	3.68	3.64	3.51	3.44	3.40	3.38	3.34	3.32
8	5.32	4.46	4.07	3.84	3.69	3.58	3.50	3.44	3.39	3.35	3.22	3.15	3.11	3.08	3.04	3.02
9	5.12	4.26	3.86	3.63	3.48	3.37	3.29	3.23	3.18	3.14	3.01	2.94	2.89	2.86	2.83	2.80
10	4.96	4.10	3.71	3.48	3.33	3.22	3.14	3.07	3.02	2.98	2.85	2.77	2.73	2.70	2.66	2.64
11	4.84	3.98	3.59	3.36	3.20	3.09	3.01	2.95	2.90	2.85	2.72	2.65	2.60	2.57	2.53	2.51
12	4.75	3.89	3.49	3.26	3.11	3.00	2.91	2.85	2.80	2.75	2.62	2.54	2.50	2.47	2.43	2.40
13	4.67	3.81	3.41	3.18	3.03	2.92	2.83	2.77	2.71	2.67	2.53	2.46	2.41	2.38	2.34	2.31
14	4.60	3.74	3.34	3.11	2.96	2.85	2.76	2.70	2.65	2.60	2.46	2.39	2.34	2.31	2.27	2.24
15	4.54	3.68	3.29	3.06	2.90	2.79	2.71	2.64	2.59	2.54	2.40	2.33	2.28	2.25	2.20	2.18
16	4.49	3.63	3.24	3.01	2.85	2.74	2.66	2.59	2.54	2.49	2.35	2.28	2.23	2.19	2.15	2.12
17	4.45	3.59	3.20	2.96	2.81	2.70	2.61	2.55	2.49	2.45	2.31	2.23	2.18	2.15	2.10	2.08
18	4.41	3.55	3.16	2.93	2.77	2.66	2.58	2.51	2.46	2.41	2.27	2.19	2.14	2.11	2.06	2.04
19	4.38	3.52	3.13	2.90	2.74	2.63	2.54	2.48	2.42	2.38	2.23	2.16	2.11	2.07	2.03	2.00
20	4.35	3.49	3.10	2.87	2.71	2.60	2.51	2.45	2.39	2.35	2.20	2.12	2.07	2.04	1.99	1.97
22	4.30	3.44	3.05	2.82	2.66	2.55	2.46	2.40	2.34	2.30	2.15	2.07	2.02	1.98	1.94	1.91
24	4.26	3.40	3.01	2.78	2.62	2.51	2.42	2.36	2.30	2.25	2.11	2.03	1.97	1.94	1.89	1.86
26	4.23	3.37	2.98	2.74	2.59	2.47	2.39	2.32	2.27	2.22	2.07	1.99	1.94	1.90	1.85	1.82
28	4.20	3.34	2.95	2.71	2.56	2.45	2.36	2.29	2.24	2.19	2.04	1.96	1.91	1.87	1.82	1.79
30	4.17	3.32	2.92	2.69	2.53	2.42	2.33	2.27	2.21	2.16	2.01	1.93	1.88	1.84	1.79	1.76
40	4.08	3.23	2.84	2.61	2.45	2.34	2.25	2.18	2.12	2.08	1.92	1.84	1.78	1.74	1.69	1.66
50	4.03	3.18	2.79	2.56	2.40	2.29	2.20	2.13	2.07	2.03	1.87	1.78	1.73	1.69	1.63	1.60
60	4.00	3.15	2.76	2.53	2.37	2.25	2.17	2.10	2.04	1.99	1.84	1.75	1.69	1.65	1.59	1.56
120	3.92	3.07	2.68	2.45	2.29	2.18	2.09	2.02	1.96	1.91	1.75	1.66	1.60	1.55	1.50	1.46
200	3.89	3.04	2.65	2.42	2.26	2.14	2.06	1.98	1.93	1.88	1.72	1.62	1.56	1.52	1.46	1.41
500	3.86	3.01	2.62	2.39	2.23	2.12	2.03	1.96	1.90	1.85	1.69	1.59	1.53	1.48	1.42	1.38
1000	3.85	3.01	2.61	2.38	2.22	2.11	2.02	1.95	1.89	1.84	1.68	1.58	1.52	1.47	1.41	1.36

DEGREES OF FREEDOM FOR DENOMINATOR

APPENDIX (F)   Critical Values of the *F* Distribution   Alpha = .025

DEGREES OF FREEDOM FOR NUMERATOR

	1	2	3	4	5	6	7	8	9	10	15	20	25	30	40	50
1	647.8	799.5	864.2	899.6	921.8	937.1	948.2	956.7	963.3	968.6	984.9	993.1	998.1	1001	1006	1008
2	38.51	39.00	39.17	39.25	39.30	39.33	39.36	39.37	39.39	39.40	39.43	39.45	39.46	39.46	39.47	39.48
3	17.44	16.04	15.44	15.10	14.89	14.73	14.62	14.54	14.47	14.42	14.25	14.17	14.12	14.08	14.04	14.01
4	12.22	10.65	9.98	9.60	9.36	9.20	9.07	8.98	8.90	8.84	8.66	8.56	8.50	8.46	8.41	8.38
5	10.01	8.43	7.76	7.39	7.15	6.98	6.85	6.76	6.68	6.62	6.43	6.33	6.27	6.23	6.18	6.14
6	8.81	7.26	6.60	6.23	5.99	5.82	5.70	5.60	5.52	5.46	5.27	5.17	5.11	5.07	5.01	4.98
7	8.07	6.54	5.89	5.52	5.29	5.12	4.99	4.90	4.82	4.76	4.57	4.47	4.40	4.36	4.31	4.28
8	7.57	6.06	5.42	5.05	4.82	4.65	4.53	4.43	4.36	4.30	4.10	4.00	3.94	3.89	3.84	3.81
9	7.21	5.71	5.08	4.72	4.48	4.32	4.20	4.10	4.03	3.96	3.77	3.67	3.60	3.56	3.51	3.47
10	6.94	5.46	4.83	4.47	4.24	4.07	3.95	3.85	3.78	3.72	3.52	3.42	3.35	3.31	3.26	3.22
11	6.72	5.26	4.63	4.28	4.04	3.88	3.76	3.66	3.59	3.53	3.33	3.23	3.16	3.12	3.06	3.03
12	6.55	5.10	4.47	4.12	3.89	3.73	3.61	3.51	3.44	3.37	3.18	3.07	3.01	2.96	2.91	2.87
13	6.41	4.97	4.35	4.00	3.77	3.60	3.48	3.39	3.31	3.25	3.05	2.95	2.88	2.84	2.78	2.74
14	6.30	4.86	4.24	3.89	3.66	3.50	3.38	3.29	3.21	3.15	2.95	2.84	2.78	2.73	2.67	2.64
15	6.20	4.77	4.15	3.80	3.58	3.41	3.29	3.20	3.12	3.06	2.86	2.76	2.69	2.64	2.59	2.55
16	6.12	4.69	4.08	3.73	3.50	3.34	3.22	3.12	3.05	2.99	2.79	2.68	2.61	2.57	2.51	2.47
17	6.04	4.62	4.01	3.66	3.44	3.28	3.16	3.06	2.98	2.92	2.72	2.62	2.55	2.50	2.44	2.41
18	5.98	4.56	3.95	3.61	3.38	3.22	3.10	3.01	2.93	2.87	2.67	2.56	2.49	2.44	2.38	2.35
19	5.92	4.51	3.90	3.56	3.33	3.17	3.05	2.96	2.88	2.82	2.62	2.51	2.44	2.39	2.33	2.30
20	5.87	4.46	3.86	3.51	3.29	3.13	3.01	2.91	2.84	2.77	2.57	2.46	2.40	2.35	2.29	2.25
22	5.79	4.38	3.78	3.44	3.22	3.05	2.93	2.84	2.76	2.70	2.50	2.39	2.32	2.27	2.21	2.17
24	5.72	4.32	3.72	3.38	3.15	2.99	2.87	2.78	2.70	2.64	2.44	2.33	2.26	2.21	2.15	2.11
26	5.66	4.27	3.67	3.33	3.10	2.94	2.82	2.73	2.65	2.59	2.39	2.28	2.21	2.16	2.09	2.05
28	5.61	4.22	3.63	3.29	3.06	2.90	2.78	2.69	2.61	2.55	2.34	2.23	2.16	2.11	2.05	2.01
30	5.57	4.18	3.59	3.25	3.03	2.87	2.75	2.65	2.57	2.51	2.31	2.20	2.12	2.07	2.01	1.97
40	5.42	4.05	3.46	3.13	2.90	2.74	2.62	2.53	2.45	2.39	2.18	2.07	1.99	1.94	1.88	1.83
50	5.34	3.97	3.39	3.05	2.83	2.67	2.55	2.46	2.38	2.32	2.11	1.99	1.92	1.87	1.80	1.75
60	5.29	3.93	3.34	3.01	2.79	2.63	2.51	2.41	2.33	2.27	2.06	1.94	1.87	1.82	1.74	1.70
120	5.15	3.80	3.23	2.89	2.67	2.52	2.39	2.30	2.22	2.16	1.94	1.82	1.75	1.69	1.61	1.56
200	5.10	3.76	3.18	2.85	2.63	2.47	2.35	2.26	2.18	2.11	1.90	1.78	1.70	1.64	1.56	1.51
500	5.05	3.72	3.14	2.81	2.59	2.43	2.31	2.22	2.14	2.07	1.86	1.74	1.65	1.60	1.52	1.46
1000	5.04	3.70	3.13	2.80	2.58	2.42	2.30	2.20	2.13	2.06	1.85	1.72	1.64	1.58	1.50	1.45

DEGREES OF FREEDOM FOR DENOMINATOR

APPENDIX (F)   Critical Values of the F Distribution   Alpha = .01

DEGREES OF FREEDOM FOR DENOMINATOR

DEGREES OF FREEDOM FOR NUMERATOR

	1	2	3	4	5	6	7	8	9	10	15	20	25	30	40	50
1	4048	4993	5377	5577	5668	5924	5992	6096	6132	6168	6079	6168	6214	6355	6168	6213
2	98.50	99.01	99.15	99.23	99.30	99.33	99.35	99.39	99.40	99.43	99.38	99.48	99.43	99.37	99.44	99.59
3	34.12	30.82	29.46	28.71	28.24	27.91	27.67	27.49	27.34	27.23	26.87	26.69	26.58	26.51	26.41	26.36
4	21.20	18.00	16.69	15.98	15.52	15.21	14.98	14.80	14.66	14.55	14.20	14.02	13.91	13.84	13.75	13.69
5	16.26	13.27	12.06	11.39	10.97	10.67	10.46	10.29	10.16	10.05	9.72	9.55	9.45	9.38	9.29	9.24
6	13.75	10.92	9.78	9.15	8.75	8.47	8.26	8.10	7.98	7.87	7.56	7.40	7.30	7.23	7.14	7.09
7	12.25	9.55	8.45	7.85	7.46	7.19	6.99	6.84	6.72	6.62	6.31	6.16	6.06	5.99	5.91	5.86
8	11.26	8.65	7.59	7.01	6.63	6.37	6.18	6.03	5.91	5.81	5.52	5.36	5.26	5.20	5.12	5.07
9	10.56	8.02	6.99	6.42	6.06	5.80	5.61	5.47	5.35	5.26	4.96	4.81	4.71	4.65	4.57	4.52
10	10.04	7.56	6.55	5.99	5.64	5.39	5.20	5.06	4.94	4.85	4.56	4.41	4.31	4.25	4.17	4.12
11	9.65	7.21	6.22	5.67	5.32	5.07	4.89	4.74	4.63	4.54	4.25	4.10	4.01	3.94	3.86	3.81
12	9.33	6.93	5.95	5.41	5.06	4.82	4.64	4.50	4.39	4.30	4.01	3.86	3.76	3.70	3.62	3.57
13	9.07	6.70	5.74	5.21	4.86	4.62	4.44	4.30	4.19	4.10	3.82	3.66	3.57	3.51	3.43	3.38
14	8.86	6.51	5.56	5.04	4.69	4.46	4.28	4.14	4.03	3.94	3.66	3.51	3.41	3.35	3.27	3.22
15	8.68	6.36	5.42	4.89	4.56	4.32	4.14	4.00	3.89	3.80	3.52	3.37	3.28	3.21	3.13	3.08
16	8.53	6.23	5.29	4.77	4.44	4.20	4.03	3.89	3.78	3.69	3.41	3.26	3.16	3.10	3.02	2.97
17	8.40	6.11	5.18	4.67	4.34	4.10	3.93	3.79	3.68	3.59	3.31	3.16	3.07	3.00	2.92	2.87
18	8.29	6.01	5.09	4.58	4.25	4.01	3.84	3.71	3.60	3.51	3.23	3.08	2.98	2.92	2.84	2.78
19	8.18	5.93	5.01	4.50	4.17	3.94	3.77	3.63	3.52	3.43	3.15	3.00	2.91	2.84	2.76	2.71
20	8.10	5.85	4.94	4.43	4.10	3.87	3.70	3.56	3.46	3.37	3.09	2.94	2.84	2.78	2.69	2.64
22	7.95	5.72	4.82	4.31	3.99	3.76	3.59	3.45	3.35	3.26	2.98	2.83	2.73	2.67	2.58	2.53
24	7.82	5.61	4.72	4.22	3.90	3.67	3.50	3.36	3.26	3.17	2.89	2.74	2.64	2.58	2.49	2.44
26	7.72	5.53	4.64	4.14	3.82	3.59	3.42	3.29	3.18	3.09	2.81	2.66	2.57	2.50	2.42	2.36
28	7.64	5.45	4.57	4.07	3.75	3.53	3.36	3.23	3.12	3.03	2.75	2.60	2.51	2.44	2.35	2.30
30	7.56	5.39	4.51	4.02	3.70	3.47	3.30	3.17	3.07	2.98	2.70	2.55	2.45	2.39	2.30	2.25
40	7.31	5.18	4.31	3.83	3.51	3.29	3.12	2.99	2.89	2.80	2.52	2.37	2.27	2.20	2.11	2.06
50	7.17	5.06	4.20	3.72	3.41	3.19	3.02	2.89	2.78	2.70	2.42	2.27	2.17	2.10	2.01	1.95
60	7.08	4.98	4.13	3.65	3.34	3.12	2.95	2.82	2.72	2.63	2.35	2.20	2.10	2.03	1.94	1.88
120	6.85	4.79	3.95	3.48	3.17	2.96	2.79	2.66	2.56	2.47	2.19	2.03	1.93	1.86	1.76	1.70
200	6.76	4.71	3.88	3.41	3.11	2.89	2.73	2.60	2.50	2.41	2.13	1.97	1.87	1.79	1.69	1.63
500	6.69	4.65	3.82	3.36	3.05	2.84	2.68	2.55	2.44	2.36	2.07	1.92	1.81	1.74	1.63	1.57
1000	6.67	4.63	3.80	3.34	3.04	2.82	2.66	2.53	2.43	2.34	2.06	1.90	1.79	1.72	1.61	1.54

Source: The entries in this table were computed by the author.

APPENDIX (t_d)

Critical Values
of Dunnett's
t Statistic (t_d)

Error df	α	Two-tailed comparisons k = number of treatment means, including control								
		2	3	4	5	6	7	8	9	10
5	.05	2.57	3.03	3.29	3.48	3.62	3.73	3.82	3.90	3.97
	.01	4.03	4.63	4.98	5.22	5.41	5.56	5.69	5.80	5.89
6	.05	2.45	2.86	3.10	3.26	3.39	3.49	3.57	3.64	3.71
	.01	3.71	4.21	4.51	4.71	4.87	5.00	5.10	5.20	5.28
7	.05	2.36	2.75	2.97	3.12	3.24	3.33	3.41	3.47	3.53
	.01	3.50	3.95	4.21	4.39	4.53	4.64	4.74	4.82	4.89
8	.05	2.31	2.67	2.88	3.02	3.13	3.22	3.29	3.35	3.41
	.01	3.36	3.77	4.00	4.17	4.29	4.40	4.48	4.56	4.62
9	.05	2.26	2.61	2.81	2.95	3.05	3.14	3.20	3.26	3.32
	.01	3.25	3.63	3.85	4.01	4.12	4.22	4.30	4.37	4.43
10	.05	2.23	2.57	2.76	2.89	2.99	3.07	3.14	3.19	3.24
	.01	3.17	3.53	3.74	3.88	3.99	4.08	4.16	4.22	4.28
11	.05	2.20	2.53	2.72	2.84	2.94	3.02	3.08	3.14	3.19
	.01	3.11	3.45	3.65	3.79	3.89	3.98	4.05	4.11	4.16
12	.05	2.18	2.50	2.68	2.81	2.90	2.98	3.04	3.09	3.14
	.01	3.05	3.39	3.58	3.71	3.81	3.89	3.96	4.02	4.07
13	.05	2.16	2.48	2.65	2.78	2.87	2.94	3.00	3.06	3.10
	.01	3.01	3.33	3.52	3.65	3.74	3.82	3.89	3.94	3.99
14	.05	2.14	2.46	2.63	2.75	2.84	2.91	2.97	3.02	3.07
	.01	2.98	3.29	3.47	3.59	3.69	3.76	3.83	3.88	3.93
15	.05	2.13	2.44	2.61	2.73	2.82	2.89	2.95	3.00	3.04
	.01	2.95	3.25	3.43	3.55	3.64	3.71	3.78	3.83	3.88
16	.05	2.12	2.42	2.59	2.71	2.80	2.87	2.92	2.97	3.02
	.01	2.92	3.22	3.39	3.51	3.60	3.67	3.73	3.78	3.83
17	.05	2.11	2.41	2.58	2.69	2.78	2.85	2.90	2.95	3.00
	.01	2.90	3.19	3.36	3.47	3.56	3.63	3.69	3.74	3.79
18	.05	2.10	2.40	2.56	2.68	2.76	2.83	2.89	2.94	2.98
	.01	2.88	3.17	3.33	3.44	3.53	3.60	3.66	3.71	3.75
19	.05	2.09	2.39	2.55	2.66	2.75	2.81	2.87	2.92	2.96
	.01	2.86	3.15	3.31	3.42	3.50	3.57	3.63	3.68	3.72
20	.05	2.09	2.38	2.54	2.65	2.73	2.80	2.86	2.90	2.95
	.01	2.85	3.13	3.29	3.40	3.48	3.55	3.60	3.65	3.69
24	.05	2.06	2.35	2.51	2.61	2.70	2.76	2.81	2.86	2.90
	.01	2.80	3.07	3.22	3.32	3.40	3.47	3.52	3.57	3.61
30	.05	2.04	2.32	2.47	2.58	2.66	2.72	2.77	2.82	2.86
	.01	2.75	3.01	3.15	3.25	3.33	3.39	3.44	3.49	3.52
40	.05	2.02	2.29	2.44	2.54	2.62	2.68	2.73	2.77	2.81
	.01	2.70	2.95	3.09	3.19	3.26	3.32	3.37	3.41	3.44
60	.05	2.00	2.27	2.41	2.51	2.58	2.64	2.69	2.73	2.77
	.01	2.66	2.90	3.03	3.12	3.19	3.25	3.29	3.33	3.37
120	.05	1.98	2.24	2.38	2.47	2.55	2.60	2.65	2.69	2.73
	.01	2.62	2.85	2.97	3.06	3.12	3.18	3.22	3.26	3.29
∞	.05	1.96	2.21	2.35	2.44	2.51	2.57	2.61	2.65	2.69
	.01	2.58	2.79	2.92	3.00	3.06	3.11	3.15	3.19	3.22

Reproduced from: C. W. Dunnett, "New tables for multiple comparisons with a control". BIOMETRICS **20**:482–491. 1964. With permission of The Biometric Society.

APPENDIX (t')

Critical Values
for Dunn's
Multiple Comparison
Test   Alpha = .05

df	NO. OF COMPARISONS								
	2	**3**	**4**	**5**	**6**	**7**	**8**	**9**	**10**
5	3.16	3.53	3.81	4.03	4.22	4.38	4.53	4.66	4.77
6	2.97	3.29	3.52	3.71	3.86	4.00	4.12	4.22	4.32
7	2.84	3.13	3.34	3.50	3.64	3.75	3.86	3.95	4.03
8	2.75	3.02	3.21	3.36	3.48	3.58	3.68	3.76	3.83
9	2.69	2.93	3.11	3.25	3.36	3.46	3.55	3.62	3.69
10	2.63	2.87	3.04	3.17	3.28	3.37	3.45	3.52	3.58
11	2.59	2.82	2.98	3.11	3.21	3.29	3.37	3.44	3.50
12	2.56	2.78	2.93	3.05	3.15	3.24	3.31	3.37	3.43
13	2.53	2.75	2.90	3.01	3.11	3.19	3.26	3.32	3.37
14	2.51	2.72	2.86	2.98	3.07	3.15	3.21	3.27	3.33
15	2.49	2.69	2.84	2.95	3.04	3.11	3.18	3.23	3.29
16	2.47	2.67	2.81	2.92	3.01	3.08	3.15	3.20	3.25
17	2.46	2.65	2.79	2.90	2.98	3.06	3.12	3.17	3.22
18	2.45	2.64	2.77	2.88	2.96	3.03	3.09	3.15	3.20
19	2.43	2.63	2.76	2.86	2.94	3.01	3.07	3.13	3.17
20	2.42	2.61	2.74	2.85	2.93	3.00	3.06	3.11	3.15
21	2.41	2.60	2.73	2.83	2.91	2.98	3.04	3.09	3.14
22	2.41	2.59	2.72	2.82	2.90	2.97	3.02	3.07	3.12
23	2.40	2.58	2.71	2.81	2.89	2.95	3.01	3.06	3.10
24	2.39	2.57	2.70	2.80	2.88	2.94	3.00	3.05	3.09
25	2.38	2.57	2.69	2.79	2.86	2.93	2.99	3.03	3.08
30	2.36	2.54	2.66	2.75	2.82	2.89	2.94	2.99	3.03
40	2.33	2.50	2.62	2.70	2.78	2.84	2.89	2.93	2.97
50	2.31	2.48	2.59	2.68	2.75	2.81	2.85	2.90	2.94
75	2.29	2.45	2.56	2.64	2.71	2.77	2.81	2.86	2.89
100	2.28	2.43	2.54	2.63	2.69	2.75	2.79	2.83	2.87
∞	2.24	2.39	2.50	2.58	2.64	2.69	2.73	2.77	2.81

| | NO. OF COMPARISONS | | | | | | | | |
df	15	20	25	30	35	40	45	50	55
5	5.25	5.60	5.89	6.14	6.35	6.54	6.71	6.87	7.01
6	4.70	4.98	5.21	5.40	5.56	5.71	5.84	5.96	6.07
7	4.36	4.59	4.79	4.94	5.08	5.20	5.31	5.41	5.50
8	4.12	4.33	4.50	4.64	4.76	4.86	4.96	5.04	5.12
9	3.95	4.15	4.30	4.42	4.53	4.62	4.71	4.78	4.85
10	3.83	4.00	4.14	4.26	4.36	4.44	4.52	4.59	4.65
11	3.73	3.89	4.02	4.13	4.22	4.30	4.37	4.44	4.49
12	3.65	3.81	3.93	4.03	4.12	4.19	4.26	4.32	4.37
13	3.58	3.73	3.85	3.95	4.03	4.10	4.16	4.22	4.27
14	3.53	3.67	3.79	3.88	3.96	4.03	4.09	4.14	4.19
15	3.48	3.62	3.73	3.82	3.90	3.96	4.02	4.07	4.12
16	3.44	3.58	3.69	3.77	3.85	3.91	3.96	4.01	4.06
17	3.41	3.54	3.65	3.73	3.80	3.86	3.92	3.97	4.01
18	3.38	3.51	3.61	3.69	3.76	3.82	3.87	3.92	3.96
19	3.35	3.48	3.58	3.66	3.73	3.79	3.84	3.88	3.93
20	3.33	3.46	3.55	3.63	3.70	3.75	3.80	3.85	3.89
21	3.31	3.43	3.53	3.60	3.67	3.73	3.78	3.82	3.86
22	3.29	3.41	3.50	3.58	3.64	3.70	3.75	3.79	3.83
23	3.27	3.39	3.48	3.56	3.62	3.68	3.72	3.77	3.81
24	3.26	3.38	3.47	3.54	3.60	3.66	3.70	3.75	3.78
25	3.24	3.36	3.45	3.52	3.58	3.64	3.68	3.73	3.76
30	3.19	3.30	3.39	3.45	3.51	3.56	3.61	3.65	3.68
40	3.12	3.23	3.31	3.37	3.43	3.47	3.51	3.55	3.58
50	3.08	3.18	3.26	3.32	3.38	3.42	3.46	3.50	3.53
75	3.03	3.13	3.20	3.26	3.31	3.35	3.39	3.43	3.45
100	3.01	3.10	3.17	3.23	3.28	3.32	3.36	3.39	3.42
∞	2.94	3.02	3.09	3.14	3.19	3.23	3.26	3.29	3.32

APPENDIX (t′) (Cont.)

Critical Values
for Dunn's
Multiple Comparison
Test   Alpha = .01

df	NO. OF COMPARISONS								
	2	3	4	5	6	7	8	9	10
5	4.77	5.25	5.60	5.89	6.14	6.35	6.54	6.71	6.87
6	4.32	4.70	4.98	5.21	5.40	5.56	5.71	5.84	5.96
7	4.03	4.36	4.59	4.79	4.94	5.08	5.20	5.31	5.41
8	3.83	4.12	4.33	4.50	4.64	4.76	4.86	4.96	5.04
9	3.69	3.95	4.15	4.30	4.42	4.53	4.62	4.71	4.78
10	3.58	3.83	4.00	4.14	4.26	4.36	4.44	4.52	4.59
11	3.50	3.73	3.89	4.02	4.13	4.22	4.30	4.37	4.44
12	3.43	3.65	3.81	3.93	4.03	4.12	4.19	4.26	4.32
13	3.37	3.58	3.73	3.85	3.95	4.03	4.10	4.16	4.22
14	3.33	3.53	3.67	3.79	3.88	3.96	4.03	4.09	4.14
15	3.29	3.48	3.62	3.73	3.82	3.90	3.96	4.02	4.07
16	3.25	3.44	3.58	3.69	3.77	3.85	3.91	3.96	4.01
17	3.22	3.41	3.54	3.65	3.73	3.80	3.86	3.92	3.97
18	3.20	3.38	3.51	3.61	3.69	3.76	3.82	3.87	3.92
19	3.17	3.35	3.48	3.58	3.66	3.73	3.79	3.84	3.88
20	3.15	3.33	3.46	3.55	3.63	3.70	3.75	3.80	3.85
21	3.14	3.31	3.43	3.53	3.60	3.67	3.73	3.78	3.82
22	3.12	3.29	3.41	3.50	3.58	3.64	3.70	3.75	3.79
23	3.10	3.27	3.39	3.48	3.56	3.62	3.68	3.72	3.77
24	3.09	3.26	3.38	3.47	3.54	3.60	3.66	3.70	3.75
25	3.08	3.24	3.36	3.45	3.52	3.58	3.64	3.68	3.73
30	3.03	3.19	3.30	3.39	3.45	3.51	3.56	3.61	3.65
40	2.97	3.12	3.23	3.31	3.37	3.43	3.47	3.51	3.55
50	2.94	3.08	3.18	3.26	3.32	3.38	3.42	3.46	3.50
75	2.89	3.03	3.13	3.20	3.26	3.31	3.35	3.39	3.43
100	2.87	3.01	3.10	3.17	3.23	3.28	3.32	3.36	3.39
∞	2.81	2.94	3.02	3.09	3.14	3.19	3.23	3.26	3.29

APPENDIX (*t'*) (*Cont.*)

Critical Values
for Dunn's
Multiple Comparison
Test   Alpha = .01

df	NO. OF COMPARISONS								
	15	**20**	**25**	**30**	**35**	**40**	**45**	**50**	**55**
5	7.50	7.98	8.36	8.69	8.98	9.24	9.47	9.68	9.87
6	6.43	6.79	7.07	7.31	7.52	7.71	7.87	8.02	8.16
7	5.80	6.08	6.31	6.50	6.67	6.81	6.94	7.06	7.17
8	5.37	5.62	5.81	5.97	6.11	6.23	6.34	6.44	6.53
9	5.08	5.29	5.46	5.60	5.72	5.83	5.92	6.01	6.09
10	4.85	5.05	5.20	5.33	5.44	5.53	5.62	5.69	5.76
11	4.68	4.86	5.00	5.12	5.22	5.31	5.38	5.45	5.52
12	4.55	4.72	4.85	4.96	5.05	5.13	5.20	5.26	5.32
13	4.44	4.60	4.72	4.82	4.91	4.98	5.05	5.11	5.17
14	4.35	4.50	4.62	4.71	4.79	4.87	4.93	4.99	5.04
15	4.27	4.42	4.53	4.62	4.70	4.77	4.83	4.88	4.93
16	4.21	4.35	4.45	4.54	4.62	4.68	4.74	4.79	4.84
17	4.15	4.29	4.39	4.47	4.55	4.61	4.66	4.71	4.76
18	4.10	4.23	4.33	4.42	4.49	4.55	4.60	4.65	4.69
19	4.06	4.19	4.28	4.36	4.43	4.49	4.54	4.59	4.63
20	4.02	4.15	4.24	4.32	4.39	4.44	4.49	4.54	4.58
21	3.99	4.11	4.20	4.28	4.34	4.40	4.45	4.49	4.53
22	3.96	4.08	4.17	4.24	4.31	4.36	4.41	4.45	4.49
23	3.93	4.05	4.14	4.21	4.27	4.33	4.37	4.42	4.45
24	3.91	4.02	4.11	4.18	4.24	4.29	4.34	4.38	4.42
25	3.88	4.00	4.08	4.15	4.21	4.27	4.31	4.35	4.39
30	3.80	3.90	3.98	4.05	4.11	4.15	4.20	4.23	4.27
40	3.69	3.79	3.86	3.92	3.98	4.02	4.06	4.09	4.13
50	3.63	3.72	3.79	3.85	3.90	3.94	3.98	4.01	4.04
75	3.55	3.64	3.71	3.76	3.81	3.85	3.88	3.91	3.94
100	3.51	3.60	3.66	3.72	3.76	3.80	3.83	3.86	3.89
∞	3.40	3.48	3.54	3.59	3.63	3.66	3.69	3.72	3.74

Source: The entries in this table were computed by the author.

APPENDIX (q)　Critical Values of the Studentized Range Statistic

$\alpha = .05$

df for error	\(r\) = Number of Steps Between Ordered Means													
	2	3	4	5	6	7	8	9	10	11	12	13	14	15
1	17.97	26.98	32.82	37.08	40.41	43.12	45.40	47.36	49.07	50.59	51.96	53.20	54.33	55.36
2	6.08	8.33	9.80	10.88	11.74	12.44	13.03	13.54	13.99	14.39	14.75	15.08	15.38	15.65
3	4.50	5.91	6.82	7.50	8.04	8.48	8.85	9.18	9.46	9.72	9.95	10.15	10.35	10.53
4	3.93	5.04	5.76	6.29	6.71	7.05	7.35	7.60	7.83	8.03	8.21	8.37	8.52	8.66
5	3.64	4.60	5.22	5.67	6.03	6.33	6.58	6.80	7.00	7.17	7.32	7.47	7.60	7.72
6	3.46	4.34	4.90	5.31	5.63	5.90	6.12	6.32	6.49	6.65	6.79	6.92	7.03	7.14
7	3.34	4.16	4.68	5.06	5.36	5.61	5.82	6.00	6.16	6.30	6.43	6.55	6.66	6.76
8	3.26	4.04	4.53	4.89	5.17	5.40	5.60	5.77	5.92	6.05	6.18	6.29	6.39	6.48
9	3.20	3.95	4.42	4.76	5.02	5.24	5.43	5.60	5.74	5.87	5.98	6.09	6.19	6.28
10	3.15	3.88	4.33	4.65	4.91	5.12	5.30	5.46	5.60	5.72	5.83	5.94	6.03	6.11
11	3.11	3.82	4.26	4.57	4.82	5.03	5.20	5.35	5.49	5.60	5.71	5.81	5.90	5.98
12	3.08	3.77	4.20	4.51	4.75	4.95	5.12	5.26	5.40	5.51	5.62	5.71	5.79	5.88
13	3.06	3.74	4.15	4.45	4.69	4.88	5.05	5.19	5.32	5.43	5.53	5.63	5.71	5.79
14	3.03	3.70	4.11	4.41	4.64	4.83	4.99	5.13	5.25	5.36	5.46	5.55	5.64	5.71
15	3.01	3.67	4.08	4.37	4.60	4.78	4.94	5.08	5.20	5.31	5.40	5.49	5.57	5.65
16	3.00	3.65	4.05	4.33	4.56	4.74	4.90	5.03	5.15	5.26	5.35	5.44	5.52	5.59
17	2.98	3.63	4.02	4.30	4.52	4.70	4.86	4.99	5.11	5.21	5.31	5.39	5.47	5.54
18	2.97	3.61	4.00	4.28	4.50	4.67	4.82	4.96	5.07	5.17	5.27	5.35	5.43	5.50
19	2.96	3.59	3.98	4.25	4.47	4.64	4.79	4.92	5.04	5.14	5.23	5.32	5.39	5.46
20	2.95	3.58	3.96	4.23	4.44	4.62	4.77	4.90	5.01	5.11	5.20	5.28	5.36	5.43
24	2.92	3.53	3.90	4.17	4.37	4.54	4.68	4.81	4.92	5.01	5.10	5.18	5.25	5.32
30	2.89	3.49	3.84	4.10	4.30	4.46	4.60	4.72	4.82	4.92	5.00	5.08	5.15	5.21
40	2.86	3.44	3.79	4.04	4.23	4.39	4.52	4.64	4.74	4.82	4.90	4.98	5.04	5.11
60	2.83	3.40	3.74	3.98	4.16	4.31	4.44	4.55	4.65	4.73	4.81	4.88	4.94	5.00
120	2.80	3.36	3.69	3.92	4.10	4.24	4.36	4.47	4.56	4.64	4.71	4.78	4.84	4.90
∞	2.77	3.31	3.63	3.86	4.03	4.17	4.29	4.39	4.47	4.55	4.62	4.68	4.74	4.80

APPENDIX (q)   Critical Values of the Studentized Range Statistic

α = .01

df for error	\(r = \) Number of Steps Between Ordered Means													
	2	3	4	5	6	7	8	9	10	11	12	13	14	15
1	90.03	135.0	164.3	185.6	202.2	215.8	227.2	237.0	245.6	253.2	260.0	266.2	271.8	277.0
2	14.04	19.02	22.29	24.72	26.63	28.20	29.53	30.68	31.69	32.59	33.40	34.13	34.81	35.43
3	8.26	10.62	12.17	13.33	14.24	15.00	15.64	16.20	16.69	17.13	17.53	17.89	18.22	18.52
4	6.51	8.12	9.17	9.96	10.58	11.10	11.55	11.93	12.27	12.57	12.84	13.09	13.32	13.53
5	5.70	6.98	7.80	8.42	8.91	9.32	9.67	9.97	10.24	10.48	10.70	10.89	11.08	11.24
6	5.24	6.33	7.03	7.56	7.97	8.32	8.62	8.87	9.10	9.30	9.48	9.65	9.81	9.95
7	4.95	5.92	6.54	7.00	7.37	7.68	7.94	8.17	8.37	8.55	8.71	8.86	9.00	9.12
8	4.75	5.64	6.20	6.62	6.96	7.24	7.47	7.68	7.86	8.03	8.18	8.31	8.44	8.55
9	4.60	5.43	5.96	6.35	6.66	6.92	7.13	7.32	7.50	7.65	7.78	7.91	8.02	8.13
10	4.48	5.27	5.77	6.14	6.43	6.67	6.88	7.06	7.21	7.36	7.48	7.60	7.71	7.81
11	4.39	5.15	5.62	5.97	6.25	6.48	6.67	6.84	6.99	7.13	7.25	7.36	7.46	7.56
12	4.32	5.05	5.50	5.84	6.10	6.32	6.51	6.67	6.81	6.94	7.06	7.17	7.26	7.36
13	4.26	4.96	5.40	5.73	5.98	6.19	6.37	6.53	6.67	6.79	6.90	7.01	7.10	7.19
14	4.21	4.90	5.32	5.63	5.88	6.08	6.26	6.41	6.54	6.66	6.77	6.87	6.96	7.05
15	4.17	4.84	5.25	5.56	5.80	5.99	6.16	6.31	6.44	6.56	6.66	6.76	6.84	6.93
16	4.13	4.79	5.19	5.49	5.72	5.92	6.08	6.22	6.35	6.46	6.56	6.66	6.74	6.82
17	4.10	4.74	5.14	5.43	5.66	5.85	6.01	6.15	6.27	6.38	6.48	6.57	6.66	6.73
18	4.07	4.70	5.09	5.38	5.60	5.79	5.94	6.08	6.20	6.31	6.41	6.50	6.58	6.66
19	4.05	4.67	5.05	5.33	5.55	5.74	5.89	6.02	6.14	6.25	6.34	6.43	6.51	6.58
20	4.02	4.64	5.02	5.29	5.51	5.69	5.84	5.97	6.09	6.19	6.28	6.37	6.45	6.52
24	3.96	4.55	4.91	5.17	5.37	5.54	5.69	5.81	5.92	6.02	6.11	6.19	6.26	6.33
30	3.89	4.46	4.80	5.05	5.24	5.40	5.54	5.65	5.76	5.85	5.93	6.01	6.08	6.14
40	3.82	4.37	4.70	4.93	5.11	5.26	5.39	5.50	5.60	5.69	5.76	5.84	5.90	5.96
60	3.76	4.28	4.60	4.82	4.99	5.13	5.25	5.36	5.45	5.53	5.60	5.67	5.73	5.78
120	3.70	4.20	4.50	4.71	4.87	5.0	5.12	5.21	5.30	5.38	5.44	5.51	5.56	5.61
∞	3.64	4.12	4.40	4.60	4.76	4.88	4.99	5.08	5.16	5.23	5.29	5.35	5.40	5.45

Source: This table is abridged from Harter, H. L., Tables of range and studentized range, *Annals of Mathematical Statistics*, 1960, 31, 1122–1147, with permission of the author and the publisher.

APPENDIX (ncF) Noncentral F Distribution Power $= 1 -$ (Table Entry)

f_e	α	.50	1.0	1.2	1.4	1.6	1.8	2.0	2.2	2.6	3.0
						ϕ					
						$f_t = 1$					
2	.05	.93	.86	.83	.78	.74	.69	.64	.59	.49	.40
	.01	.99	.97	.96	.95	.94	.93	.91	.90	.87	.83
4	.05	.91	.80	.74	.67	.59	.51	.43	.35	.22	.12
	.01	.98	.95	.93	.90	.87	.83	.78	.73	.62	.50
6	.05	.91	.78	.70	.62	.52	.43	.34	.26	.14	.06
	.01	.98	.93	.90	.86	.81	.75	.69	.61	.46	.31
8	.05	.90	.76	.68	.59	.49	.39	.30	.22	.11	.04
	.01	.98	.92	.89	.84	.78	.70	.62	.54	.37	.22
10	.05	.90	.75	.66	.57	.47	.37	.28	.20	.09	.03
	.01	.98	.92	.87	.82	.75	.67	.58	.49	.31	.17
12	.05	.90	.74	.65	.56	.45	.35	.26	.19	.08	.03
	.01	.97	.91	.87	.81	.73	.65	.55	.46	.28	.14
16	.05	.90	.74	.64	.54	.43	.33	.24	.17	.07	.02
	.01	.97	.90	.85	.79	.71	.61	.52	.42	.24	.11
20	.05	.90	.73	.63	.53	.42	.32	.23	.16	.06	.02
	.01	.97	.90	.85	.78	.69	.59	.49	.39	.21	.10
30	.05	.89	.72	.62	.52	.40	.31	.22	.15	.06	.02
	.01	.97	.89	.83	.76	.67	.57	.46	.36	.19	.08
∞	.05	.89	.71	.60	.49	.38	.28	.19	.12	.04	.01
	.01	.97	.88	.81	.72	.62	.51	.40	.30	.14	.05
f_e	α					$f_t = 2$					
2	.05	.93	.88	.85	.82	.78	.75	.70	.66	.56	.48
	.01	.99	.98	.97	.96	.95	.94	.93	.92	.89	.86
4	.05	.92	.82	.77	.70	.62	.54	.46	.38	.24	.14
	.01	.98	.96	.94	.92	.89	.85	.81	.76	.66	.54
6	.05	.91	.79	.71	.63	.53	.43	.34	.26	.13	.05
	.01	.98	.94	.91	.87	.82	.76	.70	.62	.46	.31
8	.05	.91	.77	.68	.58	.48	.37	.28	.20	.08	.03
	.01	.98	.93	.89	.84	.78	.70	.61	.52	.34	.19
10	.05	.91	.75	.66	.55	.44	.34	.24	.16	.06	.02
	.01	.98	.92	.88	.82	.74	.65	.55	.45	.26	.13
12	.05	.90	.74	.64	.53	.42	.31	.22	.14	.05	.01
	.01	.98	.91	.86	.80	.71	.61	.51	.40	.22	.09
16	.05	.90	.73	.62	.51	.39	.28	.19	.12	.04	.01
	.01	.97	.90	.84	.77	.67	.57	.45	.34	.16	.06
20	.05	.90	.72	.61	.49	.36	.26	.17	.11	.03	.01
	.01	.97	.90	.83	.75	.65	.53	.42	.31	.14	.04
30	.05	.90	.71	.59	.47	.35	.24	.15	.09	.02	.00
	.01	.97	.88	.82	.72	.61	.49	.37	.26	.10	.03
∞	.05	.89	.68	.56	.43	.30	.20	.12	.06	.01	.00
	.01	.97	.86	.77	.66	.53	.40	.28	.18	.05	.01

APPENDIX (ncF) (Cont.)

		ϕ									
		.50	1.0	1.2	1.4	1.6	1.8	2.0	2.2	2.6	3.0
f_e	α					$f_t = 3$					
2	.05	.93	.89	.86	.83	.80	.76	.73	.69	.60	.52
	.01	.99	.98	.97	.96	.96	.95	.94	.93	.90	.88
4	.05	.92	.83	.77	.71	.63	.55	.47	.39	.25	.14
	.01	.98	.96	.94	.92	.89	.86	.82	.77	.67	.55
6	.05	.91	.79	.71	.62	.52	.42	.33	.24	.11	.04
	.01	.98	.94	.91	.87	.82	.76	.69	.61	.44	.29
8	.05	.91	.76	.67	.57	.46	.35	.25	.17	.06	.02
	.01	.98	.93	.89	.84	.77	.68	.59	.49	.30	.16
10	.05	.91	.75	.65	.53	.41	.30	.21	.13	.04	.01
	.01	.98	.92	.87	.80	.72	.62	.52	.41	.22	.09
12	.05	.90	.73	.62	.50	.38	.27	.18	.11	.03	.01
	.01	.98	.91	.85	.78	.69	.58	.46	.35	.17	.06
16	.05	.90	.71	.60	.47	.34	.23	.14	.08	.02	.00
	.01	.97	.90	.83	.74	.64	.51	.39	.28	.11	.03
20	.05	.90	.70	.58	.45	.32	.21	.13	.07	.01	.00
	.01	.97	.89	.82	.72	.60	.47	.35	.24	.08	.02
30	.05	.89	.68	.55	.42	.29	.18	.10	.05	.01	.00
	.01	.97	.87	.79	.68	.55	.42	.29	.18	.05	.01
∞	.05	.88	.64	.50	.36	.23	.13	.07	.03	.00	.00
	.01	.97	.84	.73	.59	.44	.30	.18	.10	.02	.00
f_e	α					$f_t = 4$					
2	.05	.94	.89	.87	.84	.81	.77	.74	.70	.62	.54
	.01	.99	.98	.97	.97	.96	.95	.94	.93	.91	.88
4	.05	.92	.83	.78	.71	.64	.55	.47	.39	.25	.14
	.01	.98	.96	.94	.92	.89	.86	.82	.78	.67	.56
6	.05	.92	.79	.71	.62	.52	.41	.31	.23	.10	.04
	.01	.98	.94	.91	.87	.82	.76	.68	.60	.43	.28
8	.05	.91	.76	.66	.55	.44	.33	.23	.15	.05	.01
	.01	.98	.93	.89	.83	.76	.67	.57	.47	.28	.14
10	.05	.91	.74	.63	.51	.39	.27	.18	.11	.03	.01
	.01	.98	.92	.86	.79	.70	.60	.49	.37	.19	.07
12	.05	.90	.72	.61	.48	.35	.24	.15	.08	.02	.00
	.01	.98	.91	.85	.76	.66	.55	.42	.31	.13	.04
16	.05	.90	.70	.57	.44	.31	.19	.11	.06	.01	.00
	.01	.97	.89	.82	.72	.60	.47	.34	.23	.08	.02
20	.05	.89	.68	.55	.41	.28	.17	.09	.04	.01	.00
	.01	.97	.88	.80	.69	.56	.42	.29	.18	.05	.01
30	.05	.89	.66	.52	.37	.24	.14	.07	.03	.00	.00
	.01	.97	.86	.77	.64	.50	.35	.22	.13	.03	.00
∞	.05	.88	.60	.45	.29	.17	.08	.04	.01	.00	.00
	.01	.96	.81	.68	.53	.36	.22	.11	.05	.01	.00

Source: This table is abridged from Tiku, M. L., Tables of the power of the *F* test, *J. Amer. Stat. Assoc.*, 1967, **62**, 525–539, with the permission of the author and the editors.

APPENDIX (W_s)   Critical Lower-Tail Values of W_s for Rank-Sum Test for Two Independent Samples ($N_1 \le N_2$)

N_2	$N_1=1$ 0.001	0.005	0.010	0.025	0.05	0.10	$2\bar{W}$	$N_1=2$ 0.001	0.005	0.010	0.025	0.05	0.10	$2\bar{W}$	N_2
2							4						—	10	2
3							5						3	12	3
4							6					—	3	14	4
5							7					3	4	16	5
6							8					3	4	18	6
7							9				—	3	4	20	7
8						—	10				3	4	5	22	8
9						1	11				3	4	5	24	9
10						1	12				3	4	6	26	10
11						1	13				3	4	6	28	11
12						1	14			—	4	5	7	30	12
13						1	15			3	4	5	7	32	13
14						1	16			3	4	6	8	34	14
15						1	17			3	4	6	8	36	15
16						1	18			3	4	6	8	38	16
17						1	19			3	5	6	9	40	17
18					—	1	20		—	3	5	7	9	42	18
19					1	2	21		3	4	5	7	10	44	19
20					1	2	22		3	4	5	7	10	46	20
21					1	2	23		3	4	6	8	11	48	21
22					1	2	24		3	4	6	8	11	50	22
23					1	2	25		3	4	6	8	12	52	23
24					1	2	26		3	4	6	9	12	54	24
25	—	—	—	—	1	2	27	—	3	4	6	9	12	56	25

N_2	$N_1=3$ 0.001	0.005	0.010	0.025	0.05	0.10	$2\bar{W}$	$N_1=4$ 0.001	0.005	0.010	0.025	0.05	0.10	$2\bar{W}$	N_2
3					6	7	21								
4				—	6	7	24			—	10	11	13	36	4
5				6	7	8	27		—	10	11	12	14	40	5
6			—	7	8	9	30		10	11	12	13	15	44	6
7			6	7	8	10	33		10	11	13	14	16	48	7
8		—	6	8	9	11	36		11	12	14	15	17	52	8
9		6	7	8	10	11	39	—	11	13	14	16	19	56	9
10		6	7	9	10	12	42	10	12	13	15	17	20	60	10
11		6	7	9	11	13	45	10	12	14	16	18	21	64	11
12		7	8	10	11	14	48	10	13	15	17	19	22	68	12
13		7	8	10	12	15	51	11	13	15	18	20	23	72	13
14		7	8	11	13	16	54	11	14	16	19	21	25	76	14
15		8	9	11	13	16	57	11	15	17	20	22	26	80	15
16	—	8	9	12	14	17	60	12	15	17	21	24	27	84	16
17	6	8	10	12	15	18	63	12	16	18	21	25	28	88	17
18	6	8	10	13	15	19	66	13	16	19	22	26	30	92	18

APPENDIX (W_s)   (*Cont.*)

N_2	0.001	0.005	$N_1 = 3$ 0.010	0.025	0.05	0.10	$2\bar{W}$	0.001	0.005	$N_1 = 4$ 0.010	0.025	0.05	0.10	$2\bar{W}$	N_2
19	6	9	10	13	16	20	69	13	17	19	23	27	31	96	19
20	6	9	11	14	17	21	72	13	18	20	24	28	32	100	20
21	7	9	11	14	17	21	75	14	18	21	25	29	33	104	21
22	7	10	12	15	18	22	78	14	19	21	26	30	35	108	22
23	7	10	12	15	19	23	81	14	19	22	27	31	36	112	23
24	7	10	12	16	19	24	84	15	20	23	27	32	38	116	24
25	7	11	13	16	20	25	87	15	20	23	28	33	38	120	25

N_2	0.001	0.005	$N_1 = 5$ 0.010	0.025	0.05	0.10	$2\bar{W}$	0.001	0.005	$N_1 = 6$ 0.010	0.025	0.05	0.10	$2\bar{W}$	N_2
5		15	16	17	19	20	55								
6		16	17	18	20	22	60	—	23	24	26	28	30	78	6
7	—	16	18	20	21	23	65	21	24	25	27	29	32	84	7
8	15	17	19	21	23	25	70	22	25	27	29	31	34	90	8
9	16	18	20	22	24	27	75	23	26	28	31	33	36	96	9
10	16	19	21	23	26	28	80	24	27	29	32	35	38	102	10
11	17	20	22	24	27	30	85	25	28	30	34	37	40	108	11
12	17	21	23	26	28	32	90	25	30	32	35	38	42	114	12
13	18	22	24	27	30	33	95	26	31	33	37	40	44	120	13
14	18	22	25	28	31	35	100	27	32	34	38	42	46	126	14
15	19	23	26	29	33	37	105	28	33	36	40	44	48	132	15
16	20	24	27	30	34	38	110	29	34	37	42	46	50	138	16
17	20	25	28	32	35	40	115	30	36	39	43	47	52	144	17
18	21	26	29	33	37	42	120	31	37	40	45	49	55	150	18
19	22	27	30	34	38	43	125	32	38	41	46	51	57	156	19
20	22	28	31	35	40	45	130	33	39	43	48	53	59	162	20
21	23	29	32	37	41	47	135	33	40	44	50	55	61	168	21
22	23	29	33	38	43	48	140	34	42	45	51	57	63	174	22
23	24	30	34	39	44	50	145	35	43	47	53	58	65	180	23
24	25	31	35	40	45	51	150	36	44	48	54	60	67	186	24
25	25	32	36	42	47	53	155	37	45	50	56	62	69	192	25

N_2	0.001	0.005	$N_1 = 7$ 0.010	0.025	0.05	0.10	$2\bar{W}$	0.001	0.005	$N_1 = 8$ 0.010	0.025	0.05	0.10	$2\bar{W}$	N_2
7	29	32	34	36	39	41	105								
8	30	34	35	38	41	44	112	40	43	45	49	51	55	136	8
9	31	35	37	40	43	46	119	41	45	47	51	54	58	144	9
10	33	37	39	42	45	49	126	42	47	49	53	56	60	152	10
11	34	38	40	44	47	51	133	44	49	51	55	59	63	160	11
12	35	40	42	46	49	54	140	45	51	53	58	62	66	168	12
13	36	41	44	48	52	56	147	47	53	56	60	64	69	176	13
14	37	43	45	50	54	59	154	48	54	58	62	67	72	184	14

APPENDIX (W_s)   **(Cont.)**

N_2	0.001	0.005	$N_1 = 7$ 0.010	0.025	0.05	0.10	$2\bar{W}$	0.001	0.005	$N_1 = 8$ 0.010	0.025	0.05	0.10	$2\bar{W}$	N_2
15	38	44	47	52	56	61	161	50	56	60	65	69	75	192	15
16	39	46	49	54	58	64	168	51	58	62	67	72	78	200	16
17	41	47	51	56	61	66	175	53	60	64	70	75	81	208	17
18	42	49	52	58	63	69	182	54	62	66	72	77	84	216	18
19	43	50	54	60	65	71	189	56	64	68	74	80	87	224	19
20	44	52	56	62	67	74	196	57	66	70	77	83	90	232	20
21	46	53	58	64	69	76	203	59	68	72	79	85	92	240	21
22	47	55	59	66	72	79	210	60	70	74	81	88	95	248	22
23	48	57	61	68	74	81	217	62	71	76	84	90	98	256	23
24	49	58	63	70	76	84	224	64	73	78	86	93	101	264	24
25	50	60	64	72	78	86	231	65	75	81	89	96	104	272	25

N_2	0.001	0.005	$N_1 = 9$ 0.010	0.025	0.05	0.10	$2\bar{W}$	0.001	0.005	$N_1 = 10$ 0.010	0.025	0.05	0.10	$2\bar{W}$	N_2
9	52	56	59	62	66	70	171								
10	53	58	61	65	69	73	180	65	71	74	78	82	87	210	10
11	55	61	63	68	72	76	189	67	73	77	81	86	91	220	11
12	57	63	66	71	75	80	198	69	76	79	84	89	94	230	12
13	59	65	68	73	78	83	207	72	79	82	88	92	98	240	13
14	60	67	71	76	81	86	216	74	81	85	91	96	102	250	14
15	62	69	73	79	84	90	225	76	84	88	94	99	106	260	15
16	64	72	76	82	87	93	234	78	86	91	97	103	109	270	16
17	66	74	78	84	90	97	243	80	89	93	100	106	113	280	17
18	68	76	81	87	93	100	252	82	92	96	103	110	117	290	18
19	70	78	83	90	96	103	261	84	94	99	107	113	121	300	19
20	71	81	85	93	99	107	270	87	97	102	110	117	125	310	20
21	73	83	88	95	102	110	279	89	99	105	113	120	128	320	21
22	75	85	90	98	105	113	288	91	102	108	116	123	132	330	22
23	77	88	93	101	108	117	297	93	105	110	119	127	136	340	23
24	79	90	95	104	111	120	306	95	107	113	122	130	140	350	24
25	81	92	98	107	114	123	315	98	110	116	126	134	144	360	25

N_2	0.001	0.005	$N_1 = 11$ 0.010	0.025	0.05	0.10	$2\bar{W}$	0.001	0.005	$N_1 = 12$ 0.010	0.025	0.05	0.10	$2\bar{W}$	N_2
11	81	87	91	96	100	106	253								
12	83	90	94	99	104	110	264	98	105	109	115	120	127	300	12
13	86	93	97	103	108	114	275	101	109	113	119	125	131	312	13
14	88	96	100	106	112	118	286	103	112	116	123	129	136	324	14
15	90	99	103	110	116	123	297	106	115	120	127	133	141	336	15
16	93	102	107	113	120	127	308	109	119	124	131	138	145	348	16
17	95	105	110	117	123	131	319	112	122	127	135	142	150	360	17
18	98	108	113	121	127	135	330	115	125	131	139	146	155	372	18
19	100	111	116	124	131	139	341	118	129	134	143	150	159	384	19

APPENDIX (W$_s$)   **(Cont.)**

			$N_1 = 11$								$N_1 = 12$					
N_2	0.001	0.005	0.010	0.025	0.05	0.10	$2\bar{W}$	0.001	0.005	0.010	0.025	0.05	0.10	$2\bar{W}$	N_2
20	103	114	119	128	135	144	352	120	132	138	147	155	164	396	20
21	106	117	123	131	139	148	363	123	136	142	151	159	169	408	21
22	108	120	126	135	143	152	374	126	139	145	155	163	173	420	22
23	111	123	129	139	147	156	385	129	142	149	159	168	178	432	23
24	113	126	132	142	151	161	396	132	146	153	163	172	183	444	24
25	116	129	136	146	155	165	407	135	149	156	167	176	187	456	25

			$N_1 = 13$								$N_1 = 14$					
N_2	0.001	0.005	0.010	0.025	0.05	0.10	$2\bar{W}$	0.001	0.005	0.010	0.025	0.05	0.10	$2\bar{W}$	N_2
13	117	125	130	136	142	149	351								
14	120	129	134	141	147	154	364	137	147	152	160	166	174	406	14
15	123	133	138	145	152	159	377	141	151	156	164	171	179	420	15
16	126	136	142	150	156	165	390	144	155	161	169	176	185	434	16
17	129	140	146	154	161	170	403	148	159	165	174	182	190	448	17
18	133	144	150	158	166	175	416	151	163	170	179	187	196	462	18
19	136	148	154	163	171	180	429	155	168	174	183	192	202	476	19
20	139	151	158	167	175	185	442	159	172	178	188	197	207	490	20
21	142	155	162	171	180	190	455	162	176	183	193	202	213	504	21
22	145	159	166	176	185	195	468	166	180	187	198	207	218	518	22
23	149	163	170	180	189	200	481	169	184	192	203	212	224	532	23
24	152	166	174	185	194	205	494	173	188	196	207	218	229	546	24
25	155	170	178	189	199	211	507	177	192	200	212	223	235	560	25

			$N_1 = 15$								$N_1 = 16$					
N_2	0.001	0.005	0.010	0.025	0.05	0.10	$2\bar{W}$	0.001	0.005	0.010	0.025	0.05	0.10	$2\bar{W}$	N_2
15	160	171	176	184	192	200	465								
16	163	175	181	190	197	206	480	184	196	202	211	219	229	528	16
17	167	180	186	195	203	212	495	188	201	207	217	225	235	544	17
18	171	184	190	200	208	218	510	192	206	212	222	231	242	560	18
19	175	189	195	205	214	224	525	196	210	218	228	237	248	576	19
20	179	193	200	210	220	230	540	201	215	223	234	243	255	592	20
21	183	198	205	216	225	236	555	205	220	228	239	249	261	608	21
22	187	202	210	221	231	242	570	209	225	233	245	255	267	624	22
23	191	207	214	226	236	248	585	214	230	238	251	261	274	640	23
24	195	211	219	231	242	254	600	218	235	244	256	267	280	656	24
25	199	216	224	237	248	260	615	222	240	249	262	273	287	672	25

			$N_1 = 17$								$N_1 = 18$					
N_2	0.001	0.005	0.010	0.025	0.05	0.10	$2\bar{W}$	0.001	0.005	0.010	0.025	0.05	0.10	$2\bar{W}$	N_2
17	210	223	230	240	249	259	595								
18	214	228	235	246	255	266	612	237	252	259	270	280	291	666	18
19	219	234	241	252	262	273	629	242	258	265	277	287	299	684	19

APPENDIX (W$_s$)   **(Cont.)**

N_2	$N_1 = 17$ 0.001	0.005	0.010	0.025	0.05	0.10	$2\bar{W}$	$N_1 = 18$ 0.001	0.005	0.010	0.025	0.05	0.10	$2\bar{W}$	N_2
20	223	239	246	258	268	280	646	247	263	271	283	294	306	702	20
21	228	244	252	264	274	287	663	252	269	277	290	301	313	720	21
22	233	249	258	270	281	294	680	257	275	283	296	307	321	738	22
23	238	255	263	276	287	300	697	262	280	289	303	314	328	756	23
24	242	260	269	282	294	307	714	267	286	295	309	321	335	774	24
25	247	265	275	288	300	314	731	273	292	301	316	328	343	792	25

N_2	$N_1 = 19$ 0.001	0.005	0.010	0.025	0.05	0.10	$2\bar{W}$	$N_1 = 20$ 0.001	0.005	0.010	0.025	0.05	0.10	$2\bar{W}$	N_2
19	267	283	291	303	313	325	741								
20	272	289	297	309	320	333	760	298	315	324	337	348	361	820	20
21	277	295	303	316	328	341	779	304	322	331	344	356	370	840	21
22	283	301	310	323	335	349	798	309	328	337	351	364	378	860	22
23	288	307	316	330	342	357	817	315	335	344	359	371	386	880	23
24	294	313	323	337	350	364	836	321	341	351	366	379	394	900	24
25	299	319	329	344	357	372	855	327	348	358	373	387	403	920	25

N_2	$N_1 = 21$ 0.001	0.005	0.010	0.025	0.05	0.10	$2\bar{W}$	$N_1 = 22$ 0.001	0.005	0.010	0.025	0.05	0.10	$2\bar{W}$	N_2
21	331	349	359	373	385	399	903								
22	337	356	366	381	393	408	924	365	386	396	411	424	439	990	22
23	343	363	373	388	401	417	945	372	393	403	419	432	448	1012	23
24	349	370	381	396	410	425	966	379	400	411	427	441	457	1034	24
25	356	377	388	404	418	434	987	385	408	419	435	450	467	1056	25

N_2	$N_1 = 23$ 0.001	0.005	0.010	0.025	0.05	0.10	$2\bar{W}$	$N_1 = 24$ 0.001	0.005	0.010	0.025	0.05	0.10	$2\bar{W}$	N_2
23	402	424	434	451	465	481	1081								
24	409	431	443	459	474	491	1104	440	464	475	492	507	525	1176	24
25	416	439	451	468	483	500	1127	448	472	484	501	517	535	1200	25

N_2	$N_1 = 25$ 0.001	0.005	0.010	0.025	0.05	0.10	$2\bar{W}$
25	480	505	517	536	552	570	1275

Source: Table 1 in L. R. Verdooren, Extended tables of critical values for Wilcoxon's test statistic, *Biometrika*, 1963, **50**, 177–186, with permission of the author and editor.

APPENDIX (T)

Critical Lower-Tail Values of T (and their Associated Probabilities) for Wilcoxon's Matched-Pairs Signed-Ranks Test

	\multicolumn{8}{c}{NOMINAL ALPHA (ONE-TAILED)}							
	.05		.025		.01		.005	
N	T	α	T	α	T	α	T	α
5	0	.0313						
	1	.0625						
6	2	.0469	0	.0156				
	3	.0781	1	.0313				
7	3	.0391	2	.0234	0	.0078		
	4	.0547	3	.0391	1	.0156		
8	5	.0391	3	.0195	1	.0078	0	.0039
	6	.0547	4	.0273	2	.0117	1	.0078
9	8	.0488	5	.0195	3	.0098	1	.0039
	9	.0645	6	.0273	4	.0137	2	.0059
10	10	.0420	8	.0244	5	.0098	3	.0049
	11	.0527	9	.0322	6	.0137	4	.0068
11	13	.0415	10	.0210	7	.0093	5	.0049
	14	.0508	11	.0269	8	.0122	6	.0068
12	17	.0461	13	.0212	9	.0081	7	.0046
	18	.0549	14	.0261	10	.0105	8	.0061
13	21	.0471	17	.0239	12	.0085	9	.0040
	22	.0549	18	.0287	13	.0107	10	.0052
14	25	.0453	21	.0247	15	.0083	12	.0043
	26	.0520	22	.0290	16	.0101	13	.0054
15	30	.0473	25	.0240	19	.0090	15	.0042
	31	.0535	26	.0277	20	.0108	16	.0051
16	35	.0467	29	.0222	23	.0091	19	.0046
	36	.0523	30	.0253	24	.0107	20	.0055
17	41	.0492	34	.0224	27	.0087	23	.0047
	42	.0544	35	.0253	28	.0101	24	.0055
18	47	.0494	40	.0241	32	.0091	27	.0045
	48	.0542	41	.0269	33	.0104	28	.0052
19	53	.0478	46	.0247	37	.0090	32	.0047
	54	.0521	47	.0273	38	.0102	33	.0054
20	60	.0487	52	.0242	43	.0096	37	.0047
	61	.0527	53	.0266	44	.0107	38	.0053
21	67	.0479	58	.0230	49	.0097	42	.0045
	68	.0516	59	.0251	50	.0108	43	.0051
22	75	.0492	65	.0231	55	.0095	48	.0046
	76	.0527	66	.0250	56	.0104	49	.0052
23	83	.0490	73	.0242	62	.0098	54	.0046
	84	.0523	74	.0261	63	.0107	55	.0051

APPENDIX (T) (Cont.)

NOMINAL ALPHA (ONE-TAILED)

N	.05		.025		.01		.005	
	T	α	T	α	T	α	T	α
24	91	.0475	81	.0245	69	.0097	61	.0048
	92	.0505	82	.0263	70	.0106	62	.0053
25	100	.0479	89	.0241	76	.0094	68	.0048
	101	.0507	90	.0258	77	.0101	69	.0053
26	110	.0497	98	.0247	84	.0095	75	.0047
	111	.0524	99	.0263	85	.0102	76	.0051
27	119	.0477	107	.0246	92	.0093	83	.0048
	120	.0502	108	.0260	93	.0100	84	.0052
28	130	.0496	116	.0239	101	.0096	91	.0048
	131	.0521	117	.0252	102	.0102	92	.0051
29	140	.0482	126	.0240	110	.0095	100	.0049
	141	.0504	127	.0253	111	.0101	101	.0053
30	151	.0481	137	.0249	120	.0098	109	.0050
	152	.0502	138	.0261	121	.0104	110	.0053
31	163	.0491	147	.0239	130	.0099	118	.0049
	164	.0512	148	.0251	131	.0105	119	.0052
32	175	.0492	159	.0249	140	.0097	128	.0050
	176	.0512	160	.0260	141	.0103	129	.0053
33	187	.0485	170	.0242	151	.0099	138	.0049
	188	.0503	171	.0253	152	.0104	139	.0052
34	200	.0488	182	.0242	162	.0098	148	.0048
	201	.0506	183	.0252	163	.0103	149	.0051
35	213	.0484	195	.0247	173	.0096	159	.0048
	214	.0501	196	.0257	174	.0100	160	.0051
36	227	.0489	208	.0248	185	.0096	171	.0050
	228	.0505	209	.0258	186	.0100	172	.0052
37	241	.0487	221	.0245	198	.0099	182	.0048
	242	.0503	222	.0254	199	.0103	183	.0050
38	256	.0493	235	.0247	211	.0099	194	.0048
	257	.0509	236	.0256	212	.0104	195	.0050
39	271	.0492	249	.0246	224	.0099	207	.0049
	272	.0507	250	.0254	225	.0103	208	.0051
40	286	.0486	264	.0249	238	.0100	220	.0049
	287	.0500	265	.0257	239	.0104	221	.0051
41	302	.0488	279	.0248	252	.0100	233	.0048
	303	.0501	280	.0256	253	.0103	234	.0050
42	319	.0496	294	.0245	266	.0098	247	.0049
	320	.0509	295	.0252	267	.0102	248	.0051

APPENDIX (T) (Cont.)

	NOMINAL ALPHA (ONE-TAILED)							
	.05		.025		.01		.005	
N	**T**	**α**	**T**	**α**	**T**	**α**	**T**	**α**
43	336	.0498	310	.0245	281	.0098	261	.0048
	337	.0511	311	.0252	282	.0102	262	.0050
44	353	.0495	327	.0250	296	.0097	276	.0049
	354	.0507	328	.0257	297	.0101	277	.0051
45	371	.0498	343	.0244	312	.0098	291	.0049
	372	.0510	344	.0251	313	.0101	292	.0051
46	389	.0497	361	.0249	328	.0098	307	.0050
	390	.0508	362	.0256	329	.0101	308	.0052
47	407	.0490	378	.0245	345	.0099	322	.0048
	408	.0501	379	.0251	346	.0102	323	.0050
48	426	.0490	396	.0244	362	.0099	339	.0050
	427	.0500	397	.0251	363	.0102	340	.0051
49	446	.0495	415	.0247	379	.0098	355	.0049
	447	.0505	416	.0253	380	.0100	356	.0050
50	466	.0495	434	.0247	397	.0098	373	.0050
	467	.0506	435	.0253	398	.0101	374	.0051

Source: The entries in this table were computed by the author.

References

Anderson, N. H. Comparison of different populations: Resistance to extinction and transfer. *Psychological Review*, 1963, **70**, 162–179.

Appelbaum, M. I., & Cramer, E. M. Some problems in the nonorthogonal analysis of variance. *Psychological Bulletin*, 1974, **81**, 335–343.

Bakan, D. The test of significance in psychological research. *Psychological Bulletin*, 1966, **66**, 423–437.

Baker, B. O., Hardyck, C. F., & Petrinovich, L. F. Weak measurements vs. strong statistics: An empirical critique of S. S. Stevens' proscriptions on statistics. *Educational and Psychological Measurement*, 1966, **26**, 291–309.

Bishop, Y. M. M., Fienberg, S. E., & Holland, P. W. *Discrete Multivariate Analysis: Theory and Practice*. Cambridge, Mass.: MIT Press, 1975.

Blair, R. C. I've been testing some statistical hypotheses. . . Can you guess what they are? *Journal of Educational Research*, 1978, **72**, 116–118.

Blair, R. C., & Higgins, J. J. Tests of hypotheses for unbalanced factorial designs under various regression/coding method combinations. *Educational and Psychological Measurement*, 1978, **38**, 621–631.

Blair, R. C., & Higgins, J. J. A comparison of the power of Wilcoxon's Rank-Sum statistic to that of Student's *t* statistic under various nonnormal distributions. *Journal of Educational Statistics*, 1980, **5**, 309–335.

Bock, R. D. Programming univariate and multivariate analysis of variance. *Technometrics*, 1963, **5**, 95–117.

Bock, R. D., & Haggard, E. A. The use of multivariate analysis of variance in behavioral research. In D. K. Whitla (Ed.), *Handbook of Measurement and Assessment in Behavioral Sciences*. Reading, Mass.: Addison-Wesley, 1968.

Boneau, C. A. The effects of violations of assumptions underlying the *t* test. *Psychological Bulletin*, 1960, **57**, 49–64.

Box, G. E. P. Non-normality and tests on variances. *Biometrika*, 1953, **40**, 318–335.

Box, G. E. P. Some theorems on quadratic forms applied in the study of analysis of variance problems, I. Effect of inequality of variance in the one-way classification. *Annals of Mathematical Statistics*, 1954, **25**, 290–302. (a)

Box, G. E. P. Some theorems on quadratic forms applied in the study of analysis of variance problems, II. Effect of inequality of variance and of correlation of errors in the two-way classification. *Annals of Mathematical Statistics*, 1954, **25**, 484–498. (b)

Bradley, D. R., Bradley, T. D., McGrath, S. G., & Cutcomb, S. D. Type I error rate of the chi-square test of independence in R × C tables that have small expected frequencies. *Psychological Bulletin*, 1979, **86**, 1290–1297.

Bradley, J. V. *Studies in research methodology VI. The central limit effect for a variety of populations and the robustness of z, t, and F.* AMRL Technical Report 64-123, Aerospace Medical Research Laboratories, Wright-Patterson Air Force Base, Ohio, December, 1964.

Bradley, J. V. *Distribution-free Statistical Tests.* Englewood Cliffs, N.J.: Prentice-Hall, 1968.

Burke, C. J. Additive scales and statistics. *Psychological Review*, 1953, **60**, 73–75.

Camilli, G., & Hopkins, K. D. Applicability of chi-square to 2×2 contingency tables with small expected cell frequencies. *Psychological Bulletin*, 1978, **85**, 163–167.

Camilli, G., & Hopkins, K. D. Testing for association in 2×2 contingency tables with very small sample sizes. *Psychological Bulletin*, 1979, **86**, 1011–1014.

Carlson, J. E., & Timm, N. H. Analysis of nonorthogonal fixed-effects designs. *Psychological Bulletin*, 1974, **81**, 563–570.

Chase, C. I. Computation of variance accounted for in multiple correlation. *Journal of Experimental Education*, 1960, **28**, 265–266.

Clark, K. B., & Clark, M. K. The development of consciousness of self in the emergence of racial identification in Negro pre-school children. *Journal of Social Psychology*, 1939, **10**, 591–599.

Cochran, W. G., & Cox, G. M. *Experimental Designs* (2nd ed.). New York: John Wiley & Sons, 1957.

Cohen, J. The statistical power of abnormal-social psychological research: A review. *Journal of Abnormal and Social Psychology*, 1962, **65**, 145–153.

Cohen, J. Some statistical issues in psychological research. In B. B. Wolman (Ed.), *Handbook of Clinical Psychology.* New York: McGraw Hill, 1965.

Cohen, J. Multiple regression as a general data-analytic system. *Psychological Bulletin*, 1968, **70**, 426–443.

Cohen, J. *Statistical Power Analysis for Behavioral Sciences.* New York: Academic Press, 1969.

Cohen, J. Eta-squared and partial eta-squared in fixed factor ANOVA designs. *Educational and Psychological Measurement*, 1973, **33**, 107–112.

Cohen, J., & Cohen, P. *Applied Multiple Regression/Correlation Analysis for the Behavioral Sciences.* Hillsdale, N.J.: Lawrence Erlbaum Associates, 1975.

Collier, R. O., Jr., Baker, F. B., & Mandeville, G. K. Tests of hypothesis in a repeated measures design from a permutation viewpoint. Psychometrika, 1967, **32**, 15–24.

Collier, R. O., Jr., Baker, F. B., Mandeville, G. K., & Hayes, T. F. Estimates of test size for several test procedures based on conventional variance ratios in the repeated measures design. *Psychometrika*, 1967, **32**, 339–353.

Cooley, W. W., & Lohnes, P. R. *Multivariate Data Analysis.* New York: John Wiley & Sons, 1971.

Cramer, E. M., & Appelbaum, M. I. Nonorthogonal analysis of variance—Once again. *Psychological Bulletin*, 1980, **87**, 51–57.

Cramér, H. *Mathematical Methods of Statistics.* Princeton, N.J.: Princeton University Press, 1946.

Darlington, R. B. Multiple regression in psychological research and practice. *Psychological Bulletin*, 1968, **69**, 161–182.

Davidson, M. L. Univariate versus multivariate tests in repeated-measures experiments. *Psychological Bulletin*, 1972, **77**, 446–452.

Dawes, R. M., & Corrigan, B. Linear models in decision making. *Psychological Bulletin*, 1974, **81**, 95–106.

Dixon, W. J., & Brown, M. B. (Eds.) *BMDP Biomedical Computer Programs: P-series, 1977.* Berkeley, Calif.: University of California Press, 1977.

Dixon, W. J., & Massey, F. J., Jr. *Introduction to Statistical Analysis* (2nd ed.). New York: McGraw-Hill, 1957.

Dodd, D. H., & Schultz, R. F., Jr. Computational procedures for estimating magnitude of effect for some analysis of variance designs. *Psychological Bulletin*, 1973, **79**, 391–395.

Duncan, D. B. Multiple range and multiple *F* tests. *Biometrics*, 1955, **11**, 1–42.

Dunn, O. J. Multiple comparisons among means. *Journal of the American Statistical Association*, 1961, **56**, 52–64.

Dunnett, C. W. A multiple comparison procedure for comparing several treatments with a control. *Journal of the American Statistical Association*, 1955, **50**, 1096–1121.

Dunnett, C. W. New tables for multiple comparisons with a control. *Biometrics*, 1964, **20**, 482–491.

Edwards, A. L. *Experimental Design in Psychological Research* (3rd ed.). New York: Holt, Rinehart & Winston, 1968.

Edwards, W., Lindman, H., & Savage, L. J. Bayesian statistical inference for psychological research. *Psychological Review*, 1963, **70**, 193–242.

Evans, S. H., & Anastasio, E. J. Misuse of analysis of covariance when treatment effect and covariate are confounded. *Psychological Bulletin*, 1968, **69**, 225–234.

Federer, W. T. *Experimental Design: Theory and Application.* New York: The Macmillan Company, 1955.

Ferguson, G. A. *Statistical Analysis in Psychology and Education* (2nd ed.). New York: McGraw-Hill, 1966.

Fisher, R. A. On the probable error of a coefficient of correlation deduced from a small sample. *Metron*, 1921, **1**, 3–32.

Fisher, R. A. *The Design of Experiments.* Edinburgh: Oliver & Boyd, 1935.

Fisher, R. A., & Yates, F. *Statistical Tables for Biological, Agricultural, and Medical Research* (4th ed.). Edinburgh: Oliver & Boyd, 1953.

Fleiss, J. L. Estimating the magnitude of experimental effects. *Psychological Bulletin*, 1969, **72**, 273–276.

Gaito, J. Nonparametric methods in psychological research. *Psychological Reports*, 1959, **5**, 115–125.

Gaito, J. Measurement scales and statistics: Resurgence of an old misconception. *Psychological Bulletin*, 1980, **87**, 564–567.

Goldberg, L. R. Diagnosticians versus diagnostic signs: The diagnosis of psychosis versus neurosis from the MMPI. *Psychological Monographs*, 1965, **79**, (9, Whole No. 602).

Goldberg, L. R. Five models of clinical judgment: An empirical comparison between linear and nonlinear representations of the human inference process. *Organizational Behavior and Human Performance*, 1971, **6**, 458–479.

Goodman, L. A. The multivariate analysis of qualitative data: Interactions among multiple classifications. *Journal of the American Statistical Association*, 1970, **65**, 226–256.

Graybill, F. A. *An Introduction to Linear Statistical Models* (Vol. 1). New York: McGraw-Hill, 1961.

Green, P. E., & Carroll, J. D. *Mathematical Tools for Applied Multivariate Analysis*, New York: Academic Press, 1976.

Greenhouse, S. W., & Geisser, S. On methods in the analysis of profile data. *Psychometrika*, 1959, **24**, 95–112.

Guilford, J. P., & Fruchter, B. *Fundamental Statistics in Psychology and Education*. New York: McGraw-Hill, 1973.

Harris, C. W. (Ed.) *Problems in Measuring Change*. Madison, Wisc.: University of Wisconsin Press, 1963.

Harter, H. L. Tables of range and studentized range. *Annals of Mathematical Statistics*, 1960, **31**, 1122–1147.

Hays, W. L. *Statistics for Psychologists* (1st ed.). New York: Holt, Rinehart & Winston, 1963.

Hays, W. L. *Statistics for the Social Sciences* (2nd ed.). New York: Holt, Rinehart, & Winston, 1973.

Heerman, E. F., & Braskamp, L. A. (Eds) *Readings in Statistics for the Behavioral Sciences*. Englewood Cliffs, N.J.: Prentice-Hall, 1970.

Hocking, R. R. The analysis and selection of variables in linear regression. *Biometrics*, 1976, **32**, 1–49.

Hoffman, P. J. The paramorphic representation of clinical judgment. *Psychological Bulletin*, 1960, **57**, 116–131.

Hoffman, P. J. Assessment of the independent contributions of predictors. *Psychological Bulletin*, 1962, **59**, 77–80.

Hotelling, H. The generalization of Student's Ratio. *Annals of Mathematical Statistics*, 1931, **2**, 360–378.

Hovland, C. I., Harvey, O. J., & Sherif, M. Assimilation and contrast effects in reactions to communication and attitude changes. *Journal of Abnormal and Social Psychology*, 1957, **55**, 244–252.

Howell, D. C., & Huessy, H. R. A long-term follow-up of hyperkinetic and non-hyperkinetic children. Paper presented at the meeting of the Society for Epidemiologic Research. New Haven, Conn., 1979.

Howell, D. C., & Huessy, H. R. Hyperkinetic behavior followed from 7 to 21 years of age. In Gittelman, M. (Ed.), *Intervention Strategies with Hyperactive Children*. White Plains, N.Y.: M. E. Sharpe, in press, 1980.

Howell, D. C., & McConaughy, S. H. Nonorthogonal analysis of variance: Putting the question before the answer. *Educational and Psychological Measurement*, in press, 1982.

Howell, D. C., & Stacey, P. O. Orthogonal comparisons with unequal sample sizes. Unpublished mimeo, University of Vermont, 1972.

Hraba, J., & Grant, G. Black is beautiful: A reexamination of racial preference and identification. *Journal of Personality and Social Psychology*, 1970, **16**, 398–402.

Huynh, H., & Feldt, L. S. Conditions under which mean square ratios in repeated measurement designs have exact F-distributions. *Journal of the American Statistical Association*, 1970, **65**, 1582–1589.

Jette, A., Howell, D. C., & Gordon, L. R. Effect of non-interval scales on conclusions from the t-test. Paper presented at meeting of the Eastern Psychological Association. Boston, 1977.

Kapp, B., Frysinger, R., Gallagher, M., & Hazelton, J. Amygdala central nucleus lesions: Effects on heart rate conditioning in rabbit. *Physiology and Behavior*, 1979, **23**, 1109–1117.

Kendall, M. G. *Rank Correlation Methods*. London: Griffin, 1948.

Keppel, G. *Design and Analysis: A Researcher's Handbook*. Englewood Cliffs, N.J.: Prentice-Hall, 1973.

Keselman, H. J. The statistic with the smaller critical value. *Psychological Bulletin*, 1974, **81**, 130–131.

Keselman, H. J., Murray, R., & Rogan, J. Effect of very unequal group sizes on Tukey's multiple comparison test. *Educational and Psychological Measurement*, 1976, **36**, 263–270.

Keselman, H. J., & Rogan, J. C. The Tukey multiple comparison test: 1953–1976. *Psychological Bulletin*, 1977, **84**, 1050–1056.

Kirk, R. E. *Experimental Design: Procedures for the Behavioral Sciences*. Belmont, Calif.: Brooks/Cole, 1968.

Kleinbaum, D. G., & Kupper, L. L. *Applied Regression Analysis and Other Multivariable Methods*. North Scituate, Mass.: Duxbury Press, 1978.

Lewis, C., & Keren, G. You can't have your cake and eat it too: Some considerations of the error term. *Psychological Bulletin*, 1977, **84**, 1150–1154.

Lewis, D., & Burke, C. J. The use and misuse of the chi-square test. *Psychological Bulletin*, 1949, **46**, 433–489.

Lewis, H. B., & Franklin, M. An experimental study of the role of ego in work. II. The significance of task-orientation in work. *Journal of Experimental Psychology*, 1944, **34**, 195–215.

Lord, F. M. On the statistical treatment of football numbers. *American Psychologist*, 1953, **8**, 750–751.

Lord, F. M. A paradox in the interpretation of group comparisons. *Psychological Bulletin*, 1967, **68**, 304–305.

Lord, F. M. Statistical adjustments when comparing pre-existing groups. *Psychological Bulletin*, 1969, **72**, 336–337.

Maxwell, S., & Cramer, E. M. A note on analysis of covariance. *Psychological Bulletin*, 1975, **82**, 187–190.

Mayo, S. T. Towards strengthening the contingency table as a statistical method. Psychological Bulletin, 1959, **56**, 461–470.

McConaughy, S. H. Cognitive structures for reading comprehension: Judging the relative importance of ideas in short stories. Unpublished Ph.D. dissertation, University of Vermont, 1980.

McNemar, Q. *Psychological Statistics* (3rd ed.). New York: John Wiley & Sons, 1962.

McNemar, Q. *Psychological Statistics* (4th ed.). New York: John Wiley & Sons, 1969.

Melzer, K. M. Components of the judgmental process: Effects of cue presentation on IQ estimates. Unpublished M.A. thesis, University of Vermont, 1975.

Miller, R. G., Jr. *Simultaneous Statistical Inference*. New York: McGraw-Hill, 1966.

Mood, A. M. *Introduction to the Theory of Statistics*. New York: McGraw-Hill, 1950.

Mood, A. M., & Graybill, F. A. *Introduction to the Theory of Statistics* (2nd ed.). New York: McGraw-Hill, 1963.

Myers, J. L. *Fundamentals of Experimental Design* (3rd ed.). Boston: Allyn & Bacon, 1979.

Norton, D. W. Study reported in Lindquist, E. F. *Design and Analysis of Experiments in Psychology and Education*. New York: Houghton Mifflin, 1953.

Nunnally, J. C. *Psychometric Theory*. New York: McGraw-Hill, 1967.

Nurcombe, B., & Fitzhenry-Coor, I. Decision making in the mental health interview: I. An introduction to an education and research program. Paper delivered at the Conference on Problem Solving in Medicine. Smuggler's Notch, Vermont. October, 1979.

O'Brien, R. G. Comment on "Some problems in the nonorthogonal analysis of variance." *Psychological Bulletin*, 1976, **83**, 72–74.

O'Neil, R., & Wetherill, G. B. The present state of multiple comparison methods. *Journal of the Royal Statistical Society (Series B)*, 1971, **33**, 218–250.

Overall, J. E. Computers in behavioral science: Multiple covariance analysis by the general least squares regression method. *Behavioral Science*, 1972, **17**, 313–320.

Overall, J. E. Power of chi-square tests for 2×2 contingency tables with small expected frequencies. *Psychological Bulletin*, 1980, **87**, 132–135.

Overall, J. E., & Klett, C. J. *Applied Multivariate Analysis*. New York: McGraw-Hill, 1972.

Overall, J. E., Spiegel, D. K. Concerning least squares analysis of experimental data. *Psychological Bulletin*, 1969, **72**, 311–322.

Overall, J. E., & Spiegel, D. K., & Cohen, J. Equivalence of orthogonal and nonorthogonal analysis of variance. *Psychological Bulletin*, 1975, **82**, 182–186.

Pearson, E. S. The Neyman-Pearson story, 1926–34: Historical sidelights on an episode in Anglo-Polish collaboration. In F. N. David (Ed.), *Research Papers in Statistics*. London: Wiley, 1966.

Pitman, E. J. G. A note on normal correlation. *Biometrika*, 1939, **31**, 9–12.

Rosenthal, R. Combining results of independent studies. *Psychological Bulletin*, 1978, **85**, 185–193.

Ryan, T. A. Multiple comparisons in psychological research. *Psychological Bulletin*, 1959, **56**, 26–47. (a)

Ryan, T. A. Comments on orthogonal components. *Psychological Bulletin*, 1959, **56**, 394–396. (b)

Satterthwaite, F. E. An approximate distribution of estimates of variance components. *Biometrics Bulletin*, 1946, **2**, 110–114.

Scheffé, H. *The Analysis of Variance*. New York: John Wiley & Sons, 1959.

Senders, V. L. A comment on Burke's additive scales and statistics. *Psychological Review*, 1953, **60**, 423–424.

Siegal, S. *Nonparametric Statistics for the Behavioral Sciences*. New York: McGraw-Hill, 1956.

Slovic, P., & Lichtenstein, S. Comparison of Bayesian and regression approaches to the study of information processing in judgment. *Organizational Behavior and Human Performance*, 1971, **6**, 649–744.

Smith, H. F. Interpretation of adjusted treatment means and regressions in analysis of covariance. *Biometrics*, 1957, **13**, 282–308.

Snedecor, G. W., & Cochran, W. G. *Statistical Methods* (6th ed.). Ames, Iowa: Iowa State University Press, 1967.

Stevens, S. S. Mathematics, measurement, and psychophysics. In S. S. Stevens (Ed.), *Handbook of Experimental Psychology*. New York: John Wiley & Sons, 1951.

Tiku, M. L. Tables of the power of the F test. *Journal of the American Statistical Association*, 1967, **62**, 525–539.

Tukey, J. W. One degree of freedom for nonadditivity. *Biometrics*, 1949, **5**, 232–242.

Vaughan, G. M., & Corballis, M. C. Beyond tests of significance: Estimating strength of effects in selected ANOVA designs. *Psychological Bulletin*, 1969, **72**, 204–223.

Verdooren, L. R. Extended tables of critical values for Wilcoxon's test statistic. *Biometrika*, 1963, **50**, 177–186.

Wainer, H. Estimating coefficients in linear models: It don't make no nevermind. *Psychological Bulletin*, 1976, **83**, 213–217.

Wainer, H. On the sensitivity of regression and regressors. *Psychological Bulletin*, 1978, **85**, 267–273.

Walker, H. M. Degrees of freedom. *Journal of Educational Psychology*, 1940, **31**, 253–269.

Weisberg, H. I. Statistical adjustments and uncontrolled studies. *Psychological Bulletin*, 1979, **86**, 1149–1164.

Welkowitz, J., Ewen, R. B., & Cohen, J. *Introductory Statistics for the Behavioral Sciences*. New York: Academic Press, 1971.

Winer, B. J. *Statistical Principles in Experimental Design*. New York: McGraw-Hill, 1962.

Winer, B. J. *Statistical Principles in Experimental Design* (2nd ed.). New York: McGraw-Hill, 1971.

Winkler, W. H. A comparison of reality orientation and reinforcement therapy in a geriatric unit of a state hospital. Unpublished Ph.D. dissertation, University of Vermont, 1977.

Yates, F. Contingency tables involving small numbers and the χ^2 test. Supplement. *Journal of the Royal Statistical Society (Series B)*, 1934, **1**, 217–235.

Younger, M. S. *Handbook for Linear Regression*. North Scituate, Mass.: Duxbury Press, 1979.

Zeigarnik, B. Das Behalten erledgiter und unerledgiter Handliegen (The memory of completed and uncompleted actions). *Psychologische Forschung*, 1927, **9**, 1–85.

Answers to Selected Exercises

Chapter 1

1.1 Small—the set of ages of the members of a family; reasonable—the set of grade point averages of the students of a large state university; infinite—the hypothetical set of outcomes obtained by repeating an experiment an infinite number of times.

1.2 Not all students at the university have an equal chance of appearing in that course—interest and prerequisites serve as a filter.

1.3 Probably not, since it is difficult to imagine a larger group who all had an equal chance of being in this sample.

1.4 Put the name of every student in a drum, stir the contents of the drum, and draw blindly.

1.5 Measurement data—the set of scores on a scale of authoritarianism; frequency data—the number of males and the number of females classed as developmentally disabled.

1.6 Nominal—hair color; ordinal—finishing position in a race; interval—the set of dates on which students actually turn in an assigned paper; ratio—number of items correct on an exam.

1.7 Possibly a ratio scale, but not enough information is given to say with complete confidence.

1.8 This could no longer be a ratio scale, because we have no reason to expect a perfect relationship between the teacher's ability to teach and the student's knowledge of Sanskrit.

1.9 It probably says nothing about his knowledge; it says a fair amount about his motivation, and it tells us that speed is probably not an interval scale of learning.

1.10 Independent variables—good readers vs. bad readers; experimental vs. control groups; dependent variables—reading speed; pain threshold.

1.11 Sex, political affiliation, psychiatric diagnosis. **1.12** Birthweight, intelligence, driving ability.

1.13 *a.* $X_3 = 9$; $X_5 = 10$; $X_9 = 2$ *b.* $\Sigma X = 77$ *c.* $\sum_{i=1}^{10} X_i$ **1.14** *a.* $Y_1 = 9$; $Y_8 = 6$ *b.* $\Sigma Y = 57$

1.15 *a.* $\Sigma X = 77$; $(\Sigma X)^2 = 5929$; $\Sigma X^2 = 657$ *b.* $\Sigma X/N = 7.7$ *c.* The average, or, more precisely, the mean.

1.16 *a.* $\Sigma Y = 57$; $(\Sigma Y)^2 = 3249$; $\Sigma Y^2 = 377$ *b.* $\left(\Sigma Y^2 - \dfrac{(\Sigma Y)^2}{N}\right)\Big/(N-1) = 5.79$ *c.* $\sqrt{5.79} = 2.41$

1.17 *a.* $\Sigma XY = 460$ *b.* $\Sigma X \Sigma Y = 4389$ *c.* $\left(\Sigma XY - \dfrac{\Sigma X \Sigma Y}{N}\right)\Big/(N-1) = 2.344$

1.18 *a.* $\Sigma(X + Y) = (19 + 17 + \cdots + 7 + 9) = 134$; $\Sigma X + \Sigma Y = 77 + 57 = 134$
b. $\Sigma XY = 460$; $\Sigma X \Sigma Y = 4389$; $460 \neq 4389$
c. Let $C = 6$. Multiplying each number by 6 and summing. $\Sigma CX = 60 + 48 + \cdots + 12 + 42 = 462 = 6(77) = C\Sigma X$

Chapter 2

2.3 **a.** mode = 18; median = 18; mean = 18.9 **2.4** **a.** mode = 10; median = 10; mean = 10.2
2.5 range = 30; interquartile range = 3 **2.6** range = 16; interquartile range = 4
2.7 $s_X^2 = 20.214$; $s_X = 4.496$ **2.8** $s_Y^2 = 11.592$; $s_Y = 3.405$
2.10 The data for adults have a mean which is approximately half the size of the mean for the children. The same is true for the variances of the two groups.
2.11 **b.** The distribution would be negatively skewed. **c.** Either produce a car which stays tuned up or produce some cars which have much better than average gas mileage.
2.12 Bimodal, because a large number would not smoke at all and another sizable group would smoke between 1 and 2 packs/day.
2.13 **a.** mean = 21.33 **b.** standard deviation = 1.589
2.17 The missing information concerns the frequencies for individual values of X. The histogram has lumped the data into intervals which are 4 units wide.

Chapter 3

3.1 I set up the null hypothesis that last night's game was actually an NHL hockey game. On the basis of that hypothesis I expected that each team would earn somewhere between 0 and 6 points. I then looked at the actual points and concluded that they were way out of line with what I would expect if this were a NHL hockey game. I therefore rejected the null hypothesis.
3.2 **b.** Yes, that is a reasonable result. **c.** I set up the null hypothesis that my friend was telling the truth. On the basis of that hypothesis I anticipated that his time would be 35 minutes give or take a minute or two. His actual time agreed with what would be expected if H_0 were true. I therefore failed to reject the null hypothesis.
3.3 He would draw a very large number of pairs of samples from a situation in which the null hypothesis is true, calculate E on the basis of the ranges of the samples in each pair, and plot the resulting values of E.
3.4 The tabled distribution would have to have a separate cutoff point corresponding to the 5% level for all possible (reasonable) sample sizes.
3.5 You can not *prove* a null hypothesis unless you measure every single element in the population. In other words you would have to weight every single grain of sand on earth and find that the mean weight of all of these grains of sand is .013862 grams.

Chapter 4

4.1 .3989; .2420; .2420 **4.2** .1295; .0175; .0009
4.4 For $X = 2.5$, $z = -.920$, 18% of the distribution lies below $X = 2.5$; for $X = 6.2$, $z = 1.35$, 91% of the distribution lies below $X = 6.2$; for $X = 9$, $z = 3.07$, 99.9% of the distribution lies below $X = 9$
4.5 **a.** 68% **b.** 50% **c.** 84%
4.6 **a.** $964.875 \leq X \leq 985.125$ **b.** $X = 985.125$ **c.** $945.6 \leq X \leq 1004.4$
4.7 $z = (950 - 975)/15 = -25/15 = -1.67$; only 4.75% of the time would we expect a count *as low as* 950 given what we know about the distribution of other outcomes.
4.8 **b.** 15.87% **c.** 30.85%

4.9 The answers to 4.8b and c will be the same when the distributions have the same standard deviations.

4.10 $z = -1.28$; $X = \bar{X} - 1.28(\sigma) = 111.6$

4.11 $z = 1.28$; $X = \bar{X} + 1.28(\sigma) = 1884$ $z = -1.645$; $X = \bar{X} - 1.645(\sigma) = 1006.5$

4.12 **b.** $z = \dfrac{X - \bar{X}}{\sigma} = \dfrac{20 - 40}{7} = -2.86$. If our student were counting conscientiously, the probability that he would have a score as low as 20 by chance is only .0021. Since this probability is so low, I am inclined to believe that he did not count (at least not with any degree of alertness).

4.13 Multiply the raw scores by 10/7 and then add 11.43 points. (Multiplying all of the scores by 10/7 will set the standard deviation at 10, but will leave a new mean of 68.57. She needs to add an additional 11.43 to everything to bring the new mean up to 80.)

4.14 I really suggested to her that she take the set of scores and empirically (by counting) determine what score has 10% of the observations below it.

4.15 **a.** $z = -1.645$; $X = \bar{X} - 1.645(\sigma) = 76.8$ **b.** It would mean that I classify a student who falls below 76.8 as not studying, when in fact he did study.

4.16 **a.** No, I am not testing an hypothesis, I am describing something.   **b.** In Exercise 4.15 there was an hypothesis being tested, i.e., there was a H_1.

4.17 $s^2 = 15.903$; $s = 3.99$ **4.18** **a.** $\beta = .298$ **b.** $\beta = .56$ **4.19** .41 and .66

4.20 There would be no effect on α, but β would decrease with decreases in the standard deviation.

Chapter 5

5.1 Analytic—a mouse in a maze who is responding at random has a probability of .50 of turning left at a choice point; frequentistic—a mouse who has turned left on 700 out of the last 1000 trials has a probability of .70 of turning left this time (assuming no trend in the data over trials); subjective—"I would give this experiment about a 70% chance of coming up with useful results."

5.2 **a.** $\frac{1}{1000} = .001$ **b.** $\frac{2}{1000} = .002$ **c.** $\frac{3}{1000} = .003$

5.3 **a.** $\frac{1}{9} = .1111$ **b.** $\frac{2}{90} = .0222$ **c.** .0222   **d.** .0444

5.4 **b**, **c**, and part of **d**   **5.5** part **a**

5.7 The probability of 6 or more correct (out of 10) if $p = .20$ is only .0064. Thus if 6 of the 10 were correct I would conclude that they were not operating at chance (there is some cheating going on!).

5.8 At $\alpha = .05$, 5 or more correct choices would lead me to conclude that they are no longer performing at chance levels.

5.9 .010   **5.10** .036   **5.11** 24   **5.12** 12   **5.13** $\frac{1}{60}$ **5.14** 64   **5.15** 15

5.16 If $p = .50$ and $N = 20$, $p(11) = (C_{11}^{20}).5^{11}.5^9 = .16$. Since the probability of 11 correct by chance is .16, the probability of 11 *or more* correct must be greater than .16. Therefore we can not reject the hypothesis that $p = .50$ (student is guessing) at $\alpha = .05$.

5.18 $z = \dfrac{X - \mu}{\sigma} = \dfrac{X - np}{\sqrt{npq}}$

$$z = \dfrac{22 - .60(30)}{\sqrt{30(.60)(.40)}} = \dfrac{22 - 18}{\sqrt{7.2}} = 1.49; \text{We cannot reject } H_0 \text{ at } \alpha = .05.$$

Chapter 6

6.1 $\chi^2 = 11.313$; reject H_0 and conclude that students do not sign up at random.

6.2 We can not tell if students chose different sections because of the instructor, or because of the time the section meets, or for some other reason. We would *at least* need to offer all sections at the same time.

6.3 $\chi^2 = 3.4$. Since, with 4 df, $\chi^2_{.05} = 9.49$, we can not reject the null hypothesis that my daughter sorts as my theory suggests.

6.4 It only generalizes to the population of data which could be generated by my daughter. In other words, we have a random sample of her behavior. We do not have a random sample of people.

6.5 $\chi^2 = 29.35$. Since $\chi^2_{.05} = 3.84$, we can reject the null hypothesis that children chose dolls at random (at least with respect to color).

6.6 $\chi^2 = 12.24$. Again we reject H_0, but this time the departure from equality is in the opposite direction.

6.7 $\chi^2 = 34.184$. Since $\chi^2_{.05} = 3.84$, we reject the null hypothesis and conclude that the distribution of choices between black and white dolls was different in the two studies. We are no longer asking whether one color is preferred over another, but whether the *pattern* of preference is constant across studies.

6.9 *a.* A Chi-square test on these data would test the null hypothesis that the choice of the mental health center at which a person seeks help is independent of the type of problem he has. *b.* $\chi^2 = 10.305$; with 4 df $\chi^2_{.05} = 9.49$. *c.* Reject H_0 and conclude that the two variables are not independent, since $10.305 > 9.49$.

6.10 *a.* $\chi^2 = 5.153$, which is half of what it was in Exercise 6.9. *b.* The sample size plays a very important role, with larger sample sizes being more likely to produce a significant difference.

6.11 *a.* Deliberately take 10 males and 10 females and have them divide into two teams of 10 players each. *b.* Deliberately take an equal number of males and females and ask them to specify a preference among 3 types of life styles. *c.* Take a group of subjects at random and sort them by sex and by life style (categorized 3 ways).

6.12 $\chi^2 = 5.38$; $\chi^2_{.05} = 3.84$. Therefore we will reject the null hypothesis and conclude that achievement level during high school varies as a function of performance during elementary school.

6.13 *a.* $\chi^2 = 16.095$ *b.* Reject H_0. *c.* Since nearly $\frac{1}{2}$ of the expected frequencies are less than 5 I feel very uncomfortable. One approach would be to combine adjacent columns.

6.15 $\chi^2 = 5.08$; reject H_0.   **6.16** $\chi^2 = 12.753$; do not reject H_0.

6.17 We would be asking if the students are evenly distributed among the 8 categories. What we really tested in Exercise 6.13 is whether that distribution (however it appears) is the same for those who later took remedial English as it was for those who later took non-remedial English.

6.18 *a.* Because the observations are not independent. The same subjects contribute twice to the data matrix. *b.* .889 *c.* The distribution of Pro and Con scores *after* the game is independent of the distribution before the game.

6.19 *a.* $\chi^2 = 9.00$; reject H_0. *b.* If watching Monday Night Football really changes people's opinions (in a negative direction), then of those people who change, more should change from positive to negative than vice versa, which is what happened.

6.20 *a.* $\chi^2 = 12.895$ on 6 df; reject H_0. *b.* The number of days required for delivery is a function of distance, but not in a neat and readily interpretable manner.

6.21 *b.* 5 is the observed frequency. 14.3% of the deliveries in one day occur for distances of 50 miles. 16.7% of the letters mailed from 50 miles away were delivered in 1 day. 4.8% of the observations fall in this cell. *c.* The probability of a value of χ^2 greater than or equal to 12.89583 is exactly .0447.

Chapter 7

7.1 $t = 1.6$; retain H_0.

7.2 It is to insure that there are no systematic differences between the two groups other than differences in the independent variable.

7.3 $t = 2.53$; $p < .05$; reject H_0.

7.4 **a.** (1) Cavities that began during the first 6 months may not appear until the second 6-month period. (2) There might be dietary or other changes over time—especially seasonal ones. (3) Subjects may become much less conscientious over time. **b.** Half of the children should receive toothpaste X first and half should receive toothpaste Y first. Moreover, there should be a rest interval between the two 6-month periods.

7.5 $z = -1.41$. This difference is not significant.

7.6 $z = 3.14$. This college is significantly above the national average with respect to SAT scores, and its students are not a random sample from the general population of students taking the SAT.

7.7 $CI_{.95} = 490 \pm 13.86$; $CI_{.99} = 490 \pm 18.24$. We can conclude that the probability is .95 that the limits 476.14 and 503.86 include the true population mean; and that the probability is .99 that the limits 471.76 and 508.24 include the population mean.

7.8 $CI_{.95} = .889 \pm .809$. The probability is .95 that the limits .080 and 1.698 include the true difference in the mean number of cavities for the two brands of toothpaste. The corresponding 99% confidence limits are $-.289$ and 2.067.

7.9 $t = .45$; retain H_0.   **7.10** $t = -.348$; retain H_0.

7.11 The standard deviation of the difference scores is considerably larger for the data in Exercise 7.10 than for the data in Exercise 7.9. In Exercise 7.9, most people showed minor changes in behavior. In Exercise 7.10, the light smokers smoked less after the campaign, but the heavy smokers smoked even more.

7.12 $t = 2.143$; significant.

7.13 $t = 3.55$; $p < .05$; df' for Exercise 7.12 ≈ 6; df' for Exercise 7.13 ≈ 15. The differences in df' most likely depend on the relationship between the variances and the sample size.

7.14 The sample sizes might really be the more important statistic since they represent dropout rates.

7.15 For Exercise 7.12, $F = 3.96$, retain H_0. For Exercise 7.13, $F = 2.609$, retain H_0.

7.16 $t = .587$, retain H_0.   **7.17** $z = 2.24$, reject H_0 at $p < .05$.

7.21 Depending upon our final N (and therefore our final df) we will need to have a t somewhere around 2.0 to be significant. (The actual value itself depends on N, but call it 2.00.) To have a t of 2.00, we would need 98.45 subjects in each group.

Chapter 8

8.1 **a.** $\gamma = .250$ **b.** $\delta = 2.50$ **c.** power $= .71$ **8.3** 106, 125, and 169.   **8.4** .965

8.6 **a.** $N = 15.21 \approx 16$ **b.** $N = 31.36 \approx 32$

8.7 **a.** $N = 30.41 \approx 31$ subjects per group **b.** $N = 62.72 \approx 63$ subjects per group

8.8 power $\approx .30$ **8.9** power $\approx .51$

8.10 **a.** power $\approx .22$ **b.** $t = 1.185$ **c.** t is numerically equal to delta, although δ is calculated from parameters and t from statistics.

8.11 The significant t on 10 subjects, because that experiment had relatively less power and still managed to find a difference.

8.13 power $\approx .64$ **8.14** $N = 67$

8.15 He should use the Dropout Group. (You can let σ be anything you want—as long as it is the same for both calculations—and just look at the resulting values of δ.)

8.16 power $\approx .58$ **8.17** $N = 50$

8.18	Effect size	γ	one-sample t	two-sample t	correlations
	small	.20	289	1156	290
	medium	.50	47	185	48
	large	.80	19	72	20

8.19	Effect size	γ	one-sample t	two-sample t	correlations
	small	.20	121	484	122
	medium	.50	20	78	21
	large	.80	8	31	9

8.20   Not unless the underlying assumptions of the test are violated.

Chapter 9

9.2   *a.* $\hat{Y} = .0447X - 1.76$; $\hat{Y} = 2.710, 3.157, 3.604, 4.051$ *b.*   A slight change in b would make a more marked change in $\hat{Y}$ when $X = 130$ than when $X = 100$.

9.3   *b.* and *c.* 4.667, 3.333, −4.667

9.4   *a.*   .99, .71, −.99   *b.*   3 possible ways: 2 8 6 4, or 6 4 2 8, or 6 2 8 4

9.7 $a = 68.782$; $b = 11.0137$

9.8   When data are standardized, the slope equals r. Therefore the slope will be less than one (for all practical purposes) and predicted deviations from the mean will be less than actual parental deviations.

9.9   Error variance would cause many to exceed the predicted score.

9.10   *b.* $r = .738$ *c.*   Approximately 54% of the variation in grades can be accounted for by variation in number of problems solved.

9.11   *a.* $\hat{Y} = .475X + 43.2$ *b.*   A difference of 1 problem solved would lead to a predicted difference of .475 in grade. A student who solved no problems would be expected to have a grade of 43.2.

9.12   *a.* $s^2_{Y \cdot X} = \mathrm{SS}_Y(1 - r^2)/(N - 2) = 3724.5498(.445)/18 = 94.148$; $s_{Y \cdot X} = \sqrt{94.148} = 9.703$
b. $55.44 \le X \le 97.46$

9.13   *b.* $r = .811$ *c.* $\hat{Y} = .866X + .526$ *d.*   Approximately 66% of the variation in the cost of a meal ordered by the person paying the bill can be accounted for by variation in the cost of the meal ordered by the person who is not paying.

9.14   *a.* $r = .740$ *b.*   55% of the variation in Y can be accounted for by variation in X.   *d.*   The extreme scores seem to be distorting the meaning of r.

9.15 $r = -.574$; the extreme scores in fact influenced the correlation substantially.

9.16   *a.* and *b.* $t = 4.64$ **9.17**   *a.* and *b.* $t = 5.00$

9.18 $t = -2.753$. In the large university salary apparently covaries less with years of service (and more with other variables) than at the smaller school.

9.19   The faculty apparently start off at a higher initial salary, but the staff increase at a faster rate over time.

Chapter 10

10.1   *b.* $r_{pb} = -.540$; $t = -2.722$ *c.*   Performance in the morning is significantly related to people's perception of their peak periods.

10.2 b. $r_{pb} = .226$; $t = .984$ **c.** Performance in the evening is not significantly related to perceived peak periods.

10.3 It looks as if morning people vary their performance across time, but that evening people are uniformly poor.

10.4 We believe that the underlying distribution is bimodal, and not continuous.

10.5 $t = 2.725$ **10.6 b.** $r_{pb} = .214$ **c.** $r_b = .279$ **d.** Yes, because there really is a continuum.

10.7 $\hat{Y} = .202X + .0931$; when $X = \bar{X} = 2.9032$; $\hat{Y} = .680 = \bar{Y}$

10.8 They represent nothing meaningful because (1) the values (0, 1) for Ph.D. are arbitrary, and (2) no one would be admitted to graduate school with a GPA even approaching 0.00.

10.9 b. $r = .256$ **c.** $t = 1.27$, not significant **10.10 a.** $\chi^2 = 1.63$ **b.** $\phi = .256 = \sqrt{\dfrac{1.63}{25}}$

10.11 a. $\phi = .628$ **b.** $\chi^2 = 12.62$; $p < .05$ **10.12 a.** $r_s = .971$

10.13 a. $\tau = .886$ **b.** $t - 4.60$, $p < .05$ **10.14** $r_s = .891$ **10.15** $\tau = .733$

10.16 $W = .902$; $\bar{r}_s = .88$; The average pairwise correlation among judges' ranking $= .88$.

10.17 a. $\phi_c = .17$; $\phi_c^2 = .03$ **b.** Since the coefficient is not significant we can conclude that we have no reason to doubt the independence of marital status and depression.

10.18 $C = .17$, which is not significant. $C_{max} = \sqrt{1/2} = .707$

10.19 a. $\phi_c = .31$ **b.** $C = .30$ **c.** Financial security and income are not independent, but the relationship is not clearcut.

10.20 a. $\phi_c = .30$ **b.** $C = .39$ **c.** There is a significant, though nonlinear relationship between income and financial security.

10.21 They come from tables having different dimensionality.

10.22 Yes, in the sense that the income variable is an ordered variable while marital status is not.

Chapter 11

11.1

Source	df	SS	MS	F
Between Groups	2	2100.00	1050.00	40.13*
Within Groups	15	392.5	26.17	
Total	17	2492.5		

*$p < .05$.

11.2 a.

Source	df	SS	MS	F
Between Groups	1	2.2562	2.2562	1.951
Within Groups	8	9.2500	1.1563	
Total	9	11.5062		

b. $t = -1.397 = \sqrt{1.951}$ **c.** To insure that the observations were independent.

11.3 a.

Source	df	SS	MS	F
Between Groups	3	655.1429	218.381	10.778*
Within Groups	24	486.2857	20.262	
Total	27	1141.4286		

*$p < .05$.

b.

Source	df	SS	MS	F
Between Groups	1	51.5715	51.5715	1.230
Within Groups	26	1089.8571	41.9176	
Total	27	1141.4286		

Whether placement in the Usual Place produces fewer sales than placement in a Prominent Place—ignoring differences due to Known vs. Unknown brands.

11.4

Source	df	SS	MS	F
Between Groups	2	1516.10	758.05	24.01*
Within Groups	12	378.83	31.57	
Total	14	1894.93		

* $p < .05$.

11.5 a.

Source	df	SS	MS	F
Between Groups	1	1.42	1.42	.96
Within Groups	10	14.74	1.47	
Total	11	16.16		

b. t without pooling $= -.93$ **c.** t with pooling $= -.98$ **d.**   the pooled t

11.6 $\eta^2 = .196$; $\hat{\omega}^2 = .087$. I assumed a fixed model, since a random model would make no sense here.
11.7   I assume a fixed model because it would not make sense to draw rat pup ages at random. (Furthermore, notice that they are evenly spaced.)

11.8 a.

Source	df	SS	MS	F
Between Groups	2	826.8667	413.433	9.64*
Within Groups	27	1157.6619	42.876	
Total	29	1984.5289		

* $p < .05$

There are significant differences among the group means.   **b.**   The theory dealt with good vs. poor readers, but that does not appear to be a variable in the study.   **c.**   That *unselected* readers perform differently as a function of treatment condition.

11.9 I would conclude that there is likely to be a problem with heterogeneity of variance, but, more importantly, that experimental condition seems to lead to large individual differences.

11.10	*Source*	**df**	**SS**	**MS**	**F**
	Between Groups	2	413.433	206.717	4.821*
	Within Groups	12	514.512	42.876	
	Total	14	927.945		

* $p < .05$.

There are still significant differences among the groups.

11.11 I have more faith. The power of this second experiment was less, and therefore it would take a stronger effect to be significant.

11.12 **b.** The test on the MEAN is a test on H_0: $\mu = 0$.

11.14 The probability of $F \geq 10.778 = .0001$. (In this particular case p is rounded off to .0001.)

11.15 $X_{ij} = \mu + \tau_i + e_{ij}$; where μ = grand mean, τ_i = effects of treatment$_i$, and e_{ij} = unit of error for subject$_j$ in treatment$_i$.

11.16 Same as for Exercise 11.15.   **11.17** Same as for Exercise 11.15.

11.18 No, we can not speak meaningfully about an F in the analysis of variance being significantly less than 1.00. If $\sigma_\tau^2 = 0$, F is the ratio of two estimates of the same thing (σ^2) and there is no reason why one of these estimates should be appreciably smaller than the other.

11.19	*Source*	**df**	**SS**	**MS**	**F**
	Between Groups	7	43.631	6.233	7.12*
	Within Groups	264	231.264	.876	
		271	274.894		

* $p < .05$.

There are significant differences among the group means—especially comparing the first group to the others.

11.20	*Source*	**df**	**SS**	**MS**	**F**
	Between Groups	6	2.767	.461	<1
	Within Groups	64	42.282	.661	
	Total	70	45.049		

It indicates that the significant difference that we found in Exercise 11.19 was due to the fact that the first group differed from the others.

Chapter 12

12.1 $SS_{Contrast_1} = 900$; $SS_{Contrast_2} = 1200$

12.2 For $\alpha = .05$: Per Comparison $= \alpha = .05$; Per Experiment $= 2\alpha = .10$; Experimentwise $= 1 - (1 - \alpha)^2 = .0975$.

12.3 $F = 1.95$; This was a waste of time because we only have two groups and thus the overall F is equivalent to the F on the contrast.

12.4 $q = -1.976$; $t\sqrt{2} = -1.976$

12.5

	143	146	64	99	L	$\dfrac{L^2}{n\Sigma a_i^2}$	F
a.	1	1	−1	−1	126	567.00	27.98
b.	1	−1	1	−1	−38	51.57	2.55
c.	1	−1	−1	1	32	36.57	1.80
						655.14	

d. The first contrast compares known vs. unknown brands. The second contrast compares usual vs. prominent locations. The third looks at what we will refer to in Chapter 13 as the interaction of brand and location.

12.6 $SS_1 = 900$ $F_1 = \dfrac{900}{26.17} = 34.39$ $t = 5.86$; reject H_0

$SS_2 = 1200$ $F_2 = \dfrac{1200}{26.17} = 45.85$ $t = 6.77$; reject H_0

12.7

	GROUPS				
	2	**3**	**1**		
	30	48	75	r	W_r
30	—	18	45*	3	32.21
48		—	27*	2	26.64
75			—		

The difference between Treatments 1 and 2 is significant, as is the difference between Treatments 1 and 3.

12.8 Tukey$_b$: $W_3 = 32.21$, $W_2 = 29.42$; Tukey$_a$: $W_3 = W_2 = 32.21$. For both of these tests, only the difference between Treatments 1 and 2 is significant.

12.9 To carry out this test in the most exact manner we generate a table of differences among *means*, a table containing df' for each pairwise comparison, and a table of the critical value of $\bar{X}_i - \bar{X}_j$ for each pair of means. We then compare the critical values against the obtained mean differences. The results show that Group 1 differs from all other groups and that Group 5 differs from all other groups. The remaining pairs of means are homogeneous.

12.10 We use the same procedures as in Exercise 12.9, except q_r is taken as the average of q_r and $q_{max\,r}$. The results are the same as for Exercise 12.9.

12.11 $F_{obt} = 113.26$ and 61.57, respectively. The critical value of $F = 10.76$. Thus both contrasts are significant.

12.13 If you are willing to sacrifice using a common error term, you simply run the relevant t tests but evaluate them at $\alpha' = \alpha/c$.

Chapter 13

13.1 a.

Source	df	SS	MS	F
Pay	1	3.8281	3.8281	10.43*
Sex	1	.0781	.0781	<1
Pay × Sex	1	3.4032	3.4032	9.27*
Error	16	5.8750	.3672	
Total	19	13.1844		

* $p < .05$.

There is a significant effect for who is paying and a significant P×S interaction.

b. $X_{ijk} = \mu + \alpha_i + \beta_j + \alpha\beta_{ij} + e_{ijk}$

13.2 a.

Source	df	SS	MS	F
Parity	1	13.0667	13.0667	3.35
Size/age	2	97.7333	48.8667	12.54*
Parity x Size	2	17.7333	8.8667	2.28
Error	54	210.4000	3.8963	
Total	59	338.9333		

* $p < .05$.

b. There was a significant effect due to Size, with Full term dyads (mother-infant pair) showing the best interaction and low birth weight dyads with mothers under 18 showing the worst.

13.3 It is hard to believe that mothers who are less than 18 years old and have had at least their second child don't differ in many respects from the rest of the mothers.

13.4 This would be a relevant consideration if you averaged across all primiparous mothers and took this average as some sort of measure of the typical primiparous dyad. The LBW < 18 group plays a disproportionate role relative to its size in the population. If you treat cell means separately and realize what is going on, there should be no problem.

13.5 a.

Source	df	SS	MS	F
Site	2	356.0444	178.0222	6.07*
Delay	2	188.5778	94.2889	3.22
S×D	4	371.9556	92.9889	3.17*
Error	36	1055.2000	29.3111	
Total	44	1971.7778		

* $p < .05$.

b. $X_{223} = \mu + \alpha_2 + \beta_2 + \alpha\beta_{22} + e_{223}$

13.6 a. $\hat{\alpha}_1 = 3.9778$ (if A refers to Site) **b.** $\hat{\beta}_3 = 2.8445$ $\quad \hat{\alpha\beta}_{11} = 1.3553 \quad \hat{\alpha\beta}_{23} = 1.7555$

13.7 **a.** $SS_{delay\ at\ neutral} = $ 1.2 $F < 1$
$SS_{delay\ at\ A} = 254.8$ $F = 4.35^*$
$SS_{delay\ at\ B} = 304.53$ $F = 5.19^*$
$\overline{\qquad 560.53}$

     $^* p < .05.$

b. $560.53 = SS_D + SS_{SD}$

13.8 **a.** $SS_{size\ at\ primip.} = $ 18.2000

     b. $SS_{size\ at\ multip.} = \dfrac{97.2667}{115.4667} = SS_{size} + SS_{P \times S}$ **c.** $115.4667 = SS_{size} + SS_{P \times S}$

13.9

Source	df	SS	MS	F
Sex	1	6.242	6.242	11.65*
Group	7	13.259	1.894	3.53*
S×G	7	3.697	.528	<1
Error	219	117.427	.536	
Total	234			

$^* p < .05.$

13.10   No. The method of classification *forces* some of the cell sizes to be small.

13.11

Source	df	SS	MS	F
Parity	1	11.2358	11.2358	2.68
Size	2	85.8264	42.9132	10.26*
P×S	2	15.4556	7.7278	1.85
Error	49	205.0013	4.1837	
Total	54			

$^* p < .05.$

13.12

Source	df	SS	MS	F
Reputation	1	567.000	567.000	27.98*
Location	1	51.571	51.571	2.55
R×L	1	36.571	36.571	1.80
Error	24	486.286	20.260	
Total	27	1141.429		

$^* p < .05$

13.13   They are the same—as they should be.

13.14

Source	df	SS	MS	F
Hospital	1	552.544	552.544	24.57*
Treatment	1	288.300	288.300	12.82*
H×T	1	107.339	107.339	4.77
Error	11	247.417	22.492	
Total	14	1195.600		

$* \, p < .05.$

13.15 a.

Source	df	SS	MS	F
Hospital	1	350.017	350.017	15.56*
Treatment	1	350.017	350.017	15.56*
H×T	1	107.332	107.332	4.77
Error	11	247.417	22.492	
Total	14			

$* \, p < .05.$

b. Note that the interaction and the error terms have remained the same, but there have been substantial changes in the main effects.

13.16 No, because the sample sizes are arbitrary and don't reflect relative frequencies in the population. If they did reflect the relative frequency in the population you *might* want to let sample sizes influence the analysis—but probably not.

13.17 $\eta^2 = .29, .01,$ and $.26;$ $\hat{\omega} = .26, —,$ and $.22$ **13.18** $\eta^2 = .04, .29,$ and $.05;$ $\hat{\omega}^2 = .03, .26,$ and $.03$

13.19

Source	df	SS	MS	F
CS	1	185.008	185.008	16.72*
Int	2	78.017	39.008	3.53*
Exp	3	103.025	34.342	3.10*
C×I	2	.017	.008	<1
C×E	3	217.825	72.608	6.56*
I×E	6	.050	.008	<1
C×I×E	6	.050	.008	<1
Error	96	1062.008	11.0626	
Total	119	1646.000		

$* \, p < .05.$

There are significant differences due to each of the main effects and there is a significant CS×Experience interaction, with a tendency for more trials required for learning when the CS is a familiar one.

13.20 Knowing what is happening at each level of each variable doesn't really tell you about differences in the differences themselves.

13.23 $SS_{\text{main effects}}$ refers to the total variation accounted for by one or the other (or both) of the individual main effects. $SS_{\text{explained}}$ is the total variation which can be accounted for in some way.

Chapter 14

14.1 a. $X_{ij} = \mu + \pi_i + \tau_j + \pi\tau_{ij} + e_{ij}$ or $X_{ij} = \mu + \pi_i + \tau_j + e'_{ij}$

b.

Source	df	SS	MS	F
Between Subjects	7	189112.5		
Within Subjects	16	5400.0		
Session	2	1918.75	959.375	3.858*
Error	14	3481.25	248.661	
Total	23	194512.5		

* $p < .05$.

c. There is a significant difference among the session totals, with scores increasing as a function of experience.

14.2 a. $t = 1.19$ **b.** $F = 1.41$; $\sqrt{F} = \sqrt{1.41} = 1.19$

14.3

Source	df	SS	MS	F
Between Subjects	19	106.475		
Groups	1	1.225	1.225	< 1
Ss within groups	18	105.250	5.847	
Within Subjects	20	83.500		
Trials	1	38.025	38.025	15.259*
T×G	1	.625	.625	<1(=.251)
T×Ss within groups	18	44.850	2.492	
Total	39	189.975		

* $p < .05$.

There is a significant change from baseline to training, but it does not occur differentially between the two groups.

14.4 a. $t = -.501$ **b.** $t^2 = .251 = F$ for the interaction **c.** A t test on the difference scores is asking whether the baseline-training differences are themselves different across groups. This is exactly what an interaction tests.

14.5 a.

Source	df	SS	MS	F
Between Subjects	29	159.733		
Groups	2	11.433	5.716	1.04
Ss within groups	27	148.300	5.490	
Within Subjects	30	95.000		
Trials	1	19.267	19.267	9.44*
T×G	2	20.633	10.316	5.05*
T×Ss within groups	27	55.100	2.040	
Total	59	254.733		

* $p < .05$.

c. Reinforcement or attention are sufficient to produce a change from baselines performance, but the additional control group demonstrates that this change is real and not one which would have happened anyway.

14.6 *a.*

Source	df	SS	MS	F
Between Subjects	9	67.200		
Groups	1	34.134	34.134	8.26*
Ss within groups	8	33.066	4.133	
Within Subjects	20	100.667		
Problems	2	66.467	33.233	48.63*
$P \times G$	2	23.266	11.633	17.02*
$P \times S$s within groups	16	10.934	.683	
Total	29	167.867		

* $p < .05$.

b. No

14.7 *b.* $\hat{e} = .771$

14.8 Yes; the separate within group covariance matrices are roughly equal and the assumption of a constant (pooled) covariance matrix seems reasonable given the sample sizes.

14.9 *a.* and *b.*

$$SS_{\text{group at add}} = .9 \qquad F < 1$$
$$SS_{\text{group at subt}} = 3.6 \qquad F = 1.96$$
$$SS_{\text{group at mult}} = 52.9 \qquad F = 28.86*$$
$$SS_{\text{prob at calc}} = 78.533 \qquad F = 57.47*$$
$$SS_{\text{prob at non-calc}} = 11.200 \qquad F = 8.20*$$

* $p < .05$.

14.10 *a.*

Source	df	SS	MS	F
Between Subjects	19	164.933		
Age	1	29.400	29.400	7.35*
Readers	1	68.267	68.267	17.067*
$A \times R$	1	3.267	3.267	<1
Ss within groups	16	64.000	4.000	
Within Subjects	40	88.667		
Items	2	60.400	30.200	51.4*
$I \times A$	2	0.000	0.000	<1
$I \times R$	2	.933	.467	<1
$I \times A \times R$	2	8.533	4.267	7.26*
$I \times S$s within groups	32	18.800	.5875	
Total	59	253.600		

* $p < .05$.

14.11 *a.* $SS_{\text{reading at child}} = 50.7 \qquad F = 12.675*$

b. $SS_{\text{items at adult good}} = 4.133 \qquad F = 3.52*$

14.13 There would be a very decided lack of independence among items due to the fact that an increase in one category would necessitate a decrease in another—i.e., the subject would have less opportunity to draw from all categories.

14.14 *a.*

Source	df	SS	MS	F
Between Subjects	14	69.433		
Group	2	7.233	3.617	<1
Ss within groups	12	62.200	5.183	
Within Subjects	45	117.5		
Time	1	60.000	60.000	109.09*
T×G	2	7.900	3.950	7.18*
T×Ss within groups	12	6.600	.550	
Place	1	26.667	26.667	43.24*
P×G	2	1.433	.717	1.16
P×Ss within groups	12	7.400	.617	
T×P	1	4.267	4.267	28.44*
T×P×G	2	1.433	.717	4.78*
T×P×Ss within groups	12	1.800	.150	
Total	59	186.933		

* $p < .05$.

14.16 There are many simple effects. One example is the simple interaction effect of T×G at Work. $SS_{T×G \text{ at work}} = 7.267$ $F = 10.38^*$.

14.17 *b.* The F for MEAN is a test on H_0: $\mu = 0$. *c.* $MS_{\text{within cell}}$ is the average of the cell variances.

14.19 From Exercise 14.10, $MS_{\text{within cell}} = (64.000 + 18.800)/48 = 1.725 = MS_{\text{error}}$ in Exercise 14.19.

Chapter 15

15.1 *a.* A difference of $+1$ degree in temperature (all other things equal) will produce a difference of $-.01$ in perceived quality of life. A difference of \$1000 in median income is associated with a $+.05$ difference in perceived quality of life (again, all other variables held constant). Similarly for the other values of b. The intercept has no practical interpretation here. *b.* 4.92 *c.* 3.72

15.2 A difference between two cities of 1 standard deviation in temperature will be a difference of $-.438$ standard deviations in perceived quality of life, and so on for the other variables.

15.3 Temperature ($t = -1.104$)

15.4 *a.* $\hat{Y} = .605\text{RESPON} - .334\text{NUMSUP} + .486\text{ENVIR} + .070\text{YRS} + 1.669$
b. $\beta' = [.624 \ -.311 \ .514 \ .063]$

15.5 *a.* ENVIR *b.* The gain in prediction from adding the additional variables is less than the loss in power due to the increase in p relative to N.

15.6 .28096

15.7 As the correlation between them decreases, the higher will be the squared semi-partial correlation of each variable with the criterion. Thus each will add more previously unexplained variation.

15.8 If two variables are highly correlated, one variable adds relatively little if the other is in the equation. Which of these two variables will carry the most weight for a particular set of data is heavily dependent on chance.

15.15 a. .6215, .7748, .8181

15.16 It has no meaning in that we have data on the entire population (the 10 districts).

15.17 The gain in R^2 is not sufficient to offset the loss in degrees of freedom.

15.18 It plays an important role through its correlation with the residual components of the other variables.

15.19 The correlation between Y and $\hat{Y}$ would be .646 instead of .818.

15.20 Within the context of a multiple regression equation, we can not look at one variable alone. The slope for one variable is only the slope for that variable when all other variables are held constant.

Chapter 16

16.1

Source	df	SS	MS	F
Treatments	2	57.733	28.867	9.31*
Error	12	37.200	3.100	
Total	14	94.933		

* $p < .05$.

16.2 a. $\alpha_1 = 2.467$ $\alpha_2 = -0.133$ $\hat{Y} = 2.467X_1 - 0.133X_2 + 5.733$ **b.** $R^2 = .608 = \eta^2$

16.3

Source	df	SS	MS	F
Treatments	2	79.010	39.505	14.919*
Error	18	47.657	2.648	
Total	20	126.667		

* $p < .05$.

16.4 a. $\alpha_1 = 2.403$ $\alpha_2 = .06$ $\hat{Y} = 2.403X_1 + .06X_2 + 5.797$ **b.** $R^2 = .62$

16.6

Source	df	SS	MS	F
Sex	1	65.333	65.333	7.73*
SES	2	338.667	169.333	20.03*
S×S	2	18.667	9.333	1.10
Error	42	355.000	8.452	
Total	47	777.667		

* $p < .05$.

16.7 **a.** Because we have equal ns, and therefore the variables are orthogonal—i.e., they don't account for overlapping portions of the variance. **b.** This will not be true with unequal ns.

16.8

Source	df	SS	MS	F
Sex	1	60.015	60.015	7.21*
SES	2	346.389	173.195	20.80*
S×S	2	21.095	10.547	1.27
Error	35	291.467	8.328	
Total	40			

* $p < .05$.

16.9 It is larger because in Exercise 16.8 some of the variation accounted for by SES was shared with Sex and the interaction, and thus not included in SS_{SES}.

16.10 $\hat{\mu} = 13.4167$; $\alpha_1 = 1.167$; $\beta_1 = -3.167$; $\beta_2 = -.167$; $\alpha\beta_{11} = .833$; $\alpha\beta_{12} = -.167$

16.11 Using means of means: $\mu = 13.675$; $\alpha_1 = 1.231$; $\beta_1 = -3.717$; $\beta_2 = .350$; $\alpha\beta_{11} = .478$; $\alpha\beta_{12} = .544$

16.12 If we are actually dealing with unweighted means, SS_A and SS_B will be zero because means of means are all 7 for rows and columns.

16.16

Source	df	SS	MS	F
Covariate	1	1716.288	1250.678	55.806*
Treatments	2	652.923	326.461	14.567*
Error	11	246.522	22.411	
Total	14	2615.733		

* $p < .05$.

16.18 **a.**

Source	df	SS	MS	F
Covariate	1	2979.129	2979.129	133.617
Metering	1	172.697	172.697	7.746*
Treatment	2	1120.872	560.436	25.137*
M×T	2	8.246	4.123	<1
Error	23	512.799	22.296	
Total	29	4796.700		

* $p < .05$.

16.20 44.825 54.049 61.031
       41.154 49.508 54.831

16.21	Source	df	SS	MS	F
	Metering	1	197.633	197.633	5.64*
	Treatment	2	1086.467	543.233	15.50*
	M×T	2	6.066	3.033	<1
	Error	24	841.200	35.050	
	Total	29	2131.366		

* $p < .05$.

Chapter 17

17.1 It is a random process, which prevents the incorporation of systematic bias. It also leaves the statistical formulae unaffected. The major difficulty is that for a given experiment the presence or absence of a significant effect may be determined by the flip of a coin.

17.2 The Wilcoxon Rank-Sum Test has a broad null hypothesis dealing with the equality of populations. The t test has a much narrower null hypothesis dealing with population means.

17.3 The Wilcoxon Matched-Pair Signed-Rank Test deals with the null hypothesis that the distribution of difference scores is symmetrical about zero. The null hypothesis for the corresponding t test deals specifically with the mean of that distribution (having *assumed* its shape).

17.4 (1) Our statistical tests are concerned with the numbers that we use, not their relationship to the objects they measure. (2) In Monte Carlo studies it has been shown that the conclusions actually drawn from the data with respect to statistical significance are essentially unchanged whether the data are ordinal or interval.

17.5 Because t has already assumed that there are no differences with respect to variability or shape, and thus rejection of H_0 can only mean that the means are different.

17.6 *a.* $W'_s = 23$; $W_{.025} = 27$ *b.* I would reject H_0 and conclude that older children include more inferences in their summaries.

17.7 *a.* $W_s = 53$; $W_{.025} = 68$; reject H_0. *b.* Subjects in the lesion group take longer to learn, as the theory predicted.

17.8 $z = -3.15$ **17.9** $W_s = 53$; $W_{.05} = 72$; again reject H_0.

17.10 *a.* $T = 8.5$; $T_{.025} = 8$; retain H_0. *b.* We do not have sufficient evidence to reject H_0 and say that there is a reliable increase in hypothesis generation over training. (Here is a case where the method of breaking ties is critical.)

17.11 *a.* $z = -1.94$. We would come to the same conclusion. *b.* The answers agree quite well. They don't agree better because N is small.

17.12 *a.* $W_- = 46$; $W_{.025} = 52$. *b.* I would reject the null hypothesis and conclude that first-born children are more independent.

17.14 $z = -2.20$, which agrees with our earlier conclusion.

17.15 $H = 5.124$; $\chi^2_2(.05) = 5.99$; do not reject H_0. **17.16** $H = 6.757$; $\chi^2_2(.05) = 5.99$; reject H_0.

17.17 $\chi^2_F = 9.04$; $\chi^2_2(.05) = 5.99$; reject H_0—the truancy rate improved.

17.18 We would not be able to take the relative magnitudes of the differences into account.

17.19 These are exactly equivalent tests.

17.20 $\chi^2_F = 9.0$; $\chi^2_2(.05) = 5.99$. We can reject the null hypothesis and conclude that people don't like tea made with used tea bags.

Index

A

Different ways to make a z-score

$$Z = \frac{X - \mu_X}{\sigma_X}$$

$$Z = \frac{(\bar{X}_1 - \bar{X}_2) - (\mu_1 - \mu_2)}{\sigma_{\bar{X}_1 - \bar{X}_2}}$$

$$Z = \frac{\bar{X} - \mu_{\bar{X}}}{\frac{\sigma_{\bar{X}}}{\sqrt{n}}}$$

$$Z = \frac{X - np}{\sqrt{np(1-p)}} \quad \text{when } X \text{ is a binomial}$$
$$np = \text{mean}$$

Confidence Intervals

$$\bar{X} \pm \frac{Z\sigma}{\sqrt{n}} \qquad \hat{p} \pm \frac{Z\sigma}{\sqrt{n}}$$

independent t $\quad (\bar{X}_1 - \bar{X}_2) \pm t \sqrt{\frac{s_1^2}{n_1} + \frac{s_2^2}{n_2}}$

dependent t $\quad \bar{d} \pm t \frac{s_d}{\sqrt{n}}$

Glossary of Important Symbols

Greek Letter Symbols

α	level of significance
α_i	treatment effect for ith level of A
β	probability of a Type II error
β_i	standardized regression coefficient; treatment effect for ith level of B
γ	effect size
δ	noncentrality parameter
η	correlation ratio
μ, μ_X	population mean
$\mu_{\bar{x}}$	mean of the sampling distribution of means
ρ	population correlation coefficient
σ, σ_X	population standard deviation
$\sigma^2, \sigma_X^2, \sigma_e^2$	population variance
Σ	summation notation; variance-covariance matrix
τ	Kendall's tau
τ_j	treatment effect for the jth treatment
ϕ	phi coefficient; noncentrality parameter
ϕ_C	Cramérs Phi
χ^2	chi-square
χ_F^2	Friedman's χ^2
ω^2	Omega squared

English Letter Symbols

a	intercept; number of levels of variable A
b, b_i	regression coefficient—slope
C	contingency coefficient
df	degrees of freedom
e_{ij}	unit of error associated with subject i in treatment j
E(MS)	expected mean square
EW	experimentwise error rate
F	F statistic
GM	grand mean